FORENSIC TOXICOLOGY

Mechanisms and Pathology

FORENSIC TOXICOLOGY

Mechanisms and Pathology

Robert H. Powers
Dorothy E. Dean

CRC Press
Taylor & Francis Group
Boca Raton London New York

CRC Press is an imprint of the
Taylor & Francis Group, an **informa** business

CRC Press
Taylor & Francis Group
6000 Broken Sound Parkway NW, Suite 300
Boca Raton, FL 33487-2742

First issued in paperback 2021

Version Date: 20150917

ISBN 13: 978-0-367-77794-4 (pbk)
ISBN 13: 978-1-4665-8194-4 (hbk)

Visit the Taylor & Francis Web site at
http://www.taylorandfrancis.com

and the CRC Press Web site at
http://www.crcpress.com

Contents

Preface

Forensic Toxicology: Mechanisms and Pathology was designed to accompany and complement a course in forensic toxicology on which the authors have collaborated for a number of years. The course itself has evolved and grown to focus on basic toxicology, the mechanism of action of drugs, and the physiological and pathological consequences of drug or toxin exposure. The contents of the course, and hence this text, reflect the perspectives and viewpoints of a forensic pathologist (Dr. Dean) and a forensic toxicologist (Dr. Powers) and are built on the understanding that the fields of forensic toxicology and forensic pathology are not at all exclusive, but to a great extent mutually dependent, and information and insight from each field can be of use and benefit to the other.

In developing a textbook for our forensic toxicology students, we wanted to introduce the general concepts of toxicology, but from a forensic perspective. We also wanted a book that reflected our interest in the importance of understanding both the mechanistic basis of action and the physiologic and pathologic consequences of the drugs and poisons we encounter as forensic toxicologists. Finally, we wanted a broadly accessible presentation of toxicologic issues that might be of use to forensic pathologists, lawyers, or other professionals with an interest in a forensic toxicologic perspective on casework.

We believe that forensic toxicology is, like many scientific fields, dynamically responding both to technological advances and to changing roles and expectations of those with expertise in the field. In the last 20 years an explosion of computer-based advances has produced—primarily in various mass-spectrometry-based instruments—a tremendous capability to identify and accurately quantitate a wide variety of drugs and toxins in complex biological matrices. In recent years the forensic community has also had to deal with a corresponding increase in the number of synthetic drug analogs.

In parallel with this increased analytical capability and expanded field of target analytes, there is also an increasing involvement on the part of many forensic scientists with efforts to explain the meaning of their results, in both the legal and medical arenas. More importantly, there is an increasing expectation on the part of the end users of our findings—for example, lawyers, medical personnel, judges, and juries—that the toxicologist will be able to explain what the drugs do and how they do it in a readily comprehensible manner. However, providing useful answers to questions of the meaning of toxicologic results requires a generalized understanding not only of the analytical findings and the underlying scientific basis, but also of the implication of those findings in the context of a specific case. Being able to function in such a role, often bridging the gap between the legal, forensic, and medical communities, requires a broad scope of knowledge of multiple disciplines. This melding of case-specific analytical data with an understanding of meaning of results in casework is not new, and the best of our field have always been those knowledgeable toxicologists whose ability to offer valid and relevant opinion in complex cases has been well recognized. To function effectively in this environment, the forensic toxicologist should be as comfortable discussing ion ratios in a mass-spectrometry analytical scheme, as he or she is discussing the mechanism of action of a drug on a biochemical scale, that has led to physiologic consequences in a particular case.

Our forensic toxicology class has also grown and changed, and we now leave much of the analytical aspects of toxicology to other courses. Our focus is the consequences of drug exposure: mechanistically at the molecular level, in terms of how the drugs affect the biochemistry of the body; physiologically in respect to the effects on the body as a functional system; and pathologically in terms of postmortem forensic toxicology and the challenges associated with explaining the role a drug may have played in causing or contributing to a death.

Forensic toxicology is a fascinating field, and we hope that this text can serve as a vehicle for students and others interested in toxicologic questions to explore the discipline, and perhaps be a basis for further interest, research, and possibly even a career.

Authors

Robert H. Powers completed his PhD in biochemistry at Michigan State University under Dr. Steven Aust, working on the mechanism of dioxin, PCBs, and similarly acting toxins. Dr. Powers has directed several forensic toxicology laboratories throughout the country and has recently retired from that role to become an associate professor at the University of New Haven (UNH), Department of Forensic Sciences, where he has taught forensic toxicology at the graduate level for more than 10 years. Research projects at UNH now include the effect of ethanol on phase I and phase II metabolism of selected drugs and drug classes, decompositional drug metabolism and postmortem changes, and glycoprotein-based species differentiation.

Dr. Powers is board certified as a Fellow of the American Board of Forensic Toxicology and is active as a consultant for civil and criminal cases, with a particular focus on questions of drug involvement in death cases and drug and alcohol impairment.

Dorothy E. Dean obtained her medical degree from the University of Toledo Medical Center in Toledo, Ohio, in 1993, acquired additional training in anatomic and clinical pathology at the University of Cincinnati, and completed a fellowship in forensic pathology at the Hamilton County Coroner's Office in Cincinnati, Ohio. Dr. Dean is board certified in anatomic, clinical, and forensic pathology and is currently a deputy medical examiner in Summit County (Akron), Ohio. Prior to her medical training, Dr. Dean was a high school math and physics teacher.

Dr. Dean is a member of several professional organizations including the American Academy of Forensic Sciences and the National Association of Medical Examiners. She is a member of the federal Disaster Mortuary Operational Response Team (DMORT) and its Ohio counterpart (OMORT). Her special interests include teaching medical students and medical residents, identification of unidentified remains, and evaluating drug- and poison-related deaths.

I Fundamentals

Introduction

1

Toxicology is the study of the harmful or adverse effects of chemicals on living systems. It is not necessarily a discrete, easily definable or limited discipline, in that aspects of toxicology are an important part of nearly all of the life sciences, from basic mechanistic biochemistry, through nearly all the medical fields to environmental and epidemiological sciences. Even historians and anthropologists can deal with questions of poisonings, the manner in which drugs and medicinal (and poisonous) materials were used in history, or even environmental contamination events. In turn, toxicologists can address an extremely wide variety of questions, ranging from assessing the basic toxic potential of newly developed pharmaceutical agents, determining the mechanism of action or metabolic fate of a new "designer drug," attempting to understand the connection between an industrial pollutant and an ecosystem impact, identifying a toxic contaminant in a food product, or determining the role a drug or poison may have played in a death. In essence, the arena for toxicology studies or examination comprises all aspects of the interaction between chemicals and living systems.

One might reasonably ask, then, what exactly is *forensic* toxicology? A glib answer (though containing some truth) is that forensic toxicology is simply "toxicology done in a forensic manner." It is not so much the sample or sample type that determines "forensic" status or not, but rather the purpose for which the analytical result will be used. Forensic toxicology analyses and results are differentiated from similar testing done in a nonforensic setting by the degree of documentation, validation, and quality control that is routinely part of the forensic analytical process. Forensic analyses are performed with the expectation that they may be used as evidence in a legal forum and may therefore be challenged, from the adversarial perspective that characterizes our judicial system. In many cases, forensic laboratories are accredited, a process that provides a demonstrated level of performance and is increasingly expected of forensic laboratories. Ultimately, it is not only the analytical findings, but the documentation of calibrators and controls, instrumental operating conditions, sample chain of custody, laboratory accreditation, etc., that allow a court (and the legal "other side") to evaluate the credibility of the findings.

Forensic toxicology, then, differs from other analytic disciplines really only in the degree of documentation and efforts to provide traceability for all aspects of the analytical process, such that the validity of the analysis and the results can be evaluated after the fact. This concept can be readily observed in the contrast between an alcohol determination in a hospital clinical toxicology laboratory, versus the same analysis in a forensic toxicology setting. In the clinical laboratory, the analysis will often be performed on an automatic analyzer using an enzymatically based method. Controls will be run on some periodic basis (usually at the beginning of a shift), and calibration of the instrument will be performed according to a specific timetable or on an as-needed basis. Samples are prepared and analyzed one at a time, in response to a specific need and request as a function of patient care, and without co-prepared calibrators or controls. This approach and methodology is demonstrably perfectly adequate and reliable for the clinical setting. In contrast, however, the corresponding analysis in the forensic laboratory is generally based on discrete batches containing multiple samples, for which the instrument is independently calibrated, and containing batch-specific controls prepared contemporaneously with the samples. In the clinical setting, the emphasis is on speed, and reliability is established with a validation process that examines and demonstrates between- and within-run variation and variability. In the forensic setting, the focus is somewhat less on the speed of analysis, and reliability is demonstrated by batch-specific documentation of calibration, controls, and instrumental performance. Both approaches are valid, useful, and appropriate for their specific purpose. On occasion, forensic analyses are utilized in a clinical setting, and similarly, clinical results may be entered as evidence in legal proceedings.

Forensic toxicologists, like their clinical counterparts, often have the opportunity to utilize their knowledge from many varied disciplines including analytical chemistry, pharmacology, physiology, anatomy, and biochemistry to understand the role that drugs, poisons, or toxins may have played in their casework. In addition to analytical results, other information such as medical records, autopsy reports, case documentation, investigation findings, and other information may be used to help resolve issues in the criminal or civil justice system. Common questions for toxicologists range from a determination of whether there has been past drug use (workplace drug testing), if an individual was impaired due to the presence of a particular drug (performance toxicology), or if a specific drug or toxin played a role in the death of an individual (postmortem toxicology). Issues regarding the presence of and concentration of drugs can of course simply be considered as analytical challenges. Beyond simple toxin exposure or drug usage, however, questions about the implications of drug exposure or usage necessitates an understanding of the mechanism of action of the drug, its fate in the body, and the corresponding physiological implications.

Forensic toxicology evolved as a discipline, primarily in postmortem and forensic laboratories as an application of the developing fields of chemistry and analytical chemistry, as scientists were called upon to determine if drugs, poisons, or toxins were present in casework samples. The challenge of developing accurate and reliable methods for the detection and analysis of drugs and poisons in complex biological matrices, that can then be presented and defended in court, has been and remains a rewarding discipline for students and practitioners alike. While the foundation of the field lay in classical analytical and "wet chemical" methods, tremendous advancements have been made over the past several decades in the capabilities of the instrumentation available to toxicology laboratories (primarily based on mass spectrometry) to determine what drugs or poisons may be present in a particular sample, and to provide an accurate quantitation thereof. For many drugs, the process of identification and quantitation, even from unusual and challenging matrices, is now often a well-characterized and even routine process.

As suggested above, what remains following the determination of the presence of a specific drug, toxin, poison, or mix thereof is of course, the deceptively simple question: What does it mean? While many texts, tables, and articles present therapeutic, toxic, and lethal levels of drugs, all too often such information may be of only limited utility in actual casework, in that the specific circumstances of a case can make the generalized guidance of less relevance or value. For example, polydrug exposures (quite common in forensic casework) can make interpretation of toxic levels particularly difficult, in that multiple "therapeutic" levels may add up to toxic or even lethal effects. To adequately address the challenging questions regarding the meaning of analytical findings, the forensic toxicologist requires an in-depth knowledge of the mechanisms by which drugs work in the body, as well as how they are absorbed, distributed, metabolized, and eliminated. Equally important to an appreciation for toxin effects at the molecular level is an understanding of the basic operation of the organ systems upon which toxic effects are mediated.

The implications of the presence of a drug in a forensic sample may be considerably different in a case of driving under the influence (DUI) or drug-facilitated sexual assault (DFSA), where functional impairment is a key issue, as opposed to a death case, where the question of effect is on a somewhat more basic level—could the drug or drugs present be an explanation for the death? An understanding of the impact that a drug may reasonably have had will be of considerable and perhaps critical importance to investigating agencies or the forensic pathologists who must ultimately determine the cause and manner of death. The common ground is that those using toxicologic information often need more than simple numbers and a reference to a published table. A therapeutic level of an opiate, as an example, might still produce (particularly in combination with a low level of ethanol) a significant degree of impairment.

The ability of the forensic toxicologist to understand the basis for the actions of drugs and poisons and to communicate effectively regarding these mechanisms and effects is an increasingly valued skill. Those who depend upon our forensic qualitative and quantitative analyses can often also benefit from our toxicologic perspective on a case, the conclusions we draw, and ultimately our understanding of what the analytical results may really mean in a specific case-related context.

In toxicology laboratories focusing on DUI, DFSA, and related crimes, there is often good communication between toxicologists and attorneys in the criminal justice system (both prosecution and defense). Both sides (or plaintiff and defense in the civil arena), in addition to the judicial system in general, benefit when the laboratory and its scientists can be trusted to provide unbiased, reliable scientific information, including analytical results and opinions or interpretations of those results. Similarly, in the postmortem setting it is not uncommon for forensic pathologists and toxicologists to discuss the meaning of toxicology results, often in particularly difficult and challenging cases. In death cases the pathologist has the ultimate responsibility of determination of cause and manner of death but may benefit from an additional perspective regarding the role that drugs may or may not have played in the case. Clearly, the involvement of the toxicologist at the beginning of the case can also benefit the process of test selection, thereby helping to ensure that the appropriate information is available for the case pathologist.

There is, of course, a wealth of interesting and challenging problems and issues to be addressed within the purely analytical aspects of forensic toxicology. There is an increased expectation that the analyst will be asked to appear in court to explain the scientific basis for both their findings and their reasons for accepting those findings as valid and reliable. The general public (from which our juries are drawn) has an increased awareness of the role and function of crime lab analyses due at least in part to the popularity of forensically oriented television shows (the so-called CSI effect). Recent Supreme Court decisions (*Melendez-Diaz v. Massachusetts* (2008); *Crawford v. Washington* (2004)) have clarified the legal responsibility for analysts to be available to present and explain their findings at trial. Further, the variety and scope of drugs we are challenged to identify and quantitate continues to increase, as reflected in appearance and influx of the so-called synthetic cannabinoids in recent years, as well as the various other designer drugs such as the cathinones and tryptamines. Questions of structure and function are becoming increasingly common and important in the judicial system. There is an increasing realization that simple two-dimensional structural similarity between molecules is an inadequate basis to assume functional similarity. The responsibility of the toxicologist to be able to understand and explain the mechanistic implications of structure and pharmacologic activity is becoming ever more important.

Despite the challenge of new analytes, and new technologies of detection and quantitation, we have chosen to leave analytical topics and questions out of this book. While some analytical issues are discussed in relation to specific topics, we take as our starting point for much of our consideration an identified, quantified analyte.

There are a number of different areas or specialties within forensic toxicology. The need for toxicologic analysis as part of a thorough postmortem examination for drugs and poisons is obvious, as well as in cases of driving under the influence of drugs or alcohol. However, the whole arena of preemployment drug testing, having grown out of the military's drug-testing program, represents a huge volume of forensic analyses that has been the impetus for tremendous scientific gains in methodology and equipment for testing, as well as for the laboratory certification and inspection processes. It is no exaggeration to suggest that the National Institute on Drug Abuse (NIDA) drug-testing laboratory certification program (now the National Laboratory Certification Program [NLCP]) set the standard for forensic laboratory inspection and certification programs, albeit for a limited group of analytes. A broader-scope analog, the American Board of Forensic Toxicologists (ABFT) laboratory accreditation program, extends the concept of good forensic practices to multiple drugs and types of laboratories, emphasizing process, procedures, and documentation.

So where to begin? Since toxicology is the study of the effects of drugs, poisons, chemicals, etc. on living systems, we might think about those effects from a forensic perspective, or more specifically, attempting to link the identification (and perhaps quantitation) of a specific compound to a given physiologic response, for example, intoxication, narcosis, or even death. In the context of criminal investigations, we're used to thinking in terms of *means, opportunity, and motive*. In the forensic toxicology world, it is more appropriate to think in terms of *drug, dose, and mechanism*. To explain or understand a given physiologic response or condition, we must have a drug present that is capable of causing that response, but perhaps more importantly, a dose in the body adequate to explain the phenomenon. Finally, we believe that to invoke a particular drug or poison as an explanation for a response, a mechanism must be identified, or at least reasonably inferred, linking the drug to a biochemical response and ultimately to the physiology or pathology we identify as having been caused by the drug.

Our interest and emphasis in this book is to help students see the action of drugs in the biochemical, pharmacologic, and physiologic contexts of molecular action, leading to the critically important perspective of pathologic and behavioral consequences. Like the class from which it is derived, this book is divided into segments covering first, basic toxicologic concepts, including toxicokinetics; then the major organ systems, including basic physiology and anatomy, and the consequences of toxin action; and finally the major toxin types (e.g., opiates, alcohol). We also wished a mechanism to share case examples from the authors' experience, often incorporated in the class discussions, and therefore we have included a number of such cases as a means of illustrating ideas from the text. Questions and topics for discussion are included with chapters to facilitate further exploration and research.

In class, beyond the linear sequence of chapters and topics, we devote a considerable amount of time to side topics that hopefully facilitate understanding of the topic, represent useful knowledge, or may simply be of interest. We have attempted to achieve a similar approach in this text, in that we have included sidebars that allow for an expanded discussion or other topics of use or interest.

We hope that *Forensic Toxicology: Mechanisms and Pathology* will provide an interesting introduction to the field for both undergraduate and graduate students.

A Selected History of Forensic Toxicology

2

Contents

2.1 Introduction

Toxicology, or the study of the mechanisms and effects of compounds deleterious to living systems, began in a sense with the process by which prehistoric peoples learned to distinguish poisonous from edible plants, and similarly, to avoid poisonous or venomous animals as a matter of self-interest. Early societies learned to utilize naturally available materials for a variety of purposes, including medicinal, religious, recreational, and of course, as poisons.

The history of toxicology, prior to the advent of modern analytical methods, is often viewed as a history of poisons, poisoning events and often stories of the poisoners themselves. Until the establishment of scientific methodology and the development of chemistry and the biological sciences, anecdotal and historical information was often the limit of what was available. From a forensic perspective, in the absence of a scientifically based analytical capability, there was only a limited ability to associate a particular drug or poison with a death. Nevertheless, a comprehensive history of the use of poisons for personal or political motivations (including warfare; see Sidebar 2.1) would cover many volumes. Similarly, an exploration of the development of the biological and physical sciences, and ultimately the paths that led to modern analytical chemistry, pathology, and toxicology and their forensic analogs, would also be huge. In this brief introduction to the field, we will mention a few selected events to convey a sense of the evolving and developing processes that have led to the current state of the art. The reader is encouraged to delve more deeply into some of the fascinating events and personalities that are part of the history of poisons, toxins, forensic sciences, and the basic understanding of the sciences underlying our discipline.

SIDEBAR 2.1 POISON ARROWS

Poisoned arrows (and other edged weapons) have figured largely in myth and legend, and in reality, they have been used essentially around the world, with different societies and regions incorporating different toxicologic agents as the base. In fact, *toxikon* is the Greek root word from which we derive our modern words of intoxicate, toxidrome, and of course toxicology, made of the Greek words, *toxikon* and *logia*. *Toxikon* was used by the Greeks to describe the poison into which they would dip the tips of their arrows, *logia* refers to the study of or science of a topic. Greek archers made use of the paralytic effects of extracts of the hellebore plant among other poisons. Ancient Chinese texts reference the addition of aconite to their arrows, and the same poison is recorded in the Indian text *Rig Veda*, written circa 1100 BC. Hunters in Africa have used a variety of different poisons ranging from the East African highlands, where oubain is extracted from the bark of the species *acokanthera* trees, to the Kalahari desert in South Central Africa, where natives crush the larvae of beetles (genus *Diamphidia*) that contain a poison causing hemolysis in the bloodstream of the wounded animal. In the rainforests of Central and South America, natives have fashioned curare-laced arrow tips and dipped their arrowheads in the toxic exudates of tree frogs belonging to the family Dendrobatidae. Alkaloids released from these aptly named "poison dart frogs" include epibatidine and batrachotoxin, some of the most potent neurotoxins in the world.

Forensic toxicology has evolved as a function of the development of the natural sciences and the application of the scientific method to forensic questions and issues in specific cases. With the beginnings of an understanding of atomic and molecular structure, and the introduction of wet chemical analysis, followed later by an explosion of instrumental techniques, the field of forensic toxicology has grown into a complex discipline with considerable capabilities for the detection and quantitation of poisons and toxic compounds.

2.2 Ancient Egypt

The ancient Egyptians had an extensive knowledge of plant and animal poisons, as indicated in fragments of documents preserved from that era. The Ebers Papyrus (circa 1550 BC), named after the Egyptologist George Ebers, contains a compendium of medical knowledge of that time period, including descriptions of various maladies and their possible treatments. The document describes remedies using opium, henbane, castor oil, peppermint, tamarisk, meadow saffron, and many other plant-based therapies. Inorganic species, such as iron, antimony, mercury, and lead compounds, are also identified as therapeutic agents. Another document, the Brooklyn Papyrus (named for the museum in which it is housed), delineates the poisons associated with various species of snakes, scorpions, and spiders of the region. Other documents of the period make reference to "the penalty of the peach," a reference to the ability of cyanogenic glycosides (found in the pits of peaches and apricots) to generate cyanide during the digestive process that the ancient Egyptians used as a method of execution.

2.3 Ancient Greece

Some of the knowledge of poisons the ancient Greeks possessed is well documented, including records

Figure 2.1 *The Death of Socrates.* (Metropolitan Museum of Art; Jacques Louis David [French, Paris 1748–1825 Brussels].)

detailing various poisons being used in weaponry and medicine and, as with the Egyptians, a means of state-sanctioned execution. The philosopher Socrates, sentenced to death in 399 BC, chose to drink a mixture prepared from the spotted hemlock (containing the potent neurotoxin coniine) as his means of execution. The hemlock solution was also provided by the state to those citizens who professed a desire to commit suicide. Curiously, references to criminal poisonings are rare in Greek writings, despite the relatively common use of poisons in society. Nevertheless, the Greek physician and teacher Hippocrates (often called the "father of medicine") required his students to swear in his "Hippocratic Oath" that they would "give no deadly medicine to anyone if asked," suggesting that the concept of using medicines as poisons was well understood. Hippocrates was also a supporter of plant-based therapies for treatment of both disease and poisoning (Figure 2.1).

2.4 Ancient Rome

Poisons and poisoners played a significant role in Roman military activities as well as the larger society. Roman legions were reputed to coat their weapons with "serpents' blood" to act as a poison, although, as snake blood does not contain the poisonous compounds that characterize the various poison venoms, this might have been more for the psychological effect on opposing forces. In this time period King Mithridates of Pontus, also known as the "first experimental toxicologist," lived and studied various poisons and their effects. Mithridates attempted also to develop a universal antidote (see Sidebar 2.2).

SIDEBAR 2.2 KING MITHRIDATES AND THE UNIVERSAL ANTIDOTE

One of the more fascinating figures in the history of toxicology has to be Mithridates VI Eupator Dionysius, king of Pontus (a region of present-day Turkey), who reigned during 120–63 BC. He became nominally king, along with his brother, around the age of 12, when his father, Mithridates V, was killed—perhaps by his mother and probably by poison. The brothers were too young to rule, so their mother wielded their authority as reagent, along with the jointly ruling king, Laodice VI. Apparently an attack was made on young Mithridates VI, and he went into hiding in the countryside. With consideration for the means by which his father had perished, and recognizing that the political intrigues of the court were to be a way of life apparently for him as well, he began to ingest small doses of various plant and animal poisons in order to build up resistances to any poison. Eventually Mithridates successfully returned to his throne; ousted Laodice VI, his mother, and brother; and as sole ruler began an even more intensive study of poisons and ways by which they could be counteracted. Mithridates is often referred to as the first experimental toxicologist, although the studies on the effects of poisons and the effectiveness (or lack thereof) of antidotes he performed utilized human subjects: criminals, prisoners, and slaves of his court. He is credited by legend to have developed an all-encompassing universal antidote, called "Mithridatum," that he would consume daily.

His knowledge of poisons not only kept him safe from would-be successors but also served him well in his battles with the Romans. It is described that his warriors used poisoned arrows against Roman invaders to great effect. Another account comes from near the end of the Third Mithridatic Wars, during which King Mithridates was being pursued by the great Roman general Pompey. Mithridates came to a region having vegetation he knew well and ordered his men to collect honey in jars and display them along the road he knew Pompey's armies would travel. Mithridates knew that honey from this region would have been made of rhododendron nectar and therefore be quite toxic. (Rhododendron nectar contains grayanotoxin, a sodium channel-blocking agent that would have been concentrated in the honey, accounting for its toxic nature.) After consuming the sweet syrup, the Roman soldiers began to experience nausea, dizziness, bradycardia, and vomiting, at which point Mithridates led a charge and slaughtered several Roman squadrons. Eventually, Pompey would defeat King Mithridates in 66 BC, and some of his greatest spoils of war were the antidote recipes of Mithridates, which he brought back to Rome, where they were translated into Latin for the benefit of the Roman imperials. (Such recipies seem no longer to exist, however.) Shortly after his defeat, Mithridates fled to Crimea, where heartbroken at his defeat and the betrayal of his son, he wished his life to end. The exact details of Mithridates's death are not known, although there are two unquestioned details: first, that he died by a sword (*whose* sword varies on the historian); and second, that he did not die by poison. After watching his wife and children succumb to the poison he provided them to avoid torture, he himself tried by the same manner, but his legendary antidote regimen protected him to the very end, even when he would have preferred it to fail (Figure 2.2).

A group of poisoning deaths of married Roman citizens (hence, males) of ~330 BC was attributed by the historian Livy (59 BC–17 AD) to a group of the wives of the victims, arranged with the goal of property acquisition for their members (thereby documenting the historical antecedent of a common theme of poisoning that continues to this day). When questioned about their suspected involvement in the deaths, several of the wives claimed that chemical mixtures found in their possession were actually therapeutic medicines. Given the opportunity to drink the "medicinal potions" as a means of demonstrating the validity of this argument as an alternative to facing the court system, many of the participants chose the former and quickly died. One could suggest that by so doing, the accused avoided an (arguably) even worse fate at the hands of the Roman law and the various possibilities for execution. The investigation eventually led to the convictions of more than 150 accomplices in the first recorded poisoning trial in Roman history.

Poisoning became especially prevalent during the civil wars in Rome, so much so that in 82 BC the emperor Sulla issued *Lex Cornelia*, an edict that carried harsh class-specific punishments for those involved in poisonings: those of noble birth would suffer the loss of their property or banishment, while those of lower status would be killed in the Colosseum. Despite the potential legal consequences, poisoning continued to be used by members of both high and low society, including the imperial families (see Sidebar 2.3). Emperors of Rome would look to the physician and philosopher Galen of Pergamon (129–199 AD) as a source for both medical advice and treatment and for antidotes for poisoning, both real and suspected.

Figure 2.2 King Mithridates, *The Royal Toxicologist*. (Robert Thom, 1915–1979; from *Great Moments in Pharmacy* series.)

SIDEBAR 2.3 POISON AND THE GREAT CAESARS

Poison apparently played an important role in the succession of the Julio-Claudian dynasty, the Caesars. Caesar Augustus died in 14 AD, poisoned, many believe, by his wife, Livia. When feeling ill (and hence, possibly poisoned) Augustus was in the habit of eating only figs that he picked from a specific tree at his personal villa. According to legend, Livia initiated the process by arranging some tainted food and then ended the scheme by painting Augustus's figs with "belladonna," a potent anti-cholinergic neurotoxin (atropine). Her motive was to ensure the succession of her son Tiberius (having already dispatched of Augustus's two sons and true heirs). Tiberius was succeeded by the infamous Caligula, who was murdered by his own Praetorian Guard in 41 AD, to be succeeded by Claudius. The death of Claudius by poison (mushrooms, by legend) was orchestrated by his wife Agrippina (also his niece) in 54 AD, although there is debate on who actually performed the act. One of the suspected killers was a woman named Locusta, who would become the court poisoner of Claudius's successor, the Emperor Nero, who gave her pardon in exchange for her lethal services on his behalf. Locusta was responsible for the death of Britannicus, son of Claudius, and Nero's younger half-brother in an attempt to eliminate any opposition to his throne. Locusta was rewarded for this deed by Nero with vast country estates and a school for her to teach her deadly craft.

The death of Britannicus highlights the cunning and skill of Locusta. Since Britannicus was a person of the upper class (also the emperor's half-brother), he employed tasters that would screen his food and drink by sampling it before he himself ate or drank—the best safeguard against poisons of the day. To circumvent this defense, Locusta had the goblet of wine for Britannicus warmed prior to being served. The warmed wine passed the tasters' testing, and Britannicus took the goblet and drank, only to find the wine too hot for his comfort. The goblet was then handed back to a servant, who poured in cold water to cool the mixture. Locusta had dissolved a poison in the water, and shortly after drinking, Britannicus began to gasp for air and convulse. He died and was hastily buried that night, only days before his fourteenth birthday.

Galen was a significant figure in the medical history of medicine, who advanced the teachings of Aristotle and Hippocrates with the study of anatomy, physiology, and pharmacology to become the preeminent physician of Rome. His medicinal preparations from plants came to be called "galenicals." Galen espoused the belief that an imbalance of the "four humors" (fluids: blood, yellow bile, black bile, and phlegm) was the cause of diseases. Galen also prepared antidotes with multiple ingredients called "theriacs" that were (according to legend) based on captured recipes from King Mithridates.

2.5 Dark Ages and Medieval Period

The fall of Rome, around 476 AD, marked the beginning of a long period of regression of learning and scientific inquiry in Western Europe. The study of medicinal topics essentially ended as monks simply copied Greek and Roman treatises rather than experimenting and adding new research and knowledge to the field. Significant contributions were made, however, by scientists in the Islamic realm, including the *Al-Qanun fi al-Tibb*, or *The Canon of Medicine*, written by Ibn Sina (latinized as Avicenna, 980–1037), who taught in the Persian Empire in present-day Iran, and is recognized as a major influence on science and medicine of the period. The *Canon* is a multivolume encyclopedia covering anatomy, physiology, pathology, and pharmacology and was based on many of the principles of Galen along with novel additions by the author, including observations on mercury and arsenic poisoning.

Scientific inquiry began to be renewed in the Western world with the Renaissance. The Italian professor of medicine Petrus de Abano (1257–1316) summarized Greek and Arabic writings on toxins in his book *De Venemis*. De Abano classified known poisons as well as various strategies that could be used to help neutralize a poisonous ingestion. In other parts of Italy, however, the knowledge of poisons was taught not for healing but for more nefarious purposes. The study and use of poisoning as a means to gain status and power became a sort of cult phenomena, and "schools of poisoning" became especially active in Venice and Rome between the fifteenth and seventeenth centuries. In Venice, the infamous "Council of Ten" arranged poisonings for political purposes on a contractual basis, while the Borgia's la Cantarella (a poison based on arsenic; see Sidebar 18.1) was used to dispatch the political and religious enemies of their family in Rome. Around 1650, Madame Giulia Toffana, operating in Naples and later Rome, flourished as a professional poisoner and teacher of her lethal art with her eponymous (also arsenic-based) poison, Acqua Toffana. Madame Toffana is thought to be responsible for the deaths of Pope Pius III and Pope Clement IV, among many others of lower station. In 1533, Catherine de Medici, born of Italian royalty, married the French King Henry II and is believed to have brought the Italian knowledge of poisons to her new country. In France, poisoning became increasingly recognized as a problem, ultimately leading to the creation of the "Chambre Ardente" (Star Chamber), a tribunal convened specifically for poisoning cases, in 1679. Within three years it had brought charges against 442 people. The most infamous of those convicted was a woman known as La Voisin, who started as a poor midwife and began to make and sell potions, mostly arsenic based, to high-society French women, including a known mistress of the king at the time, Louis XIV.

The Renaissance brought about a shift in philosophy, as scientists began to rely less on mysticism, magic, and alchemy, and more on objective investigation and experimentation as the basis for understanding the natural world. One of the key scientists to support this shift was Paracelsus, born as Theophrastus Bombastus von Hohenheim. Paracelsus was one of the first scientists to directly study the effects of poisons on animals in a systematic fashion. He used mercurial compounds for the treatment of syphilis, an approach that brought him into conflict with the members of the medical community, who claimed he was using poisonous prescriptions. His response, articulated in his *Third Defense*, has become a basis upon which modern toxicology rests: "What is there that is not poison? All things are poison and nothing without poison. Solely the dose determines that a thing is not a poison" (Figure 2.3).

While Latin remained the preferred language of the scientific intelligentsia, *A Mechanical Account of Poisons in Several Essays* was written by Richard Mead and published in English, appearing in 1708. Mead was a physician at St. Thomas Hospital in London and wrote regarding poisonous snakes, spiders, and scorpions;

Figure 2.3 Paracelsus. (Originally painted by Quentin Metsys [c. 1465-1530].)

poisonous minerals and plants; opium; and finally, contaminated water and air from various sources.

2.6 Dr. Addington and the Case of Mary Blandy

The utilization of chemical analysis and experiment in the legal arena was of course inevitable as the sciences grew, developed, and expanded in analytical capability. An early example of the use of what would now be considered wet chemical techniques is a case from the mid-1700s in southeast England, involving an unmarried 30-year-old woman, Mary Blandy. A Scottish army officer, William Cranstoun, believed Mary would inherit a small fortune and pursued a relationship with her, despite having a wife and child in Scotland (whom he disavowed). Cranstoun's apparent affections were returned, but Mary's father forbade the relationship upon learning of the existing marriage. Cranstoun is alleged to have provided Mary with a powder that he promised "would eliminate her father's objections to the marriage." Mary obediently began to add this powder to her father's food, and soon, as advertised, her father's objections ended, albeit along with his life. Mary Blandy was brought to trial at Oxford in 1752, charged with the murder.

A local physician, Dr. Anthony Addington, had been provided some of the powder, which had been recovered from the father's food for examination. Dr. Addington observed that the material appeared to be white arsenic (arsenic trioxide), including a milk-white color and gritty texture. He performed a number of tests on the material, including flame, color, and precipitation. Addington's results were consistent with those generated by a known sample of arsenic, in particular, a garlic smell, and white fumes when burned (considered to be characteristic of arsenic trioxide). Dr. Addington ultimately offered testimony that he believed the powder from the food to be white arsenic, and as a consequence, Mary Blandy was convicted of murder and hanged. Cranstoun escaped English law and fled to France. This case represents one of the first records of scientific evidence being presented in order to prove homicidal poisoning.

Developments in chemistry continued to lay groundwork for the use of scientific evidence in the legal system, particularly regarding arsenic. In 1786, Dr. Samuel Hahnemann described a process of exposing acidified samples to hydrogen sulfide gas, yielding the yellow arsenic trisulfide, in his book *Poisoning by Arsenic: Its Treatment and Judicial Investigations.*

The ability of carbon (as charcoal) to reduce the highly toxic arsine gas in a heated glass tube, producing an elemental arsenic "mirror" upon cooling, was reported in 1787 by Johann Metzger. In 1806, Valentine Rose, a professor at the Berlin School of Medicine, demonstrated the presence of arsenic in gastric contents collected from a suspected poisoning victim. Rose treated the liquid with potassium carbonate, calcium oxide, and nitric acid, yielding arsenic trioxide (As_2O_3, normally in the form of As_4O_6, and hence As^{+3}), which was then passed over heated charcoal as per the Metzger test. The formation of the characteristic mirror was considered as evidence of the presence of arsenic. While these early tests were of course of somewhat questionable reliability (as might be expected based on the inherent variability of the reagents, reaction vessels, and conditions used), they nevertheless can be seen as laying a foundation for the forensic sciences we pursue today.

2.7 Orfila, the Father of Forensic Toxicology

Mathieu Joseph Bonaventure Orfila is often referred to as the founder of toxicology as a recognizable discipline. He was born in April 1787, on the island of Majorca, off the eastern coast of Spain. Following studies in Valencia, Barcelona, and Madrid, Orfila eventually earned a medical degree in Paris in 1811 and began practice and

Figure 2.4 Joseph Bonaventure Orfila 1787–1853. (Lithograph by Alexandre Collette, 1814–1876.)

teaching. The unreliable, inconsistent, and often siply erroneous results produced by the chemical tests for poisons was an important issue for Orfila. In later years, he wrote: "The central fact that had struck me had never been perceived by anyone else. My first words were these: Toxicology does not yet exist." Orfila believed that the best way to be certain that a particular poison had been used in a case was to have a clear understanding of its effects, which could only be accomplished (at that time) by the observation of consequences of exposure in animal experiments. Animal studies soon followed, and Orfila ultimately developed an important concept of drug distribution. In 1813, he summarized his findings from animal experiments and classified his information in *Traites de poisons* (*Treatise on Poisons*). In this text, poisons were assigned to one of six categories (later condensed to four): acrid, corrosive, astringent, stupefying, narcotico-acrid, and septic. Orfila also summarized the chemical tests employed for the detection of common poisons. The volume served to define the field, and earned Orfila the title of "Father of Forensic Toxicology" (Figure 2.4).

Orfila was named the professor of medical jurisprudence at the Paris Medical School in 1819 and became dean of the Medical School in 1830. Orfila testified for the first of many times as an expert witness in 1824, ultimately becoming famous for his testimony in the courtroom, one of the first "celebrity" expert witnesses. In 1839, Orfila became the first person to extract arsenic from a tissue other than the stomach, using a variation of a test developed by an English scientist, James Marsh.

2.8 The Marsh Test

James Marsh, a chemist assistant to Michael Farady at the British Royal Military Academy, came to the issue of testing for arsenic poisoning almost by chance. In November 1832, in Kent, England, 20-year-old James Bodle was accused of and tried for the arsenic poisoning of his grandfather, George Bodle. It was believed that young James had grown tired of waiting for his grandfather's death to inherit his farm, and apparently decided to hasten the process by adding arsenic to the family coffee pot. The coroner examining the case needed a chemist to evaluate the evidence and approached the well-known and respected scientist Faraday (later to be known for his work with the relationship of electricity and magnetism) with the problem. Faraday's workload was such that he passed the case to his assistant, James Marsh (1774–1846), who also worked as an ordnance chemist for the British Navy at the Royal Arsenal in Woolwich. Marsh used the standard method of arsenic detection at the time: the precipitation of arsenic sulfide, and was able to demonstrate the presence of arsenic in the coffee. However, by the time Marsh testified, his evidence had deteriorated, and the jury, unconvinced by the results Marsh presented, acquitted Bodle. (A decade later, Bodle confessed to the poisoning.)

In response to the outcome of the case, Marsh pursued the development of a more reliable test, based on the work of Carl Wilhelm Scheele, a Swedish pharmacist. Scheele had, in 1775, discovered the ability of arsenic trioxide to form arsine gas (AsH_3, which has a characteristic garlic-like odor) in the presence of nitric acid and zinc. Marsh constructed an apparatus that would allow detection of any arsine gas formed by treatment of samples with the zinc/nitric acid mixture. A sample, suspected of containing arsenic, was placed into a vessel with zinc and nitric acid. Any arsenic present in the sample would be reduced by the zinc, then combined with acidic protons, yielding arsine gas, AsH_3. Combustion of the hydrogen-arsine mixture would deposit elemental arsenic as either a silvery mirror (on glass) or a black deposit (on a ceramic surface). The magnitude of the deposition was proportional to the amount of arsenic present in the sample.

Marsh published a description of his test in October of 1836 in the *Edinburgh Philosophical Journal*, claiming to be able to detect as little as 0.02 mg of arsenic. One year later, in 1837, a student of Orfila, Jon Jacob Berzelius of the Karolinska Institute in Stockholm, modified the test so that it could be reliably used in a quantitative manner, based on the evaluation of known standard amounts of arsenic (Figure 2.5).

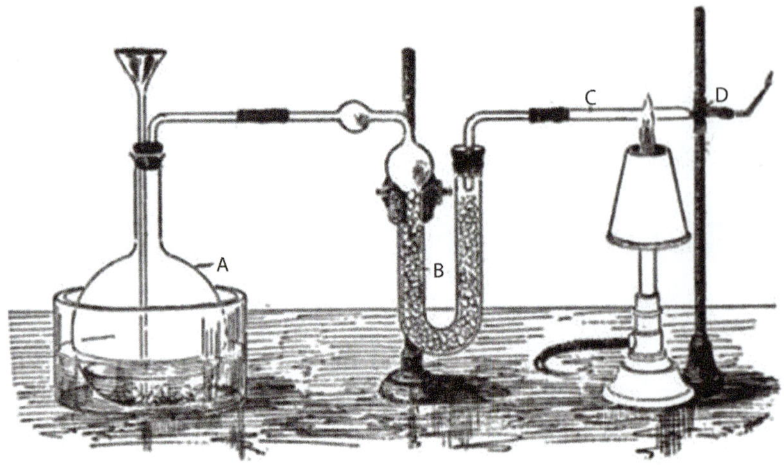

Figure 2.5 Apparatus for the Marsh test. In Marsh's approach, material (e.g. tissue, gastric contents, emesis) potentially containing arsenic would be digested (A) with arsenic-free zinc and hydrochloric acid, liberating arsine (AsH_3) and Hydrogen (H_2) gases. The evolved gases would pass through a calcium chloride drying tube (B) into a heated glass tube (C), and ultimately released through a small orifice (D). Combustion of arsine in the hydrogen flame allowed the reduction of As^{3+} to the elemental form, and its deposition as an arsenic mirror on cool surfaces. (Adapted from Hugh McMuigan, 1921. *An Introduction to Chemical Pharmacology*, Philadelphia: P. Blakiston's Son & Co.; page 397. https://en.wikipedia.org/wiki/Marsh_test#/media/File:Marsh_test_apparatus.jpg)

2.9 The Lafarge Case

Four years after first being published, the Marsh test played a significant role at the center of an important case in Tulle, France. The highly publicized trial of Marie Lafarge was the prime focus of the media of the day and the center of attention for the French public who kept the courthouse filled. Foreshadowing trials to come, the defendant became a celebrity, and forensic examinations of the evidence became the major points of contention in the trial and ultimately determined the result.

In the fall of 1840, Marie Lafarge was charged with murdering her husband by poisoning with arsenic. Prosecutors had information that Lafarge had bought rat poison (in the form of arsenic trioxide) and servants' testimony claiming to have seen Marie pour a powder into her dying husband's food. Nevertheless, the prosecutors wanted chemical proof of the poison either from food taken from the decedent's bedside or from stomach contents, and preferably both. Local chemists were charged with the analytical task, and they eventually reported finding arsenic in both the food and gastric contents tested, using a sulfur precipitate test (like the one that frustrated Marsh).

The defense attorney had corresponded with Orfila regarding the testing used in this case and read his comments in the matter aloud in court—to the effect that the results in the case were not credible and that the test itself had been shown to be unreliable. Orfila had further indicated that in his opinion, only the results of a Marsh test should be considered a valid demonstration of the presence of arsenic in a poisoning case. The court then ordered the analysis be repeated using the Marsh test. The original chemists were not able to demonstrate the presence of arsenic, and so the second analysis was unsuccessful (at least from the perspective of the prosecution).

The prosecution (equally familiar with Orfila's opinions) also cited the Parisian expert and presented to the court Orfila's expectation that poisons (e.g., arsenic) were distributed throughout the body and would not solely be found in the stomach. In addition, he offered a logical explanation for the absence of arsenic in gastric samples, simply that much, if not all, of the poison in the stomach had been expelled as emesis. The prosecutor further claimed that the only way to prove that indeed arsenic was not present was to demonstrate its absence in major organs of the body. The court concurred, but once again, following the exhumation and testing of new samples using the Marsh approach, the local chemists were unable to detect arsenic in the samples.

The prosecution made a final request, based on a belief that the provincial chemists, having never before utilized the Marsh test, had somehow failed to perform the test in a proper manner. He requested that Orfila himself be summoned from Paris to perform testing to definitively ascertain the presence or absence of arsenic. The defense, having introduced Orfila into the trial in the first place, could not object. Orfila then agreed to travel from Paris to Tulle in order to conduct the tests, only adding to the public interest in the case. Orfila tested not only the organs of the deceased but also the soil in which the body was buried, in recognition of the natural occurrence of arsenic in soil as a crustal element and the importance of establishing a background or baseline level of an analyte before interpreting any other results. Orfila announced he had detected the presence of arsenic in the tissues of Lafarge (soil was eliminated as the arsenic source) and that the false results previously reported were not the fault of the Marsh test itself but rather faulty execution of the test by the original chemists. In a last desperate effort, the defense summoned another expert, François-Vincent Raspail (see Sidebar 2.4), to refute Orfila's testimony. However, Raspail failed to arrive in time to present an alternative explanation for the results, and the jury deliberated for only one hour before finding Marie guilty. She was sentenced to life imprisonment but was ultimately released from incarceration shortly before her death in 1852 (Figures 2.6 and 2.7).

SIDEBAR 2.4 ORFILA AND RASPAIL

François-Vincent Raspail was a well-known and respected French chemist who was often an opponent of Orfila in scientific and legal matters. Raspail often criticized lectures and articles of Orfila consistent with the nature of scientific discourse of the day. Raspail was expecting to appear on behalf of Marie Lafarge following Orfila's first appearance in that famous case, but due to a combination of illness and ill-luck (he heard rumors that Lafarge had been acquitted and spent an extra night to rest), he did not arrive in time to testify prior to the completion of the trial. Nevertheless, Raspail remained in Tulle and learned that three tests had been performed on Lafarge's organs in Tulle by Orfila and his assistants. The first two examinations, using the same local reagents used by the chemists in previous tests, demonstrated no appreciable amounts of arsenic from the samples. However, when Orfila switched to reagents brought with him, metallic arsenic was detected. Raspail then inquired of the whereabouts of the chemicals used in Orfila's Marsh tests and was told that the local pharmacist was in possession of them, save "his potash, his zinc, and the nitrate of potash by means of which he obtained the deposit on the third plate." Curiously enough, Orfila had returned to Paris with these reagents. Believing Orfila's reagents to have been contaminated, he wrote to the presiding judge with his misgivings about the evidence at one point, saying, "Give me anything you like—your own armchair—and I will find arsenic in it." (Marsh himself had cautioned at the end of his 1836 landmark paper that a false positive could be observed if the zinc used in the test was contaminated with traces of arsenic.)

The ongoing rivalry between Orfila and Raspail may have been based on science, but politics were a factor as well. Orfila was a member of the French aristocracy and a staunch conservative, while Raspail was an ardent socialist, to the point that he had served time in jail for protesting, and ran for the presidency. Raspail was self-taught and believed that medicine should be shared with the poor, in contrast to the legendary Orfila, who had been trained in universities throughout Europe. In his memoirs, a Parisian police commissioner recounts a conversation he had with Orfila shortly after the Lafarge trial. According to the commissioner, Orfila stated that if Raspail had arrived before the jury deliberations had completed, Madame Lafarge would have been exonerated, not because of the science but because of the public support for the young wife and the certainty that Raspail would have used that to his advantage in swaying the jury.

Figure 2.6 Marie Lafarge. Deutsch: Marie Lafarge, ge. Capelle (1816–1852) französische Giftmörderin Lithographie von Gabriel Decker, um 1850. (https://commons.wikimedia.org/wiki/File:Narie_Lafarge_Litho.JPG)

Figure 2.7 François-Vincent Raspail. (https://en.wikipedia.org/wiki/Fran%C3%A7ois-Vincent_Raspail#/media/File:Fran%C3%A7ois-Vincent_Raspail_01.jpg)

2.10 The Reinsch Test

In 1841, a German chemist, Hugo Reinsch, further refined testing for arsenic by placing the sample or tissue in question in hydrochloric acid in the presence of a piece of copper foil. The solution allowed the electrolytic reduction of arsenic by copper, and deposited or "plated out" the elemental arsenic on the foil. This test was easy to perform and quickly replaced the Marsh test among practicing toxicologists. Many other metals reacted in a similar fashion, yet the color and nature of the metal deposit allowed the experienced analyst to distinguish between species. The utility of the Reinsch test was such that it was still being used as a quick screen for heavy metal poisoning in some laboratories well into the 1950s and 1960s.

2.11 Isolation of Alkaloid Poisons and Count Bocarmé

The increased analytical capability represented by the Marsh and Reinsch tests had an effect on the practice of poisoning, in that the ability of chemists to identify the presence of some species (e.g., arsenic, bismuth, mercury) suggested that other, nonmetallic compounds might be better choices for the poisoner who wished their crime to remain undetected. As concern shifted toward plant-based poisons, chemists were required to attempt to isolate these natural compounds from corpses, a task difficult enough from the plant sources themselves, and made considerably more difficult in the forensic environment prior to the development of sensitive analytical equipment.

The basis for the identification of organic compounds was primarily purification, usually via extraction and recrystallization. Using such approaches, morphine was first isolated from the poppy plant in 1804, strychnine from *nux-vomicus* seeds in 1819, and coniine from hemlock in the same year. Nicotine was isolated from tobacco in 1828 and the aconitine from monkshood in 1832. The increasing ability of analytical chemists to isolate specific compounds represented the beginning of forensic analysis for these and many other compounds.

The first alkaloid to be isolated from a human decedent began with a Belgian wedding in 1843. Count Hippolyte Visart de Bocarmé had fallen in love with Lydie Fougnies, a daughter of a merchant, and believing her family to be wealthy, quickly married her. The count and his new wife lived a life of extravagance, quickly exhausting their savings and Lydie's inheritance; however, the couple had an eye on the rest of the family wealth. In the fall of 1850, when Lydie's brother Gustave planned a visit to announce his engagement, they recognized a threat in that if Gustave married, his share of the inheritance could never be claimed, even in the event of his death. The couple set in motion a plot to murder Gustave during his visit.

During dinner, servants heard screaming and rushed into the dining room to find Gustave writhing in agony, with the count apparently attempting to pour vinegar down his throat. The count curiously ordered Gustave washed in vinegar and moved upstairs, where he soon died. The local magistrate was alerted by the serving staff and took custody of the body. The organs were eventually brought to a chemist, Jean Servais Stas, a student of Orfila. His first tests produced a smell that convinced him he was dealing with an organic poison, and with further work, he was able to isolate a substance that smelled like tobacco. Stas eventually extracted nicotine from tissues with an acidic alcohol solution. A large supply of tobacco leaves and exhumed corpses of animals upon which Bocarmé had apparently practiced were enough to convince the court, and convict the count of the murder of his brother-in-law. Surprisingly, Lydie was acquitted, but Bocarmé was executed by guillotine in July 1851.

The Stas method was modified in 1856 by Friedrich Julius Otto, who was able to remove organic contaminants by making the initial acidic alcohol solution alkaline, then extracting alkaloids with ether or chloroform.

Figure 2.8 Jean Servais Stas.

The Stas-Otto method was eventually employed for the successful detection of colchicine, caffeine, coniine, quinine, morphine, atropine, and strychnine (Figure 2.8).

2.12 Development of Forensic Toxicology in Europe

Advances in both practical and theoretical chemistry and physics in the 1800s made possible the development of analytical techniques applicable to biological materials. Robert Bunsen (of the Bunsen burner) and Gustav Kirchoff of the Heidelberg Institute discovered flame emission spectrometry for the identification of mineral elements in 1859. While progress in elemental analysis was being made, similar advances in the isolation and identification of alkaloids were being accomplished.

The development of color and precipitation tests was essential to identify these newly isolated alkaloids. The work of German-born pharmacist Johann Draggendorff and his assistants Edward Marquis and Karl Friedrich Mandelin achieved considerable success, with reagents and color tests associated with their names still in use today. One issue with these tests was discovered by the Italian chemist Francesco Selmi, who noted that postmortem products can cause false positives in color tests. For this reason, direct animal testing was still used as a valid forensic method for proof of alkaloid exposure into the early 1900s.

The use of animals as sensitive indicators of the presence of organic toxins was extensively explored in the late 1800s and early 1900s. In 1864, professor Auguste Tardieu at the University of Paris helped prove the presence of digitalis toxin by injecting a frog with extracts from a victim suspected of poisoning. He then observed the reactions of the injected frog compared with the symptoms in frogs injected with digitalis. Frogs were similarly used by the English physiologist Marshall Hall in the mid-1800s to visualize the violent effects of miniscule amounts of strychnine. The German chemist Friedlieb Runge, investigating the mydriatic (dilating) effects of atropine, suggested using the eyes of cats as a means of the detection of atropine, while in 1911 another German, Walter Straub, described the characteristic S-shaped mouse tail seen in mice exposed to morphine (a response still used in opioid research). Sometimes the animal species involved was none other than *Homo sapiens*, and such was the case when toxicologist Thomas Stevenson, in 1880, tasted a small amount of an extract from a poisoned victim and experienced numbness in his tongue, leading to him conclude the presence of aconitine. (The practice of similarly testing suspected cocaine is still occasionally employed by field personnel.)

An important turning point in the field was made by a research associate of François Magendie at the Collège de France in Paris, Claude Bernard, who began to view poisonings from a physiological and biochemical standpoint. They were able to determine the mechanism of carbon monoxide as a substitute for oxygen on hemoglobin and curare as a motor neuron poison, with no effect on sensory nerves.

2.13 Forensic Toxicology in the United States

Toxicology was also developing in the United States with the European ideas and texts as models shaping the practices of American scientists. The first book published in the United States pertaining to symptoms and treatment of poisoning was *A Practical Treatise on Poisons* in 1848 by O.H. Costill. In 1867, Theodore Wormley generated the first American text discussing the detection of poisons in organic tissues, *The Micro-Chemistry of Poisons*. John Reese, a professor of medical jurisprudence in Philadelphia, produced *Manual of Toxicology* in 1874, followed a decade later by *Text Book of Medical Jurisprudence and Toxicology*.

2.13.1 The Bizzare Case of Dr. Buchanan

In 1892, a scandalous trial, notable for the extent to which scientific testimony and demonstration were central to the process, focused on several elements of toxicology in a courtroom of New York City. Dr. Robert

Buchanan was arrested for the murder of his wife, Anna Sutherland, a brothel madam whose cause of death was originally listed as a brain hemorrhage. The circumstances of the event and the subsequent behavior of Dr. Buchanan were suspicious to an enterprising reporter, Ike White of the *New York World*, who began to investigate this increasingly suspicious death.

Through interviews with associates of the doctor, White learned of the fascination Dr. Buchanan had with an earlier trial of a New York medical student, Carlyle Harris, several years prior, who was charged with and convicted of murdering his wife. Her death (suspiciously) had also been originally linked to brain hemorrhage; however, the constricted, miotic pupils allowed scientists to identify morphine as the true cause of her death.

White approached the doctor responsible for Anna's autopsy and inquired about the possibility of a morphine overdose, but the doctor said that Anna did not have the pinpoint pupils characteristic of an opiate overdose victim. White recalled a colleague who suffered from an eye ailment and would return from a physician visit with large, dilated pupils, a consequence of eye drops containing atropine. White then interviewed the nurse who had watched over Anna in her last days, who informed him that she clearly recalled seeing Dr. Buchanan administering eye drops to his dying wife on several occasions. Armed with these "coincidences," White was able to convince the coroner to exhume the body for the purpose of toxicological testing. A well-recognized American toxicologist, professor Rudolph Witthaus, found lethal amounts of morphine in the body and informed the prosecution that atropine would indeed reverse the pupil constriction characteristic (meiosis) of morphine overdose. Dr. Buchanan was subsequently arrested for murder.

Buchanan's trial began in March 1893, with the display of the prosecution killing a cat with morphine and then adding atropine drops to the dead cat's eyes, masking the classic opiate pinpoint pupils. The defense, however, had a demonstration of their own and showed that the color test Witthaus employed could produce false positives due to "cadaveric alkaloids." With that impeachement of the analytical findings, the defense might have won the case. However, Dr. Buchanan was allowed to testify, and his attitude and inconsistencies in testimony allowed the prosecution to prevail. Dr. Buchanan was convicted and sentenced to death.

Witthaus eventually showed that the chemicals used in the defense's demonstration were contaminated, thus resulting in the false positives, and this information contributed to the failed appeal on behalf of Dr. Buchanan, who was executed in 1895. One year previous, Witthaus collaborated with a New York City attorney named Tracy Becker in publishing *Medical Jurisprudence, Forensic Medicine and Toxicology* in four volumes.

In 1918, Dr. Charles Norris became the first medical examiner of New York City. Prior to this point, deaths were investigated by coroners, who were occasionally corrupt and rarely had any medical training. Dr. Norris hired Dr. Alexander O. Gettler and created the nation's first forensic toxicology lab (see Sidebar 2.5). In so doing, Dr. Norris ushered in a new era of forensic medicine (Figure 2.9).

SIDEBAR 2.5 GETTLER'S LAB: THE BIRTHPLACE OF AMERICAN FORENSIC TOXICOLOGY

Alexander Oscar Gettler (1883–1968) was born in Austria-Hungary before immigrating to Brooklyn, New York, in 1889. Determined to go to college, but from a family that couldn't afford tuition, he worked as a ferry ticket agent while attending classes at the College of the City of New York. He then enrolled at Columbia University, where he earned his master's degree in 1910, and two years later, his doctorate degree in biochemistry. He became a clinical chemist at the Bellevue Hospital pathology laboratory, where he was approached by Dr. Charles Norris to perform chemical analysis for the newly formed medical examiner's office. Along with his hundreds of research studies and publications, Gettler's testimony helped to convict the guilty and exonerate the innocent based on sound scientific principles. An inveterate gambler who was never an arm's length from a cigar, Gettler would work at his laboratory for just over four decades before retiring at the age of 75.

Gettler's other great legacy was his commitment to educating future chemists and toxicologists. Even when he was actively cultivating and directing the nation's first forensic toxicology laboratory, Gettler continued to teach chemistry at Bellevue Medical School (now New York University). He started a graduate program in 1935 and his students would go on to become lab directors at toxicology laboratories throughout North America. Dr. Gettler's students would contribute greatly to the forensic literature in their own right and included, among many others, Henry Freimuth, Abraham Freireich, Sidney Kaye, and Irving Sunshine. His influence is evident even to this day as the Alexander O. Gettler Award and Irving Sunshine Award are annual prizes conferred to forensic toxicologists by the Toxicology Section of the American Academy of Forensic Science.

Figure 2.9 Dr. Norris (left) and Dr. Gettler (far right), circa 1922–1923.

Dr. Gettler was a dedicated scientist who was proficient at inventing new methods and pushing existing current methods to their limits of sensitivity. From arsenic to carbon monoxide, cyanide to radium, Gettler was constantly experimenting and augmenting the literature on postmortem toxicology.

Gettler and Norris saw firsthand the dark side of Prohibition (of ethyl alcohol) in 1921, as thousands of people were brought into the morgue after consuming methanol as a substitute for ethanol. Gettler was one of the first to relate the amount of alcohol in the brain to a person's degree of drunkenness and published the first scientific scale of intoxication in 1927 in an article titled "Alcohol Content in Human Brains."

Instrumental methods of analysis would supplant colorimetric methods as the twentieth century exploded with advancements in electronics, beginning with simple vacuum tubes before World War I, more complex electronics in the years prior to World War II, and with the appearance and use of the transistor in the 1950s and 1960s, evolving toward integrated circuits, computers, and ever more powerful analytical instrumentation.

2.13.2 Innovations in Alcohol Testing

Erik Widmark became professor and head of the Department of Medical and Physiological Chemistry at the University of Lund in Sweden in 1921. Applying his previous work on developing a method to detect acetone concentrations in blood, Widmark published a microdiffusion-based method for the quantitative analysis of ethanol in fingertip blood in 1922. Ten years later, Widmark's landmark monograph on the medicolegal aspects of ethanol was published, defining the

Figure 2.10 Erik Widmark.

pharmacokinetic constants relating the amount of ethanol absorbed and distributed with a determined ethanol concentration (Figure 2.10).

In 1938, University of Indiana professor Rolla Harger invented the Drunkometer, the first reasonably stable breath testing instrument. The device consisted of balloon and color-changing solution of potassium permanganate and sulfuric acid. The Drunkometer set the stage for the development of specialized instrumentation for the testing of alcohol in breath, leading ultimately to the current variety of computerized devices, and the nearly universal acceptance of breath alcohol testing as a valid indication of the blood alcohol level of an individual, and hence, their degree of impairment (Figure 2.11).

In 1939, Indiana became the first state to enact a law on driving while intoxicated (DWI). The original limit for

Figure 2.11 Rolla Harger's Drunkometer. (State Archives of Florida.)

blood alcohol content (BAC) was set at 0.15 g/dL, almost twice that of today's national standard. The independent experiments of Butcher and Redetzki in Germany and the Swedish scientists Bonnichsen and Theorell led to the development of the first enzymatic analysis (using alcohol dehydrogenase) of ethanol in 1951. In 1954, Robert Borkenstein invented the first portable breathalyzer that is the basis for the breathalyzers still used today.

2.14 The Age of Chromatography

In March 1903, M. S. Tswett first published his observations on the separation of plant pigments, which he called chromatography. The method remained without significant impact for almost three decades until 1938, when thin-layer chromatography was first described. The first liquid–liquid partition chromatography was described in 1941, and in 1952, a monumental step was taken with the adaption of gas as a mobile phase, and gas chromatography (GC) was described as a method to separate and identify fatty acids. In 1960, Douglas Lucas in Canada would publish the first use of gas chromatography as a member of the forensic field when he used GC to analyze petroleum product residues in a suspected arson case. By the late 1960s GC was being used for the forensic detection of alcohol in blood. In the 1960s, modern high-performance (high-pressure) liquid chromatography (HPLC) was developed with the forensic applications starting to appear in the early 1970s.

In 1976, gas chromatography coupled to a mass spectrometer (GC/MS) was evaluated for the first time for forensic purposes by the British scientists Zoro and Hadley, with one of their applications discussed being the detection of drugs in toxicology cases. In the same year, Dubowski first described the use of headspace gas chromatography to quantitate alcohol in biological fluids. The development of atmospheric pressure ionization sources—both chemical and electrospray—paved the way for the first commercial tandem liquid-chromatograph to mass spectrometer to be introduced in 1989.

Enzymatic assays are used extensively by toxicology labs across the world for primary drug screenings. The first such assay was the radioactive immunoassay (RIA) published by Berson and Yalow in the late 1950s. Nonradioactive variants (e.g., enzyme multiplied immunoassay technique/enzyme immunoassay [EMIT/EIA]) debuted in 1971 and soon largely replaced RIA as these new kits required no radioactive components. Much of the impetus for the immunoassay-based testing was a response to a need for large-scale rapid drug-screening methods for the US Army, after coincident with the Vietnam War in the late 1960s into the early 1970s, the first EMIT kit was produced in 1972.

2.15 Impact of Mass Spectrometry

The explosion that has occurred in the field of analytical instrumentation as a function of computerization has been mirrored in the myriad of applications within the forensic toxicology laboratory. While GCMS has been the staple analytical tool for most analytes, more and more laboratories are using LCMS as well as MS-MS technologies on a routine basis. Time-of-flight and other MS technologies may be expected to see more utilization in the laboratory in the coming years.

Perhaps the greatest change in the analytical process is not so much a change at all, in that the goal of the instrumental advances has always been, What drugs are present, if any, and how much is there? The purpose for the question was always focused on the implications of the presence of a drug, which we can rephrase as simply, What does it mean? With the increased analytical capability, the question of how this matrix for this (or indeed any) drug can be analyzed is less of an issue. However, the essential question of what it means remains the key challenge for the forensic toxicologist now, as it always has in the past.

TOPICS FOR DISCUSSION

1. Should forensic toxicology be considered a stand-alone discipline? Why or why not?
2. The expansion of the capabilities of DNA testing have severely impacted many forensic disciplines. What could be effects of continued development and capability in this area of forensic toxicology?
3. Much of our knowledge of the effects of poisons and toxins have been from ethically undefensible activities. Should such knowledge be utilized? Why or why not?
4. Forensic science was once at the forefront of scientific investigation and experimentation and was closely linked to state-of-the-art theory, instrumentation, and equipment. Is that still the case? Why or why not?
5. What has been, and what will be, the effect and impact of the designer drugs, (including the synthetic marijuanas) on forensic toxicology (both performance, e.g., DUI, and postmortem)?
6. Consider the prohibition and legalization of drugs (including ethanol). Are we moving toward more or less legalization of recreational

drugs? Is that a good or bad thing? (Differentiate between drug classes as appropriate.)

Bibliography

Eckert WG. Historical development of forensic sciences. In: Eckert WG, editor. *Introduction to Forensic Sciences.* 2nd rev. ed. New York: CRC Press, 1997.

Lane RW, Borzelleca JF. Harming and helping through time: The history of toxicology. In: Hayes AW, editor. *Principles and Methods of Toxicology.* 5th rev. ed. New York: Informa Healthcare, 2008.

Sunshine I, editor. *Was it a poisoning?: Forensic Toxicologists Searching for Answers.* Distributed by National Medical Sciences Inc., Copyright Irving Sunshine, 1998.

Trestrail JH III. *Criminal Poisoning.* Totowa, NJ: Humana Press, 2000.

Watson KD. Highlights in the history of toxicology. In: Wexler P, editor in chief. *Information Resources in Toxicology.* 3rd rev. ed. New York: Academic Press, 2000.

Wennig R. Forensic toxicology. In: Satoh T, editor. *Environmental Toxicology and Human Health, in Encyclopedia of Life Support Systems, Developed under the Auspices of the UNESCO.* Oxford, UK: EOLSS Publishers. [http://www.eolss.net]

Toxicity and Toxidromes

3

Contents

3.1 Introduction

Toxic has become a term used to describe a negative or detrimental impact or effect for subjects that can be far removed from medical, or even biochemical systems, as in *toxic assets*. For the toxicologist, pathologist, or physician, toxicity is an expression of damage, direct or indirect, to a living system elicited by a chemical of either endogenous or exogenous origin. We attempt to understand and explain the effects of toxic compounds in terms of their specific biochemical mechanism of action and ultimately the physiological and pathological consequences to the body.

There is often a general belief that a toxic compound is dangerous at any level or concentration, that simple proximity to the material corresponds to exposure, and that any exposure corresponds to a likelihood of a toxic response. However, the actual concentration or amount of a drug or poison to which a person might be exposed is equally as important as its capability to cause harm. It is simplistic but nevertheless important to recognize the dose required to elicit a toxic response, and that exposures need not necessarily automatically be above that threshold level.

Linking a toxic compound to a specific biological response should not be done without an understanding of the mechanistic basis of the toxic action. It is of course a human foible to confuse causation with coincidence, and sometimes the presence of a potentially toxic drug is linked to a death or other injury response, even in the absence of consistent evidence to that effect.

As was noted in Chapter 1, it has long been recognized that the difference between a drug (implying a beneficial pharmaceutical compound) and a toxin, or poison (capable of causing injury, damage, or even death), is merely a function of dose. We therefore draw no distinction between drug, poison, (chemical) species, toxin, or any other word that signifies a unique chemical structure, and will use the terms synonymously throughout the text.

3.2 Three Prongs of Toxicity

For a chemical to be justifiably linked to a specific condition or toxic consequence, three elements of toxicity must be present: exposure, dose, and mechanism, as shown in Figure 3.1. (We do of course acknowledge that there are toxic/poisonous compounds for which the mechanism of action is unknown or not yet completely characterized.) We expect that the mechanism of toxic action must be explainable within the current understanding of biochemistry, physiology, and pathology. In short, "magic" is generally not an acceptable explanation for the mechanism of a toxic response.

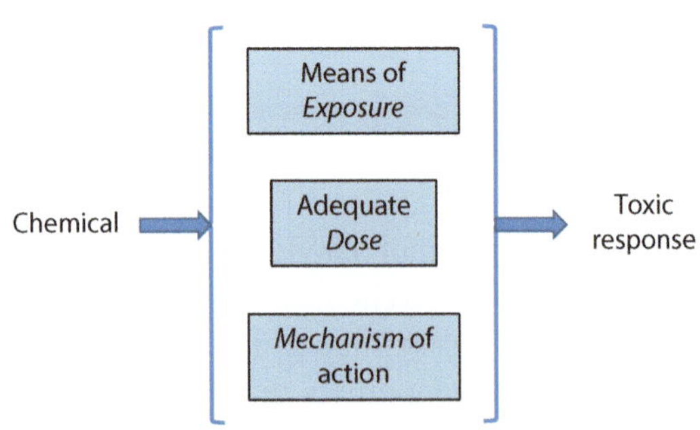

Figure 3.1 Three elements of toxicity.

3.2.1 Exposure

It is not uncommon for the general public to equate the simple proximity to a toxic compound with risk of toxic consequences, even in the absence of an actual mechanism of exposure. Examples are many, from asbestos in buildings to lead in pewter goblets and paint. In these cases, the potential toxin may indeed be present in the surrounding environment, but in the absence of a mechanism of active uptake into the body (such as exposure to dust from the uncontained demolition or decomposition of asbestos insulation, or the deliberate ingestion of lead-containing paint chips), there can be no toxic response. On the other hand of course, there are many examples of supposedly safe materials that have indeed presented a means of toxin delivery. Examples here would include lead-based gasoline additives (no longer used), numerous industrial chemicals that have found their way into foodstuffs (e.g., melamine), and a number of drugs that have been introduced into general use and then subsequently recalled (e.g., Thalidomide, Fen-Phen, Vioxx). The nature of chemical reactions requires that proximity to a toxin is not enough; exposure to the chemical is needed for a basis for direct reaction between the toxic compound and the biomolecules of the living system.

3.2.2 Dose

An important concept in toxicology is that concentrations of a drug or toxin can be in an individual for which there is no detectable biochemical response (the no observable effect level [NOEL]). Most drugs operate via interactions with biomolecules, and those interactions are a function of concentration. For example, while a level of 200 ng/mL of (free) morphine in the blood can be lethal to an adult human, 20 ng/mL will perhaps have a mild analgesic effect in very sensitive people, but 2 ng/mL would not be expected to elicit any responses at all. The response to the drug is related to the ability of morphine to bind to and activate several specific opiate receptors, and as noted above, the extent of that binding is a kinetically driven function of the concentration of the drug. It stands to reason, then, that the concentration of morphine in the blood can be so low that binding to the opiate receptor is not of a magnitude adequate to activate the receptor. As with therapeutic, desirable interactions, so too with toxic interactions. For a toxic response, while exposure to a drug is a necessity for causing a toxic response, the dose must be adequate to cause the biochemical reactions underlying toxicity.

3.2.3 Mechanism

Explaining the toxic response of a person to a particular drug requires an understanding of the underlying biochemistry and physiology of the body, specifically how exactly the presence of the toxin affects the operation of biomolecules, thereby distorting the normal system physiology. An understanding of the underlying mechanism of operation of the toxin can be particularly useful when dealing with multiple drugs or attempting to determine the role that a drug or combination of drugs may have played in a particular case or circumstance.

3.3 Multiple Drug Effects

As noted above, the potential for combined effects when multiple drugs are present in the body can provide a significant challenge for the toxicologist. There is often the suggestion that drugs producing similar effects must "multiply" each other's effects. While one might reasonably expect that morphine and oxycodone, two opiate agonists, would indeed act together, no such mechanistic interaction would be expected between a combination of morphine and fluoxetine, one being a central nervous system (CNS) depressant, the other a selective serotonin reuptake inhibitor (SSRI). From the standpoint of receptor binding, morphine and fluoxetine are mechanistically distinct, and therefore no interaction would normally be expected between the two species. The terminology normally used to describe drug interactive effects are additive, synergistic, potentiation, and antagonistic. A numerical approach to a representation of the different effects is presented in Figure 3.2.

3.3.1 Additive Effects

Additive effects can be expected when two species operate via the same mechanism (e.g., bind to the same receptor). Two separate opiate species or two different benzodiazepines would be expected to exhibit simply additive effects. Similarly, ethanol, a generalized CNS depressant, would be expected to have an additive effect on other CNS depressants, such as barbiturates, benzodiazepines, and opiates, although not a function of a similar mechanism of action in the body. Mechanistically unrelated toxins can also result in additive effects.

3.3.2 Synergistic Effects

In a synergistic effect, the presence of a second drug acts to enhance or multiply toxicity by a mechanism linked to, but distinct from, the action of the first drug. An example is the combination of a monoamine oxidase inhibitor (MAOI; e.g., Meclobamide) and a selective serotonin reuptake inhibitor (SSRI; e.g., fluoxetine), the combination of which can result in a potentially life-threatening "serotonin syndrome" (see Sidebar 7.7). The consequences of a synergistic combination of drugs are greater than would be expected on a simple additive basis.

3.3.3 Potentiation

In some cases, the presence of an innocuous or otherwise nontoxic species increases the expression of toxicity caused by another agent. An example is the inhibition of acetaldehyde dehydrogenase by disulfiram, thereby increasing the concentration of acetaldehyde following ethanol ingestion and the headache associated with that

Additive:

Drug A + Drug B;
$2 + 4 = 6$
The combined effect of drugs with *additive* effects is approximately equal to the sum of the individual effects associated with the dose of each.

Potentiation:

Drug A + Drug B;
$0 + 4(\times 4) = 16$
The effect of a nontoxic species, able to amplify or increase the effect of a toxic agent is referred to as *potentiation*.

Synergy:

Drug A + Drug B;
$2 \times 4 = 8$
The combined effect of *synergistic* drugs is greater than the sum of the individual effects associated with each drug.

Antagonism:

Drug A + Drug B;
$-2 + 4 = 2$
The ability of a nontoxic agent to block, limit, or otherwise interfere with the ability of a drug to elicit a response normally associated with a dose or concentration is *antagonism*.

Figure 3.2 Drug interactions.

compound. In the absence of alcohol, disulfiram itself is innocuous, and as such, it is used as an adjunct in helping alcoholics deal with their addiction by providing negative reinforcement. The toxicity of acetaminophen (APAP) can be considerably enhanced by the induction of a cytochrome p-450 isozyme by isoniazid, thereby enhancing the rate at which the toxic metabolite of APAP, N-acetyl-p-quinoneimine (NAPQI), is formed, with the consequence of severe and occasionally fatal liver damage.

3.3.4 Antagonism

A drug antagonist, in general terms, is simply a compound (e.g., another drug) that blocks or limits the effectiveness of a specific drug. Such an effect is usually mediated by a process of competitive binding between the antagonist and the receptor, or enzyme binding site to which the drug would normally bind, producing the desired physiologic effect. Using the "lock and key" analogy, an agonist (the drug that works the system) fits the lock and works the mechanism. On the other hand, the antagonist, or the "wrong key," fits the lock but cannot work the mechanism. However, the presence of the wrong key in the lock blocks a potentially functional key. The classic example of antagonism is the morphine structural analog naloxone, which despite strong affinity for the opiate receptors, is unable to elicit the physiological responses of morphine or related compounds. In fact, the ability of naloxone to "outcompete" morphine for the active sites of the receptors is the basis for its use as an emergency treatment for opiate overdose, with an almost instantaneous reversal of symptoms.

3.4 Descriptions of Toxicity, or Toxic Potential

3.4.1 Fundamental Issues

3.4.1.1 Concentration Units

Many disciplines deal with questions of toxicity, toxins, and toxic response. The units for the expression of drug or poison concentration can differ quite markedly between fields as shown in Table 3.1. Practitioners quickly become adept at converting between the common units regularly used in their field, and it is important that the toxicologist be conversant with the conventions of various disciplines.

3.4.1.1.1 Environmental Environmental toxins can be as varied as pesticide residues, naturally occurring elements or compounds, organic and inorganic industrial compounds in soil and on or in foodstuffs, or appearing as contaminants in wildlife. Environmental toxins can also be airborne as gases or as particulate materials. Environmental toxin concentrations are often expressed in units of parts per million (ppm: µg/g, mg/kg; 1×10^{-6}, or mg/L), parts per billion (ppb; ng/g, µg/kg; 1×10^{-9}), or parts per trillion (ppt; pg/g, ng/kg; 1×10^{-12}) as commonly used units. For gases and airborne materials, common units are milligrams (mg), micrograms (µg), nanograms (ng), or picograms (pg) per cubic meter. Particular applications or subdisciplines may have their own standard or expected units.

3.4.1.1.2 Medical Within the medical world, drug concentrations are usually expressed as µg, or ng/mL, although occasionally (most notably with ethanol) units of mg/dL (dL = 100 mL) are used. A blood ethanol of 100 mg/dL is equivalent to 0.1 g%.

3.4.1.1.3 Postmortem Postmortem work is essentially medical in nature. Nevertheless, the common convention is to express drug concentrations as mg or µg/L, rather than the µg or ng/mL more routinely used in the medical setting. Drug levels in tissues are normally expressed as ng, µg, or mg drug per g or kg of tissue.

3.4.1.1.4 Legal Within the legal environment, the units used in a case may vary based on the way a particular law is written and the legal practice and precedent for the type of case being tried. The preferences of the trial judge may be a consideration as well. Experts presenting opinion regarding that key issues will generally agree on a common terminology for the units to be utilized. For example, in a medical malpractice case, where the key issue revolves around the level of a particular drug, the discussion will usually be in terms of µg or ng/mL. If the case then involves a death, and the key question is regarding the potential for a drug to have caused or contributed to that death, the discussion will most likely involve units of mg/L. Ethanol

Table 3.1 Example Units

Analyte	Environmental	Medical	Postmortem	Legal
Ethyl alcohol	PPM (air)	mg/dL	g/100 mL	gram % (as weight/volume)
Morphine	N.A.	ug/mL	mg/L	Case-dependent
Arsenic	PPB (water)	ug/g	mg/kg	Case-dependent
Carbon monoxide	PPM (air)	% Carboxy-hemoglobin	% Carboxy-hemoglobin	Case-dependent

remains an interesting exception to this rule. Hospitals normally report ethyl alcohol as mg/dL, while most state DUI regulations and laws utilize g/dL (g/100 mL, g/%). (Most hospitals use serum as the basis for ethanol determination, and a serum alcohol requires a small correction to reflect a "whole blood" concentration; see Chapter 12, "Alcohols.")

3.4.1.2 Unexpected Effects

3.4.1.2.1 Hypersensitivity A number of drugs are able to elicit an allergic response in some people, the magnitude of which may be as mild as simple itching. More serious expressions can include hives, nausea, or even death. (*Anaphylaxis* is a very severe allergic reaction, usually with rapid onset, and can cause death.) An allergic response requires an initial exposure to the drug to establish antibody production, which is then expressed at some future time when another exposure to the drug occurs. In some cases, the process of becoming sensitized to a drug can take years of repeated exposures. *Hypersensitivity* is perhaps somewhat of an unfortunate choice in that an individual who possesses more of a particular type of receptor upon which a drug binds than the general population might also be described as hypersensitive without any implication of an allergic response.

3.4.1.2.2 Idiosyncrasy Some individuals respond to a drug in an unusual or unexpected manner, perhaps even the exact opposite of the normal response. An example of such an idiosyncratic behavior is excited or nervous behavior following administration of a CNS depressant drug (e.g., a barbiturate or a benzodiazepine). A classic example of an idiosyncratic effect is demonstrated by the effective treatment of many hyperactive children or children with attention-deficit disorder with either amphetamine or related CNS-stimulant drugs. The paradoxical calming effect of these drugs often can allow affected children to function on a more normal level with their peers in a classroom situation.

3.4.1.2.3 Side Effects Many substances cause effects other than only those desired. Many side effects are relatively innocuous for most people, such as the drowsiness that accompanies a number of over-the-counter (OTC) cold medications (e.g., diphenhydramine or dextromethorphan). There are circumstances when side effects may be of forensic significance, such as (with the OTC cold medications noted above) when the CNS depression caused by cold medication affects the ability to safely drive a motor vehicle or operate machinery. Side effects can be considerably more significant to the point of limiting the use of the medication (such as the cardiotoxicity associated with some anthroquinone antibiotics).

3.4.1.3 Classic Descriptions of Toxicity

3.4.1.3.1 Categories of Toxicity The classic categories used to describe toxins and toxicity are not rigorously defined, with labels ranging from "essentially safe" to "extremely toxic," as shown in Table 3.2. In the absence of a rigorous definition, the categories are only of limited quantitative use but are able to convey a general sense of the risk associated with specific toxins, which is defined in terms of the dose required to produce injury.

3.4.1.3.2 LD_{50}, ED_{50} One of the basic questions that toxicologists have had to deal with historically was simply how to compare one toxin with another. How too could different dosages be compared? The key to the resolution of such questions lies in the essential nature of the biologic response. Drugs (with very few exceptions) exert their effects by means of receptor- or enzyme-mediated processes (essentially, binding to an active site on a biomolecule). The concentration-dependent interaction between the toxin and the biomolecule through which the toxic response is mediated is then the basis for toxicity. Since at and below a certain concentration there will be essentially no binding (and hence, no effect…), and at a certain concentration an increase will cause no increase in effect (all possible binding sites are occupied already), then dose versus response can be represented with a *sigmoid curve*, as shown in Figure 3.3.

One of the original means of comparison of toxicity was to look at the midpoint of that biological response curve, with the response in question being the death of the test animals. The parameter identified was the concentration of drug that produced death of half of the test group, within the defined test interval. This "lethal dose for 50%," abbreviated as LD_{50}, became (and remains) a standard basis for comparison of toxicity, at least among laboratory or test animals.

The LD_{50} is a measure of the central point of a sigmoid curve and, as such, is simply one specific example of an effective dose (ED) for 50% of a test population, for a particular measured parameter (in this case, lethality). One can compare drugs easily with other ED

Table 3.2 Categories of Toxicity

Toxicity Rating	Rat LD_{50}, (Oral; mg/kg)	Adult Human LD_{50}; Oral (Estimated)	Toxin
Essentially safe	>15,000	>1 Qt.	Water
Slightly toxic	5000–15,000	~300 g	Ethanol
Moderately toxic	500–5000	~4 g	Nicotine
Very toxic	50–500	~200 mg	Cyanide
Extremely toxic	5–50	~200 ug	VX nerve gas
Supertoxic	<5	~200 ng	Botulinum

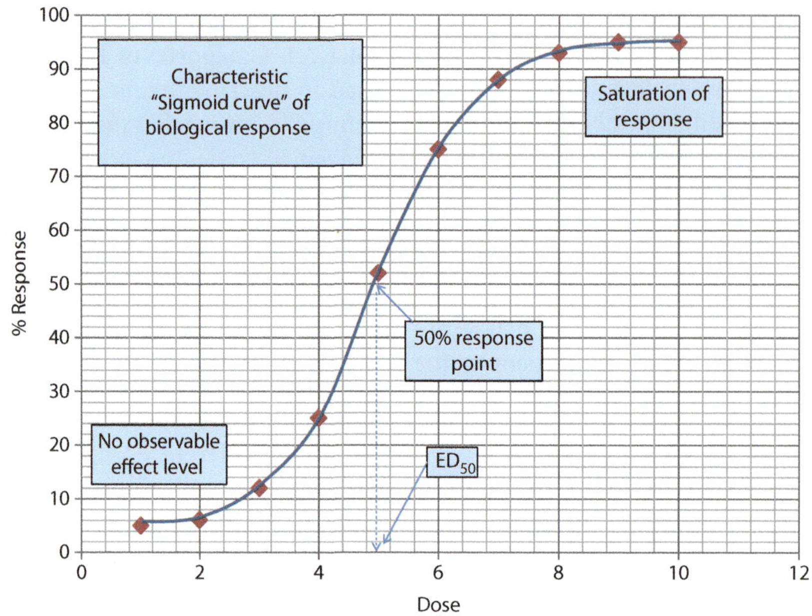

Figure 3.3 Sigmoid curve (typical sigmoid biological response curve).

parameters, as long as the target value can be measured or quantitated. Any point on the sigmoid curve for comparison, for example an ED_{10} or ED_{90}, can readily be used. However, because the maximal slope is achieved at the midpoint of the curve, the ED_{50} is the most sensitive measurement point. For example, the ED_{50} for slurred speech associated with alcohol ingestion is ~0.17 g/dL (fortunately, a large difference from the LD_{50} of somewhere above 0.5 g/dL). The sigmoid curve, as characteristic of receptor-mediated processes, proceeds from a no-observable effect level (NOEL) to a saturation of response. Interestingly, biochemical processes and phenomena that are functionally related (e.g., by receptors or other related binding processes) must have parallel dose-response curves. However, unrelated processes and phenomena *may* have parallel dose-response curves.

3.4.1.3.3 Therapeutic Index The magnitude of the difference between a therapeutic level of a drug and a toxic or potentially lethal level can be quite useful as a relative indication of drug safety. Clearly, a drug for which the therapeutic level is well below a concentration associated with toxic symptoms is safer than a drug where the distinction between such levels is less. The ratio of the toxic (or lethal) dose to the therapeutic dose is defined as the *therapeutic index*. Consider a drug for which the midpoint of the therapeutic range is 200 μg/L, and the low end of the lethal range is characterized as 800 μg/L. The therapeutic index for the drug would therefore be ~4. A classic definition of therapeutic index is toxic dose/therapeutic dose. A somewhat more rigorous definition would be LD_{50}/ED_{50}.

3.4.2 Measuring and Describing Toxicity

Toxins or poisons can be characterized and described in a number of ways. The actual levels or concentrations of a particular toxic species in the environment can be measured (e.g., air, water, and soil) or, in a less direct manner, the concentrations and effects of such compounds on the flora and fauna of that environment. Similarly, we can examine populations of plants or animals statistically to identify trends or hotspots that may be indicative of a toxic exposure, even without a particular toxin being identified. Finally, we can examine individual symptoms, behaviors, and toxin levels in an effort to understand a particular or suspected toxic event.

3.4.2.1 Measuring and/or Describing the Environment

Environmental toxicology is a broad and fascinating discipline with an essentially unlimited potential for important questions and problems that need to be resolved. While the realm of forensic toxicology is often focused on medicinal and recreational drugs, any compound capable of negative impacts on living systems is within the realm of environmental toxicology. The potential for environmental impacts of man-made chemicals, or consequences of activities to be addressed within the legal system, can generate a forensic aspect to many analyses or research projects.

Recognition of the potential for man-made compounds to be released into both the workplace and the environment has led to the generation of *exposure limits*, describing levels above which particular compounds or chemical species are reasonably expected to present a toxic risk. Exposure limits have been generated by a number of different agencies, primarily with regard to environmental and industrial environments and toxins.

3.4.2.1.1 American Conference of Governmental Industrial Hygienists The American Conference of Governmental Industrial Hygienists (ACGIH) was formed before World War II as the National Conference of Governmental Industrial Hygienists, changing to ACGIH in 1946. The organization remains focused on a number of industrial health issues, including the agricultural industry. Of particular interest to the toxicologist are the tabulations of threshold limit values (TLVs) and biological exposure indexes (BEIs). TLVs represent a concentration of a chemical to which a worker may be exposed for a working lifetime, with no expectation of adverse effects. BEIs are simply measurable chemical or biochemical markers of exposure at or below the TLV. TLVs and BEIs published by the ACGIH represent guidelines or recommendations and are not regulations. Nevertheless, they can provide useful information regarding exposures and toxicity of industrial chemicals.

3.4.2.1.2 Occupational Safety and Health Administration The Occupational Safety and Health Administration (OSHA) was established in 1970 as an agency within the Department of Labor. The enabling legislation allows OSHA to create and issue health and safety regulations for the workplace. As such, OSHA is both a regulatory and enforcement agency. While much of OSHA activity is focused on physical parameters and industrial safety, considerable efforts are expended to deal with chemicals and their toxic potential in workplace settings. Most significantly for the toxicologist are limits on chemical exposure, characterized as permissible exposure limits (PELs). PELs are normally expressed as time-weighted averages (TWAs), but may also be presented as short-term exposure limits (STELs). Other useful limits to be aware of are immediate danger to life and health (IDLH) and threshold limit value—ceiling (TLV-C). IDLH is a fairly clear descriptor, and TLV-C serves to define an upper limit of safe exposure in specific circumstances.

3.4.2.1.3 National Institute for Occupational Safety and Health The research arm of OSHA, the National Institute for Occupational Safety and Health (NIOSH) is focused on recommendations for workplace safety and is therefore closely related to the regulatory side. Both OSHA and NIOSH were created in 1970 with the Occupational Safety and Health Act. NIOSH does not engage in enforcement activities but rather provides information and alerts regarding newly identified or recognized occupational hazards.

3.4.2.1.4 Odor Threshold Odor threshold is an interesting parameter in that people generally associate or correlate the degree to which an odor is disagreeable with an expectation of toxicity. Such a link is clearly valid for many noxious compounds, where the sense of smell can be a reliable indicator of potential hazard. However, for many other compounds, the level at which they can be detected by odor is already potentially hazardous or even lethal (e.g., phosgene). Similarly, some compounds humans find particularly disagreeable (e.g., putrescine, cadaverine, and skatole) present no significant toxic hazard.

3.4.2.2 Epidemiological Studies

The evaluation of populations for abnormal levels of disease, expression of toxic symptoms, or other definable symptomology has a long history of successfully identifying environments or locations with an unexpected or previously unrecognized toxic potential. Such studies can be useful in either identifying an unanticipated exposure to a recognized toxin or chemical agent, or of the identification of a region or population with unexpected levels of a particular disease or symptoms. Such identification of "population clusters" can ultimately lead to the recognition of a previously unrecognized toxin or hazardous location (e.g., Agent Orange, or dioxin, from defoliants used in Vietnam; "Love Canal" an industrial waste dump site in upstate New York).

3.4.2.3 Individual Symptoms/Behaviors

3.4.2.3.1 Medical Evaluation

The evaluation of a patient's medical condition as part of an emergency response, triage, or routine medical examination or treatment can provide a tremendous amount of information useful for the toxicologist. (See Section 3.5.)

3.4.2.3.2 Field Sobriety/Drug Effects Testing In the world of forensic toxicology, considerable resources are devoted to the prosecution of DUI cases, whether the impairment is caused by alcohol or other drugs. Commonly, in such cases, the behavior of the driver in question will be evaluated to some degree. Depending on the circumstances, this evaluation might be the administration of the Standardized Field Sobriety Tests or a more exhaustive evaluation of physiological parameters performed by a drug recognition expert. In some cases, only a limited description of the driving behavior, resulting in the detention of the suspect, or their behavior during the arrest process may be available. Often, the behaviors can be used in conjunction with testing to support or refute the contention of impaired driving. Other cases may have no characterization of driving ability other than the fact that a collision occurred.

3.4.2.4 *Characterization of Toxin Levels*

Historically, blood drug levels have been qualified as subtherapeutic, therapeutic, toxic, or lethal. While the designations are not absolute, this system is widely used within the medical, postmortem, and toxicologic communities. It is also generally understood that for many drugs, the commonly published values may not represent exact and clear boundaries between categories. A level of morphine, for example, that may provide analgesia in one individual may cause potentially life-threatening respiratory depression in another. Unfortunately, within the legal world, the designations are often (albeit incorrectly) considered as being absolute, with the implication that a subtherapeutic level of a drug can never provide any of the desired effect, and similarly, a level in the so-called toxic range must cause toxic symptoms. Unfortunately, the converse argument is often raised as well, that a drug level in the therapeutic range cannot have contributed to either undesirable side effects (e.g., impairment of driving ability) or (in the extreme) the death of an individual. Hence, for the toxicologist, the classification of drug levels as subtherapeutic, therapeutic, toxic, or lethal may be a useful guide, as an indicator of what might be the subject's toxicologic status, but should not be viewed as an absolute predictive basis for the response of the individual to the drug in question.

3.5 Medical Response

The response of medical personnel to a toxin-related illness can provide a great deal of useful information to the toxicologist attempting to understand the extent to which drugs or poisons may have contributed to the underlying illness. While the toxicologist may not be trained as a physician, the benefits of being familiar with the medical approach to toxic events can be of tremendous benefit.

3.5.1 Clinical Evaluation and Response

The approach of the medical community to an emergency, traumatic, or otherwise life-threatening situation is generally characterized as *evaluation, stabilization, management*, with evaluation being a dynamic and ongoing process that may change as information (e.g., history, laboratory findings) and patient responses to either stimuli or treatment are assessed. The specific treatment sequence in any case will vary with circumstance, patient, and physician. However, the assessment of the patient and the documentation of the evaluation/treatment process can provide useful information to the eventual evaluation of the role of a drug or poison in the event. Admittedly, while the quality of the documentation can vary between facilities and individuals, the general practice of extensive record-keeping and notes in the medical records can provide a wealth of useful information for the toxicologist.

3.5.1.1 *Evaluation/Stabilization*

Of primary importance in the emergency medical situation are the control of bleeding and ensuring that the patient is able to breathe and has adequate cardiac and CNS function (including control of seizures, if present). Addressing these areas will usually trump any further assessment procedures.

3.5.1.2 *Emergency Medical Technician Response*

The role of the emergency medical technician (EMT) usually involves a rapid evaluation of initial signs and symptoms and the establishment of priorities for patient stabilization. That first assessment and documentation of a potentially dynamic situation may be particularly useful in the determination of the time course of the effects of a drug or toxin. Vital signs will be collected or commented upon (e.g., pulse, respiration, blood pressure, assessment of consciousness). EMT documentation may be particularly useful in DUI cases with injured drivers who may have been impaired by drugs or ethanol at the time of the accident. In such cases, there may be no standard evaluation of behavior or driving ability by law enforcement personnel, and the EMT evaluation may be an important basis for a legal determination of impairment (or lack thereof).

3.5.1.3 *Consciousness Assessment*

The mental status of the patient is routinely assessed and is often documented by the Glasgow Coma Scale, or GCS (see Sidebar 3.1). The essence of this evaluation is a measure of the motor, verbal, and eye-opening response of the patient, with a numerical scale for each parameter and the overall sum serving as a general indication of the patient's mental status. The normal GCS score is 15.

SIDEBAR 3.1 GLASGOW COMA SCALE

The Glasgow Coma Scale (GCS) reflects an evaluation of consciousness and was initially introduced in 1974 at the University of Glasgow in Scotland as a means of evaluating cases of head injury. The assessment is now widely used by medical personnel as a means of documenting the mental status of a patient. The GCS provides an objective, reproducible way to assess the neurological condition of a patient. The scale ranges from a low score of 3, reflecting deep unconsciousness, to 15,

Table 3.3 Glasgow Coma Scale

Parameter	Result	Score
Eye response	No response	1
	Open to pain	2
	Open to command	3
	Open spontaneously	4
Verbal response	No sounds	1
	Incomprehensible	2
	Inappropriate words	3
	Confused speech/disoriented	4
	Talking/oriented	5
Motor response	No response	1
	Extension to pain	2
	Flexion to pain	3
	Withdraws from pain	4
	Localizes to pain	5
	Obeys command	6

representing normal function, as the sum of assessment scores of eye, verbal, and motor responses to stimuli, as shown in Table 3.3.

3.5.1.4 *History and Physical Examination*

The patient history and physical examination findings should be clearly documented in the medical records of the patient. While perhaps not of particular interest in acute toxicity cases, when there are questions regarding potential overdose, the medical history of an individual and information about their medications may be of great use. The basic vital signs, pulse rate, blood pressure, respiration rate, and temperature, can be as useful to the toxicologist in trying to understand the role a toxin may have played in a case as they are to the clinician in trying to provide care for the patient.

3.5.2 Patient Monitoring and Clinical Laboratory Testing

In many cases, whether the subject is living or dead, there may be records of medical care and testing available for evaluation. A familiarity with the generally monitored parameters, as well as clinical testing, at least in a general sense, is an useful skill for the toxicologist. A working knowledge of the meaning of several key test results can facilitate an understanding of the role that drugs or toxins may have played in the case. An example of a typical metabolic panel of testing is shown in Table 3.4.

Medical records generally contain a considerable amount of information, some of which may be relevant to the determination of the role a particular toxin may have played in the case. Consider a death in a hospital, several hours after the IV administration of a narcotic analgesic (e.g., morphine or hydromorphone). While a reasonable question may be raised regarding the role such drug may have played in the death, a chart annotation reflecting a routine check of the patient, including a respiration rate of 18 bpm (breaths per minute) taken one-half hour prior to the death would strongly suggest that the narcotic analgesic did not play a significant causative or contributory role (depressed respiratory rate is a characteristic effect of an overdose level of opiates; the normal respiratory rate suggests that overdose levels were not achieved). Clinical laboratory tests can provide useful system-based, objective, and reproducible information regarding cardiac damage and function (troponin, creatine kinase, EKG monitoring), hepatic damage (AST and ALT enzymes), renal function (urea nitrogen, creatinine), pulmonary status (pH, pCO_2, pO_2, bicarb, O_2 saturation), metabolic disturbance or metabolic poisons (anion gap, serum osmolality), as shown in Table 3.5.

Table 3.4 Clinical Testing; Typical Metabolic Panel

Analyte	Normal Range (Serum)
Sodium	(133–145 mmol/L)
Potassium	(3.3–5.1 mmol/L)
Chloride	(96–108 mmol/L)
Bicarbonate	(22–29 mmol/L)
Anion gap	(9–16 mmol/L)
Glucose, random	(70–105 mg/dL)
Urea nitrogen	(6–20 mg/dL)
Creatinine	(0.5–1.2 mg/dL)
Calcium	(8.4–10.2 mg/dL)
ALT (alanine aminotransferase)	(0–41 U/L)
AST (aspartate aminotransferase)	(0–38 U/L)
Alk phos	(39–117 U/L)
Total bilirubin	(0–1 mg/dL)
Total protein	(6–8.3 g/dL)
Albumin	(3.4–4.8 g/dL)
Albumin:globulin ratio	(0.6–1.5)
Magnesium	(1.6–2.4 mEq/L)
Phosphate	(2.4–4.5 mEq/L)
Lipase	(30–210 IU/L)
Serum osmolality	(289–308 mOsm/kg)
Amylase	(30–110 IU/L)

3.5.3 Toxidromes

A toxidrome is simply a collection of symptoms, characteristic or typical of a particular type of drug, toxin, or poison, generally reflecting a common underlying mechanism. The pattern of symptoms can guide the clinician toward treatment and the toxicologist toward identification of a specific drug or toxin. Some toxidromes can be easily defined, such as the opiate toxidrome, while

Table 3.5 Clinical Testing; Examples of System-Based Tests

Electrolytes and hydration	Sodium, potassium, chloride, bicarbonate, glucose, blood urea nitrogen (BUN), anion gap, creatinine
Liver function	Albumin, ammonia, total protein, alanine amino transferase (ALT), aspartate amino transferase (AST)
Kidney function	Albumin, bun, calcium, creatinine, magnesium, urinary protein
Cardiac function	Creatinine phosphokinase, troponin, creatine kinase-myocyte fraction
Coagulation	Partial prothromboplastin time (PTT), prothrombin time (PT), platelet count

others tend to be a little less well characterized and may share some symptoms with other toxidromes. The utility of this approach is that the medical response need not be drug-specific but can be toxidrome-specific. Hence, with a case of opiate poisoning, an opiate antagonist can be utilized, with no need for the specific identification of morphine, hydrocodone, methadone, or some other opiate. With regard to analysis, an understanding of the toxidrome can help guide the analytical process. For example, if a sympathomimetic amine (SMA) were suspected, the analyst might ensure that the method utilized could identify relatively small, volatile compounds, such as amphetamine, methylenedioxyamphetamine (MDA)/methylenedioxymethamphetamine (MDMA), and pseudoephedrine. The characteristics of six different toxidromes are described below.

3.5.3.1 *Cholinergic*

The cholinergic toxidrome is caused by drugs or poisons that result in an elevated level of the neurotransmitter acetylcholine (ACh) or other acetylcholine receptor agonists at nicotinic and muscarinic receptors. The expression of symptoms can vary somewhat, depending on the ratio of nicotinic versus muscarinic stimulation. The syndrome is characterized by CNS depression, seizures, hypertension, agitation, delirium, miosis (pinpoint pupils), fasciculations (muscle twitching), tremors, bradycardia, and coma. Cholinergic poisoning can be fatal and is the mechanism of action of organophosphate and carbamate insecticides, and a number of nerve gases. (e.g., VX and Sarin) The symptomology of the cholinergic toxidrome can be characterized by the mnemonic SLUDGE, salivation, lacrimation, urination, defecation, gastric sounds, emesis.

3.5.3.2 *Anticholinergic*

The anticholinergic toxidrome is caused by the presence of acetylcholine receptor antagonists (e.g., atropine, succinylcholine). Symptoms include dry mucus membranes, dry/warm and flushed skin, tachycardia, urinary retention, mydriasis (dilated pupils), constipation, seizures, and decreased or absent gastric sounds. Myoclonus (spasmodic muscle contractions) may be present as well. An old mnemonic for the toxidrome runs: "Hot as a hare, blind as a bat, red as a beet, mad as a hatter, dry as a bone, bowel and bladder lose their tone, and the heart runs on alone." The classic anticholinergic poison atropine is found in the "deadly nightshade" plant.

3.5.3.3 *Sympathomimetic*

The symptoms of the sympathomimetic toxidrome are basically those of an overabundance of stimulatory neurotransmitters. Psychotropic responses may include anxiety and delusion concurrent with physical symptoms including diaphoresis (excessive perspiration), hyperreflexia, mydriasis (pupil dilation), piloerection (goose bumps), and seizures. There may be serious cardiac issues associated with this toxidrome, including arrhythmias, tachycardia, and hypertension. Examples of substances that may cause this toxidrome include stimulants such as amphetamines and cocaine, as well as many of the newer synthetic drugs such as mephedrone and related species currently being sold as bath salts.

3.5.3.4 *Opiate*

Opiate toxicity is characterized by CNS and respiratory depression and miosis (pinpoint pupils). Pulmonary edema is characteristic, and as the toxic response deepens, there is a progressive deepening of coma, bradycardia, hypotension, hypothermia, respiratory acidosis, and death. While the classic opiates (morphine, codeine, and thebaine) are natural alkaloids, a number of semi-synthetic opioids bind to the same receptors as does morphine and are therefore capable of causing the same toxidrome. These opioids (e.g., hydrocodone and hydromorphone, oxycodone and oxymorphone) are structurally quite similar to morphine. A number of structures, apparently quite different from morphine (at least in the common 2-D representations), are nevertheless able to adopt a 3-D configuration similar to morphine, bind to the receptors, and thereby function as opiate agonists (e.g., meperidine, propoxyphene, fentanyl). Opiate toxicity can be readily reversed by opiate receptor antagonists such as naloxone, and such reversal is diagnostic of the toxidrome.

3.5.3.5 *Hallucinogenic*

The symptoms of a hallucinogenic toxidrome reflect an impact on CNS function such that perception of reality is significantly distorted. Hallucinations are most commonly visual but may also be auditory or involve other senses as well. Hallucinations may be accompanied by seizures, paranoia, panic, and self-destructive behavior (e.g., trying to fly). Lysergic acid diethylamide (LSD) is an archetypal hallucinogenic agent; however, hallucinations have been associated with some SMAs as well. Phencyclidine and ketamine are examples of dissociative anesthetics and often also classified as a hallucinogenic, primarily as a function of their ability to produce a sense of separation of the consciousness from the corporeal body of the user.

THC, or marijuana, is also currently commonly classified as a hallucinogen (and we will treat it as such in this text). However, the classification is somewhat unsatisfactory, in that the drug is not commonly associated with hallucinations and certainly has some sedative activities. It is not inconceivable that with the increased activities of legalization (or at least tolerance of use), and the appearance of more functional analogs of the drug, that a new category of "cannabimimetics" may come into common use.

3.5.3.6 *Sedative-Hypnotic*

The symptoms of sedative-hypnotic toxidrome are consistent with a depressant effect on the CNS system. These include a progressive, dose-dependent lack of muscle control coordination and cognitive ability, ultimately leading to coma and potentially death, as respirations and cardiac functions are depressed and then cease. Other symptoms associated with this type of toxin include confusion, stupor, delirium, and slurred speech. This syndrome can be caused by a wide variety of agents, with ethyl alcohol being the archetype and most commonly encountered. Some other compounds and drug classes causing the sedative-hypnotic toxidrome are the benzodiazepines, barbiturates, γ-hydroxybutyric acid (GHB), marijuana (THC), and methaqualone. Interestingly, while most sedative-hypnotic compounds are effective as anticonvulsants, some actually lower the seizure threshold and may facilitate or cause seizures when present at toxic levels.

3.5.4 Antidotes

Antidotes are chemicals that by the nature of their biochemical action negate, inactivate, block, or otherwise reverse the actions of specific toxins in the body. A number of examples of antidotes are shown in Table 3.6. Some compounds act directly to block the toxic response, such as the opiate antagonist naloxone. Opiates affect their physiologic response by binding to and activating specific receptors in the body. Naloxone, while structurally quite similar to the archetypal opiate morphine, can bind to the opiate receptors, but its structure does not allow the receptor to carry out the biological transformations that would result in opiate toxicity. While bound to the receptor, naloxone blocks opiate binding and is "protective." The reversal of opiate toxic effects by naloxone can be extremely rapid and seem almost miraculous. However, the serum half-life of naloxone is shorter than most opiates. Therefore, the opiate-intoxicated patient must be monitored for recurring symptoms and redosed accordingly until the opiate is metabolized.

Table 3.6 Antidote Examples

Condition	Antidote
Organophosphate insecticide or nerve gas	Atropine/pralidoxime
Acetaminophen	N-acetylcysteine
Benzodiazepines	Flumazenil
Carbon monoxide	Hyperbaric oxygen
Cyanide	Amyl nitrite
Digoxin	Digoxin fab antibody
Ethylene glycol	Ethanol
Heavy metals	Chelating agents, e.g., EDTA
Iron	Desferoxamine
Opiates	Naloxone
Serotonin syndrome	Cyproheptadine

Antidotes can also act indirectly, as is the case with n-acetylcysteine, used to treat an overdose of acetaminophen. A toxic metabolite of acetaminophen is conjugated (and thereby detoxified) by reaction with glutathione. In cases of severe acetaminophen exposure, the body's supply and ability to regenerate glutathione can become depleted. N-acetylcysteine stimulates the production of glutathione and can directly conjugate with the toxic metabolite (N-acetyl-p-quinonimine) as well.

3.5.5 Decontamination

There are a number of processes for both internal and external toxin decontamination. *Internal decontamination* is normally used in reference to materials that are still present in the lungs or GI tract. Once a toxin has crossed into the circulation, *biotransformation*, *metabolism*, and *elimination* are more commonly used terms to describe the removal of toxins from the body. Decontamination of the external surfaces of the body can be a trivial issue of soap and water, or an extremely serious problem, in the case of transdermally absorbed toxins, such as organophosphate insecticides and nerve agents. Decontamination protocols are dependent upon the toxic agent, and the materials (such as binders and surfactants) that may also be present. Removal of materials from the GI tract can be accomplished by a number of mechanisms. Induction of emesis (vomiting), while historically an accepted practice, is no longer considered a viable method for decontamination because of the risk of complications, including aspiration of emesis with the possibility of asphyxiation or subsequent chemically induced bronchopneumonia. More accepted is the practice of orogastric lavage (stomach pumping), which consists of passing a tube into the stomach and repeated withdrawing of the contents by suction, with sequential rinsing. Obviously, orogastric lavage is not effective if compounds have passed on to the intestine. Another approach to detoxification is to pass a solution of activated charcoal into the stomach. This material has a large capacity for binding organic materials, thereby precluding their absorption into the body.

Whole bowel irrigation is a mechanism for the removal of toxins that have progressed beyond the stomach. Other techniques for removing toxins from the body include ion trapping, in which the pH of the urine is adjusted to favor the ionized form of toxic species, thereby precluding their resorption by the body and enhancing their rate of elimination in the urine; and dialysis and hemoperfusion, which can directly remove toxins from the blood, driven by gradient-based diffusion across semipermeable membranes.

REVIEW QUESTIONS

1. Briefly distinguish between potentiation, additive, synergistic, and antagonism effect between drugs.
2. Both short-acting benzodiazepines and inhaled anesthetic gases can be used to provide anesthesia. Benzodiazepines can be used medically in the outpatient setting and for dental procedures; however, inhaled anesthetics (e.g., halothane) must be utilized by a trained anesthesiologist. Briefly discuss a reasonable basis for the distinction in terms of therapeutic index.
3. Briefly distinguish between a hypersensitive, an idiosyncratic, and a side effect reaction to a drug.
4. Consider an experiment in drug design. A new opiate analgesic has been developed, and an experiment to determine its effectiveness has been designed. The parameter being tested is a variation of a "hot pad" test in which a rat is placed on a surface just warm enough to be uncomfortable for the animal. If the rat moves off the hot pad within 4 seconds of being placed, the response is considered no analgesia. More than 4 seconds is considered analgesia. Based on structure activity information, an effective dose was expected to be ~50 μg/kg. Eight groups of 20 rats each were tested. Group, dose (ug/kg), and number of animals displaying analgesia were as follows: 1, 0, 0; 2, 15, 1; 3, 30, 4; 4, 40, 13; 5, 50, 17; 6, 60, 19; 7, 75, 20; 8, 100, 20. Based on this data, what would you estimate the ED_{50} for analgesia of the new compound to be?
5. Glucose is regularly employed as a quick fix for insulin-induced hypoglycemia. Would you consider that an antidote? Why or why not?

TOPICS FOR DISCUSSION

1. Discuss the status of unregulated herbal medications with regard to the potential for unexpected toxic consequences.
2. Should heavy metals be considered as a toxidrome? Why or why not?
3. Should emergency medical personnel evaluation of intoxication be used in the legal system? Why or why not?
4. What key symptoms can be used to differentiate the toxidromes discussed in the text?
5. Many people are concerned with the risks associated with industrial chemicals and food additives. Identify a compound of concern and evaluate the reality of risk, based on realistic estimates of dose and exposure mechanisms.

Bibliography

Adams JG, editor. *Emergency Medicine.* 1st ed. Philadelphia: Saunders/Elsevier, 2008.

Brent J, Phillips SD, Wallace KL, Burkhart KK, Donovan JW. *Critical Care Toxicology: Diagnosis and Management of the Critically Poisoned Patient.* 1st ed. St. Louis: Mosby, 2005.

Dart RC, editor. *Medical Toxicology.* 3rd rev. ed. Philadelphia: Lippincott Williams & Wilkins, 2004.

Fenton JJ. *Toxicology: A Case-Oriented Approach.* Boca Raton, FL: CRC Press, 2002.

Marx JA, Hockberger RS, Walls RM. *Rosen's Emergency Medicine: Concepts and Clinical Practice, v. 3.* 6th rev. ed. Philadelphia: Mosby/Elsevier, 2006.

Nelson LS, Lewin N, Howland MA, Hoffman R, Goldfrank L, Flomenbaum N, editors. *Goldfrank's Toxicologic Emergencies.* 9th rev. ed. New York: McGraw Hill Medical, 2011.

Toxicokinetics

4

Contents

4.1 Introduction

One can think of toxicology as being a science focusing on the abnormal or altered functions of the body as a drug or a poison interacts with or distorts the normal chemical processes. These interactions produce physiologic and pathologic consequences that would not normally arise in the absence of the drug. Toxicology is, in essence therefore, a study of "broken biochemistry." The consequences of drug or toxin action are expressed as a function of the physical actions and responses of the body and are therefore physiologic and pathologic. The factors controlling the magnitude of the effects of drugs are pharmacologic. Toxicology is therefore a unifying science in that aspects of many disciplines are involved and essential in nearly all aspects of the field:

Mechanism: Biochemical
Expression: Physiologic/pathologic
Magnitude: Pharmacologic

4.2 Basic Definitions

Some useful basic definitions are

Pharmacokinetics: the biochemical fate of drugs in the body and the biochemical processes affecting that fate

Pharmacodynamics: the impact of the drug on the physiologic and biochemical processes in the body

Toxicokinetics: pharmacokinetics of drugs and poisons

4.3 Fate of Drugs and Poisons in the Body

Many of the interpretative issues that the forensic toxicologist has to deal with involve questions about the amount of drug that was in a body at a particular time. Often the amount that has been delivered into the body (by whatever means) is known, but sometimes not. Nevertheless, in many cases, useful information or inferences can be derived based on what information is known, deduced or hypothesized based on an understanding of what can happen to drugs and toxins as they pass through and interact with living systems. The fate of drugs in the body is commonly viewed as the sum of the processes of *absorption* (the processes by which drugs and poisons are brought into the blood and cells of body), *distribution* (the processes by which drugs and poisons are moved around the body and taken up into organs and tissues), *metabolism* (the processes by which drugs and poisons are biochemically altered or broken down), and *elimination* (the processes by which drugs and poisons are removed from the body). The sum of these processes is often abbreviated as ADME.

4.4 Blood as the Central Factor

Excluding localized effects (such as a response to a chemical irritant, e.g., an acid or caustic burn on the skin), for a toxin to have an effect on the body, it must achieve transit into the blood. The blood provides the transit mechanism for the drug to reach the target tissue(s). There are numerous ways to get chemicals into the body, the most common being ingestion or injection. Inhalation can be both an effective way to deliver drugs to the body and a means for unwanted toxins to reach the bloodstream. Inhalation is often an exposure route for environmental toxins (e.g., carbon monoxide) as well as deadly poisons such as nerve gas (e.g., the organophosphate sarin). The common factor for virtually all the absorptive mechanisms is that the only way into the body involves transit across one or more functional cellular membrane systems, ultimately reaching the circulating blood. Further, the only route for many drugs to the tissues they affect following transit in the blood is membrane transit into the target tissue. It is important to bear in mind that for many drug species (those ionized at physiologic pH), an energy barrier (the charge on the cellular membrane) precludes the passage of a drug from the blood into the cells of a target tissue, and in the absence of an energetically favorable way past that barrier, no net transit from the blood will occur (see Sidebar 4.1).

SIDEBAR 4.1 MEMBRANES: STRUCTURE AND FUNCTION

Membranes, in the most simplistic sense, separate the interior of cells and cellular organelles from the exterior of those structures. The basic membrane structure is a two-layer system, composed of phospholipids, with various protein and glycoprotein functional inclusions. Typical membrane composition is ~50% of the volume of the cell. The hydrophilic phospholipid "heads" form the membrane exterior and interior face, while the hydrophobic lipid "tails" form the interior space of the membrane, as shown in Figure 4.1. Membranes are biochemically dynamic, acting to transport materials in and out via specific transport proteins and thereby actively controlling the influx and efflux of biological molecules, maintaining a charge on the membrane (localized variations in the membrane charge form the basis of neurotransmission) and facilitating cell–cell communication. The cellular membrane is the location of active receptor molecules that, when activated by a molecule that "fits" the receptor, can produce a biochemical response. Membranes also contain pores through which water is able to traverse. From a toxicologic perspective, four key features stand out. First is the *aquaporin* pore structures that allow equilibration of water in and out of the cell (and an equally facile route for small molecules of similar polarity, e.g., methanol and ethanol). Second is the membrane charge, and mechanisms associated with maintenance of that charge (and in the neurological system, is the point of action of a great number of toxins). Third is the receptor functions, and again, many toxins act via cell membrane receptors. Finally, the recognition and uptake of a number of drugs by membrane uptake molecules is the mechanism by which cells can achieve the concentrations of drugs necessary to carry out biotransformation and elimination of the drug.

4.5 Routes in, Routes Out

The sum total of motion of drugs into, around, and through the body is characterized in the acronym ADME, as outlined above: absorption, distribution, metabolism, elimination. These processes are discreetly definable, but functionally contemporaneous in that all can occur at the same time. As soon as a drug starts to appear in the blood as it is absorbed into and distributed around the body, it becomes available for uptake by or (depending on the ionic character of the drug) diffusion into cells. Similarly, as soon as a drug appears in a tissue with the necessary enzymatic systems for its chemical transformation or breakdown, those biochemical processes can begin as well (see Chapter 5). Finally, to the extent that the drug can be excreted, either unchanged or altered by the processes of metabolism and biotransformation, the process of elimination occurs. Absorption tends to be completed more rapidly than distribution, metabolism may continue long after the drug has been initially distributed around the body, and elimination

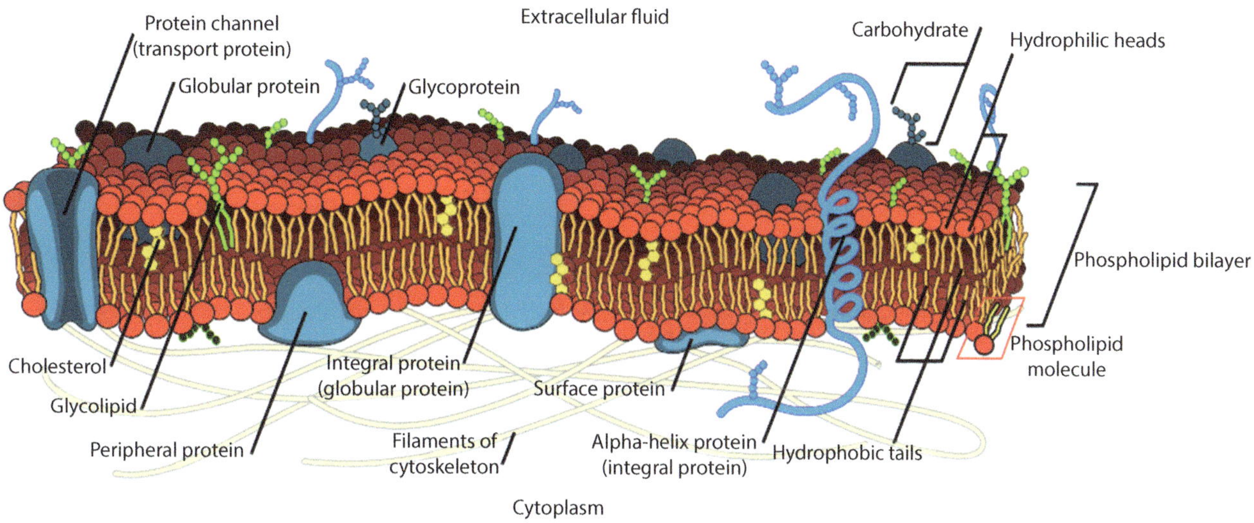

Figure 4.1 Cellular membrane. (Mariana Ruiz Villarreal; public domain.)

goes on until the drug has been completely removed from the body.

4.5.1 Absorption

4.5.1.1 Mechanisms of Absorption

Cells can receive drugs or toxins from an extracellular matrix in a number of ways (be it blood, air, gastric fluid, or other medium). Materials coming into the cell from a higher concentration may simply diffuse into the cell downgradient (depending on their electronic structure) or transit membrane pores if small enough. Molecules for which the energy required to transit the membrane exceeds the driving force of the concentration gradient or are being actively concentrated by a specific tissue must be brought into the cells by special transport mechanisms. Larger size particles, either solid or liquid, are actively engulfed by special cells to facilitate the uptake and transport of materials into cells of the body.

4.5.1.1.1 Passive Transport Perhaps the most intuitive and obvious mechanism of drug transfer into the cell is simple diffusion of a drug through the cellular membrane into the cellular interior. This process is known as *passive transport* and is essentially concentration and solubility driven diffusion. The absorption of tetrahydrocannabinol (THC) into cells, and ultimately its preferential concentration in hydrophobic regions of the body, is a reflection of its neutral, lipophilic character. One important point to note is that diffusion based on solubility is somewhat of a one-way street, in that the diffusion coefficient is simply a function of concentration and solubility. Hence, a drug that is preferentially distributed into lipophilic tissues in life has no reason to "leave" those tissues after death, unless the nature of those tissues is changed. Drugs that are concentrated as a function of passive transport do not then generally exhibit postmortem redistribution (a phenomenon wherein drugs concentrated in specific tissues during life reequilibrate in the body after death; see Section 4.5.2.1.2.2).

4.5.1.1.2 Filtration Filtration, the motion of molecules through specific membrane pores, is analogous to passive transport in that the rate of the process is driven by gradient-based diffusion. Generally, the pores (actually, specific proteins creating a channel in the cellular membrane) are small enough such that molecules >100 dal are excluded. The classic example of this phenomenon is the equilibration of ethanol in the total body water, which occurs because ethanol is able to transit the aquaporin family of transmembrane water channels. The process is totally driven by gradient-based diffusion, and after distribution has occurred throughout the body, redistribution is a process of equilibration as ethanol is metabolized in the liver.

4.5.1.1.3 Special Transport (Receptor Mediated)

4.5.1.1.3.1 Active Transport The specific binding and subsequent transport of drugs into the cellular body is a complex and fascinating area of protein and glycoprotein function. Such transport uses energy (usually in the form of ATP) to bring molecules into the cell against a concentration gradient (see Sidebar 4.2). This energy-dependent function allows certain drugs to be concentrated in specific tissues. This protein-mediated transport process provides the cell with a mechanism to bypass the membrane charge, which makes the simple diffusion of ionic species energetically unfavorable. This

SIDEBAR 4.2 DRUG UPTAKE PROTEINS

Much of the early investigation into drug uptake was focused on the *ATP binding cassette* group of proteins, a superfamily of transporters that function to translocate a variety of materials into cells and cellular organelles. These transmembrane proteins use the energy of ATP hydrolysis as the driving force for the conformational changes that allow a drug binding on the exterior face to be brought to the interior of the cell by simply a shape change of the protein. Recently a number of other membrane transport protein families have been identified, including two "solute carrier" groups, capable of transport of type 1 (small) organic anions, cations, and zwitterions (containing both positive and negative charges on different parts of the molecule) and type 2 (large) organic cations. The significance for the toxicologist may be twofold. First, the dedicated transport mechanisms reflected in specific membrane-based transport protein provides elevated basis for the concentrations of drugs in specific tissues (e.g., liver). For enzymatic processes, such concentrations may be essential to achieving biotransformation of the drug, depending on the Km (a measure of the ability of a drug to bind to an enzyme catalytic site) of the enzyme capable of carrying out the rate-limiting step of metabolism. If the blood concentration at therapeutic (or even toxic) levels is less than the Km, then an appreciable biotransformation rate cannot be achieved and elimination of the unmodified drug will be the only mechanism for alleviation of the toxic response. If, on the other hand, the drug can be translocated into cells containing the enzymes necessary for catalysis, at concentrations near or above the Km, then biotransformation can play a significant role in the modification or elimination of the drug. Such concentration then also plays a significant role in building up the antemortem gradient which, after death, may reequilibrate throughout the body in the process we refer to as postmortem redistribution. Finally, as the genetics of the transporters and their drug specificity become increasingly elucidated, we may find in the expression of specific transport proteins an additional genetic factor affecting the way in which we as individuals handle, process, and eliminate certain drugs. Along these lines, the ability of compounds to inhibit drug transport may also provide some additional explanation for drug–drug interaction by mechanisms other than agonism or antagonism of drug receptors.

mechanism can build up the concentration of drugs within tissues to a degree considerably larger than is present in the blood, and is therefore the mechanism by which the body achieves the high ratio of some drugs between tissues and the blood.

4.5.1.1.3.2 Facilitated Transport In contrast to the energy-utilizing mechanism described above, facilitated transport provides glycoprotein binding and a protein-mediated route into the cell for specific drugs, but does not use energy and does not occur against a concentration gradient.

4.5.1.1.4 Endocytosis Endocytosis is a complex multistep process whereby molecules binding to specific proteins on the cellular surface become "engulfed" in an inward folding pit in the cellular membrane. This section of membrane becomes internalized in the cell, ultimately dissociating from the membrane proper, and becoming a vesicle within the cell, called an *endosome*. While the process can occur at the molecular level, it can also occur on a larger scale, allowing the cell to ingest solids and liquids, in processes known as phagocytosis and pinocytosis, respectively.

4.5.1.2 Factors Affecting Absorption

The rate of absorption of a drug or toxin is dependent upon a large number of factors involving the drug, the delivery mechanism, and the tissue(s) serving as a barrier to absorption. Some of the most significant factors are the degree of blood perfusion and the ability of the drug to diffuse or be transported across the barrier membranes. For any drug to transit a membrane based on diffusion, there will be a number of determinants for the rate of passive flux, including (but not limited to) molecular size, the pH of the region, pK of the drug, amount of exposed area, concentration, and lipophilicity of the drug. Protein-based transport will be affected by the number and nature of transport molecules, the affinity of the drug for those proteins, and the availability of energy to facilitate the transport process.

4.5.1.2.1 Factors Affecting Absorption from the Gastrointestinal Tract The most common manner of dosing of drugs and medicinal compounds is probably formulations provided in pills, capsules, or tablets. However, numerous factors affect the degree to which a drug will be absorbed from the GI tract and subsequently appear in the general circulation. Most drug delivery systems are designed so that the drug survives transit through the stomach and is liberated in the small intestine, where the bulk of absorption occurs. The rate of gastric emptying can affect the rate in which a drug reaches the circulation. The rate of pill, tablet, or capsule dissolution and solubilization of the contents will also affect the amount and rate at which a drug will be absorbed. The intestinal wall is biochemically active, and the ability of the drug to survive enzymatic activity there will also be a factor in the amount of drug reaching the circulation.

4.5.1.2.2 Factors Affecting Absorption from the Lungs Delivery of drugs to the lungs can result in rapid and effective transfer of a significant amount of drug to the bloodstream in a very short time period. The lungs can be viewed as a physiologically optimized system for the diffusion-based transit of small molecules to and from the gaseous (air) to liquid (blood) phase. More specifically, oxygen is transferred downgradient into the blood, while carbon dioxide diffuses downgradient out of the blood and into the air in the lungs. Small neutral molecules can be effectively introduced into the blood via this route, as well as larger, more complex molecules such as cocaine, nicotine, THC, inhaled anesthetics, and so forth. The lungs combine a high surface area with a rapid and efficient blood turnover, thus maximizing the concentration gradient between inhaled air/drug and the blood. Factors limiting drug delivery are a function of the basic capacity of the lungs themselves, including the surface area of the diffusible surface, volume, and rate of gaseous turnover (respiratory rate). A compromised pulmonary system (e.g., as a consequence of edema, emphysema, or asthma) will be less able to readily transfer oxygen in and carbon dioxide out, and correspondingly less able to serve as an effective transit medium for other drugs and other compounds contained in the inspired air. In a general sense, larger functional surface area and rapid blood turnover facilitates absorption of drugs from the inspired air.

4.5.1.2.3 Factors Affecting Absorption from the Skin Transdermal absorption is generally the least effective means of getting a drug into the body. Any drug must cross several cell layers in the skin to reach the blood. The skin comprises both a physical barrier (dead and desiccated cells—the *stratum corneum*) and a biochemical barrier (the living cells of the epidermis, dermis, and vasculature wall). Factors that will be significant (albeit highly variable) in affecting the degree and rate of absorption include the lipid solubility of the drug, the degree of hydration of the skin, and the availability of surface-active agents, or solvents (e.g., dimethylsulfoxide [DMSO], acetone, dichloromethane, ethanol) that may serve to facilitate the diffusion of drug through the skin into the blood. Transdermal drug delivery systems attempt to minimize the variability of the process and to provide a controlled rate of transfer. Several transdermal drug delivery systems have been commercially used for such diverse drugs as scopolamine, nicotine, morphine, and fentanyl.

4.5.1.3 *Drug Delivery Mechanisms*

Each of the many methods for getting a drug into the body has its advantages and disadvantages. However, the ability to provide a well-characterized dose of a drug in the body is an essential part of modern pharmaceutical-based medicine. From a toxicologic perspective, knowledge of the mechanism by which a particular drug was delivered may be useful in forming conclusions regarding likely or possible levels in the body at some time after the dose.

4.5.1.3.1 Pills, Potions, and Elixirs (Tablets and Oral Formulations) Perhaps the easiest way to get a drug (or toxin) into the body is to swallow it. Pills were originally made by hand and were generally spherical. The term *pill* has stuck, however, and is now used colloquially to describe tablets, capsules, and caplets, all of which are designed to deliver a standardized or at least characterized amount of drug on a per unit basis. From a toxicologic perspective, the advantage of commercially prepared medicines, be they tablets, capsules,* or caplets, is the expectation of a readily identified and well-characterized dose. Oral formulations, if in their original containers, are equally easily identified. Some of the more interesting dose-delivery systems include lollipops containing drugs, indwelling drug pumps (see Sidebar 4.4) and aerosolized drug delivery units. Historically a number of elixirs have been used as drug vehicles for which the high percentage of alcohol may have been a factor in their commercial success.

4.5.1.3.2 Injections The most immediate and direct mechanism for delivery of drugs into the body is injection. Most commonly used are intramuscular and intravenous (often via an indwelling catheter or IV line). Intravenous administration produces a direct and immediate concentration of drug in the circulating blood, whereas with intramuscular, the drug must

* Capsules are generally formed of gelatin and contain a medication dose in powdered form. Capsules can be taken apart and the contents amended, adulterated, or switched entirely. Capsules are no longer used to formulate over-the-counter (OTC) medications because of a poisoning event that occurred in 1982. Specifically, Tylenol capsules in the Chicago area were contaminated with potassium cyanide, resulting in a number of deaths. No culprit was ever definitively identified. As a result, caplets became the preferred delivery formulation for OTC medications, and the US Food and Drug Administration adopted stringent packaging safety regulations.

pass through multiple membranes and pores to reach the circulation. Direct arterial injection also achieves essentially instantaneous transfer of a drug from outside the body to the inside, but in contrast to an IV dose, the blood is headed away from the central core and "distribution center" (the heart) toward the periphery. Other injection sites can include subcutaneous, intradermal, directly into cavity spaces, (e.g., the peritoneal, or abdominal cavity) or cerebral-spinal fluid (CSF).

4.5.1.3.3 Inhalable Preparations Delivery of drugs via an inhaler is well accepted, particularly for such medical issues as asthma, and is the basis for much of general anesthesia. The relatively quick transit of inhaled drugs into the bloodstream makes inhalation an effective means of drug delivery. Inhalation is a significant route for many poisons including cyanide, pesticides, and of course nicotine and the carcinogenic compounds associated with smoking. The advantage of this delivery system is that an almost instantaneous dose of drug can be delivered with a minimum of inconvenience on the part of the user. The circulation from the lung leads back to the heart, then via arterial flow throughout the body, bypassing hepatic first-pass metabolism (see Sidebar 4.3). A disadvantage of this system can be the irregularity of delivery (which of course is just fine for as-needed medications such as asthma inhalers).

SIDEBAR 4.3 FIRST-PASS METABOLISM

One aspect of the mechanism by which drugs can be delivered into the system is the phenomenon known as *first-pass* metabolism. Basically, this is simply a function of whether or not the drug must pass through the liver (the primary organ for the breakdown of foreign substances—e.g., drugs—in the body) before being distributed throughout the circulation. Drugs that are ingested and pass through into the intestine are absorbed into the vascular system and then flow, via the portal vein, into the liver. Depending on the drug, there may be essentially no breakdown of the drug in the liver, or conversely, there may be extensive metabolism and loss of an effective medication (from one perspective) and detoxification of a potentially dangerous substance (from another perspective). The susceptibility of drugs to first-pass metabolism is the reason some drugs are only given IV and some abused drugs are generally only insufflated or injected (e.g., cocaine, heroin). Interestingly enough, even though most drug metabolism occurs in the liver, there is a considerable capability for the lungs to carry out some metabolic reactions, and there can be first-pass metabolism there as well (although the term is normally used with reference to the liver).

4.5.1.3.4 Transdermal: Salves and Patches Transdermal drug delivery systems are elegantly simple mechanisms to achieve a (more or less) controlled, topical administration of a drug. Commonly referred to as a *patch*, this approach has been used for a variety of drugs, including scopolamine for motion sickness, fentanyl and morphine for analgesia, nicotine, clonidine, methylphenidate, among many others. There are several approaches to the drug delivery, including single or multiple layers containing drug, a fluid reservoir or a semisolid suspension contained in an adhesive structure, and a semipermeable membrane placed next to the skin, through which the drug diffuses. The advantage of such systems is a relatively consistent delivery of the drug over a long time period. In addition, depending on the location of the device, the drug may reach the heart prior to the liver and, as such, not be subject to the first-pass metabolism that characterizes drugs entering the body through the GI tract. Of interest and concern to the toxicologist is the potential for an excessive amount of a drug to be delivered in a manner inconsistent with the anticipated medical use. This may include either deliberate or accidental overdose. The essential simplicity of the transdermal devices provides some safeguard against malfunction, in a general sense, but such innocent actions as placing a heating pad over the device and placement of multiple devices, or even extraction of the contents for abuse purposes, can result in inappropriate and even overdose levels.

4.5.1.3.5 Alternate Drug Delivery Systems The field of drug delivery is continually growing and developing. More drugs can be expected to be available in nontraditional delivery mechanisms, and consideration of the variability in delivery may be significant in understanding drug levels in individual cases. While continued growth and change can be expected in trans- and subdermal methods, many variations of implantable drug delivery systems (pumps) are available, wherein the drug reservoir lies within the body and delivers the drug at a constant rate, or at a specific schedule, and can usually be recharged externally. Knowing that such a system is in place can be of great significance when attempting to determine cause and manner of death. For example, a high level of a drug in the blood after death may not be the result of an overdose during life, but rather simply a reflection of continued action of the pump after death (see Sidebar 4.4).

SIDEBAR 4.4 INTRATHECAL MORPHINE PUMP

A number of years ago we had the opportunity of working on an interesting case involving an apparent lethal overdose of morphine. The decedent was a 57-year-old female who weighed just over 200 lbs. and had suffered chronic back pain. The woman had a long history of opiate use (no indication of any abuse problems) and at the time of her death was receiving morphine via an indwelling intrathecal morphine pump, which delivered morphine directly to the space around the spinal cord. Her medical history was significant for a number of cardiac issues, such that a sudden cardiac event would not have been an unreasonable explanation for her death. However, a postmortem femoral blood morphine level was determined to be ~2.0 mg/L, and there was approximately a day between death and autopsy. No clear anatomic cause of death (COD) was determined at autopsy. Approximately three days prior to the death, the morphine pump had been refilled, a process by which morphine is essentially injected directly into a reservoir fill port on the device via syringe. The family concluded that the physician responsible for the pump had overfilled the device, causing it to deliver excessive amounts of morphine, resulting in the overdose and death. No flaw in the device was identified, nevertheless, a significant lawsuit was initiated.

Our involvement in the case was relatively brief. In essence, we asked the question: "Who turned off the pump?" The answer, of course, was no one, and so a reasonable explanation for the death was that in the time between the (presumably cardiac-event caused) death and the removal of the pump at autopsy, enough morphine had been delivered into the central lower abdominal region to diffuse to the point where femoral blood was collected, leading to the elevated level.

4.5.1.4 Bioavailability

Bioavailability is simply the proportion of a drug dose that actually reaches the circulation. The bioavailability of an IV- or intra-arterially (IA)-injected drug will be (at least at the time of injection) 100%. Other factors and processes will start to diminish that number immediately, but nevertheless, the reasonable expectation is that all of the drug contained in an IV or IA injection reaches the bloodstream relatively instantaneously. This 100% injection value provides a point of comparison for the evaluation of the efficiency of other methods of drug delivery.

4.5.1.4.1 Measures of Bioavailability

4.5.1.4.1.1 Blood Drug Level One commonly used measure of bioavailability is simply the concentration of that drug in blood or serum. The underlying (but often inaccurate) assumption is that the concentration of drugs is relatively stable, representing a steady state in the body. With the dynamic and overlapping processes of absorption, distribution, metabolism, and elimination, a single blood level of a drug, while representing a legitimate snapshot of drug concentration at that point in time, is not terribly useful in generating a comprehensive picture of drug level in the individual over a longer period. Such single-point information may be all that is available in many cases (with the additional problem that some cases will also have blood drug levels determined in samples collected after death—these with their own, special set of potential problems and confounders). It is important to recognize that a single measured time point may not provide a true reflection of the ongoing drug status of the individual, particularly if unabsorbed materials remain in the GI tract or if the individual was redosed shortly after the sample is collected. The blood level may represent a peak value, and that fact may be of considerable significance in many cases, for example, driving under the influence (DUI) and drug-facilitated sexual assault (DFSA). The key point is that in the absence of dosing information, the prudent toxicologist should be cautious and thoughtful about the conclusions they may draw based on a single point of blood drug information.

4.5.1.4.1.2 Area under the Curve A parameter commonly used in clinical toxicology (although somewhat less frequently in forensic toxicology) is a plot of blood drug concentration versus time, which can provide a useful expression of the availability and concentration in the body. The area of such a figure is known as the *area under the concentration curve* or simply *area under the curve*, abbreviated AUC. AUC is the integrated concentration versus time area. This very useful value provides both an opportunity to evaluate different doses and dose patterns in a patient in a clinical setting, yet also provides a basis for determination of changes in the ability of an individual to absorb, metabolize, and eliminate a drug. AUC is reflective of effective exposure to a drug and provides the basis for comparison within and between dosage schemes (e.g., pill vs. injection). When used in comparison to IV/IA measurements (100% bioavailability) one can calculate the fraction of a dose that

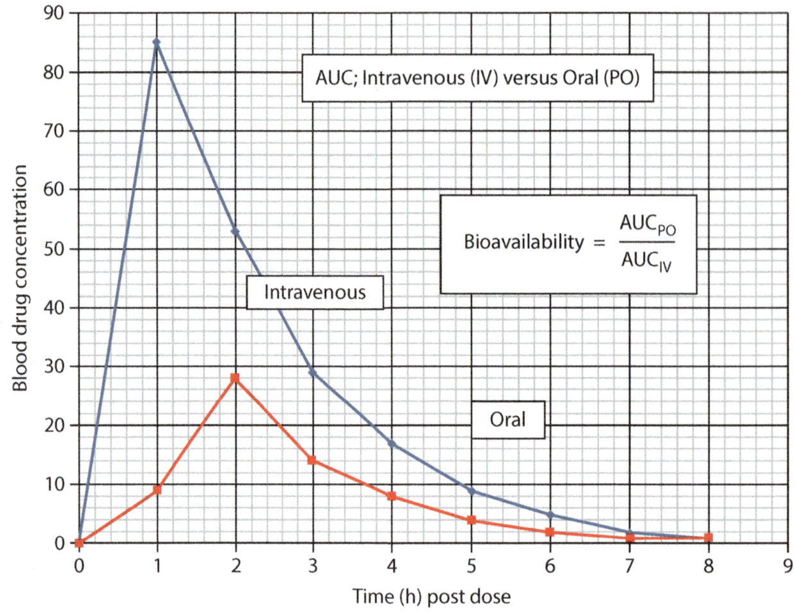

Figure 4.2 Area under the curve (AUC); IV versus oral dose.

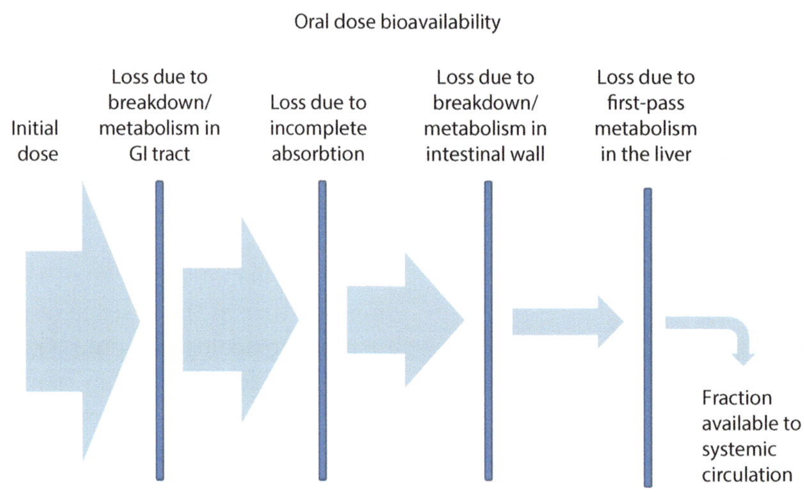

Figure 4.3 Function of progressive losses.

will arrive in the blood. AUC also works well as a means for consideration of the factors that affect the amount of drug in the vascular space and available to the body (Figures 4.2 and 4.3).

4.5.1.4.2 Factors Affecting Bioavailability Of course, many factors will affect the bioavailability of a drug. Clearly, the initial release of a drug from its ingested form will be a significant factor, and this initial liberation process is often incorporated along with absorption, distribution, metabolism, and elimination in consideration of the fate of drugs in the body (hence, in many texts, LADME is used as an acronym for the processes).

4.5.2 Distribution

Drugs in the circulation do not, as a general rule, remain limited to the blood. To some extent, and dependent on the nature of the drug, there will be either diffusion into cells, or specific drug uptake mechanisms will act to bring drugs into cells throughout the body. The extent to which these processes will occur and the tissue-specific differences between drugs and drug uptake can reflect a number of complex biochemical processes. The potential differential distribution and concentration of drugs within the body is a factor to carefully consider when making inferences based on their analytical findings.

4.5.2.1 Distribution Processes

As with absorption, the processes by which distribution around the body occurs can be generally grouped as passive, diffusion-based, and the more active, receptor-mediated transit. Initially, immediately after introduction of a drug, distribution around the body will be determined by blood flow, including both pattern and velocity. After a relative equilibrium has been achieved in the blood by mixing, the primary factors affecting distribution will be a function of the affinity the specific drug has for a particular tissue, or the ability of the tissue to internalize the drug via specific uptake mechanisms. The processes of distribution are relatively rapid, compared to absorption, metabolism, and elimination.

4.5.2.1.1 Diffusion Diffusion is the motion of a substance away from a region of high concentration to a region of lower concentration. The magnitude of net motion is a function of concentration and the energy required to transit from one region to another. The underlying basis for the diffusion is molecular motion, a function of mass and temperature. From a biochemical perspective, molecules can be expected to diffuse within the cellular or extracellular matrix, dependent upon their solubility. Molecules may diffuse across such barriers as cellular membranes, as long as the energy available for that motion exceeds that required to transit the barrier. In the case of nonpolar, lipophilic molecules, this does not generally present too significant a limitation on cellular uptake, and such molecules readily diffuse into lipophilic spaces, such as adipose tissue. In contrast, the energy required to facilitate the diffusion of a charged species across a (charged) cell membrane might be higher that can be overcome by the concentration gradient, and for those compounds, diffusion does not then represent a viable mechanism for transit into the cell.

4.5.2.1.2 Drug Uptake by Target Tissues After distribution, relatively few drugs have an equivalent concentration in tissues and blood, nor is the distribution of drugs in tissues uniform. The explanation for the uptake of drugs from the blood by tissues was thought to be primarily a function of simple diffusion, and indeed that explanation is clearly valid for a number of drugs, particularly those that are not ionized at physiologic pH. Lipophilicity has long been cited as a basis for tissue uptake, and indeed, that factor is predominant for such drugs as THC and other neutral, hydrophobic species. However, a key factor in the process of diffusion of a drug across a cellular membrane is that the *energy of solvation* released by the physical movement of the drug across the membrane barrier must be greater than the energy required for that transit. Of course, the process is also driven by, and is a function of, the concentration of the drug in the extracellular fluid (meaning the blood). In many cases, the push provided by the concentration of the drug in solution, coupled with the pull of the solvation energy, is adequate to explain the uptake of drugs by a gradient-driven, diffusion-based process. However, bear in mind that there is a charge on the membrane of cells, and the diffusion-based explanation does not provide an adequate basis for the uptake of charged molecules across a charged membrane. (The energy required for the charged species to transit the membrane is not overcome by the combination of solvation energy in the more lipophilic region and the driving force provided by a concentration gradient outside of the cell.) Most of the drugs in use are ionized at physiologic pH, and as such, there must be an alternate mechanism to explain their uptake and concentration in specific tissues.

4.5.2.1.2.1 Uptake Proteins Specific membrane-bound proteins, capable of transporting either organic anions or cations, have been identified, and their existence and wide distribution addresses the energy issue involved in transmembrane transport of ionic species. The significance of such transporters to the toxicologist is that they provide a reasonable biochemical mechanism to explain the uptake and concentration of ionized molecules on a tissue-specific basis. As noted above, while the uptake and concentration of neutral, lipophilic species in adipose or other lipophilic tissue is readily explainable based on diffusion, the transit of ionized species into tissues presents more of a theoretic issue and requires a mechanistic explanation beyond simple diffusion.

4.5.2.1.2.2 Postmortem Redistribution The phenomenon of postmortem redistribution (PMR) has been recognized for a number of years within the community of toxicologists working in support of medical examiners. Unfortunately, the apparently variable and unpredictable nature of PMR has led to skepticism on the part of many individuals as to the magnitude and even the occurrence of the phenomena. Further, there was not a well-articulated basis for the movement of drugs after death from regions in which they had been concentrated in life. Indeed, if one looks only at diffusion-based distribution, there is little reason for a neutral, hydrophobic molecule to move from a lipid-rich location to anywhere else in the body, in the absence of a kinetically understandable driving force. However, the vast majority of drugs with the potential for significant concentration in the liver and other organs in the body achieve those antemortem concentrations, despite the energy barrier imposed by the membrane charge,* by the process of drug transport proteins. Death, and its concomitant loss of that membrane charge and disruption of membrane continuity, presents an opportunity for drugs to then diffuse out of tissues that they could not diffuse into during life. This gradient-based diffusion leads then to an increase of drug in the blood in regions of the body near where drugs are concentrated in life, hence, near the liver, heart, lungs—the central cavity. This view also explains why some cases have significant differences between blood drawn from a peripheral blood source and heart blood, and in other, seemingly similar cases, no such difference. The process is essentially chaotic (in the mathematical sense) in that the factors affecting the magnitude and to an extent direction of drug diffusion from, for example, the liver are multifactorial and unpredictable. A commonly held view among many forensic toxicologists is that it is impossible to reliably interpret drug concentrations drawn postmortem from central vessels (the aorta, vena cava, pulmonary tree, etc.).

4.5.2.1.3 Blood–Brain and Placental Barriers

4.5.2.1.3.1 Blood–Brain Barrier The blood–brain barrier (BBB) is a euphemism describing the physical limitation of diffusion of drugs from the blood into the tissues of the central nervous system (CNS). In this region, the intercellular spaces that are a part of normal vessel structure are blocked by endothelial cell "tight junctions." Hence, there are no pores or openings in the endothelial membrane. The consequence of this structural distinction in the vasculature is that an additional cellular wall barrier (with associated electrical charge) is in place around the capillary and vessel walls, restricting the diffusion-based transit of ionized molecules into the brain. The route in, therefore, for any charged molecules important to the function of the brain (e.g., glucose) is accomplished with specific transport proteins. Similarly, no charged organic species can easily transit from the blood into the brain, in the absence of specific transport molecules. Interestingly, once lipophilic or neutral molecules enter the brain, they may be metabolized to more polar species (e.g., cocaine to benzoylecognine), and these metabolites of some species can become more concentrated in the brain than in the blood.

4.5.2.1.3.2 Placental Barrier The placenta is an organ derived from fetal and maternal tissues that serves as the interface between the fetus and the mother at the uterine wall. The placental barrier provides a physical separation between the maternal and fetal circulation, yet allows the transfer of nutrients into the fetal circulation and metabolic byproducts (e.g., O_2 and CO_2, respectively) back to the maternal circulation. Neutral molecules can readily diffuse across the placental barrier, and while lacking the tight junctions characterizing the BBB, the placental barrier does serve as an effective block to ionized species. The placenta is heavily populated with transport proteins, thereby allowing a route in for important biomolecules, as well as a number of compounds, including drugs and pharmaceuticals that are potentially toxic to the developing fetus.

4.5.2.2 Compartments

The differential distribution of drugs around the body lends itself to the concept of "compartments," which are defined as identifiable locations where drug concentrations are achieved by distinct equilibrium with other regions. Both real and conceptual locations can be considered as compartments. The transit of drugs into or out of compartments reflects equilibrium processes, dependent upon the circumstances of the moment. Similarly, there may be transitions *within* compartments that are also equilibrium processes (which may also therefore be viewed as sub-compartments; Figure 4.4).

4.5.2.3 Volume of Distribution

The volume of distribution (V_d) is an artificial but useful concept. Simply put, it is the volume of blood that would be required to explain the concentration of a drug in the body, *assuming there was no distribution beyond the blood volume.* V_d equates the amount of a drug ingested with the concentration observable in the blood. V_d is normally expressed on a liters per kg body mass basis, with a range of from ~0.2 L/kg to ~40 L/kg. A second important assumption is that there has been a single-dose event, patently false in the case of an ongoing therapeutic regimen. The formula for V_d is quite simple:

$$V_d = \frac{\text{Amount of Drug (mg)}}{\text{Blood Concentration (mg/L)} \times \text{Body Weight (kg)}}$$

The utility of this concept lies in inferences that can be drawn based on the relationship between dose ingested and blood level. If for example, a blood level

* The energy required to move an uncharged molecule across a membrane (e.g., from the exterior [C_1] to the interior [C_2]) can be described by Ficke's law of diffusion: $\Delta G' = 2.3\ RT\ \mathrm{Log}\ (C_2/C_1)$. When $\Delta G'$ is negative, the solute molecule can cross the membrane without the need for additional enegy input. However, when the membrane is charged, an additional electrostatic has to be figured in, yielding $\Delta G' = 2.3\ RT\ \mathrm{Log}\ (C2/C1) + ZF\Psi$, where Z is the species charge, F is the Faraday (23.062 kcal/v-mole), and Ψ is the membrane potential, in volts. Hence, in the presence of a membrane charge, a significant energy barrier to transmembrane transit may exist. A positive value of $\Delta G'$ suggests that energy must be expended to cause transmembrane transit.

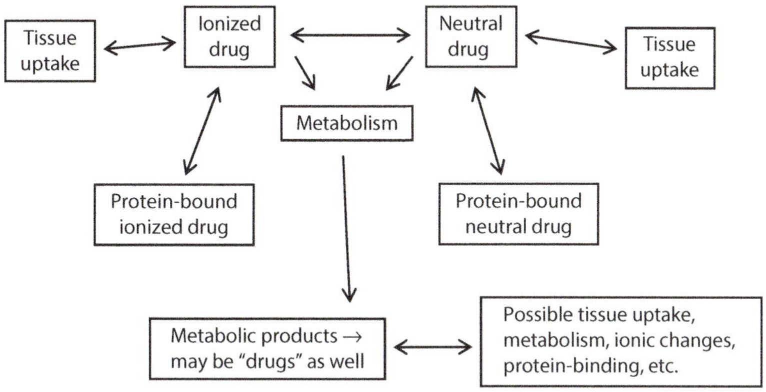

Figure 4.4 Possible transitions within the vascular compartment.

of a drug is known, the amount of drug ingested can be inferred. If there is an estimate of the underlying drug level, the amount of elevation consequential to a repeated dose can be estimated. Similarly, if the amount of drug ingested is known, an expected maximal blood level can be calculated. As with all pharmacokinetic calculations, some uncertainty is involved in all such relationships, and inferences from V_d calculations should be carefully considered, with the inherent uncertainty of the process candidly reflected as well (Table 4.1 and Figure 4.5).

4.5.2.3.1 Factors Affecting Magnitude of V_d Factors that tend to increase the uptake of a drug from the blood into the tissues will correspondingly increase the V_d. Hence, the more lipophilic a drug is, the more partition into lipophilic tissues is favored, and the blood:tissue equilibrium shifts to the right with a corresponding increase in the V_d. Similarly, to the extent that a tissue (or tissues) expresses specific transport proteins and mechanisms to facilitate uptake, there will be a corresponding decrease in the blood concentration of the drug and also an increase in the V_d. Protein binding (e.g., to serum albumin) has an interesting effect in that

Table 4.1 Volume of Distribution Examples

Drug	~V_d, L/kg
Ibuprofen	0.2
Ethanol	0.6
Ethylene glycol	0.8
Pentobarbital	0.85
Acetaminophen	0.9
Alprazolam	1.6
Cocaine	2.3
Morphine	3.5
Amphetamine	4.4
Phencyclidine	6.2
Amitriptyline	8
Heroin	25

What would be the amount of hydromorphone (HM) necessary to explain a blood concentration of 37.5 ug/L in a 193 lb male? (assuming a single-dose event, and 100% bioavailability)?

Given; $\text{Volume of distribution } (V_d) = \dfrac{\text{Amount of drug (mg)}}{\text{Blood conc.} \times \text{Body weight (kg)}}$

and; $193 \text{ lb} \times 0.454 \text{ kg/lb} = 87.6 \text{ kg}$, and; $37.5 \text{ ug/L} = 0.0375 \text{ mg/L}$

and; $\text{HM } V_d = 2.9 \text{ L/kg}$. Then; $2.9 \text{ L/kg} = \dfrac{\text{mg HM}}{0.0375\text{mg/L} \times 87.6 \text{ kg}}$

So; $\text{mg HM} = 2.9 \text{ L/kg} \times 0.0375 \text{ ug/L} \times 87.6 \text{ kg}$
$= 9.5 \text{ mg}$

Figure 4.5 Volume of distribution—example calculation.

such binding tends to keep a drug in the vascular compartment, with a correspondingly low V_d. The means of measurement of the drug is key: if the total drug is measured in the blood (as is commonly done in forensic toxicologic processes), then the effect of protein binding will be undetected. More accurately, to the extent that protein binding will tend to reduce partition of the drug out of the vascular space, V_d will be lowered. If, on the other hand, free drug is measured, the (artificially) elevated V_d due to loss of the drug to protein binding will become apparent.

4.5.2.3.2 Practical Application of V_d calculations By knowing the blood level, a V_d calculation can allow an estimate of the amount of drug taken. V_d is often used to provide an indication as to whether an individual was ingesting a drug in accordance with a particular therapeutic regimen or if the level observed represents an accidental or deliberate overdose. Sometimes the relationship is improperly used with postmortem drug levels to determine or suggest the magnitude of an antemortem ingestion, despite the uncertainties associated with such levels. The importance of understanding the limitations and inherent uncertainties of applications of this calculation can hardly be overestimated. In a classic example of "garbage in, garbage out," the calculation of the amount of drug ingested, when based on a flawed drug level determination (e.g., a level artificially elevated by the process of postmortem redistribution), can lead to significantly erroneous conclusions. However, with appropriate care and consideration of the potential limitations, confounders, and uncertainties attendant to such calculations, V_d information can in some cases provide useful and valid information.

One of the main sources of uncertainty underlying V_d calculations, particularly as applied in forensic casework, is the degree to which the blood value used is a valid and accurate reflection of a true antemortem value. To the extent that a level has been overstated (e.g., is reflective of postmortem redistribution rather than of a true antemortem blood level), the inferences regarding the number of pills (or other dose) required to reach a particular level would be elevated and, while perhaps numerically accurate, would nevertheless be significantly misleading in regard to the case as a whole. A second source of uncertainty is the degree to which the drug is present in the body prior to the ingestion or dose in question. An inherent assumption of the V_d calculation is that the drug level is a consequence of a single-dose event. One could conceivably use the V_d to determine the difference between an underlying, presumably steady-state level (recognizing that the term *steady state* is a misnomer, merely describing a consistent range in which the drug level alternates between dose events) and a specific-dose event, but again, an awareness of the magnitude of uncertainty in the process is essential. Finally, there is the variation between individuals with regard to the V_d value for any specific drug. Published values represent averages, and many of the tabular presentations do not present ranges or any statistical basis on how best to use the variable. In summary, while V_d calculations can be useful and facilitate understanding in some cases, great care should be taken to ensure that conclusions reached are legitimate. An example V_d calculation in spreadsheet format is presented in Figure 4.6.

Vol. dist., blood level, pills ingested for: Oxycodone

Subject: **Doe, John**	Gender:	m
	Race:	w
	Age:	52
	Weight:	224
Body weight in kg (lbs x .4536 kg/lb) =		101.61 kg
Blood/plasma drug level (mg/L):		0.857
Volume of distribution: (V_d)	High	3.7
	Mean	2.75 L/kg
	Low	1.8
Mg ingested: (Based on blood level and BW) (Single dose event assumed)	High	322.184 mg
	Mean	239.461 mg
	Low	156.738 mg
Pill/tablet amount:		40 mg
"Minimum Number Ingested" (Based on Vd's noted above)	High	8
	Mean	6
	Low	4

Figure 4.6 Spreadsheet calculation for V_d.

4.5.3 Elimination

The primary route out of the body for most drugs and their metabolites is elimination via the urine. As noted in Chapter 5, the end result of most metabolic processes is a molecule with more polar character and greater water solubility than the original starting species. The increased aqueous solubility facilitates partition into the blood, therefore increasing the amount of drug that will ultimately be filtered by the kidneys and eliminated from the body in the urine. Clearly the physiology of the kidney (addressed in Chapter 10) will affect the magnitude and rate at which compounds can be eliminated, and the process is most effective with non-protein-bound, water-soluble molecules. Molecules with molecular weights greater than roughly 400 daltons can also be eliminated across the hepato-biliary border into the bile and eventually the feces. This process (as described in Chapter 9) is dependent upon specific transport proteins.

4.5.3.1 Elimination Parameters

A number of important kinetic parameters can be used in describing the processes of elimination. A summary of which is provided in Table 4.2. While extensive kinetic calculations are not normally required of forensic toxicologists, there are enough cases where a knowledge and facility with such values can be of considerable use. The toxicologist may have to deal with cases in which such calculations have been employed in clinical assessment, and a familiarity with the values may be beneficial.

4.5.3.2 Elimination Kinetics

4.5.3.2.1 Zero Order When the rate of elimination of a drug is independent of the drug concentration, that process is a *zero-order* reaction. Increasing concentrations of substrate do not increase the rate of reaction. A classic example is the oxidation of ethyl alcohol by the enzyme alcohol dehydrogenase (ADH). When the alcohol concentration of the body is greater than ~0.02 g/dL (equivalent to roughly one drink in an average-sized

Table 4.2 Kinetic Parameters and Equations

Parameter	Abbreviation	Description	Formula
Concentration	C_x	Concentration (mass/volume) of a drug at time x; o = initial, t = time t.	
Zero-order equation		Relates the concentration of a drug undergoing zero-order elimination at (elapsed) time t to the rate constant and concentration at time 0.	$C_t = -kt + C_o$
First-order equation		Relates the concentration of a drug undergoing first-order elimination at (elapsed) time t to the rate constant and concentration at time 0.	$\ln(C_t) = -kt + \ln(C_o)$
Half-life	$t_{1/2}$	Relates the time required for the concentration of a drug to be reduced by half to the elimination constant, k.	$t_{1/2} = \ln(2)/k$
Elimination rate constant	k	Relates the first-order half-life of a drug to the rate of elimination.	$k = \ln(2)/t_{1/2}$
Clearance	CL	Reflects the volume of blood cleared of drug per unit time.	$CL = V_d(k)$

individual), the enzyme is binding, reacting, and releasing the products as fast as possible. The reaction is saturated, and having more substrate (alcohol) available will not increase the rate of reaction. The rate for a zero-order reaction is simply the amount of drug lost per unit time (e.g., for alcohol, ~0.02 g/dL/hr). The rate equals k, the rate coefficient, equal to the negative rate of change of the drug over time. The zero-order rate equation is therefore $C_t = -kt + C_o$, where C_t is the concentration at time t, and C_o is the initial concentration. Half-life is not a constant in zero-order processes, and the plot of concentration versus time is a straight line (Figure 4.7).

4.5.3.2.2 First Order In first-order elimination, the rate of elimination is a function of the concentration of the drug. Most drug elimination can be described as first order. The rate of elimination is equal to k(C), where C is the concentration of the drug. The first-order rate equation is $\ln(C) = -kt + \ln(Co)$. Half-life and k are related by $t_{1/2} = \ln(2)/k$. The equation is often presented as $C_t = C_0e^{-kt}$. A plot of concentration versus time will be a curve of decreasing negative slope, but the half-life of a first-order reaction is a constant, and hence, a constant fraction of drug is eliminated from the blood per unit time (Figure 4.8).

4.5.3.2.3 Michaelis–Menton Kinetics The Michaelis–Menton approach to the understanding of enzyme kinetics represents a milestone in biochemistry. The importance and significance of the Michaelis–Menton equation, which relates reaction velocity with a characteristic (for each enzyme) and substrate concentration to the field of biochemistry (and many other related disciplines), simply cannot be overstated. One of the inherent properties of the equation is that it relates reaction rate as a zero order becomes first order, as substrate is depleted.

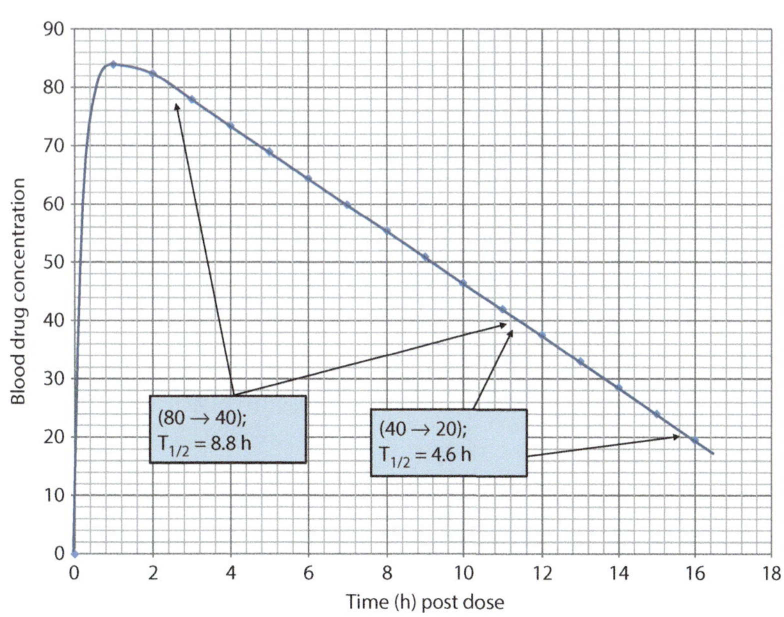

Figure 4.7 Example of zero-order kinetics.

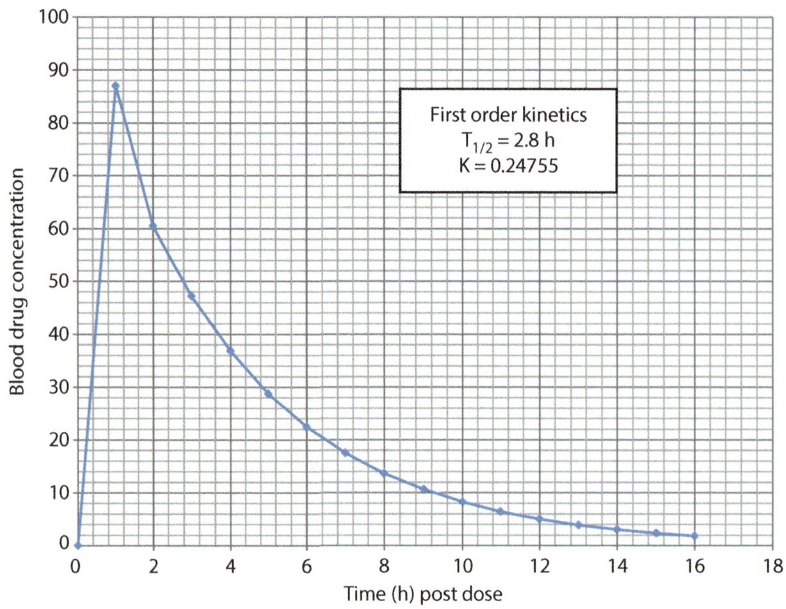

Figure 4.8 Example of first-order kinetics.

The phrase *Michaelis–Menton kinetics* has come to mean a scenario where neither zero-order nor first-order kinetics are appropriate to describe the reaction, but rather there is a mix of order, as the concentration of drug (or enzyme substrate) becomes low enough such that first-order kinetics dominate.

4.5.3.2.4 Clearance The ability of the body to remove a drug can be expressed as *volume of blood* from which the drug has been removed per unit time. Another way of thinking of this parameter is simply that if a drug is at a specific concentration in the blood at time 0, and a lower concentration at time t, for the concentration of the drug in the blood to remain the same, the volume of blood containing the drug must be smaller. The difference in volume is the blood that has been cleared of the drug. This can be of significance because if the body is less able to clear a drug, then the steady-state level achieved for a specific dose regimen will be raised, which may have toxicologic significance. Clearance is commonly considered in clinical toxicology situations, but less so in forensic. Nevertheless, this parameter can be of utility in forensic toxicology cases, particularly when determining possible explanations for toxic or lethal levels of drugs.

4.5.3.3 Multiple Dose Considerations

While single-ingestion events are common enough, often a drug level must be considered in light of an ongoing dose regimen. Multiple ingestions of a drug result in a continuous rise and fall of drug concentrations in the blood, rising to a point where the elimination rate of the drug equals the ingestion rate. This point is called *steady state* but is a misnomer in that the concentration in the blood continues to rise and fall between peak and trough values. It is important to recognize that a single blood drug level, in the absence of time-of-dose information, may be reflective of any point between the peak and trough value and may be misleading with regard to the average level of the drug in a case.

REVIEW QUESTIONS

1. "Marijuana brownies" have been a popular means of ingestion of THC. Would you expect "heroin brownies" to be an effective drug delivery system as well? Why or why not?
2. Would you expect a difference in AUC for a drug injected in the femoral vein versus the antecubital fossa (vein in the arm)? If so, why?
3. What barriers must smoked "crack cocaine" pass through to reach target molecules in the brain?
4. Consider a drug that is over 95% bound to serum albumin. Explain why the volume of distribution of this drug determined in terms of free drug is drastically different compared with the V_d when talking about total drug.
5. Would a drug that is positively charged at physiological pH be expected to have a larger or a smaller V_d than a neutral drug? Why?

6. The half-life of a drug that follows zero-order elimination kinetics increases, decreases, or remains constant if the concentration of that drug is increased?
7. Oxazepam was found experimentally to have a first-order elimination rate constant of 0.041 per hour. If a 30 mg pill was ingested, how much will remain in (a) 10 hours and (b) 24 hours?
8. The following nicotine study was conducted in rats. The rats were given a 0.1 mg/kg injection of nicotine. Blood was collected at time points listed below with the mean plasma concentration determined by LC/MS.

Time after Dosing (min)	Mean Plasma Nicotine Concentration, C (ng/mL)
20	21.0
30	18.5
60	12.5
120	5.8
180	2.7

   a. Sketch a graph relating the variables. Is nicotine elimination zero or first order?
   b. Calculate the half-life of nicotine in this study, if possible.
   c. If the experiment were to continue, how much nicotine would be left after a total of three half-lives had passed since initial dosing?
9. Morphine is found to have a half-life of 3 hours in a patient. This patient is given 20 mg IV morphine. Using this information, calculate how much time passes until 85% of this dose has been eliminated.

TOPICS FOR DISCUSSION

1. Therapeutic drug monitoring (TDM) is a clinical technique that clinicians use in dosing patients with certain drugs. Blood samples are taken at frequent intervals to quantitate serum levels of the drug to keep the drug in a therapeutic range but not a toxic range. Explain why medical marijuana (active agent THC) is a poor choice for TDM.
2. Explain why the following sentence is at least in part correct: Drug metabolism is not initiated until absorption and distribution is completed.
3. Back-extrapolation of alcohol from a known point to a prior time (using zero-order kinetics) is a not-uncommon practice in forensic toxicology. What additional problems would you anticipate in attempting a similar activity with a drug eliminated via first-order kinetics?

Bibliography

Duffus JH, Worth HGJ, editors. *Fundamental Toxicology for Chemists*. Cambridge, UK: Royal Society of Chemistry, 1996.

Kalant H, Grant DM, Mitchell J, editors. *Principles of Medical Pharmacology*. 7th rev. ed. Toronto: Saunders Elsevier, 2007.

Rang HP, Dale MM, Ritter JM, Flower RJ, Henderson G, editors. *Rang and Dale's Pharmacology*. 6th rev. ed. Philadelphia: Churchill Livingstone/Elsevier, 2007.

Renwick, AG. Toxicokinetics. In: Hayes AW, editor. *Principles and Methods of Toxicology*. 5th rev. ed. New York: Informa Healthcare, 2008.

Walsh CT, Schwartz-Bloom RD. *Levine's Pharmacology: Drug Actions and Reactions*. 7th rev. ed. New York: Taylor & Francis, 2005.

Biotransformation

5

Contents

5.1 Introduction

Many of the drugs, poisons, toxins, or other exogenous compounds that enter the body are chemically modified prior to their eventual elimination. These structural changes often facilitate or hasten the removal of chemicals from the body by making them more water soluble, and therefore more readily subject to elimination in the urine. In many cases, the structural changes serve to make the compound less toxic, such as the hydrolysis of the methyl ester of cocaine to form benzoylecgonine, or the attachment of a glucuronic acyl residue to morphine, yielding morphine glucuronide. In some cases, however, the metabolic product is actually more toxic than the original molecule, such as the formation of a toxic quinone-imine metabolite from acetaminophen (NAPQI; N-acetyl para-quinonimine), which can damage the liver and kidney, or formic acid from methanol, to which the optic nerve is particularly sensitive. Chemical changes that produce more toxic species are called *activation* reactions; those that render compounds less toxic are considered to be *deactivation* reactions. While metabolic transformations can occur throughout the body, much of the breakdown of xenobiotics takes place in the liver. In a general sense, the purpose of metabolic transformations can be thought of as twofold: to decrease the toxicity of exogenous compounds, and to enhance their aqueous solubility (thereby shortening their residence time in the body). Knowledge of the metabolic fate of a drug in the body can help the toxicologist evaluate and understand the significance of their analytical findings in the overall context of a case.

5.2 Metabolism

The term *metabolism* is often used with reference to the chemical changes the body makes to both exogenous and endogenous molecules. For our purposes the process might be more accurately referred to as *biotransformation*, which can then be defined as the structural change or modification of a drug or chemical (xenobiotic or endogenous) within a biological system.

Biotransformations are almost exclusively a function of enzymatic reactions, that is to say, the specific chemical transformations are enzymatically catalyzed and, in the absence of the enzyme, would not proceed (at least at temperatures compatible with life). Enzymatic reaction pathways can be saturated by an overabundance of substrate relative to the amount of enzyme present. Some enzymes or enzyme systems can be induced, meaning that more copies of the molecule are synthesized in response to exposure to the particular substrate. Enzymatic reactions can also be inhibited, in that molecules other than the normal substrate can compete for catalytic binding sites on the enzyme, limiting the available sites for the catalytic process. Inhibition can also be achieved by a limitation on the availability of substrates, co-substrates, or other factors necessary for the enzymatic reaction. Enzymes are protein molecules and, as such, are sensitive to pH, tonicity, temperature, and the microenvironment in which they exist within the cytoplasm or cellular organelle. Determination of the optimal parameters for enzyme function is one of the basic processes of enzyme characterization. Many different types of reactions can be carried out enzymatically in the body; examples of reaction types and enzyme classes are presented in Table 5.1.

Table 5.1 Example Biotransformation Reactions

Reaction	Example Substrate
Hydroxylation	Acetonitrile
Aromatic	Phenytoin
Aliphatic	Secobarbital
Epoxidation	Carbamazepine
Dealkylation	Codeine
N-Oxidation	Desipramine
S-Oxidation	Chlorpromazine
Deamination	Amphetamine
Desulfuration	Thiopental
Dehalogenation	Halothane
Reduction	Carbon Tetrachloride
Glucuronidation	Glucuronosyl Transferases
Sulfation	Sulfotransferases

5.2.1 Why Metabolize?

The ability of the body to detoxify a wide variety of compounds comes with an "opportunity cost" in the diversion of resources to generate the biochemical machinery capabable of such reactions. Clearly, to the extent that an organism can either detoxify or shorten the residence time of a potentially harmful compound in the body represented an evolutionary advantage, and is expressed in the complex and elegant systems capable of performing such reaction. Simply enhancing the aqueous solubility of a compound will tend to shorten the time it spends in the body, since in most organisms there is a relatively rapid flux of water through the body, and water-soluble species are eventually eliminated in the urine. Many toxins are at least somewhat lipophilic, and metabolic transformation often has the effect of increasing the polarity of the molecule and, thereby, its overall aqueous solubility. In short, metabolic transformations that enhance the aqueous solubility of compounds increase the rate at which the modified chemicals are eliminated from the body in the urine.

5.2.2 Metabolic Transformations Are Enzymatic Processes

Enzymes are proteins that act as biochemical catalysts by lowering the activation energy required to allow a specific reaction to proceed. The action of enzymatic catalysis allows both simple and complex reactions that would not otherwise proceed to be carried out at normal body temperatures.

Enzyme action can be thought of as the combination of substrate (S) with enzyme (E), forming an enzyme-substrate complex (ES), which then undergoes a chemical change or rearrangement, producing a short-lived intermediate enzyme-product complex (EP), which rapidly dissociates, yielding unchanged enzyme and product; (E) + (P). Hence:

$$E + S \rightarrow ES \rightarrow (EP) \rightarrow E + P$$

The enzyme itself is not affected or functionally changed by the process and will continue to catalyze the reaction as long as the kinetics remain favorable and the required substrates and co-factors are present.

Enzymes and enzyme systems may be quite complex. Enzymes may contain metals that can play a role in the catalytic process, usually acting to facilitate electron transfer to or from the substrate molecule. Nonproteinaceous co-factors may also facilitate or participate in the reaction process, such as nicotinamide adenine dinucleotide (NAD), thiamine pyrophosphate (TPP), or coenzyme A (CoA). Protein molecules, including enzymes, are sensitive to the parameters of the solution in which they exist, and enzyme function can be significantly affected by such variables as pH, ionic or salt concentration, and temperature. The ability of an enzyme to catalyze a reaction is a function of (among other things) an adequate concentration of substrate, since binding of the substrate to the enzyme will be kinetically driven. Conversely, there is some (high) concentration of substrate, which essentially serves to maintain substrate bound to the enzyme active site. In such situations, the flux of substrate through the enzyme is maximal; as soon as the EP complex dissociates, yielding free enzyme (E), and then another molecule binds to the active site, forming a new ES complex and starting the reaction sequence again. In these conditions, the enzyme is operating at the fastest possible rate, or maximal velocity of substrate through the enzyme, often referred to as V_{max}. A plot of substrate concentration versus enzyme velocity exhibits a characteristic shape, showing a saturation of enzyme and a corresponding limited rate as substrate concentration increases (Figure 5.1).

An elegant and effective expression of enzyme activity was proposed in 1913 and is known as the Michaelis-Menten Equation. This view of enzyme activity, and the inferences from it, has provided the basis for much of our understanding of both enzyme-catalyzed reactions and of the kinetics of numerous other biochemical processes that are driven or controlled to some extent by the binding of one molecule to another. (The derivation of the Michaelis–Menten equation from the generalized expression noted above is both elegant and straightforward and can be found in nearly all biochemistry texts.)

The Michaelis–Menten equation relates the initial reaction rate (V_0) to the substrate concentration [S]. The maximal rate the enzyme can achieve (in a given set of conditions) is V_{max}. The Michaelis constant, (K_m), reflects the substrate concentration at which the reaction rate is ½ V_{max} and is a measure of the affinity of the enzyme for its substrate in a manner analogous to the Kd of protein receptor binding.

Michaelis–Menten equation:

$$V_0 = \frac{V_{max}[S]}{K_m + [S]}$$

As noted above, a typical substrate-velocity plot will exhibit a characteristic hyperbolic shape. Interestingly, a number of useful transformations of the equation can be used with experimental data. In one case, a simple inverse of the equation yields an equation of a straight line, in which velocity (actually, 1/velocity), when plotted against substrate concentration (actually, 1/[S]), generates a plot with an x-intercept of $-1/K_m$, and y-intercept of $1/V_{max}$, and a slope of K_m/V_{max}.

$$\frac{1}{V_0} = \frac{K_m}{V_{max}[S]} + \frac{1}{V_{max}}$$

Such a plot can allow a researcher to determine if a chemical affects the binding site of an enzyme

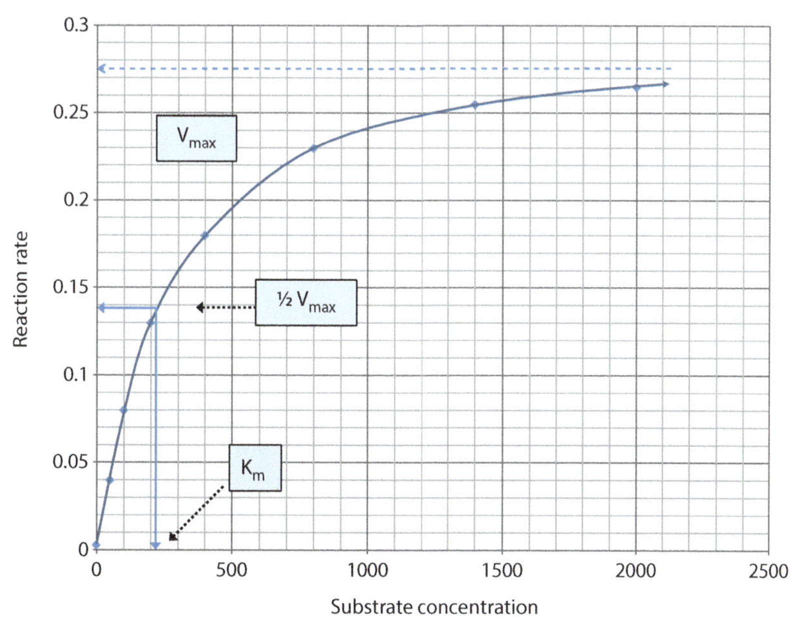

Figure 5.1 Enzyme substrate-velocity plot. A plot of the rate of an enzyme reaction (initial velocity) versus the amount of substrate present at the start of the reaction. V_{max} is the maximal rate the enzyme system could achieve, and the substrate concentration at half that velocity (1/2 V_{max}) corresponds to K_m, or the enzyme-specific Michaelis–Menten constant.

(by changing K_m) or the function of an enzyme (by changing V_{max}).

The derivation of the Michaelis–Menten equation is an elegant exercise, describing a specific time in an enzyme-catalyzed reaction when the concentration of substrate has not been appreciably altered by the action of the enzyme. The derivation is based on several assumptions, including that the reaction is irreversible, the product does not bind to the enzyme, the concentration of enzyme-substrate complex does not change, and as soon as the product is formed it is dissociated from the enzyme.

5.2.3 Limitation of Enzymatic Processes

Because of the nature of the enzymatic process, specifically the binding of the substrate to the active site and often the requirement for co-factors or co-substrates, factors can affect the rate of enzymatic catalysis beyond the substrate concentration and the amount of enzyme. Enzymatic processes can be saturated, induced, inhibited, and limited.

5.2.3.1 Saturation of Enzyme Catalysis

Since the process of an enzymatically catalyzed reaction involves (at a minimum) the binding of the substrate to the active site of the enzyme with such binding being driven by concentration, then clearly, a concentration of substrate exists that corresponds to the active site of the enzyme being occupied essentially 100% of the time. As soon as the catalyzed reaction is completed and the substrate (now the product) molecule is released, another substrate molecule binds to the active site. In such conditions, the enzyme reaction is proceeding as fast as possible, and the only limitation on the reaction rate is the amount of enzyme. Such conditions are referred to as zero order, in that the rate of disappearance of substrate is independent of the substrate concentration (at least until enough substrate has been reacted so that the concentration is no longer saturating). The common example we see of this phenomena is simply the oxidation of ethanol by the enzyme alcohol dehydrogenase. In the range of above 0.02 g/dL, and below 0.35 g/dL, the elimination rate of ethanol tends to be linear, reflecting the saturation of the enzyme, and hence, zero-order kinetics. Below ~0.02 g/dL, the enzyme is no longer saturated, and the rate becomes a function of substrate concentration. Above 0.35 g/dL, other enzyme systems participate in the catalytic process and contribute to the elimination rate in a nonlinear fashion.

5.2.3.2 Enzyme Induction

One interesting feature of enzymes is that more enzyme can be produced as a response of the body to the presence of substrate. This process is called induction, and again, ethanol is a good example of the phenomena. Experienced drinkers generally have produced more alcohol dehydrogenase than their nondrinking counterparts, and as such can have elimination rates considerably larger than those of uninduced individuals. The main groups of enzymes involved in drug metabolism (the cytochrome P450s) are also subject to induction, and this process can have a significant impact on levels of drug that will result from a specific dose. Enzyme induction can be an important factor to consider when trying to determine the relationship between drug levels and administered dose.

5.2.3.3 Inhibition of Enzymatic Processes

The activity of an enzyme is a direct consequence of the physical binding of a substrate molecule to a specific, active site on the enzyme. Clearly, molecules other than the substrate may have an affinity for the same site and, by binding there, can block the ability of the enzyme to bind the actual substrate, resulting in an inhibition of activity. Inhibitors can be either medicines or poisons, depending on the nature of the reaction being inhibited and the physiological consequences of that action. A classic example is the action of organophosphate nerve gases, which inhibit the action of the enzyme acetylcholinesterase. This enzyme is found in cholinergic neural junctions and catalyzes the hydrolytic cleavage of the excitatory neurotransmitter acetylcholine into acetate and choline. By blocking the action of the enzyme, an excess of acetylcholine remains in the neural junction, making a small release of neurotransmitter (perhaps not enough to have triggered an action potential in the postsynaptic neuron or muscle fiber) effectively larger and thereby triggering the response. The consequences can be catastrophic for an organism, leading to the expression of the potentially fatal cholinergic syndrome.

Inhibition of enzymes can be of different types, depending on the nature of the interaction between the inhibitor and the enzyme. If the inhibitor competes directly with the substrate for the binding site that forms the active site of the enzyme, the inhibitor is referred to as a *competitive* inhibitor. If, on the other hand, the inhibitor binds somewhere else on the enzyme, affecting its structure and hence catalytic ability, without affecting the ability of the substrate to bind, the interaction is called *noncompetitive* inhibition. Finally, there is *uncompetitive* inhibition, a consequence of an inhibitor that binds to the enzyme-substrate complex, thereby affecting both the ability of the substrate to bind to the enzyme and the ability of the enzyme to catalyze the reaction.

Evaluation of the substrate-velocity plot of an enzyme (as noted in Section 5.2.2) in the presence and absence of an inhibitor allows a determination as to the exact nature of the inhibition. A change in the y-intercept suggests an effect on V_{max}, and hence a noncompetitive inhibitor. Similarly, a change in the x-intercept suggests an effect on the binding of the substrate to the enzyme as reflected in Km and a competitive inhibitor. An effect on both would suggest an uncompetitive inhibitor (Figure 5.2).

5.2.3.4 Limitation of Enzymatic Processes

Many enzymatic processes depend on more than simply the presence of the substrate and the enzyme itself. Co-factors can provide or remove electrons (e.g., NAD+, NADH) or whole substituent groups. Co-substrates may be required and must be present for the reaction to proceed. If the availability of co-factors or co-substrates is limited, then the availability of substrate or even its ability to bind to the active site (e.g., no inhibitors are present) may no longer be the determining factor for the reaction.

5.2.4 Drug–Drug Interaction

The fact that the rate of elimination of a drug from the body can depend on the rate of enzymatic processes and that those processes are subject to the factors noted above points out the potential for drug–drug interaction. Obviously, if two drugs elicit effects by the same mechanism, perhaps serving as agonists for the same receptor system, then one would expect an additive effect when in the body at the same time. Similarly, the blocking of the mechanism of action by one drug can be the basis for the action of an antidote (e.g., in a morphine overdose, the binding of naloxone to the opiate receptors blocks the action of the drug).

However, there can be more subtle interactions, based on the induction or inhibition of enzyme systems. Consider the effect of a drug that induces an enzyme responsible for the biotransformation of a particular therapeutic drug from an active to an inactive species. As the amount of enzyme increases, the rate of elimination of the therapeutic drug will increase, and the AUC for a given dose will decrease. In contrast, if the enzymatic action produces a potentially toxic species, then the rate of production of the toxic compound will increase, even though the dose of the therapeutic agent has remained unchanged. Similarly, and in contrast to the induction of enzymes, is the inhibition of biotransformation enzymes by specific drugs. Inhibiting an enzyme responsible for the elimination of a drug will increase the AUC of that drug. Depending on the drug and circumstances, the resulting elevated concentration can have toxic consequences. There are numerous examples of drug–drug interactions, and the forensic toxicologist should consider the potential for unexpectedly elevated (or lowered) levels of a given species to be the consequence of either induction or inhibition of biotransformation systems in their efforts to understand specific case circumstances.

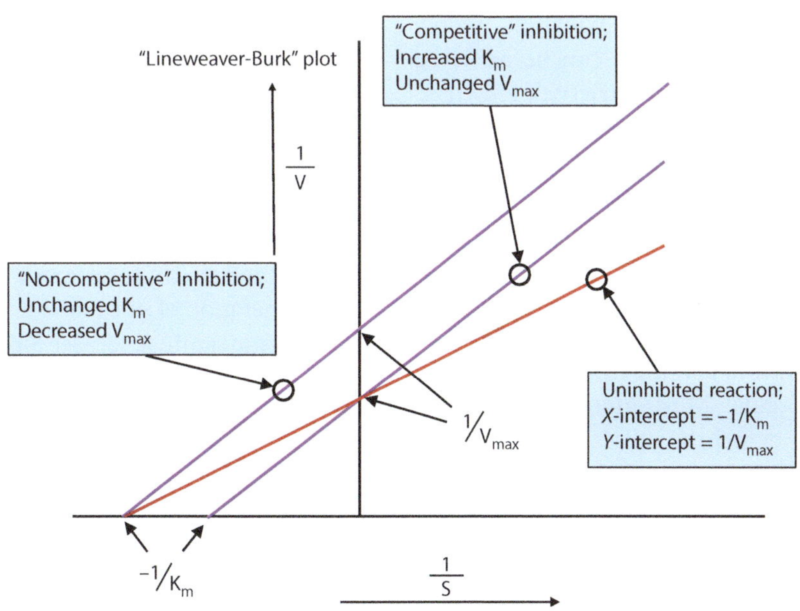

Figure 5.2 Lineweaver–Burk plot. In this presentation, 1/V is plotted versus 1/S, reflecting a linear transformation of the Michaelis–Menten equation. In this plot, the y-intercept is equal to $1/V_{max}$, and the x-intercept is equal to $-1/K_m$.

5.3 Phase I and Phase II Reactions

Biotransformation reactions are generally categorized into two broad categories, phase I and phase II reactions. Phase I reactions may be thought of as enhancing or increasing the reactivity of the molecule (*activation* is reserved for a specific purpose, addressed below) in that these reactions introduce reactive sites on otherwise unreactive molecules. An example is simply the hydroxylation of benzene to form phenol. Phase II reactions involve the conjugation of drugs (or their phase I metabolites) with water-soluble molecules such as glucuronic acid. The end result of the conjugation process is a significantly more water-soluble or hydrophilic species than was the original molecule. The enhanced water-solubility of the phase II metabolite favors partition into the aqueous phase (hence, the blood), leading to filtration and elimination in the kidney. The combination of the processes, then, is that a relatively hydrophobic but toxic molecule undergoes a phase I reaction, introducing a reactive site on the molecule and then a phase II reaction, adding on a polar, hydrophilic group. The end result is a more hydrophilic species than was the original molecule, significantly increased solubility in the blood and much more readily removed in the urine. Hence, the net result is a lower half-life and diminished AUC for the drug.

5.3.1 Phase I Reactions

Phase I reactions can be quite varied with the generalized end point of a molecule with a new reactive site or group having been introduced. Oxidation, reduction, or hydrolytic phase I reactions can be achieved with substrate molecules by a wide variety of enzymes. The classic or archetypal phase I reaction would be the introduction of a hydroxyl group on an otherwise unsubstitued aryl hydrocarbon (as noted in the benzene/phenol example cited above). The enzyme systems responsible for these transformations can be cytosolic or membrane bound and can be found throughout the body, although some tissues (particularly the liver) have a relatively high amount and play a significant role in the detoxification of molecule. Most mono-oxygenations are catalyzed by either cytochrome P450s (CYPs) or flavin monooxygenase (FMO) enzymes. Both systems are localized on the endoplasmic reticulum (EPR), a network of lipoprotein membranes running throughout the cell and contiguous with many cellular organelles. The EPR and the associated functional enzyme systems may be isolated from cells as *microsomes* or the *microsomal fraction* (Table 5.2).

Table 5.2 Example Phase I Reactions and Enzymes

Reactions	Enzymes
Hydroxylation	Cytochrome P450s
Epoxidation	Flavin monooxygenases
Dealkylation	Prostaglandin synthetases
Oxidation	Molybdenum hydroxylases
Desulfuration	Alcohol/aldehyde dehydrogenases
Dehalogenation	Esterases/amidases
Reduction	Epoxide hydrolases
Dehydrogenation	Multiple dehydrogenases
Hydrolysis	Multiple hydrolases

5.3.1.1 Cytochrome P450s

The major enzyme system involved in phase I transformations are the isozymes of cytochrome P450s. These iron-containing heme proteins catalyze a wide variety of reactions and are responsible for the vast majority of metabolic transformations that are of significance to the disposition of drugs in the body. The nomenclature as "P450" arose as a historical reference to the absorption maxima of the "CO-binding pigment of the microsomal fraction"—so named before the enzymatic capability of the material was recognized. Originally thought to be a single protein, this group of isozymes has now been characterized in more than 400 specific forms and comprises a superfamily of enzymes. The significance of this enzyme family can hardly be overstated, and it has been estimated that the CYP enzymes account for more than 70% of the specific reactions involved in drug biotransformation.

5.3.1.1.1 Basic Reaction The archetypal CYP phase I reaction can be described in the following generalized equation: $RH + O_2 + NADPH + H^+ \rightarrow ROH + NADP^+ + H_2O$, with NADPH being regenerated by the action of NADPH reductase. The essence of the catalytic process involves the transfer of electrons on and off the central iron atom in the enzyme, and ultimately, the oxidation (loss of electrons) from the substrate. The mechanism of the reaction is of interest both because of the potential nonspecific nature of the reaction (hence the wide variety of reactions catalyzed by the enzyme system) and the potential for the generation of side reactions that may themselves be of toxicologic significance (see Sidebar 5.1).

SIDEBAR 5.1 CYP450 MEDIATED REACTION SEQUENCE

The oxidation of a substrate molecule can be thought of as beginning (as shown in Step 1 in Figure 5.3), with the binding at its active site of an oxidized P450 molecule forming a P450(Fe+3)-substrate complex.

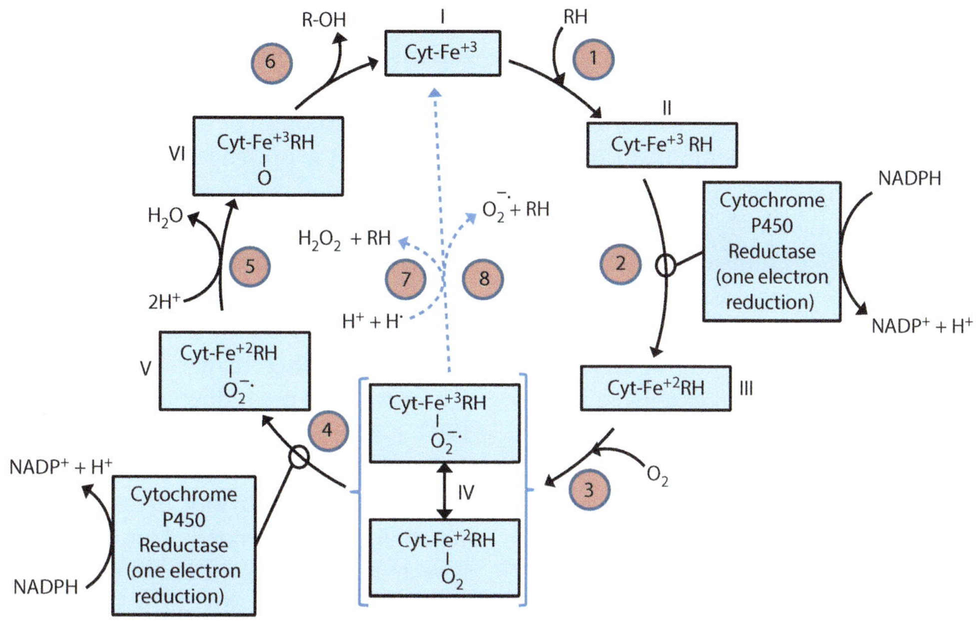

Figure 5.3 Oxidation of substrate RH by CYP450 molecule. (1) Binding of substrate (RH) to oxidized P-450 molecule (I). (2) Reduction of complex II by NADPH/CYP450 reductase (heme iron to +2). (3) Binding of O2 to complex III. (4) Reduction of complex IV by NADPH/CYP450 reductase (heme iron to +2) to complex V. (5) Dismutation of complex V, yielding one molecule of water and the ternary substrate-oxidized P450-oxygen complex VI. (6) Decomplexation of complex VI, with insertion of oxygen atom in the substrate C-H bond. (7) Radical-mediated reductive decomplexation of complex IV, releasing the substrate and hydrogen peroxide. Decomplexation of complex IV, releasing substrate and superoxide.

A single electron is transferred from the oxidation of NADPH to cytochrome P450 reductase and thence to the P450-substrate complex, reducing the heme iron to the +2 state. The P450 (Fe+2)-substrate complex binds a single molecule of oxygen, forming a complex that can be thought of as either a ferric complex (Fe+3) binding superoxide (O2–) or a ferrous complex (Fe+2) binding an oxygen molecule. Oxidation of an additional molecule of NADPH and transfer of the electron to the P450 complex via CYP450 reductase "locks" the complex as a ferric-superoxide binding complex. The complex subsequently dismutates a molecule of water, yielding a single oxygen-P450-substrate complex, which undergoes bond reconfiguration, with the result of the insertion of the oxygen atom in the C-H bond. The new bond structure favors decomplexation, as oxidized substrate and oxidized CYP450. The ferrous/ferric/oxygen/superoxide complex can also break down, yielding either hydrogen peroxide (following a free-radical reaction with an available hydrogen atom) or superoxide. In either case, the unoxidized substrate molecule is released as well.

In addition to the classification scheme for the CYPs themselves, there are general classes of types of ligands for CYP450s, type 1 and type 2. Type 1 ligands are able to bind to a relatively hydrophobic site on the enzyme in proximity to the central heme iron atom. However, type I ligands are unable to serve as ligands for the heme iron and are therefore available as substrates for monooxygenation reactions. In contrast, type 2 ligands interact directly with the heme iron, usually via sterically unhindered nitrogen complexing directly with the iron atom. Such molecules are usually inhibitors of P450 activity (e.g., SKF-525A and ethylisocyanide).

Cytochrome P450s are present in essentially all tissues, although the liver has the highest concentration, as would be expected considering its role as the primary organ for protecting the body against foreign compounds. The specific pattern of isozymes present will vary in individual tissues, depending on the metabolic role of the CYP450s in that organ. Isozymes present in the kidney and adrenal cortex, for example, tend to be somewhat more oriented toward synthetic reactions than degradative. Of the multiple isozymes present, seven (at least) are of particular interest in regard to drug metabolism: CYP1A2, CYP2C9, CYP2D6, CYP2C19, CYP2E1, CYP3A4, and CYP3A5 (see Table 5.3).

5.3.1.1.2 Genetic Considerations Levels of specific CYP isozymes can vary considerably, depending on the genetic makeup of the individual. The CYP2D6 isozyme is of particular significance for the toxicologist in that it plays a role in the metabolism of many psychotropic and other drugs of medicinal and forensic significance. There can be a great degree of variability between individuals in the amount of 2D6 expressed as a function of genetic polymorphism or the number of copies of the gene for the enzyme. Poor metabolizers have little or no 2D6 function, intermediates have a level between poor and the normal extensive metabolizer. Individuals with multiple copies of the gene expressed, and hence an abnormally high rate of 2D6 activity, are referred to as ultrarapid metabolizers. An understanding of the metabolic capability of the individual may be of significance in attempting to determine the underlying basis for either the apparent lack of activity of a specific drug or, in contrast, an apparent overdose event or expression of particular sensitivity. The levels of other CYP isozymes may be similarly affected by genetic makeup; the degree of expression, reflecting metabolic capability, may be of significance in the interpretation of forensic casework.

5.3.1.1.3 Induction, Inhibition, and Drug–Drug interactions The amount of specific CYP isozymes present in an individual may be significantly affected by induction, the response of increased enzyme synthesis in response to the presence of substrate. The early work on CYPs suggested that there were two general classes of the enzyme family (referred to at that time as cytochrome P450), one induced by phenobarbital (PB) and the second induced by 3-methylcholanthene (3MC), a planar aromatic hydrocarbon. It is now understood how extensively drugs other than the specific isozyme substrate can cause isozyme induction. The induction typified by 3MC is actually on CYP1A2, and for PB on 2B6, 2C9, and 3A4,5 and 7. The significance here is that the induction of an isozyme by one drug may increase the rate of metabolism of a second drug, thereby decreasing the expected area under the curve for a specific dose. While such considerations are normally the realm of the clinical toxicologist, it is important for the forensic toxicologist to understand the potential for unexpectedly high rates of metabolism based on enzyme induction by drugs other than the medication of interest.

Similarly, some drugs can inhibit CYP-catalyzed metabolism of other species, and the magnitude of such inhibition can in some cases be quite significant (Table 5.3).

Table 5.3 Example CYP450 Isozymes and Substrates

• CYP2D6 • Tricyclic compounds – (e.g., amitriptyline and clomipramine) • SSRIs – (e.g., fluoxetine and paroxetine) • Opioids – (e.g., oxycodone and tramadol) • Antipsychotics – (e.g., thioridazine and perphenazine) • β-Blockers – (e.g., metoprolol and propranolol) • Some Antiarhythmics – (e.g., flecainide and mexiletine) • Miscellaneous compounds – (e.g., amphetamine, metoclopramide, promethazine, chlorpheniramine)	• CYP2C19 • Tricyclic compounds – (e.g., amitriptyline and clomipramine) • Some atypical antipsychotics – (e.g., citalopram and moclobemide) • Anti-seizure medications – (e.g., phenobarbital and phenytoin) • Miscellaneous compounds – (e.g., opranolol, carisoprodol, progesterone, coumadin)	• CYP3A4 • Tricyclic compounds – (e.g., amitriptyline and clomipramine) • SSRIs – (e.g., citalopram and sertraline) • Misc. antidepressants – (e.g., mirtazapine and trazedone) • Antipsychotics – (e.g., haloperidol and quietiapine) • Opioids – (e.g., codeine and methadone) • Benzodiazepines – (e.g., alprazolam and diazepam) • Z-drugs – (e.g., zopiclone and zolpidem) • Calcium channel blockers – (e.g., diltiazem and quinidine) • H1-receptor agonists – (e.g., terfenadine and quinidine) • Miscellaneous compounds – (e.g., cafeine, cocaine, destromethorphan, lidocaine propranolol, coumadin)
• CYP2E1 • Anesthetics – (e.g., halothane and isoflurane) • Solvents – (e.g., benzene and dimethylformamide) • Miscellaneous compounds – (e.g., acetaminophen, ethanol, theophylline, zopiclone)	• CYP1A2 • Tricyclic compounds – (e.g., amitriptyline and clomipramine) • Some atypical antipsychotics – (e.g., olanzapine and clozapine) • Miscellaneous compounds – (e.g., haloperidol, caffeine, melatonin, cyclobenzaprine, fluvoxamine, naproxen, acetaminophen, verapamil, coumadin)	

5.3.1.2 *Flavin-Containing Monooxygenases*

The flavin-containing monooxygenases (FMOs) represent another oxidative enzymatic system, analogous to the CYPs, with a spectrum of substrates generally containing a nitrogen or sulfur atom that is somewhat nucleophilic. The FMO reaction uses molecular oxygen, reducing one atom to water, and the other serves to oxidize the substrate molecule. In contrast to the CYPs, there are relatively few FMOs, five gene families, each with a single enzyme. The FMO system can have an activity overlapping that of the CYPs, but the system is not inducible by xenobiotic drugs. Oxidations of forensic interest include amphetamine and related compounds, desipramine, ephedrine, propranolol, amitriptyline, benzphetamine, bupivacaine, methylphenyltetrahydropyridine, phenothiazine, promazine, thioridazine, and related species.

5.3.1.3 *Cytosolic Enzymes*

A number of enzymes are capable of performing oxidations in the cytosol. Examples are the broad family of dehydrogenases, of which perhaps alcohol and aldehyde dehydrogenase are of the greatest significance for the toxicologist. Both oxidative enzymes can use either NAD^+ or $NADP^+$ as electron acceptors, although the reaction is faster with NAD^+. Curiously enough, n-butanol is the most rapidly metabolized species of the alcohols (highest Vmax). Xanthine oxidase, another cytosolic oxidase, is significant in metabolism of purines.

The monoamine oxidases are mitochondrial flavoproteins (containing a derivative of riboflavin, either FAD, flavin adenine dinucleotide, or the mononucleotide analog FMN). While in general this group of enzymes degrades primary, secondary, and tertiary amines (with reaction rates in that order), MAOs are perhaps best known in the forensic toxicology for their role in the degradation of neurotransmitters, specifically serotonin. The ability of certain drugs to inhibit this action accounts for a class of antidepressant drugs known as *monoamine oxidase inhibitors* (MAOIs). Interestingly enough, these enzymes are relatively inactive on species with a methyl group on the β-carbon, and as such, molecules like ephedrine and phenylpropanolamine are not effective substrates.

A related enzyme is *diamine oxidase*, which is a widely distributed copper-containing enzyme, preferentially active on alkyl diamines. Cadavarine, a five-carbon chain diamine, and putrescine, its four-carbon analog, are the preferred substrates. Diamines with a carbon chain longer than eight carbons are not substrates for the enzyme.

5.3.2 Phase II Reactions

Phase II reactions can considerably increase the aqueous solubility of a molecule by conjugating an active group of a molecule with a hydrophilic group such as glucuronic acid, sulphate, or amino acids. Type I reactions combine an activated conjugating agent (e.g., uridine diphosphoglucuronic acid [UDPGA]) with the substrate to produce the final species (sulfates and glycosides). Type II reactions use an activated substrate, which is subsequently combined with an amino acid to form the final product.

5.3.2.1 *Glucuronidation*

Glucuronidation is responsible for most of the phase II products of interest to the forensic toxicologist. The archetypal glucuronidation involves the reaction of a hydroxyl group with UDPGA, producing an O-glucuronide, and is catalyzed by a *UDP glucuronosyl transferase* (of which there are many types). O-glucuronidation can be accomplished with a number of different substrate types besides alcohols, including carboxylic acids and unsaturated ketones (capable of keto-enol tautomerism). The reaction of UDPGA with the aglycone is an SN2-type, with inversion (UDPGA is alpha, hence the glucuronide product is beta). UDP glucuronosyl transferase is a membrane-bound protein, isolated in the microsomal fraction as a single protein ~59 Kdal. The enzyme is specific for UDPGA, and other UDP sugars are inactive (Figure 5.4).

While the formation of O-glucuronides is commonly encountered, N-, S-, and C-glucuronides can also be formed. N-glucuronides can be formed from carboxyamides, sulphonamides, and primary, secondary, and even some basic tertiary amines. S-glucuronides can be formed from both aliphatic and aromatic thiols and dithiocarboxylic acids. C-glucuronidation would be expected to be energetically unfavorable but can occur in some 1,3-dicarboxylic compounds.

5.3.2.2 *Sulphation*

The addition of a sulfonate group to an alcohol or amine, forming a sulfate ester ($R-OSO_3^-$), is catalyzed by a family of related cytosolic sulfotransferases and can be used in a wide variety of xenobiotics as well as endogenous substrates. The sulfo group is donated from the activated 3′-phosphoadenosine-5′phosphosulfate (PAPS) (Figure 5.5).

5.3.2.3 *Methylation*

Amines, hydroxyl, and sulfhydryl groups can be directly methylated by the action of specific methyltransferase enzymes. The methyl group is initially located on an activated sulfur atom in S-adenosyl methionine, which

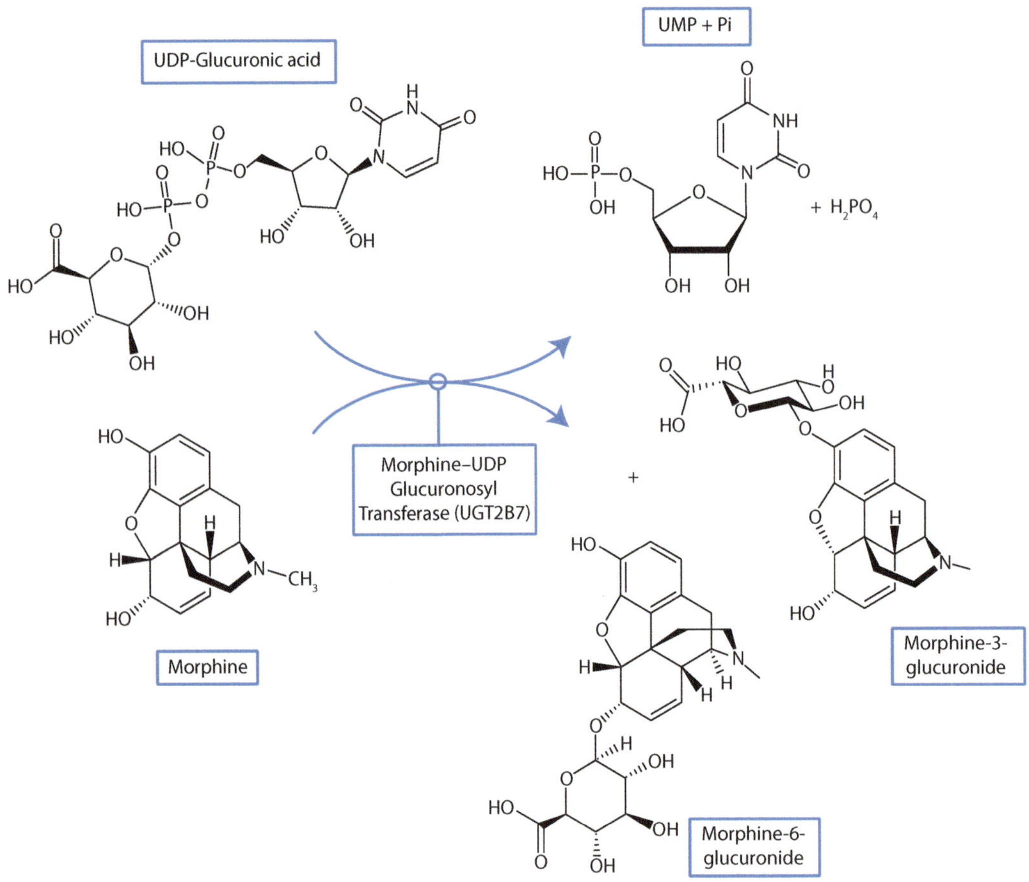

Figure 5.4 Formation of morphine 3- and morphine 6-glucuronide via morphine glucuronosyl transferase.

becomes S-adenosyl homocysteine (see Figure 5.6). Phase II reactions generally increase the aqueous solubility of the substrate; however, in the case of methylation, there can be a decrease in hydrophilicity. Nevertheless, the methylated products are generally less reactive, and hence, the reaction is deactivating. The process can result in the biomethylation of some elements, such as the formation of methylmercury by bacterial species, a process of considerable environmental and toxicological significance.

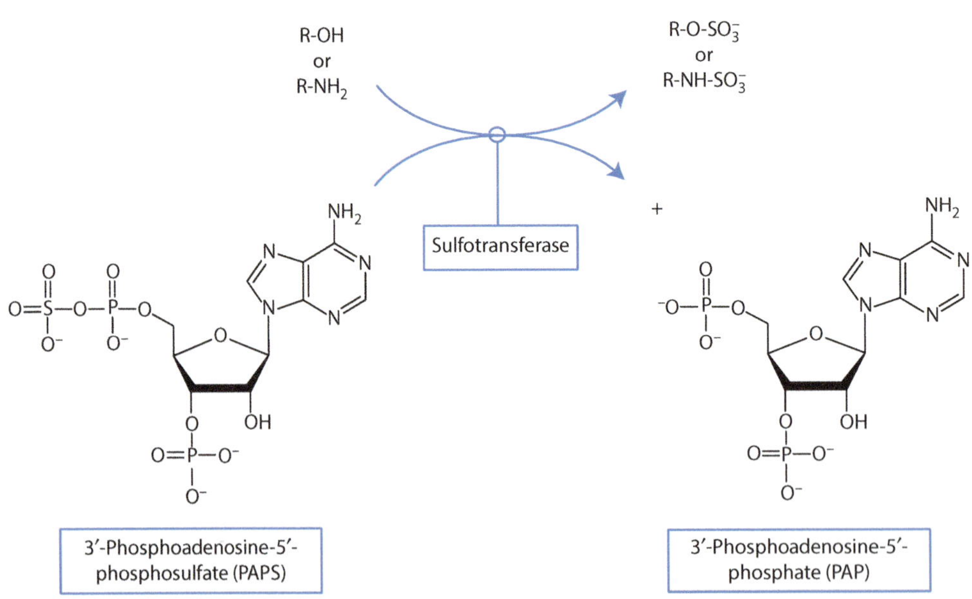

Figure 5.5 General scheme of sulfation of hydroxyl or amine-containing substrates.

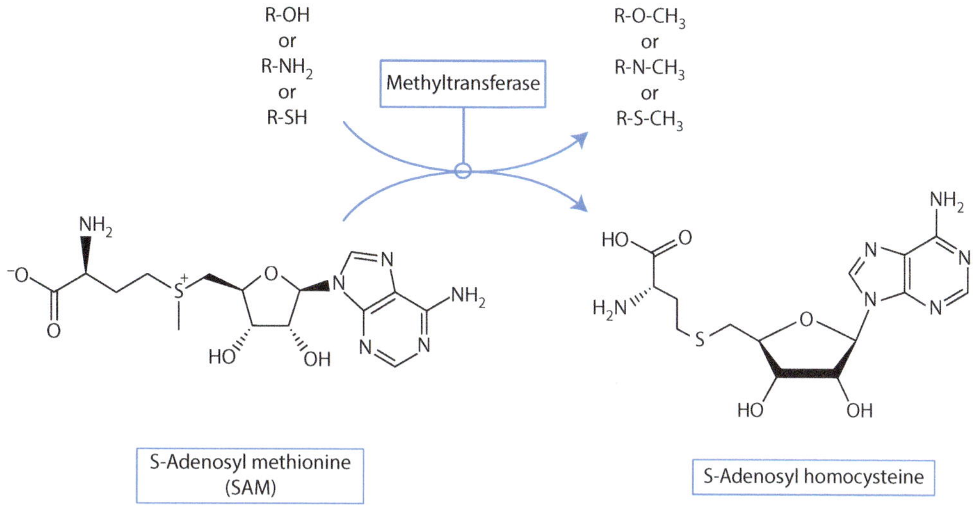

Figure 5.6 General scheme of methylation by SAM-methyltransferase.

5.3.2.4 *Acetylation*

A wide variety of nitrogenous compounds (and some O- and S- species) can be conjugated via acetylation, including aromatic primary amines, hydrazines, hydrazides, sulphonides, and some primary aliphatic amines. The reaction is generally of two types, either a reaction with an activated conjugating agent (acetylCoA), or the xenobiotic is activated and conjugated by reaction with an amino acid. The O- and S-acetyltransferases (also cytosolic) are less commonly encountered.

Acetylation via acetylCoA: The activated co-factor acetylCoA is formed by the condensation of acetate and coenzyme A, catalyzed by CoA-acetyltransferase. The acetylation of a drug is catalyzed by a cytosolic N-acetyltransferase, the levels of which are genetically determined, with the population divided into fast or slow acetylators depending on their genetic makeup. A number of drugs are significantly metabolized by the acetylation process (e.g., isoniazid, hydralazine, procainamide, phenelzine, dapsone, and a number of sulfonamides) and important kinetic parameters associated with the drug (e.g., $t_{1/2}$ and AUC will be affected by the conjugation ability of the recipient molecule).

5.3.2.5 *Amino Acids*

Exogenous carboxylic acids, including arylacetic acids, aromatic, and aryl-substituted carboxylic acids, can be activated to form S-CoA derivatives via the action of mitochondrial ATP-dependent ligases. The activated species can then react with amino acids, generally glycine or glutamate. The formation of hippuric acid from toluene is an example of the process, as shown in Figure 5.7. Interestingly, analogous reactions with bile

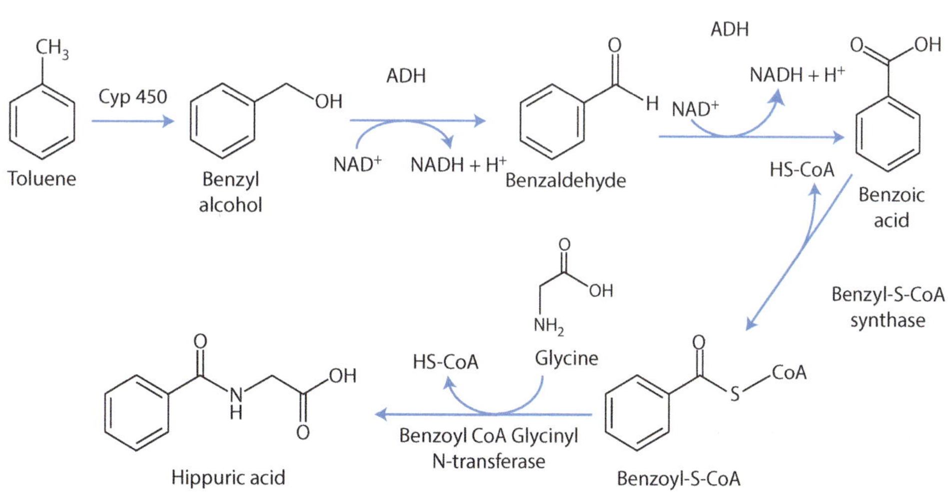

Figure 5.7 Formation of hippuric acid from toluene, via conjugation with glycine.

acids can also generate conjugated species via the action of a bile acyl:CoA ligase and cytosolic bile-acyl-coA amino acyl n-acetyltransferase.

5.3.2.6 Glutathione

Glutathione (GSH) is a tripeptide composed of cysteine, glutamic acid, and glycine. The central cysteinyl side-chain presents a nucleophilic sulfhydryl group that can form conjugates with a wide variety of xenobiotic electrophilic species, such as alkyl, aryl and aralkyl halides, alkenes, and aryl and alkyl epoxides. Nonenzymatic addition reactions may occur with free radicals and other reactive intermediates and play an important role in limiting oxidative or free-radical damage to cells. Conjugation between GSH and xenobiotic species is achieved by a glutathione S-transferase, which has been described as active in both cytosolic and microsomal cellular fractions.

5.3.2.7 Mercapturic Acids

A number of compounds able to form GSH conjugates can undergo further enzymatic modification, resulting in the formation of mercapturic acids, which are the N-acetylcysteinyl conjugates of xenobiotics. The initial step is the formation of the GSH conjugate, which is then hydrolyzed at the g-glutamyl bond by g-glutamyl transferase. The glycine moiety is removed by hydrolysis, and acetate is added by an acetyl CoA acyl transferase.

5.4 Reactive Metabolites

Not all biotransformations produce less toxic or less reactive species. In some cases, molecules of significantly greater toxic potential are produced as a consequence of phase 1 reactions or other enzymatic transformations. The biochemical transformation of xenobiotics to reactive (or more so) species is commonly referred to as metabolic activation or bioactivation. Such reactions are the initial event in many examples of chemically induced toxicity. Recognition of the ability of reactions in the body to produce significantly more toxic species was based on a number of compounds, one of which was DAB (N,N-dimethyl-4-aminoazobenzene), a recognized hepatocarcinogen in rats. DAB metabolites bind covalently to proteins and nucleic acids in the cell, and that covalent binding was found to be an essential part of the carcinogenic process. An example that is commonly dealt with in forensic casework is the production of NAPQI (N-acetyl para-quinonimine) from acetaminophen, a process that has been directly responsible for many fatalities associated with acetaminophen overdose.

Reactive intermediates are generally electrophiles, reacting with cellular nucleophiles, for example, nucleic acids, proteins, and specific molecules such as glutathione. Many reactive intermediates are able to reduce oxygen, thereby leading to the generation of superoxide and, subsequently, more reactive oxygen radical species, a process that can lead to oxidative damage or lipid peroxidation.

Products of phase I enzymatic reactions can be more reactive and more toxic than the original substrate molecule. Activating enzymes is more a description of a specific reaction process and product than a class of enzymes. As an example, CYPs normally act as detoxifying agents but, depending on the substrate, can produce potent toxins, mutagens, teratogens, and carcinogens. Reactive intermediates are generally classified with regard to how long-lived they are in the cell. Ultra-short-lived metabolites are so reactive that they generally bind to the site of their formation, the enzyme catalytic site. As a consequence of such binding, they inactivate the enzyme. The molecule giving rise to such a species often referred to as "suicide substrates." Short-lived metabolites either remain in the cell or last long enough only to travel to nearby cells. Long-lived metabolites are reactive intermediates that are able to be remain unreacted long enough to move away from the cells in which they were formed and travel around the body. (e.g., a number of carcinogenic species).

The formation of reactive intermediates will be dependent upon a number of factors, including the amount of enzyme capable of forming the species, the availability of the substrate molecules, and any co-factors necessary for the reaction. The amount of the effect generated by a certain level of substrate will be a function of these factors, as well as the presence of any inhibiting agents, and the degree to which detoxification mechanisms can function.

REVIEW QUESTIONS

1. What characterizes and distinguishes the two types of transformation reactions?
2. Enzyme production can be enhanced as a consequence of toxin exposure. What is this process, and how can it be helpful? How can it be deleterious?
3. How does in general, each type of biotransformation process affect the target molecule in terms of polarity? Solubility? Why is this important?
4. Describe the three types of enzymatic inhibitors.
5. What distinguishes the FMO system from the CYP system?
6. What is a "suicide substrate?"

TOPICS FOR DISCUSSION

1. Can the presence of an inhibitor change the kinetics of an enzymatic reaction? How?
2. Components in grapefruit juice have been shown to inhibit intestinal cytochrome P450 isozymes, specifically the CYP3A4 family. Research this phenomenon and explain how this interaction can lead to fatal consequences.
3. Pharmacogenetics is a burgeoning field of study where drugs are prescribed based on genetic typing of certain enzymes to predict how fast a drug will clear a patient's body. What are some advantages and disadvantages of this approach?
4. It has been suggested the CYP system evolved, or at least adapted, in response to combustion products in the atmosphere. Is this reasonable?
5. What are the assumptions required for the derivation of the Michaelis–Menton equation? Why are they important?

Bibliography

Kemper RA, Hayes JR, Bogdanff MS. Metabolism: A determinant of toxicity. In: Hayes AW, editor. *Principles and Methods of Toxicology*. 5th rev ed. New York: Informa Healthcare, 2008.

Lieberman M, Marks A. *Mark's Basic Medical Biochemistry: A Clinical Approach*. 3rd rev. ed. Philadelphia: Wolters Kluwer Health/ Lippincott Williams & Wilkins, 2009.

Mozayani A, Ramon LP. *Handbook of Drug–Drug Interactions: A Clinical and Forensic Guide*. Totowa, NJ: Humana Press, 2004.

Nelson DL, Cox MM. *Lehninger Principles of Biochemistry*. 6th rev. ed. New York: W.H. Freeman, 2013.

Pratt CW, Cornely K. *Essential Biochemistry*. 2nd rev. ed. Hoboken, NJ: Wiley, 2011.

Postmortem Toxicology

6

Contents

6.1 Introduction

We have chosen to include a separate chapter on postmortem toxicology because this particular subject, like that of driving under the influence, often involves efforts on the part of the toxicologist beyond simply determination of what drugs may be present and the amounts thereof, but also what those findings mean in the context of the overall cases. In postmortem considerations, the question is what role (if any) did the drug play in the death? While seemingly simplistic, the question cannot generally be resolved by reference to a table of postmortem drug levels, or some formula to convert such values to antemortem levels, or amount of drug that had been ingested. In these cases, viewing the results from a perspective of understanding of the actions of the drugs that have been found, with a critical eye to the uncertainty associated with inferences based on postmortem toxicologic results, the toxicologist can sometimes offer valuable insight and interpretation for a case. It is toward sharing some of the challenges and issues facing the toxicologist in the postmortem world that this chapter is focused.

The goal of a forensic postmortem examination is to determine the cause and manner of death (COD and MOD) in cases where the death was unexpected, suspicious, unattended, the result of criminal activity, or no physician is willing to sign the death certificate. Such cases become the legal responsibility of either a coroner or medical examiner (both systems are in use in the United States), depending on the local jurisdiction.* It is these offices that ultimately have the responsibility for

* The role and position of coroner arose in the sixteenth century in medieval England, with the dual responsibility of holding inquests on individuals who had died by accident or violence, and maintaining the rights of the crown with regard to tax and property matters. In modern days, the coroner is an elected official, responsible for issuing death certificates. Coroners may be trained medical personnel (e.g., forensic pathologists [FPs]), but in many jurisdictions are not. Many coroners' offices either have FPs on staff or send cases as appropriate to neighboring jurisdictions for autopsy procedures by such trained personnel. In contrast, a medical examiner is usually an appointed office, and the function is generally provided by an FP.

the death certificate. Regardless of the organizational structure, forensic death investigations and autopsies will generally be performed by trained forensic pathologists (FPs). (For simplicity, we will refer to the responsible person as the medical examiner [ME] and the organization as the ME office.)

In many cases, the role that drugs or poisons may have played in the death represents an essential question for the case FP and therefore requires a reliable analysis of samples collected at autopsy (and perhaps at the scene as well, depending on case circumstances). Information regarding what drugs were present (and occasionally absent), in the decedent can be significant factors in the determination of COD and MOD. In such cases, there may be extensive and specific toxicologic analysis and interpretation. Final reports in these cases are often held until completion of the analytical work as "pending toxicology results." These cases, where the drugs present may have played a role in the death, can present unique and interesting challenges for the forensic pathologists and toxicologists.

The need for reliable chemical analysis of samples collected after death has long been a driving force within the field of toxicology, with a unique set of challenges that serve to make this subdiscipline a fascinating field in its own right. An understanding of the postmortem processes (potentially including examination, autopsy, embalming, cremation, as well as the complex and chaotic process of decomposition) to which the body may be subjected after death is essential for the toxicologist to appreciate and fully use the information they provide, and to communicate their findings in a useful manner to the case pathologist. It is also important for the toxicologist to understand that biochemical changes occurring in the postmortem interval may also impact their toxicological findings, from the artifactual generation of target analytes (e.g., ethanol; γ-hydroxybutyric acid [GHB]) to the reequilibration (postmortem redistribution) within the body of drugs that were, prior to death, concentrated in specific organs or tissues. The primary subject of this chapter is the postmortem context from which our toxicological samples are derived and to which our analytical findings and inferences must relate.

6.2 Forensic Postmortem Examinations

The concept of an in-depth invasive examination of a dead body may be a curious or a repulsive thought for many people uninitiated to the medical field. The justification for the practice is the potential for significant information regarding the death to become available during the complex examination called the autopsy. Traditionally, the examination of the deceased was termed *necropsy* derived from the Greek words for corpse (*nekros*) and view (*opsis*). This term is currently more commonly used for the postmortem analysis of animals. *Autopsy* is used to describe the examination of human remains, again from the Greek words for self (*autos*) and view, yielding *autopsy* or *see for one's self*. An autopsy, or the dissection and examination of the body, is the primary mechanism by which the FP gains the information they require to determine the cause and manner of death.

6.2.1 Role of the Medical Examiner

The role of the ME is to ensure that if there is information important for society to be gained from the death (e.g., that a crime has been committed), that this information is acquired in a scientific and forensically defensible fashion. The jurisdiction of the medical examiner or coroner is defined by law as extending over cases wherein the death in question is potentially nonnatural (homicide, suicide, or accident), may have been the result of a crime, or for which there is no physician willing or available to sign the death certificate. The decision as to whether a specific case falls in the jurisdiction of a particular office, and how then to proceed, is the responsibility of either the ME or the forensic pathologist who will take responsibility for the case, and who will ultimately sign the death certificate.

An autopsy can be requested by family members in cases not initially accepted by the ME office, and in many cases such requests will be honored. In some cases, an autopsy for medical purposes may be performed by hospital personnel if the ME has declined to take jurisdiction. Cases handled in this manner are usually those in which the decedent's medical problems are documented, but the family wants to know more information about those diseases and the final cause of death. Similarly, requests to not perform or to limit the extent of an autopsy are generally honored if possible, recognizing that the responsibility of the ME is to the community, not just to the family of the deceased.

The practice of a formalized death investigation by medical personnel trained in forensic practice has become standard in many Western countries. Forensic pathology is a medical specialty that focuses on gaining an understanding of how and why an individual died, and practitioners have received specialized training allowing them to determine COD and MOD in the medicolegal arena. The forensic pathologist uses information derived from the death scene, other investigation results and documents (e.g., medical records), as well as the examination/autopsy procedure itself as an opportunity to gain information about the deceased and their death. The goal of the pathologist is to determine or confirm the identity of the decedent and determine COD and MOD. The process involves the documentation of the nature and extent of injuries and disease, or lack thereof, as well as any medical intervention that may have occurred, whether in an emergency or routine treatment setting.

Death investigations may lead to the recognition that a crime has occurred or that a previously unrecognized disease process was responsible, or in contrast, that the death was a reasonable consequence of natural disease processes. Clearly, it is in the interest of society to recognize homicides and other crimes or circumstances including medical error or malpractice. It is equally important to recognize when a death has not been caused by criminal action, negligence, or malpractice. Postmortem examinations often play a significant role in establishing the basis for legal claims in the civil arena, as COD and MOD findings may impact insurance payments or become a basis for lawsuits. Ultimately, the death certificate and the information contained in the autopsy report become available for use in criminal and civil court proceedings, and the pathologist or toxicologist may play a major role in explaining their findings and opinions within the judicial system.

6.2.2 Scene Investigation

The investigation of a death that has been accepted by the ME office will almost always include some degree of scene investigation, usually by personnel specifically trained for that process (medicolegal investigators). Scene investigation can be brief and perfunctory or, in the case of an apparent or suspected homicide, can be or become crime scenes and may be extensive and complicated. Many crime scenes require considerable expertise from investigative personnel. Information from this process can be of considerable use and interest to the toxicologist, including such information as medical history and prescription information, clinical and medication history just prior to death if the decedent was hospitalized, medications present (and pill counts), temperature of the body, illicit drugs found at the scene, and other information that may help guide the toxicologic investigation.

6.2.3 Types of Postmortem Examinations

The case pathologist has a range of possible approaches for the examination of the body of the decedent, and the nature and extent of the postmortem evaluation may vary, depending on the nature and circumstances of the case. Not all cases accepted into an ME office will receive an autopsy. COD and MOD can be determined and a death certificate completed in a case without an autopsy if, in the opinion of the ME or case pathologist, such an examination is not necessary. Some cases may then be satisfactorily resolved by a simple evaluation of medical records; others may require an examination of the outside of the body only; and some will need a full autopsy examination. Toxicology testing, either on specimens obtained postmortem or on samples collected prior to death by medical services, may be tested, depending on case circumstances.

6.2.3.1 Records Review

A comprehensive review of medical records, coupled with pertinent investigative information, may provide the case pathologist with adequate information with which to satisfactorily resolve a case even without the actual examination of the deceased person. This approach might be employed in several types of situations, with the common factor being no significant expectation or evidence of criminal activity related to the death. For example, if a person died after a week of hospitalization following an apparent drug overdose, with hospital drug testing consistent with the clinical course and diagnosis, the body of the deceased may not be autopsied. Toxicology testing may still be requested if samples are available.

6.2.3.2 External Examination

In cases where the decedent has a documented medical history, a recognized disease process that may reasonably have been fatal, and there are no concerns regarding foul play, the pathologist may choose to limit their examination to the outside of the body (variably called an external examination, view, inspection, etc.). Blood samples from the deceased will often be collected in such cases for routine toxicological examination, and as with a records review case, hospital toxicology laboratory findings will be reviewed and considered as part of the evaluation of the case. An external examination may also be adequate in cases where the decedent's regular treating physician is not available to sign the death certificate, but an explanation of the death may be reasonably ascertained based on history and medical records.

6.2.3.3 Autopsy

An autopsy, being an invasive, in-depth dissection and medical examination of the decedent, is, when coupled with competent scene/case investigation and comprehensive toxicologic evaluation, the most thorough and reliable method for conclusive determination of the cause and manner of death in cases coming under the jurisdiction of the ME. It may seem unnecessary to perform an autopsy in cases where the cause and manner of death are apparently obvious, such as a drug overdose, a traumatic motor vehicle accident, or even a gunshot wound homicide. There may, however, be more questions or issues regarding the death than simply, what was the final mechanism? For example, in the case of an apparent drug overdose, the death may have been the consequence of unusually concentrated, or even contaminated illicit materials (e.g., highly concentrated heroin, or a "club drug" containing synthesis by-products). Not uncommonly, a different drug may be found in the body than what was represented or available as a prescription to the decedent. An overdose of prescription medications may represent an inadvertent consequence of a prescribed dose or a conscious departure from the prescription regimen (e.g., a suicide). In motor vehicle crashes or other accidents, drugs found in the crash victims, and particularly the driver, may be significant with regard to impairment considerations. A homicide victim may have been impaired or affected by drugs at the time of their death, which may impact the interpretation of the event. The information that may be generated during a death investigation can have very significant legal consequences, depending on the nature of the case.

The autopsy process can provide information about preexisting medical issues and the extent to which such conditions may have contributed to the death. Toxicology testing can provide information about drugs that may have affected the decedent at the time of death, even to the point of being the major causative factor. One of the more frequent, unexpected findings in forensic medicine is the toxicologist's detection of apparently high levels of one or more prescription medications in the bloodstream of a person for whom they were (or in some cases not) prescribed. Often in such cases, the death scene and case history do not suggest an overdose, and foul play is not suspected. The pathologist may or may not detect significant disease at autopsy, and as such, the cause and manner of death may be related to the drugs present in the decedent.

6.2.4 Findings and Reports

The findings and opinions of the ME, including the autopsy and toxicology results, are contained in a summary report detailing the assessment of cause and manner of death that is issued after all relevant examination results (including toxicology testing) have been obtained and considered. Such reports are public records and are readily available (with the exception of those regarding victims of homicides) after the resolution or adjudication of the case. Prior to the release of the report, only agencies directly involved in the case (e.g., law enforcement, prosecutor, and defense team) will have access to autopsy findings, toxicology results, and associated opinions. Autopsy reports may also be used by a medical service attempting to correlate clinical information with autopsy findings (e.g., hospital morbidity and mortality review panels). Autopsy reports are regularly requested by family members, often for resolution of insurance matters. This varied array of users necessitates that pathologists write reports in typical medical language with either explanatory notes for any specialized language, or a distillation of findings in an "opinion" section, allowing nonmedical personnel to readily understand the findings and conclusions.

6.2.5 Autopsy Process

The autopsy procedure is a complex and complete physical examination of the body, accompanied by thorough documentation and photographs. The process begins with an examination of the outside of the decedent's body. Clothing, personal effects, and medical devices (e.g., IV lines) and their specific locations are documented in the autopsy report. After the assessment of the outside of the body, the pathologist examines the inside of the body, including the condition of the internal organs and tissues. During the process, the individual organs are removed, weighed, and their condition noted in an overall or "gross" sense. Gastric and intestinal contents are examined (often pills or pill fragments are recovered). Samples of body fluids and organs are taken and reserved for toxicologic, microbiologic, and microscopic analysis. Microbiologic analysis can confirm or identify disease processes that may not be immediately apparent upon gross exam (e.g., myocarditis). Microscopic analysis of tissue sections can allow the pathologist to identify the characteristic pathologic signs of many disease processes, including coronary artery stenosis, pulmonary embolism, and emphysema, along with various forms of liver toxicity (e.g., cirrhosis). Items of potential evidentiary value recovered during the process are retained, including medication patches (on or in the body), pills, tablets (or fragments), projectiles, bullets, and so forth. The usual autopsy procedure includes examination of the head, thorax, abdomen, and pelvic organs. Occasionally, a partial autopsy will be performed, limiting the examination to one or several body regions, usually in response to a religion-based objection to the autopsy process. In any case, the nature and extent of any injury and natural diseases is noted and documented.

Autopsy reports are generally divided into sections separating evidence of injury from documentation of natural diseases. For example, if the decedent has been shot through the chest involving the heart, the path of the bullet will be documented in the "Evidence of Injury" section. The "Internal Examination" section of the report will detail the medical condition of the heart, describing features such as the patency of the coronary arteries, the thickness of the ventricular walls, and the circumference of the valves.

6.3 Role of the Toxicologist in Postmortem Forensic Examinations

Toxicologic examination of samples collected during autopsy or received from a hospital (having been collected prior to death) are a routine part of the postmortem forensic examination process. Historically, some toxicologists had participated in sample collection; however, this practice is increasingly unusual, and most often samples are collected by medical or morgue personnel. Consideration of toxicology findings results is an essential part of the process of determination of cause and manner of death.

6.3.1 Samples and Sampling

Body fluids reserved for postmortem forensic toxicology testing are generally collected in a standardized, specific manner within each office or jurisdiction. As in all forensic processes, there is an expectation of clear and accurate sample labeling, documentation of chain of custody, and proper storage of the samples. Blood is the most commonly used postmortem sample and is generally collected from either a central source (heart or large vessels proximate to the heart) or a peripheral source, one outside the central trunk of the body (usually the femoral vein, as the largest vein distant from the central body organs).

Occasionally blood will be collected from the subclavian vein (located just beneath the clavicle, or collarbone) and considered as peripheral. From a medical perspective, subclavian blood does contain venous blood returning from the periphery; however, from a postmortem toxicologic perspective, its location in the chest cavity makes it a central source. Some facilities routinely collect blood from both central and peripheral sites and may use central blood for screening purposes and peripheral for any quantitative analysis that may be required.

In some ME offices, heart blood may be collected, presumably from the heart using a large bore needle and inserting it into the torso through the intact skin. While blood samples may indeed be readily obtained with this method, the specific sample site and integrity of the sample may be subject to question. The use of heart blood for the determination of drug levels (even if properly collected) may provide questionable or potentially misleading quantitative results as a function of postmortem redistribution (see Section 6.3.3.2). In some cases, "blood" from the chest cavity is collected for analysis. Such fluid may be of questionable toxicologic value because of its undefined character.

A number of other sample types may be collected routinely as a function of the practice of individual pathologists or ME offices. Urine samples are collected in many offices, via direct extraction from the bladder by a suprapubic tap or from a Foley catheter pouch. Urine samples often contain drugs that had been present in the blood prior to death and can therefore provide potentially useful information about the time prior to the death. However, it is essential to bear in mind that drug concentrations in urine are not necessarily indicative of antemortem drug concentrations, and great care should be taken regarding any conclusions drawn based on urine drug analysis. Any quantitative inference drawn from drug concentrations in urine samples will require extraordinary justification and rational. Vitreous humor (VH), on the other hand, can be a particularly useful sample (see Sidebar 6.1). Bile is occasionally collected and submitted for analysis; however, because of the mechanism of its generation, the ability of bile to be reflective of the drug composition is somewhat compromised (many drugs may not be significantly excreted in the bile). Sections of tissues are often submitted and analyzed, particularly in cases of suspected overdose. Most often collected and analyzed are gastric contents, liver, kidney, brain, spleen, and lung.

SIDEBAR 6.1 VITREOUS HUMOR TESTING

Vitreous fluid (vitreous humor [VH]), the aqueous fluid in the eyeball, can be a particularly useful forensic sample, maintained in a somewhat protected space within the body. VH is readily and often routinely collected at autopsy using a small-gauge needle and a 5 mL syringe. VH samples can often be collected even in cases of severe trauma or from cases with some degree of decomposition. Because of its location, drug concentrations present in VH are not likely to have been affected by postmortem redistribution. Drugs present in VH may be reasonably assumed to have been present in the blood at the time of death. In the case of alcohol, VH levels seem to lag somewhat behind the blood level, and this relationship is often used to infer whether an individual's blood alcohol concentration (BAC) was rising or falling at the time of death. VH is used as a blood substitute for analysis of electrolytes (with some caution, particularly with regard to potassium, due to the rapid loss of intracellular potassium after death).

6.3.2 Scope of Testing

Postmortem toxicology testing is driven by need, standard practice, case circumstance, and information available. Most offices use a standard menu or panel employed for analysis of postmortem samples in general. If a specific case warrants a particular or unusual analysis, then the laboratory either performs it or arranges for such an analysis to be performed. This process is most commonly used in cases when heavy metal poisoning is suspected, as instruments capable of detection of a broad spectrum of metals and metalloids (e.g., ion-coupled plasma-mass spectrometry [ICP-MS]) are not common in forensic toxicology laboratories.

6.3.2.1 Screening

Many laboratories employ a routine postmortem drug screen panel, consisting of an analysis for ethanol (and other volatiles) and immunological screening for a number of common pharmaceutical and illicit drugs. Ethanol (volatiles) screening procedures (usually headspace-GC, with simultaneous injection onto two different columns and detectors) are adequately qualitatively and quantitatively rigorous to provide reportable results. However, immunologic procedures are presumptive and are not an adequate basis upon which to report the presence of a drug in the absence of additional confirmatory procedures, usually a combined chromatographic and mass spectrometric method (e.g., GCMS, LCMS, or LCMSMS).

Immunologic screening panels can vary somewhat between laboratories but commonly include amphetamines, barbiturates, benzodiazepines, cocaine, marijuana, and opiates, as shown in Table 6.1. PCP, methadone, and oxycodone are often included, and regionally common drugs may be incorporated in the panel as well. Commonly, when there is no suspicion of drug involvement in the death, negative findings in the screening panel will represent the extent of toxicologic testing. If, on the other hand, drug involvement in the death is a possibility, a more comprehensive GCMS or LCMS screen may be used to identify potentially important drugs or toxins that may be present, as shown in Figure 6.1. Such chromatographic approaches are more labor intensive and costly than the immunological methods but have the advantage of being able to identify a larger, essentially unlimited group of drugs.

Table 6.1 Example Immunoassay Drug Screen Panel

Amphetamines	Amphetamine, methamphetamine, MDA, MDMA, some cross-reactivity with other SMAs
Barbiturates	Extensive group cross-reactivity
Benzodiazepines	Extensive group cross-reactivity
Cocaine	Cocaine and benzoylecgonine
Methadone	Methadone
Opiates	Opiates (morphine, codeine, variable cross-reactivity with other opiates, and semisynthetic opioids)
Oxycodone	Oxycodone (some cross-reactivity with structurally similar semisynthetic opioids)
THC	THC and THC-COOH, some cross-reactivity with other related species
PCP	Phencyclidine

The MS-based screening procedures are normally set up with a standard set of calibrator and control drugs to facilitate quantitative reporting for those particular species. If a drug is identified in a sample that is included in the calibrator and controls for the procedure, the results may at that point be reportable, depending on the quality control parameters for the batch. It is not unusual, however, for compounds to be identified only by spectral match with reference to one of the many mass spectral libraries available. In such a case, most laboratories will report identification "by library spectral match" for compounds *not* of significance to the case in question. For compounds of forensic significance in casework, the standard practice is to acquire a valid reference standard and reanalyze the sample in a batch with appropriate control and calibrators for the compound of interest, even for a qualitative result.

6.3.2.2 Quantitative Analysis

The standard practice for quantitative analysis is based on use of a mass spectrometer, with a gas or liquid chromatograph (GC or LC) providing some degree of analyte separation prior to the mass spectrometer (MS) stage, hence GCMS or LCMS. (This statement may soon be rendered moot in light of recent advances in time-of-flight (TOF) and other MS-based technologies.) Instruments utilizing multiple MS sections, MSMS techniques, can provide significantly enhanced sensitivity and selectivity.

GCMS analyte-specific procedures can be dedicated to several species (e.g., cocaine and benzoylecgonine, or opiates) and use selected-ion monitoring for sensitivity. The combination of retention time comparison to known reference material, and characteristic molecular fragmentation pattern and ratios (again compared with reference standards) provides a rigorous basis for qualitative identification based on two separate physical

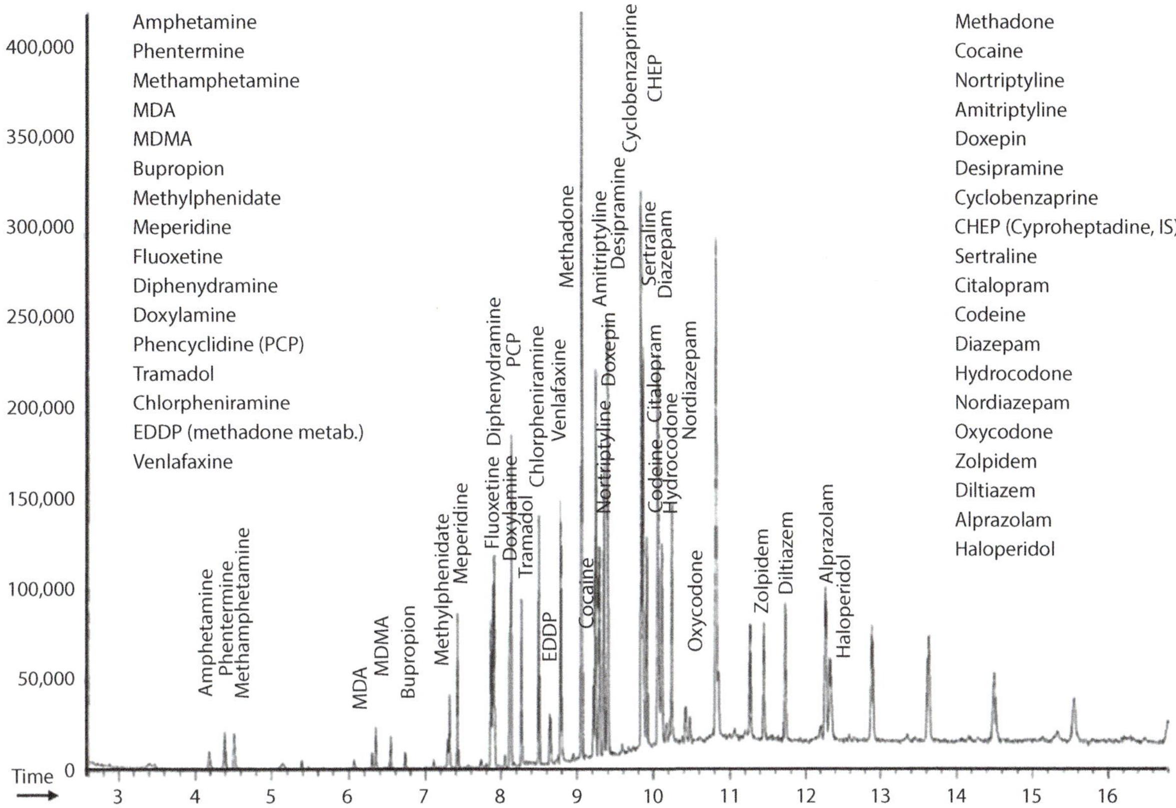

Figure 6.1 Total ion chromatogram; basic drug screen calibrator.

properties (overall size and shape and electrical configuration of the molecule, leading to interaction with the chromatographic column and hence retention time, and the internal bond structure, leading to a characteristic fragmentation pattern and generation of specific ions in a particular ratio). The probability that two different complex molecules (that are not an optical isomeric pair) would generate identical results in such a system is exceedingly small.

Quantitative analysis is a function of the inclusion of appropriate matrix-based calibrators and proper controls of the specific analyte to allow reporting. While peripheral blood samples are preferred, the circumstances of postmortem testing occasionally require that less-than-optimal sample materials be used. In overdose cases, or those where there may be a question as to whether a drug was present in overdose levels, tissue samples may also be analyzed. Liver is most commonly examined, with brain, lung, kidney, and spleen occasionally tested as well. In some offices, tissues are routinely tested in any case of suspected overdose. Interestingly enough, in a case where the drug has only been present in the body for a matter of minutes (e.g., a suicidal ingestion of a drug new to the user), there may not be adequate time for tissue levels to rise to those normally seen in overdose of individuals who are acclimated or are otherwise regularly exposed to the drug. In such cases, the relatively low tissue levels might be somewhat misleading. It is worth once again emphasizing the great potential for uncertainty in the application of quantitative analytical results (however accurate in the particular sample), to an inference of antemortem levels of the drug.

6.3.2.3 *Specialized Toxicology Testing*

Most ME laboratories have some capability for specialized or specific tests that, while not used on a regular or routine basis, are nevertheless validated and available for application in cases as necessary. Specific tests will vary between laboratories, but examples are typically cyanide, GHB, and some of the synthetic cannabinoids and newly appearing amphetamine analog-type designer drugs. As noted above, many ME laboratories also use commercial laboratories that maintain a capability for uncommon tests for the analysis of analytes that are not currently within the testing scope.

6.3.3 Challenges and Confounders of Postmortem Testing

Problems and difficulties that can arise with the analysis of biological samples for postmortem testing are easily divided in two general categories: analytical and interpretive. Clearly, the ability to detect and accurately quantitate drugs in the postmortem setting is an essential and limiting factor in the use of toxicology to facilitate an understanding of the cause and manner of death. However, equally important is recognition of the potential uncertainties and limitations associated with those determinations when trying to explain or understand antemortem behavior, based on results from postmortem samples.

6.3.3.1 *Analytical Challenges*

The analytical challenges faced by the forensic toxicologist tend to be a function of the nature and/or the amount of sample available for analysis. In many cases, there is an ample supply of blood, urine, and even vitreous fluid, such that multiple tests can be run, with confirmatory procedures as necessary. Often the samples are of excellent condition, having been collected shortly after (or in the case of some hospital samples, shortly before) death, and in appropriate tubes for preservation (e.g., fluoride/oxalate, gray tops). In contrast to such cases, samples can sometimes be of limited volume, of undefined composition (e.g., fluid collected from decomposed or partially decomposed bodies), or significantly contaminated by nonbiological materials. Such samples may not behave in the extraction and analytical schemes as well as the typical sample materials or indeed as the corresponding control materials used. Occasionally only tissue samples may be available, and they may not be of a consistency that is easily handled (e.g., desiccated, decomposed, or otherwise degraded), or the only samples available have been collected from an embalmed body (see Sidebar 6.2).

SIDEBAR 6.2 EMBALMED, ENTOMBED, OR BURIED REMAINS

Occasionally, a case will arise in which the COD and MOD are questioned, and the only recourse is a reexamination of the body. In such cases, the body may be disinterred and re-autopsied, or new samples may be collected for toxicologic analysis. Unfortunately, the fluid collected in such circumstances often looks like blood and has been mistaken as such by more than one laboratory. Ethanol is often a component of embalming fluids. Even if there is no indication that samples were derived from an embalmed decedent, the appearance of methanol, isopropanol, and acetone in addition to ethanol should be strongly suggestive. Clearly, any conclusion regarding ethanol in a sample derived from an embalmed body is not defensible.

The analysis of "blood" and body tissues from embalmed remains can pose a serious problem for the toxicology laboratory. Most laboratories will decline to analyze samples from embalmed bodies, but occasionally a case may arise where the simple demonstration of the presence of a drug or poison as having been present will provide useful forensic information. (Failure to demonstrate a drug in such circumstances is not necessarily definitive proof that the drug had not been present.) During the embalming process, the venous blood is pushed out of the body forcefully via a catheter that has been inserted into the vascular system. Embalming fluid may also be injected into the organs of the torso with a trochar (a form of tube, or cannula). Therefore, drugs or volatile compounds in the blood and vascular system are effectively removed (and some degree of extraction from tissues occurs during the perfusion/draining process as well). However, drugs remaining in the tissues will, after the embalming process, diffuse into the aqueous/organic embalming fluid that has been perfused throughout the system, in a variation of the postmortem redistribution process. As might be expected, analytical procedures performed on samples derived from an embalmed body, while potentially qualitatively useful, have a considerable uncertainty associated with any quantitative drug findings, and inferences based on concentration of drugs are likely to be meaningless.

6.3.3.2 *Interpretive Challenges*

Perhaps the biggest challenge that forensic toxicologists deal with is the expectation that a quantitative drug value identified in a postmortem sample is necessarily reflective of antemortem levels of the drug. Unfortunately, the lay public and even many medically trained personnel accept this "common sense" assumption. There can be a significant educational hurdle to be dealt with in communicating to such individuals that postmortem drug levels may not be indicative of the antemortem levels an individual experienced just prior to their death, and indeed may vary significantly from those levels.

6.3.3.2.1 Postmortem Redistribution The historic view that drugs distribute uniformly throughout the body has changed and evolved considerably, as an increasing body of evidence has demonstrated differences in drug concentrations between blood collected from the central cavity or heart (as has been historic practice) and blood collected from a peripheral source, such as the femoral vein. These differences (with peripheral drug levels being generally less than central) can be of great magnitude but are not necessarily predictable, sometimes varying considerably between apparently similar cases. There has been, understandably, some reluctance to accept the concept that there could be a redistribution process occurring after death that may effectively invalidate, or at least call into serious question, the concentrations of drugs determined in postmortem samples. However, with increasing experimental documentation of the differences between central and peripheral blood, and as the identification of specific transport proteins and systems provided a mechanistic basis for understanding the difference between blood and organ drug levels postmortem, the phenomenon of *postmortem redistribution* (PMR) has become well recognized and accepted in the toxicologic community.

In short, drugs that have become concentrated in some tissue or tissues, due to specific uptake mechanisms in the cell to facilitate their concentration in tissues during life, could (and do) redistribute or equilibrate throughout the body once the mechanistic basis for creating and maintaining that concentration stops, shortly after the time of death.

Simple diffusion of drugs ionized at physiological pH (hence, most drugs) into tissues is limited by the electrostatic charge on the cell membrane, and such species become concentrated in specific tissues by the action of membrane transport proteins (whereas non-ionized species are able to diffuse across the membrane). After death, the ATP-dependent membrane charge on cells disappears, and the membrane becomes increasingly compromised as autolysis (the failure of cellular structures as degradation enzymes catalyze membrane molecular breakdown) proceeds. As the energy barrier to diffusion of ionized species disappears, and membrane structure becomes increasingly degraded, previously concentrated drugs are able to transit the degrading cell membrane, and equilibrate as a function of gradient-driven diffusion. The complex process is essentially chaotic in nature, meaning that the degree of PMR in a specific case is generally unpredictable.

In the antemortem state there is no expectation of a differential in drug values between peripheral and central blood samples because blood continues to circulate, and cellular membranes (and membrane potential) are maintained. Given a long enough interval after death, adequate to allow equilibration of drugs throughout the body based on diffusion, one would also expect no differential between peripheral and central blood drug levels. (PMR, therefore, represents a dynamic transitional state between equilibria and is not, even on a case-specific basis, amenable to description by statistical parameters. Average PMR or central:peripheral ratios, while potentially instructive, can also be grossly misleading.) The concentration of drugs in a sample collected postmortem will depend on the extent to which a particular analyte had been concentrated antemortem, the location of the *diffusion front* (the leading edge of a diffusion process) of the drug in the region around the tissue in which it had been concentrated, and finally, the location from which the particular sample had been drawn. Obviously, if the sample has been collected beyond the diffusion front, the drug level will not be affected by PMR. It is important to note that PMR may be a major factor in cases where drugs present had only been used at therapeutic levels. In fact, it is not uncommon that a routine therapeutic drug will be attributed to a causative or contributory role in a death, despite the lack of clinical history or pathologic corroborative evidence to support such a conclusion based on artificially elevated concentrations in a postmortem heart blood sample.

In contrast, it can equally be problematic to assume that elevated blood levels, even from heart or central blood samples, must necessarily be reflective of PMR. In cases where exposure to the drug has occurred in a naïve individual, and death ensues shortly after exposure, there may simply not have been adequate time for an antemortem concentration of the drug to build up in tissues. In such cases, there may be no antemortem gradient and no basis for PMR.

The key point for the toxicologist is that because of all the variables potentially impacting the magnitude of PMR in a particular case, it can be nearly impossible to predict the magnitude of redistribution that will be reflected in a given a sample. Therefore, it is also nearly impossible to reliably predict an antemortem level of a drug, based on a postmortem sample drawn from a region subject to PMR (e.g., the central cavity). While peripheral blood sources (e.g., femoral vein) may provide a much-reduced expectation for PMR elevation, the practical toxicologist will take great care in attempting to infer an antemortem level from a drug level determined in a sample that may reflect some degree of PMR. Providing a reasonable explanation of the process and its consequences to forensic pathologists who must use toxicologic analytical findings (and on occasion, to the legal community) can represent an important task and challenge.

6.3.3.2.2 Decomposed Samples Decomposition poses additional complications regarding toxicologic analysis in that the supply of usable specimen may be limited, and the composition of samples can be significantly different (e.g., more viscous) than normally analyzed. Because of the nature of the decompositional processes (reflecting microbial metabolism), the potential for matrix effects and the appearance of microbial metabolic products in extraction procedures increases (see Sidebar 6.3). Drug levels from decomposed bodies can be very difficult to interpret because of the potential for postmortem redistribution, loss due to microbial activity, potential concentration due to dehydration (which may lead to artificially high and potentially misleading drug levels), *in situ* contamination, and so forth. In a practical sense, any inference beyond simply the identification of the drugs present may be questionable, and further, the absence of expected or suspected drugs may not be truly indicative that the drug was not taken prior to, and indeed, may have caused or contributed to the death.

SIDEBAR 6.3 ETHANOL IN DECOMPOSED CASES

Ethanol can be produced in significant amounts during the process of decomposition by bacterial fermentation of native sugars, and levels in excess of 0.1 g/dL have been reported. Because ethanol is water soluble and not specifically concentrated in any tissue, it is generally not subject to postmortem redistribution, and a central blood sample (e.g., from the heart) would be expected to provide a result as valid as one drawn from a peripheral source. (An antemortem concentration of ethanol in the stomach can, however, provide a reservoir from which postmortem redistribution, in a sense, can occur.) In practical terms, microbial production of ethanol via fermentation processes will also produce other short-chain alcohols and aldehydes, and a characteristic pattern of decompositional products can be readily recognized via headspace GC (Figure 6.2). Nevertheless, attempts to distinguish between antemortem ingestion and postmortem production of ethanol in decomposed remains must be carefully considered. While such a distinction may be important for the determination of cause and manner of death, and perhaps to answer ancillary questions, the inherent uncertainty in the process is considerable, and a strong opinion should be accompanied by good data and sound reasoning (and perhaps a corroborative analysis of a VH sample).

6.3.4 Pediatric Cases

The pediatric population is recognized as representing a significant challenge for the toxicologic community. In essence, the pharmacologic parameters associated with drugs in adults cannot automatically be applied to children as if they were merely miniature adults. While drug absorption, distribution, metabolism, and elimination follow the same general patterns in children, the *rates* of these processes can vary significantly from the adult. The adage "children are not just small adults," popularized by toxicologists with extensive experience in this area is particularly apt and care should be taken in drawing any conclusions regarding drug levels in the pediatric population when using toxicologic parameters developed from an adult population.

Neonates and children have a higher percentage of body water than adults, so drugs that are distributed in

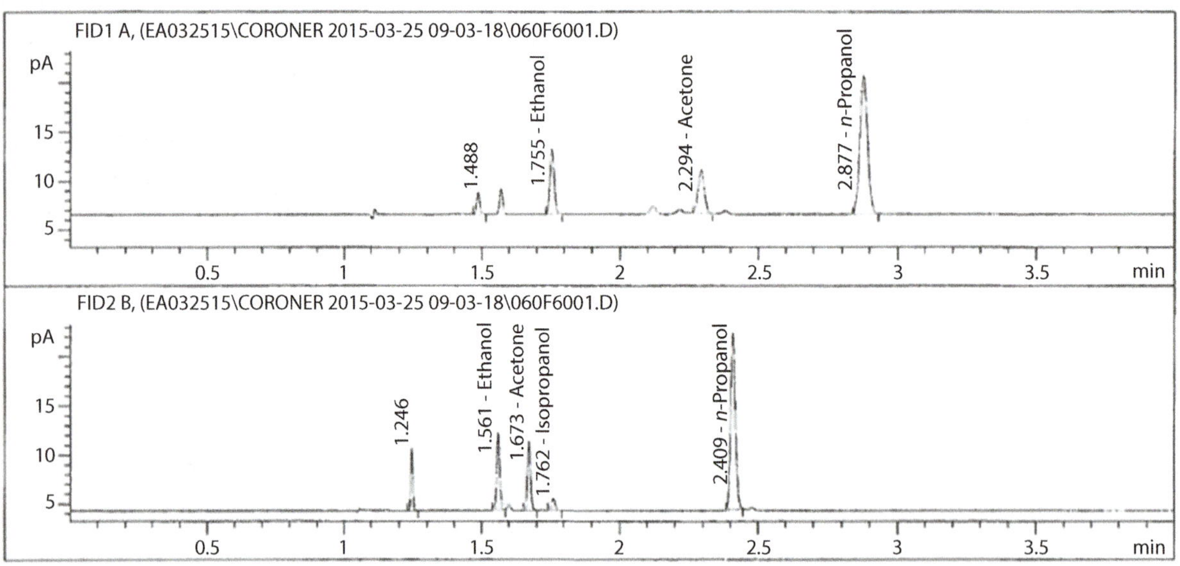

Figure 6.2 Ethanol and related volatile compounds in a decomposed sample. (Courtesy of Dr. John Wyman, Cuyahoga County Medical Examiner's Office, Cleveland, Ohio.)

body water will have a somewhat larger effective volume of distribution in young patients than they will in adults. Likewise, protein binding can be less than in adults, yielding a higher active (free, unbound) drug concentration in circulation than would be found in an adult with a similar weight-based dose. Metabolism of many drugs occurs in the liver by cytochrome P450 enzymes. In children, the expression of these various metabolizing systems may not be at levels expected in adults, resulting in significantly slower elimination rates than would be expected in the adult population. Neonates and infants have a lower glomerular filtration rate (GFR) than do adults, and drugs eliminated via kidneys may have a lower elimination rate than expected in adults. (Neonatal GFR is only about 50% of that of adults but usually approaches adult rates by the end of the first year of life.) Another adage that might be of use in the consideration of such cases is "pathology trumps toxicology" with the interpretation that the medical evidence in a case, being medical history and records, clinical parameters, and ultimately autopsy findings provide the best information as to the physiological processes in the individual. Toxicologic findings may support or help explain those findings, but ultimately, the expression of toxicity is a function of physiology and pathology.

6.3.5 Geriatric Cases

The geriatric population also presents issues for the toxicologist to consider regarding the interpretation of drug levels. As with the pediatric population, the same basic pharmacologic processes continue to operate in older patients as in adults; however, rates of such processes may be affected as organs become less efficient as a function of the normal aging process, or are affected by disease. Often, older adults can have digestive issues resulting in either rapid or slow absorption of drugs. Elderly patients often have a lower percentage of muscle mass and body water and a higher percentage of body fat. Drugs that distribute in body water will have an effectively lower volume of distribution for these patients. Liver function may be impaired leading to significant effects on metabolism and elimination. Elderly people more commonly have some compromised kidney function, with a reduced GFR, leading to a longer half-life, AUC, and blood concentration for some drugs. The geriatric population also tends to take more medications than younger adults, complicating any interpretation of toxicologic findings and raising the potential for drug–drug interactions. The relatively large doses of analgesics used in the hospice setting may also raise concerns and issues in some cases. In many laboratories, postmortem opiate levels in hospice care patients are reported without quantitative values.

REVIEW QUESTIONS

1. Would you consider that from a toxicologic perspective, a blood sample collected from the subclavian vein is peripheral (versus central)? Why or why not?
2. In an investigation of an apparent oxycodone overdose, hospital screening was negative. What do you conclude?
3. Given a sample that is apparently blood, how would you resolve the question as to whether it actually is fluid collected after embalming?
4. A hospital patient received an opiate injection 3 hours prior to death. Heart blood levels of the drug are consistent with an opiate-based death. What one clinical parameter do you want to know to resolve whether the opiate concentration is valid? (Think opiate toxidrome…)
5. What *scene* investigative parameter would you be interested in knowing, if postmortem findings included MDA and MDMA, and sympathomimetic amine toxicity was being considered? (Think sympathomimetic toxidrome…)

TOPICS FOR DISCUSSION

1. Could alcohol in the stomach at the time of death be a source for postmortem redistribution? If so, how?
2. Vitreous electrolyte values are often considered in postmortem cases, except for potassium. What is the mechanistic basis for the exclusion?
3. Would you expect THC to be the subject of postmortem redistribution? Why or why not?
4. Do you believe that opiate or other end-of-life care medications should be quantitatively reported in hospice cases? Why or why not?
5. Toxicologic findings show the presence of amitriptyline at about three times therapeutic levels in an elderly decedent, and a question of suicide has been raised. What do you want to know to help resolve the issue?
6. Standard practice in postmortem cases is to collect blood in gray top tubes, containing fluoride and oxalate. What is the role of each in the preservation of the sample?
7. It has been suggested that average values of PMR can be used as a basis for estimation of antemortem drug levels. Could this process be valid in some cases?

Bibliography

DiMaio V, DiMaio D. *Forensic Pathology.* 2nd ed. Boca Raton: CRC Press, 2001.

Dolinak D, Matches E, Lew E. *Forensic Pathology Principles and Practice.* New York: Elsevier, 2005.

Knight B. *Forensic Pathology.* 2nd ed. London: Arnold, 1996.

Mozayani A, Raymon L, editors. *Handbook of Drug Interactions: A Clinical and Forensic Guide.* Totowa, NJ: Humana Press, 2004.

Spitz WU, editor. *Spitz and Fischer's Medicolegal Investigation of Death.* 4th ed. Springfield, IL: Charles C. Thomas, 2006.

Organ System Toxicology

II

Neurotoxicology

7

Contents

7.1 Introduction

The ability of drugs, toxins, and poisons to affect the nervous system lies at the base of much of the casework of the forensic toxicologist. From the mild euphoria generated by a low level of ethyl alcohol, to the cardiotoxic effects of the classic poisons such as aconite and atropine, so many of the drugs we deal with as either recreational, therapeutic, or toxic agents exert their primary effects on the body via an interaction with some aspect of the nervous system. Familiarity with the mechanism of action of a toxin on specific biomolecules is an essential part of the process of understanding the overall toxicity of the drug. A practical understanding of the functionality of the underlying system, in this case the complex, interwoven network of communicating cells we call the nervous system, is important too, if not equally essential.

With an incredibly complex interconnected network of cells, the nervous system performs a multiplicity of tasks that both keep us alive and enrich our lives. Neurons, nerves, and the nervous system provide a basis for the receipt of information from the outside world and control of multiple biological functions in the body, as well as the basis for consciousness, thought, language, and emotions.

7.2 Anatomy

The nervous system can be anatomically divided into two major parts: the central nervous system (CNS), composed of the brain and the spinal cord, and the peripheral nervous system (PNS), serving to connect the CNS to the body as a whole and the outside

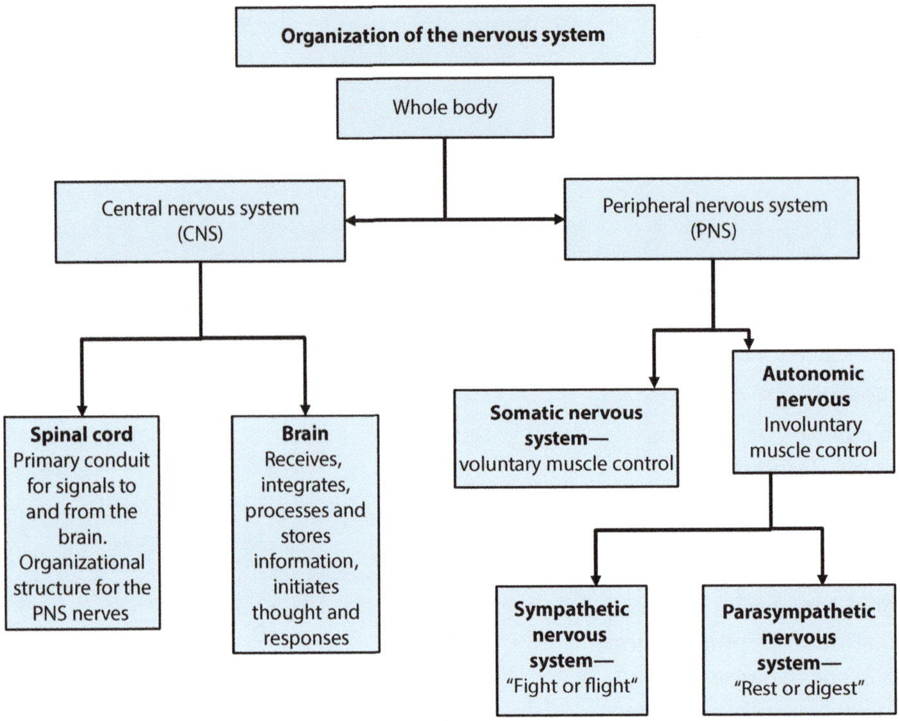

Figure 7.1 Organization of the nervous system.

world as shown in Figures 7.1 and 7.2. The nerves of the CNS send and receive information only from other nerves and do not directly connect to other body parts (muscles, skin, intestines, etc). The majority of structures we call nerves are actually part of the PNS, even if their cell bodies lie within the brain or spinal cord. The PNS is further divided into the somatic and autonomic systems. The somatic PNS innervates skin, joints, and skeletal muscle and provides the basis for voluntary muscle movements; while the autonomic system innervates smooth muscle of internal organs and blood vessels, cardiac muscle, and glands. Within the autonomic nervous system, the balance between the sympathetic and parasympathetic system largely determines the activity levels for the various functions of the body, from cardiac activity to secretion of digestive enzymes.

Ganglia are structures composed primarily of neurons and serve to provide interconnections between the nervous systems and also function as organizational points for nerves within the body. Nerve fibers that connect the CNS to ganglia are *preganglionic*, and the nerves then leading from the ganglion to the innervated organ or muscle are *postganglionic*. Ganglia can be further interconnected with other ganglia in a complex system known as a *plexus* (e.g., the solar plexus, or technically the celiac plexus, located at the base of the sternum, and comprised of a number of other ganglia in the abdomen).

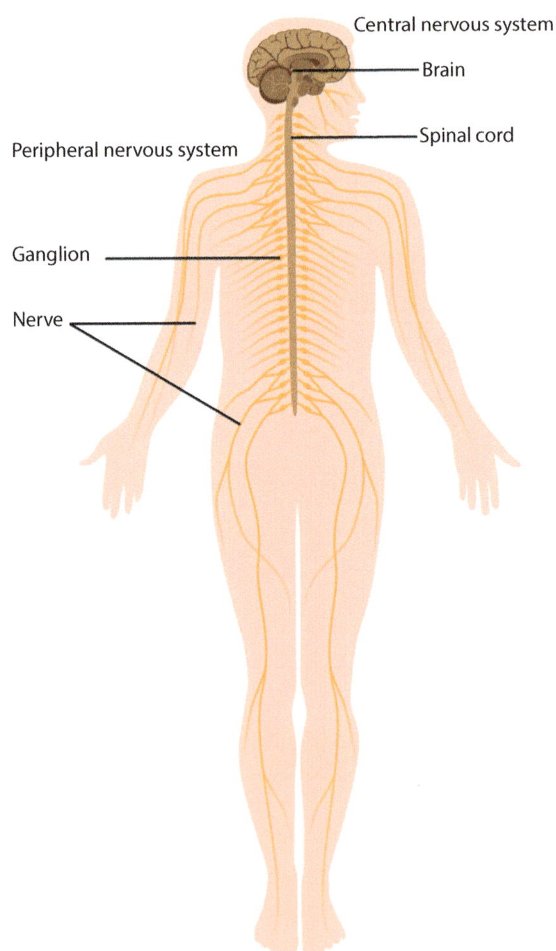

Figure 7.2 Central and peripheral nervous system.

7.3 Physiology

The basic, essential element of the nervous system is a single neuron. Nerves are then (at least as a colloquial term) a collection of integrated neurons (e.g., the vagus nerve; see Figure 7.3). The nervous system incorporates both neurons and supportive cells functioning in various capacities (Glial cells).

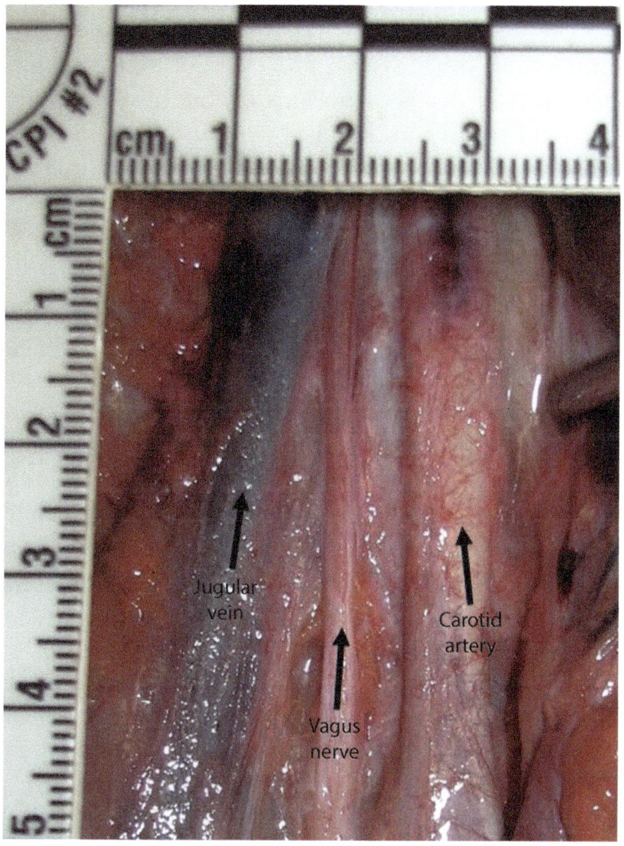

Figure 7.3 Vagus nerve, *in situ*.

7.3.1 Neurons

A neuron is the basic cellular component of the nervous system and is capable of receipt, integration, and propagation of signals. Neurons consist of a cell body, or *soma*, containing the nucleus and cellular organelles; *dendrites*, which are branching processes extending from the soma that serve to receive incoming signals from other neurons, or sensory inputs and another process; the *axon*, which serves to propagate a signal to either another nerve cell or muscle cell (Figure 7.4).

While neurons can have many branching dendrites, each contains only a single axon. Axons are in many cases surrounded by a protective myelin sheath, which serves to insulate the axon and allow a more rapid propagation of the nerve signal down the length to the axon terminal. Signal propagation at the axon terminal proceeds from one neuron to another across the *synapse*, or space between the cells, as a chemical rather than an electrical signal. The synapse may be between the axon terminal and either dendrites or soma of a nerve cell or of a nerve or muscle cell.

Neurons, while sharing the same basic structure, can be generally classified as sensory, motor, or interneurons. Sensory neurons provide the basis for the translation of physical phenomena to a nervous signal that can then be received and processed in the brain. Motor neurons provide communication with muscle fibers, allowing the conscious control of movement and the unconscious control of heartbeat, breathing, and a host of other processes dependent on some degree of regulation (e.g.,

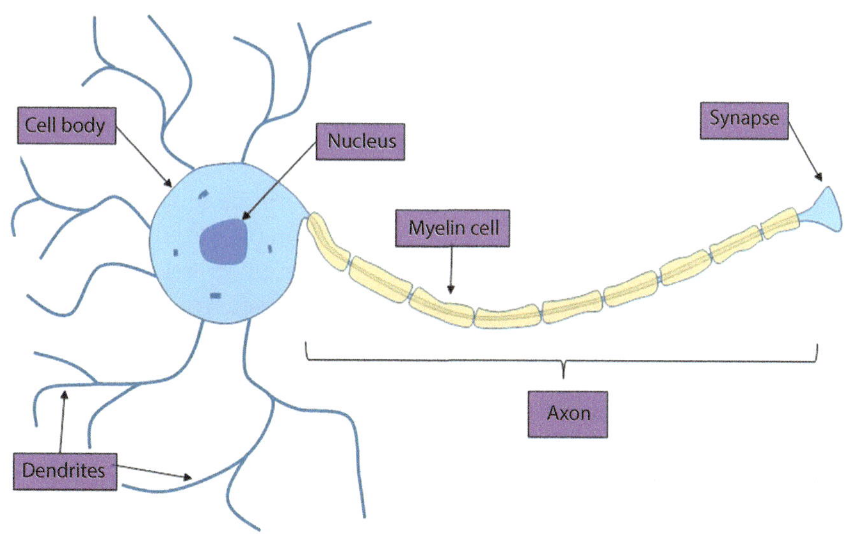

Figure 7.4 Basic neuron structure.

glandular secretions). Finally, interneurons simply communicate from one neuron to the next, promulgating signals throughout the nervous system. Interestingly, it is the activity of the interneurons that provide the basis of thought, emotion, and reaction.

7.3.2 Glial Cells

Glial cells serve in an essentially supportive role for the neurons. Oligodendrocytes form the axonal myelin sheath within the CNS, and Schwann cells perform the same function in the PNS. Microglial cells are phagocytotic cells within the CNS, performing a protective function; and finally, astrocytes serve in a biochemical supportive role and also participate in formation of the blood–brain barrier.

7.4 Neurotoxicologic Responses

The nervous system can be damaged in a number of ways. Direct physical damage can occur as a function of trauma or disease. There can also be a biochemically mediated effect on a cellular function by either an interference with cellular processes or signal propagation. Neurotoxic damage can be caused by overinduction response of the nervous system as well, in the sense of causing nerves to initiate or propagate signals inappropriately.

7.4.1 Susceptibility of the Nervous System

In some ways, the nervous system is more susceptible to the effects of toxins than are other tissues or organs. Neurons have a limited ability to regenerate, and a very large surface area:cellular volume ratio. Metabolically, the activity of neurons is relatively limited, with the activity of the cells being exclusively focused on information transfer. However, several defensive mechanisms are active to help protect neurons. The CNS is protected somewhat by the blood–brain barrier. This barrier is simply a function of the filling of the pores and spaces between the cells of the vasculature by cellular projections from astrocytes, making a continuous, nonporous surface. Drugs or toxins must therefore cross cell membranes to achieve transit into the CNS from the vasculature. Such a barrier is only a minimal limitation on the diffusion of nonionized, lipophilic materials. However, since most drugs are ionized as physiological pH, transmembrane diffusion is energetically unfavorable, and many drugs cannot reach the CNS in the absence of specific transport mechanisms. Another significant protection at the level of the individual neuron is the myelin sheath, surrounding and protecting the axonal processes extending a significant distance away from the cell body. Finally, within the cell itself, many common protective enzymes, such as catalase, superoxide dismutase, and others, are also present in the neurons, providing some degree of internal protection against biochemical degradation.

7.4.2 Manifestations of Neurotoxicity

Unlike some other disease processes, or toxic reactions, the effects of drugs or poisons on the nervous system tend to be readily discernible by either the affected individual or those around them. The effects of a toxin on neurotransmission can be immediate and dramatic, such as a lack of motor coordination, or on a more extreme scale, the paralysis of the breathing and cardiac muscles, with death quickly following. More subtle effects, such as may be caused by psychotropic drugs, can be perceived by users as euphoria, mood alteration, or hallucinations. Indeed, the ability of some drugs to provide a slight change in mood or overall outlook is the basis of the multimillion-dollar industry in antidepressant drugs. Cognitive abilities may also be impacted as either a transitory or permanent effect of neurotoxins, the classic example being of course ethyl alcohol, whose neurotoxic effects are (at least in nonchronic, and nonfatal doses) temporary.

Types of nerve damage can be generally classified as either a *neuronopathy*, or direct toxicity to the neural cell; *axonopathy*, damage to the axonal process; *myelinopathy*, damage to the myelin sheath of the axon; or *transmission toxicity*, a blockage or interference with the normal processes of neurotransmission.

Sites within the neuron may also be targets of toxic action; such effects can be as varied as the biochemical process that take place. In a general sense, there can be effects on aspects of normal intracellular biochemistry, including the processes that serve to transport biomolecules within the cell (of particular significance in nerve cells because of the physical distance between the cell body and the extended cellular processes). Membranes, either within the cell or the external cell membrane, can become compromised and "leaky." Many toxin actions are expressed in relation to *neurotransmitters* (NTs, chemicals used in nerve signal propagation), which can be affected in multiple ways, including effects on the biochemical reactions underlying synthesis, storage, and release. Interference with the ability of the cell to break down NTs can generate toxic consequences as well. A number of neurotoxins interfere with the normal release of NT molecules, and the effect on NT reuptake by neurons following the signal process is a mechanism for the action of many therapeutic drug actions (and recreational drugs as well). Finally, toxins can directly impact the cellular receptors for NTs on either the sending or receiving neuron (see Sidebar 7.1).

The nervous system has a limited ability to regenerate or repair damage. In a practical sense, transection damage to an axonal process can often be repaired as the nerve cell extends pseudopod-like processes through the remaining neural tube, to reinnervate tissues. Nerve cell regeneration is an active topic of research.

7.5 Neurotransmission

The propagation of a nerve signal is often discussed as if it was an electrical current being carried or sent along the nerve, and thence from one nerve to the next as if the cell itself was an electrical wire or conductor. The reality, however, is somewhat different and considerably more complex. Rather than a current or even a localized flux of electrons, the nerve signal is actually the propagation of a region of "depolarization" of the cell membrane along the nerve, and down the axon toward the next nerve or muscle cell. Perhaps more accurately described as a region of temporary membrane polarity reversal, it is this process of transitory change of the charge on the cellular membrane, and then reversion to the normal resting state, that provides the basis of nerve signal propagation through the neuron and along the axonal process to the junction of the next nerve or muscle cell. Hence, while not reflective of an electrical current per se, signal transmission within the nerve is a function of electrical charge. However, at the junction between nerve cells or between nerve and muscle cells, the mechanism of signal propagation changes from charge to chemical.

The intracellular junction, called a synapse, is where the signal is transmitted from one cell to another as a function of the release and diffusion of NTs across the space between cells. Subsequent binding of NTs to specific receptors initiates the depolarization of the downstream or postsynaptic neuron, or the contraction of a muscle cell. An understanding of the processes involved is essential for a thorough comprehension of the mechanism of action of many different drugs and toxins.

SIDEBAR 7.1 NEUROTRANSMITTERS

Neurotransmitters (NTs) are simply the biomolecules responsible for promulgating a nerve signal, either excitatory or inhibitory, across a synaptic space. Most NTs are synthesized in the neuron and packaged in *NT vesicles* prior to their release in response to a wave of depolarization reaching the synapse. The process of inclusion of NT molecules in the presynaptic vesicles is mediated by specific transport proteins, which can be the target for some toxic molecules. Almost all NTs are subject to some degree of presynaptic reuptake, following release into the synaptic space. This allows for a lower background level of NT when the next release event occurs and also preserves the NT molecules for multiple use.

NTs are commonly grouped into monoamine, amino acids, peptides, and other structures. While most commonly thought of in terms of the well-recognized acetylcholine (see Sidebar 7.4), glutamate, N-methyl-d-aspartate receptor (NMDA; see Sidebar 7.2), gamma-amino butyric acid (GABA), dopamine, serotonin, and epinephrine, there is a large and varied group of molecules functional as NTs. From complex polypeptides (e.g., substance P, functioning in certain types of pain neurotransmission) to small gaseous molecules such as nitric oxide, hydrogen sulfide, and carbon monoxide, there is a tremendous variety and specificity of NTs. Some example molecules are presented in Figure 7.5.

SIDEBAR 7.2 NMDA RECEPTOR

The N-methyl-d-aspartate receptor (NMDA receptor) is a type of ionotropic glutamate receptor, for which NMDA is an activating ligand. The receptor requires multiple ligand binding for activation (normally NMDA or glutamate and glycine in two separate binding loci). Activation of the receptor allows calcium ions into the cell, thereby leading to a hypopolarization, or excitatory change. A number of compounds act as NMDA receptor anatgonists, most commonly used for induction of anesthesia in animals, the common example being ketamine. Ketamine and a number of similarly acting compounds, such as PCP and nitrous oxide, are also used as illicit recreational drugs. Some synthetic opioids, such as meperidine, methadone, propoxyphene, and tramadol, appear to have some degree of NMDA antagonist activity. A classic response to the NMDA receptor antagonists is a dissociative anesthesia, where the user experiences an out-of-body experience associated with the analgesia. Some degree of amnesia is often also a consequence of use. Ketamine and related compounds have been used in cases of DMSA (Figure 7.6).

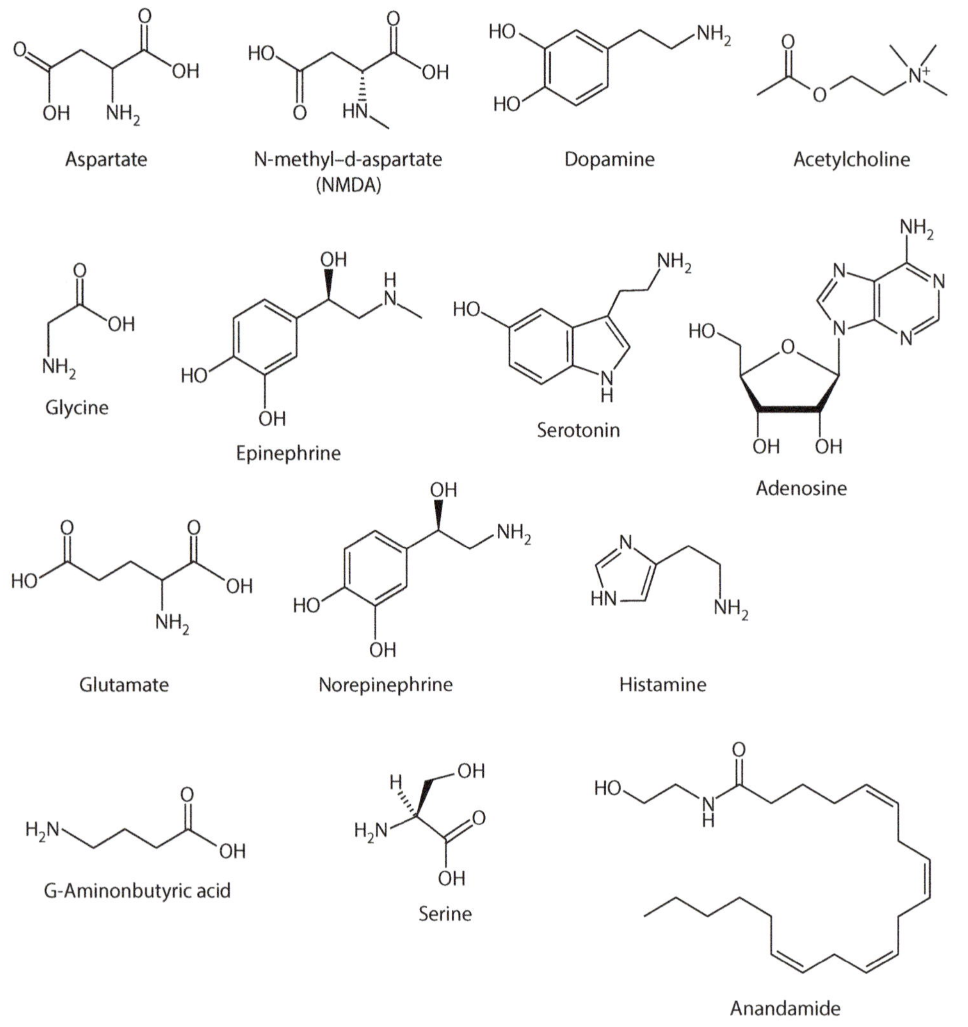

Figure 7.5 Example neurotransmitters.

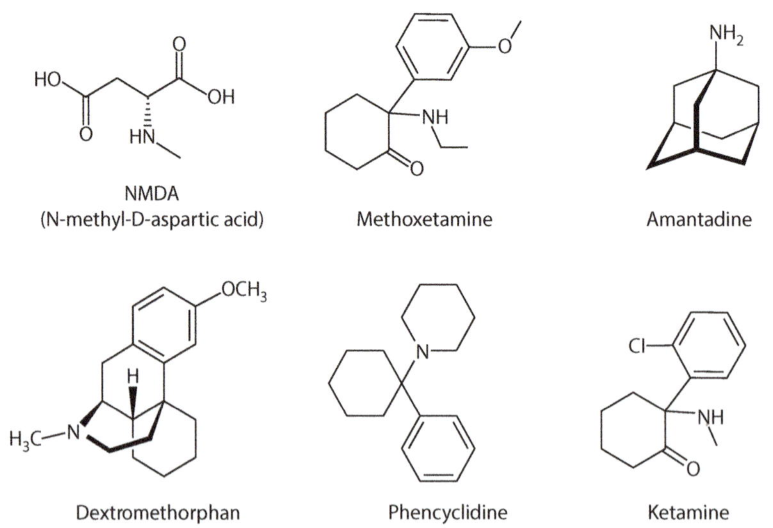

Figure 7.6 NMDA antagonists (NMDA, ketamine, PCP, meperidine, tramadol).

7.5.1 Neuronal Membrane Potential

All cells in the body maintain a small electrical potential on their outer membrane. This potential provides the energy for many of the transport processes that serve to move molecules into and out of the cell. While the magnitude varies between cell types, the cellular membrane of the neuron maintains, in its resting state, a potential of ~70 mV relative to the outside of the cell (the resting potential). Cellular membrane potential is generated and maintained by the action of the sodium-potassium ATPase ion pump and specific potassium channel proteins, which allow the transit of potassium ions out of the cell. The ion pump moves three sodium atoms out of the cell, hydrolyzes one ATP molecule, and brings two potassium ions into the cell with every cycle, yielding the net removal of one positive charge (see Sidebar 7.3). This process concentrates potassium on the intracellular side of the membrane; however, the potassium channels allow gradient-driven diffusion of potassium out of the cell, driving the interior of the cell more negative. The ultimate limitation to the egress of potassium is the electrostatic potential, with potassium leakage essentially terminated when the membrane potential reaches ~80 mV.

SIDEBAR 7.3 SODIUM-POTASSIUM ATPase

The sodium-potassium ATP-driven transport pump (Na^+-K^+ ATPase) is a transmembrane transport protein, which acts to remove three sodium ions from within the cell and, in the same cycle, allows two potassium ions to enter. The activity of this transporter is essential to establishing and maintaining the cellular membrane potential and gradients of extracellular sodium and intracellular potassium. The action of the pump is essential to reestablish of the membrane potential following neuron depolarization. Blockage or interference with the activity will preclude the cell from returning to the resting state, able to accept and promulgate a new signal. The protein acts by binding three sodium ions and a molecule of ATP on the intracellular side of the membrane. ATP is hydrolyzed, with the phosphorylation of an aspartate residue (key to function of the protein), and release of ADP. The phosphorylation and sodium binding leads to a conformational change, allowing the release of the sodium ions into the extracellular space. Two extracellular potassium ions are bound, causing dephosphorylation of the aspartate residue and another conformational shift, closing access to the extracellular side and opening intracellularly. The dephosphorylated protein has a low affinity for potassium ions, which are then released into the cytosol, and the cycle can begin again, depending on the availability of sodium ions (Figure 7.7).

The African arrow poison *ouabain* functions to block the activity of the Na-K ATPase by binding to the extracellular portion when phosphorylated. In so doing, the cell is blocked from reestablishing the membrane potential, ultimately leading to paralysis and death. The cardiac glycosides (e.g., digoxin, oleandrin, and related molecules) act in a similar fashion, but their activity is limited primarily to the myocardium (Figure 7.8).

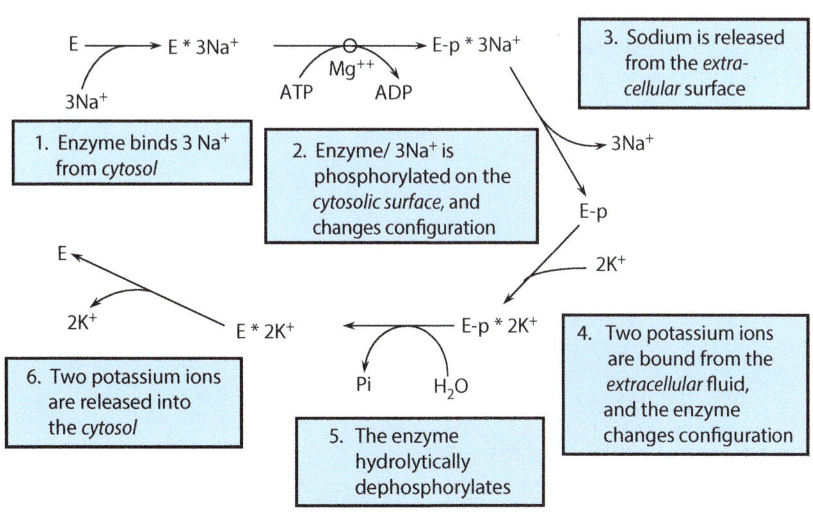

Figure 7.7 Sodium-potassium ATPase cycle.

SIDEBAR 7.4 NICOTINIC VS. MUSCARINIC ACETYLCHOLINE RECEPTORS

Acetylcholine is a primary NT, active in both the sympathetic and parasympathetic systems and in multiple tissues. The two types of acetylcholine receptors are muscarinic and nicotinic. In structural terms, muscarinic receptors are G-coupled protein receptors (activating a second messenger within the cell, potentially leading to multiple cellular functions, rather than directly acting, e.g., on an ion channel), while nicotinic receptors are ligand-gated ion channels. They can be found on both sides of the synaptic space (presynaptic and postsynaptic). Both muscarinic and nicotinic receptors are located in the CNS and autonomic nervous systems, while only nicotinic receptors are found at neuromuscular junctions. Both the sympathetic and parasympathetic systems are cholinergic (utilizing acetylcholine as NT) at the preganglionic level. In the sympathetic system, the postganglionic NT is norepinephrine; while in the parasympathetic system, the NT remains acetylcholine.

Muscarinic Receptors

The muscarinic type of acetylcholine receptors were so named for their ability to bind both acetylcholine and muscarine, a toxic alkaloid found in a number of poisonous mushroom species, particularly of the Amanita family. Muscarinic receptors are *metabotropic* receptors, also often referred to as G-protein coupled receptors, which function within the postsynaptic cell by activating a second messenger (usually cAMP or cGMP), which in turn activates or inactivates enzymes and other cellular molecules, leading to reactions or sequences of reactions and changes within the cell. Muscarinic receptors are found in the organs innervated by the autonomic, parasympathetic system and in the CNS itself. There are five subclasses of muscarinic receptors, M_{1-5}.

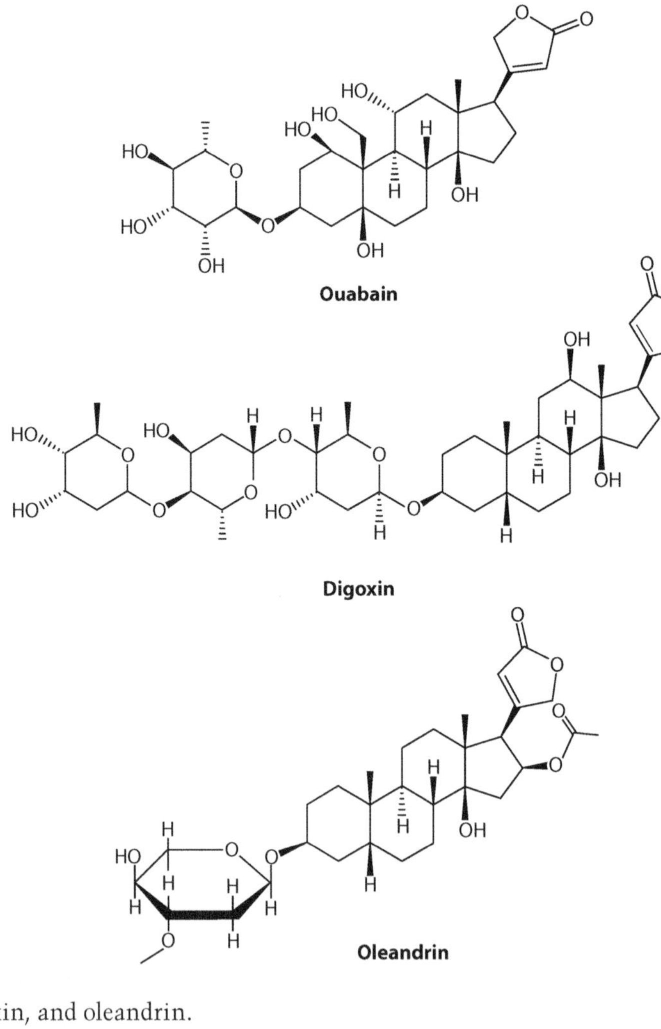

Figure 7.8 Ouabain, digoxin, and oleandrin.

The M_2 receptor is of particular interest from a toxicologic perspective, in that activation lowers conduction velocity at the sinus and atrioventricular nodes, resulting in a lowered heart rate.

Nicotinic Receptors

Nicotinic receptors are ligand-gated sodium ion channels. Activation by ligand (acetylcholine) binding induces a conformational change, which allows gradient-driven entry of sodium ions into the postsynaptic cell which, depending on signal magnitude, may result in subsequent depolarization of the postsynaptic membrane. Nicotinic receptors can be generally divided into subtypes, with one type (N_m) found at neuromuscular junctions, and the other (N_n) found in the CNS at both cholinergic and adrenergic ganglia.

7.5.2 Propagation of Depolarization

As noted above, nerve signals are actually regions of depolarization traversing the length of the neuron, from the dendrites or the soma where the signal was initially received, along the axon to the synapse at the terminal end of the axon. The initial step in propagation of depolarization is the response of voltage-sensitive sodium channels (or voltage-gated) to polarity reversal (e.g., influx of sodium ions) in their vicinity as the wave of depolarization approaches. These channels are normally closed in the resting state. In response to depolarization, the sodium channels open, allowing sodium to enter the cell, driven by both the concentration and voltage gradient. This massive influx of sodium reverses the membrane potential and triggers the opening of adjacent voltage-gated sodium channels. The magnitude of the potential shift in the membrane is to ~ +40 mV intracellularly. As this potential is reached, the voltage-gated sodium channels close and voltage-gated potassium channels open (similar to the sodium channels, the voltage-gated potassium channels are normally closed at resting potential). At this point, potassium rapidly exits the cell, again driven by both a concentration and voltage gradient. The egress of potassium reverses the membrane potential back toward the original negative on the inside, positive outside the cell; however, the potential is "overshot" by 10 mV or so. At this point, while the membrane potential is of the correct polarity, the localized ion concentration is reversed in relation to the normal resting state, with sodium on the inside, potassium on the outside. The normal operation of the sodium-potassium ion pump, combined with the potassium channels, allows the cell to reestablish the normal ionic balance. While the process of ionic rebalancing is occurring, the cell is unable to propagate depolarization and is considered refractory until the membrane potential is reestablished. It is important to note that the slight temporal delay between the opening of the sodium and potassium channels, caused by a differential voltage sensitivity, is the basis for the unidirectional propagation of depolarization from the dendrites and soma, toward the axon and synapse (Figure 7.9).

7.5.3 Events at the Synapse

The transition of the wave of depolarization progressing along the neuron from an electrical to a chemical signal, across the synaptic space to a new neuron or muscle cell, and initiation of depolarization is a complex and fascinating biochemical process. It begins in the region of the synapse with voltage-gated calcium channels, which, in response to a localized depolarization, allow the influx of calcium ions into the neuron. In the cell, calcium combines with *calmodulin*, a calcium-binding protein. The calcium-calmodulin complex binds to and activates the phosphorylating enzyme, kinase II. Activated kinase II is then able to phosphorylate NT storage vesicles, the functional signal allowing the "docking" and fusion of those vesicles with the cellular membrane in the synapse and the release of NT into the synaptic space.

Following the release of NTs from the vesicles into the synaptic space, the molecules diffuse into the synapse, and some bind to and activate ligand-gated sodium channels on the postsynaptic surface. These NT receptors then allow the gradient-driven flux of sodium into the postsynaptic cell, causing a localized membrane polarity reversal and, if the magnitude of sodium influx is adequate, trigger the opening of voltage-gated sodium channels. With the transition to voltage-gated sodium channels, the whole depolarization cycle starts again, moving away from the synapse, through and along the neuron. If the postsynaptic cell is muscle, the processes of contraction are initiated.

The magnitude of the sodium influx is critical to the process of propagation of depolarization. A sufficient amount of sodium must reach the inside of the cell to achieve a depolarization adequate to trigger the voltage-gated sodium channel. The degree of depolarization necessary for this to occur as measured in voltage at the cellular membrane is called the *action potential* (Figure 7.10).

7.5.4 Inhibitory Neurotransmission

The processes of neurotransmission discussed above are focused on excitatory neurotransmission, resulting in the propagation of a nerve signal or causing muscle

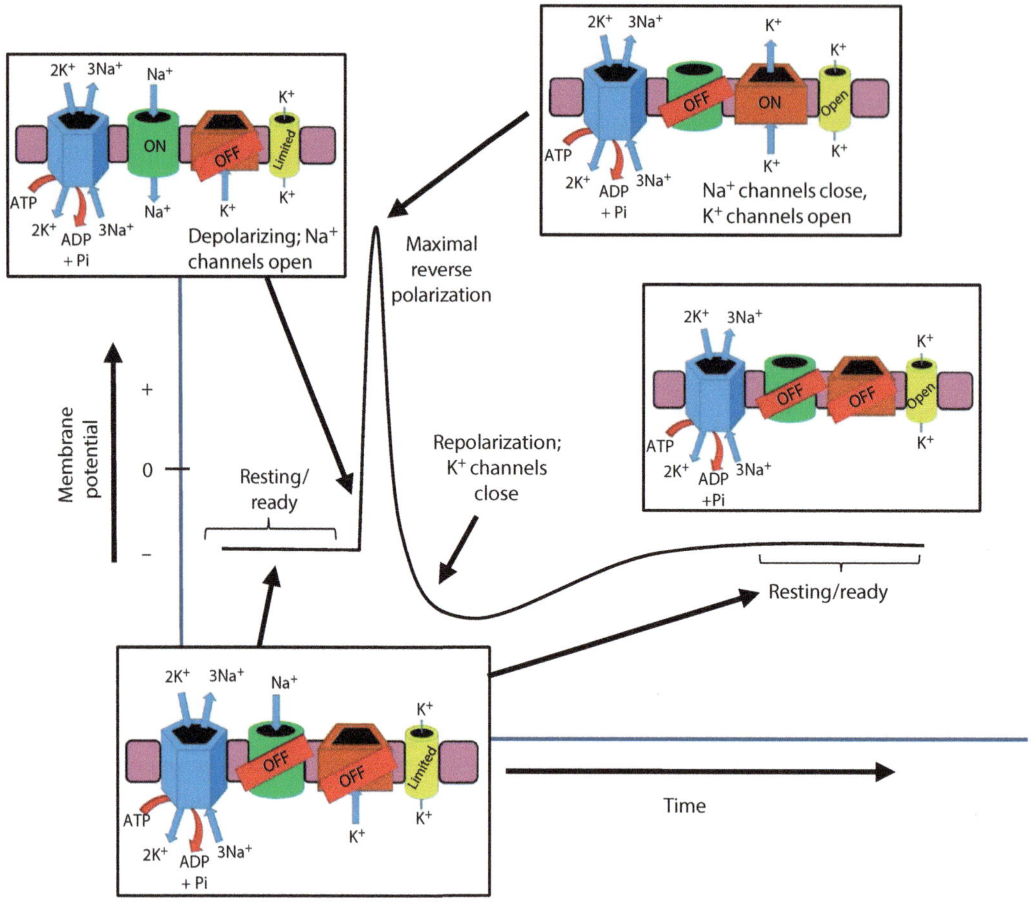

Figure 7.9 Propagation of depolarization.

contraction. There is, however, the need to be able to desensitize the system, both at the cellular and at the larger organ and indeed whole organism level. It is a common misconception to envision the nervous system as being either on or off; however, we exist on a continuum of CNS activity, normally transitioning in a day from sleep, through various degrees consciousness and mental excitation, and ultimately back to sleep. The inhibitory functions of the CNS result in the downregulation of the system, allowing sleep. Taken to extremes, these same inhibitory processes can produce anesthesia, coma, and ultimately death.

Mechanistically, the inhibitory process is quite simple. The primary inhibitory NT is gamma-amino butyric acid (GABA), and its receptor is a ligand-gated *chloride* receptor. (Another significant inhibitory NT is glycine, active

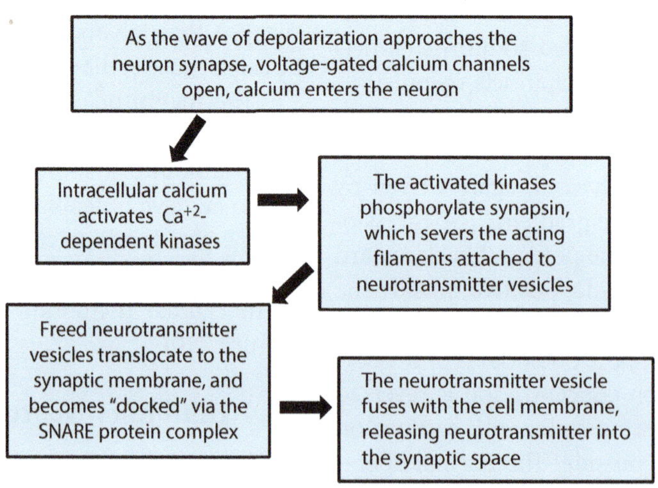

Figure 7.10 Events at the synapse.

in the spinal cord alone; see Sidebar 7.6.) Thus, when an inhibitory neuron releases GABA at the synapse, it binds to its receptor on the postsynaptic nerve surface and allows chloride ions to enter the cell. Since chloride has a negative charge, such influx causes a localized hyperpolarization of the postsynaptic neuron, thereby requiring a

SIDEBAR 7.5 THE GABA RECEPTORS

GABA is the primary inhibitory NT in the body. (Glycine plays an analogous role in the spinal cord; see Sidebar 7.6.) GABA action is mediated by the $GABA_A$ receptor, which is a ligand-gated chloride channel, opened in response to GABA binding. The significance of the $GABA_A$ receptor is that it contains multiple ligand-binding sites for compound types other than its endogenous agonist, GABA. The receptor complex contains (separate) binding sites for benzodiazepines and barbiturates, capable of increasing chloride flux through the receptor in the presence of agonists. There is also a binding site in the ion channel of the complex, which allows for direct antagonism of the receptor by such molecules as picrotoxin.

The receptor generally comprises five subunits—two alpha, two beta, and a gamma—which span the cell membrane. The (non-GABA) pharmaceutical binding sites are associated with the α-subunit, while the GABA site is on the beta subunit, and hence, there are two GABA-binding sites/receptors. Agonist binding to the GABA site results in opening of the chloride ion channel. Nonendogenous agonists of the GABA site include muscimol and ibotenic acid (psychoactive alkaloids found in a number of mushrooms in the Amanita family). $GABA_A$ agonists are sedative hypnotics due to the hyperpolarization such compounds cause in the postsynaptic membrane, generating an overall inhibitory response (Figure 7.11).

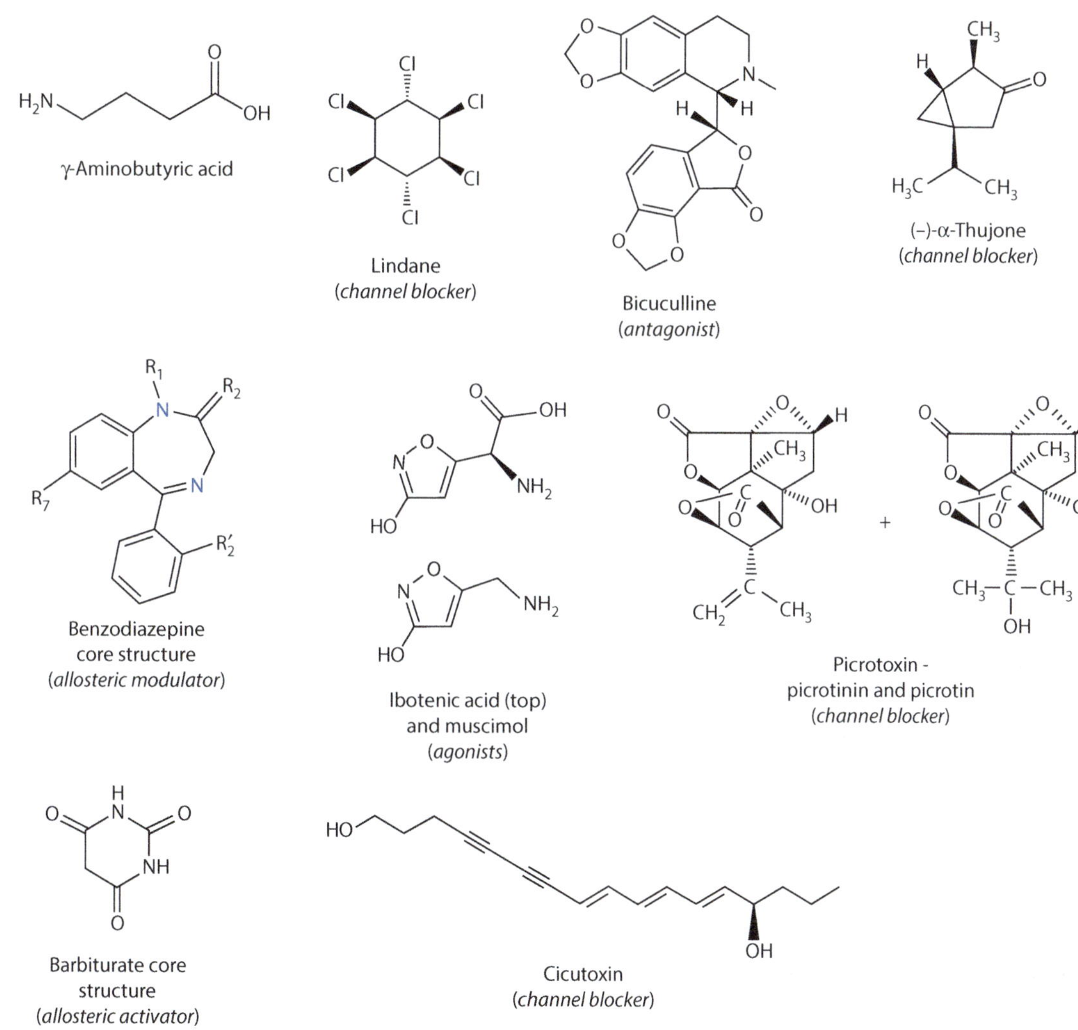

Figure 7.11 $GABA_A$-active compounds.

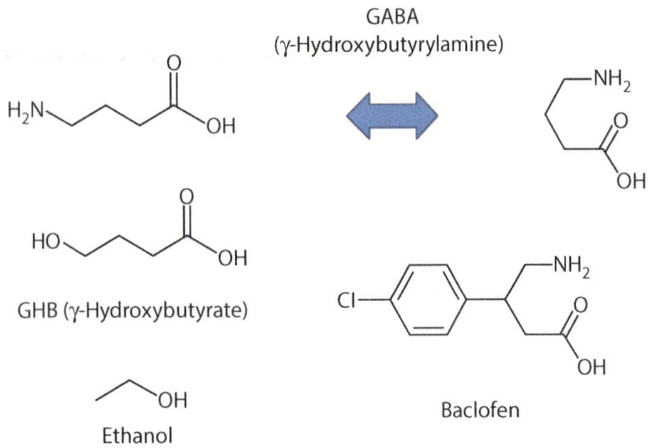

Figure 7.12 $GABA_B$-active compounds.

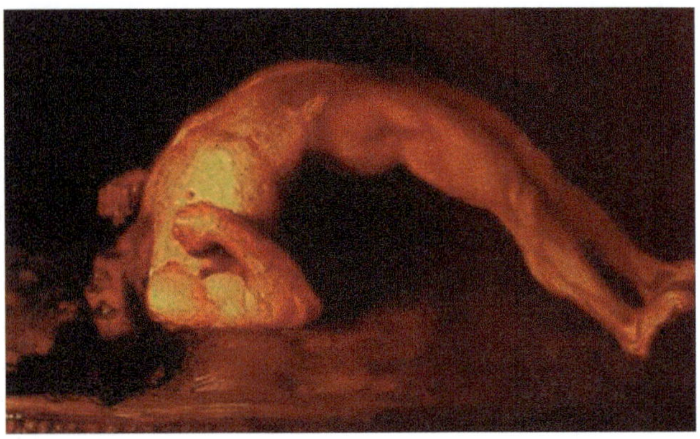

Figure 7.13 Ophisthatonic seizure. (*Opisthotonus (Tetanus)*, Charles Bell [1809]; in the Royal College of Surgeons, Edinburgh.)

larger excitatory signal (with associated sodium influx) to allow the action potential to be reached (Figure 7.14).

Antagonists of the $GABA_A$ site decrease the frequency of ion channel opening, as well as the average open duration and therefore act as de-inhibitors, producing excitation of the nervous system. Carried to extremes, the consequences of such drugs can be seizures/convulsions, coma, and death. Examples of such drugs are bicuculine, found in Dutchman's pipe, and lindane (hexachlorocyclohexane), a chlorinated hydrocarbon insecticide no longer in use. Similar effects are produced by compounds able to act as agonists at the picrotoxin binding site, located in the central ion channel of the receptor complex. Picrotoxin, (found in a southeast Asian plant, Indian berry), and functionally analogous compounds, for example, cicutoxin (found in water hemlock) and thujone (a traditional component of Absinth, a liqueur containing an extract of wormwood), are able to block or limit chloride flux without affecting ligand binding to the GABA site.

The benzodiazepines, a popular class of antidepressant drugs, act as allosteric activators of the receptor, increasing the duration of ion channel opening in response to GABA binding. Benzodiazepine binding does not in itself activate the receptor but only enhances the response of the system to endogenous GABA (as released by the presynaptic, inhibitory neuron). This is in contrast to the barbiturates, which, while not ligands for the GABA site, are able to cause chloride channel opening in response to binding at the barbiturate site. Barbiturates have a considerably greater toxic potential than the benzodiazepines, particularly in combination with other CNS depressants, such as ethyl alcohol or opiates. A number of famous people have died as a consequence of barbiturate overdose (or barbiturate/ethanol combinations), including Marilyn Monroe, Judy Garland, Jimi Hendrix, and Dorothy Kilgallen.

A second GABA receptor was identified (designated $GABA_B$) with studies showing a GABA-dependent inhibitory effect, despite the presence of the $GABA_A$ inhibitor, bicuculine.

The $GABA_B$ receptor is a metabotropic, or G-protein coupled, receptor, linked to potassium channels. Activation of the $GABA_B$ receptor results in a gradient-driven hyperpolarization of the neuron and, as such, is an inhibitory response. Activation of the $GABA_B$ receptor has been suggested as one aspect of the mechanism of ethanol action in the body. Baclofen was found to mimic GABA under these conditions as well and is now the classic $GABA_B$ agonist and is currently used to treat muscle spasticity in cases of spinal cord injury, cerebral palsy, and multiple sclerosis (Figure 7.12).

When the $GABA_B$ receptor is activated, a series of intracellular reactions occur, including cyclic-AMP activation that ultimately results in the opening of postsynaptic potassium channels, allowing for the efflux of potassium from the postsynaptic neuron. This loss of potassium drives the membrane potential of the neuron more negative, thus inhibiting the neuron. This hyperpolarized neuron requires an influx of a larger number of sodium ions, compared with a noninhibited state, in order for the postsynaptic response to initiate a nerve signal.

Presynaptic inhibition results from $GABA_B$ receptors decreasing calcium conductance in the presynaptic neuron. Voltage-gated calcium channels are inhibited as a result of $GABA_B$ activation and the resulting decreased amount of calcium ions entering the neuron results in less phosphorylation of docking proteins involved in neurotransmitter vesicle docking and release. With less excitatory neurotransmitters, such as glutatmate, in the synapse, the magnitude of the potential is less and the postsynaptic neuron remains unfired (Figure 7.12).

SIDEBAR 7.6 GLYCINE, THE GLYCINE RECEPTOR, AND THE ACTIVITY OF STRYCHNINE AND TETANUS

The glycine receptor is a ligand-gated chloride channel, serving a function similar to the $GABA_A$ receptor. This system, however, is localized and limited to the spinal cord. The limited role of glycine as a spinal cord–specific inhibitory NT was proposed in 1965. Strychnine, one of the most commonly recognized poisons, acts on this receptor as a high-affinity antagonist, with a Kd of 30 nM for the receptor, much lower (reflecting greater affinity) than the endogenous ligand, glycine (10uM). As might be expected from an inhibitory NT antagonist, the action of strychnine is as a convulsant, causing contraction of the muscles controlled through the spinal cord. Antagonist action at the glycine receptor causes a characteristic seizure, classified as opisthotonic, a consequence of contraction of the musculature controlled through the spinal cord, leading to asphyxia due to the spasmodic contraction of the diaphragm and intracostal muscles. Because the action of the glycine receptor is essentially limited to the spine, individuals suffering from the toxic actions of a glycine receptor antagonists are presumably awake and aware of their condition until losing consciousness as a function of anoxia. Tetanus toxin (tetanospasmin) causes a similar reaction but by a different mechanism. Specifically, tetanospasmin interferes with the release of glycine (and GABA) from the presynaptic neurons (Figure 7.13).

7.6 Ion Channel Toxins

Ion channel toxins affect the normal propagation of nerve signals by interfering with the function of the proteins allowing ion flux into or out of the nerve cell as a depolarization wave passes along the cell. Mechanistically, this can occur by either blocking the normal function of the channel (e.g., opening or closing) or physically obstructing the channel itself, precluding binding of the ion at the appropriate time. Sodium, potassium, and calcium channel blocking agents exist, and the toxic consequences of each can be fatal. Interestingly, examples of each are also used therapeutically. The indication of the use of such drugs in a medical history of a patient may provide information relative to the overall cardiovascular state of the individual, and such information may be of considerable use in efforts to determine the extent to which a drug or toxin played a causative or contributory role in a particular case.

7.6.1 Sodium Channel Agents

An archetypal agent of this class is tetrodotoxin and is the toxic agent in Fugu, or pufferfish, a sushi delicacy. (Specialized training is required of chefs who prepare Fugu to ensure that the served portions do not contain any of the toxin.) Tetrodotoxin blocks the pore opening of the voltage-gated sodium channel, thereby preventing any depolarization of the nerve cell. The net result of tetrodotoxin poisoning is respiratory paralysis. In mechanistic contrast, the toxin aconitine (from the monkshood plant) essentially holds the sodium channel in an open state, such that

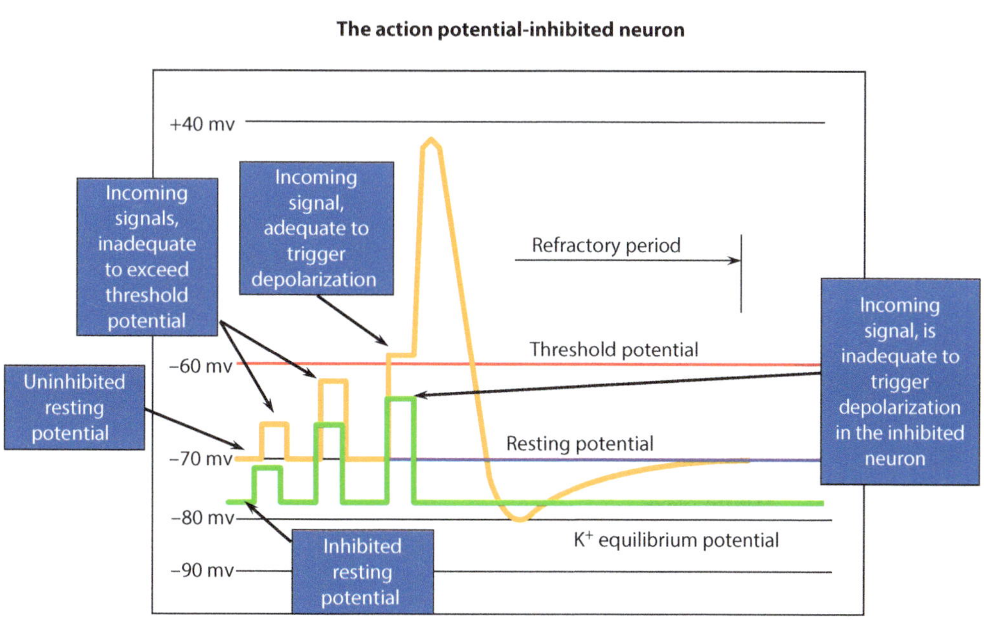

Figure 7.14 Uninhibited versus inhibited action potential trace.

the membrane is precluded from properly repolarizing, again leading to muscular paralysis. A related poison, known as batrachotoxin, is characterized as one of the most potent of the nonpeptidal neurotoxins and is derived from poison-arrow frogs. Batrachotoxin acts like tetrodotoxin, producing a depolarization of the neuron, thereby precluding the neuron from signaling muscle contraction (Figure 7.15).

7.6.1.1 Antiarrhythmic Sodium Channel Agents

A number of effective antiarrhythmic agents function on the sodium channel: Type 1a (slows nerve conduction) examples are quinidine and procainamide; Type 1b agents are (beat) frequency dependent, examples being lidocaine and mexiletine; and Type 1c agents are the most potent and cause a pronounced depression of depolarization rate, slowing conduction, examples being flecainide and propafenone. The utilization of these agents may be indicative of a life-threatening cardiac event or condition, and any association of toxicity with other drugs or pharmaceutical agents on board should be considered from that perspective.

7.6.1.2 Local Anesthetics

While the use of local anesthetics is usually without consequence, many of these compounds function as sodium channel blocking agents, but rather than acting on the outside of the neuronal membrane, they are taken up and act intracellularly. Mechanistically, these agents bind to the inside of the sodium channel, blocking influx of sodium and thereby preventing depolarization. While normally introduced locally, the inadvertent administration of such agents (e.g., bupivacaine, etidocaine, ropivocaine) into a vascular return can have rapid and potentially devastating consequences, as the drug can induce a cardiac failure that is not responsive to normal resuscitative efforts.

7.6.2 Potassium Channel Agents

Potassium channel blocking agents are generally utilized in the treatment of specific cardiac arrhythmias, with their main effect being a prolongation of the time required for repolarization. Examples are amiodarone and sotalol. Potassium channel blockers are associated with an increased risk of *torsades de pointes* (an abnormal cardiac rhythm, discussed in Chapter 8).

7.6.3 Calcium Channel Agents

Calcium channel blocking agents are most commonly utilized as antihypertensive agents (e.g., amlodipine, verapamil, diltiazem). The limitation on influx of calcium results in a decrease in cardiac contractility and also relaxation of the vascular smooth muscles in the arterial vessels. This relaxation caused a decrease in peripheral vascular resistance and an overall drop in blood pressure.

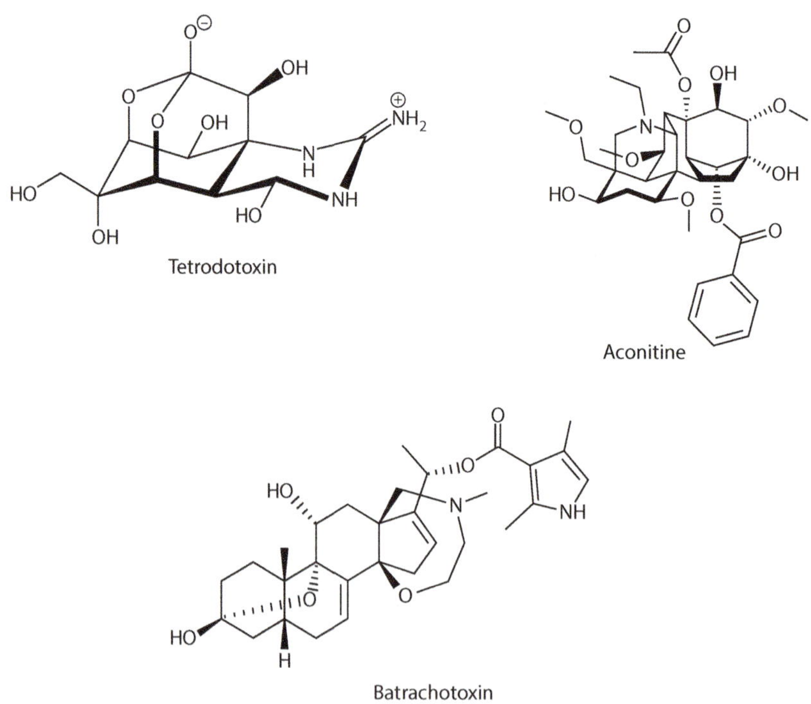

Figure 7.15 Tetrodotoxin, aconitine, batrachotoxin.

7.7 GABA Receptor Inhibitors and Agonists

The GABA receptor provides the basis for a mechanism of downregulation of the excitatory level of the nervous system and hence of the body overall. GABA receptor agonists are among the most common medications currently prescribed worldwide. There are specific, separate binding sites on the receptor for benzodiazepines, barbiturates, and some steroids. Ligand binding to these sites result in a hyperpolarization of the neuron. There is also a binding site in the chloride channel of the receptor (the picrotoxin site), agonists of which cause a corresponding decrease in the amount of chloride transiting the ion channel (e.g., picrotoxin, bicuculline, pentylenetretrazol). As such, binding of agonists to the picrotoxin site is excitatory, and the consequences can be convulsions or seizures.

There is an interesting functional difference between the benzodiazepine and barbiturate binding sites. Agonist binding to the barbiturate site directly activates the receptor, allowing for enhanced chloride influx into the neuron. In contrast, benzodiazepines are able to serve only as allosteric agonists, enhancing only the activity of the receptor to endogenous GABA. This simple distinction is the underlying basis for the relative safety of benzodiazepines, as compared with the barbiturates as a group.

7.8 Neural Body Toxins

Toxins that are directly cytotoxic to the neuron are referred to as neural body toxins. A number of well-recognized toxic species act on the neurons and are able to cause neuronal death. An example is cyanide, which if present at levels inadequate to cause an acute cardiac-based death can nevertheless impact cellular respiration in neurons, leading to cellular death preferentially to other tissue cells that may be somewhat more metabolically able to withstand the biochemical stress. A number of metal species are also able to bind to structural proteins and act as cellular enzyme inhibitors, with toxic consequences (e.g., arsenic, lead, mercury).

A classic example of a neuronal body toxin is methylphenyltetrahydropyridine, MPTP. More accurately, MPTP is the nonneurotoxic precursor to the toxic cationic species N-methyl-4-pyridin-1-ium (MPP+). MPTP, as a lipophilic, uncharged species is able to cross the blood–brain barrier and enter neurons, where it is oxidized to the aromatic cationic species by the action of a monoamine oxidase. MPP+ is toxic primarily to dopaminergic neurons in the substantia nigra of the brain and can cause symptoms of Parkinson's disease. MPTP can be produced as an accidental by-product in the manufacture of methylphenylpropionylpiperidine (MPPP), a synthetic opiate analog related to meperidine, ketamine, and PCP (Figure 7.16).

7.9 Toxins That Attack Myelin

Toxins that attack the myelin sheath around axons can cause significant problems with neuronal conduction. Not only does the neuron become exposed, but in the absence of the insulating effect of the myelin, the localized charge associated with the depolarization process can diffuse somewhat away from the neuron, resulting in a diminution of signal and slower transmission time.

A number of chemical toxins can either cause a breakdown in the myelin or impair its formation, including lead, some copper compounds, organotin species, and tellurium. A classic example of toxins able to act in this manner are the tri-alkyl tin compounds, typified by triethyl tin, which can cause a dissociation of the myelin from the neuron, leading to vacuolization

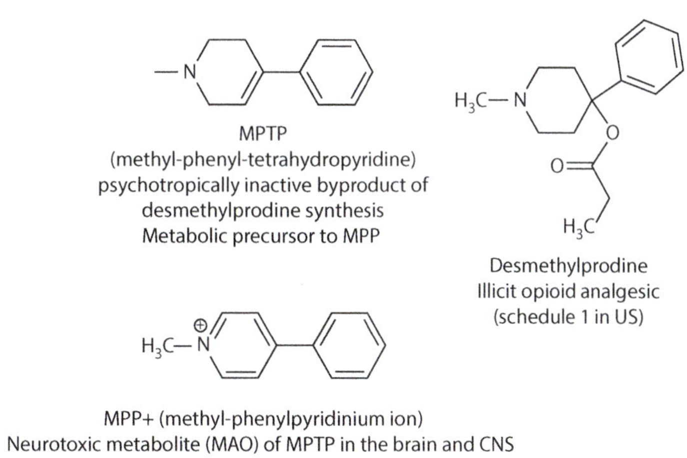

Figure 7.16 MPTP, MPP+, and desmethylprodine.

of the axon-myelin complex, affecting the ability of the nerve to propagate an action potential, as noted above. Another metal leading to a similar endpoint but via a different mechanism is tellurium, which generates a demyelinating polyneuropathy, most likely as a function of the inhibition of the enzyme squalene epoxidase, which represents the rate-limiting step in sterol biosynthesis. Inhibition of this enzyme can affect the ability of the body to form the molecules of the myelin sheath. A more common demyelinating toxin is *hexachlorophene*, used as a general bacteriocidal agent and as a topically applied antiseptic. If ingested, hexachlorophene can cause significant vacuolization within the CNS.

7.10 Toxins That Attack Axons

Microtubules provide an intracellular mechanism for transport of important biomolecules within the neuron. Molecules that are able to interfere with microtubule operation can compromise the ability of the cell to transport NTs from the vicinity of the soma to the synapse, as well as other important cellular constituents, including membrane proteins. Longer neurons, with therefore longer microtubules, are more sensitive to the effects of toxins affecting them, and physical effects are noted in the longer limbs. A classic example of a compound toxic specifically to microtubules is the common industrial intermediate acrylamide. Another compound with a similar endpoint is tri-ortho cresyl phosphate (TOCP), which, while acting as an organophosphate inhibitor of acetylcholinesterase, also acts as a neurotoxin causing axonal damage. TOCP has been the cause of several mass toxicity events, one associated with its use as an adulterant of solutions intended to bypass the prohibition laws of the 1930s, and again in 1959 as a consequence of contaminated cooking oil. As a consequence, a peripheral neuropathy affecting long axons can affect the ability of an individual to raise and control the foot during walking, producing a characteristic gait referred to as a Jake walk, named for Ginger Jake, a drink which was the source of the toxin for many individuals.

7.11 Toxins That Affect Synaptic Function

The effects of neurotoxins on synaptic function are usually considered in terms of an interference with the normal release of NTs, in response to a depolarization event. Interference with voltage-gated calcium channels could therefore be considered in this category, representing the initiation of the process leading to NT release.

A number of toxins, in particular the sympathomimetic amines (e.g., amphetamine, methamphetamine, cocaine, and related compounds), affect the levels of NT in the synaptic space by acting as inhibitors of the NT reuptake process. Several of these species also affect the packaging of NT molecules within the presynaptic neuron (more specifically discussed in Chapter 15). Many of the currently popular antidepressants function as selective serotonin reuptake inhibitors, acting to increase the levels of serotonin in the synaptic space.

Tetanus toxin is related to botulism toxin (discussed in Section 7.12, "Cholinergic Toxins," below) and is released by the bacterium *Clostridia tetani*. The action of this toxin action is restricted to the inhibitory neurons using GABA and glycine as NTs. In consequence, the response to tetanus toxin is muscle contraction, which can lead to paralysis and ultimately asphyxia and death. The toxin consists of a 150 kDal protein with a heavy (100 kDal) B-chain and light (50 kDal) A-chain linked by a disulfide bond. The heavy chain binds to the neuronal membrane of peripheral neurons and facilitates the translocation of the protein into the cell. The toxin is then transported, in a retrograde fashion, along the axon until reaching CNS inhibitory neurons. In the inhibitory neurons, the disulfide bond is cleaved, releasing the light chain, which functions as a zinc-containing endopeptidase, targeting the vesicle-associated membrane proteins (VAMP; specifically, synaptobrevin is cleaved). The VAMP facilitates binding of the NT vesicle to the presynaptic membrane as part of the release process in response to depolarization. Tetanus toxin therefore inhibits the release of NTs (GABA and glycine), producing spastic paralysis, or inappropriate musculature contraction (often in response to small stimuli).

SIDEBAR 7.7 SEROTONIN SYNDROME

Serotonin syndrome is a potentially serious drug reaction that is, in essence, simply a consequence of an excess of serotonin in the nervous system, or more specifically, an inappropriate excess of serotonin in the synaptic space. Causes may vary from drug interactions, overdose of pharaceuticals, or use of recreational drugs. Initially recognized as a consequence of co-administration of monoamine oxidase inhibitors (MAOIs), and selective serotonin reuptake inhibitors (SSRIs), the effect can be caused by any combination of pharmacologic events that interfere with the normal metabolism (including synthesis, reuptake, storage, and release) of serotonin.

Administration of an SSRI alone, even at levels well above therapeutic, seems inadequate to generate serotonin syndrome in healthy individuals, and the magnitude of the therapeutic index characteristic of these drugs emphasizes the large difference between the therapeutic and potentially toxic range. A number of drugs other than SSRIs affect serotonin storage, release, and reuptake and have been associated with serotonin syndrome (primarily sympathomimetic amines, such as methamphetamine and MDMA; see Chapter 15).

Serotonin syndrome has a rather complex combination of symptoms and can be mistaken for other illnesses in some people. Diagnosis often depends on evaluation of symptoms, combined with consideration of history, and in some cases, evaluation of toxicologic information. Currently, no readily available laboratory tests can be used to confirm the diagnosis.

The symptoms of serotonin syndrome are often described as a clinical triad including cognitive effects (mental status changes: headache, agitation, confusion, hallucinations and coma), autonomic effects (involuntary hyperactivity: shivering, sweating, hyperthermia, hypertension, tachycardia, nausea, diarrhea), and somatic effects (neuromuscular abnormalities: myoclonus, hyperreflexia and clonus, and tremor). In severe cases, the combination of tachycardia, hypertension, and hyperthermia may be life-threatening. Other potential complications, primarily a consequence of hyperthermia, include metabolic acidosis, rhabdomyolysis, seizures, renal failure, and disseminated intravascular coagulation (DIC; see Sidebar 9.3).

Both SSRIs and MAOIs act as antidepressants by the common mechanism of increasing the amount of serotonin available in the synaptic space. The effect is to increase the magnitude of the postsynaptic signal generated by serotonergic neuron in response to depolarization. The two types of drugs achieve this end result by different mechanisms. SSRIs inhibit the ability of the presynaptic serotonin reuptake transport proteins to reinternalize serotonin from the synaptic space, thereby increasing the concentration available to bind to postsynaptic receptors. MAO is an enzyme that acts to catalyze the breakdown of serotonin into 5-hydroxyindolacetic acid. Inhibition of this enzyme increases the intracellular concentration of serotonin, and hence the amount of serotonin incorporated into the presynaptic NT vesicles. Fusion of the NT vesicles and release of serotonin into the synaptic space will therefore involve more serotonin than would be released in the absence of the MAO inhibitor.

One of the more common causes of serotonin toxicity was the result of the combination of an MAO inhibitor and an SSRI. Most MAO inhibiting drugs are irreversible, so that recovery after the medication has been discontinued can take many weeks. In many cases, an MAO inhibitor would be discontinued in favor of an SSRI. Unfortunately, during the transitional period, even though the MAO inhibitor had been discontinued, the effect on the breakdown of serotonin continued. That continuation of the MAO inhibition effect, in combination with increased serotonin levels in the synapse due to the inhibition of reuptake, was adequate, in some cases, to cause serotonin toxicity, and could even present a risk of a life-threatening episode (Figures 7.17 and 7.18).

7.12 Cholinergic Toxins

A number of drugs target cholinergic neurons, and their actions can produce either a cholinergic or an anticholinergic syndrome. Either can, in the extreme, prove to be fatal. While a number of compounds act via the acetylcholine receptors, as either agonists or antagonists, other species can either affect the enzyme responsible for breaking down acetylcholine in the synaptic space or directly affect acetylcholine release. The NT acetylcholine is synthesized within the neuron, by the action of choline acetyltransferese on choline and the activated form of acetic acid, acetyl CoA.

A number of compounds affect ACh release into the synapse. Botulism, or botulinum poisoning, is mostly due to contaminated food that has been improperly canned

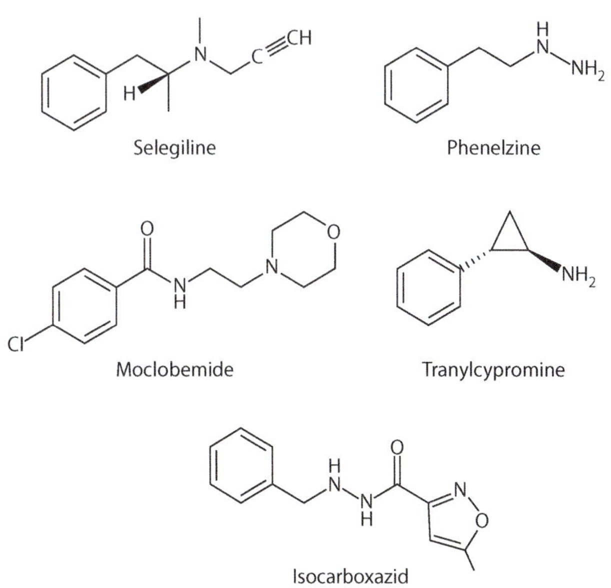

Figure 7.17 Example MAOs.

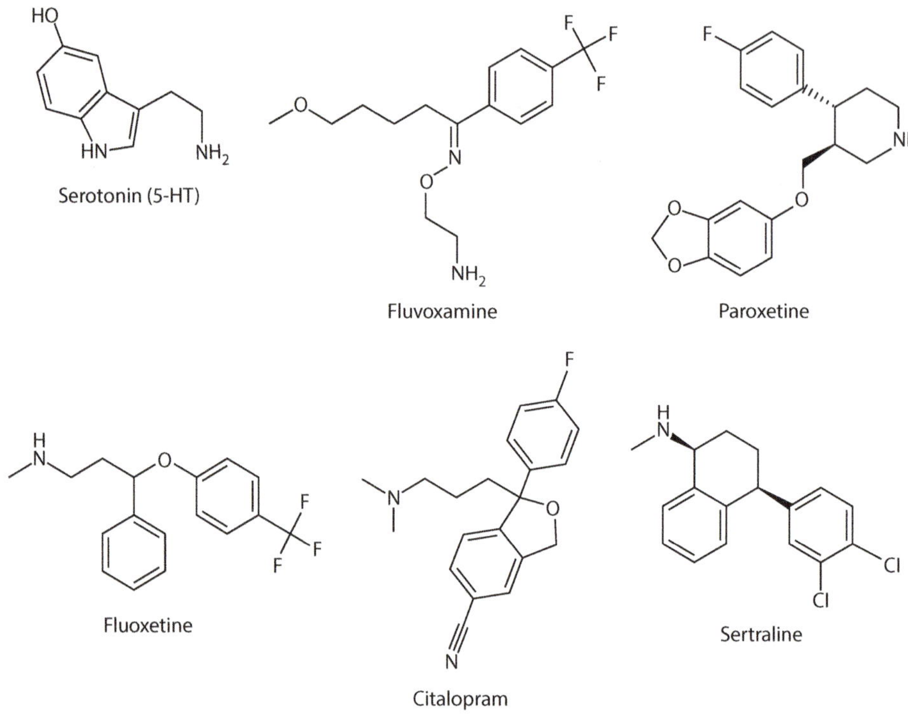

Figure 7.18 Example SSRIs.

or preserved and is caused by a group of toxic molecules produced by the anaerobic bacterium *Clostridium botulinum*. These toxins functionally inhibit the release of acetylcholine at the synapse of cholinergic neurons. The effect of the toxin is to produce muscular paralysis, and in some cases, atrophy. Botulinum toxin is one of the most poisonous compounds known, yet nevertheless, in the form of Botox, it has recently received considerable use in the cosmetic field as the basis for removal of wrinkles from the face.

Another example is latrotoxin, characteristic of spiders of genus *Latrodectus*, or the "widow" spiders (e.g., black widow), which causes the inappropriate release of ACh into the synaptic space. The experimental drug vesamicol inactivates a vesicular ACh transport protein, responsible for incorporation of ACh molecules into the presynaptic vesicle. Hemicholine acts by blocking the presynaptic reuptake of choline by a specific choline transport protein. Other well-known toxins include South American arrow poisons (curare), poison hemlock (coniine), and muscle relaxants or paralytics (e.g., vecuronium, pancuronium, and succinyl choline) used in surgical procedures (see Chapter 17).

REVIEW QUESTIONS

1. Briefly describe the organization of the neuronal system. Account for CNS, PNS, and somatic, autonomic, sympathetic, and parasympathetic aspects.
2. Briefly discuss the protections of the nervous system, at the level of the system (CNS), the cellular environment, and within the cell itself.
3. What are the distinctions between axons and dendrites?
4. What is the blood–brain barrier (physically and functionally), and how is it formed?
5. Describe the processes by which the cellular membrane potential is generated.
6. What is the sequence of events that results in the propagation of depolarization along the axon?
7. What is the sequence of events that results in the propagation of depolarization across a synapse?
8. What is the mechanism by which inhibitory NTs affect neurotransmission?
9. Briefly explain why neurotransmission cannot proceed in reverse.

TOPICS FOR DISCUSSION

1. Would you expect the effects of a CNS stimulant (e.g., cocaine) to cancel out the effects of a CNS depressant (e.g., alcohol)? Why or why not?
2. To what extent is an individual experiencing a seizure responsible for their actions? How about a drug-induced seizure? What factors weigh in your consideration?
3. What would you expect the physiological consequences of a breakdown in the blood–brain barrier to be?

Bibliography

Brodal, P. *The Central Nervous System: Structure and Function*. 3rd rev. ed. New York: Oxford University Press, 2004.

Conn MP, editor. *Neuroscience in Medicine*. 3rd rev. ed. Totowa, NJ: Humana Press, 2008.

Gilman AG, Rall TW, Nies AS, and Taylor P, editors. *Goodman and Gilman's The Pharmacological Basis of Therapeutics*. 8th ed. New York: McGraw-Hill, 1990.

McCorry LK. *Essentials of Human Physiology for Pharmacy*. 2nd Ed. Boca Raton, FL: CRC Press, 2009.

Squire LR, Berg D, Bloom FE, Du Lac S, Ghosh A, Spitzer NC, editors. *Fundamental Neuroscience*. 3rd rev. ed. Boston: Elsevier, 2008.

Cardiac Toxicology

8

Contents

8.1 Introduction

All lethal rapidly acting toxins ultimately affect the function of the heart, either directly via effects on the cardiac muscle or the nerve signals controlling contraction, or indirectly by affecting the availability or utilization of oxygen. Longer-acting agents can affect the biochemistry of the body in such a manner so that the heart is no longer able to function. In either case, the cessation of the heartbeat has long (and reasonably so) been considered the hallmark of death. Many postmortem cases can be clearly related to cardiac effects, either by the actions of a toxin (in the absence of natural disease) or natural disease (in the absence of a toxin). However, the challenge the pathologist and toxicologist often face is to understand and evaluate the role that drugs or toxins may have played in a case, against a background of some degree of underlying disease or pathologic condition. An understanding of the actions of a drug in a case, particularly those with a direct cardiac effect, can be facilitated by a corresponding appreciation for the condition of the heart. An understanding of cardiac function, as well as anatomy and physiology, disease states, and some characteristic pathology, is therefore often useful and perhaps even essential for the toxicologist. This chapter focuses on the basic structure and function of the heart and the mechanisms of actions of a number of toxins, with consideration of the factors that toxicologists may be interested in or may find helpful in their casework. While the toxicologist need not bring a physician-level understanding to the disease states of the heart, it is important to be able to interpret the effects of drugs or toxins in the context of any underlying disease or pathology.

8.2 Anatomy and Physiology

8.2.1 Normal Anatomy

The heart is situated in the thoracic cavity just about in the middle of the chest. Normally, the heart is angled somewhat to the left, and people usually feel their heartbeats somewhere just to the left of the midline of the sternum. Normal adult heart size is between 300 and 375 g, slightly smaller in females.

The heart functions solely as a pump to circulate blood around the body. Anatomically, the heart consists of two separate, two-stage coordinated pumps, a left and right atrium and ventricle. The first-stage atria serve to receive and collect blood coming into the heart and then deliver it to the second-stage ventricles. The ventricles then pump the blood out of the heart to the lungs or the rest of the body. The right side of the heart receives oxygen-depleted blood from the body and pumps it to the lungs. The left side receives oxygenated blood from the lungs, and delivers it, via arterial flow, throughout the body. The left ventricle is the largest and most powerful chamber of the heart, because of the size of the vascular space into which the blood is delivered and the inherent backpressure of that network. Blood does not mix from one side to the other in the heart, and flow is in one direction only, atrium to ventricle. Entry to each of the chambers is controlled by valves. The overall function of the heart and, hence, blood flow is controlled by coordinated muscular contraction of the myocardium and the action of the valves (Figures 8.1 through 8.4).

The contraction of the ventricular myocardium of the heart, known as *systole*, pushes blood into the arterial system. *Diastole* is the relaxation of the heart, allowing blood to return from the body to the atria. The start of the heartbeat cycle occurs as venous blood, received into the right atrium from the vena cava, and oxygenated blood, received in the left atrium from the pulmonary veins, is pumped into the right and left ventricles, respectively, with atrial contraction. Ventricular contraction follows, with deoxygenated blood being delivered to the lungs from the right ventricle via the pulmonary arteries and oxygen-enriched blood delivered to the rest of the body via the aorta. The left ventricular contraction represents the most energetic effort of the heart, needed to generate the pressure required to deliver blood throughout the body, returning ultimately to the right atrium (Figure 8.5).

8.2.2 Normal Electrophysiology

The heart is under the neuronal control of the vagus nerve (cranial nerve X), but it also has its own electrical system. The heart can beat on its own for a few minutes after a person is brain dead or the spinal cord has been severed at the neck.

The beating of the heart is a consequence of rhythmic, coordinated nerve signals originating in the sinoatrial node (SA node), located in the right atrium near its junction with the superior vena cava. The SA node is a specialized groups of myocytes that function as the epicenter of electrical control of the myocardium by generating the normal sinus rhythm and is therefore the natural pacemaker of the heart. Neuronal stimulation of the cells in the SA node causes contraction of the atrial myocardia (both left and right) in a coordinated way by sending a nerve signal to the myocardial cells, as a wave of depolarization (as described in Chapter 7). In contrast to nerve cells, though, as the myocardial cell depolarizes, an influx of calcium ions through voltage-gated

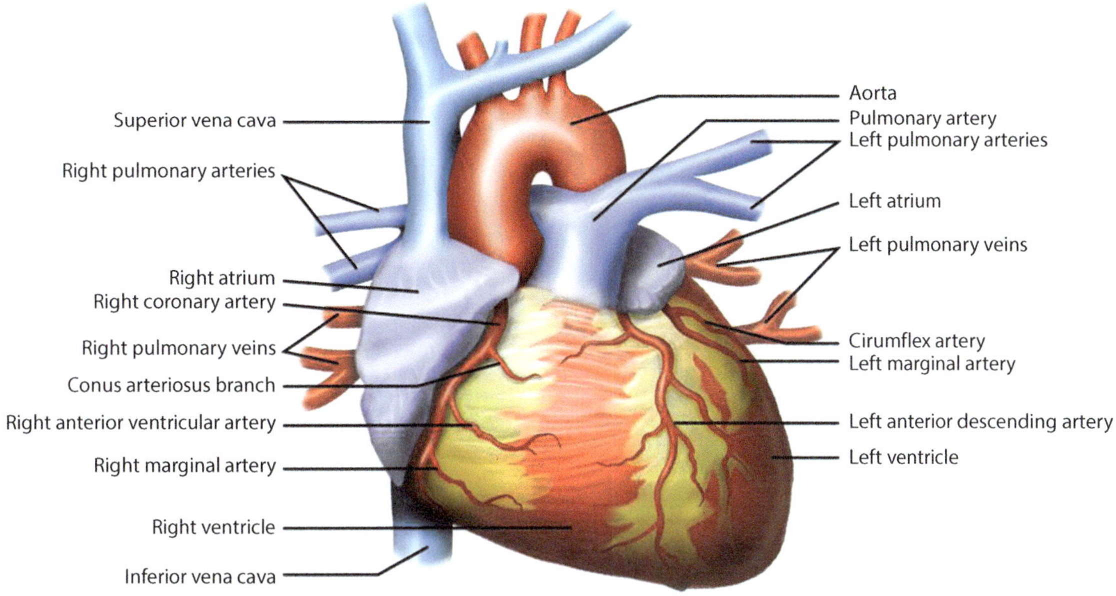

Figure 8.1 Stylized human heart. (Retrieved from Wikipedia Commons April 2, 2015. Image made available and published under the Creative Commons Attribution-Share Alike 3.0 Unported license by user and author Ties van Brussel. Original upload date March 10, 2013. License can be found here and no changes were made to the image: http://creativecommons.org/licenses/by-sa/3.0/legalcode.)

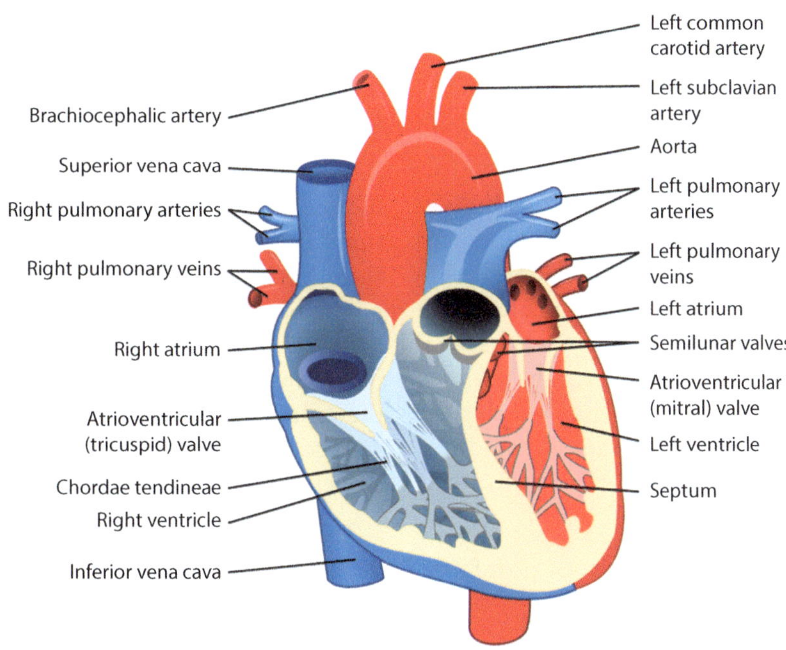

Figure 8.2 Heart diagram. (Retrieved from Wikipedia Commons April 2, 2015. Image made available and published under the Creative Commons Attribution-Share Alike 3.0 Unported license by user and author ZooFari. Original upload date March 2010. License can be found here and no changes were made to the image: http://creativecommons.org/licenses/by-sa/3.0/legalcode.)

calcium channels both sustains the depolarization and facilitates further calcium release from within the sarcoplasmic reticulum of the cell, an essential part of the contractile response.

Contraction of the atria also stimulates the atrioventricular (AV) node, located between the atria and ventricles. The AV node delays and then stimulates contraction of the ventricles, transmitting the signal through specialized neurons, the His bundle and Purkinje fibers. This delay between atrial and ventricular contraction is essential to allow for blood to flow into the relaxed ventricles during atrial contraction. The

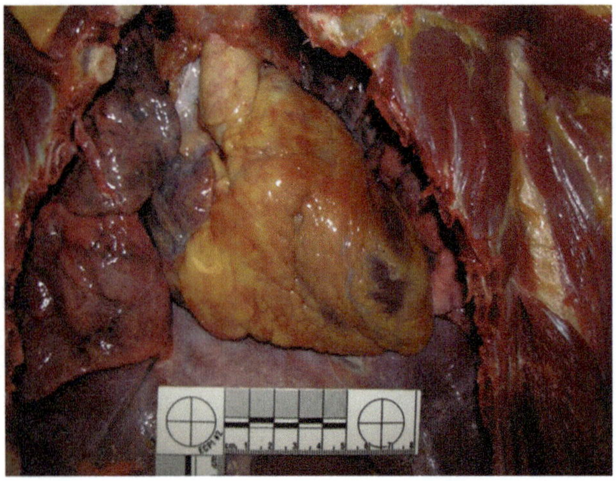

Figure 8.3 Heart *in situ*. Open chest cavity displaying the normal relationships of the heart, the lungs, and the diaphram. Note that the apex heart is directed to the left side of the body.

delay is also the basis for the characteristic two-stroke "lub-dub" sound of the heartbeat. Any disturbance in the normal progression of the signals in the heart can cause a subsequent error in the timing or function of contraction, which may then affect the force, rate, or rhythm of the heart (Figure 8.6).

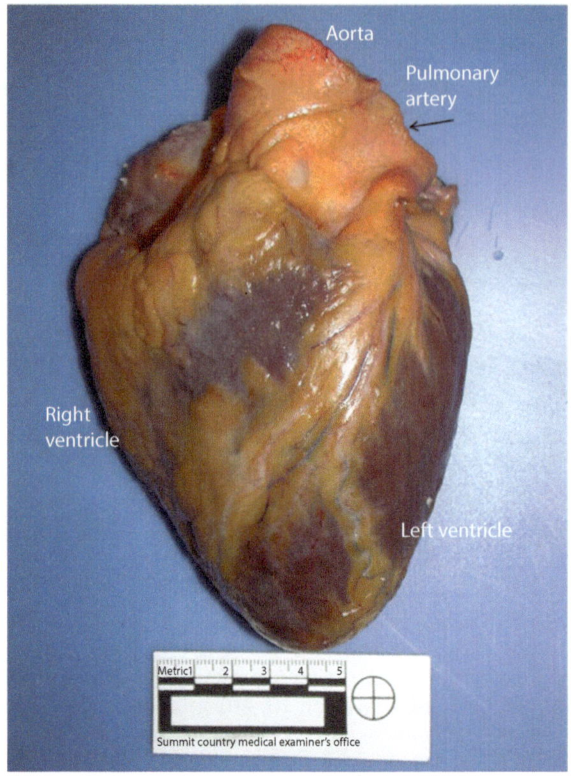

Figure 8.4 This 350 gm heart is of the usual size for an average-sized adult. Some major landmarks are labeled. It usually sits in the chest with the apex directed slightly toward the left side of the body.

8.2.3 The Electrocardiogram

Changes in membrane potential of the myocardium as a consequence of de- and repolarization induce currents that can be detected through the skin by electrode sensors and recorded as an electrocardiogram (EKG). The EKG is a plot tracing cardiac-related electrical charge at various points on the skin over time, generally recorded on graph paper or presented on a digital display. By convention, each 1 mm square in the horizontal direction (*X*-axis) represents 0.04 seconds (5 squares make 0.2 seconds). Each 1 mm square in the vertical direction (*Y*-axis) represents 0.1 mV. At least two electrodes (leads) are required to acquire an EKG, but tracings can be made from multiple leads, generating more detailed information reflecting activity in different sections of the heart. A three-lead EKG can record activity in the anterior and lateral regions of the heart, whereas a 12-lead diagnostic EKG can record the posterior portion as well (Figures 8.7 and 8.8).

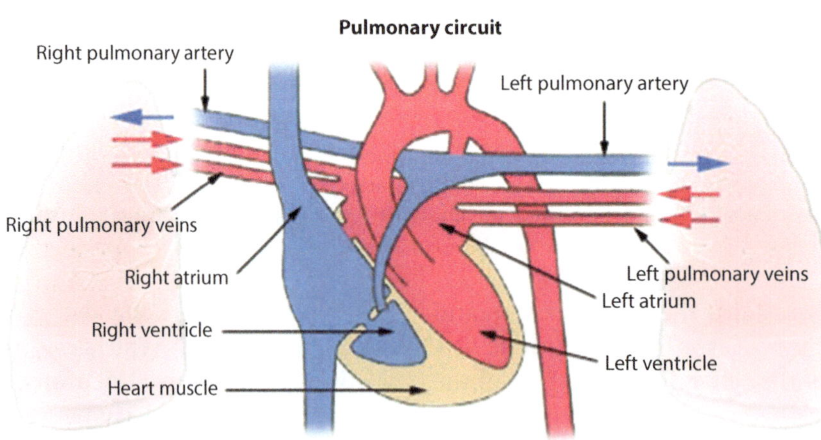

Figure 8.5 Diagram of blood flow to and from the lung.

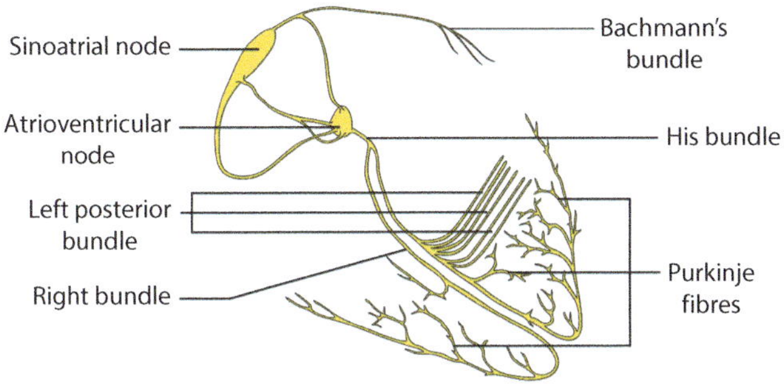

Figure 8.6 Cardiac conduction system. (Retrieved from Wikipedia Commons April 2, 2015. Image made available and published under the Creative Commons Attribution 3.0 Unported license by user and author Madhero88. Original upload date April 29, 2010. License can be found here and no changes were made to the image: http://creativecommons.org/licenses/by-sa/3.0/legalcode.)

Depolarization of the myocardium starts at the SA node and causes the contraction of both atria. This depolarization is observable on the EKG as the P wave. As depolarization proceeds to the AV node, the signal is slowed, allowing time for blood from the atria to fill the ventricles. This delay is observable as a flat line following the P wave. The myocardium of the atria is thin, containing much less muscle mass than that of the ventricles, and the repolarization current for the atria is not generally visible on the EKG. The signal then passes through the bundle of His with its left and right branches, and within the interventricular septum through specialized conduction cells (Purkinje fibers) into the myocardium of the left and right ventricles, causing contraction of both ventricles. This process (depolarization and contraction of the ventricular myocardium) is seen as the QRS complex on the EKG. The Q wave represents the initial signal from the SA node, which may be small or not visible. Ventricular depolarization is observable as the R and S wave and ventricular repolarization is represented by the T wave. The space between the S wave of the QRS complex and the T wave is called the ST segment. The ST segment is important because any positive deviation away from the horizontal may indicate myocardial ischemia (lack of oxygen) or infarction (myocardial injury). Individuals trained and experienced in reading and interpreting EKGs can derive a significant amount of information about the status of the heart and the nature of any abnormalities, rhythym issues, or tissue damage (see Sidebar 8.1; Figure 8.9).

8.2.4 Clinical Assessments of Heart Condition

An understanding of the condition and cardiac history of a patient or decedent can be of tremendous importance to the toxicologist in trying to understand the role a drug may have played in a case. In many cases where a drug is present, even at a concentration capable of eliciting a toxic response, the underlying cardiac

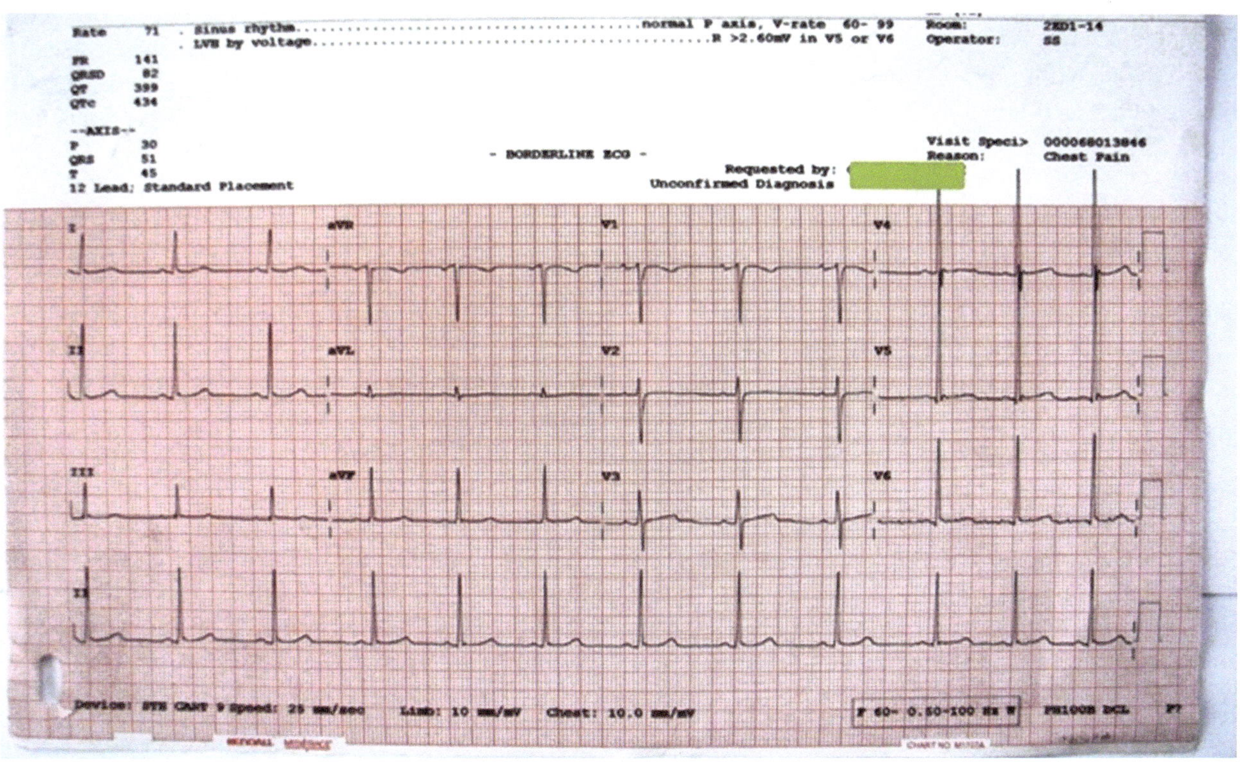

Figure 8.7 This EKG strip was run on a young man with chest pain. By EKG, he has normal sinus rhythm, but his left ventricle is enlarged.

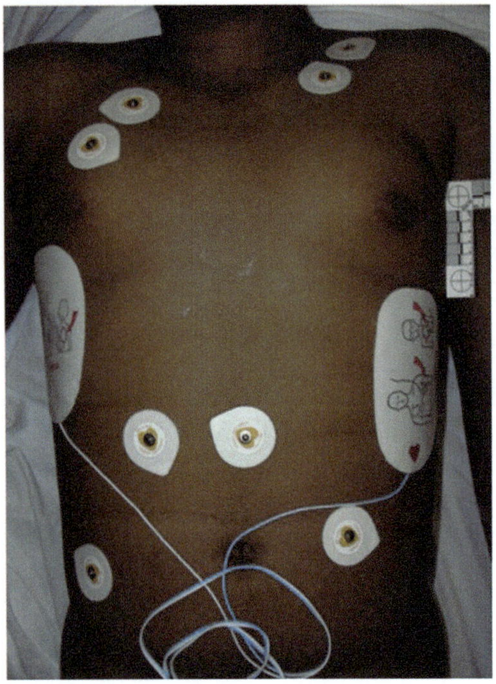

Figure 8.8 EKG contact points and leads in place.

SIDEBAR 8.1 IONIC BASIS FOR THE ELECTROCARDIOGRAM WAVE FORMATION

Changes in membrane potential in the myocardium occur as a consequence of de- and repolarization (essentially a reversal of the normal polarization of the cellular membrane). Because of the number of cells doing essentially the same thing at the same time, the magnitude of the electrical change in the region of the heart can be detected through the skin by electrode sensors and recorded as the electrocardiogram, or EKG. The contraction of the heart walls is driven by progressive depolarization traveling along the cell membranes of the cells that make up the heart (called contractile myocardial cells or contractile myocardium) in a manner analogous to nervous transmission. At rest, the uncontracted cells have a net charge across the membrane (negative inside, positive outside), reflecting the resting potential. Sodium is in excess on the outside of the cells, potassium on the inside (see Sidebar 8.2). In response to depolarization, the sodium channels in the membrane open, and sodium enters the cell driven by the concentration gradient, reducing the net negative charge on the inside of the cell. This sudden change in membrane potential of multiple cells is reflected in the steep slope of the upstroke on the EKG. The myocardial action potential is

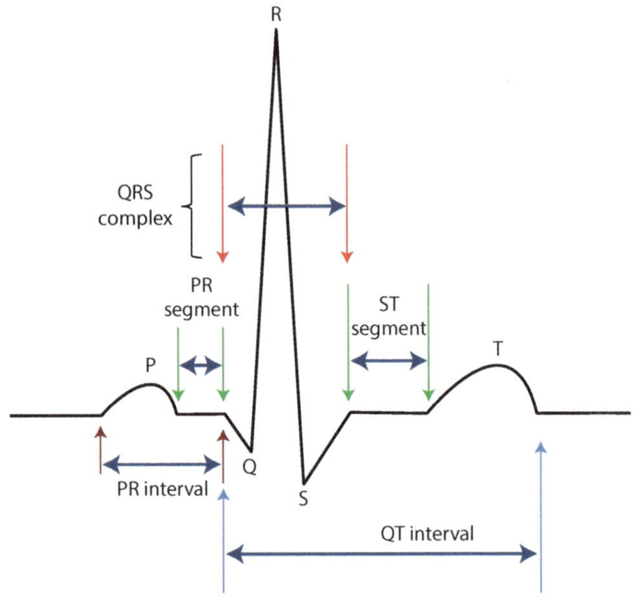

Figure 8.9 Normal sinus rhythm.

longer than the neuronal, primarily because of the influx of calcium, through channels that are somewhat slower to open. Therefore, the action potential appears more like a plateau than a peak. Potassium efflux, driven by voltage and concentration gradient, contributes to the repolarization of the cell. The normal balance between sodium–potassium and the membrane potential is restored by the action of the sodium–potassium ATPase. The processes of repolarization, because of the synchrony between so many cells in the myocardium, is reflected in the EKG downstroke (Figure 8.10).

condition and circumstances of the death or the medical condition of the patient may suggest that the drug did not contribute. (Conversely, in some cases, an unexpected drug finding can lead to a reassessment of what had been considered a sudden fatal cardiac event.) Many civil lawsuits are initiated based on the presence of drugs in a concentration presumed to be toxic, without consideration of the underlying disease state of the individual. Teasing out a true antemortem drug level and considering the contribution of an underling disease in the new illness can be a challenging undertaking that can have significant legal and financial consequences for the principals in such cases.

Clinicians assess multiple aspects of cardiac health by using a combination of pulse rate, EKG, blood pressure, and other clinical parameters in addition to medical history. Many details of the specific rhythm of the heart and various abnormalities or disease states can

SIDEBAR 8.2 A POTASSIUM POISONING?

A number of years ago, we were asked to evaluate a case in which a ~60-year-old moderately obese male with a considerable history of medical issues, including apparent progressive congestive heart failure, had died during surgery for multiple coronary bypass grafts. Unfortunately, after the operation, one of the operating room staff had offered an opinion to the family members to the effect that the patient's potassium levels had become "too high." He further opined that the patient "must have been given potassium by mistake." Clearly, such an opinion can lead directly to the legal system and civil action (if not criminal). Resolution of the case, though, was relatively straightforward (as are so many apparent "poisonings"). The "elevated" potassium level that was reached during the operation of ~10 mEq/L was certainly quite high (normal levels are ~4.2 mEq/L) and not at all consistent with normal physiology. Such a level, if achieved during life, would indeed represent a significant and immediate medical emergency. However, it should be recalled that after death of a cell, or multiple cells, that the sodium–potassium pump, the action of which maintains the "sodium on the outside, potassium on the inside" gradient of ions and associated membrane potential, stops. In consequence, as the cell membrane loses its functional capability, sodium moves into the cell, driven by the gradient between the exterior and internal concentrations, and similarly, potassium rushes out.

In this case, the patient was losing cardiac muscle, and was indeed dying on the table. As a consequence, his serum potassium levels became elevated, not because of a mistaken (or more sinister motive) injection of potassium but because he was losing myocardium, and potassium was leaking out of compromised, dead, and dying cells. The important point here is that postmortem blood electrolyte levels are often unreliable and should be used and considered with great care. It is generally expected that after death samples will show low sodium, high potassium, reflective of the process described above, only occuring with all the cells in the body. Nevertheless, forensic pathologists will often collect and evaluate vitreous fluid for some electrolytes and glucose. Even with this often well-protected matrix, great care must be used in interpretation.

be diagnosed with the EKG. Contractile strength and peripheral resistance in the arteries of the limbs can be assessed with blood pressure monitoring.

A more detailed evaluation of heart state and disease can be accomplished by an echocardiogram, which measures the heart in motion by using ultrasonography. During this procedure, both wall motion and valve mechanics can be assessed, as well as wall thickness and the circumferences of the valve annuli.

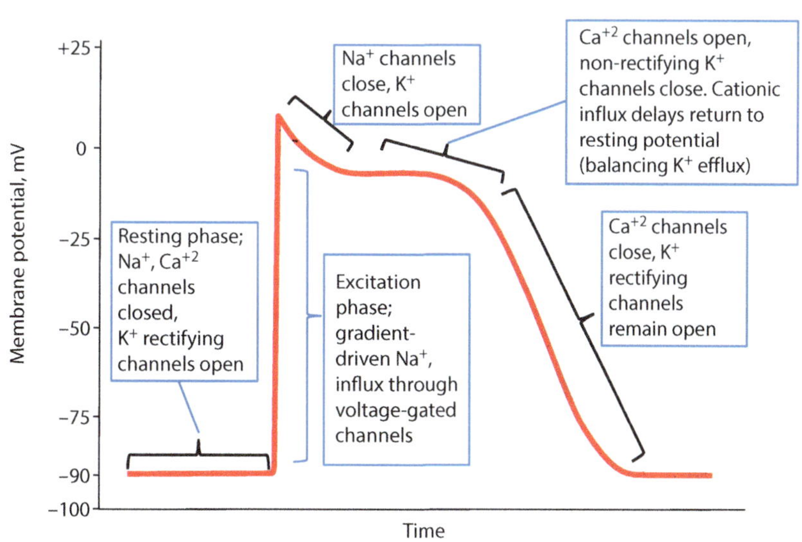

Figure 8.10 Cardiac action potential.

8.3 Disease States

8.3.1 Hypertrophy

The heart responds to stress, such as a chronic or recurring hypertension, by increasing the size of cells comprising the myocardium. (In general, an increase in the size of cells is *hypertrophy*, and increase in number is *hyperplasia*. Usually the tissue is specified, as in myocardial hypertrophy.) An increased size of myocardial cells is considered a disease state in that an enlarged heart signifies a compensatory reaction of the body to recurrent stress. For example, in response to chronic hypertension (such as may be caused by vascular constriction and increased resistance to arterial flow), the left ventricular myocardium will become larger and thicker as a result, reflecting ventricular hypertrophy. Similarly, if there is increased resistance to flow into or within the lungs, the walls of the right ventricle will exhibit hypertrophy.

Ventricular wall thickness is routinely measured during a forensic autopsy, with normal thickness (approximately 1 cm from the mitral valve) of ~1.3 cm and up to 1.6 cm. A thickness of 1.7 cm or more is generally considered hypertrophic. Similarly, the right ventricular wall should only be up to 0.3 cm in an adult at autopsy. With rare exceptions, cardiac hypertrophy is indicative of an individual who has had a chronic disease or underlying condition generating stress on the heart for months to years prior to the discovery of the enlargement (Figures 8.11 and 8.12).

The presence of myocardial hypertrophy in a case may be of significance in the evaluation of the role of drugs, in that the enlarged heart is somewhat more susceptible to fibrillation, rhythm disturbance, or sudden cardiac event (any of which may lead to death) than normal. While chronic hypertension is not uncommon in older individuals, the occurrence of a significantly enlarged heart may also be indicative of chronic stimulant use. Regardless of the etiology, a markedly enlarged heart is, in many cases, an adequate explanation for a sudden cardiac death and should not be ignored, even in light of the presence of drugs or other potentially toxic agents. (This is not to say that such findings are of greater significance than the presence of drugs, but rather, that the evidence of myocardial hypertrophy may increase the chance that the death was not necessarily a drug-related event or may suggest an increase susceptibility to certain toxic agents. The enlarged heart, as evidence of underlying disease, becomes an important factor to consider in the evaluation of the role drugs or toxins may have played in a particular case.)

Cardiac weight is a key parameter determined at autopsy. Anatomists, physiologists, and pathologists have studied organ weights as compared to body height, body weight, body mass index, race, gender, and age, without arriving at a definitive consensus for "normal." Historically, cardiac enlargement was considered to be a heart weight of greater than 350 g, but such a rule of thumb does not take into account the size of the person. In a practical sense, the determination of cardiac enlargement will be performed by a treating physician while the patient is still alive or by a pathologist at

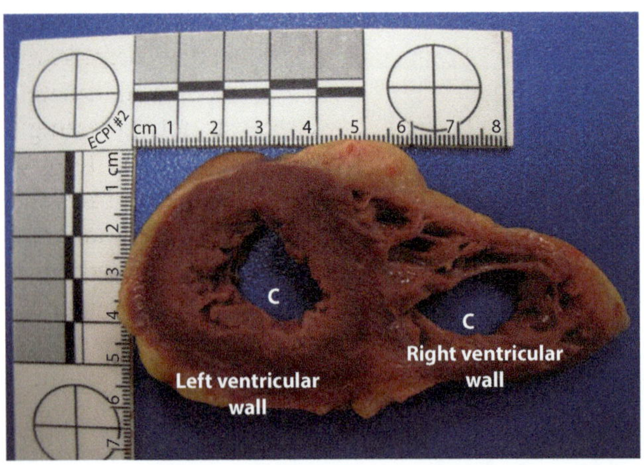

Figure 8.11 A transversely oriented section from a 350 gm heart. The left ventricle is on the left side of the photograph; the right ventricle is on the right. The myocardium is of the usual red-brown color and was relatively firm. The ventricular chambers (where the blood goes, indicated by the letter c) are of the usual size, neither compressed nor dilated.

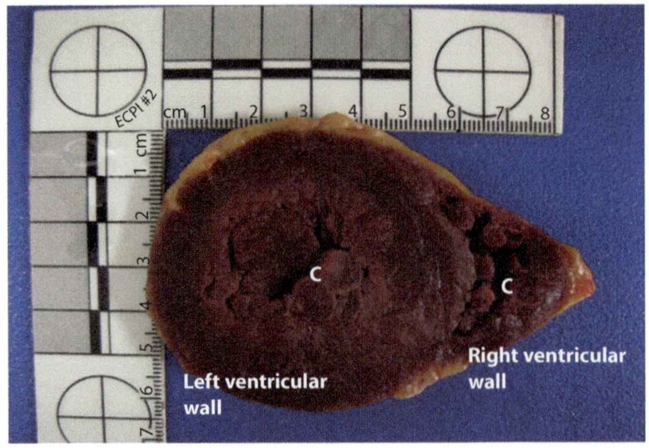

Figure 8.12 A transversely oriented section from a 500 gm heart. The left ventricle is on the left side of the photograph; the right ventricle is on the right. The myocardium is of the usual red-brown color and was relatively firm. There are no areas of grossly evident ischemia. However, the myocardium of both walls and of the interventricular septum is markedly thickened due to the prolonged extra work required of the heart in the patient with hypertension. The ventricular chambers (where the blood goes, indicated by the letter c) are very compressed because the muscle is so thick.

autopsy. The toxicologist can make use of heart weight and the physician/pathologist determinations and opinions as part of their own evaluation of a case (while recognizing that the legal authority and responsibility for the determination of cause and manner of death rests with the case pathologist).

8.3.2 Ischemia and Infarction

The myocardium receives oxygen and nutrients via the coronary arteries, which arise directly from the aorta. Disruption in blood flow, such as may be caused by stenosis (narrowing) of the arterial lumen or spasm of the arterial wall, can cause tissue ischemia (a restriction in flow of blood and hence the availability of oxygen to a tissue). An ischemic condition can be followed by infarction (tissue death due to a localized lack of oxygen) if blood flow is not quickly restored. Ischemia is the classic heart attack or myocardial infarction. At autopsy, the degree of stenosis of the coronary arteries (right; left anterior descending, or LAD; and circumflex) will routinely be noted. Significant stenosis in the cardiac arteries increases the likelihood of a cardiac event having been caused by ischemia rather than some other cause, such as a therapeutic or recreational drug (Figures 8.13 through 8.16; see Sidebars 8.3 and 8.4).

8.3.3 Rate Abnormalities

In the resting adult, the normal heart rate is between 60 and 100 beats per minute (BPM); readings outside this range are usually considered abnormal. Tachycardia is a condition in which the heart rate is too fast, and bradycardia, in contrast, describes an abnormally slow heart rate. Athletes and other people in good physical condition may have a normal resting heart rate below 60 bpm. Tachycardia can be caused by stimulant drugs, such as sympathomimetic amines, and bradycardia can be caused by CNS depressants, such as benzodiazepines, various narcotics (e.g., opiates), and alcohol.

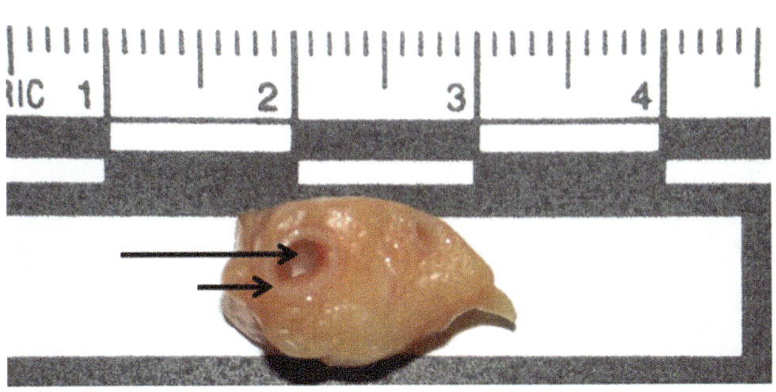

Figure 8.13 Section of normal coronary artery in epicardial adipose tissue.

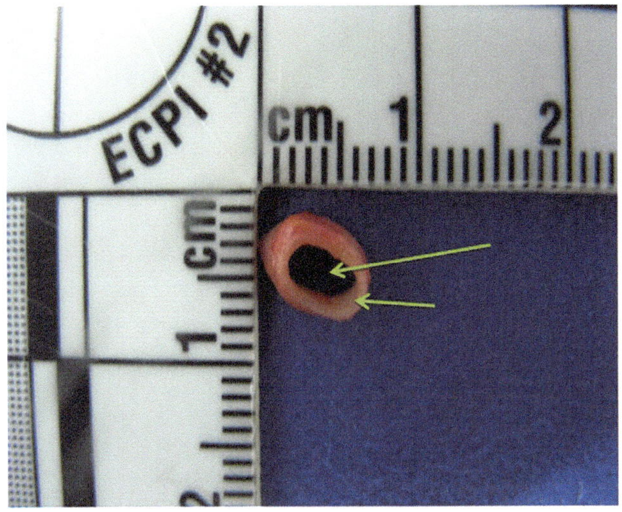

Figure 8.14 Normal coronary artery dissected away from epicardial adipose tissue. The thin wall (short arrow) is embedded in the epicardial adipose tissue. The lumen (long arrow pointing to the empty space) is widely patent. There is no atherosclerotic plaque.

8.3.4 Rhythm Disturbance

Disturbance in the progression of a conductive signal from the SA node through ventricular contraction can cause a variation from the normal cardiac rhythm. Arrhythmia, or dysrhythmia, reflects an abnormal beat frequency. Tachycardia is too rapid rhythm, bradycardia too slow. There are three main mechanisms for disordered rhythm: inappropriate origin of a contractile signal from cells not contained within the SA node, appearance of the normal signal at the SA node but at an inappropriate time, and finally, an abnormal or backward progression of the contractile wave through the myocardium (known as a reentry pathway). Reentry pathways may cause dysrhythmic contractions and inadequate ventricular filling.

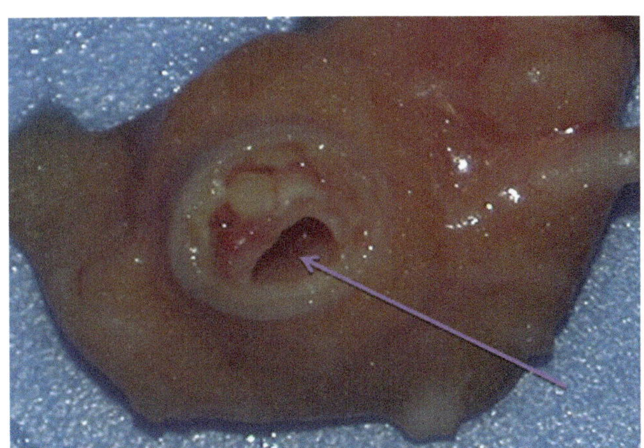

Figure 8.15 Coronary artery plaque with hemorrhage into the plaque. The residual lumen (arrow) is only about 25% of the original lumen.

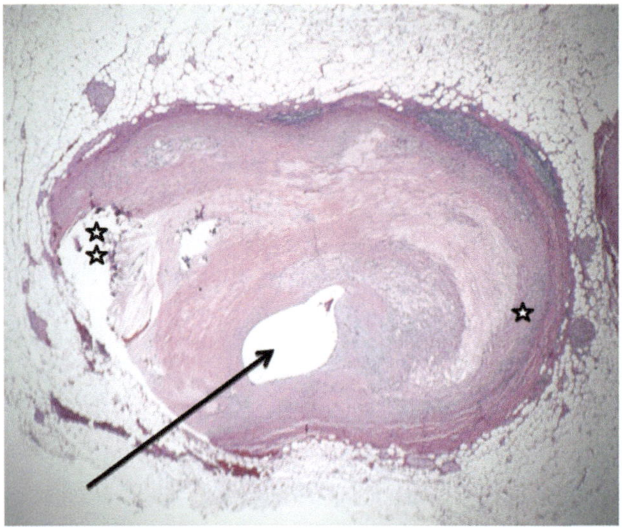

Figure 8.16 Coronary artery atherosclerosis, microscopic view, 2×. This coronary artery is significantly narrowed by fibrous tissue (*) and dystrophic calcification (**). The residual lumen (open space indicated by the arrow) is very small.

Anti-arrhythmic drug therapy may be used to ameliorate these conditions, usually sodium- or calcium-channel blockers or β-blockers (β_1-adrenergic antagonists) with the goal of adjusting the propagation of the depolarization wave through the myocardium to allow for coordinated, effective contraction of the atria and the ventricles. (Na^+, Ca^+, and β_1-adrenergic antagonists are discussed in Section 8.4, below).

8.3.4.1 Atrial Fibrillation

Atrial fibrillation (AF) is chaotic, uncoordinated, often rapid contraction of the atria that does not allow proper filling of the ventricles, and may result from an underlying heart disease, such as hypertension, or may arise spontaneously. AF is not usually life-threatening but may be associated with unpleasant symptoms such as fatigue, shortness of breath, and perceptible heart

SIDEBAR 8.3 ACUTE CARDIAC DEATHS: THE PATHOLOGIST'S PERSPECTIVE

Sudden cardiac-related deaths in adults are often called heart attacks by the general public, whether the consequence of a fatal arrhythmia or ischemic anoxia (loss of oxygen to tissues). While a sudden arrhythmic event may not leave clear pathologic evidence, an anoxic event of 20–30 minutes will cause necrosis of the myocardium, and if the patient survived long enough, the myocardial ischemia will become visible as dark mottling of the muscle tissue. In some cases, a sudden cardiac death may be pathologically evaluated and diagnosed, but in other circumstances (a sudden dysrhythmia leading to asystole), there may not be clear pathologic indication of the nature of the cardiac event (Figure 8.17).

In the case of a patient who died suddenly and for whom a cardiac death is suspected, the pathologist will weigh the heart, examine the myocardium and coronary arteries, and measure the thicknesses of the walls and the valve circumferences. The degree of stenosis apparent in the coronary arteries can be particularly helpful in evaluating the potential for a death to be the consequence of an ischemic event. Similarly, ventricular wall thickness can be used to evaluate cardiac hypertrophy. An enlarged heart, one in which the myocardium is hypertrophic, is at risk for an abnormal electrical signal transmission that may lead to a fatal dysrhythmia (considered by many people to be a sudden heart attack). An abnormality in one or more valves may also cause a dysrhythmia. Consideration of history, in particular of cardiac-related conditions (e.g., Long QT syndrome) may be informative as well.

As noted above, evidence of an acute myocardial infarction can often be detected, depending on the survival time following the ischemic event. While the time period is variable, myocardial necrosis can be detected grossly with a postevent survival time of as short as 4–12 hours after the ischemic event. If the patient survives 24 hours or more, coagulation necrosis of the myocardium acquires an abnormal appearance progressing from dark mottling with a yellow-gray center to yellow-tan, softened tissue. Longer survival times allow some degree of healing to occur and can be observed in the form of white scar tissue. Patients who die very shortly after their ischemic event (e.g., survival time <~30 min) will not have had time to develop visible changes in the myocardium, and necrosis will be undetectable, even by light microscopy. However, wavy fibers may be observed in microscopic sections from individuals who survived as little as 30 minutes beyond the ischemic event.

In summary, sudden cardiac-related deaths can often present a diagnostic challenge for the forensic pathologist and may often be diagnosed only by inference, relating the outcome (sudden death) to the underlying pathology, enlarged heart, coronary arterial stenosis, or other underlying medical condition.

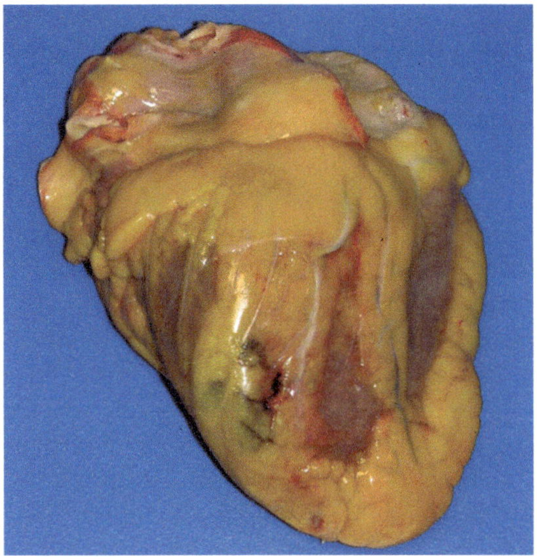

Figure 8.17 The red-purple area in the left ventricular free wall of this heart is a ruptured myocardial infarction. The peak time for rupture is approximately 4 days after the infarction. This patient was a chronic cocaine user.

palpitations. Chronic atrial fibrillation can progress into ventricular fibrillation, with its higher risk of serious consequences, including death. AF is commonly treated pharmacologically, often with β-blocking agents.

SIDEBAR 8.4 ACUTE CARDIAC DEATHS: THE TOXICOLOGIST'S PERSPECTIVE

Diagnosis of an acute cardiac death is plainly not the business of the toxicologist. However, identification of the presence of a drug of poison that could be an explanation for such a diagnosis is clearly of benefit to the case pathologist. What can be a bit more problematic for the toxicologist is teasing out the contribution that drugs or pharmaceuticals (and even abused drugs) may have or have not made, particularly when the levels or amounts ingested are not adequate for a direct cardiac event.

It can be useful, in many cases, for the toxicologist to at least understand the implications of the medical history of the decedent, specifically in relation to the potential for the death to be cardiac related rather than a toxic consequence of drug ingestion. As an example, consider a case in which an individual who was prescribed oxycodone died in hospital care ~6 hours after receiving his last dose of oxycodone. Evaluation and consideration of the case may be significantly affected by knowledge that the patient did or did not have an extensive history of cardiac problems.

8.3.4.2 Ventricular Fibrillation

Analogous to AF, ventricular fibrillation (VF or V-fib) is a condition in which the ventricles do not contract in a rhythmic, coordinated manner, and as such are often described as "quivering" rather than pumping in a normal fashion. As a consequence, blood is not effectively expelled into the pulmonary artery or the aorta, and the organs and tissues become ischemic, due to the lack of adequate oxygen. Ventricular fibrillation is a serious and often rapidly fatal condition.

8.3.4.3 Long QT Syndrome and Torsades de Pointes

Long QT syndrome is a phenomenon whereby the time between the start of ventricular contraction and the completion of ventricular repolarization is abnormally long. Long QT syndrome can be either acquired or congenital and represents a slowing of the electrical signal through the myocardium, or a delay in repolarization of the ventricles. The problem associated with Long QT syndrome arises when the atria contract prior to the completion of the ventricular refractory period, which are then unable to respond at the correct time. Long QT syndrome can be asymptomatic or ultimately fatal, depending on its severity and the occurrence of an associated rhythm disturbance. Persons with Long QT syndrome are at an increased risk of a sudden, potentially terminal cardiac event. A number of drugs are associated with causing this condition in various classes (e.g., erythromycin, quinidine, and methadone).

Torsades de pointes is a related, albeit relatively rare, rhythm disturbance caused by an electrical signal beginning in the ventricle and leading to ventricular tachycardia (200–250 bpm). Often only a transient phenomena, the condition may be fatal if prolonged, because the ventricle cannot empty or refill completely. Torsades de pointes can be perceived by the patient ("my heart is going too fast") based on pulse rate and may be confirmed by EKG. This condition is so named based of the EKG appearance showing a gradual change in rhythm, with an electrical pulse progressing above and then below the isoelectric line and lengthening of the QT interval, hence the "twisting of the points." Some drugs can have the (unusual) side effect of causing torsades de pointes, for example, quinidine, used as an antidysrhythmic.

8.3.5 Cardiomyopathies

The term *cardiomyopathy* refers to a primary disease of the heart muscle regardless of etiology, as long as it is not secondary to another condition. (Hence, cardiac hypertrophy from chronic hypertension would not be considered a cardiomyopathy, but myocarditis—an inflammation of the heart muscle—would be.) Cardiomyopathies can be difficult to classify because the source of heart muscle diseases can be diverse, sometime overlapping, and sometimes not known. Cardiomyopathies are catagorized by the functional derangement produced: restrictive, hypertrophic, dilated, and arrythmogenic.

Restrictive cardiomyopathy refers to disease states in which the heart is not free to relax completely within the pericardial sac. The ability of either the left or both ventricles to fill is restricted, most commonly by deposition of material (e.g., amyloid, a protein aggregate; fibrosis; or scar tissue) in the muscle, often caused by an inflammatory process. This condition is the least common of the three patterns in the United States, but more often seen in tropical regions.

Hypertrophic cardiomyopathy refers to an enlarged heart. This is by far the most common cardiomyopathy encountered in the United States. It is characterized by thickening of the walls and microscopic evidence of myocyte disarray (a chaotic arrangement of myocytes in contrast to the normal orderly bundle arrangement). There is also an increase in fibrous tissue around each myocyte. The entire heart may not be affected; for example, the tissue involved may be only the interventricular septum (asymmetrical septal hypertrophy), the left ventricular free wall (excluding secondary causes of hypertrophy such as hypertension), or the right ventricular free wall. Hypertrophic cardiomyopathy may be reflective of a genetic component, with about 50% of affected people expressing an inherited form.

Dilated cardiomyopathy refers to a condition whereby the chambers of the heart are enlarged. Causes can include genetic abnormalities and other underlying cardiomyopathies. This condition is characterized by some degree of left ventricular dysfunction, reduced systolic force, and symptoms of congestive heart failure (edema, effusions, fatigue, low oxygen saturation, etc.). Echocardiographic imaging is a noninvasive technique that allows diagnosis without further muscle damage. Peripartum-associated cardiomyopathy is a sudden, unexplained dilatation of the left ventricle near the end of pregnancy or in the early postpartum period, which can be a cause of sudden death.

Arrythmogenic cardiomyopathy refers to the progressive deposition of adipose or fibroadipose tissue in the ventricular myocardium. The appearance of such noncontractile cells in the myocardium can cause a conduction defect. This condition should not be confused with the limited deposition of fat cells in the right atrium with age, a natural progression of the aging process that is not arrythmogenic.

8.3.6 Tamponade

Tamponade is a fluid buildup in the pericardial sac, which prevents the heart from filling completely. As fluid influx into the pericardial sac continues, the space available for each subsequent ventricular expansion becomes smaller, ultimately preventing adequate filling of the ventricles. Cardiac tamponade is usually caused by a rapid accumulation of blood from a ruptured myocardial infarction or a rupture in the aorta contained within the sac (Figure 8.18).

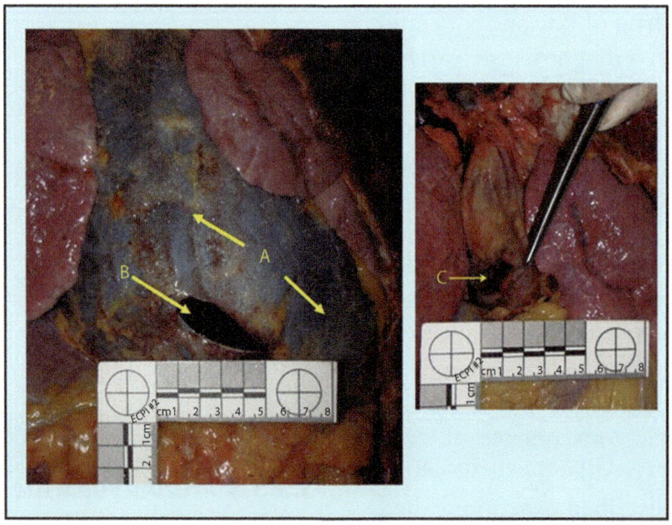

Figure 8.18 Cardiac tamponade: This example of cardiac tamponade came from a 39-year-old, 235 lb., 6′1″, apparently healthy and very athletic-looking male who had been experiencing vertigo for about 24 hours prior to being found dead in bed. At autopsy, his pericardial sac (A) was under tension with 830 mL of liquid and coagulated blood. A dissection in the descending aorta progressed in a retrograde fashion, causing the collection of blood in the pericardial sac (hemopericardium) (B). The origin of the dissection was in the intima of the descending portion, the blood tracked through the media of the aortic root and broke through the adventitia at the weakest place (C).

8.3.7 Inflammation

Inflammation of the myocardium can be incidental and asymptomatic, debilitating, or even in some cases fatal. A variety of different viruses, bacteria, or fungi can attack the myocardium, but the most commonly occurring pathogens are viruses. These are ubiquitous and usually not contagious from person to person. The heart may also become inflamed as an abnormal response to some drugs (e.g., epinephrine). While not a toxicologic issue directly, the presence of myocarditis (usually determined postmortem by microscopic examination of multiple heart sections) is in many cases an adequate explanation for death. This is not to suggest, however, if myocarditis is present, that it necessarily was a causative or contributory factor. Nevertheless, the role or potential role of a drug in a case should be considered in light of such findings.

8.3.8 Heart Failure

The term *heart failure* or *congestive heart failure* (CHF) generally refers to a poorly functioning heart. The result is a low ejection fraction (that portion of ventricular blood ejected during systole) and fluid buildup in body cavities (pleural, pericardial, peritoneal effusions) because of inadequate blood flow through the body. This may be considered an end-stage disease whose only therapy is symptomatic, implementation of a pacemaker, or a transplant. A number of pharmaceutical approaches are used to ameliorate the symptoms of CHF, including angiotensin-converting enzyme inhibitors, β-blockers, and diuretics. (Although CHF is considered an end-stage disease, this term does not refer to the speed at which the disease progresses nor the life expectancy of the patient. Many people live for many years with diagnosed CHF when provided with appropriate treatment and care.)

8.3.9 Valvular Diseases

Four valves in the heart prevent backflow of blood during contraction. The aortic and pulmonic valves are semilunar valves composed of cusps resembling half-moons, located in the pulmonary artery and aorta, respectively (see Figure 8.2). The other two (mitral and tricuspid) are atrioventricular valves that separate the atria from the ventricles on the left and the right sides, respectively. Normally functioning valves are smoothly operating structures whose elements are controlled by muscles of the myocardium (for the atrioventricular valves) and the annulus and other supporting structures for the two semilunar valves. If any of these key elements is diseased, the valves may fail to close completely, leading to regurgitation of blood during systole and eventual fibrosis of the endocardium as a response to the high-pressure flow past the leaky valves. The valve cusps and leaflets may also become diseased on their own, which may lead to formation of scar tissue or perforations. Consequences of such issues may be anywhere in the spectrum from inconsequential to devastating, depending upon the type and severity of the condition. Valvular disease may also include secondary changes in the heart including fibrosis, myocardial hypertrophy, and heart failure.

8.4 Mechanisms of Therapy

Therapeutic mechanisms of cardiac drugs are as variable as the underlying disease states the drugs are designed to treat. The goals of therapy are to treat patients with heart disease while minimizing any adverse effect on lifestyle. Nevertheless, many cardiac drugs can be toxic in excess, often as a consequence of simply too much of an effect that at lower concentrations of the drug would be therapeutic. The potential for therapeutic drugs with no abuse potential to be lethal in overdose should not be overlooked by the toxiciologist.

8.4.1 Inhibition of Na-K ATPase

The sodium–potassium ATPase normally functions to maintain the charge on the cellular membrane by exchanging three intracellular sodium ions for two extracellular potassium ions, driven by the concurrent hydrolysis of an ATP molecule with each cycle of the pump. Pharmacologic control of sodium flux allows some control of contractility of the heart. Drugs such as digitalis work by inhibiting the action of the ion pump, resulting in a slightly increased intracellular concentration of sodium ion, and hence a slight hypopolarization of the cell membrane. Because sodium and calcium are exchanged across the cell membrane, the decrease in the sodium gradient across the membrane makes the efflux of calcium from the cell less favorable (thereby increasing the intracellular concentration of calcium). Calcium plays an essential role in muscle contraction. With depolarization, more calcium is available for release and the heart can contract more forcefully, a *positive inotropic* effect.

8.4.2 Sodium Channel Blockers

Sodium channel blockers act in a manner like local anesthetic agents, inhibiting the progression of nerve signals. Blocking, or functional inhibition, of the voltage-gated sodium channels on the nerve diminishes or precludes the progression of the depolarization signal. The prototype agent of this class is lidocaine, also used as a local anesthetic. Blocking sodium channels on the myocardium makes the cells harder to excite (raises the threshold for excitation) and therefore slows the propagation of the impulse. Obviously, overuse of sodium channel blockers can cause complete cessation of electrical impulse propagation and heart block. Both saxitoxin and tetrodotoxin block the extracellular side of the channel, whereas some local anesthetics (e.g., bupivacaine) block the inside of the channel.

8.4.3 Calcium Channel Blockers

Calcium channel blockers inhibit calcium from entering myocardial cells and vascular smooth muscle cells. This translates into decreased contractility, decreased AV nodal conduction, and decreased heart rate (slower conduction = slower rate). Additionally, these drugs have a peripheral effect of vasodilation, lowering blood pressure. There are two major categories of drugs in this class: dihydropyridines (e.g., amlodipine and nifedipine) and the nondihydropyridines (e.g., diltiazem and verapamil). The former has more of an activity on the myocardium, and the latter has more of an effect on the periphery. These drugs are used as antihypertensive agents and to reduce the probability of ischemic events.

8.4.4 Potassium Channel Blockers

Potassium channel blockers block or restrict the efflux of potassium with a resultant prolongation of ventricular repolarization. The prototype medication is amiodarone and is used to treat ventricular tachycardia or ventricular fibrillation. Because these drugs do not act on the sodium channel, depolarization and contraction are not affected. Other examples of drugs in this class are ibutilide, dofetilide, and sotalol.

8.4.5 Adrenergic Receptor Blockers

Adrenergic receptors are differentially expressed on many cell membranes throughout the body (see Table 8.1). Drugs formulated to inhibit the adrenergic nervous system were originally used to treat hypertension because of their vasodilating capability and act by blocking the vasoconstrictive effects of epinephrine and norepinepherine on α and β receptors. Some differential specificity can be exhibited by individual drugs, allow targeting for specific purposes, for example, hypertension or asthma.

The β_1-adrenergic receptors are expressed primarily on the myocardial cell membrane. This specialization is useful for therapy in that some drugs are selective β_1-adrenergic receptor blockers. When used, such agents inhibit catecholamine-mediated contraction (cardiac contractility) and slow conduction from the SA and AV nodes. Examples of drugs in this class are atenolol and propanolol. Administration of a β_1-adrenergic receptor antagonist (β-blocker) shortly after a person has an ischemic myocardial event or a diagnosed myocardial infarction has been shown to reduce patient mortality.

Long-term use of β-blockers can also be an effective treatment for hypertension because of the action in reducing the force of the contraction of the left ventricle.

β_2-adrenergic receptors are located on the vascular membrane and bronchial smooth muscles. Blocking these receptors allows bronchial and vessel relaxation. Some β-blockers are nonselective, meaning they inhibit both β_1 and β_2 receptors, for example, propranolol.

α receptors are found on vascular smooth muscle and, when blocked, cause vasodilation of arterioles. Alpha receptors are also found on bronchial smooth muscle and can be used to treat asthma by opening the bronchioles as well as reduce afterload (back pressure on the heart), reducing cardiac oxygen demand. Examples of α-antagonists are prazocin and theophyllin. Alpha receptors also have subtypes, and different pharmacologic profiles may be expressed by selective drugs.

Table 8.1 Adrenergic Receptors: Location and Function

Receptor	Location	Function
α_1	Arterioles and veins	Constriction
	Heart	Inotropy
	Bladder sphincter, pilomotor	Contraction
	Pupils	Dilation (mydriasis)
α_2	Arterioles	Constriction
	Heart	Inotropy
	Various cell membranes	Oppose potassium influx
	Kidney	Sodium retention
	Platelets	Aggregation
	Presynaptic noradrenergic cells	Reduce norepinepherine release
β_1	Heart	Inotropy and chronotropy
	Kidney	Renin release
β_2	Arterioles and bronchi	Dilation
	Heart	Inotropy and chronotropy
	Islet cells (pancreas)	Insulin release
	Various cell membranes	Allow potassium entry
	Uterus	Relaxation
	White blood cells	Inhibition of margination
	Presynaptic nonadrenergic cells	Enhance norepinepherine release

8.4.6 Nitrates

Nitrates (e.g., nitroglycerine, isosorbide nitrate) act as vasodilators, and their effect on the coronary arteries results in enhanced blood flow to the myocardium. The mechanism involves conversion to nitric oxide by an aldehyde dehydrogenase. Nitric oxide binds to and activates guanylate cyclase, resulting in increased levels of cyclic guanosine monophosphate (cGMP), a cellular second messenger analogous to cyclic adenosine monophosphate (cAMP). cGMP acts on the vascular endothelium of the coronary arteries in the heart as well as the peripheral veins, thereby reducing preload (venous or loading pressure going into the heart) and reducing overall myocardial oxygen demand. Mechanistically, cGMP appears to activate protein-dependent kinases (phosphorylating enzymes). Nitrates can reduce afterload by dilating peripheral arterioles, are especially useful in patients with congestive heart failure, and are often used as a response to angina attacks.

8.4.7 Angiotensin-Converting Enzyme (ACE) Inhibitors

ACE inhibitors are a commonly prescribed group of antihypertensive. ACE inhibitors are often used in therapy for patients with acute myocardial infarction because of a protective effect on blood vessel endothelium (and can therefore help prevent damage to the myocardium after an ischemic attack). ACE inhibitors reduce the propensity for atherosclerotic plaque formation primarily by an antiproliferative and antimigratory effect on inflammatory cells (see Sidebar 10.4).

8.5 Common Toxins

8.5.1 Cocaine and Other Sympathetic Amines

Sympathetic amines, cocaine in particular, and amphetamine-related drugs (e.g., methamphetamine, methylenedioxyamphetamine [MDA], methylenedioxymethamphetamine [MDMA], etc.) are widely used illicitly (see Chapter 15). In addition to the psychotropic effects that drive the extensive illegal trade in the drug, cocaine is an effective local anesthetic with vasoconstrictive actions that tend to keep the anesthetic effects localized. Historically, cocaine has been used in dental and surgical procedures; however, such use now is extremely unusual. The cardiotoxic effects of cocaine and similar species are a function of the transient but pronounced hypertension associated with use. Cocaine is a norepinephrine reuptake inhibitor and, as such, is an alpha and beta receptor agonist by the indirect mechanism of causing increased norepinepherine concentration in the synaptic space. Cocaine causes increased peripheral vascular resistance, increased constriction of coronary arteries, and increased rate and force of contraction of the myocardium. Chronic increased constriction of peripheral vessels and coronary artery increases the likelihood of atherosclerosis. Multiple episodes of cocaine-induced vasoconstriction can cause damage to the intima of the vessel, making it more susceptible to plaque formation. Sympathetic stimulation also has arrythmogenic potential (Figure 8.19).

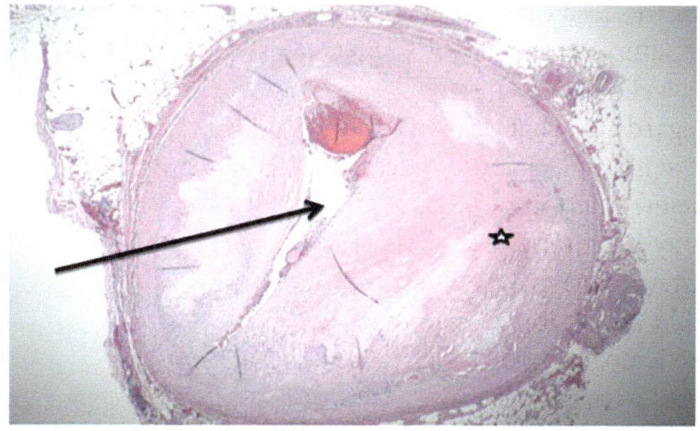

Figure 8.19 Coronary artery atherosclerosis, microscopic view, 2×. This coronary artery is significantly narrowed by fibrous tissue (*). The residual lumen (open space indicated by the arrow) is very small. There is some blood in the lumen (red material). This artery came from a 38-year-old man who was a chronic cocaine user.

The onset of action of cocaine is almost immediate following exposure, and with a relatively short half-life in the body, the duration of action is generally one hour or less. The presence of cocaine in blood at autopsy is often considered by many pathologists to provide an adequate explanation for death (particularly in the absence of another, more compelling cause). The vasocontrictive potential of the primary cocaine metabolite benzoylecgonine is often unrecognized and should also be considered as a contributory factor in acute hypertension in some cases (even though the compound is apparently without psychotropic activity).

8.5.2 Nicotine

Nicotine is an indole-alkaloid compound derived from the tobacco plant. It is used as an organic insecticide and is a toxic and addictive component of tobacco sold for human use. When inhaled or absorbed through the skin or mucosa, nicotine can reach the brain in under half a minute. The half-life in blood is about 2 hours.

Nicotine activates the splanchnic sympathetic nerves leading to the medulla of the adrenal gland, thereby stimulating the release of epinephrine and norepinepherine into the bloodstream. The increased release of epinephrine and norepinephrine is the basis for the addictive potential.

Nicotine has a myriad of negative effects on the body, both short term and long term. Nicotine causes vasoconstriction and increased heart rate. Over time, increased peripheral resistance and increased heart rate cause long-term increase in cardiac oxygen demand, leading to hypertension and atherosclerosis. Nicotine is a significantly toxic drug, with an LD_{50} in many species less than that of strychnine.

8.5.3 Digoxin/Digitalis

Digoxin is a purified cardiac glycoside derived originally from the foxglove plant, which has an extensive history in folk medicine as a cure for "dropsy" (congestive heart failure). Foxglove is native to Europe, Asia, Australia, and Africa and is a common garden plant (as an introduced species) in the United States. The dramatic flower stems are white, yellow, pink, or purple and grow on a stalk between 2.5 and 8 feet tall.

In therapeutic doses, digoxin slows and strengthens the heartbeat. Overdose can be fatal, and foxglove has a history as a source of an effective poison, in addition to use in folk medicine. Mechanistically, the cardiac glycosides inhibit the sodium–potassium ATPase, resulting in elevated intracellular calcium concentrations. (The sodium gradient, generated by the Na-K ATPase, provides the driving force for calcium removal via a sodium–calcium antiport transporter.) Elevated intracellular calcium affects the ability of the myocardium to properly relax prior to a new contraction event.

The cardiac glycosides are generally rather large, nonthermolabile compounds, and as such are not amenable to analysis by GCMS. Demonstration of the presence of such compounds may be difficult in some poisoning cases. However, with the increasing availability of HPLC-MS, comprehensive analysis in suspected poisonings becomes much more feasible. There are a number of sources of cardiac glycosides, including lily of the valley and species of yew, discussed below.

8.5.4 Doxorubicin

Doxorubicin is an anthracycline antibiotic and antineoplastic agent that has been used in treating some lymphomas, bladder cancer, and some cancers of the breast. Like many chemotherapeutic agents, it acts on actively replicating cells, either limiting replication or killing the cell. Mechanistically, the drug acts as a DNA intercalating agent (meaning the drug lies within the DNA coil), affecting the normal actions of enzymes, e.g., topoisomerase II, on the DNA molecule and inhibiting the replication process.

Side effects of anthracycline use are predominantly expressed in active tissues, for example, hair follicles, gastrointestinal mucosa (leading to the hair loss and GI upset characteristic of treatment). An additional side effect, unrelated to the DNA actions, is expressed on myocardial cells. High levels of doxorubicin can cause dilated cardiomyopathy and congestive heart failure by a decline in mitochondrial phosphorylation, in a dose- and duration-dependent manner. The quinone structure of the drug allows for redox cycling of electrons from NADH or NADPH, ultimately reducing iron III to iron II and leading to the generation of active oxygen species (e.g., superoxide and hydroxyl radical), which in turn can result in lipid peroxidation and oxidative stress. Oxygen radical toxicity can cause myofibrillar loss and vacuolization of myocyte cytoplasm.

8.5.5 Tricyclic Antidepressants

Tricyclic antidepressant agents (TCAs) have been on the commercial market since the early 1950s. These drugs have been traditionally used to treat clinical depression and are still widely used but have become progressively less popular in comparison to the newer benzodiazepines and selective serotonin reuptake inhibitors (SSRIs). Clinical use of the drugs has expanded to the treatment, or at least amelioration of, cluster headaches. TCAs work as serotonin and norepinephrine reuptake inhibitors, thereby producing elevated neurotransmitter levels in the synaptic space. Interestingly, TCAs also can act as sodium and calcium channel blockers in high levels, with the potential of causing a potentially fatal arrhythmia. This effect on ion channels is the basis for the often lethal toxicity associated with overdose.

TCAs are also one of the classic compounds with which the process of postmortem redistribution was identified, with significantly lower levels often determined in postmortem samples collected from a peripheral source (e.g., femoral vein) as compared to central blood (collected in or in the vicinity of the heart). As with all such compounds, great care should be taken with the interpretation of postmortem drug levels, particularly if taken from a nonperipheral source. Amitriptyline and imipramine are the most commonly seen TCAs, along with their metabolites, nortriptyline and desipramine, respectively.

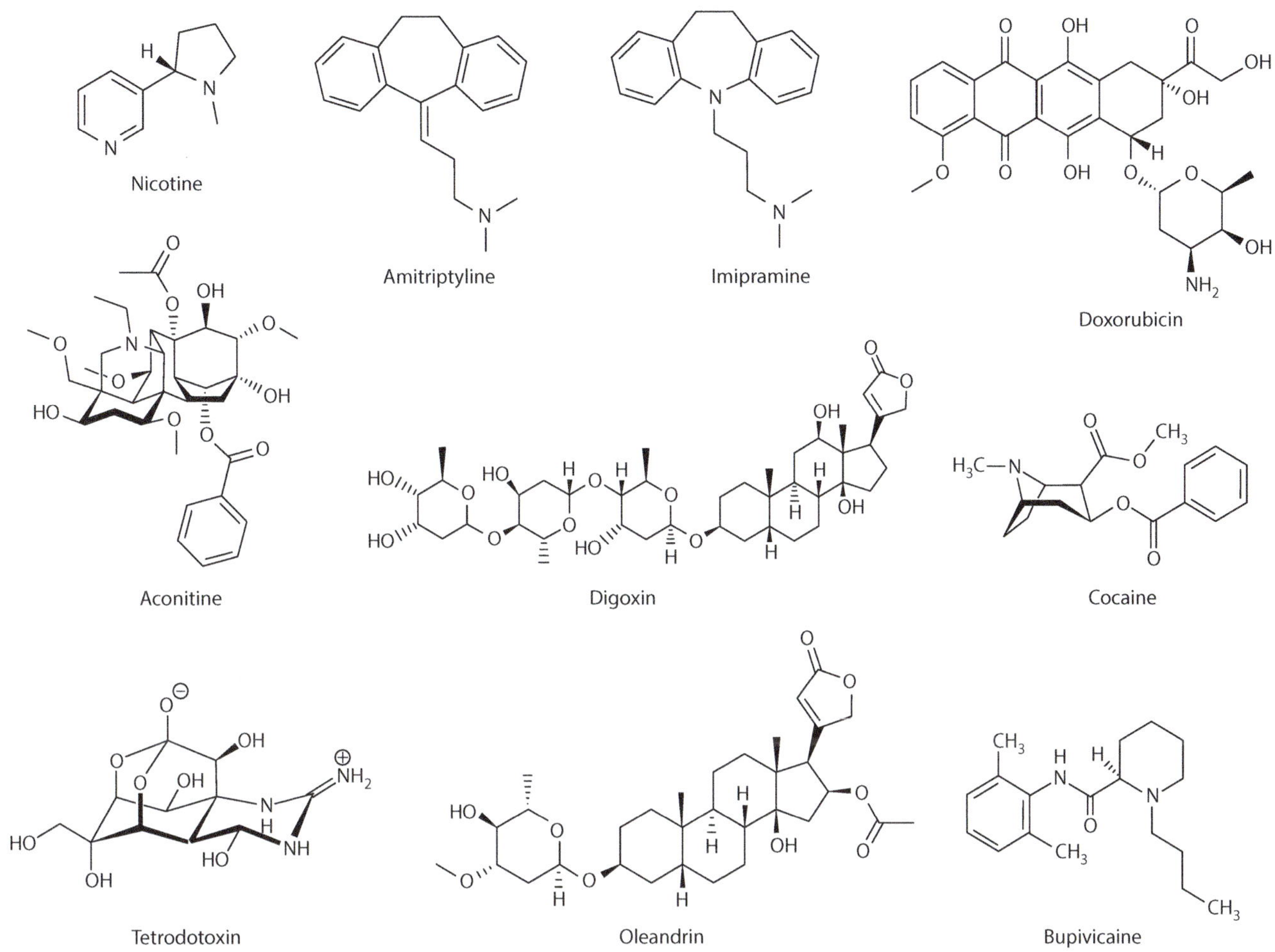

Figure 8.20 Example cardiac toxins.

8.6 Uncommon Toxins (Figure 8.20)

8.6.1 Aconitine

Aconitine is a derivative of the Aconitum plant, also called devil's helmet and monkshood. It has been used historically in herbal medicine as an antipyretic and an analgesic, but with a very narrow therapeutic index. Aconitine has a long and colorful history as a poison (see Sidebar 8.5). The mechanism of action is relatively straightforward: aconitine binds to the alpha subunit of voltage-gated sodium ion channels in muscle and nerve cell membranes, causing the channel to remain open longer than the normal response. Aconitine therefore causes prolonged depolarization and affects the ability of the cell to repolarize as well, thereby increasing the refractory period of the neuron. At a high enough dose, the neuron becomes functionally blocked or paralyzed. While the effect of aconitine (muscular paralysis) is the same as such molecules as the classic sodium channel blockers, mechanistically there is a distinction in that aconitine holds the channels open, while such molecules as tetrodotoxin block the opening and action of the channel. Both lidocaine and tetrodotoxin have been used to treat aconitine-exposed patients.

The clinical effects of aconitine can be variable and include several tissues and organ systems. Paresthesia of the face, lips, and extremities may be seen, as well as hypotension, bradycardia, chest pain, ventricular arrhythmias, abdominal pain, nausea, vomiting, diarrhea, sweating, and dyspnea.

SIDEBAR 8.5 MONKSHOOD AND ACONITINE

Monkshood is a perennial plant that grows to about 3 feet at full maturity, commonly with dark blue petals (though the flowers can also be white, purple, yellow, or pink). The potentially deadly nature of the plant has been long recognized by both Eastern and Western societies, with reference in early and Greek and Roman times and earlier in the Eastern civilizations. The medicinal potential of the plant has been also used with incorporation into both Chinese traditional medicine and Ayurvedic healing.

Monkshood and the toxic alkaloid aconitine are the primary reason for the notoriety of the plant. Aconitine has been used as a poison and a component of poisons throughout recorded history. Even in mythology the drug has appeared, as the poison by which Medea attempts to kill Theseus. It is also incorporated into works of fiction (both literary and staged; e.g., Harry Potter, Shakespeares' Henry IV, some classic movies of the vampire/wolfman/Dracula genre, and even television with episodes of *Dexter* and the *NCIS-Los Angeles* series).

Fiction may often embellish reality, but with aconitine, the real-life use of the poison has occurred in many homicides up to and including modern times as well as in accidental poisonings. With this in mind, aconitine can serve as a practical reminder of the potential for toxins and poisons to appear in forensic casework that are somewhat removed from the routine group of drugs and pharmaceuticals regularly encountered. As is often the case, the circumstances of a poisoning or toxic event, including clinical data (if available), can be of use in understanding the nature of the potential causative agents, which can then inform both the analytical process and the consideration of linkage of any identified compounds to symptoms. In short, symptomology, clinical chemistry, pathology, and forensic toxicology should be linked in a web of mechanistic consistency.

8.6.2 Tetrodotoxin

Tetrodotoxin is a very potent sodium ion channel blocker, effectively preventing nerve signal propagation by blocking the ability of voltage-gated sodium channels to open in response to depolarization. Tetrodotoxin is found in some species of fish, notably the sushi delicacy fugu (pufferfush) and some octopuses. The animals probably acquire the toxin as a consequence of the action of symbiotic bacteria (species of *Pseudomonas*, *Vibrio*, and *Pseudoalteronomas).* Tetrodotoxin is about 100 times more toxic than cyanide and is easily absorbed through the skin, though ingestion is the usual route of exposure. Symptoms are rapid and include muscular paralysis, apnea (from paralysis of the diaphragm), and cardiac failure.

8.6.3 Grayanotoxins

Grayanotoxins are a group of structurally related toxins derived from rhododendron and related species (although not all rhododendron species are toxic). These toxins also function as sodium channel blockers and were formerly called *rhodotoxin* because the honey made by bees collecting nectar from the rhododendron bush can be toxic. The leaves and flowers also contain grayanotoxin. *Rhododendron ponticum*, native to Turkey, has been associated with toxic honey for centuries. Other plants that produce grayanotoxin and are well-recognized for their toxic potential are the mountain laurel and the sheep laurel. Grayanotoxins are not particularly potent, and clinical effects last only about 24 hours (dose dependent). Therapy is not usually required.

8.6.4 The Yew Plant

The yew plant (*Taxus baccata*) is a popular, hardy landscape plant, forming dense treelike bushes that may grow to be quite tall or may be successfully trimmed to mimic shrubbery. The plant has a long history of use as a basis for poisons in England and northern Europe. Nearly all parts of the yew plant contain the very potent calcium channel blockers taxine A and B. Ingestion of the toxin can lead to a potentially fatal bradycardia. Symptoms of exposure can develop rapidly following ingestion. Extracts from the yew plant have been used as herbal heart medications, although not with the success of the digitalis-based medications. The anticancer drug Taxol is prepared from either the Pacific or European yew.

8.6.5 Lily of the Valley

The lily of the valley, *Convallaria majalis*, is a common, popular ground cover with fairly broad, pointed leaves and a short stalk of white bell-like flowers opening in spring. Despite its innocuous appearance, all parts of the plant are poisonous, containing the toxic glucosides (a combination of a glucose and another functional group, connected via a glycosidic bond) convallarin and convallarotoxin. Both are considered to be cardiac glycosides and act by inhibition of the sodium–potassium ATPase, thereby affecting the ability of the neuron and myocardium to reestablish and maintain the membrane potential after a depolarization event. Overdose symptoms are bradycardia and dysrhythmia, potentially leading to ventricular fibrillation and death.

8.6.6 Oleander

Oleander (*Nerium oleander*) is a landscape plant grown naturally in tropical and subtropical regions and contains the toxic cardiac glycoside oleandrin. All parts of the plant are toxic but have been used medicinally to treat congestive heart failure. Oleandrin, like the other cardiac glycosides, inhibits the NA-K ATPase. Adults appear to be less vulnerable to the toxic effects than are children and small animals.

REVIEW QUESTIONS

1. Briefly describe the flow of blood through the body, specifically with regard to the chambers of the heart.
2. Describe the physiological significance of the P, Q, R, S, and T waves on the electrocardiogram.
3. Name two key measurements performed at autopsy that can assist in assessing cardiac health.
4. What is the mechanism of action of digitalis? What are the consequences for intracellular ions?
5. What might be a reasonable physiologic consequence of chronic cocaine use, and why might such a consequence occur?
6. Your forensic pathologist colleague calls and says he thinks he has a case that's an amitriptyline overdose, with a serum level well into the toxic range. To help assess the case, what do you want to know, and why?
7. What may be the significance of a medical history of prolonged QT syndrome in the evaluation of a possible fatal overdose case?
8. Why may an overdose of an adrenergic β-blocker be fatal?

TOPICS FOR DISCUSSION

1. Consider the role and function of the Purkinje fibers. What would the consequences be if they failed to perform?
2. Consider the relationship between aconitine and tetrodotoxin. What biochemical parameters would help determine if one compound could be used to treat exposure to the other?
3. Would amitriptyline or cocaine be more dangerous to a person with Long QT syndrome, and why?
4. What would the consequences of a venous bolus dose of potassium be to the heart?
5. How could a history of CHF be a confounder in an overdose case?
6. Historically, an effective diet drug combination (Fen-Phen) was associated with long QT syndrome in some individuals. Was the decision to remove the drug from the marketplace correct?

Bibliography

Aaronson PI, Ward JPT, Connolly MJ. *The Cardiovascular System at a Glance*. 4th rev. ed. Walden, MA: Wiley Blackwell, 2012.

Bell DR. The electrical activity of the heart. In: Rhoades RA, Bell DR, editors. *Medical Physiology: Principles for Clinical Medicine*. 3rd rev. ed. New York: Lippincott Williams & Wilkins, 2009.

The Heart. In: Martini FH, Nath JL, editors. *Fundamentals of Anatomy and Physiology*. 8th rev. ed. New York: Pearson Benjamin Cummings, 2009.

Kang YJ. Toxic responses of the heart and vascular system. In: Klassen CD, editor. *Casarett and Doull's Toxicology: The Basic Science of Poisons*. 8th rev. ed. New York: McGraw-Hill, 2013.

McCorry LK. *Essentials of Human Physiology for Pharmacy*. 2nd ed. Boca Raton, FL: CRC Press, 2009.

Hepatotoxicity

9

Contents

9.1 Introduction

The liver is one of the largest and most important internal organs in the body, serving as the major source for the synthesis of essential biomolecules, processing of nutrients for energy, essential elements, and for the metabolic transformation of both endogenous and exogenous chemicals. Metabolic products can exit the hepatocyte directly into either the bloodstream or be excreted into the biliary system. The liver has multiple endocrine functions (release of chemicals into the body, e.g., albumin, lipoproteins, triglycerides, hormones, and metabolic intermediates) as well as exocrine functions (e.g., the formation and secretion of bile).

The impact of either chronic or acute toxic insult to the liver can be devastating, leading potentially to a progressive deterioration of hepatic function, liver failure, and ultimately death. The ability of the toxicologist to understand and appreciate the status of hepatic function can be important in many forensic cases, in terms of either the impact of an acute toxin or in the determination of the extent to which a functionally challenged liver may have played in the role of the actions of drugs or other toxins.

9.2 Anatomical Description

9.2.1 Gross Description

The liver is a reddish-brown organ, generally ~1500 g in adults, normally situated on the right side in the abdominal cavity just below the diaphragm. Anatomically, the liver is divided into two major lobes, left and right, the latter being significantly larger. The two minor lobes, situated on the posterior surface, are termed the *quadrate* and the *caudate*. The distinction between lobes is only physical, in that there is no functional distinction or differentiation between the different lobes (Figure 9.1).

The functional cells within the liver are hepatocytes, and each borders the bloodstream on one side and a bile canaliculus on another. A network of supportive material, made up of collagen and glycoprotein, provides a crosslinked fibrous network (the reticular matrix) supporting the overall structure. While the majority of the surface of the liver is unattached, a portion is connected to the abdominal wall by ligaments.

In contrast to other organs in the body, the blood supply for the liver is twofold. Most blood (~75%+) reaching the liver is venous in origin, arriving via the portal vein and carrying nutrients from the GI tract and metabolic products and intermediates from throughout the body. Significantly, as venous return, blood in the portal vein is deoxygenated. However, in addition to the venous flow, a supply of oxygenated blood reaches the liver from the hepatic artery, a branch of the celiac trunk from the aorta.

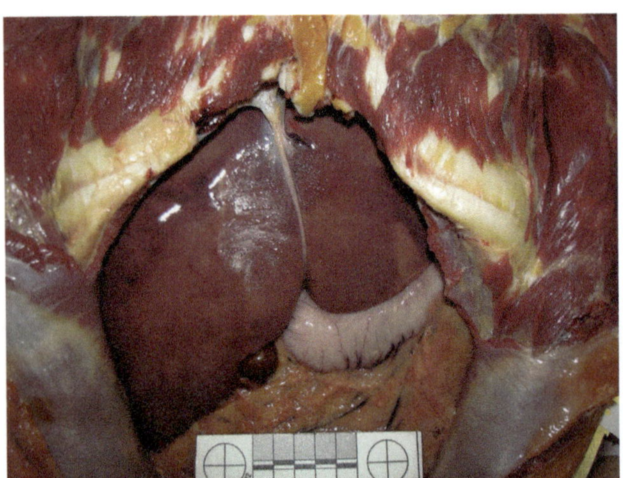

Figure 9.1 Normal liver, *in situ*: Open abdominal cavity displaying the normal relationship of the liver to the bottom of the rib cage. Notice that the liver is red-brown and shiny.

The portal venous and hepatic arterial blood combine in the channels between hepatocytes (the hepatic sinusoids) as the blood flows toward the central vein. Blood flow in the liver is directly in contact with a surface of the hepatocytes, facilitating transit of materials, both in and out of the blood. Because of the relatively large surface area comprising the channels of blood flow, the intravascular pressure in the liver is low. Ultimately, blood flow out of the liver is from the central vein into the inferior vena cava, then via the vena cava to the right atrium of the heart. The *bile canaliculus* parallels the sinusoid on the other side of the hepatocytes. Bile flow proceeds toward the portal vein and hepatic artery, joining the bile duct system at that point. The combination of the portal vein, hepatic artery, and bile duct are referred to as the *portal triad*. The network of bile ducts lead to the gallbladder, located on the undersurface of the liver, between the left and right lobes. The gallbladder and the bile ducts transport bile acids, salts, and other products important to the digestive process to the intestinal lumen (Figures 9.2 through 9.4).

9.2.2 Microscopic Descriptions

The three general approaches in which the basic functional structure of the liver is commonly described, differing in the perspective on which the description is based, are as follows: the classic liver lobule, the liver acinus, and the portal lobule. A useful description of hepatic toxicity or disease may contain location-specific information presented in terms of one of these three approaches.

9.2.2.1 The Classic Lobule

The classic liver lobule is considered as a hexagon, with the central vein in the middle and a portal triad at each of the vertices. While human liver exhibits the classic lobule to the trained eye, it is not as easily visualized as in some other species with more pronounced connective tissue structure (e.g., pig). Nevertheless, the landmarks in the human liver can be easily seen and recognized by light microscopy. The expression of hepatic cellular toxicity is often described in terms of the two main features of this model, the central vein (centrilobular) or the portal triad (periportal). These regions can be distinguished in terms of oxygen tension, in that the periportal region, located close to the hepatic artery, will tend to have a greater access to oxygen and hence intracellular oxygen tension than cells located closer to the central vein, or centrilobular. The toxicologic implication is that toxins whose effect can be ameliorated by the availability of energy or oxygen-dependent processes will be more

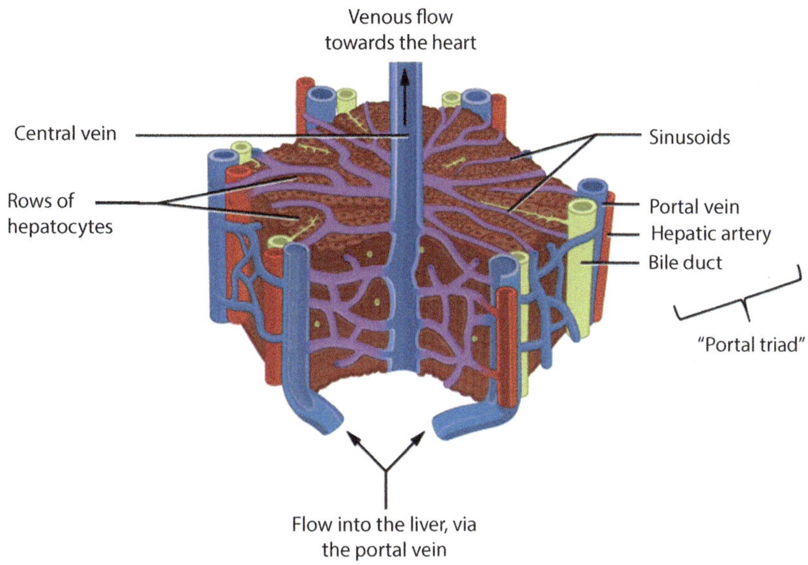

Figure 9.2 Basic structural diagram showing direction of blood and bile flow. (Retrieved from Wikipedia Commons April 9, 2015. Image made available and published under the Creative Commons Attribution 3.0 Unported license by OpenStax College—Anatomy & Physiology, Connexions Web site. http://cnx.org/content/col11496/1.6/. Original upload date June 19, 2013. License can be found here and only the bottommost image was used with some modification to the illustration labels: http://creativecommons.org/licenses/by/3.0/legalcode.)

likely to cause an effect in the low-oxygen centrilobular regions. A classic example is the centrilobular toxicity characteristic of acetaminophen poisoning (Figure 9.5).

9.2.2.2 The Liver Acinus

The liver acinus is the smallest functional unit of the organ, with a complete blood supply, and may be considered as a central axis comprising a terminal branch of the portal vein, hepatic artery, and bile canaliculus surrounded by regions of progressively less oxygenated regions of hepatocytes. The "zones" within the acinus are based on the degree of oxygenation of the blood. Concentric rings of hepatocytes are considered around the portal triad. The central zone is (zone 3) farthest from the hepatic artery and is therefore the least oxygenated region. In contrast, the region closest to the portal triad, and hence the hepatic artery and the source of oxygenated blood, is zone 1, normally reflecting the highest oxygen tension. Zone 2 lies in between and defines a region of intermediate oxygen tension. The metabolic capability of the hepatocyte is, to a great extent, determined by its energy source and hence the availability of oxygen. Zone 3 hepatocytes are most susceptible to toxic stress, and this is the region with cells that often appear swollen and fragmented in early liver damage.

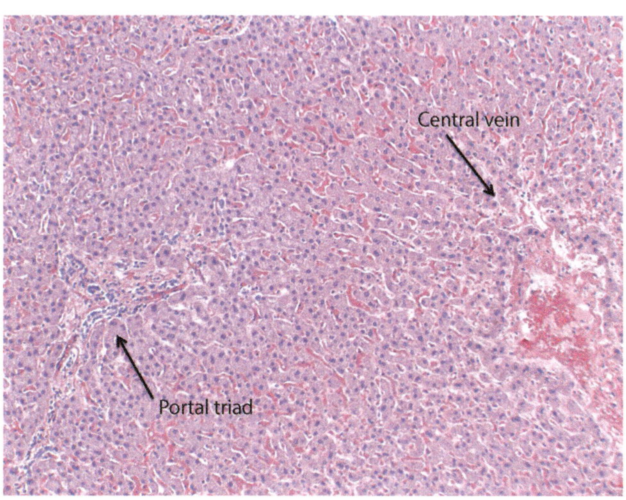

Figure 9.3 Normal liver, 10×.

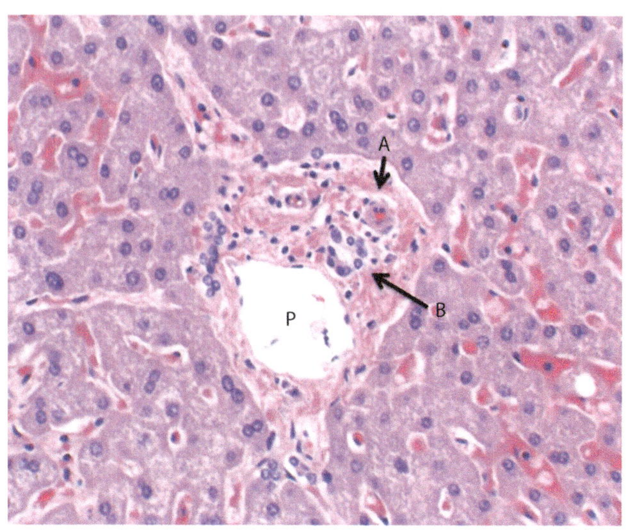

Figure 9.4 Normal liver, 20×, showing the features of the portal triad: the portal vein (P), the bile duct (B), and a branch of the hepatic artery (A).

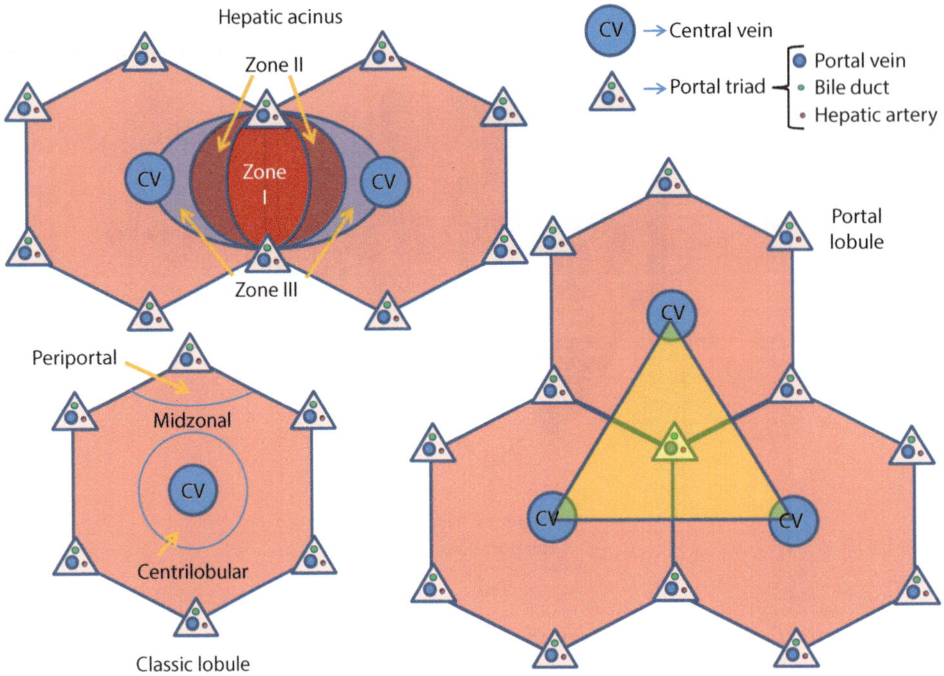

Figure 9.5 Classic lobule, acinus, and portal lobule.

9.2.2.3 The Portal Lobule

The underlying concept of the portal lobule is based on the exocrine function of the liver, including bile production and drainage. The central feature is the bile duct contained within the portal triad. Bile flows toward the portal triad within the bile canaliculi into the bile duct, to the common bile duct (a feature large enough to be seen grossly) and eventually into the gallbladder. The portal lobule can be viewed as a triangle with a portal triad in the center and central veins at each of the vertices.

9.3 Physiological Processes

The liver performs multiple vital functions and is essential to life. While the functions of the lungs, kidneys, and even heart can be performed artificially for some time, there is as yet no artificial liver, and the only option in the case of a seriously diseased or nonfunctional liver is transplant. The intracellular functions of hepatocytes are numerous, complex, and varied. Generally, these processes are subdivided into four major categories: energy and nutrient processing, *de novo* synthesis of molecules, detoxification of blood, and excretion of bile for lipid digestion.

9.3.1 Energy and Nutrient Processing

The liver serves as the major site of catabolic reactions in the body, breaking down nutrients and generating common metabolic products that can be further oxidized for energy or utilized as synthetic intermediates. The major energy-producing pathways of the body are based on the oxidation of glucose, and the liver is essential for normal glucose metabolism.

Hepatocytes take up sugars and other nutrients from the blood that were absorbed in the intestines. Glucose is the basic sugar molecule around which the body's energy processes function. Other sugars are converted into glucose for the oxidative, energy-generating process known as *glycolysis*. To the extent that excess sugar is available, it is stored as the polysaccharide glycogen. Glucose can be readily liberated from glycogen in response to the needs of the body. Blood glucose levels are controlled through the actions of the hormones insulin, which facilitates glucose uptake and utilization, and glucagon, which helps to mobilize glucose from glycogen. Glucose can also be generated from more basic molecules as needed (gluconeogenesis).

In addition to glucose metabolism, the breakdown, oxidation, and synthesis of lipids represent another important series of energy storing and mobilization reactions that also occur primarily in the liver. Lipids serve as high-energy storage molecules in the form of fatty acids, mono-, di-, and triacylglycerols. Fatty acids can provide energy equivalents via hydrolysis, as well as the basis for many structural components of the body (e.g., cholesterol, steroids, and related molecules). Lipid molecules are distributed around the body from the liver, secreted as a combined molecule of lipid and protein, as a lipoprotein or lipoprotein complex. Lipoproteins are grouped into four general categories: chylomicrons, VLDL, LDL, and HDL. The acronyms stand for very low density lipoprotein, low-density lipoprotein (so-called bad cholesterol), and high-density lipoprotein ("good" cholesterol). As its name suggests, HDL is the densest molecule of the four and contains the highest percentage of protein. The lipoprotein complex as initially secreted by the liver is in the form of VLDL, and as the molecule delivers lipid materials to cells, the composition of the complex changes, through LDL and ultimately HDL.

Chylomicrons are the least dense of the lipoproteins, having the least amount of protein. Lipid absorbed from the intestines that had been eaten as food is in the form of cholesterol and triglycerides that are converted to chylomicrons by intestinal cells. Chylomicrons are absorbed by hepatocytes where the lipids are released and processed by the hepatocyte. When the VLDL fraction is high in plasma, the plasma can appear turbid in the test tube (sometimes called fatty plasma).

9.3.2 Synthesis of Biomolecules

The importance of the synthetic role of the liver can hardly be overstated. While synthetic reactions do occur to some extent throughout the body, the bulk of the routine processes of synthesis of essential biomolecules (proteins, glycoproteins, lipoproteins, hormones, enzyme cofactors, etc.) for transport, storage, or other functions occurs in the liver. (For example, fibrinogen and nearly all blood coagulation factors are produced by hepatocytes and released into the blood as needed, as are those factors that act as inhibitors of the process.) The essential role of protein synthesis for the cell, the organ, and the body is emphasized by a number of toxins associated with mushrooms, and the deadly poison ricin (see Section 9.6.2.2 and Sidebar 9.1).

SIDEBAR 9.1 RICIN AND ABRIN

Ricin and abrin are two proteinaceous plant-derived toxins. While ricin has received considerable notoriety for its potential as a large-scale poisoning agent, both toxins have a deadly potential. Both toxins consist of two protein subunits, linked with disulfide bridges, and only a slight difference in molecular weight between the two compounds. (Ricin is composed of a 32 Kdal α-chain and 34 Kdal β-chain, while the abrin α- and β-chains are 30 and 35 Kdal, respectively.) Ricin is found in the castor plant and is concentrated in the castor bean. (Castor oil does not contain appreciable quantities of ricin.) Castor beans, if ingested whole, are not toxic, in that the seed coat survives the digestive process and the toxin is not released. On the other hand, either a broken seed coat or the act of chewing will release the toxin, with potentially devastating consequences. Ricin was used in the 1978 assassination of the Bulgarian dissident Georgi Markov, who was shot in the leg with a small pellet containing ricin, and died several days later. Abrin is contained in seeds of the rosary pea, found in the southeastern United States. All parts of the plant are toxic.

The target of both proteins is the ribosome, a cellular organelle that functions in protein synthesis. Eukaryotic ribosomes are composed of two components, a small (40S) and large (60S) subunit. The intact ribosome functions by translocating along an mRNA molecule, serving as a base upon which tRNA delivers amino acids in the sequence coded in the mRNA, thereby synthesizing the amino acid core of a functional protein. The B of the toxin chain serves to bind to the cellular membrane, initiating the process of endocytosis, internalizing the molecule into the cell and more specifically into the endoplasmic reticulum. The A-chain is dissociated, which then binds to the 60S ribosomal subunit, blocking the protein synthetic function.

The symptoms of ricin poisoning are dependent upon the route of exposure. The organs and tissues that are the earliest affected are the ones that are the first exposed. Hence, with an inhalation exposure, the respiratory system is first affected; following ingestion, the GI system and the liver become the primary target. Venous injection normally affects the liver primarily, perhaps the most sensitive of the organs, as a function of its role in synthesis and delivery of many proteins. Regardless of the exposure mechanism, symptoms can begin to be expressed after a few hours, and death by multiorgan system failure is certain in 36–72 hours if the dose is large enough.

9.3.3 Detoxification

Biotransformation of foreign materials, via phase I and II reactions (Chapter 5), is one of the major functions of the liver. Most of the enzymes involved in such biochemical modifications are located or at least present in significant amounts in the liver. To facilitate this process, the liver is able to effectively concentrate xenobiotics intracellularly, in part because of the extensive surface area of hepatocytes exposed to the blood. The ability of the liver to concentrate drugs and toxins in the hepatocyte is essential, in that the levels of drugs that may be routinely reached in the blood can be less than the Km for the transforming enzymes, and a mechanism for concentration of the drug is important to achieve a significant rate of enzymatic catalysis. (The CYP450s can have relatively high Km values, often in the micromolar range.) Concentration of the substrate provides a kinetic driving force for the reactions, or more accurately, for the binding of the substrate to the enzyme. Drug uptake by the hepatocyte must be achieved against the electrostatic opposing force of the membrane charge. Several families of generalized membrane transport proteins provide the mechanistic basis for the process. It is then this glycoprotein-mediated, energy-dependent concentration process, functional against an electrochemical gradient, that provides the basis for the antemortem concentration of drugs. After death, with the loss of the cellular membrane charge and functional failure of the membrane itself, the gradient-driven diffusion of drugs out of the liver and throughout the body provides the mechanism for the phenomena recognized as *postmortem redistribution*.

9.3.4 Bile Formation and Elimination

Bile is a dark green to yellowish-brown fluid produced in the liver and stored in the gall bladder. Bile is a mixture of mostly water, bile salts, and other molecules, generally >400 dal, that are transported across the hepatobiliary membrane (between the hepatocyte and the bile canaliculi). Bile is released into the duodenum in response to food passing from the stomach into the intestine, where it facilitates absorption of ingested foodstuffs. Bile salts act as surfactants, emulsifying lipids by forming micelles (spherical molecular aggregates with hydrophobic materials on the inside and the hydrophilic molecular portions on the outside). Lipids in the micelles are available for enzymatic breakdown, thereby making the molecular constituents available for absorption and use by the body. The presence of bile facilitates not only lipid absorption but also such important hydrophobic materials as vitamins A, D, E, and K. Bile formation and excretion also provide a mechanism for the body to eliminate the breakdown products of hemoglobin (biliverdin and bilirubin).

Bile salts are formed in the liver by the oxidation of cholesterol to cholic and chenodeoxycholic acid. Both molecules can then be conjugated with either glycine or taurine as the amino conjugates are secreted into the bile canaliculi. Microbial dehydration and deconjugation can subsequently occur, yielding deoxycholic and lithocholic acid, respectively. All four of these compounds can be resorbed in the intestine and reused, in a process known as *enterohepatic circulation*, of some significance for the forensic toxicologist (see Sidebar 9.2).

The main bile pigment is bilirubin, an orange-yellow heme breakdown product. The average lifetime of a red blood cell is ~120 days, and following hemolysis, the heme molecules are oxidized in the liver, spleen, and bone marrow, initially to a green pigment, biliverdin, by heme oxygenase, a process that liberates the iron atom in the ferrous state. Biliverdin is reduced to bilirubin by the action of biliverdin reductase in a NADPH-dependent reaction, yielding the more stable bilirubin. Some bilirubin circulates in the blood bound to albumin as delta-bilirubin. Bilirubin reaches the hepatocyte by passive diffusion and active transport, where it becomes conjugated to glucuronic acid, and transported across the hepatobiliary border into the bile canaliculi. Unconjugated bilirubin cannot pass into the bile canaliculi. Conjugated bilirubin is water soluble and may either be excreted or reabsorbed and undergo further processing.

SIDEBAR 9.2 ENTEROHEPATIC CIRCULATION

Bile acids can be resorbed in the intestine after fulfilling their role in lipid absorption. Resorbed bile acids are returned to the liver in the blood, cross into the hepatocytes, and are eventually retransported across the blood-hepatocyte border in a process of *enterohepatic recirculation*. Conjugated drug species can follow a similar path, in that after excretion into the bile, the conjugated forms can by hydrolyzed back to the glucuronic acid and aglycone (free drug) by the action of microbial glucuronidases present in the bacterial constituents of the intestine. Free drug can then be resorbed and reappear in the blood. As an example, morphine can be readily glucuronidated in the liver and subsequently excreted across the hepatobiliary membrane into the bile, ultimately reaching the intestine. Some of the excreted morphine glucuronide can then be deconjugated by the bacterial glucuronidases. The extent of such deconjugation can have a significant impact on the circulating levels of morphine in an individual, particularly if their medical regime includes circumstances such that the composition of the intestinal flora is significantly altered (e.g., a significant antibiotic protocol). Clinical toxicologists are generally well aware of the potential for enterohepatic circulation to affect the functional levels of some drugs in the body.

9.3.5 Storage

The liver functions as a significant storage depot of blood, numerous biomolecules, and nutrients, for example, vitamins, glucose (in the form of glycogen), and iron. The process of glucose storage and release from the polysaccharide glycogen is an active and essential mechanism for the maintenance of blood glucose levels. Vitamins A and D are highly lipophilic, and the liver can store enough for several months. Vitamin K, an essential lipid-soluble vitamin and co-factor for coagulation, is also synthesized and stored in the liver, although only about a 4-day supply. The liver is also the repository of about a year or more supply of vitamin B_{12}. The essential (and highly bioactive)* element iron is also stored in the protein, ferritin.

9.4 Types of Hepatic Injury

Injury to hepatocytes can cause reduced or impaired function at the biochemical level, or injury to the point of cell death. Consequences of toxic effects may lead to significant reduction of hepatic function, liver failure, and ultimately, death (see Sidebar 9.3).

SIDEBAR 9.3 LIVER FAILURE

Liver failure, as *acute* or *fulminant* (occurring rapidly following the appearance of hepatic disease or toxic insult), is a medical emergency requiring immediate treatment, possibly involving a liver transplant. Acute liver failure is characterized by destruction of over 80% of the hepatocytes, and such a loss of hepatocytes is generally well in excess of the liver's ability to regenerate. Hepatocyte functional impairment impacts the broad scope of metabolic function, including glycolysis and gluconeogenesis, mobilization of energy reserves, protein synthesis, and synthesis of coagulation factors. Patients in such conditions are quite ill and may become comatose and jaundiced. Bruising, as a function of the loss of coagulation factors, may become evident on the limbs and torso. Any intravascular (IV) catheter site may bleed profusely around the catheter and in the subcutaneous tissue. Not surprisingly, disseminated intravascular coagulation (DIC)† may also ensue, characterized by limited or absent coagulation factors and elevated PT (prothrombin time), and PTT (partial thromboplastin time). Liver function tests (e.g., hepatic enzyme levels in serum) will be very high in early hepatic failure as hepatocytes lyse and release their cytosolic contents into the blood. Total protein and albumin in the serum are usually low, reflecting decreased synthesis. Treatment of fulminant hepatic failure depends upon the cause. Sometimes therapy can only be supportive (fluid replacement, replacement of coagulation factors and red blood cells, respiratory support, etc.). The severity of this medical emergency is such that in many cases, even with aggressive and competent care, the patient may still die.

9.4.1 Hepatocellular Death: Apoptosis and Necrosis

Apoptosis is a process of programmed individual cell death that is a normal cellular function and usually beneficial to the organism, in that it provides a mechanism

* The bioactivity of iron is a function of the relative facility with which it can participate in redox reactions, cycling between the +2 (ferrous) and +3 (ferric) valance state, accepting or donating electrons as appropriate. In this role, iron is an essential core feature of such proteins as the cytochromes (e.g., cytochrome c reductase, reducing NAD+ to NAD) and the proteins of the electron transport system in the mitochondria. In another capacity, the ability of iron as part of the hemoglobin tetramer to gently bind oxygen in one (oxygen-rich) area of the body and then release it in another (oxygen-poor) area is (arguably) the basis for much of the vertebrate life on this planet. Iron availability in the body is tightly controlled, because of the ability of ferrous iron to easily donate an electron to molecular oxygen, forming superoxide and potentially leading to other active oxygen species, such as hydroxyl radical OH, and other free-radical species capable of initiating lipid peroxidation and cellular macromolecular damage. Iron is transported within the body (e.g., following absorption in the intestine) as ferric iron by the protein transferrin and is stored in the protein ferritin. Iron toxicity can be a serious and even fatal condition. Treatment often involves the use of the chelating agent desferrioxamine, which (unlike some other similar agents) does not allow the chelated iron atom to redox cycle while bound.

† *Disseminated intravascular coagulation* (DIC) is the consequence of the disruption of the normal clotting process. This can occur in response to the activation of the clotting process, consuming clotting factors and platelets, or the failure of the liver to produce the factors. Ultimately, bleeding can occur throughout the body. The formation of small blood clots can result in a compromise of tissue blood flow, leading to multiple organ damage.

for the renewal of tissue components. This mechanism of cellular regeneration and renewal, and associated rates of cellular death, is organ and tissue-specific. In response to cellular death by apoptosis, a localized phagocytosis of cellular fragments and debris is initiated to engulf the cellular remnants in an organized and controlled manner. The normal process of apoptosis is not, therefore, of significance in an acute toxicologic sense.

In contrast to the regular death and replacement of cells reflected in the process of apoptosis, *necrosis* is defined as the death of cells or groups of cells in a tissue or organ caused by factors that are apart and distinct from normal cellular functions. Factors capable of causing cell death include infection, temperature extremes, toxin action, reduction in blood flow, anoxia, and trauma. The damage reflected by cell and tissue necrosis may be repairable but is nevertheless detrimental to the organ and the body as a whole and is indicative of a response or reaction to a chemical or physiologic challenge.

Necrosis is an irreversible process and, depending on the magnitude of damage, may eventually involve disruption of membrane integrity, leakage of intracellular components to the extracellular space, and the induction of an uncontrolled inflammatory response, which can cause further damage to neighboring cells. Localized phagocytosis may be inadequate for cleanup; therefore, necrotic debris consisting of intracellular constituents and partially degraded products as well as intact and lysed inflammatory cells can accumulate. Necrotic regions in tissues or organs may be readily recognizable by either gross or microscopic examination at autopsy, and information generated in this manner can be extremely useful when correlated with toxicology results.

Necrosis may be described as focal, zonal, diffuse, or massive. Focal necrosis suggests that a limited number of cells have died; zonal necrosis implies more cells and some sort of regional association. Diffuse necrosis involves even more cells, but not in a specific zone, and massive necrosis implies the extensive death of multiple cells.

The liver has significant regenerative capabilities. Damaged or necrotic cells can be replaced within the reticular matrix. However, depending on the magnitude of damage, fibrotic infiltration (scarring) may occur by the replacement of cellular debris with connective tissue. A small degree of fibrosis can be inconsequential. Larger amounts of hepatocellular damage can result in bands of fibrosis that can then actually isolate hepatocytes from their blood supply, causing further liver damage. When allowed to progress to the extreme (e.g., advanced cirrhosis), this process can result in liver failure, potentially leading to death.

9.4.2 Cholestasis and Jaundice

Cholestasis is a blockage of the flow of bile from the liver into the duodenum (by way of the gallbladder) and is characterized by the accumulation of bile pigment in the hepatocyte. Cholestasis can be obstructive, the consequence of a physical blockage in the flow of bile to the intestine (e.g., gallstones, or tumors of the biliary tree), or metabolic in the sense of an interference with the biochemical processes of formation or transport. Although it is usually not evident grossly, bile can be seen microscopically in a cholestatic liver as small yellow or brown spherules of intrahepatocellular pigment. When severe, the liver can take on a deep green-brown color. Ultimately, bile components, including bile pigments such as bilirubin, can appear in the blood and tissues, giving a yellowish tinge to the body and most notably the sclera of the eyes (commonly referred to as jaundice). A common cause of this condition is the inability of the hepatocytes to conjugate plasma bilirubin due to hepatocellular damage. In such cases, normal bilirubin production from hemoglobin breakdown occurs at a higher rate than the remaining functional hepatocytes can process, and bilirubin then escapes across the blood:hepatocellular border. In such cases, hepatic enzyme levels in the serum may be elevated due to hepatocellular damage, and both conjugated and unconjugated bilirubin can be detected (Figure 9.6).

9.4.3 Fatty Liver (Steatosis)

Large amounts of lipids are stored in the liver in various forms, including fatty acids, triacylglycerols, and other lipophilic carbohydrate forms. The liver functions to metabolize fatty acids for energy, as synthetic intermediates, and to synthesize triglycerides, cholesterol, and related compounds. A small amount of lipid in some hepatocytes is of no clinical significance. However, large amounts can have a significantly negative effect and are normally an indication of an ongoing disease, toxic insult, or metabolic derangement. Normal liver contains only about 5% by weight of lipid, mostly in the form of triglycerides. In contrast, fatty livers are large, yellow, greasy, soft, and can contain 50% or more by weight of lipid (Figure 9.7).

Microscopically, small amounts of lipid are contained in small intracellular, nonmembrane-bound droplets. This appearance is called microvesicular steatosis (fatty degeneration). In contrast, larger amounts of lipid, coalesced into small unattached droplets (nonmembrane bound), constitutes macrovesicular steatosis. In some cases, the droplets may be large and numerous

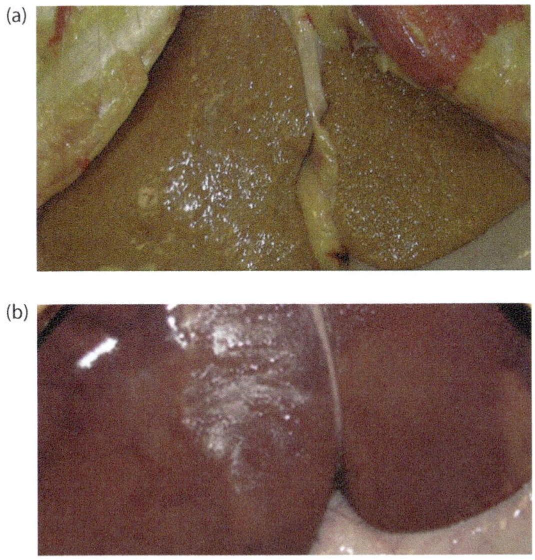

Figure 9.6 Cholestatic versus normal liver, *in situ.* (a) Liver *in situ* from a jaundiced decedent; (b) normal liver *in situ.*

enough to displace the nucleus (normally centrally located) to the periphery of the cell. Steatosis is readily visible by light microscopy. Usually, steatosis is nonuniform, often concentrating in zones 2 and 3 in alcoholics and zones 1 and 2 in some people in consequence to hepatotoxin exposure, but the location of the steatosis is not reliably diagnostic.

Steatosis is a reversible process, and although the presence of large amounts of lipid is abnormal, with recovery from the underlying insult, the condition can regress in a matter of days to weeks. There is very little if any hepatocyte necrosis or inflammation associated with steatosis, and biochemical tests of hepatocellular enzymes are usually in the normal reference ranges (Figures 9.8 and 9.9).

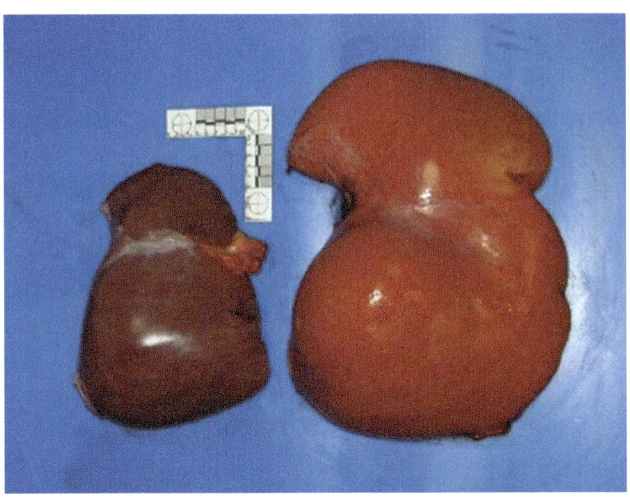

Figure 9.7 Size comparison between a normal 1800 gm liver and an enlarged, fatty, 3000 gm liver.

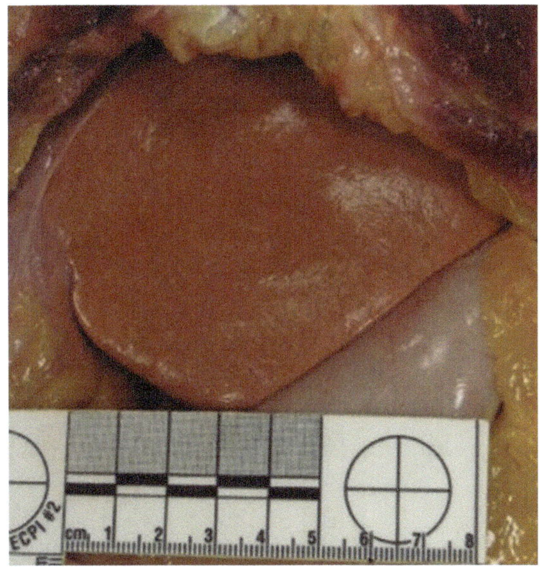

Figure 9.8 Steatotic liver, *in situ.*

9.4.4 Cirrhosis

Cirrhosis is the generalized process of hepatic fibrosis that has progressed to the point where isolated nodules of hepatocytes lose their direct connection to the blood supply. Cirrhosis is more of a response to a chronic toxic or physiologic insult than a disease in and of itself. As the liver is impacted by the toxic agent (e.g., alcohol), necrotic hepatocytes can be replaced by fibrous tissue. As fibrotic material occupies progressively more space within the liver, the physical structure becomes distorted, with the potential for significant effects on blood flow. A slight limitation in the ability of oxygenated blood to reach the hepatic sinusoids can have a major impact on the hepatocytes in that region, eventually resulting in their death. As the disease progresses, fibrotic tissue can eventually encircle, obstruct, and cause whole groups of hepatocytes to die. Necrotic products can further

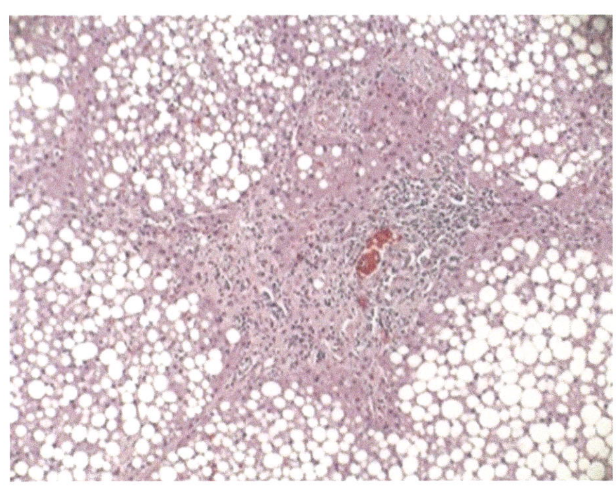

Figure 9.9 Steatotic liver, 10×.

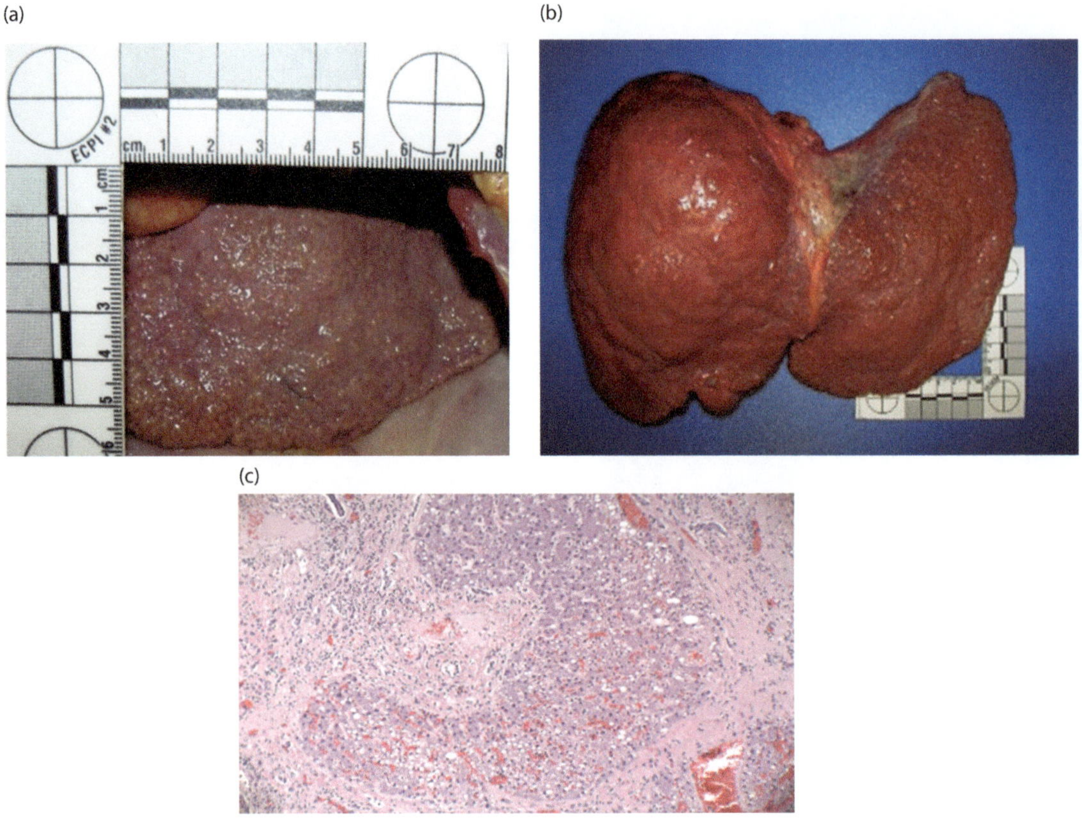

Figure 9.10 (a) Micronodular cirrhosis, *in situ*; (b) micronodular cirrhosis, gross; (c) micronodular cirrhotic liver, 10×.

impede hepatic function by providing physical blockage within the liver. The development of cirrhosis can take years as the disease progresses with ever-decreasing liver function and capability. Cirrhosis is often cited as a causative or contributory factor to death. Evidence of cirrhosis (as may be indicated in an autopsy report) should suggest impaired hepatic function, which may be of use in consideration of the role a particular toxin may have played in a death. Grossly, the cirrhotic liver is composed of small nodules resembling cobblestones ranging in diameter from several millimeters up to about 1 cm (Figure 9.10).

9.4.5 Disease States

9.4.5.1 Hepatitis

Hepatitis, or the inflammation of the liver, is a generalized descriptive term. Hepatitis may be caused by a number of factors, including infection (e.g., viral or bacterial hepatitis) or toxic insult. The disease may be chronic or acute. At autopsy, there may be no hint of underlying pathology upon gross examination. Microscopically, however, inflammatory cells (neutrophils, lymphocytes, macrophages, and eosinophils) may be apparent in the liver tissue.

One of the most common noninfectious causes of hepatitis is chronic alcohol exposure. The initial consequence of such exposure is steatosis. Further consequences of alcohol toxicity can cause damage to cellular membranes, necrosis, and an inflammatory response triggered by cellular death. The combination of an inflammatory response with steatosis is referred to as *steatohepatitis*.

Infectious viral hepatitis can be caused by a variety of agents. This group of diseases affects primarily the liver and is distinct from viruses with other systemic targets but also coincidentally may cause hepatocellular damage. Historically, the causative viruses have been named alphabetically. Currently, at least five different viruses are identified. Hepatitis A and E are self-limiting, requiring no antiviral treatment, and are primarily caused by viruses in contaminated water and food (the so-called fecal–oral route). Individuals infected with these viruses are contagious to other people only for as long as they are ill. In contrast, hepatitis B, C, and D are caused by bloodborne viruses. These forms of the disease may be transmitted intravenously by shared needles, accidental needle punctures, or exposure to infected body fluids by some other mechanism. Infections with hepatitis B, C, and D can become chronic and may be contagious to other people for the life of the patient. Hepatitis C infection is correlated with a high risk of hepatocellular carcinoma; however, there is apparently less risk with hepatitis B and D. Diagnosis of the specific viral agent in a hepatitis case is made serologically by the detection of specific immunoglobulin (IgM and IgG) in the serum. Currently, vaccines are available to prevent the infection by hepatitis A and B viruses, but not C–E. Pathologically, infections with hepatitis C can cause lymphocytic aggregates around the portal triad. Such aggregations are a characteristic feature of this virus, as a function of intracellular edema and cellular rupture caused by the infection, and are readily recognizable on microscopic sections.

Bacterial, fungal, and parasite infections can also be present in the liver. These are systemic infections that also colonize hepatocytes and cause an inflammatory response. They may be detected serologically in the living person and can be confirmed based on evaluation of autopsy materials.

9.4.5.2 Diabetes

Diabetes, more properly known as diabetes mellitus, is a metabolic disease in which the body is not able to maintain control of blood glucose levels in a normal manner. While not a toxic response per se, an overdose of insulin could certainly be considered a poisoning. It is important for the toxicologist to have an understanding of the diabetic process and the implications that the presence of the disease may have in understanding a particular case. A rather simplistic view is that insulin facilitates the uptake of glucose from the blood and its utilization in cells, including storage in the form of a polysaccharide, glycogen. Glucagon is a hormone that stimulates the liberation of glucose from glycogen. The balance between insulin, glucagon, and the dietary intake of glucose and its precursors is the basis for the maintenance of blood glucose in the normal range.

The usual laboratory reference value for blood glucose is between 70 and 110 mg/dL. Diabetes, often characterized (and diagnosed) by hyperglycemia, or an excess of glucose in the blood, can be caused by a failure of the body to produce insulin. This condition is referred to as type 1 diabetes and is managed by providing the insulin required, either by injection or pump. Type 2 diabetes is characterized by an impairment of the ability of the body to respond to insulin.

One of the common consequences of diabetes treatment can be the occurrence of low blood sugar, or hypoglycemia. The symptoms of hypoglycemia can include impaired judgment and cognitive function, ataxia, dysphoria, lightheadedness, visual disturbances, slurred speech, seizures, and ultimately coma and death. Commonly, the cause of hypoglycemia is an injection or dose of insulin not accompanied by a dietary source of glucose. In other words, the biochemical mechanism for glucose uptake and utilization from the blood is activated, but no source of glucose is provided. In these cases, blood glucose can drop precipitously and represent a potentially lethal medical emergency. (The brain has an absolute requirement for a constant supply of glucose for metabolism and proper function.) Fortunately, hypoglycemia is readily resolved when a glucose source is provided. However, as noted above, the symptoms of hypoglycemia can resemble alcohol or drug intoxication. Mistaking hypoglycemia for intoxication could present serious complications for an arrestee, and as such, law enforcement personnel are usually well trained in this area. (Emergency medical assistance will normally be requested if a suspected DUI driver is thought to possibly be suffering from diabetes-associated hypoglycemia.) Further complicating this issue is the fact that alcohol ingestion tends to exacerbate diabetes-associated hypoglycemia, and there can clearly be cases in which the impaired behavior reflects both the presence of alcohol and a lowered blood glucose level.

9.5 Liver Function Tests

Clinically, the function of the liver can be assessed by measuring the concentration of hepatic enzymes, proteins, and metabolic products in serum, or by the collection of some tissue via a liver biopsy. Serum measurements are generally preferable to a biopsy; however, examination of actual tissue does allow the pathologist, and hence the treating physician, the benefit of a direct examination for the presence of steatosis, fibrosis, or even a potential malignancy.

Hepatocyte injury, damage, and necrosis, with subsequent cell membrane leakage or disruption, can result in the appearance of normally intracellular components in the blood. Many such materials, as well as those reflecting the normal metabolic functions of the liver, can be readily measured in the laboratory. Such liver function tests can be grouped into two general categories: those evaluating the metabolic and synthetic functions of hepatocytes, and those evaluating the ability of the liver to conjugate and eliminate biomolecules into the biliary tree.

Two hepatic enzymes commonly evaluated in a clinical panel are aspartate aminotransferese (AST, also known as SGOT), and alanine aminotransferase (ALT, also known as SGPT). Hepatocellular necrosis causes a marked rise in serum levels of AST and ALT, and serum levels of these enzymes can be sensitive indicators of hepatocellular stress, injury, damage, or necrosis. Some differences between ALT and AST are worth noting.

ALT occurs predominantly in the liver and is a cytoplasmic enzyme. Therefore, leakage into the blood is a good marker for hepatocyte injury. In contrast, AST can also be found in myocytes, red blood cells, and the kidney. However, AST is primarily contained within the mitochondria. Mild hepatocyte injury that destroys only the cell membrane but leaves the mitochondria and other cellular organelles mostly intact will cause an increase in serum ALT more so than AST. Severe injury that also results in organelle destruction will cause a rise in AST. The serum half-life of ALT is about 2 days, significantly longer than that of AST (about 17 hours).

Other hepatic enzymes may also be detectable in serum, in the case of hepatocellular injury or toxic response. Lactate dehydrogenase (LDH) is located in the cytoplasm of many cells and levels can be elevated with mild liver cell injury. Elevated lactate levels have been suggested as potentially interfering with serum enzymatically based ethanol quantitative measurements (such as are used in hospitals). However, lactate is not a particularly good substrate for alcohol dehydrogenase. The presence of lactate and LDH could conceivably generate enough NADH to potentially interfere with an enzymatically based assay, but levels of lactate and LDH would have to be quite significant to generate a signal comparable to ethanol in the reaction mix generally used in hospital assays. The presence of lactate, LDH, or both does not interefere with the analysis of ethanol and related molecules by headspace gas chromatography, the generally accepted forensic methodology for such testing.

9.5.1 Other Hepatic Function Measures

The hepatocyte is the only body cell with biochemical capability to convert ammonia to urea. An elevation of serum ammonia is considered to be an indication of severe liver/hepatocellular injury. Many proteins are made exclusively in the liver, such as albumin, and many others primarily so. Serum protein levels in general (serum albumin in particular) can be an important gauge of liver function. As hepatocyte function becomes increasingly impaired, unconjugated bilirubin levels in the serum rise as well. However, protein and bilirubin values must be used with caution and should not be used alone to diagnose or infer liver disease.

9.6 Hepatotoxins

Hepatotoxins are simply those compounds that significantly or primarily affect the liver. Because of the great number of biochemical reactions that occur in hepatocytes, nearly all enzymatic- or pathway-specific metabolic toxins will affect the liver. Clearly, many volumes could be devoted to all the different potential hepatotoxic agents. However, hepatotoxins can be generally categorized in a number of ways. One approach is separation by mechanism of action: directly affecting the structure of the cell or its organelles (direct toxin) versus those that affect specific metabolic pathways (indirect toxins). Another approach to categorize toxins is to describe which cell in the liver is damaged (hepatocyte, bile duct epithelium, blood vessels, etc.). Perhaps the most simplistic approach is to consider common versus uncommon or unusual toxins, an approach used in this brief overview.

9.6.1 Common Hepatotoxins

Perhaps the two most common hepatotoxins are ethyl alcohol and acetaminophen. Either can be fatal in excess, and yet represent some of the most commonly used drugs throughout the world. The combination of the two exacerbates their toxic potential, even to the point of fatality.

9.6.1.1 Acetaminophen

Acetaminophen (APAP, paracetamol) is a nonsteroidal anti-inflammatory drug (NSAID) popularly marketed both alone and in combination with other drugs as an analgesic and antipyretic. It has weak anti-inflammatory properties and is therefore relatively ineffective in treating inflammatory conditions. It is inexpensive and readily available as an over-the-counter medication. Acetaminophen is rapidly and virtually completely absorbed from the stomach and small intestine. Plasma half-life is approximately 2 hours. Unlike the other NSAIDs, APAP has a considerable potential for toxicity in overdose. The combination of ready availability, effective absorption, and toxic potential contributes to the use of APAP in suicidal efforts.

The mechanism of therapeutic action of APAP is a centrally mediated (hypothalamus) blockade of prostaglandin production via inhibition of prostaglandin-endoperoxide synthase (otherwise known as cyclooxygenase, COX).

APAP is primarily metabolized in the liver by three pathways (two phase II conjugations and a phase I activation reaction), and the remainder is excreted unchanged into the urine. APAP is readily conjugated with either UDP-glucuronic acid via a glucuronosyltransferase, or PAPS (phosphoadenosine phosphoryl sulfate) via a sulfotransferase. The conjugated forms of APAP are highly water-soluble, and readily eliminated in the urine. Cytochrome P450 oxidation generates an active

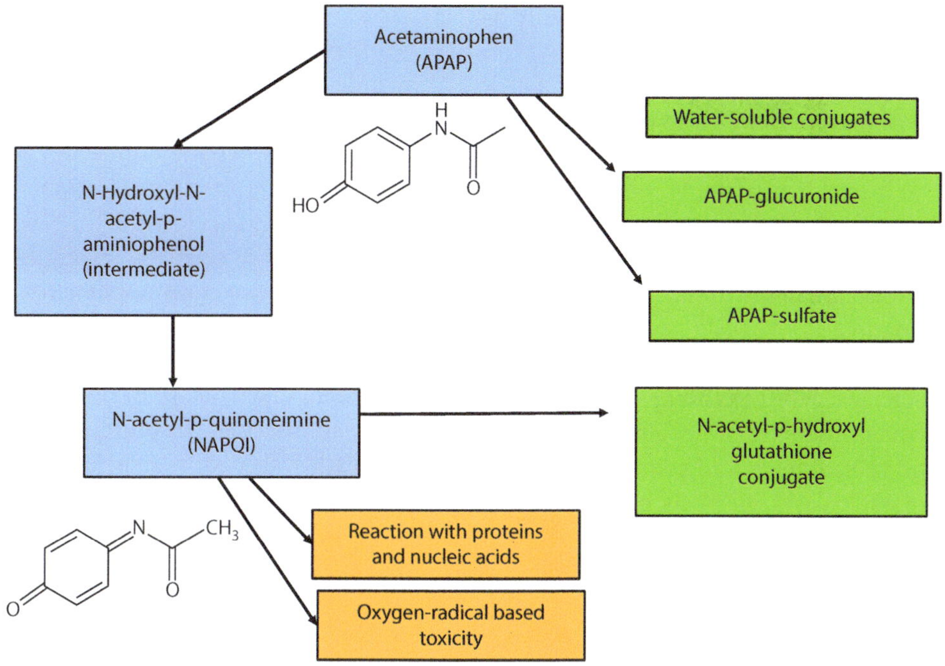

Figure 9.11 APAP toxicity, structural diagram.

intermediate compound, N-acetyl-p-quinoneimine (NAPQI). It is the formation of this species which can lead to toxic consequences. NAPQI can be conjugated with glutathione and eliminated, but to the extent that the body generates more than can be eliminated (or overwhelms the ability of the hepatocyte to synthesize or regenerate glutathione), the molecule can form covalent bonds with cellular macromolecules and can also serve as a basis for the initiation of oxygen radical toxicity, leading to lipid peroxidation and membrane damage. In therapeutic doses in healthy people, the metabolism of APAP progresses smoothly, including conjugation and elimination of the ~10% of the ingested dose that is oxidized to NAPQI (Figure 9.11).

In the case of an overdose or when the patient has some degree of existing liver damage or functional compromise, the rate of generation of NAPQI can exceed the body's ability to conjugate and eliminate the molecule. Depending on the degree of excess, hepatocellular damage to the point of necrosis can occur. The key factor is the ability of the body to synthesize glutathione (GSH), an energy-dependent process. In cases of APAP toxicity those hepatocytes that are the most energetically limited (e.g., by the relative lack of oxygen) will most likely be susceptible to toxic consequences. In other words, those cells most vulnerable are those furthest from the oxygen source, the hepatic artery. APAP toxicity is often expressed as a *centrilobular hepatic necrosis*, reflecting the impact on the cells located further from the hepatic artery (Figure 9.12).

In cases of APAP poisoning, the patient may initially feel only mildly ill with nonspecific symptoms. Eventually, depending on the magnitude of damage, the patient becomes very ill as hepatic damage, and ultimately liver failure, proceeds. Death ensues if the degree of hepatic damage is severe enough (see Sidebar 9.4).

Treatment in such cases often depends upon the stage at which the patient presents. An effective and specific antidote, N-acetylcysteine can be given, which acts as a conjugate analog of glutathione. If provided early enough, the combination of conjugation with available glutathione and N-acetylcysteine can prevent or

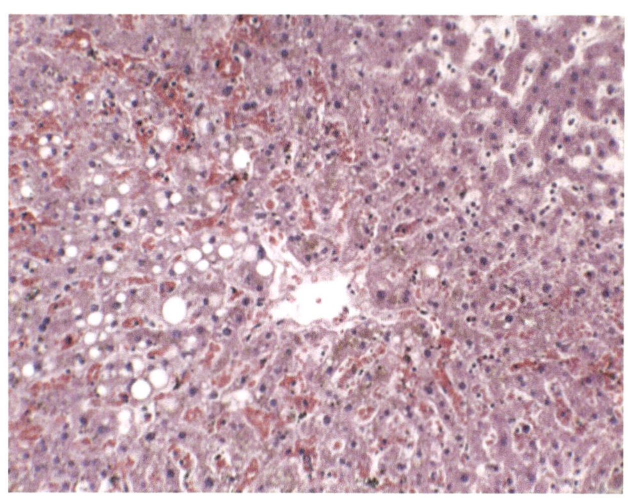

Figure 9.12 Centrilobular hepatic necrosis, characteristic of acetaminophen toxicity.

ameliorate the degree of toxicity that would normally be associated with a particular level of APAP.

The relationship between the amount of APAP ingested, the time of that ingestion, and the serum level provides a basis for the prediction of hepatocellular damage. There is a well-established nomogram (Rumack-Matthew nomogram) for predicting hepatic injury based upon this data. Clinicians can also follow the patient with serial serum measurements to monitor the degree of metabolic elimination.

At autopsy following an APAP-related death, the liver is enlarged, soft, and pale. Microscopically, the classic lesion is necrosis of the ring of hepatocytes around the central hepatic vein, zone 3, and sometimes zone 2 hepatocytes. In massive cases, necrosis can be present throughout the liver.

SIDEBAR 9.4 AN UNEXPECTED OVERDOSE

A number of years ago, we were consulted regarding a ~150 lb, ~50-year-old white female who had been transported to an emergency room in a critically ill condition. The patient had nausea and bouts of emesis. Clinical testing indicated she was acidotic (pH ~6.9) with elevated AST and ALT. She was tachycardic, but with regular sinus rhythm. She was tachypneic, with 28 BPM, and disoriented. Her other vital signs were BP 80/42, temperature 96.9°F, and O_2 sat 98%. Initial assessment considered acute pancreatitis, with shock and possible renal failure. An unspecified toxicity was considered. An APAP serum level of 87 mg/dL was reported, and the case was reassessed in light of that finding. The patient was started on N-acetylcysteine, however, after several days of ICU treatment, she died.

The patient's past medical history included chronic lumbosacral pain for which she was prescribed Vicodin (750 mg APAP, 7.5 mg hydrocodone) on an as-needed basis, not to exceed 4/day. There was no indication the patient abused her medication. Autopsy findings showed a heart weight of 420 g, with <20% stenosis of coronary arteries and no indication of infarction. There was slight left ventricular hypertrophy. The liver was ~1400 g, pale brown, and unusually soft. There was mild steatosis, and upon microscopic examination, centrilobular necrosis without inflammation. The kidneys exhibited ~10% glomeruli sclerosed, with no inflammation or fibrosis, some loss of nuclei, and some sloughing of tubular epithelium.

The medical examiner findings in the case included a diagnosis of hydrocodone and acetaminophen intoxication. The cause of death was cited as acute hepatic failure due to hydrocodone and acetaminophen intoxication. The manner of death was ruled accidental.

This was a relatively straightforward, albeit tragic case of acetaminophen toxicity. The legal issue in the case revolved around whether the Vicodin, as prescribed by the treating physician, had been taken as prescribed. (The underlying argument was that the prescription was flawed and the death was a consequence of malpractice.) The case was rather simply resolved in the following manner. There was no positive opiate screen result upon hospitalization (although it should be noted that screen assays are generally not particularly sensitive to the semisynthetic opiates). The clinical picture upon arrival was consistent with APAP toxicity and not at all consistent with an opiate overdose. Finally, opiates are not hepatotoxins.

A rough estimate of the number of Vicodin tablets required to generate the serum APAP level was determined using Vd (bearing in mind that the 87 mg/L was an antemortem and therefore a presumably reliable value, but also considering the case did not represent a single-ingestion event; new doses of APAP were ingested prior to the complete elimination of the previous dose, thereby complicating the picture). This calculation resulted in a number well in excess of what had been taken by the patient. In retrospect, it became apparent that the patient had been experiencing pain, despite her use of Vicodin. Presumably cautious regarding overuse of her opiate prescription, she had been augmenting the Vicodin with APAP OTC formulations, and in this manner acquired the resulting APAP levels beyond the ability of her liver to detoxify the NAPQI metabolite.

9.6.1.2 Alcohol

The immediate, short-term effects of alcohol are related to its ability to act as a CNS depressant. However, alcohol is cytotoxic, and chronic exposure can ultimately cause fatty changes in the liver, leading to a cirrhotic endpoint (see Chapter 12).

9.6.2 Uncommon Hepatotoxins

Many elements and molecules with an acute toxic potential affect the liver, from poisons with a long history, such as arsenic and cyanide, to medicines in regular use with the potential for hepatotoxic effects, such as chlorpromazine and allopurinol. Many plants contain unusual hepatotoxic structures such as the toxin of the immature fruit of the ackee plant, hypoglycin, containing a methylenecyclopropyl group. There are of course multiple and various mushroom toxins, with varying degrees of hepatotoxicity, and an equally diverse group of bacterial compounds. Industrial chemicals are also well represented, with such compounds as the synthetic intermediate vinyl chloride. Nevertheless, frank toxicity as a consequence of toxin exposure remains relatively uncommon. This in itself can pose a challenge both for the medical community, in the difficulty of recognizing a toxic exposure as a potential underlying mechanism for a particular set of symptoms, and for the toxicology laboratory, as an exercise in analytical chemistry, identifying a toxic agent that may not be a regular analyte of the laboratory.

9.6.2.1 Carbon Tetrachloride

Carbon tetrachloride (CCl_4) used to be a relatively commonly used chemical cleaner (both in the dry-cleaning industry and at home for spot cleaning), but different materials have replaced it in the United States. Historically, CCl_4 was used as a refrigerant, as a pesticide component, and in fire extinguishers. Its use has been all but abolished since the 1980s or so because of its negative effects on the ozone layer in the atmosphere. It has never been used medicinally. However, CCl_4 has been and is still occasionally (rarely!) abused as an inhaled hallucinogen, can be accidentally absorbed through the skin, and can be accidentally ingested. Carbon tetrachloride is nonpolar and readily lipid soluble. About 50% of ingested, inhaled, or absorbed carbon tetrachloride is eliminated unchanged in the urine. The remainder is metabolized by the P450 enzyme system into a trichloromethyl free radical. As a free-radical species, it can initiate lipid peroxidation, resulting in cellular damage, and depending on the amount ingested, cause cytotoxity analogous to APAP poisoning, including the centrilobular distribution of necrotic cells (reflective of the availability of GSH and the ability of the body to synthesize the molecule).

9.6.2.2 Mushroom Toxins

Mushrooms have been the source of toxins from prehistoric times, in both accidental and deliberate circumstances. Accidental poisoning occasionally occurs when people harvest mushrooms and mistakenly pick a toxic species. Mushroom identification can be difficult, in that many mushroom species have a similar appearance, especially when they are still small. About 100 species of mushrooms are toxic to humans and other mammals, but only a relatively small number are potentially fatal. Dose-dependent symptoms range from mild GI upset to death consequential to liver and kidney failure. In many cases, no symptoms appear until after serious organ damage has occurred. As might be expected, ingestion of potentially poisonous mushrooms constitutes a medical emergency. Treatment is often aimed at reducing the absorption of toxins by gastric lavage and activated charcoal if the ingestion has been recognized early enough.

The toxins associated with the deadly species of mushrooms are most often the *amanitins*. Amanitin is an eight–amino acid cyclic peptide and is the most deadly of the *amatoxins* (found in such aptly named species as the death cap and destroying angel). The oral LD50 of α-amanitin has been estimated at 0.1 mg/kg. Mechanistically, the toxin binds into the bridge helix in a molecule of RNA polymerase II. In so doing, the ability of the cell to synthesize mRNA from the DNA template is impaired. The net effect is a nonspecific inhibition of protein synthesis, with lethal consequences to the cell (Figure 9.13). (As might be expected, the effect on protein synthesis is symptomologically similar to that caused by the ribosomal poisons ricin and abrin.)

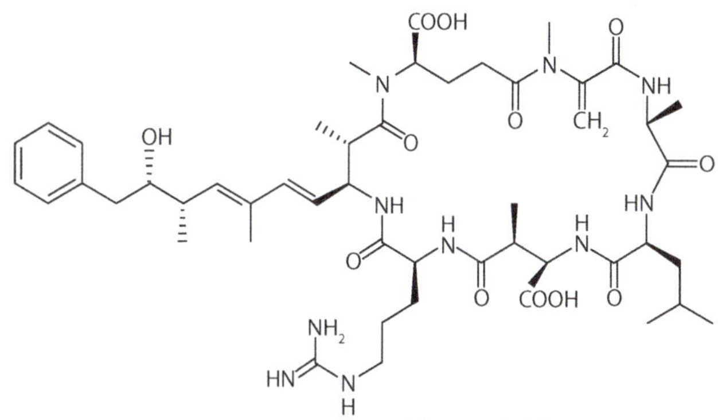

Microcystin LR

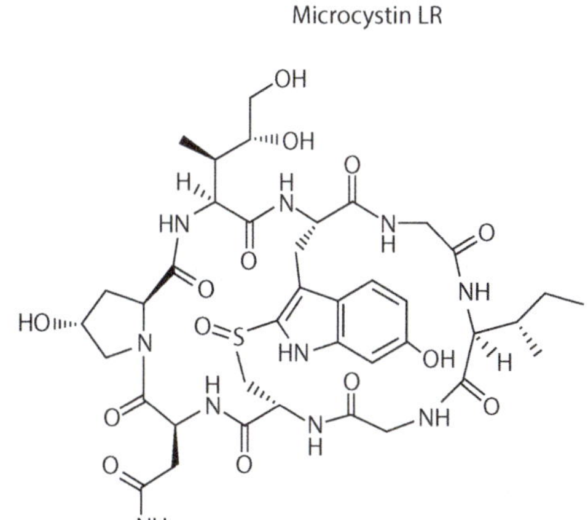

α-Amanitin

Figure 9.13 Microcystin LR and α-Amanitin.

9.6.2.3 Microcystins

Blue-green algae, also called cyanobacteria, often grow in stagnant and slow-moving bodies of water. Most of the bacterial species are harmless to people, but some produce large cyclic peptide toxins called microcystins, some of which act as hepatotoxins. Microcystins are released into the water from algal cells that have ruptured, and may be absorbed by fish and wildlife and also by people swimming or exposed to contaminated water.

Microcystins are cyclic polypeptides made up of seven amino acids, which act on the cells of mammals and fish by inhibiting protein phosphatases (Figure 9.3). These enzymes normally function to cleave phosphate from proteins, a common step in many biochemical pathways. The accumulation of phosphorylated proteins is believed to be the mechanism by which microcystins damage hepatocytes. The most commonly seen consequences are nausea, vomiting, and some degree of hepatic failure.

9.6.2.4 Bromobenzene

Bromobenzene is one of the components that can be used in the illicit manufacture of phencyclidine (PCP) and provides an interesting example of toxicity following enzymatic activation. The toxic action of bromobenzene is similar to that of acetaminophen in that it causes centrilobular hepatic necrosis resulting from the formation of reactive metabolites that can directly interact with vital cellular components, and serve as the source of active oxygen species leading to lipid peroxidation and *oxygen-radical* type toxicity.

Bromobenzene is readily oxidized by CYP isozymes to either the 2,3- or 3,4-arene oxide, and either of these species is able to covalently bind with cellular macromolecules, leading to a toxic effect (as are several other metabolites that can be produced). Both species are also substrates for the action of epoxide hydrolase, forming intermediate dihydrodiols, which may ultimately lead to the formation of either 2- or 4-bromoquinone. The quinone compounds can be conjugated with glutathione (GSH), thereby eliminating the toxic potential. However, in the absence of adequate GSH reserves or synthesis capability, these species can serve as the source of electrons for the formation of active oxygen species, leading to lipid peroxidation. As with acetaminophen, the ability of the body to generate GSH is oxygen dependent, and therefore the centrilobular regions of the liver will be the least capable of generating adequate GSH to detoxify the quionone species, leading to the expression of centrilobular hepatic necrosis as a pathologic consequence of toxicity (Figure 9.14).

9.6.2.5 Warfarin

Warfarin is an anticoagulant that was originally developed as a pesticide targeting rats and mice and is still used for that purpose. While warfarin remains a popular rodenticide, a number of related compounds have

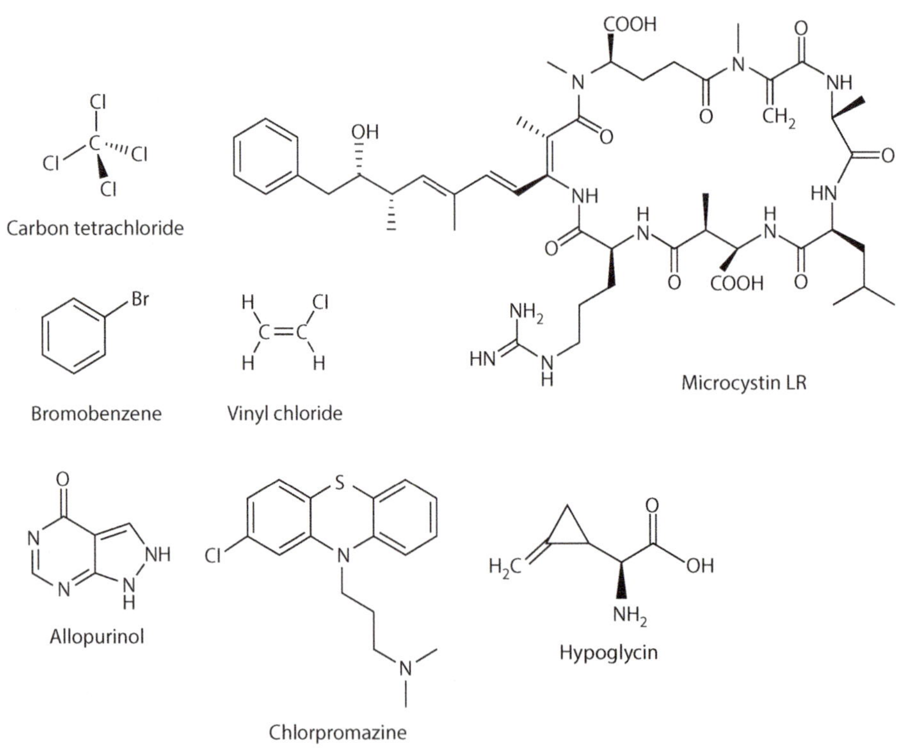

Figure 9.14 Example hepatotoxins.

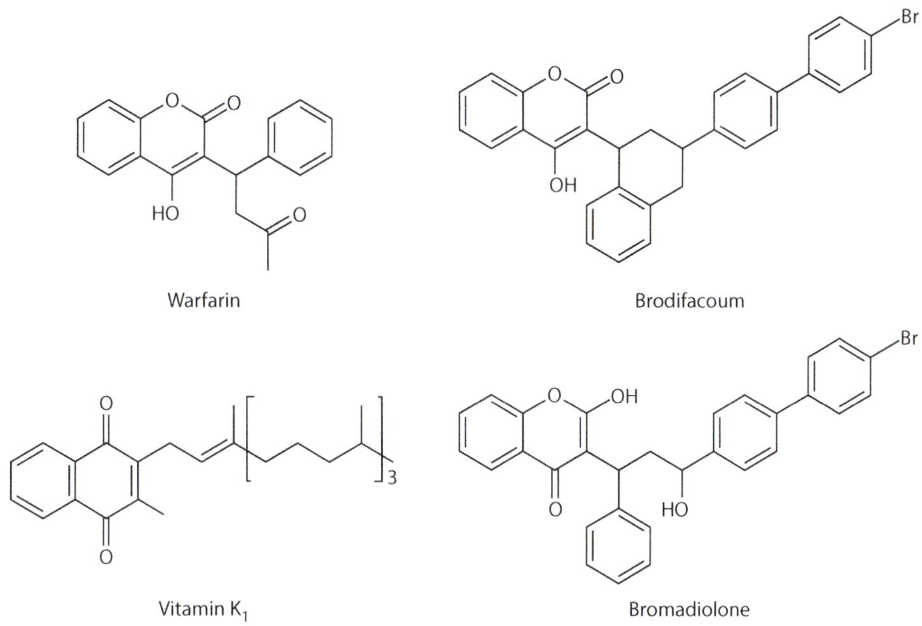

Figure 9.15 Warfarin and related compounds.

been developed with a similar mechanism of toxicity and with a similar potential for mammalian toxicity (e.g., brodifacoum, dicoumarol, bromadiolone; see Figure 9.15).

The toxic action of these drugs is a consequence of their inhibition of the clotting function of the blood, resulting in lethal internal hemorrhage in affected animals. In the 1950s, it was recognized that nontoxic levels of the drug could potentially provide an effective means for the prevention of undesired clot formation, and warfarin (as Coumadin) has since become commonly prescribed as an oral anticoagulant. Warfarin is sometimes (incorrectly) referred to as a blood thinner by nonmedical personnel, due to its effect on slowing the rate of clot formation.

Mechanistically, warfarin and related compounds inhibit the vitamin-K dependent enzyme vitamin K epoxide reductase, which recycles vitamin K for clotting factors II, VII, IX, and X and proteins C and S. (For this reason, infusions of vitamin K are a therapeutic mechanism for a warfarin overdose.) Vitamin K is present in the diet, especially in leafy vegetables.

Pharmaceutical uses of warfarin include atrial fibrillation and clotting disorders. Fibrillation can cause turbulent flow inside the chamber, which can result in clot formation that may then break free and migrate to the brain, resulting in a stroke. An anticoagulant regimen can prolong the clotting process and allow the body's own mechanisms to prevent inappropriate clot formation during fibrillation. Clotting disorders are a group of abnormalities that cause a person's blood to clot abnormally quickly. These disorders most commonly reflect a problem with synthesis of one or more of the factors controlling the rate of coagulation, thereby increasing the risk of pulmonary thromboemboli or ischemic injury to tissues. Individuals who have received mechanical heart valves may also be prescribed warfarin or a related compound to avoid clot formation.

Overdoses of warfarin or one of its analogs can be fatal, whether the source of the drug is pharmaceutical or a rodenticidal preparation. Treatment, when possible, is with a combination of vitamin K and replacement of coagulation factors in the form of plasma replacement or transfusion (Figure 9.15).

REVIEW QUESTIONS

1. Briefly highlight the similarities and differences between ricin and α-amanitin (e.g., effects, structures, mechanisms).
2. Contrast the classic versus portal lobule in terms of oxygen tension and nutrient availability.
3. Mechanistically distinguish the effects of carbon monoxide and cyanide on the liver.
4. Would a course of a broad-spectrum antibiotic be expected to affect the AUC for Ritalin? Morphine? Why or why not?
5. What impact would you expect cirrhosis to have on the ability of the liver to metabolize drugs by CYP450 pathways?
6. What is the relationship (if any) between chronic alcoholism and hypoglycemia?
7. Why doesn't hemoglobin generate superoxide?

TOPICS FOR DISCUSSION

1. Should acetaminophen be available as an OTC medication? Why or why not?
2. Discuss how the architecture and biochemistry of the liver facilitates drug elimination.
3. Should patients suffering from cirrhosis be candidates for liver transplant? Why or why not?

Bibliography

Fenton JJ. *Toxicology: A Case-Oriented Approach*. Boca Raton, FL: CRC Press, 2001.

Jaeschke H. Toxic responses of the liver. In: Klassen CD, editor. *Casarett and Doull's Toxicology: The Basic Science of Poisons*. 8th rev. ed. New York: McGraw-Hill, 2013.

Liver metabolism. In: Lieberman M, Marks A, editors. *Mark's Basic Medical Biochemistry: A Clinical Approach*. 3rd rev. ed. Philadelphia: Wolters Kluwer Health/Lippincott Williams & Wilkins, 2009.

Reichl FX and Ritter L, editors. *Illustrated Handbook of Toxicology*. Stuttgart: Thieme, 2011.

Suchy FJ. Hepatobilliary function. In: Boron WF, Boulpaep EL, editors. *Medical Physiology*. 2nd rev. ed, updated. Philadelphia: Saunders-Elsevier, 2012.

Kidney Toxicology

10

Contents

10.1 Kidney General Overview: Anatomy, Physiology, and Basic Functions

The kidneys are structurally and functionally complex organs whose primary role is the filtration of the blood and elimination of water and water-soluble materials. In addition, the kidneys perform a number of vital regulatory and hormonal functions within the body. Normal kidney function is required for the body to maintain blood pressure, blood volume, and electrolyte homeostasis, and to provide a mechanism for the body to rid itself of potentially toxic materials, whether derived from routine and natural biochemical processes or from materials foreign to the body. Kidney failure is as serious a medical emergency as heart, lung, or liver failure. Kidney stones, or the formation of organic or mineral deposits in the kidney can also represent a potentially serious medical issue (see Sidebar 10.1).

Mechanistically, the kidneys act by filtering the blood, then selectively resorbing specific materials from the filtrate, based on the dynamic needs and physiologic state of the body. This combination of unselective (other than by molecular weight or size) filtration followed by selective reabsorption allows not only for the mass elimination of waste materials but also for the retention

SIDEBAR 10.1 KIDNEY STONES (NEPHROLITHIASIS)

Kidney stones (nephrolithiasis) can occasionally cause some degree of renal failure. The most common symptom of kidney stones is extreme pain as the stones or parts thereof transit the ureters. Considerable pain can be associated with tissue stretching during this process. If stones have not migrated to the distal collection system, they may still cause localized renal failure by causing back pressure into the cortex.

of important biomolecules such as glucose and amino acids. Control over the reabsorption of water and salts is the mechanism by which the kidneys play a major role in the regulation of pH, electrolyte balance, and blood pressure.

A number of biologically important molecules are synthesized in the kidney. These include the hormone calcitriol, which promotes the absorption of dietary calcium in the GI tract; erythropoietin, which controls the production of red blood cells; and the enzyme renin, which plays a key role in control of blood pressure in the body.

The human body normally has two kidneys located in the posterior portion of the peritoneal (abdominal) cavity on either side of the spine. Each kidney is approximately 150 g in an adult, and roughly 12 × 7 × 3 cm in overall size with the characteristic kidney bean shape. A great deal of functional redundancy is built into the renal system, and a person can maintain normal function with only the partial use of one kidney. The kidneys are highly perfused and receive a significant proportion of the total blood output from the heart.

The effects of either toxins or disease processes can impact filtration, elimination, and resorption, as well as other functions of the kidneys, with potentially devastating effects to the body. The consequences of kidney failure are expressed as inadequately regulated blood volume or content, inappropriate electrolyte levels within the body, and a failure to properly eliminate metabolic products, drugs, and toxins. Initially, this condition is *renal insufficiency* and as it progresses in severity, *renal failure*. While patients can live without any kidney function by undergoing frequent blood dialysis (several times weekly), they often do not feel well. Renal dialysis can substitute for the excretory functions and some of the regulatory functions of the kidney but cannot entirely substitute for all the regulatory and hormonal functions inherent to the organ system.

As with the state of cardiac and hepatic function, it may be important in a particular case for the toxicologist to understand the functional capacity of the kidneys in order to fully appreciate or evaluate the role a drug or toxin may have played in affecting the body, including possibly causing or contributing to a death (Figures 10.1 through 10.3).

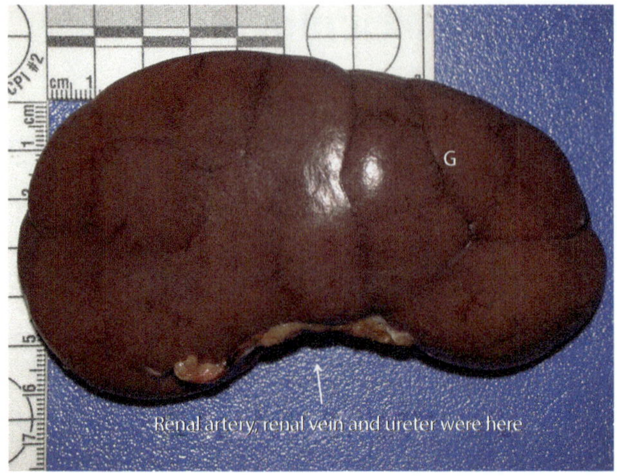

Figure 10.1 A ~150 g normal kidney, showing the typical smooth, red-brown surface. The renal artery, the renal vein, and the ureter have been severed close to the organ. The grooves in the surface (G) are remnants of fetal lobulations.

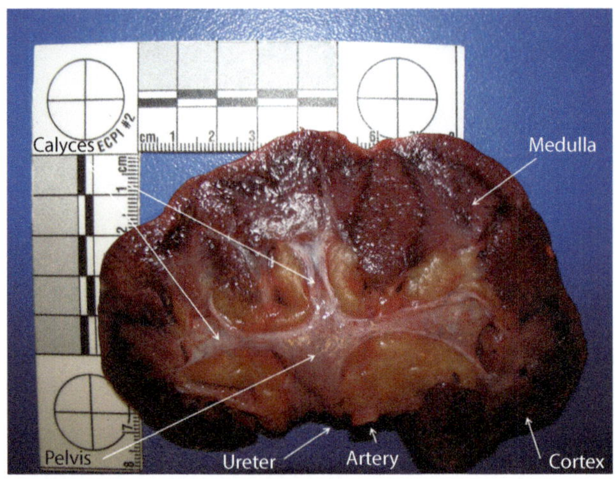

Figure 10.2 Bisected kidney; the cortex, medulla, calyces, renal pelvis, ureter, and renal artery are visible.

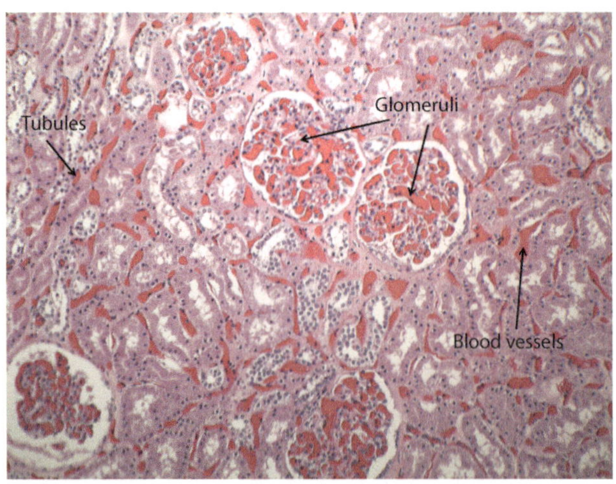

Figure 10.3 Normal kidney cortex at 10×. Glomeruli, tubules, and blood vessels are labeled.

10.2 Excretion

The excretory function of the kidney can be subdivided into three major parts: filtration, reabsorption, and secretion. The rate of renal excretion for any species can be simply expressed as excretion rate = filtration rate − reabsorption rate + secretion rate.

10.2.1 Filtration

Excretion of water, metabolic waste products, and toxins is the primary essential function of the kidneys. The basis for the process is the filtration of blood and the subsequent concentration of the filtrate and selective reabsorption of some filtrate materials. The end result of the filtration/reabsorption process is urine, stored in the bladder after formation. Urine can be thought of, in the absence of infection or other medical issue, as a sterile ultrafiltrate of the blood. (Nevertheless, many laboratories handle urine as potentially infectious material, using universal biological precautions.) As a material derived from the blood, and to some extent reflective of the content, the value of urine in a medical sense has been recognized from the earliest days of scientific medicine. Color, odor, and volume were important parameters for physicians to examine, and the extent to which urine is used in modern clinical testing emphasizes the value of this material as a diagnostic tool.

The basic functional unit of the kidney is the *nephron*, composed of a vascular portion (blood flow and filtering component), and a tubule system into which the filtrate flows, providing the necessary surface area for the concentration and reabsorption of materials. Arterial blood reaches the nephron from short renal arteries branching directly off the abdominal aorta. The renal arteries (traversing the kidney in arcs, hence *arcuate arteries*) are large vessels and carry a large volume of blood. Arterial blood, via the afferent arteriole, traverses a network of specialized capillaries forming the roughly spherical glomerulus (where filtration actually occurs) and exits via the efferent arteriole, becoming venous blood in the process and eventually joining into the renal vein. The glomerulus, or filtering element, is contained within the Bowman's capsule, the lumen of which serves to collect the filtrate and represents the start of the tubule system. The glomeruli are microscopically recognizable in the renal cortex as small, pink balls within a capsule (Figure 10.3). A significant volume of plasma passes through the glomerular pores into the Bowman's capsule, leading into the proximal tubule. The normal glomerular pore size is such that materials of greater than ~35 Kdal are retained in the unfiltered blood.

The vesicular pores, or *fenestra*, of the glomerular capillaries allow small solutes and water, but not larger molecules, to traverse the capillary membrane by the actions of hydrostatic and oncotic pressures. The effective cutoff for the filtration process corresponds to a small protein or protein fragment (see Sidebar 10.2). At the stage of Bowman's capsule, the fluid is an ultrafiltrate of blood and traverses a contiguous tubule that extends into the renal medulla, then back into the cortex, forming the *loop of Henle*. The proximal tubule is closest to the glomerulus and is convoluted, maximizing surface area. The section of the tubule returning from the loop of Henle is referred to as the *distal convoluted tubule* (DCT) from which concentrated filtrate (now essentially urine) flows into the small tubules of the macroscopic collecting system that coalesce into successively larger tubes, which finally form the ureter, and ultimately to the urinary bladder. The ureters (one from each kidney) transit from the renal pelvis to the bladder, where urine is stored until evacuated through the urethra. There is no further concentration of urine after it leaves the kidney (Figure 10.4).

In normal adults, the volume of filtrate generated from the blood and appearing in the Bowman's space—the *glomerular filtration rate* (GFR)—is about 100 mL/min (of which ~99 mL is resorbed back into the blood), decreasing slightly with age. The ultrafiltrate at this point is essentially an aqueous mix of ions, some small proteins, amino acid salts, and organic molecules. There is therefore normally very little protein and virtually no cellular elements in the filtrate. The rate of filtration is dependent upon renal blood flow and pressure and is controlled by the constriction and relaxation of the afferent and efferent arterioles and overall blood pressure of the body.

SIDEBAR 10.2 NEPHROTIC SYNDROME

When the glomerular capillaries become inappropriately permeable (e.g., pore size increases, and hence the molecular weight [mw] cutoff for filtration goes up), protein that would normally be retained in the blood can be filtered into the Bowman's space and then to the urine. The consequence is proteinuria, which can readily be determined by urinary protein levels. The condition is called *nephrotic syndrome*. In some cases, the glomerular capillary membrane may become selectively permeable to certain proteins. An example of this condition is when immunoglobulin A (IgA) is allowed to be excreted, a condition clinically termed *IgA nephropathy* (a condition of glomerular mesangial cells. Accumulation of IgA stimulates an immune response, which leads to scarring, further damaging the kidney).

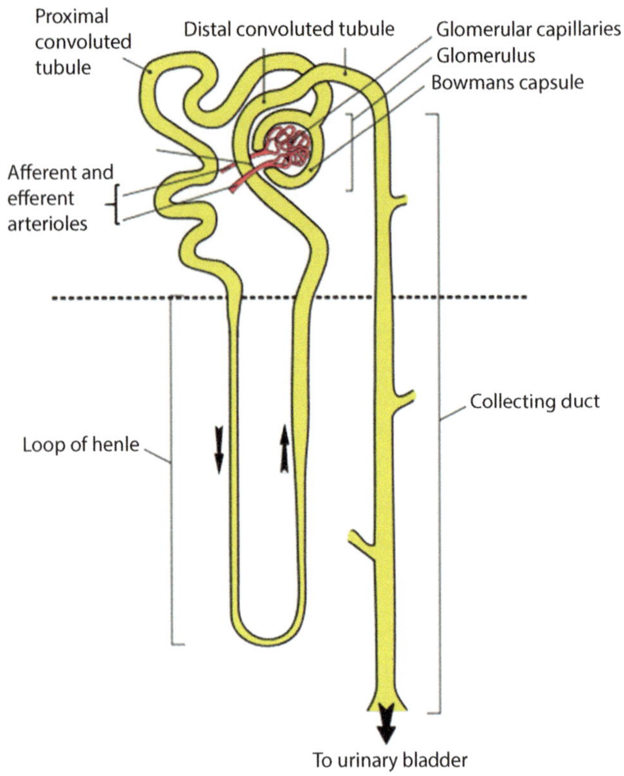

Figure 10.4 Simplified nephron structure. (Retrieved from Wikipedia Commons April 2, 2015. Image made available and published under the Creative Commons Attribution-Share Alike 3.0 Unported license by user and author Yosi I. Original upload date December 25, 2007. License can be found here and no changes were made to the image: http://creativecommons.org/licenses/by/3.0/legalcode.)

10.2.2 Reabsorption (Tubular Reuptake)

Filtration in the kidneys is selective only in terms of molecular size, and many important or useful materials, such as glucose, amino acids, ions, and other biomolecules, could be lost in the filtrate. However, there is a significant amount of reabsorption that occurs after the filtration process, allowing some control over what is maintained by the body. Reabsorption occurs in the collecting system, primarily from the proximal convoluted tubule (PCT). While some reabsorption can occur by diffusion, most molecules are brought into the proximal tubule cells by specific transport proteins (both active and passive transport processes). Water is able to readily transit the cellular membranes, and the degree of aqueous reabsorption will depend primarily on osmotic pressure, in turn related primarily to sodium concentration. The degree to which a specific molecule will be reabsorbed is a function of concentration, resorption mechanism, and filtrate flow.

Specific solutes can be transported back to the peritubular capillary (the blood) either between tubular epithelial cells or across their membranes (transmembrane transport being normally facilitated by specific transport proteins, e.g., organic acid transporters, etc.) This system is further complicated by some ion co-transport, for example, sodium and bicarbonate. If scarring or other damage to renal tubules is present, reabsorption is hampered and the body loses some of its ability to recover and return important biomolecules, water, and inorganic ions to the blood (see Sidebar 10.3).

Water, sodium, chloride, potassium, calcium, and bicarbonate are primarily reabsorbed in the loop of Henle. Pharmacologically, diuresis (loss of fluid from the body) may be controlled by drugs that inhibit NaCl reabsorption in the loop of Henle. These loop diuretics (e.g., furosemide) act by inhibiting a chloride-sodium-potassium symport protein. By precluding the hypertonicity of the loop cells compared to the lumen, osmotically-driven reabsorption of water is limited.

SIDEBAR 10.3 ACUTE TUBULAR NECROSIS

Acute tubular necrosis (ATN) simply reflects the death of cells in the tubular epithelium. Depending on the underlying cause for the cellular damage and the degree to which the kidney is affected, the tubules may recover. However, if the damage is adequate, kidney failure can ensue as a serious, potentially fatal condition.

ATN can be caused as a direct consequence of the action of nephrotoxic drugs (e.g., ethylene glycol) or toxins on the epithelial cells, or by such causes as reduced perfusion prior to the kidney (hence ischemic injury), damage to the glomeruli, physical damage to the tubules or interstitium of the kidney, or other injury including kidney stones. The clinical diagnosis of acute tubular damage (which is ATN) is based on the detection of clumps of tubular epithelial cells in the urine. Because the collection system is long and narrow, any cellular debris will be packed together and appear in the urine as a small group, seen in urine microscopy as "casts."

10.2.3 Secretion

A number of substances can be eliminated from the body by secretion from the tubule epithelial cells, via specific transport proteins into the tubule lumen. Examples include morphine and related drugs, as well as some of the opioids, penicillin, digoxin, tubocurarine, atropine, paraquot, and others. Interestingly, a number of conjugated species can also be secreted, including some glucuronides, glycine conjugates, and sulphates. The process can be significant in the elimination of particular species and may be impacted by kidney functional impairment or disease, resulting in unexpectedly high levels of the drug.

10.3 Blood Pressure Control

A second important function of the kidney is the regulation of blood pressure and tonicity. By excreting water, controlling ionic concentration by excretion and reabsorption, and impacting artery and arteriole constriction, the kidneys maintain the body's total amount of water and help keep electrolyte concentration and blood pressure within a relatively narrow physiologic range.

Cells in the region of the afferent arteriole function as baroreceptors, responsive to low-perfusion blood pressure, which is normally reflective of systemic blood pressure. In response to low pressure, the enzyme renin (also known as angiotensinogenase) is produced in the smooth muscle cells surrounding the arterioles going to and from the glomerulus, the afferent and efferent arterioles, respectively. Renin has no direct physiologic action on its own but is an enzyme that cleaves angiotensinogen (made in the liver) to an intermediate compound angiotensin I. Angiotensin I is further cleaved by angiotensin-converting enzyme (ACE) to angiotensin II, which has a vasoconstrictive effect, thereby elevating blood pressure. Angiotensin II stimulates the secretion of aldosterone from the adrenal cortex, causing increased reabsorption of sodium and water into the blood. Renin secretion is also increased with increased sympathetic tone and reduced Na^+ and Cl^- in the blood. The renin-angiotensin-aldosterone system causes constriction or relaxation of arterioles, stimulates the release of antidiuretic hormone and thirst reflex, and contributes to the reabsorption of sodium and chloride by the proximal tubule.

The enzymatic conversion of angiotensin I to angiotensin II provides a very selective mechanism for the therapeutic control of blood pressure, specifically by inhibiting the activity of ACE. A class of drugs known as ACE inhibitors (see Sidebar 10.4) has become increasingly popular in recent years as a reliable means for hypertension control (e.g., captopril, lisinopril, enalalpril).

SIDEBAR 10.4 ANGIOTENSIC-CONVERTING ENZYME INHIBITORS

Angiotensin-converting enzyme hydrolyzes two amino acyl residues from angiotensin I, generating angiotensin II, a potent vasoconstrictor. ACE inhibitors have several clinical uses, the most common being use as an antihypertensive agent. The hypotensive effect also reduces the pressure at the afferent glomerular artieriole and the intraglomerular pressure, thereby reducing the rate of protein filtration. ACE inhibitors are therefore also a treatment for nephritic syndrome. (Distinct from nephrotic syndrome, nephritic syndrome involves some degree of inflammation, damage to the capillaries, and leakage of red blood cells into the urine.) ACE inhibitors are also used for patients with hypertension and kidney damage from diabetes mellitus (DM).

ACE inhibitors can have a very rare but potentially fatal side effect, *angioedema*. Angio(neurotic) edema is a nonimmunologically mediated swelling of mucus membranes, particularly of the mouth and the tongue. The cause is not an allergic reaction but a side effect of the agent, leading to inhibition of breakdown of the vasodilator bradykinin. Excessive circulating bradykinin can cause leaky vessels and intracellular fluid to leak into tissues. Treatment is airway control, discontinuation of the ACE inhibitor, and interestingly, epinephrine.

Diuretics are compounds that increase the rate of production of urine, usually by limiting resorption of ions, thereby maintaining the osmotic pressure for water from the tubule epithelial cells toward the filtrate. Diuretics can be prescribed for hypertension and some types of heart disease. Some diuretics function by affecting the pH of the urine (making it more basic), and can therefore facilitate the elimination of acidic species via ion trapping (the acidic species is increasingly ionized as the pH is elevated and is therefore more likely to stay in the aqueous filtrate). A number of different types of diuretics, such as loop diuretics (discussed above), thiazides, and thiazide-like diuretics (e.g., hydrochlorothiazide, chlorthalidone, metolazone, chlorothiazide), directly inhibit the sodium-chloride symport, limiting resorption of both sodium and chloride; and carbonic anhydrase inhibitors (e.g., acetazolamide, methazolamide, dichlorphenamid) limit bicarbonate sodium and chloride reabsorption. Osmotic diuretics (e.g., mannitol, isosorbide, glycerine) simply increase the osmolarity of the filtrate, decreasing the volume of water that would be reabsorbed in the absence of the osmotic force.

10.4 Hormone Production

10.4.1 Erythropoeitin

Erythropoietin (Epo-E) is a hormone necessary for the production of red blood cells (RBCs) and is primarily synthesized by interstitial fibroblasts near the peritubular capillaries. Epo-E stimulates the maturation of proerythrocytes in bone marrow stem cells, thereby forming mature red blood cells. Epo-E synthesis is influenced by blood oxygen concentration; and in a low-oxygen environment (e.g., high altitude), Epo-E production is stimulated and increases within minutes to hours. However, the number of RBCs will not be measurably increased until the cells are made from stem cells in the bone marrow and reach circulation, a process that takes about five days. People who go from a low lying, coastal area to an elevated environment will generally need about five days at least to acclimate to the reduced amount of available oxygen in the atmosphere. (Athletes take advantage of this phenomenon by training at high altitudes for increased endurance and enhanced oxygen transport capability.) Some elite athletes have supplemented their training program with exogenous Epo-E to cause extra stimulation of RBCs for better endurance. (The use of Epo-E is banned in many sports.)

Patients with chronic renal failure are often anemic even though they may have healthy bone marrow and no reason for accelerated red cell destruction. Their anemic condition can be a consequence of an inability of their kidneys to make enough Epo-E to stimulate adequate RBC maturation. Patients on renal dialysis are often severely anemic and may require red blood cell transfusions to maintain adequate oxygen-carrying capacity. In the fetus, the liver produces some Epo-E, but production from the adult liver is minimal.

10.4.2 Calcitriol

Calcitriol (1,25-dihydroxycholecalciferol or 1,25-dihydroxyvitamin D_3) is the hormonally active form of vitamin D and is produced in proximal tubule cells. Calcitriol functions to increase the level of calcium available in the blood by promoting its GI absorption and increasing the level of reabsorption in the renal tubules. The hormone is necessary for adequate calcium deposition and bone health. Patients with renal failure or who are on renal dialysis usually do not have enough vitamin D for calcium balance, and supplements may be needed.

Mechanistically, calcitriol binds to a specific receptor (vitamin D receptor), and the resulting ligand-receptor complex translocates to the nucleus and promotes the expression of a gene coding for a calcium-binding protein (Calbindin D), which facilitates calcium uptake in the intestine. Interestingly, increased calcium transport across the intestine is matched with the counter-ion phosphate to maintain electrical neutrality.

10.4.3 Gluconeogenesis

The kidneys are able to synthesize glucose (gluconeogenesis) from amino acids and other precursors as a response to low blood levels, in a manner analogous to the liver. The kidney uses lactate and glutamine as a source of pyruvate, which is then carboxylated to oxaloacetate, phosphorylated to phosphoenolpyruvate, and then by (essentially) reversing the reactions of glycolysis, forming glucose. While originally thought to be a function of prolonged energy deficit, gluconeogenesis in the kidney may play a more routine role in the overall glucose homoestasis in the body, augmenting the major role occupied by the liver in this function.

10.5 Clinical Measurements of Renal Function

It is neither practical nor necessary to obtain a biopsy of the kidney to assess its function. Blood analyses in concert with a thorough physical examination of a patient will usually reveal sufficient information for the clinician to be able to make a diagnosis and treat any problems that arise. The blood tests involved in assessing renal function are primarily based upon the kidneys' excretory ability.

Measuring the blood pH and the levels of urea, sodium, potassium, chloride, bicarbonate, creatinine, and nitrogen gives a good estimate of how well the kidneys are functioning because the kidney is the primary organ in maintaining these levels. In renal insufficiency or failure, there will be a deviation from the reference range in some or all of the components. When medical history or clinical records are available, information regarding renal function can be of use in determining the possible role and action of drugs or other poisons. Some blood values used by clinicians to assess renal function are as follows.

10.5.1 Blood Urea Nitrogen (BUN)

Urea (H_2NCONH_2) formation is the primary mechanism for elimination of waste nitrogen, as a molecule that is considerably less potentially toxic or damaging than ammonia (NH_3). Urea is formed in the urea cycle, in which two molecules of ammonia, generated from protein oxidation, are transferred onto a carbonyl group. Urea is primarily generated in the liver, but the kidney is also active in the process. Urea is readily dissolved in the blood, filtered in the kidney, and ultimately excreted in the urine. Urea also plays a role in the control of blood pressure, by reabsorption into the region around the distal tubule in the ascending loop of Henle. This causes a localized hyperosmolarity, driving water reabsorption. The reabsorbed urea can be reexcreted by the urea transporter 2 system, a process controlled by antidiuretic hormone, providing some biochemical control over the process. This mechanism allows the body to generate a hyperosmotic urine. Normal blood urea ranges are ~2.5–6.7 mmol/L.

10.5.2 Creatinine

Creatine phosphate (phosphocreatine) is a metabolic intermediate that serves as a source of high-energy phosphate bonds in skeletal muscle and brain. Creatinine is the dephosphorylated product and is produced at a relatively constant rate in the body. Creatinine is excreted by the kidney, primarily by glomerular filtration, but some tubular secretion also occurs. Blood levels of creatinine rise as renal filtration rate falls. Serum creatinine level is a commonly used indicator of renal function but is usually elevated only in consequence to a functional deficit and is not particularly useful in detection of early kidney disease. Urine creatinine may be checked during standard urine drug tests as an evaluation as to whether the sample has been diluted.

10.5.3 Glomerular Filtration Rate (GFR)

GFR reflects the sum of the filtration action of all the millions of glomeruli in both kidneys and thereby provides an estimate of how much blood is passing through the glomeruli each minute. Clinical evaluation of GFR is really monitoring the ability of the kidneys to filter and eliminate solutes. When performing serial measurements, the test can determine the progression and magnitude of renal disease or the effectiveness of treatment and the healing process. GFR measurement (see Sidebar 10.5) can also be a useful parameter for isolation of specific renal functions from problems occurring in the postnephron tubule system (e.g., kidney stones).

SIDEBAR 10.5 CLINICAL MEASUREMENT OF GFR

Renal filtration of physiologic components is actually a multiphasic process. Ions and so forth can be filtered and reabsorbed many times before they are actually eliminated in the urine. A true measure of GFR would require determination of a substance that was only filtered and was not subject to resorption. An example of this type of compound is *inulin*, a 5-sugar polysaccharide fructan. Determination of the clearance rate (filtration) of inulin provides a convenient means of determining the GFR. Inulin is inert in the body, causing no physiologic response, and is therefore safe to administer to patients, even those with compromised renal function. Inulin is used extensively experimentally and commonly in a clinical setting. In contrast, the naturally occurring compound creatinine (a breakdown product of creatine phosphate) approximates the same single-filtration properties as inulin and is produced by the body at a relatively constant rate. As such, GFR can be directly measured, in that the amount appearing in the urine, compared with the concentration in the blood reflects the volume of blood that has passed through the glomerulus. The amount excreted per unit time, expressed as a volume of blood containing that amount, reflects the glomerular filtration rate.

GFR can be measured as follows:

volume filtered = amount excreted

$$\text{GFR} = \frac{\text{Rate of urine flow} \times \text{urine[inulin]}}{\text{Plasma[inulin]}}$$

$$\text{GFR} = \frac{\text{Rate of urine flow} \times \text{urine[creatinine]}}{\text{Plasma[creatinine]}}$$

A quick assessment of GFR can be accomplished by simple measurement of plasma creatinine, as accumulation of creatinine in the blood outside of normal levels suggests that glomerular filtration is compromised.

10.6 Examples of Toxins

10.6.1 Heavy Metals

All of the heavy metals (e.g., lead, mercury, cadmium, chromium) are proximal tubule toxins, in addition to the toxicity caused to other systems within the body (see Chapter 18). A common mechanism for the elimination of metallic species is their chelation by a small, cysteine-rich protein, *metallothionine*. The metal-metallothionine complex is filtered by the kidneys as a mechanism for the elimination of the element.

Toxic levels of metallic species can accumulate in and ultimately destroy the renal tubules cells, often representing an irreversible injury. The consequences to the tubular epithelium affects all processes, reabsorbtion of water, ions, and organic molecules, causing an acid-base disturbance (metabolic acidosis) and hypophosphatemia (low blood phosphates).

The symptoms of metal exposure are nonspecific, yet clinical testing can indicate the damaged organ system. Beta 2 microglobulin is a small molecule that, while filtered in the glomerulus, should normally be reabsorbed in the proximal tubules and returned to the blood in normal, healthy kidneys. Detection of the molecule in the urine can be an early and sensitive marker for kidney damage but is nonspecific in that levels will increase in any condition where tubules are damaged.

10.6.2 Aminoglycosides

Aminoglycosides (e.g., streptomycin, gentamycin) are antibiotics that act as protein synthesis inhibitors. Unfortunately, they are also one of the more common causes of drug-induced nephrotoxicity. The aminoglycosides are filtered by the glomeruli and are taken up by proximal tubular cells, resulting in tubular necrosis. The degree of toxicity is a function of both dose and duration of treatment.

10.6.3 Chemotherapeutic Agents

A number of chemotherapeutic agents (e.g., cisplatin, carboplatin, mitomycin, methotrexate) have significant nephrotoxic potential that may be expressed (depending on the specific drug) in distinct areas of the kidney. An example is cisplatin, a widely used chemotherapeutic agent but with a considerable potential for kidney toxicity. Cisplatin is an alkylating agent and, as such, affects growing or metabolically active regions of the body, such as the tubular epithelium. Mechanistically, cisplatin is filtered but is, to some extent, taken up and concentrated in proximal tubular cells, presumably as a function of organic cationic transporters, and leading ultimately to the disruption and death of the cell. Because of the injury, there can be a concomitant inflammatory response, leading to further damage.

10.6.4 Hexachorobutadiene

Hexachlorobutadiene (HCBD; $Cl_2C = C(Cl)C(Cl) = CCl_2$) is a chlorinated compound functionally similar to toluene in its uses as an industrial solvent, primarily for other halogenated compounds. HCBD has been used as an herbicide. As might be expected from aliphatic halogenated species, HCBD can readily form radical species and serve as an initiator lipid peroxidation. The toxic response to HCBD does include fatty liver, but the compound also causes necrosis of epithelial cells in the kidney, a *necrotizing nephritis* that can lead to renal failure.

10.6.5 Aristolochic Acid

The Aristolochiaceae family of plants includes wild ginger and a wide number of species. As a group, they are often referred to as Dutchman's pipe or pipevines. Species have been used in herbal medicines since the Egyptians, Greeks, and Romans, as well as in oriental medicine. In 2001, the US Food and Drug Administration issued a health alert warning about traditional or folk medicines or dietary supplements that may contain aristolochic acid, noting that such products were associated with "permanent kidney damage, sometimes resulting in kidney failure that has required kidney dialysis or kidney transplantation." These species may also have significant carcinogenic potential.

Aristolochic acid exposure appears to be primarily a function of herbal remedies, mostly for dietary purposes, but also for skin conditions (e.g., eczema), hepatitis, arthritis, rheumatism, and for analgesia. Exposure causes an extensive interstitial fibrosis, with atrophy and loss of proximal tubules.

The compound can readily form a lactam, as a condensation between the carbonyl carbon and the nitro group nitrogen. The intermediate for this formation, an aristolactam nitrenium ion, appears to be able to interact directly with DNA, forming covalent adducts. This process might be related to the carcinogenic effects associated with the compound.

10.6.6 Orellanine

Orellanine is a nephrotoxin, isolated in 1962 from a mushroom, *Cortinarius orellanus*, a process started with an investigation of a small epidemic in Poland in the early 1950s. The structure of the molecule, strikingly different from other mushroom toxins, was determined to be a bipyridine dioxide, with a (stable) tautomeric form of an amine oxide. Structurally related to diquat and paraquat, these species can participate in redox reactions, resulting in the formation of radical oxygen species capable of initiating lipid peroxidation and related reactions.

One of the unusual aspects of orellanine is the relatively long time between exposure and expression of symptoms, reported in some cases to be as long as 3 weeks and minimally 2–3 days. Early symptoms are similar to flu (nausea, vomiting, abdominal distress, headache). Symptoms of renal failure follow (thirst, frequent urination, perirenal pain), ultimately followed by full renal failure, and death in the absence of successful treatment (Figure 10.5).

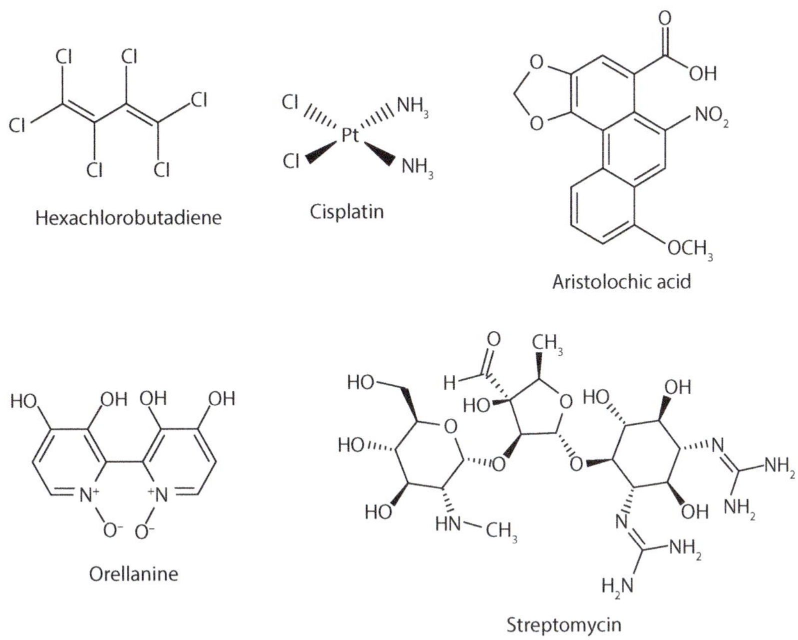

Figure 10.5 Example kidney toxin structures.

REVIEW QUESTIONS

1. What is the glomerular filtration cutoff? What would be the consequences if it were lower or higher?
2. Discuss the immediate threat to life caused by kidney failure.
3. Discuss the factors affecting filtration rate.
4. What is the mechanism by which loop diuretics affect blood pressure?
5. Would you expect a salt ingestion to affect blood pressure? Why or why not?

TOPICS FOR DISCUSSION

1. Hypertension is one of the more commonly treated medical conditions in the adult population. What are the main mechanisms for pharmacologic control of hypertension?
2. What are the long-term consequences of renal dialysis?
3. What would the main utility of catabolic enzymes such as CYPs be in the kidney? Of what use would phase II enzymes be?
4. How reflective of blood drug concentrations would you expect urine to be (both qualitatively and quantitatively)?

Bibliography

Giebisch G, Windhager E. Glomerular filtration and renal blood flow. In: Boron WF, Boulpaep EL, editors. *Medical Physiology*. 2nd rev. ed, updated. Philadelphia: Saunders-Elsevier, 2012.

Lash LH. Principles and methods for renal toxicology. In: Hayes AW, editor. *Principles and Methods of Toxicology*. 5th rev. ed. New York: Informa Healthcare, 2008.

Schnellmann RG. Toxic responses of the kidney. In: Klassen CD. *Casarett and Doull's Toxicology: The Basic Science of Poisons*. 8th rev. ed. New York: McGraw-Hill, 2013.

Tanner GA. Kidney function. In: Rhoades RA, Bell DR, editors. *Medical Physiology: Principles for Clinical Medicine*. 3rd rev. ed. New York: Lippincott Williams & Wilkins, 2009.

Urinary system. In: Patton KT, Thibodeau, GA. *Anatomy and Physiology*. 7th rev. ed. St. Louis: Mosby-Elsevier, 2010.

Pulmonary Toxicology

11

Contents

11.1 Introduction

The lungs are the relatively simple organs that provide the necessary surface area and mechanism by which the body is able to absorb oxygen from the atmosphere and eliminate carbon dioxide. The uptake and utilization of oxygen is a biochemically elegant process that, quite simply, provides the basis for life. During respiration, oxygen diffuses across the alveolar-capillary membrane in the lungs and is transported throughout the body (bound to hemoglobin*), and as a gas dissolved in the aqueous matrix that is the blood, ultimately diffuses into the tissues of the body. Reduction of molecular oxygen in the energy-generating processes of oxidative phosphorylation, ultimately producing water and carbon dioxide, provides the energy to support the body.

The process of respiration, while essential for life, also presents one of the major routes into the body for potentially toxic or pharmacologically active species. At a normal breathing rate of ~20 breaths per minute, ~10L of air is internalized and ultimately exhaled. While in the lungs, diffusion-based exchange of gaseous molecules can occur between the inspired air and the blood circulating in close proximity to the membranes of the air sacs. Particulate materials as well as aerosolized liquid droplets can be inspired, and the lungs therefore represent a significant potential mechanism for the delivery of drugs and toxins to the body.

Failure of respiration can occur as a consequence of damage or functional failure of lungs themselves; or of the airways providing flow to and from; or by interference with the transport, delivery, or utilization of oxygen in the body. Indirectly, either neural or muscular paralysis can result in respiratory failure, also with potentially fatal consequences. Respiratory depression, as caused by opiates or other CNS depressants, can have an obvious impact on the availability of oxygen for tissues, but further on blood pH and hence on the ability of numerous functions dependent upon hydrogen ion concentration to operate properly.

Inhalation is a rapid means for getting a drug into the body, and smoking remains an extensive habit in our society, both for tobacco and as a means of ingesting a number of abused drugs, including marijuana (and its synthetic analogs), cocaine and amphetamines, opium, PCP, and others. In industrial situations, the lungs are often the main route of toxin exposure, as has been historically demonstrated by the mesothelioma (a form of lung cancer) associated with breathing of asbestos dust in shipyards, and black lung disease from coal mine workers. Poison gas was used extensively in World War I, and while similar weapons were not used in World War II, a number of compounds developed for that conflict remain a threat and may have been used in some conflicts and at least one terrorist attack. The civil war in Syria (2013) has had numerous anecdotal suggestions of the use of sarin and related nerve agents.

Evaluation of lungs during the autopsy process can provide a significant amount of information regarding the nature of a death, beyond such obvious conditions as pneumonia. Lung weights, collected at autopsy, can have use in the evaluation of potential overdose, as can the presence, nature, and extent of edema. Microscopic examination of the lungs can reveal a history of drug abuse by the presence of pill fragments. Evaluation of the airway can reveal considerable information about the nature of a fire-related death.

11.2 Anatomy and Physiology

11.2.1 Anatomy of the Lungs

The lungs (Figure 11.1) are situated in the chest in the *thoracic cavity*, the space defined by the diaphragm and the rib cage, containing the heart, and the space in which the lungs expand and contract during the breathing process. The lungs are separated from each other in the front (anteriorly) by a soft tissue loosely attached to the sternum, the *anterior mediastinum*. In the middle of the chest, the lungs are separated by the heart, trachea, esophagus, and aorta. The separation of the lungs is important because air, blood, or other fluid that goes into one lung cavity is isolated, while the other lung may remain unaffected and able to function. A breach of the air-tight seal of the lung cavity, allowing air flow into the pulmonary space (*pneumothorax*), of one lung does not necessarily collapse the other lung.

Normal combined lung weight is 700–800 g in a normal-sized adult and is proportional to weight. Heavy lungs can indicate a disease process or a toxic exposure. The extra weight in heavy lungs is usually due to accumulated blood, pus (as a consequence of infection), or fluid (edema). Blood within the vasculature of the lungs usually accounts for about 40–50% of the weight of lungs at autopsy.

The lungs are extensions of the trachea, which branch into two main-stem bronchi, then into bronchioles, and ultimately ending in small airspaces known as alveoli. The structure of the airways is provided by a cartilaginous framework that serves to hold the trachea and bronchi open. Smaller airways, 1 mm in diameter or less, are called bronchioles and do not have cartilage. The

* Hemoglobin (Hb) is a tetrameric iron-containing protein (total of ~64 kDal) with the primary function of facilitating transport of oxygen from the lungs throughout the body. Each of the subunits contains an iron atom in a heme group (iron bound in a porphyrin heterocyclic ring), and each can bind and transport one oxygen molecule. A saturated Hb molecule, then, carries four oxygen molecules in the bloodstream. The heme iron in Hb must be in the ferric state (+2) for the molecule to bind oxygen—and in so doing, shares an electron with oxygen generating a partially oxidized iron (toward ferrous) and a partially reduced oxygen (toward superoxide O_2). (Protonation of the oxygen molecule at this stage leaves the heme iron in the ferric state, and the molecule is *methemoglobin*, incabable of binding oxygen. The enzyme methemoglobin reductase reactivates the molecule by reducing the iron back to the ferrous state.)

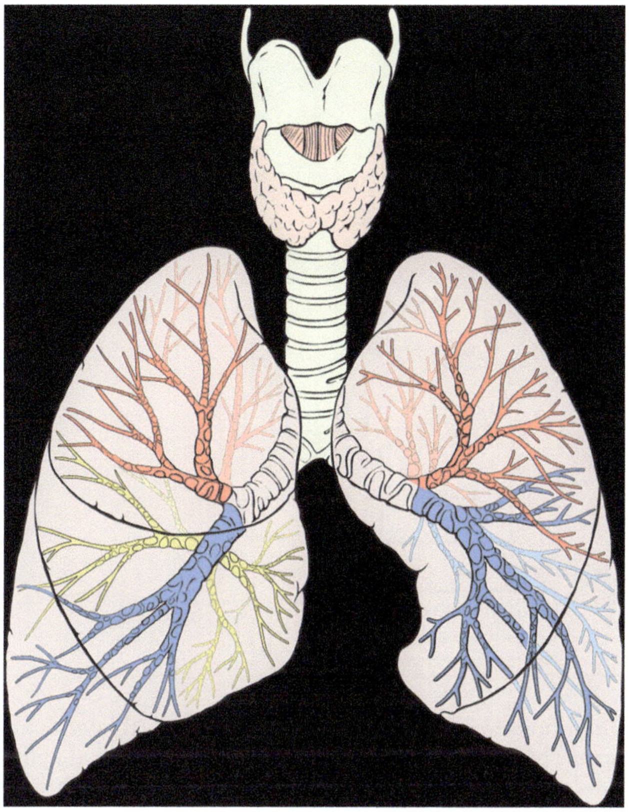

Figure 11.1 Diagram of the lungs. (Retrieved from Wikipedia Commons April 2, 2015. Image made available and published under the Creative Commons Attribution 2.5. Generic license by user and author Patrick J. Lynch, medical illustrator and C. Carl Jaffe, MD, cardiologist. Original upload date December 23, 2006. License can be found here and no changes were made to the image: https://creativecommons.org/licenses/by/2.5/legalcode.)

end of the airway is the terminal respiratory unit called the alveoli, which resemble (microscopically) bunches of grapes on a stem. There are about 3×10^8 alveoli in each lung, with total surface area of about 1 m^2/kg of body weight (roughly the area of a tennis court).

The tissues and space around the alveoli are known as the interstitium. Oxygen and carbon dioxide are exchanged between inspired air in the alveoli and blood in the capillary lumen. That gaseous exchange across the alveolar membrane is a simple diffusion process, reflecting a drive toward equilibrium between the oxygen-rich, carbon dioxide-poor inspired air, and the carbon dioxide-rich, oxygen-poor blood in the alveolar capillaries.

The lungs receive blood from two sources for two different purposes. The arterial blood supply for the lung tissues arises from branches of the thoracic aorta. This aortic blood warms the incoming air and provides oxygen to the trachea, bronchi, and other support structures of the lungs. The oxygen-depleted blood supply for gas exchange in the alveoli comes from the pulmonary artery and its branches, directly from the right ventricle of the heart. In contrast to the other arteries of the body, the pulmonary arteries serve to transport deoxygenated blood. Oxygenated blood returns to the left ventricle via the pulmonary veins.

11.2.2 Physiology of Breathing

Breathing is primarily controlled centrally at the level of the brain stem and is usually an unconscious, involuntary action. Motor impulses from the brain stem send neural signals to the phrenic nerve (at the level of cervical vertebrae 3 through 5) to stimulate the diaphragm and intercostal muscles to move in a coordinated manner, expanding the chest and thoracic space, thereby causing negative pressure in the pleural cavities and drawing air into the lungs. Upon exhalation, the muscles contract the chest up and in, expelling air from the lungs. Breathing can be controlled voluntarily by using the diaphragm, intercostal, and abdominal muscles. Paralysis of either muscular action or the ability of the neurons to promulgate signals of neuronal control can, depending on severity, cause depressed respiratory capability, anoxia, and death.

The airway itself begins with the mouth and nasal passages, the latter being lined with a ciliated epithelium and mucosal goblet cells, the function of which is to trap incoming particles and preclude their reaching deeper areas in the airway and lungs. The bronchi are similarly lined with ciliated epithelium, and the action of the cilia serves to help remove particulate matter by wafting such materials up and out of the lungs. Interestingly, the bronchioles are lined by simple, unciliated cuboidal epithelial. Particulate and droplet materials small enough to traverse the bronchioles and reach the alveoli are ultimately removed by phagocytosis or pinocytosis, respectively. Large particles in the inspired air (e.g., 5 um and larger), tend to be trapped in the upper airway, nasal cavity, and pharynx. Particles in the 1–5 um range stay suspended in the air and can impinge on the trachea, bronchi, and bronchioles, and are wafted up and out of the pulmonary tree by the action of the ciliated epithelia (the "bronchociliary elevator"). Particles smaller than 1 um can reach the alveoli. A further protective mechanism in the lungs is provided by the *Clara cells*, nonciliated cells that produce and secrete a number of proteolytic enzymes. Clara cells are also metabolically active, containing a number of cytochrome P450 enzymes, and are therefore capable of participating in a number of biotransformation processes (Figure 11.2).

The bronchioles, alveolar ducts, and alveoli remain open due in part to the action of *surfactant*, a soaplike mixture of glycoproteins that coats cells of the airway

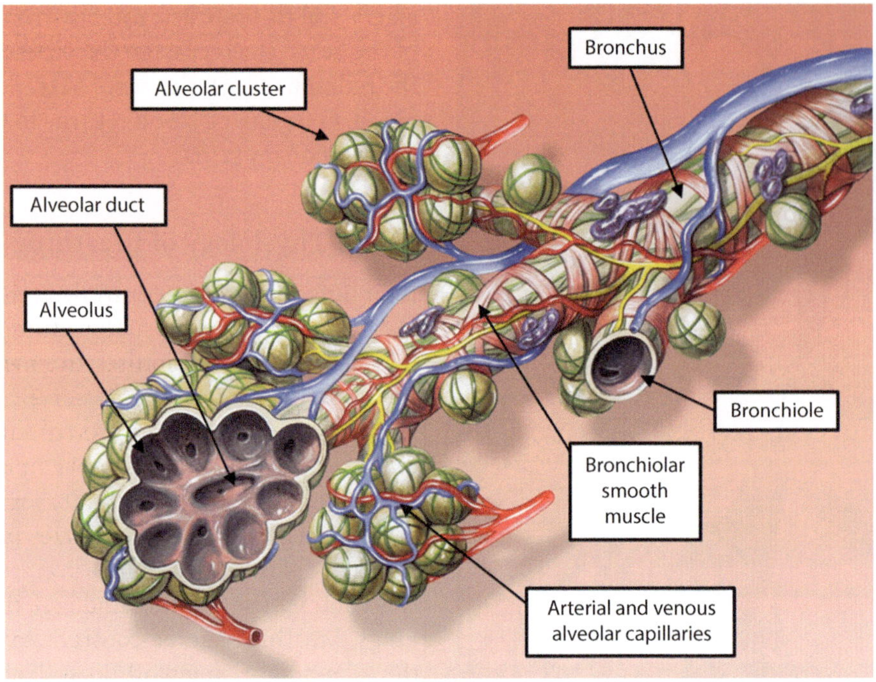

Figure 11.2 Bronchial anatomy. (Retrieved from Wikipedia Commons April 2, 2015. Image made available and published under the Creative Commons Attribution 2.5. Generic license by user and author Patrick J. Lynch. Original upload date December 23, 2006. License can be found here and image was modified with addition of labels to the image: https://creativecommons.org/licenses/by/2.5/legalcode.)

and reduces surface tension. The net effect is to make the cells less "sticky" and less likely to collapse. Damage to the cartilaginous framework of the airway or loss of surfactant production can cause collapse of the lungs, which are virtually impossible to reinflate without external support. (The ratio between two major components of pulmonary surfactant, lecithin and sphingomyelin, determined in amniotic fluid, has been used as an assessment of fetal maturity.)

11.2.3 Clinical Assessment of Pulmonary Function

In many cases, a clinical assessment of pulmonary function can provide useful information regarding the health of an individual, particularly in light of a toxin exposure. Such relatively simple measurements as breath rate and volume can still be critical in evaluating toxic exposures or suggestions of overdose. The air capacity of the lungs at various stages of inflation can be a very useful parameter for assessment of lung function (Figure 11.3). Normal breath volume is ~0.5 L. The total lung capacity (TLC) in an adult is ~6 L. Residual air (functional residual capacity, FRC) is the air left in the lungs after a normal, voluntary exhalation and is ~2.5 L. The residual volume (RV) is the air left over after a complete and forceful exhalation, with normal volume of just over a liter, as the lungs cannot be voluntarily completely emptied of air. Clinicians can also get a rapid assessment of real-time lung function by assessing oxygen saturation of red blood cells using *pulse oximetry*. Simply put, the pulse oximeter detects what percentage of the arterial hemoglobin is oxygenated, ranging from low to 100%, with a normal range of ~95–99%. If the "pulse ox" is not as high as needed, supplemental oxygen may be administered. Oxygenation may be tested continuously with a monitor on the finger (pulse oximetry devices sense oxygenated blood close to the surface of the skin) (see Sidebar 11.1).

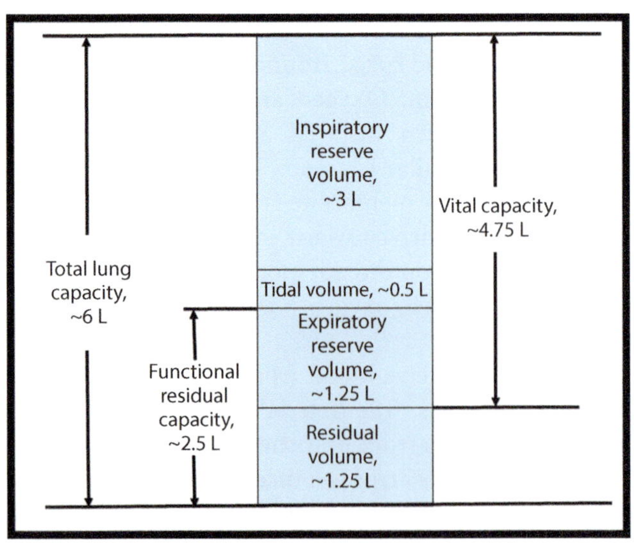

Figure 11.3 Capacity of the lungs.

SIDEBAR 11.1 CHRONIC OBSTRUCTIVE PULMONARY DISEASE

Chronic obstructive pulmonary disease (COPD) is a progressive disease of the lungs that describes a diminished functional capacity to move air in and out and to facilitate the exchange of gases (e.g., oxygen and carbon dioxide) between the inspired air and the capillary blood at the level of the alveoli. COPD generally is reflective of some degree of two conditions: chronic bronchitis, resulting in inflamed airways with mucus generation, and emphysema. From a toxicologic perspective, COPD is indicative of some degree of impairment of an individual's overall health and may make them more susceptible to the effects of particular toxic agents than would otherwise be expected.

11.3 Disease States

The lungs, like most of the rest of the body, respond to injury in only a few ways: inflammation, disintegration (structure of alveoli and alveolar walls is destroyed), cellular death (necrosis), or formation or infiltration of fibrotic tissue (scarring). Disease processes in the lungs can be considered as bronchial, parenchymal, or interstitial. Significant medical issues can be caused by material foreign to the lung, such as clots or clot fragments reaching the lungs (see Sidebar 11.2), or inhaled or injected materials (see Sidebar 11.3).

11.3.1 Bronchial Diseases

The archetypal disease affecting the tracheobronchial tree (trachea and bronchi) is bronchial asthma, usually just called asthma. Asthma is essentially an inappropriate contraction of smooth muscle surrounding the bronchioles, thereby narrowing the airways and restricting the flow of air to and from the alveoli. The severity of asthma in an individual may vary, with some patients only mildly affected and some affected very seriously. In some cases, the asthma attacks can be so severe that the available airway space is not sufficiently open to allow adequate gas exchange to maintain minimal oxygenation of tissues. This phase is called *status asthmaticus* and without medical attention can be a fatal condition (Figure 11.4).

Asthma is characterized by exacerbations and remissions that cycle over the course of a day to several days, and lung function may be normal for weeks or months between episodes. The physiologic cause of asthma is an inappropriate or unusually sensitive response to airborne irritants in the trachea and the bronchi. Asthma

SIDEBAR 11.2 PULMONARY THROMBOEMBOLI

Pulmonary thromboemboli, or blood clots to the lungs, are a very serious, potentially fatal (and very rapidly so) condition in which thrombi form in a distal location and migrate to the pulmonary arterial tree. Risk factors for the formation of thromboemboli include venous stasis from any means, hypercoagulable states, and injury. Thrombi that form in the lower extremity or pelvis (sometimes the upper extremity) veins may dislodge and migrate through the heart with the blood en route to the lungs. The large diameter of these once-thrombi cause them to lodge in and block the smaller vessels. Clot fragments may occlude larger vessels as well. The direct consequence of pulmonary thromboemboli is a restriction in the amount of blood that may be oxygenated and returned to the body. Small thromboemboli may heal without consequence, but thromboemboli in the proximal arterial tree (the main pulmonary trunk) are generally fatal without therapy. Dyspnea (shortness of breath) is the most frequently expressed symptom, and tachypnea (rapid breathing) is the most frequent early sign of massive, proximally located pulmonary thromboemboli. Small, peripheral thromboemboli may cause pleuritic pain, cyanosis, and dyspnea. The diagnosis is difficult because there are many conditions that mimic pulmonary thromboemboli including cardiac ischemia and bronchopneumonia.

SIDEBAR 11.3 FOREIGN BODIES IN THE LUNGS

Small materials can become trapped in the network of fine vessels in the lungs and obstruct blood flow. When a blood clot (thrombus) breaks up, fragments of the clot may act in this manner. As noted above, if the amount of material is enough, blood flow through the lungs can be essentially stopped, and the victim dies of pulmonary embolism. Some individuals who abuse drugs will inject crushed pills or pill fragments directly into their veins (thereby avoiding first-pass metabolism in the liver and increasing the effective dose). Pills and tablets are not formulated for such intravenous administration, and no matter how finely crushed or powdered, can result in insoluble particles being trapped in the alveolar capillaries. These materials are often readily apparent in microscopic analysis and appear as crystals, often polarizable, in the interstitium (framework) of the lungs. Sometimes, inflammatory cells will surround and engulf the material and may even coalesce into cells with multiple nuclei. While these crystals are usually inconsequential, they are a useful marker for intravenous drug abuse and may be of value in gaining an understanding of a case. In some cases, a large burden of such materials can significantly attenuate blood flow, contributing to a localized ischemia.

may also be triggered by exercise and even therapy for other diseases (e.g., β-blockers for hypertension) as well as emotional response to fright or danger. Most people recover completely after an attack of asthmatic airway obstruction with inhalent therapy (that act to relax bronchial contraction) and removal of the triggering irritant.

The use of inhaled β-agonists as an immediate treatment for bronchial asthma is now a common and effective mechanism of asthma therapy (e.g., metaproterenol, terbutaline, albuterol). The availability of such medications in convenient, metered, inhalable dosing units has allowed many asthma sufferers to pursue many activities they would be otherwise precluded from. A rare side effect, *paradoxic bronchospasm*, can occur with this therapy, wherein instead of breathing in the asthmatic being eased by use of the drug, the bronchial musculature constricts further. Paradoxic bronchospasma can be a potentially serious, life-threatening event.

Asthma, when active at the time of death, can be readily recognized at autopsy and is characterized pathologically by hyperinflated lungs, mucus deposition in the trachea, and the proximal bronchial tree. Microscopically, mucus and, often, sloughed epithelial and inflammatory cells can be observed. The basement membrane of the bronchioles (small bronchi) is generally thickened with an increased number of epithelial mucosal cells present. Inflammatory cells (mostly eosinophils and lymphocytes) are present in the submucosa and the epithelium.

11.3.2 Parenchymal Diseases

Inflammatory diseases of the lung include pleurisy (inflammation of the pleura—the outer lining of the

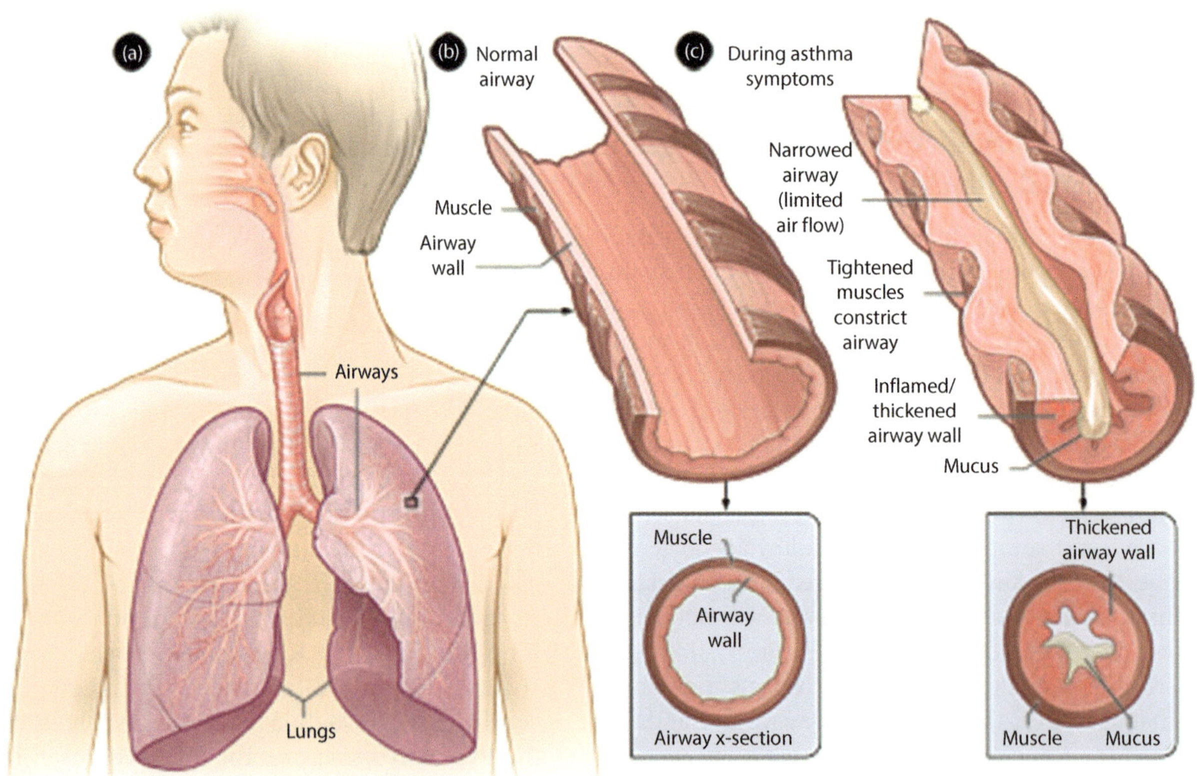

Figure 11.4 Asthma—diagram of bronchiolar constriction (U.S. Department of Health and Human Services, www.nhlbi.nih.gov/health/health-topics/topics/asthma/)

lungs and the inner lining of the chest wall), pneumonitis (inflammation of the lung, without infection; see Sidebar 11.4), and pneumonia (inflammation of the lung associated with infection). The migration of inflammatory cells to areas of injury is one of the natural responses of the body in response to infection or toxic insult. Inflammation can also cause airway edema, *pulmonary edema* (exudation of intracellular fluid in the spaces between the cells). Edema causes a reduction in the effective diameter of the lumen of the airways and may completely fill alveoli, rendering them nonfunctional for gas exchange. Edema may be cleared by diuresis, but recovery is dependent upon the severity of the edema and the underlying disease process, and the effectiveness of treatment. Pulmonary edema can become so severe that the patient dies essentially from anoxia. Extensive pulmonary edema is characteristic (but not diagnostic) of respiratory depression-related deaths (such as may be caused by an opiate overdose; see Sidebar 11.5).

One of the most common causes for the pulmonary edema is congestive heart failure: the heart cannot develop enough pressure to force blood into the arterial system. Blood backs up in the heart, contributing to enlargement and dilatation of the left ventricle. Eventually, blood backs up into the pulmonary venous system. The lungs become less compliant, resistance in the small pulmonary vessels increases, and an increased lymphatic flow occurs. The back pressure

SIDEBAR 11.4 PNEUMONIA: LOBAR AND BRONCHIAL

Pneumonitis is an inflammation of lung tissue; it becomes a pneumonia when caused by infection and coupled with an exudate, filling alveoli. Infection of the lungs is a common and often obvious finding at autopsy, but the etiology (causation) may be subtle and not initially apparent. There are a myriad of potential causes of lung infections (bacterial, viral, protozoal, fungal) and also numerous factors that can predispose a person to such infections.

Pathologically, pneumonia is divided into two general types: bronchopneumonia and lobar pneumonia. Lobar pneumonia is an infection initially confined to one lobe of the lung. (The lungs have five lobes: three on the right side and two on the left.) Lobar pneumonia is generally an infectious process caused by a specific organism, usually *Strep. pneumoniae*, but other organisms have been implicated. Lobar pneumonia can be fatal if left untreated, and lobar pneumonia can be a fatal condition.

Bronchopneumonia, while possibly expressed in only one lobe, may also occur in multiple areas. It is caused by successive infection of the conductive airways. It usually occurs in the young, the old, and the otherwise unhealthy. There are numerous potential causes and predisposing conditions, such as congestive heart failure, and as such, the presence of bronchopneumonia itself is not necessarily instructive. Bronchopneumonia is not uncommon among the drug-abusing community, thought to be a function of the opiate-based supression of the gag reflex, leading to aspiration-based pneumonia.

In contrast to lobar pneumonia, bronchopneumonia is an inadequate cause of death, and an underlying cause must also be identified, for example, bronchopneumonia due to complications of congestive heart failure.

SIDEBAR 11.5 NONCARDIOGENIC PULMONARY EDEMA

Congestive heart failure is one of the most common causes for pulmonary edema. However, it has long been recognized that pulmonary edema can be associated with heroin ingestion or an opiate overdose in an individual who was not expressing heart failure. Such edema can be noted in terms of elevated lung weights and pathologists' observations. While the exact mechanism of pulmonary edema has not been elucidated, the underlying cause may be related to localized hypoxemia and acidemia. In consequence to an opiate overdose, capillary walls become porous and some of the liquid portion of blood seeps out into the alveoli from the capillaries. The liquid portion mixes with the air in the alveoli, forming foam. This foam can be either white (early stages) or pink-tinged as red blood cells also move into air spaces. Foam exudes from the mouth and nose and can be seen microscopically as pale pink (eosinophilic) material in alveoli. From a toxicologic perspective, one expects a pathologic finding of significant pulmonary edema in opiate overdose cases in which the decedent lived for some time following exposure to the drug. The absence of such a finding might reasonably raise questions about the validity of the conclusion of the death being a function of an opiate overdose.

causes the capillaries and lymphatics to become leaky and fluid accumulates in the alveoli. Patients become hypoxic and experience an increased sense of effort to breathe. If left untreated, hypoxia can worsen, leading to respiratory acidosis and becoming a life-threatening condition.

Acute respiratory distress syndrome (ARDS) is a very serious condition caused by pulmonary edema, a function of permeability of the alveolar capillaries. ARDS is characterized by sudden respiratory failure and is a potentially serious response to acute lung injury from either direct pulmonary toxins, systemic medical diseases, or in some cases toxins affecting other parts of the body. Impairment of pulmonary function is readily apparent clinically—the patient is hypoxic with difficulty breathing. Treatment is supportive and aimed at the cause of ARDS, and mechanical ventilation may be required to maintain oxygenation of tissues until the underlying condition is addressed.

11.3.3 Interstitial Diseases

The tissues and space around the alveoli of the lungs, including the support molecules, or "scaffolding," that supports the cellular structure and open airspace, is the *interstitium* of the lungs. The classic and perhaps most common disease of the interstitium is pulmonary emphysema, a disease process whereby the walls of alveoli are damaged or destroyed. Emphysema is usually the result of a toxic insult, usually chronic smoking, although it can also be a consequence of a genetically inherited condition (e.g., alpha-1 antitrypsin deficiency). Only a short duration or a light smoking history is required for lung damage to start to occur. Along with the wall of the airway, the capillaries lining the alveoli can also be affected. The end result of irritation or toxic insult is the formation of fibrotic scar tissue. Fibrosis is irreversible and renders the airways useless to gas exchange, ultimately resulting in nonfunctional alveolar space incapable of oxygen and carbon dioxide exchange, and once destroyed, these tissues are unable to regenerate. A patient with emphysema must be considered as having a compromised ability to provide oxygen to body tissues, and may as such be more susceptible to toxic or therapeutic agents affecting respiration or cellular utilization of oxygen (Figure 11.5).

Two of the more commonly encountered conditions in end-stage lung disease are emphysema and idiopathic pulmonary fibrosis. The former is characterized by enlargement of air spaces and the latter with dense scar tissue. Both conditions may be diagnosed by imaging studies and lung biopsy.

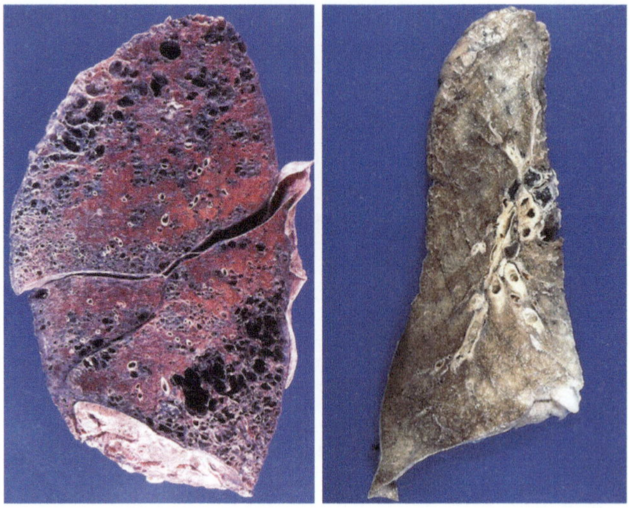

Figure 11.5 Emphysema.

11.4 Asphyxia

Asphyxia is the process by which a person has become unconscious or died as a result of insufficient oxygen reaching the brain and other vital organs. Asphyxia can result from hypoxia or anoxia. Hypoxia implies that some oxygen, but an inadequate amount, is being supplied to the body or tissue. Anoxia means that no oxygen is available or utilization is blocked at the molecular level.

The supply of oxygen can be limited or blocked in numerous ways, including mechanical methods such as hanging, strangulation, smothering, crushing, or restriction of movement of the torso (expansion and contraction of the chest) and obstruction or occlusion of the airway by foreign material. Asphyxia can also result from the displacement of oxygen from the air supply. Injury, such as pneumothorax (air in the pleural cavity), can cause atelectasis (partial or total collapse of the lung), affecting the ability to breathe and resulting in either transitory hypoxia or asphyxia.

In contrast to the mechanisms of physical asphyxia, some toxins can directly interfere with the body's ability to absorb, transport, or utilize oxygen and are referred to as *chemical asphyxiants*. Examples of these chemical asphyxiants are some of the most well-known toxins and poisons, such as cyanide, carbon monoxide, and hydrogen sulfide. Some chemicals cause a physical asphyxia as a consequence of their caustic action on the tissues of the airway, with subsequent edema and blockage of oxygen transfer at the alveolar level (e.g., phosgene, acid fumes, smoke, etc.). Changes in the structure or oxidation state of hemoglobin can also affect the oxygen-transport ability of the body (see Sidebar 11.6).

SIDEBAR 11.6 METHEMOGLOBIN AND METHEMOGLOBINEMIA

Methemoglobin is the oxidized-iron form of hemoglobin, containing ferric iron (Fe^{+3}), rather than the normal ferrous (Fe^{+2}) form. Methemoglobinemia can be expressed as a genetic disorder or an acquired condition. An enzyme normally present in red blood cells (methemoglobin reductase) functions to convert methemoglobin to hemoglobin by reducing the ferric iron to the ferrous form. A genetic deficiency in this enzyme can be inherited in an autosomal recessive pattern. Heterozygotes (people with only one abnormal gene for the enzyme) have lower levels of the enzyme but are physiologically normal. They may, however, become hypoxic before normal people if exposed to chemicals capable of oxidizing ferrous iron. Homozygotes (people with two defective genes for the enzyme) tend to have methemoglobin levels as high as 50%. In an effort to compensate, the body may produce more red blood cells, causing polycythemia.

The other cause of methemoglobinemia is caused by a structural abnormality in the hemoglobin molecule itself. Several possible alterations in either the alpha or the beta chains of the hemoglobin molecule can cause a change in the preferential oxidation state, allowing methemoglobin to remain in that form rather than to be converted to hemoglobin.

Acquired forms of methemoglobinemia are caused by exposure to oxidizing drugs and compounds that oxidize the hemoglobin ferrous iron to the methemoglobin form (various nitrites and nitrates, quinones, and sulfonamides).

11.4.1 Interference with Cellular Utilization of Oxygen

11.4.1.1 The Biochemistry and Physiology of Respiration

Aerobic respiration is a biochemical process using oxygen as an electron acceptor in order to generate energy, primarily in the form of adenosine triphosphate (ATP), and reducing capability in the form of NADH, NADPH, and $FADH_2$. The key reactions of the process are the breakdown of glucose (glycolysis) and the subsequent oxidation of pyruvate in the mitochondria in the Krebs cycle. An essential part of the process is the transfer of electrons along a series of proteins, with a final transfer being to an atom of oxygen. This *electron transport chain*, while forming the final sequence of events in the energy generation from glycoloysis, is nevertheless crucial, and interruption of the flow of electrons can terminate the ability of the cell to generate the energy required for function. From a toxicologic perspective, therefore, the potential of certain compounds to interrupt this process by blocking the utilization of oxygen qualifies such species as *chemical asphyxiants*.

The process of breathing provides a mechanism for rapid exchange and equilibration of the gases oxygen and carbon dioxide with the outside environment. There is no "reservoir" of oxygen within the body (beyond that temporarily bound to molecules of hemoglobin). There is a reservoir of carbon dioxide in a sense, in that CO_2 in the aqueous media of the body exists in equilibrium with H_2CO_3, HCO_3^-, and HCO_3^{-2}. In fact, the dynamic equilibrium of these compounds, and the rate at which the reaction is driven toward or away from carbonate by the concentration of carbon dioxide (thereby either liberating or removing H+ from solution), provides an essential pH buffering system for the body (Figure 11.6).

The physical mechanism of breathing requires the use of musculature, specifically, the diaphragm,

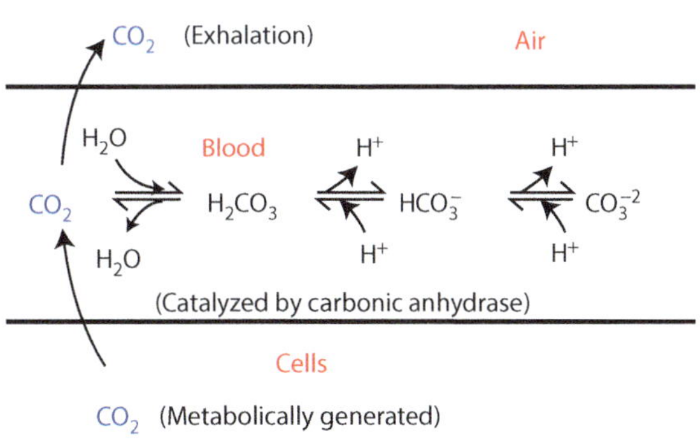

Figure 11.6 Equilibrium between gaseous and solvated CO_2, H_2CO_3, HCO_3^-, and HCO_3^{-2}.

intercostal muscles of the chest, and abdominal muscles during forced exhalation. Paralysis of these muscles (such as by the actions of neurotoxins) can result in asphyxia simply by restricting the body's ability to exchange pulmonary air with that of the environment. Similarly, compounds that inhibit respiratory function by direct action on the central nervous system system (e.g., opiates) by restricting the magnitude or frequency of respiratory efforts can produce hypoxia and a respiratory acidosis as the body's inability to remove CO_2 increases the concentration of H+ in the blood.

11.4.1.2 Cyanide

Cyanide, like strychnine and arsenic, is one of a relatively few deadly poisons that are well known in the general public. Cyanide has been used as a chemical warfare agent, a means of both mass and individual suicide, an execution agent (perhaps most infamously in the Nazi concentration camps in World War II), and as an agent of both mass and individual homicidal poison. Cyanide has also been responsible for countless deaths as a component of toxic gas mixtures in both residential and commercial building fires.

Cyanide, as cyanide ion (CN^-), interferes with the ability of cells to utilize oxygen by inhibiting one of the final proteins of the electron transport chain just prior to the reduction of an oxygen molecule oxygen. This reduction of molecular oxygen is the energy basis for the life of the cell and ultimately the organism as a whole. Specifically, CN^- inhibits the action of cytochrome C oxidase, which in normal operation transfers four electrons to one molecule of oxygen, along with four protons, thereby generating two water molecules. Like CO, cyanide binds to the ferrous iron atom within the protein and thereby precludes the transfer of electrons to molecular oxygen. This molecular block terminates the electron-transport chain and stops the ATP-generating processes dependent upon the reduction of oxygen (oxidative phosphorylation).

Inhalation of gaseous cyanide can cause death within minutes by producing hypoxia/anoxia at the cellular level. Blocking utilization of available oxygen produces chemical (as opposed to physical) asphyxia. At toxic but nonfatal doses, cyanide can cause coma, seizures, apnea, and cardiac arrhythmias.

Cyanide, either as a free ion (CN^-) or as a substituent group (–CN), is a rather ubiquitous molecule. The relatively small quantities we routinely ingest dietarily or by smoking are readily metabolized to thiocyanate by the mitochondrial enzyme rhodanese (thiosulfate cyanide sulfotransferase), and then eliminated by the kidney.

Cyanide toxicity can also result following the ingestion of *cyanogenic glycosides* such as amygdalin (contained in peach and apricot pits—CN^- is released from the glycosidic form during digestion). Other exposure routes, either accidental or deliberate, may utilize either gaseous cyanide or various salt forms (e.g., sodium or potassium cyanide). All are equally toxic, as a function of the liberation of CN^- ion in the body. The lethal level of cyanide in the blood is considered to be ~3 mg/L.

Cyanide gas may be produced from the burning of cyano-group containing materials such as some types of foam rubber and other man-made material as well as some animal products. In a house fire, inhaled cyanide may actually cause death before inhalation of carbon monoxide can form a substantial amount of carboxy-hemoglobin.

Cyanide poisoning may not be recognizable at autopsy, particularly in cases where there is some degree of underlying disease that may be, in the absence of suspicion of foul play, considered as the cause of death. In some cases, morgue staff may detect the presence of cyanide by an almond-like odor. Roughly one-third of the population is capable of smelling cyanide and associate the smell with almonds or bitter almond. However, just as in carbon monoxide poisoning, the blood and therefore livor mortis has a bright red color, which may also raise the suspicions of the case pathologist.

Testing for cyanide, while relatively straightforward by a number of methods, is not generally performed as part of a normal postmortem panel, and in the absence of suspicion, the compound may be overlooked in some cases. While unusual in forensic work, cyanide salts are available and may indeed be found in either suicide or homicide cases. Interpretation of blood cyanide levels can be difficult because many people have a detectable baseline level of cyanide in blood. The amount of cyanide and thiocyanate (SCN^-) found in serum, saliva, and urine are dependent on personal habits and genetic traits, with smokers having two to three times the levels detected in nonsmokers.

Treatment of inhaled cyanide poisoning is generally supportive only, because of time constraints (meaning that because of the rapid action of toxin, there may be no time for treatment with an antidote regimen). An effective treatment regimen (albeit more applicable to ingested cyanide) is treatment with nitrite (e.g., amyl- or sodium-) compounds, which oxidize a portion of the hemoglobin molecules to methemoglobin (Fe^{3+}), which very effectively binds cyanide, and kinetically "liberates" cyanide from cytochrome oxidase. Thiosulfate treatment then facilitates formation of thiocyanate, which can be readily eliminated.

11.4.1.3 Hydrogen Sulfide

Hydrogen sulfide (H_2S) is a relatively common industrial intermediate and by-product used in coking and refining and is a side product of many natural gas wells. It is a potent CNS depressant, readily capable of causing death. Hydrogen sulfide is mechanistically similar to cyanide in that it complexes with cytochrome iron, thereby inhibiting cellular respiration. Hydrogen sulfide has a characteristic "rotten eggs" smell and can be detected by humans at concentrations well below any toxic threshold. However, the compound serves to deaden that sense fairly quickly, such that prolonged exposure may occur as the victim becomes less aware of the potential danger. Hydrogen sulfide is not commonly encountered in the forensic toxicology world, perhaps because the odor of the toxin serves as an effective warning well below potentially toxic concentrations. However, hydrogen sulfide has been used as a means of suicide, a trend that seems to have started in Japan around 2008 or earlier. In essence, sulfur-containing compounds are mixed with an acidic solution, releasing H_2S gas. Some large-scale poisoning events occurred in Japan and several successful suicide events have occurred in the United States as well.

11.4.2 Interference with Transport/Absorption—Carbon Monoxide

Carbon monoxide (CO), well recognized as a potential poison, is a colorless, odorless gas that is not an irritant to mucus membranes. CO is a normal component of the air we breathe, comprising less than 0.001% of atmospheric gas (albeit apparently rising) and is normally a product of the incomplete combustion of hydrocarbons. CO is a small molecule and is easily transferred from the lungs to the blood across the alveolar-capillary membrane. CO is another example of a chemical asphyxiant in that it blocks the ability of the body to utilize molecular oxygen, although in a manner very different from cyanide or hydrogen sulfide. CO has a much higher affinity for the oxygen-binding site on the hemoglobin (Hb) molecule than does oxygen itself (250–300 times greater). When present in significant concentration, it preferentially binds to Hb, forming carboxyhemoglobin (COHb), and thereby removes that oxygen binding/transport site from availability for O_2 transport. Because of the high affinity, CO is only slowly displaced by O_2 and eliminated by exhalation (depending on the ambient atmospheric composition).

The binding of CO to one of the hemoglobin subunits of the Hb molecule affects the other three oxygen-binding sites and increases their affinity for molecular oxygen. This tighter O_2 binding also results in a less facile release in the low-oxygen regions of the body. (CO binding to hemoglobin shifts the Hb-O_2 dissociation curve, as shown in Figure 11.7.)

In short, CO occupies O_2 binding sites and causes molecular oxygen to bind more tightly to the remaining sites it does occupy. The net result is less oxygen available to distribute to tissues and a less efficient transfer to the tissues upon delivery. From here, it replaces oxygen on hemeproteins or is (eventually) eliminated unchanged from the lungs. A number of other molecules similar to oxygen can also bind on the hemoglobin molecule, including cyanide (CN^-), sulfur monoxide (SO), nitric oxide (NO), sulfide (S^{2-}), and hydrogen sulfide (H_2S). All of these species can limit oxygen binding and transport, thereby causing hypoxic or anoxic toxic effects.

There are many possible sources of carbon monoxide exposure. Some of the most common include motor vehicle exhaust, either unvented in an enclosed space, or in vehicles with leaky or faulty exhaust systems. Carbon monoxide can also build up in occupied facilities from faulty or defective heating systems. CO poisoning is not uncommon in colder climates in winter months when supplemental heating devices can be used in inadequately ventilated situations. In some situations, nonspecific symptoms of fatigue and headache

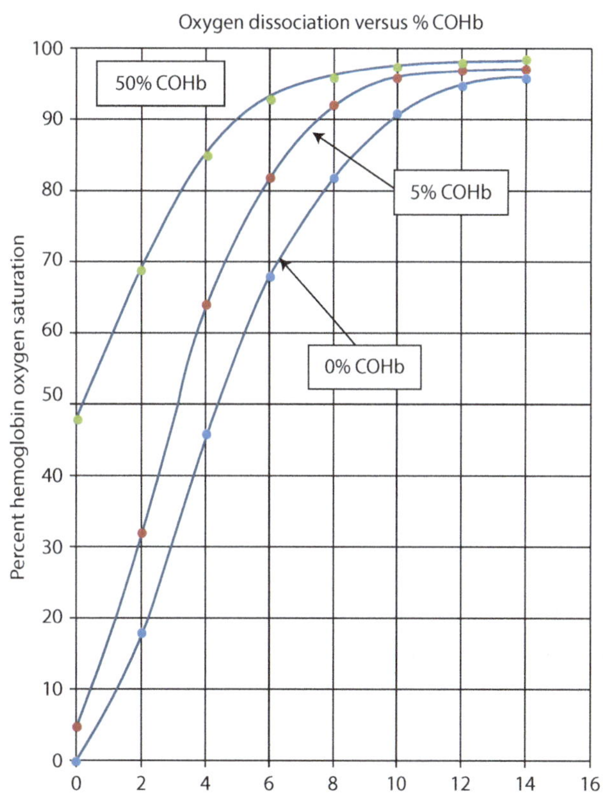

Figure 11.7 Hemoglobin-oxygen dissociation curve versus percent carboxyhemoglobin.

may occur over the course of months or years. One of the more well-recognized means of potentially toxic CO exposures is combustion fumes and smoke. CO can represent a significant component in smoke from residential or other fires and is often the cause of death in such events, even in the absence of thermal or burn injuries.

The symptoms of carbon monoxide poisoning are the same as those for other types of asphyxiation: headache, nausea, confusion, blurry vision, and loss of consciousness. However, the exposed patient may also complain of gastrointestinal disturbances and muscular cramping. Consequences of exposure are related to dose, which in turn is a function of the concentration of CO in the air mixture and the time of exposure. Table 11.1 shows the relationship between concentration of CO in the air, time of exposure, and symptomatic consequences.

The medical (or postmortem) diagnosis of carbon monoxide intoxication is simply a function of the determination of the percentage of COHb in venous blood in a deceased person.

Typical COHb concentration in nonsmokers is ~1–3%, whereas smokers tend to have an average value of ~5–8% but can reach as high as 15%. The inhalation of exhaust fumes usually causes death when the level is in the range of 40% COHb or so, but people who die in a structural fire may accumulate levels as high as 80% COHb before they succumb.

Table 11.1 CO Concentration and Consequences of Exposure

CO Concentration	Exposure Consequences
35 ppm (0.0035%)	Headache, possible dizziness following prolonged exposure.
100 ppm (0.01%)	Mild headache following 2 or more hours of exposure.
200 ppm (0.02%)	Headache within 2–4 hours of exposures, impact on judgment and cognitive capabilities.
400 ppm (0.04%)	Frontal headache within 1–2 hours. Effects on cognition and judgment.
800 ppm (0.08%)	Pronounced headache, dizziness, nausea, possible seizure in less than an hour. Unconsciousness possible in less than 2 hours.
1600 ppm (0.16%)	Pronounced headache, dizziness, nausea, possible seizure, tachycardia in less than 1/2 hour. Death possible in less than 2 hours.
3200 ppm (0.32%)	Onset of symptoms within 10 minutes or less. Death possible in less than 1/2 hour.
6400 ppm (0.64%)	Onset of symptoms within minutes. Death possible in 15 minutes.
12,800 ppm (1.28%)	Unconsciousness ensues after several breaths. Death in minutes.

A strict interpretation of CO toxicity based on COHb laboratory values with rigid cut-off points is not necessarily valid. Different measurement techniques can produce somewhat different values (and the toxicologist should become familiar with the ranges of COHb percentage generally associated with death in their laboratory). In a larger sense though, a CO exposure represents an additional physiologic stress on an individual and lower levels of CO exposure may have more serious consequences in some patients than would normally be expected. Patients with an increased demand for oxygen, such as those with native pulmonary or cardiac disease, and people with an increased metabolism, such as pregnant women, infants, and fetuses (CO also easily crosses the placenta), have a lesser ability to tolerate an increase in the inhaled carbon monoxide than do healthy individuals without such complicating factors.

The preferred method for treatment of CO toxicity, following removal from the contaminated atmosphere, is hyperbaric oxygen, with 100% oxygen at atmospheric pressure being the next best thing. Breathing room air reduces the percentage of COHb by about half in roughly 5 hours. Breathing 100% oxygen reduces that time to less than 1 hour. In a hyperbaric chamber, the time to reduce COHb by half is further reduced to about 15 minutes, thereby hastening recovery substantially.

From a toxicologic perspective, major CO exposures, and hence elevated COHb levels, are regularly encountered in fire victims and in suicide cases where exposure to automobile exhaust is the source of the CO. When elevated CO levels are obtained in cases in which drugs (e.g., opiates or CNS depressant) are present, developing an opinion on the combined role of drugs and CO effects can present a significant challenge (see Sidebar 11.7).

SIDEBAR 11.7 TWO CARBON MONOXIDE DEATHS

Despite the fact that carbon monoxide is well-recognized as a potentially toxic agent, there are still toxic exposures that could have readily been avoided. One recent case involved a 35-year-old male whose hobbies included the meticulous care of an expensive sports car. He habitually ran the engine in his garage and kept notes on the vehicle's performance. On a winter day, he ran the engine as usual, but kept the garage door closed against the harsh winter air. He was eventually discovered by his girlfriend, who had gone to look for him as he missed an appointment. Upon entering, she noticed a strong smell of vehicle exhaust and found the victim in a kneeling position between two of his cars. Thinking that he was overcome and still alive, she tried to roll him over on his back. She put two pillows under his head to cushion him from the concrete. The body, however, was in strong rigor mortis—elbows and knees flexed—with cherry red livor mortis present anteriorly. Autopsy procedure revealed only hypertensive cardiovascular disease (heart weight 490 gm, left ventricular hypertrophy, wall thickness 1.8 cm). The subsequent toxicologic evaluation revealed a COHb level of 75.8%. The cause of death was determined to be carbon monoxide intoxication and the manner of death was ruled accidental.

Auto exhaust has often been used as a means of suicide, and various arrangements for directing the flow of gas into the vehicle cabin have been used, such as a hose from a clothes dryer, etc. As noted above, simply running vehicles in a closed space also generates levels of CO adequate to cause death. One recent example was a 53-year-old male who had suffered from depression for many years. He was found dead in his vehicle by his wife, with the car engine ignition key in the "on" position. No suicide or farewell notes were recovered; however, a healed incised wound on the anterior aspect of the right forearm was consistent with a history of at least one previous suicide attempt. The only noticeable feature at autopsy was the intense pink hue of the livor mortis. COHb was determined to be 82%. Cause of death was determined to be carbon monoxide intoxication, and the manner of death was certified as suicide.

11.4.3 Caustic Action within the Airway: Mechanism, Symptoms, Pathology

Inhalation of caustic agents (e.g., hydrochloric and other acid fumes, ammonia, and caustic mists or dusts) has the common pathologic and physiologic consequences of epithelial tissue damage, with the corresponding edema. The exact nature and magnitude of toxic consequences will depend on the agent, the magnitude of exposure, and to an extent the underlying health of the exposure victim. Often such cases can be seen as a combination of a caustic and an asphyxial event. From a toxicologic perspective, there may be little in terms of testing to support obvious pathologic findings of necrosis and edema in the airway and lungs (however, scene evidence may be corroborative and even compelling).

Somewhat less obvious (although certainly now well recognized) are the irritant or caustic action of such species as asbestos, coal dust (e.g., anthracite coal dust), and silica dust. One common feature of exposure to these agents is that cigarette smoking tends to exacerbate the potential for toxicity by affecting the efficiency of the ciliated cells lining the bronchioles. This action, limiting the ability of the lungs to clean themselves, has the effect of increasing the area under the curve for the inhaled toxin.

11.4.3.1 Smoke Inhalation

Smoke inhalation is commonly cited as a cause of death. The mixture of hot gases, soot, and particulate matter comprising smoke can indeed quickly cause death, either by the presence of chemical asphyxiants (e.g., CO or CN), by anoxia in an oxygen-depleted environment, or by the caustic damage generated by the associated thermal injury. COHb formation is a marker of smoke inhalation but may not be the sole cause of death. People who have significant medical disease, especially cardiac and respiratory disease, will succumb to the physiological stress of smoke inhalation faster than healthy people.

Pathologists routinely request a COHb determination on deceased people who have been found in a burned structure, even if there is no evidence of smoke inhalation at autopsy (see Sidebar 11.8). Such an analysis may further support a conclusion that the victim did not breathe smoke or soot, and was therefore dead prior to the fire.

SIDEBAR 11.8 PATHOLOGY OF SMOKE INHALATION

The proximal and midportions of the airway (trachea and bronchi) are lined by ciliated epithelium, which comprise one of the first lines of defense against injury from inhaled agents. Ciliated cells have cell processes (*cilia*) projecting from them that provide a mechanical sweeping of the airway. The ciliated epithelium is fairly delicate and responds to insult (e.g., chronic smoking) by reverting to a nonciliated columnar epithelium. Eventually, the cells can transform to a flat cellular form, squamous epithelium. This transitional process between cellular forms is *metaplasia* and is considered as an initial step toward neoplasia (an abnormal cell growth, potentially a transitional phase leading toward cancer). Metaplasia can be reversed when a person quits smoking, depending on the extent of cellular transformation and damage. Smokers, especially those with a long history of inhalation, generally do not have ciliated respiratory epithelium. A significant consequence of this is a limitation in the ability of the lungs to remove particles, which may be a factor in the development and expression of the toxic response to environments with inhalable, potentially toxic materials.

Cases involving an acute "smoke" inhalation from fire-related deaths are not at all uncommon in the toxicology laboratory. The mixture of smoke and hot gases from a fire scene can be acutely caustic to the airway as a function of temperature, causing tissue necrosis and even charring, along with the deposition of soot and other inhaled materials in the airway as shown in Figure 11.8. (The presence of such materials in the airway may be of use to the case pathologist in determining if the decedent was dead prior to being reached by the fire.) The hot gas mixture can also contain a significant amount of carbon monoxide and may contain other toxic species, such as cyanide.

11.5 Oxygen Blockage and Displacement

Simple displacement of the fraction of oxygen (roughly 20%) in the air required to maintain life with another, even nontoxic gas can be as lethal as an efficient chemical asphyxiant. Virtually any gaseous mixture can asphyxiate, and many different gases have been associated with both accidental deaths and, in many cases, suicides. Understanding what gaseous mixture may actually have been available in a given situation can pose significant challenges, as can the task of demonstrating the presence of a suspected gas in a postmortem sample. In some cases, e.g., propane, or other flammable gases, detection, and even quantitation (in terms of blood saturation) may be relatively straightforward. In other cases, for example, helium or even nitrogen asphyxiation (*toxicity* would be an inappropriate term), demonstration of the causative agent may pose some analytical difficulties.

In many cases (particularly suicides), the physical layout of the scene, including a gas source, may be clearly indicative of the asphyxiant agent. In other scenarios, for example, industrial accidents, there may be more of a question as to the nature of the breathable mixture, and even with regard to the oxygen content of that gas mixture. While such questions may seem superfluous, the difference between a 6% and a 14% oxygen atmosphere may have, in some circumstances, significant legal ramifications (see Sidebar 11.9).

11.5.1 Hypoxic Environments

Hypoxic environments, those in which oxygen is either absent or at levels inadequate to maintain consciousness, are often confused with a toxic gas mixture. As such, cases when death or incapacitation has resulted from such a circumstance can still come to the forensic toxicologist, usually as examples of suicide or accident.

Humans require a minimum level of oxygen in inspired air to maintain cerebral and cardiac function. The usual concentration of atmospheric oxygen is approximately 20%. When the concentration falls to approximately 10%–15%, judgment and coordination are impaired; loss of consciousness occurs at about 8%–10% and death is ultimately inevitable below 8% oxygen concentration.

Industrial accidents can result from an individual unknowingly entering an airspace with limited or absent oxygen, such as a large reaction vessel, tank or tank car, storage space, or dedicated work room. However, the potential for hypoxic environments is as widely varied

(a) (b)

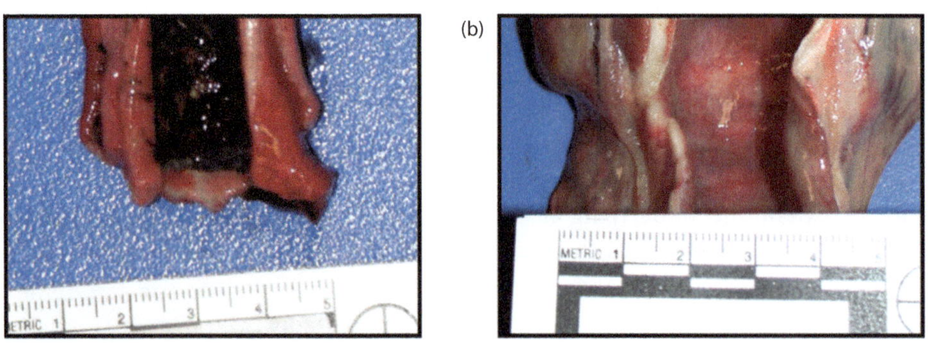

Figure 11.8 Soot in the airway following a death during a house fire (a). Note also that the mucosa of the trachea is reddened, caused by carboxyhemoglobin in the blood and by irritation of the mucosa by the hot gasses in the fire. A normal airway (b) is shown for comparison.

SIDEBAR 11.9 THREE ANOXIC DEATH CASES

Suffocation by Plastic Bag

While suffocation by plastic bag can be accidental, this mechanism can also be employed by an individual in a suicidal effort. In a recent case of an elderly male with multiple serious medical problems, the victim was apparently quite determined as he had placed a plastic bag over his head and secured it with a neck tie. When his caregiver found his body in his bed in his secure residence, she pulled the bag loose and attempted resuscitation, unsuccessfully. The autopsy procedure revealed severe arteriosclerotic and hypertensive cardiovascular disease. Neither drugs of abuse nor ethyl alcohol were detected in autopsy blood samples.

Inhalation of Helium Gas

Inhalation of an inert gas in an anoxic environment is occasionally encountered. An example is the case of a 39-year-old man who killed himself by securing a plastic bag over his head into which he ran tubing from a canister of helium. The decedent was discovered when the cleaning service could not open the door. The manager of the hotel used a passkey and cut the inside safety chain to gain entry and then found the decedent with a plastic bag tightly secured around his neck and still inflated. The victim was declared dead by responding emergency medical personnel, and the medical examiners' office was notified. The helium tank was almost empty and the valve was in the "on" position. After a thorough investigation of the scene of death as well as his apartment and a complete autopsy, the cause of death was determined to be asphyxia by oxygen displacement. The manner of death was ruled suicide.

Solvent—Huffing

On a cold December day a sanitation worker found the body of a middle-aged-appearing man on the conveyor belt inside an industrial recycling plant. The body was relatively free of trauma and fully clothed. He was later identified by fingerprint comparison, having been arrested two weeks before (having been found unresponsive inside a storage room of a local business establishment with a plastic bag next to his face; observers had noted a strong odor of glue coming from his body). The investigative information revealed that the items on the conveyor belt around the body of the deceased had come from a small section of the city and were able to be tracked back to a certain dumpster. The man was last seen by a friend at his residence the evening before he was found dead, which is in the same neighborhood as is the dumpster. At autopsy, this 46-year-old male was determined to have had only minor injuries, compatible with minor antemortem blunt trauma or perimortem damage during transportation. The most notable characteristic was a cluster of hard, dry, white-gray material adherent to his hands. Because of the known history of glue sniffing, a toxicology analysis with emphasis on volatile compounds was performed with the following results: ethanol—9.0 mg/dL (0.09 g/ dL), acetaldehyde—1.5 mg/dL, toluene—9.3 ug/mL (reporting limit 0.30 ug/mL). Postmortem peripheral blood in a sodium fluoride tube was used for the analyses. The testing was negative for other compounds. The only other significant autopsy finding were hypertensive cardiovascular disease (heart weight 475 gm, left ventricular hypertrophy, wall thickness 1.9 cm) and pulmonary emphysema. Because of the nature of where and how he was found, it is reasonable to conclude that he was exposed to low environmental temperatures at least for some time. Hypothermia may have contributed to his death, at least to some degree.

as the gases and gas mixtures that can be generated or used in an industrial setting.

Suicidal use of hypoxia is not uncommon, most frequently seen in the form of a plastic bag with an inert gas supply, thereby displacing the breathable air. Helium, nitrogen, and propane have been used, but again, the potential is limited only by the availability of the compressed gas.

11.5.2 Physical Asphyxia

In contrast to chemical asphyxia, mechanical or physical asphyxia is a process by which the air or oxygen supply is physically prevented from reaching the body or the cells. Examples are hanging, strangulation, and suffocation. While the pathologist may see the effects of a restricted blood return from the head (e.g., petechial hemorrhages), such findings are absent in chemical asphyxia deaths.

11.5.3 Huffing Solvents and Aromatic Hydrocarbons

"Huffing," or the deliberate inhalation of volatile compounds, is not a particularly common form of drug abuse, but neither is it so rare as not to be occasionally encountered. Accidental exposures to volatile compounds, most commonly in industrial situations, can also produce toxic consequences ranging from mild headaches to serious debilitation and even death. Toxicologic analysis in huffing/inhalation cases is critical to an association of death with the use of a particular potentially toxic agent. Scene investigation may also suggest what agent was used and thereby guide testing. A wide variety of compounds can be used in huffing scenarios, and industrial exposures are limited only by the scope of the chemical processes involved. Materials used in huffing can be found in a myriad of commercially available and relatively inexpensive products. Examples include spray paints and other aerosolized products, glues, paint, various solvents, paint strippers, gasoline, and other fuels. Huffing effects tend to be short-lived, lasting generally only 5–15 min.

The practice of huffing can cause significant damage to the brain over time, specifically to the white matter (probably related to the high lipophilicity of most organic volatile solvents and related compounds). Clinical symptoms associated with huffing can include a range of effects ranging from acute euphoria to the subacute consequences of white matter damage (ranging from tremor, to ataxia, cognitive impairment, dementia, and amnesia). Fatal consequences of huffing or solvent exposure can be due to oxygen displacement (and hence asphyxia) or a cardiac arrythmia (either brady- or tachy-), leading to an acute cardiac event. Tachyarrhythmias are the classic presentation, with the arrhythmia presumed to arise in the myocardium, possibly having been sensitized by an increase in native catecholamines consequential to the solvent exposure.

11.6 Common Toxins

11.6.1 Nicotine

Nicotine is an acetylcholine receptor agonist with a stimulatory effect at small doses, and is potentially acutely toxic in high doses. The major route of exposure is tobacco smoking. Currently, patches and gum containing nicotine are readily available. Nicotine, particularly in combination with smoke (e.g., cigarette smoking), is an irritant and inflammatory agent, particularly in the respiratory system. Nicotine-related vasoconstriction can have a negative impact on gas exchange and may thereby exacerbate asthma. Smoking can cause chronic bronchitis, and prolonged use of tobacco can lead to progressive pulmonary damage, expressed as emphysema. Nicotine also damages or inhibits the *mucociliary elevator*, thereby prolonging the residence time in the body of materials that would normally be removed from the lungs.

11.6.2 Ammonia Gas

Ammonia (NH_3) is a major industrial and agricultural chemical widely available in liquid form, has a high vapor pressure, and readily forms ammonium hydroxide with any available water molecules. When in contact with skin, mucus membranes, or alveolar surfaces, the conversion to the caustic form readily causes tissue necrosis. Breakdown of cells causes local inflammation and massive edema, eventually leading to scarring. If ammonia gas is inhaled in toxic concentrations, the mucosa and the lung parenchyma may be destroyed, leaving the exposed individual at risk for rapid death.

11.6.3 Chlorine Gas

Chlorine is a gas at room temperature, and while rarely encountered in any significant quantity in normal environments, it is a widely used industrial chemical, and industrial or transport exposures represent the majority of toxicologic events. When inhaled, it combines with body water to form hydrochloric and hypochlorous acid, causing irritation, cellular damage, and necrosis, leading to a potentially fatal edema. Chlorine gas was used extensively in World War I, paving the way for more toxic agents such as phosgene.

11.6.4 Sulfur Dioxide

Sulfur dioxide is released in the burning of oil and coal and is primarily used as an industrial intermediate in the production of sulfuric acid. In small concentrations, it may be used to preserve dried fruit and other foodstuffs. Upon inhalation, it forms sulfuric acid, with damaging effects on the lungs, resulting in irritation, inflammation, and edema. As with other agents causing such effects, the degree of response, potentially including death, will be a function of the magnitude and duration of exposure.

11.6.5 Ozone

Ozone (O_3) is a gaseous oxygen allotrope (an alternate molecular form; in this case, O_3 instead of the more common O_3), much less stable than its O_2 counterpart. It has a sharp odor, similar to but (at least at low concentrations) less disagreeable than chlorine. It is a powerful oxidizing agent, with extensive use in multiple industrial applications. This oxidizing potential can result in damage to mucosal and respiratory tissues if inhaled, producing irritation, inflammation, and edematous response as seen with other inhaled toxic species. Unlike the agents that form acidic or basic species in the lungs, ozone is capable of reacting directly with organic double bonds and also serves as a generating species for oxygen free radicals, leading to lipid peroxidation and oxygen radical toxicity.

11.6.6 Nitrogen Dioxides

Nitrogen dioxide (NO_2 and related compounds NO_x) can be formed from combustion of fuel and is also present in tobacco smoke. NO_2 is toxic, causing pulmonary edema and inflammation with adequate exposure. Long-term exposure has been linked to lung cancer. NO_2 has an acrid odor and is easily detected at low concentrations, and therefore inhalation exposure can generally be avoided. However, prolonged exposure to even low concentrations (e.g., 4 ppm) can dull the sense of smell, leading to the potential for a toxic exposure. Pulmonary edema can appear as long as several hours following exposure to a fatal concentration. The primary source for NO_2 is internal combustion engines, which generate various oxidized nitrogen species, NO_x. These various NO_x species are significant contributors to both industrial and automobile-generated smog.

11.7 Uncommon Toxin Examples

11.7.1 Phosgene

Phosgene ($COCl_2$) is a liquid used as an industrial intermediate in the production of some plastics and pesticides. At room temperature it readily vaporizes to a gas more dense than air, with an odor said to be of newly mown grass or hay. It is extremely toxic if inhaled, hydrolyzing upon contact with water to hydrochloric acid, causing tissue damage and potentially massive pulmonary edema, often resulting in death. It was first used as an agent of chemical warfare in World War I and found to be more effective than chlorine gas alone.

11.7.2 Silicon

Elemental silicon is relatively inert and poses no real health risk. However, the crystalline form of silicon dioxide can be very toxic if inhaled, causing an intense inflammatory reaction, edema, and fibrosis, and is now referred to as silicosis. Inhalation of silicon dioxide over time has also been linked to lung cancer. The usual mechanism for exposure is occupation related, for those individuals who regularly inhale crystalline silica dust. Acute silicosis can cause shortness of breath, cough, fever, and even cyanosis. Silica particles can be small enough so as to reach the alveolar sacs in the lungs, ultimately to be taken up by macrophages via phagocytosis. This process sets off an inflammatory response, resulting in the stimulation of fibroblasts, and eventually, the fibrosis and nodular lesions characterizing the disease.

11.7.3 Asbestos

Asbestos is a term used for some fibrous forms of silicate, which has been used extensively in various construction applications primarily as thermal insulation. Asbestos is fireproof and easily molded and applied to complex surfaces (e.g., pipes). Asbestos was once very commonly used, but due to strict regulation it has become essentially obsolete for almost all applications. Thus, current exposure circumstances are unlikely to be of the chronic nature that has characterized so many of the cases of asbestos-related disease in the past.

The cause of the toxic response is the potential for small particles of asbestos to become trapped in the lung, causing inflammation and fibrosis. Pathologists can recognize asbestos particles as brown beaded rods associated with or embedded within mononuclear inflammatory cells without the use of special stains. The mineral is also carcinogenic and has been linked to mesothelioma and other lung cancers.

11.7.4 Paraquat

Paraquat is a nonselective contact herbicide widely used throughout the world. Mechanistically, paraquat readily accepts and shunts electrons from photosynthesis onto molecular oxygen, in a redox cycle, forming oxygen radical species and regenerating the original molecule. Damage to the plant tissues, cellular molecules, and membranes is due to the action of active oxygen species, such as superoxide, hydroxy and peroxy radical, and lipid peroxy intermediates, with the subsequent molecular damage. Paraquat is also toxic to human beings, with a similar mechanism, utilizing NADH or NADPH as the electron source and generating initially superoxide and ultimately other active oxygen species capable of forming lipid peroxides and other oxidized

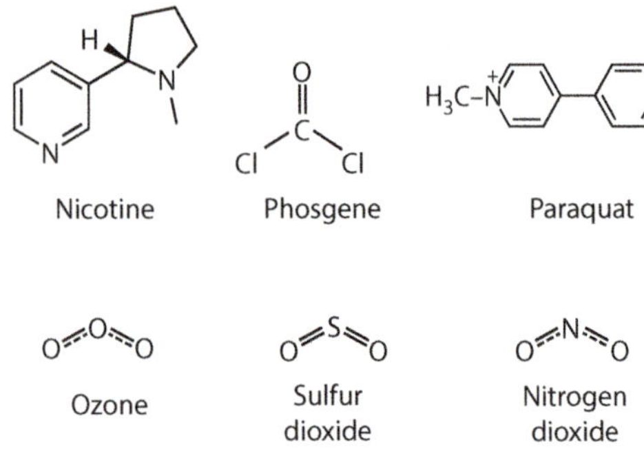

Figure 11.9 Paraquat and examples of pulmonary toxins.

molecules. The lungs seem to be particularly sensitive to paraquat toxicity, even following an oral ingestion with expression of significant cellular damage, formation of fibrotic tissue, and onset of ARDS (Figure 11.9). Kidney and liver damage can also occur, but the lungs seem to be the primarily affected tissue. Overall, the risk of damage is greatest by inhalation, followed by ingestion, then dermal absorption. Interestingly, paraquat ingestion has been used as a suicide agent in developing countries because it is effective, available, and cheap. Similarly, paraquat has also been implicated in a number of homicides.

REVIEW QUESTIONS

1. How does drug uptake in the lungs differ from the same processes in the liver?
2. What is the effect of nicotine on lung physiology?
3. What would be the reasonable physiological consequences of hyperventilation?
4. What is the sequential pattern of pulmonary tissue response to chronic toxic insult?
5. Name two diseases that could be exacerbated by inhaled toxins.
6. How is ammonia gas toxic to the lung?
7. What medical problems might a maintenance worker experience while working in a long traffic tunnel? What would the symptomology be? Postmortem finding?
8. Why would the CO elimination rate be dependent upon atmospheric composition?
9. Both CO and CN are chemical asphyxiants. How are they different?
10. CO saturation of 40% is often seen in car exhaust suicides. Fire deaths can show up to 80%. Why the difference?

TOPICS FOR DISCUSSION

1. Discuss how asthma, interstitial, and alveolar lung diseases affect the rate of absorption of inhaled toxins.
2. What might the role of smoking be with regard to black lung disease and asbestosis?
3. Should smokers be eligible for lung transplants?

Bibliography

Boron W. Acid-base physiology. In: Boron WF, Boulpaep EL, editors. *Medical Physiology*. 2nd rev. ed, updated. Philadelphia: Saunders-Elsevier, 2012.

Leikauf GD. Toxic responses of the respiratory system. In: Klassen CD. *Casarett and Doull's. Toxicology: The Basic Science of Poisons*. 8th rev. ed. New York: McGraw-Hill, 2013.

Physiology of the respiratory system. In: Patton KT, Thibodeau, GA. *Anatomy and Physiology*. 7th rev. ed. St. Louis: Mosby-Elsevier, 2010.

The respiratory system. In: McConnell II TH, Hull KL. *Human Form, Human Function: Essentials of Anatomy and Physiology*. New York: Lippincott Williams & Wilkins, 2011.

Valentine R, Kennedy GL. Inhalation toxicology. In: Hayes AW, editor. *Principles and Methods of Toxicology*. 5th rev. ed. New York: Informa Healthcare, 2008.

Toxins, Drugs, and Drug Classes

III

Alcohols
Ethanol, Methanol, and Related Compounds

12

Contents

12.1 Introduction

Ethanol; the only poison that does not require subterfuge for administration

Ethyl alcohol is probably the most significant drug for the forensic toxicologist, as evidenced by its status as an automatic analyte for postmortem, driving under the influence (DUI), drug-facilitated sexual assault (DFSA), postaccident, and even most presumed or suspected cases of poisoning. While demonstrating the presence of an odd, unusual, or esoteric poison in a suspected homicide case might represent the ultimate challenge to the art and craft of the forensic toxicologist, such a case will be bracketed by hundreds if not thousands of more-or-less routine cases in which ethyl alcohol plays a major or at least a contributory role. Other alcohols, while less often encountered, are nevertheless occasionally significant analytes in forensic cases.

Alcohols are organic molecules containing a hydroxyl function (–OH). The simplest is the single-carbon alcohol methanol. The two-carbon species, ethyl

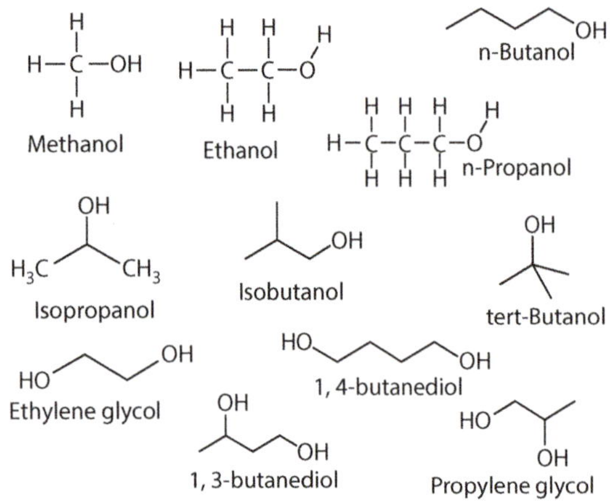

Figure 12.1 The common alcohols.

alcohol, ethanol or drinking alcohol, is also known as grain alcohol (in contrast to wood alcohol, methanol). The relatively moderate toxicity and euphorogenic effects are the basis for the extensive use of ethanol by mankind worldwide.

The other common alcohols toxicologists deal with are methanol, as noted above and shown in Figure 12.1 and Table 12.1, propyl (iso- and n-), butyl (iso, n-, and tert-), and ethylene glycol, the two-hydroxy analog of ethanol. While each has its own toxic potential, methanol, isopropanol, and ethylene glycol are most commonly encountered in forensic cases.

12.2 Ethanol

Ethanol has been and remains (at least since the repeal of Prohibition) our societies' primary legal drug, soporific, analgesic, and narcotic. Alcohol plays a major, if not central, role in countless social rituals and interactions, from meeting for a beer, to proposing a toast, to ringing in the New Year. The downside of the use of alcohol is of course related to both its ability to intoxicate and impair the normal cognitive and physiological functions of the body. Alcohol is estimated by some to have caused more than 100,000 deaths per year in the United States, including alcohol-related traffic crashes and other alcohol-related accidents. Alcohol abuse can be personally devastating, with considerable societal costs as well. People who abuse alcohol are more likely to have alcohol-related diseases including digestive disorders, cirrhosis of the liver, several types of cancers, and cardiovascular disease. It is nearly impossible to overstate the impact and penetration of this one drug on human society throughout the world.

Table 12.1 Low Molecular-Weight Alcohols

Compound	Formula	Mol. Wt.
Methanol	CH_3OH	32
Ethanol	CH_3CH_2OH	46
n-Propanol	$CH_3CH_2CH_2OH$	60
Isopropanol	$CH_3CH_2OHCH_3$	60
n-Butanol	$CH_3CH_2CH_2CH_2OH$	74
Isobutanol	$(CH_3)_2CHCH_2OH$	74
tert-Butanol	$(CH_3)_3CCH_2OH$	74
Ethylene glycol	$HOCH_2CH_2OH$	62

The problems associated with misuse of ethanol are certainly well recognized and appreciated, from acute issues such as drunk driving and binge drinking, to the chronic disease of alcoholism. Many treatments and support groups are available, and a myriad of laws attempt to limit or control excessive use. While some societies and cultures have successfully limited or eliminated alcohol consumption, our experience in the United States with Prohibition in the 1920s and early 1930s is recognized more for its failure to restrict access to alcohol than for any long-term success. Alcohol use remains a considerable factor in society, and hence, in the forensic world.

The analysis of ethanol, either as a component of an ingestible liquid or in biological fluids (e.g., blood or urine) is relatively straightforward. However, understanding what inferences may be properly drawn in cases that involve ethanol is an important responsibility for the forensic toxicologist, and to do so requires an understanding of the nuances of the analytical techniques employed and the metabolic processes that ethanol undergoes in the body. This process can be equally challenging for the forensic pathologist, who must in many cases determine the role, if any, that ethanol may have played as an acute toxicant or exacerbating factor contributing to a death.

12.2.1 Ethanol Pharmacokinetics

The characteristic pattern of absorption, distribution, metabolism, and elimination is as relevant to the consideration of ethanol ingestion as with any other drug. Unlike most other drugs, however, many people have a sense for both the speed of absorption and distribution, and the time required for elimination. Both blood and urine are used as forensic specimens, but the pattern of concentration versus time in each matrix differs considerably, as does their forensic utility, with blood being the most reliable indicator of the effective concentration of ethanol in the body. Breath, another commonly used forensic sample, provides a reliable measure of alcohol in the blood, urine samples considerably less so.

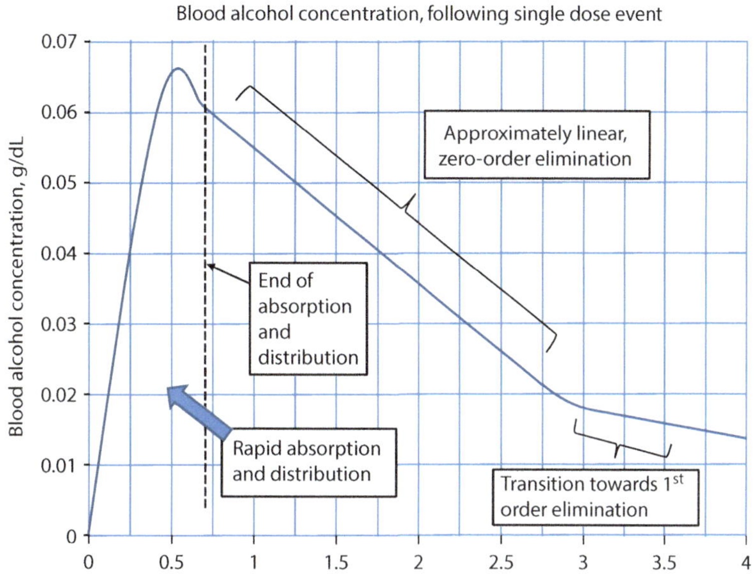

Figure 12.2 Absorption of ethanol as blood alcohol concentration versus time.

12.2.1.1 Absorption

Following ingestion, ethanol is relatively rapidly absorbed in the stomach and intestinal mucosa. As much as 20% can be absorbed through the stomach wall, but by far the bulk of absorption occurs in the small intestine. The rate of absorption is a function of concentration of alcohol, with the maximal rate of absorption occurring when the alcohol ingested is in the range of ~25% alcohol, or 50 proof. (Proof = 2 × % alcohol; hence 40% alcohol is 80 proof.)

As a general rule, absorption of one drink will raise the blood alcohol concentration of a 170–180 lb. individual by ~0.02 g/dL, within 15–40 min. or so of alcohol ingestion on an empty stomach, as shown in Figure 12.2. Food in the stomach delays transit of ingested alcohol to the intestine, where most absorption occurs, and therefore delays the time until maximal blood alcohol concentration is achieved. Taking into account concurrent metabolism, the resulting maximum blood ethanol level will be lower when there is food in the stomach than if it were empty when the person drinks. As might be expected, the blood alcohol concentration (BAC) resulting from an ingestion of alcohol is proportional to body weight (e.g., if we expect ~0.02 g/dL/drink in a 170 lb. individual, we would similarly expect ~0.026 g/dL/drink in a 130 lb. individual (.02 g/dL/drink/(130/170)) = 0.026 g/dL/drink).

So, for example, a 220 lb. male ingesting 3 standard drinks (see Sidebar 12.1) within an hour would be expected to have a BAC of ~0.045 g/dL (.02 g/dl/drink)/(220/170) = 0.0154 g/dL/drink; 3 drinks × 0.0154 g/dL/drink = 0.046 g/dL). Such rough estimations (actually a variation of the "volume of distribution" calculation; see Chapter 4) can be very useful for understanding forensic cases, including evaluating the information regarding amount and pattern of ingestion.

Consider as another example the contention raised by a (~170 lb.) drunk driver that he (or she) "only had two glasses of wine with dinner, and an after-dinner drink" and that the ingestion (in this simplistic example) ended

SIDEBAR 12.1 WHAT'S A DRINK?

Correlation of effects to dose is dependent upon knowing what the dose in a specific instance was. The dose for alcohol can vary depending on the "formulation," being beer, wine, or other liquid form. Fortunately, the more-or-less common serving measures contain roughly the same amount of alcohol. For toxicologic purposes, a "standard drink" is defined as containing ~14 g ethanol, as shown in Table 12.2.

Table 12.2 Ethanol in the Standard Drink

Drink	% Alcohol	Proof	Volume, Oz	mL EtOH	Grams EtOH
Beer	5	10	12	17.74	14
Malt liquor	7	14	8	16.56	13.1
Table wine	12	24	5	17.74	14
Fortified wine	17	34	3–4	17.59	13.9
Cordials, liqueurs	24	48	2–3	17.74	14
Distilled spirits	40	80	1.5	17.74	14

approximately one hour prior to a DUI arrest. On-scene breath testing (consistent with behavior at the scene, as well as field-sobriety testing) indicated BAC of 0.16 g/dL. Based on the three drinks (and assuming each glass of wine was actually 1.5 "standard" drinks), that would account for 4.5 drinks, and an expectation of ~0.09 g/dL as a maximal BAC. While metabolism of ethanol would normally be considered in such a case, it is readily apparent that the proffered explanation of ingestion is inadequate to explain the observed BAC in the case, and the time over which the ingestion occurred is irrelevant to that question (in this case specifically).

12.2.1.2 Distribution

Many people have noted how rapidly the effects of a drink can be felt. Ethanol is readily able to transit cell membranes, being small enough to traverse the *aquaporin* channel proteins (which allow water molecules to pass into and out of cells). As such, ethanol rapidly distributes essentially throughout all of the body water in a person, meaning that alcohol rapidly equilibrates in all the aqueous spaces in the body, such as the interior of cells, the cerebral spinal fluid, and the fluid from within the eye (vitreous humor; see Sidebar 12.2).

SIDEBAR 12.2 ETHANOL IN VITREOUS FLUID

Vitreous humor (VH), the fluid in the eye, may be readily retrieved at autopsy and has proved to be a very useful matrix for analysis. VH is maintained in a "protected space" in that it is within the tough, fibrous membranes of the eye and most of it is within the skull, shielded to some degree from physical trauma. VH is isolated from the bloodstream and is protected from the effects of hemolysis with decomposition after death. It is generally not subject to bacterial invasion and therefore often remains uncontaminated for a considerable time after death. Ethanol readily transits into the vitreous fluid, which is also readily analyzed via the same techniques used in blood. Ethanol levels in the vitreous fluid tend to lag somewhat behind those in blood and are often interpreted when they are higher or lower than corresponding blood samples, as suggesting that alcohol levels were rising (hence the decedent was in the absorption/distribution phase) or falling, respectively, and hence being eliminated. Care should be taken in such interpretations.

Interestingly, women tend to have ~5% less body water then men, and hence, their BAC tends to be just a little more, on an equivalent-dose basis, than their male counterparts. Ethanol is also able to readily traverse the blood–brain barrier, and the blood:CNS ratio is generally close to 1:1. This extensive and rapid distribution of ethanol throughout the body, without organ- or tissue-specific concentration, means that ethanol is not a good candidate for postmortem redistribution. In a sense, ethanol is already distributed or at equilibrium throughout the body at death. (An exception to this are cases where there may be alcohol in the stomach, coupled with trauma to the torso or other circumstances allowing leakage of stomach contents. Evaluation of a peripheral or vitreous sample should resolve any question about the validity of an alcohol result generated from a heart or chest blood sample.)

The rapidity with which alcohol can be distributed can be a significant factor in forensic cases. Occasionally a defense to a DUI charge will be offered, to the effect that an arrestee had ingested an amount of alcohol adequate to explain their BAC just prior to the arrest and as such their blood alcohol level was rising during the arrest process, crossing the legal threshold (0.08 g/dL) after the arrest but prior to completion of testing procedures. Indeed, such a defense may be valid in some cases. However, careful consideration of the pattern of drinking, and the rapid absorption/distribution process resulting in a maximal BAC, can often be used to either support or refute such contentions. In some cases the number of drinks that would have to be ingested to explain the determined results and the circumstances (e.g., being served in a bar) may be adequate to evaluate the explanation. (An individual claiming, for example, to have been in a bar for several hours and only ingested the seven drinks minimally necessary to explain a 0.14 g/dL BAC "just before leaving" may need some corroborative testimony or other evidence to be convincing.)

It is important from a forensic perspective to bear in mind that the extensive and rapid distribution of alcohol does not include urine. Alcohol reaches the urine as a filtrate of blood rather than as a product of rapid diffusion from the circulation.

It is also worth noting the time following ingestion of ethanol, when the absorption from the GI tract is essentially complete (or at least not contributing significantly to BAC), when ethanol levels in the blood are being lowered by both metabolic elimination and by diffusion of ethanol into tissues. This process can be described (and perhaps somewhat overstated) as a "diffusion plunge" and may be a factor in apparently elevated elimination rates for a short time period as the process of absorption is ending (see Figure 12.3).

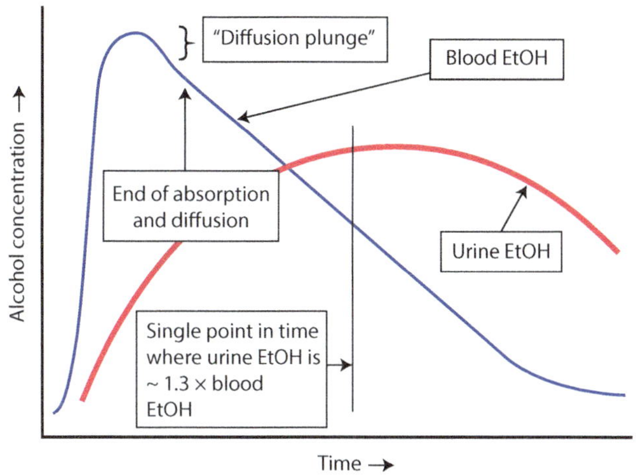

Figure 12.3 Blood versus urine ethanol concentration.

12.2.1.3 Metabolism

Roughly 90% of alcohol ingested in the body is metabolized. Most of the remainder is excreted in the urine, some is exhaled, and some volatilizes transdermally. While the exhalation route is of forensic significance (as the basis for breath alcohol testing), the volume of alcohol excreted by this route is relatively minor.

Metabolism of ethanol consists primarily of two sequential oxidation steps (see Figure 12.4) first to acetaldehyde, and second to acetate. Both steps are catalyzed enzymatically, by alcohol dehydrogenase (ADH) and acetaldehyde dehydrogenase (AADH), respectively. Ethanol catabolism does generate calories, and the relationship between alcohol and the caloric value of a drink is discussed in Sidebar 12.3.

The primary metabolic site for alcohol is the liver, but the ability to metabolize alcohol is expressed, albeit at considerably lower levels, in multiple organs throughout the body. Unlike essentially all of the drug-metabolizing systems in the body, the ability of alcohol dehydrogenase to oxidize ethanol becomes saturated at concentrations of ethanol that are relatively low, compared with the levels that are achieved by ingestion of even one or two drinks. This means that the rate at which alcohol is metabolized is a function of how much alcohol dehydrogenase is present, and it is not dependent on the concentration of ethanol. For much of the range of alcohol concentrations the forensic toxicologist is routinely called upon to deal with, the elimination can be described with zero-order kinetics and is essentially linear. More specifically, the K_m of the enzyme is equivalent to an alcohol concentration of ~0.01 g/dL (~2 mM). Therefore, at concentrations of ~0.02 g/dL and above, the enzyme is processing alcohol at the maximal possible rate (assuming the availability of the cofactor, NAD^+), limited only by the amount of ADH present.

Alcohol dehydrogenase is an inducible enzyme, which means that as the body is repeatedly exposed to a specific enzymatic substrate, more of that enzyme is produced. So, an experienced, or regular, drinker will have synthesized more ADH and therefore have a greater ability to metabolize alcohol (and hence eliminate at a faster rate) than they would have had in the absence of a drinking history.

There is a genetic component to the amount of alcohol dehydrogenase an individual starts with, or in other words, the uninduced level. Nevertheless, that amount is such that even naïve drinkers will metabolize alcohol at a rate of ~0.01 to ~0.02 g/dL/h. While two sequential samples generally allow determination of the actual rate of elimination for a particular individual at a particular time (and are the best means for determination of elimination rate), a reasonable average value commonly used for estimation purposes is ~0.02 g/dL. (Any responsible

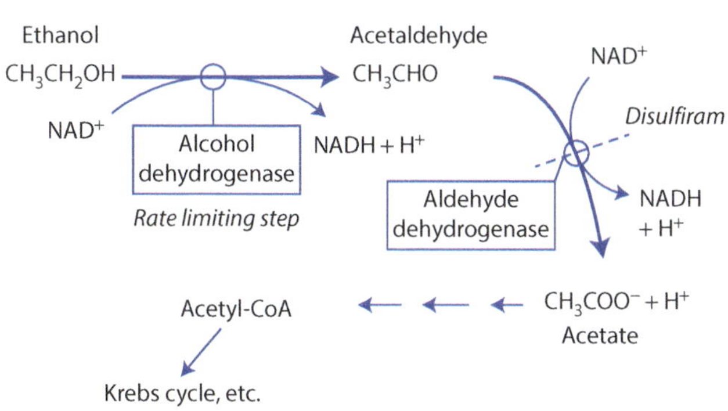

Figure 12.4 Ethanol metabolism.

SIDEBAR 12.3 ALCOHOL AND CALORIES

The contribution (or lack thereof) of alcoholic drinks to the caloric intake can be of considerable interest in some circumstances. While the caloric value of the mixtures to which alcohol can be added can in some cases be substantial, containing various syrups, sugars, and oils, alcohol itself does have a caloric value.

Consider one mole of ethanol, which is roughly equal to 46 g or about three drinks. Assuming complete metabolism, that amount would produce 2 moles NADH, which when run through oxidative phosphorylation, would yield 6 moles ATP. Also produced would be 1 mole acetyl CoA, which when run through the Krebs cycle would yield 12 moles ATP, and 1 mole ATP from substrate level phosphorylation. A rough total then is 19 moles ATP per mole ethanol. Considering ATP at ~7.3 kcal/mole, that would equal ~140 kcal/mole ethanol, or somewhere around 40 calories per drink, for the ethanol alone. In short, for most drinks, the caloric value lies in the mix, rather than the alcohol.

use of an estimated elimination rate requires the consideration of uncertainty associated with the process.)

As might be expected for a substrate present in such a relatively high concentration, there are alternate pathways for ethanol metabolism. Several enzymes can play a role in the breakdown of ethanol, specifically catalase (normally cleaving hydrogen peroxide) and a group of *mixed-function oxidases*, which represent another inducible system and may be significantly expressed in heavy drinkers. Inducible cytochrome P450 (CYP450) enzymes may also play a minor role in ethanol metabolism. However, these alternate pathways do not seem to play a significant role for alcohol concentrations less than ~0.3 g/dL or so.

Alcohol is also a substrate for (at least) two phase II conjugation reactions, specifically the formation of ethyl sulfate and ethyl glucuronide. These phase II metabolites represent relatively minor elimination pathways, at least in contrast to the amount of alcohol that is oxidized to acetate, but both compounds appear to have a half-life considerably longer than alcohol itself. Because of that longer residence time in the body, both compounds are being considered for their potential forensic significance as indicators of alcohol ingestion or alcoholism. Detection of ethyl sulfate and ethyl glucuronide has been problematic because of the low concentrations of the conjugates, but with the advent of HPLC-MS (or -MSMS) instruments, with the requisite specificity and sensitivity to regularly and reliably detect the compounds, there is increasing interest in their detection and reporting.

12.2.1.4 Elimination

The elimination processes of ethanol play a relatively minor role, compared to the rapid metabolism by oxidation. However, from a forensic perspective, both major elimination routes (breath and urine) are significant in that they provide the basis for either a confirmation of use at some time in the past (urine) or a reliable inference of BAC at the time of the test (breath). The quality of the determination of BAC from breath test is quite good, and the correlation between breath and BACs has been well established (see Sidebar 12.4).

SIDEBAR 12.4 BREATH ALCOHOL TESTING

Determination of ethanol in expired air is a well-accepted means of determination of blood alcohol concentration (BAC). Despite occasional assertions to the contrary, there is a long history of correlation studies showing the validity of the relationship. The systems used for determination are usually based in vapor-phase infrared absorption, at multiple wavelengths, thereby facilitating both qualitative and quantitative evaluations. With standard forensic practice now including a check of instrumental calibration by reference to certified gas standard materials (usually either before use in testing or, better still, before and after), the basis for legitimate scientific challenge is considerably limited.

Nevertheless, the breath alcohol determination provides only an estimate of the true BAC at the time the sample is collected. (A number of states avoid this inconvenient fact by crafting their DUI laws in terms of either a blood or breath concentration of grams ethanol/volume of blood, or volume of air, e.g., DUI defined as a BAC in excess of 0.08 g/dL blood, or 0.08 g/210 L expired breath.)

The uncertainty inherent in breath alcohol testing is not primarily the analytical uncertainty associated with the instrumental measurement. Rather, the relationship of alcohol in the blood to that of the breath is defined as the blood-breath partition coefficient (BBPC, or ratio, BBPR). This ratio reflects the partition coefficient of ethanol between blood in the alveolar capillaries and air in the alveolar spaces and has been the subject of considerable investigation and characterization. Some of the original research in the field indicated that the ratio was ~1:2100; in other words, a blood alcohol concentration of 0.1 g/dL (1 g in 1 L blood) would appear as a concentration of 1 g in 2100 L of expired breath. This value became the standard upon which breath testing was based, and the concentration of alcohol in the sample chamber (of whatever volume) was expressed for reporting purposes, in terms of weight of ethanol/210 L air (the weight of ethanol then expected in 1 dL blood [100 mL], the standard reporting convention).

However, the problem associated with this practice is twofold. First, the average BBPC of 1:2100 is an average value, and there is no way to know or reliably predict the actual BBPC of a specific individual. To the extent that a DUI arrestee's BBPC is less than 1:2100, the breath test would overstate their true BAC; and to the extent the ratio was more than 1:2100, the test would understate the true BAC. Further work has demonstrated that the average BBPC is closer to 1:2400, and so in most cases, the breath-testing process understates the true BAC.

The research on BBPC has included thousands of cases, and as such, the statistical reliability of the data is quite good. We can use both the mean value and standard deviation to make a reasonable statistical prediction for a confidence interval for any breath test result that has been calculated using the 1:2100 ratio. Using a mean value of 1:2370, and a standard deviation of 240, we can infer that 95% of the population will have a BBPC of 1:1890–1:2850. Using this range, a determined breath alcohol value can be expressed in terms of a 95% confidence interval (CI).

For example, consider a 0.120 g/210 L breath alcohol result. This result could be expressed as an expected BAC of 0.12 g/dL (95% CI = 0.108 – 0.162). While this range may seem large, in practice, it is skewed to the right because of the bias of the original calculation (based on a BBPC of 1:2100), understating the true BAC for most subjects. The practical reality then is that a breath test of 0.09 g/dL will still have a 95% CI in excess of 0.08 g/dL (and, considered from a one-tailed perspective, a probability of 97.5% that the true value is in excess of 0.08 g/dL).

In contrast to the reliability of breath alcohol values as an indicator of blood levels, while there is considerable data showing both blood and urine values (with an average of ~1.3), there is no mechanistic basis for a relationship between the two. The suggestion that a blood value can be reliably inferred from a urine value is demonstrably false; consider a 170 lb. individual 20 minutes after ingestion of two double shots. One would expect a blood alcohol of ~0.06 g/dL and rising and a urine alcohol of probably "none detected" to perhaps a 0.02 or so, yielding a urine:blood ratio of 0.3 or less. On the other end of the time scale, perhaps 4 hours later, a blood alcohol concentration of 0.01–0.02 would be reasonable, as would a urine concentration of 0.08, yielding a ratio of ~4–8, again well distant from the average ratio of 1.3 (see Sidebar 12.5). Certainly, at some point during the metabolism and elimination of alcohol, the urine:blood ratio does indeed equal 1.3; the question is of course, when? In short, in the absence of drinking history information and corroborative behavioral observations, any

SIDEBAR 12.5 FORENSIC URINE ALCOHOL SAMPLES

Urine is generally a readily available sample, commonly acquired in DUI cases in preference to blood samples, and does not require medical personnel for collection. However, the level of alcohol in such samples is not necessarily reflective of the BAC at the time of collection, despite the general assumption that it is (or at least should be). Nor, unfortunately, is such a urine level necessarily indicative of a BAC that may have been achieved at some time prior to collection. Urine is a filtration/concentration product of blood, the composition and concentration of which is dependent not only on the specific content of the blood, but also upon the state of hydration of the body, as well as the amount and distribution of electrolytes. Once formed, urine is delivered to the urinary bladder, where it stays until the person voids. While in the bladder, the urine is not actively concentrated nor diluted, except by the continued addition of more urine, which itself may be more concentrated or dilute, depending on the hydration state of the body.

The ethanol concentration of the urine being formed in the kidney will vary with the concentration of alcohol in the blood. However, since urine is being constantly produced by the body, no two samples would be expected to be identical in concentration. Two individuals of identical weight and alcohol absorption/ elimination rates, differing only in hydration status may well have markedly different profiles of urine alcohol concentration versus time, given the same amount of alcohol ingested (on a dose/weight basis). The assumption, then, that urine alcohol levels can serve as the basis for a valid extrapolation to a BAC is demonstrably false. Therefore, the detection of alcohol in a urine sample may provide a basis to *explain* impairment in an individual but does not, in and of itself, provide a basis from which to *infer* impairment.

There is a common assumption that urine alcohol levels must be numerically related to blood alcohol levels by some constant value. A value of ~1.3 to 1 is often cited as the ratio of alcohol in the urine to that in the blood, and indeed, with the accumulation of enough correlated data, an average value for that ratio can (and has often been) calculated. However, the "average" urine:blood ratio derived from correlated blood and urine data (and in fact, 1.3 is often cited) is more an artifact of data reduction than a valid representation of a physiological parameter. At some point, during the absorption/distribution/elimination of a drink or drinks, the urine alcohol:blood alcohol ratio will indeed be 1.3. The ratio of alcohol in urine to blood is a dynamic relationship, starting at 1, approaching 0 as alcohol appears in the blood but not the urine, then rising well above 1 as alcohol is eliminated from the blood but remains in the urine, and ultimately returns to 1 as complete elimination is achieved, as shown in Figure 12.3. An approach to this issue has been to have the subject donate two urine specimens, separated by some length of time (generally 30 minutes or so) with the assumption that the second sample will be more reflective of the true blood alcohol concentration at the time of collection than the first. While perhaps theoretically defensible, there may remain in a practical sense, considerable uncertainty about the true blood alcohol level in such a case.

In any forensic urine sample, the alcohol concentration may be quite close to the blood level but, conversely, may not. There does not seem to be an analytical parameter allowing an evaluation as to how valid that agreement might be, short of actually measuring blood level. In practice, the evaluation of performance, as measured by behavior, and field sobriety tests seem to provide a good basis for the evaluation of the validity of urine alcohol concentration. In short, urine drug and alcohol testing can provide an explanation for such impairment as may be demonstrable by a driver but does not in itself provide a basis for inference of impairment, in the absence of corroborative information.

inference regarding BAC or impairment based only on urine drug or alcohol levels would not be expected to be forensically defensible.

Interestingly enough, as forensic testing has become more reliable, challenges to the testing process often focus on nonanalytical issues, such as the potential for a sample to have become contaminated, problems with chain of custody, or other questions that may cast doubt on the applicability of a legitimate alcohol quantitation in a sample to a particular case or individual (see Sidebar 12.6).

SIDEBAR 12.6 SAMPLE CONTAMINATION, CHAIN OF CUSTODY, AND RELATED FORENSIC ISSUES

Forensic alcohol samples (and clinical samples being considered for forensic purposes) are not infrequently challenged with respect to their accuracy and validity. While the accuracy of the headspace-GC analysis of a particular sample on a particular batch can be demonstrated and defended by the laboratory, the underlying validity of the sample may be subject to legitimate questions. In many cases, blood samples are collected in gray-top tubes, containing sodium oxalate and sodium fluoride. The oxalate serves to prevent clotting, and the fluoride inhibits any enzymatic activity that might otherwise take place, either oxidation of ethanol or its production by fermentation processes (which would of course require a microbial contamination and the presence of an adequate fermentable substrate). A properly collected and preserved blood sample may therefore be expected to reasonably represent the alcohol concentration in the donor at the time of collection.

Samples collected in other tubes, such as serum-separator tubes, or with different preservatives may still be valid, particularly if stored under refrigerated conditions. Fermentation processes tend to produce multiple small organic molecules that readily show up during analysis. In contrast, cases in which ethanol has been ingested tend to show the presence of no other small organic molecules.

Another issue often raised with regard to blood samples is the use of "alcohol wipes" on the collection site prior to insertion of the draw needle. The implication is that some of the alcohol wiped on the surface will contaminate, and cause a false positive, or artifactually elevated result in the eventual testing. This suggestion is far fetched at best, for two reasons. First, when ethanol was actually used for the purpose of cleaning the draw site, there was not a recognizable problem with patients who would not be expected to have alcohol in them, showing a positive result. Even if only a relatively infrequent occurrence, considering the ubiquity of the alcohol test in the hospital setting, if the process could produce a contamination, it would clearly have been noticed. Second, ethanol is not the alcohol used in the antiseptic wipes, having been replaced by isopropanol many years ago.

An analogous problem can arise with samples from decomposed or partially decomposed remains. In many such cases, ethanol can be detected. In the presence of other potential microbial degradation and fermentation products, great care should be taken with regard to any conclusion regarding the use of ethanol prior to death. Clearly, in such cases, no quantitative inference should be made. Similarly, occasionally a sample may be received for analysis in a postmortem case in which methanol, isopropanol, and acetone (or some combination thereof) are present at significant levels. Usually in such cases, the medical history will include embalming.

Finally, a common challenge raised in a legal setting is with regard to chain of custody, often absent in clinical samples that have been diverted to the forensic world. The implication is of course (considering the emphasis placed on chain of custody in forensic laboratories) that in the absence of such a document, the sample could have been tampered with or may actually have been collected from someone other than to whom the sample was attributed.

Tampering with a collected sample is not a trivial matter, in that an exactly correct amount of ethanol would have to be added, so as to generate a reasonable result, and this would have to be accomplished without knowing the original concentration of alcohol in the sample. Attribution of samples in hospitals is usually not done by chain of custody but is handled with electronic documentation of identity and sample collection or transfer. In many cases, hospital documentation of sample location and activities is more thorough and complete than some chain-of-custody documents.

12.2.2 Physiological Effects of Ethanol

Ethanol functions as a central nervous system depressant. At low concentrations (<0.04 g/dL), the effects are mildly euphorogenic, and indeed, it is this perceived pleasurable response that is the basis for the popularity of the drug. As the concentration increases in the body, the magnitude of depressant effects becomes increasingly evident with diminished cognitive and motor skills, ultimately resulting in muscular paralysis, coma, and death.

12.2.2.1 Mechanism of Action

The effects of ethanol are thought to be a function primarily (if not exclusively) of the ability of the ethanol molecule to be solvated in the membranes of cells throughout the body, and by that incorporation to slightly alter (in a subtle manner) the physiology and function of those membranes. Clearly, an impact on neuronal cellular membranes, such that those membranes are just slightly less able to become depolarized, or to propagate depolarization, provides an adequate explanation for the CNS depressant effects of the drug. In short, ethanol apparently depresses the ability of neurons to function, either as aggregators or collectors of sensory information or as propagators of neuronal signals.

There is evidence suggesting that ethanol enhances $GABA_B$ receptor activity and may inhibit NMDA receptors as well. However, the relatively massive concentration of physiologically significant levels of ethanol (in the millimolar range) is so much greater than the concentrations of the neurotransmitter agonists for these receptors (micro-, nano-, and picomolar) that it is hard to argue for a ligand-mediated role of the drug (even a tiny degree of receptor affinity by a compound in such relatively high concentration would be expected to competitively preclude normal ligand binding).

As the concentration of ethanol increases, there is a corresponding decrease in nervous system function, and indeed the dose-dependent relationship is clear, with the endpoint of an overdose being mortality. There is no "saturation" of effect, since there is no receptor- or binding-site mechanism to be saturated as concentration increases. The effective target (at concentrations below those causing functional effects on motor neurons) appears to be the *reticular activating system* in the brain, located in the subcortical neuronal system: medulla, pons, and thalamus. This system is important for maintaining consciousness, respiration, cardiac rhythm, and other essential biological processes.

Tolerance to the effects of alcohol is generally expected in experienced drinkers, and an acceptance of the idea pervades common knowledge. However, while individuals certainly can acquire an enhanced rate of elimination, based on induction of ADH, a mechanistic basis for true tolerance to the effects of alcohol has not been proposed or demonstrated (see Sidebar 12.7).

SIDEBAR 12.7 ALCOHOL TOLERANCE

Much is made of "tolerance" to alcohol. It is generally assumed that heavy drinkers or alcoholics can become tolerant to the effects of alcohol, and the phenomena of tolerance is well recognized in other drugs, so logically should also be achievable with the most popular drug in our society. Unfortunately, while tolerance for many drugs can be explained by downregulation of specific receptors, a similar mechanism cannot be offered in that there is no ethanol receptor (at least none discovered to date) nor mechanism of action linked to such a receptor. In the absence of an identifiable mechanism, the perception of tolerance can be considered through another mechanism.

One evaluation of the phenomenon is readily available through the extensive correlation of BAC readings and performance on SFSTs. While there are numerous cases of relatively poor performance on SFSTs associated with a seemingly low BAC level, this is readily understood in terms of additional drugs affecting the testing subject. What is lacking is a body of cases in which a relatively normal performance on SFSTs is matched with a BAC significantly in excess of 0.12 g/dL or higher. Considering the volume of drinking that occurs in our society and the years in which many people consume multiple drinks per week, if tolerance were a significant factor, we would expect to see evidence, as suggested above. However, the data clearly show a strong correlation between BAC and impairment of behavior as evaluated by SFSTs and other measures of performance.

What is often considered tolerance, then, may actually be simply a function of induced metabolism. We often see elimination rates in DUI arrestees well in excess of 0.04 g/dL/hr, or more than twice the rate expected in inexperienced drinkers. Consider two individuals, ~180 lbs. each and identical in all respects with the exception that one is a frequent drinker (multiple drinks/day) and the other rarely drinks. Our frequent drinker has an elimination rate (due to induction of alcohol dehydrogenase) of 0.03 g/dL/hr., our infrequent drinker, 0.02 g/dL/hr. (Hence, eliminating 1.5 v. 1 drink/hour, respectively.) Assume further that they spend 4 hours together in a bar, drinking roughly 2 drinks/hour. One might roughly estimate their BAC at the end of this time as follows: Our frequent drinker would be expected to have (roughly) a final BAC of (4 hours × 2 drinks/hour – 4 hours × 1.5 drinks/hour)* 0.02 g/dL/drink of 0.04 g/dL. Our inexperienced drinker, by the same argument, 0.08 g/dL. We would expect our experienced drinker to perform more or less "to standard" on the SFSTs, but our inexperienced drinker to provide multiple clues consistent with impairment. The glib explanation is of course tolerance, but a more reasonable biochemically based explanation for the same phenomena is simply *enzyme induction.* Similar consideration should be given to comparisons between individual of different weight, bearing in mind that the BAC consequential to a drink is inversely proportional to weight.

12.2.2.2 *Effects of Ethanol, and Correlation with Blood Alcohol Concentration*

An increasing dose of ethanol produces an increased, dose-dependent depression of neuronal function. The behavioral/physiological consequences of alcohol ingestion are primarily a reflection of that functional deficit, and there can be a generalized correlation between well-recognized consequences of alcohol and BAC. Dr. Kurt Dubowski published a table reflecting those relationships in 1970, and while slightly revised over time, the "Dubowski Table" has remained a valuable tool for understanding the relationship between alcohol concentration and expressed symptoms and behaviors.

In a simplified format, a correlation table between BAC and effects can be presented as follows:

- 0.01–0.05 g/dL: Slight impairment, perceptual and emotional effects
- 0.03–0.12 g/dL: Euphoria, decreased social inhibition, decreased emotional control, decreased judgment and cognitive function, decreased fine motor skills; start of sensory-motor impairment
- 0.09–0.25 g/dL: Emotional instability, impaired perception, decreased memory, impaired coordination, impaired cognitive function
- 0.18–0.30 g/dL: Dizziness; blurred vision; slurred speech; significant impairment of cognitive, perceptual, and related functions
- 0.35–0.5 0 + g/dl: Anesthesia, coma, possible death

The DUI criteria for blood alcohol is currently 0.08 g/dL throughout the United States. A common misconception is that an individual with a BAC less than 0.08 is not significantly impaired. This is often a serious legal question in DUI cases, when the implication may be presented that if indeed the driver in question had a BAC less than 0.08 g/dL at the time of the arrest or accident, he or she was less or not at all impaired by alcohol. Nevertheless, the effects of ethanol on the body at concentrations of less than 0.08 g/dL can indeed affect the ability of an individual to operate a motor vehicle safely, as indicated in Table 12.3.

The impact of ethanol on CNS function does not have a threshold, and therefore any alcohol affects neuronal function. At low concentrations (e.g., ~0.01 g/dL), that effect may be effectively unmeasurable, and in a practical sense without impact on the ability of an individual to control a motor vehicle. However, much of the activity of driving involves the intellectual tasks of information processing and decision making, such as identifying and reacting appropriately to risks or hazardous situations in the driving environment. The impact of low levels of alcohol may be related to driving ability in a manner suggested by the Dubowski table, with respect to effects on ability to multitask, visual function and reaction, coordination, judgment, etc. (see Sidebar 12.8).

Table 12.3 Effects of Low Levels of Ethanol on Driving Skills

Blood Alcohol Concentration (g/dL)	Drink Equivalents	Impact on Driving
0.01–0.02	~1	Diminished capability for divided attention tasks. Increased reaction time. Reduced ability to perceive and process subtle visual information.
0.02–0.03	~1+	*In addition to the above*: Diminished ability to maintain smooth tracking in the roadway.
0.03–0.04	~2	*In addition to the above*: Diminished attention and focus, diminished ability to recognize and respond to hazardous or threatening situations.
0.04–0.05	~2+	*In addition to the above*: Diminished motor skill and coordination.
0.06–0.07	~3+	*In addition to the above*: Diminished capability to perceive and process information and respond in an appropriate manner to hazardous or threatening situations.
0.08–0.09	~4+	*In addition to the above*: Diminished ability to maintain concentrated attention, inappropriate speed control.

SIDEBAR 12.8 HITTING INSIDE CURVES

One of the more common crash motifs seen in DUI cases involves a vehicle hitting the inside edge of a curve, in other words, too much turn instead of too little. While a vehicle controlled by an intoxicated driver failing to negotiate a turn is readily understandable in terms of impaired consciousness or concentration, striking the inside of a curve requires a little more explanation. If we consider ethanol as a "signal attenuator" in the nervous system, then the scenario becomes explainable. As a vehicle approaches a curve, the normally functioning brain, processing the dynamic 3-D reality, recognizes the need to respond to a curve and makes an appropriate adjustment in steering, timed to coordinate with the path of the vehicle on the road. For all of us who drive, this is an automatic, almost unconscious function. In the case of the impaired driver, either there can be a delay in the recognition that a response is required, or the initial signals for small corrections do not, because of the effects of ethanol, reach the appropriate muscles and result in turning the vehicle. There is ultimately, then, as the car progresses into the curve without the appropriate change in direction, a recognition that more drastic action is called for, resulting in a major turning effort, an overcorrection, leading into a crash on the inside edge of the curve. A similar pattern of "underreaction, overcorrection" leads to the characteristic swerving down the road or weaving behavior often exhibited by impaired drivers. (Weaving due to intoxication is quite different from the often high-speed lane changes used by some drivers in an effort to pass through traffic.)

12.2.3 Alcohol Calculations and Inferences

The characteristic *volume of distribution* (Vd) of a drug may be used to relate the amount of drug determined to be present in a blood sample, to an amount of drug introduced into the body, as discussed in Chapter 4, "Toxicokinetics." The amount of alcohol in a drink of known composition can be calculated, and with the number of drinks consumed the Vd formula can be modified to include those parameters. In so doing, instead of "amount of drug" as a variable, the volume of alcoholic beverage consumed, the alcohol concentration, and the specific gravity of ethanol are used, generating the "weight of drug," within the framework of the overall calculation. The Vd is captured in the equation in the form of r, reflecting body water volume. When modified in such a fashion, the calculation is known as the Widmark equation, named for Erik Widmark, who first published the formula in 1932.*

The limitations inherent in the use of the Vd calculation remain a factor for use regarding alcohol ingestion. Nevertheless, use of such calculations can in some cases provide useful information to facilitate an understanding of a case, such as the number of drinks that must have been ingested to produce a specific BAC or an expected BAC based on a certain number of drinks.

One of the more common scenarios dealt with regarding alcohol involves the determination of the minimum amount of alcohol ingested, in light of an analytically determined BAC. For example, consider

* The Widmark formula equates the amount of alcohol consumed in terms of the number of drinks (A) to the variables of body weight (W), a constant relating the amount of water in the body (r), blood alcohol concentration at time t(C_t), the elimination rate of alcohol (b), time period over which alcohol was ingested (t), the amount of alcohol (ounces) per drink (z), and the density of alcohol is assumed to be 0.8. Hence: $A = \frac{Wr(C_t + bt)}{0.8z}$

a 170 lb. individual who claims to have had two double shots of bourbon and three beers during a 3-hour time span at a local bar. The individual was arrested for DUI approximately half an hour following his departure from the bar. One hour after that arrest, the individual receives a breath test and exhibits a 0.18 BAC. Can the arrestee's claims be evaluated? In a simplistic, rough-estimate sense, he has indicated he ingested seven drinks in 3 hours. Assuming a normal metabolic rate, we would expect he had metabolized the equivalent of about three drinks, leaving the contribution of four drinks (at ~0.02 g/dL/drink), so we would expect a BAC of ~0.08 upon leaving the bar, and ~0.07 a half hour later. An hour later, at the time of the breath test, we would expect a result in the range of ~0.05 g/dL, suggesting that his recollection of the number of drinks he actually had might be flawed.

Using the Widmark approach, and recalling that Vd = dose/(blood conc. × body weight), we can substitute and rearrange to:

$$\text{BAC}(\text{g/L}) = \text{EtOH}(\text{g})/(\text{Vd}(\text{L/kg}) \times \text{Body Weight}(\text{kg})) - \beta(\text{elimination rate}) \times \text{time}$$

Grams of ethanol in this case will be (4 × 1 oz.) × 0.4(80 proof) + (3 × 12 oz.) × 0.05 (5%) or 3.4 ounces of ethanol. Converting to milliliters, and thence to grams, (3.4 oz. × 29.6 mL/oz.) × 0.79 g/mL = 79.5 g EtOH.

Based on an elimination rate of 0.02 g/dL, our expected BAC at the end of the 3 hours in the bar would be then = [79.5 g/(0.7 L/Kg) × (170 lb/2.2 lb/Kg)] − 3 hours × 0.02 g/dL/hr; =1.46 g/L − 0.06 g/dL; =0.146 g/dL −0.06 g/dL; =0.086 in the standard measurement units.

We would expect that level to decline (b = 0.02 g/dL/hr) to ~0.076 at the time of the arrest and be in the range of ~0.056 at the time of the breath test. In short, the explanation of amount ingested does not comport with the measured value, whether estimated or calculated.

12.2.3.1 *Back-Extrapolation*

One of the more contested aspects of forensic toxicology, as relates to ethanol ingestions, is the process of *back-extrapolation*. Basically, this consists of working from a known (or inferred) BAC to an estimate of BAC at some prior time. Such calculations can be of great significance in nearly all types of cases involving alcohol, from DUI and dram shop cases (legal actions taken against a serving establishment based on damages caused by an impaired or intoxicated patron) to suicides and homicides.

As might be expected, the quality and utility of such an estimate is dependent upon the underlying assumptions made to facilitate the process. With good information and careful consideration of important limitations on the process, back-extrapolation can yield highly reliable estimates of BAC. The key limitation is that back extrapolation cannot be extended into the distribution phase, and as such, knowledge of the pattern of alcohol ingestion (or clearly identified assumptions regarding that ingestion pattern) must be known. It is incumbent upon any individual performing back-extrapolation calculations to carefully identify and consider the underlying variables and assumptions of the case, and ensure that the resulting estimates are unbiased, valid, and reasonable. Naturally, any individual performing such calculations and making such estimates should be prepared to discuss the limitations and uncertainties of the process in general, and with regard to the specific case.

The basis for back-extrapolation is simply that for any BAC greater than 0.02 g/dL and less than 0.35 g/dL, the elimination rate tends to be essentially linear, as a function of saturation of ADH. (Aldehyde dehydrogenase has a higher turnover number than ADH, and as such, oxidation of alcohol to acetaldehyde by ADH represents the limiting step in the process.) If one knows or can make a reasonable estimate of the elimination rate of the individual in question (e.g., two sequential BACs have been determined, with a known time between the samples), the time differential between the known and the target time can be multiplied by the elimination rate, and the resulting BAC added to the known value to provide an estimate of BAC at the target time. In practice, in addition to a determination of the rate of elimination, establishment of the time range in which back-extrapolation may be performed is important. Basically, absorption and distribution must be essentially completed, and as such, 30–45 min. following completion of the last drink is a commonly used rule of thumb establishing the earliest time to which back extrapolation can be performed (see Sidebar 12.9 and Figure 12.5).

SIDEBAR 12.9 BACK-EXTRAPOLATION

Consider the following case. Mr. X, a 37-year-old, 190 lb. male, has been drinking in a bar with friends following a softball game. His arrival time was ~9:30 p.m., and according to testimony, he departed the bar at ~12:30 a.m. His claim, corroborated by his friends, was that they were drinking beer, sharing pitchers. He indicates that he may have had a shot or two during the course of the evening, but that his total consumption was five or six beers total. Mr. X ordered a cup of coffee at ~12:15. At ~12:50, while en route to his home, Mr. X failed to remain in his lane, tracking a right-hand curve, with a posted speed of 45 mph. In response to Mr. X's car crossing lanes, two cars veered off the road, sustaining damage and injuries to the occupants. Mr. X crossed back into his lane, eventually going off the road and becoming stuck in a plowed field. State police and emergency medical personnel responded to the scene within minutes. Mr. X. was evaluated at the scene and, based on his performance in SFSTs and the observations of the investigating trooper, was placed under arrest for DUI at 1:20 a.m. At 2:13 and 2:36, Mr. X provided valid breath alcohol samples, which read 0.137 and 0.128 respectively. The question is simply, what was Mr. X's BAC at the time of the crash?

Whether or not back-extrapolation to the time of the crash is legitimate, is function of whether or not Mr. X was still actively absorbing and distributing alcohol at that time. Assuming Mr. X ended drinking shortly before ordering his cup of coffee, then his alcohol ingestion would have ended more than 30 min prior to the crash, making it most likely that at the time of the crash, Mr. X was in the elimination phase, and back-extrapolation to that point would be a legitimate forensic exercise. Mr. X was eliminating ethanol at a rate of 0.023 g/dL/hr; ([{0.137–0.128}/23 min] * 60 min/hr). Back extrapolating to 12:50, from the 2:13 time point, at 0.023 g/dL/hr yields an expected BAC at 12:50 of 0.17 g/dL (([{0.023 g/dL/hr}/60 min/hr] * 83 min) + 0.137 g/dL). (It might be worth noting as well that the five or six beers would not be an adequate explanation for the 0.17 g/dL BAC anticipated at the time of the crash, but that BAC would be an adequate explanation for the failure of the driver to remain in his lane and in control of the vehicle.)

12.2.4 Alcohol and Diabetes

The ingestion of alcohol in diabetics may present a medical problem in some cases. In short, the diabetic patient is constantly attempting to balance blood glucose level between the hypo- and hyperglycemic state. The ingestion of alcohol tends to exacerbate hypoglycemia.

A hypoglycemic patient is in a state of CNS depression, and distinguishing that state from alcohol intoxication may be difficult for either law enforcement or emergency medical personnel. This can be an important process, in that insulin-induced hypoglycemia is a real medical emergency that can be fatal if untreated. Similarly, hypoglycemia is occasionally offered as an explanation for behaviors that would normally be attributed to alcohol intoxication in a legal forum. Insulin-induced hypoglycemia can be quickly addressed by provision of a sugar source but can rapidly worsen in the absence of treatment. In contrast, alcohol intoxication

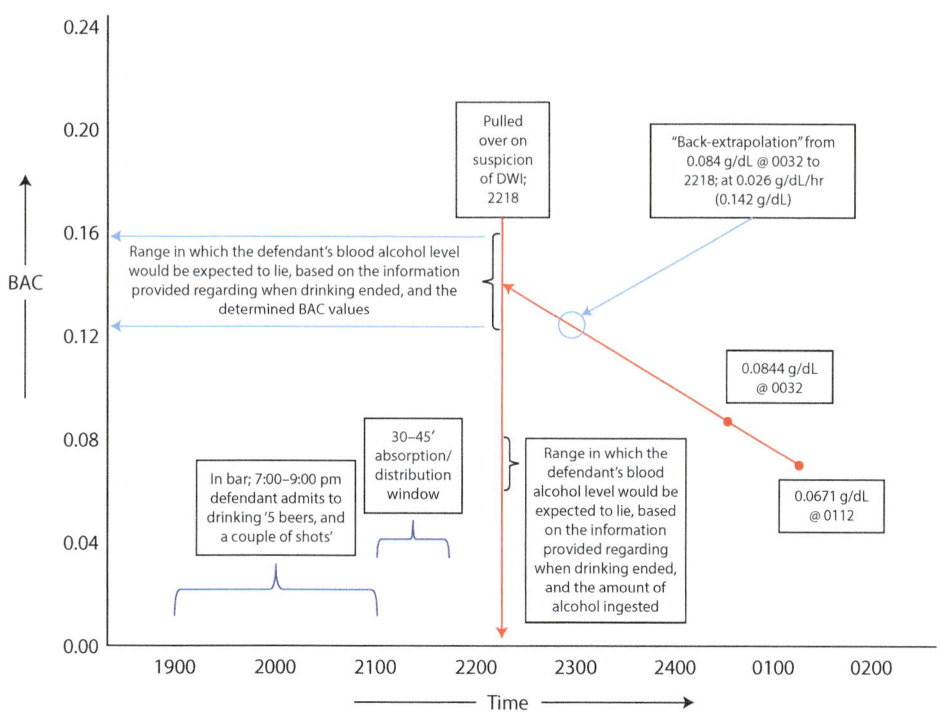

Figure 12.5 Example back-extrapolation.

progressively lessens as the body metabolizes the ethanol present.

Ethanol contributes to hypoglycemia by at least three mechanisms. The primary mechanism is a decrease in gluconeogenesis, caused as a function of the distortion of the NADH:NAD$^+$ ratio toward the reduced form, consequential to the oxidation of ethanol. The enzyme systems that play a role in gluconeogenesis are sensitive to the NADH:NAD$^+$ ratio (particularly glyceraldehyde 3-phosphate dehydrogenase and pyruvate dehydrogenase), and while the body may need the energy equivalents that would be made available by gluconeogenesis, the relative amount of NADH provides a signal to the effect that the levels are adequate and the synthetic process is inhibited.

A secondary mechanism of hypoglycemia occurs within the pancreas, a fish-shaped organ located behind the stomach, lying transversely near the midline of the abdomen. Insulin and glucagon are produced in the pancreas, and insulin release from the pancreas is enhanced to some extent by alcohol, particularly in cases of binge drinking. The mechanism by which this occurs is elusive but may be related to the action of the vagus nerve and the neurotransmitter nitrous oxide.

A third mechanism of hypoglycemia relates to nutritional deficiency. Because many chronic alcoholics do not eat a balanced diet, they may not have adequate substrates for gluconeogenesis and may have intake of complex carbohydrates inadequate to maintain their glycogen stores. Normal, healthy people with no significant medical conditions have about 24–72 hours of stored glycogen and will not experience significant hypoglycemia until they have fasted for more than a day at least. In the fasted person who drinks alcohol, there is both a lack of substrate for gluconeogenesis and impaired gluconeogenesis caused by the metabolism of alcohol.

A final complication is that at serum ethanol levels above approximately 0.1 g/dL, most people no longer recognize the symptoms of hypoglycemia. Thus, a patient with type I diabetes mellitus (an inability to produce adequate insulin in response to blood glucose levels), who usually can perceive becoming hypoglycemic, loses the ability to detect low blood sugar level and does not recognize the need to eat or otherwise get some sugar on board to correct the problem.

12.2.5 Health Effects of Chronic Ethanol Use

Alcohol dependence or alcoholism is a disease defined by the American Medical Association as a "primary chronic disease with genetic psychosocial and environmental factors influencing its development and manifestations." Alcoholism is characterized by prolonged periods of frequent or heavy drinking, the inability to control drinking once started, physical dependence manifested by withdrawal symptoms when drinking is stopped, and a variety of social and legal problems stemming from or associated with the alcohol consumption.

The chronic use of ethyl alcohol affects every organ and tissue in the body. The consequences of such use may be of relevance to the clinician and/or pathologist and may affect how the body would handle other drugs. Generally, the severity of illness is directly correlated with the extent and frequency (how much and how often) the person drinks. However, the extent to which health problems arise for any individual is a complex function of multiple factors and is not predictable based only on how much and for how long a person has been using alcohol.

Probably the most widely known and expected long-term effect of chronic drinking or alcoholism is alcoholic liver disease. This progressive expression of effects of alcohol on the liver range from accumulation of fat (steatosis), inflammation (alcoholic steatohepatitis, also called alcoholic hepatitis), and ultimately scarring and cell death (perivenular fibrosis and cirrhosis; see Chapter 9). The end stages of the disease may result in frank liver failure and death. The progression of liver damage can be more or less linear, but in practice, the findings often overlap to some degree. The status of the state of disease in the liver may be of interest to the toxicologist and the pathologist since the metabolic functions of the liver are compromised in these conditions, proportional to the severity of the disease state.

Repeated exposure to alcohol induces the synthesis of lipogenic enzymes (related to the distortion of the NADH/NAD$^+$ ratio toward the more reduced form) and inhibits triyglyceride metabolism and release of low-density lipoprotein (LDL) from hepatocytes. The net result is that abnormal amounts of lipid are stored in the hepatocytes (steatosis). This condition is noted grossly as an enlarged, greasy, pale yellow or tan-orange organ. Microscopically, lipid accumulation usually begins in the centrilobular area, because this area is less metabolically active than the more oxygenated periportal zone. The centrilobular region is less able to utilize the excess NADH produced as a consequence of ethanol oxidation. Steatosis is not unique to alcohol consumption and may be present in a variety of other conditions, including obesity, diabetes mellitus, total parenteral nutrition, and use of anticancer drugs or corticosteroids, but is nevertheless considered a risk factor for advanced, chronic liver injury. Interestingly, with regard to the alcohol-induced hepatocellular injury, two weeks to one month of abstinence can significantly reverse fatty accumulation and return the liver toward its native condition.

A fatty or steatotic liver can be further damaged by a continued pattern of ethanol consumption. The next phase involves cell death (necrosis) and acute inflammation. Grossly, the liver may look normal (firm, smooth, and red-brown) or somewhat steatotic as previously described. Microscopically, hepatocytes will contain a variable amount of lipid droplets. Groups of hepatocytes will be greatly enlarged, containing fat, water, and other accumulated products that are not exported from the cell. Necrotic hepatocytes will appear as foamy, pale cells with a very pale or absent nucleus. Necrosis triggers an inflammatory process, and a cellular infiltrate (predominately neutrophils) is often present. Inflammation generally begins in the centrilobular area, then spreads as necrosis progresses. As the necrotic regions heal, the dead hepatocytes become replaced with fibrotic scar tissue.

Clinically, jaundice can develop as bile flow is blocked and bilirubin is inappropriately released from hepatocytes into the bloodstream, causing a yellow tinge to the skin and sclerae of the eyes. Laboratory abnormalities include elevated serum bilirubin, alkaline phosphatase, and transaminase.

Fibrosis of the liver often begins with a rim of fibrous tissue around the central veins. This is also a nonspecific finding and may be seen in conditions other than alcoholic injury. Grossly, the liver may look normal or steatotic (fatty), a reflection of its microscopic appearance. Microscopically, fibrosis is evident as a pink rim (with Hematoxylin & Eosin [H&E] stain) around central veins and may be further highlighted as blue-green with special staining (Masson's trichrome). Eventually, if the hepatic degeneration continues, fibrosis will become widely spread throughout the entire organ, causing bridges of scar tissue between central veins and portal triads, which themselves become expanded by fibrosis. Clusters of hepatocytes can lose their direct connection to central veins. This extensive fibrosis is termed cirrhosis, and a liver in this condition is not capable of normal or efficient function. Such conditions require careful interpretation of drug levels in the face of compromised hepatic function.

12.2.6 Alcohol Testing

Analysis for ethanol and related volatile compounds is a relatively straightforward analytical exercise. Both screening and more definitive confirmatory approaches may be used. Endogenous alcohol, if present, is generally at such low levels as to not be a significant factor in forensic analyses (well less than 0.02 g/dL). Indirect testing for alcohol abuse is a considerably less straightforward proposition, and considerable efforts have been expended in attempting to discern a clear parameter that would correlate to routine alcohol abuse (see Sidebar 12.10).

SIDEBAR 12.10 BIOCHEMICAL MARKERS OF ALCOHOL ABUSE

Because of the extent to which regular abuse of alcohol can be a detrimental factor in a person's life, and the risk such individuals represent to society in some cases (e.g., repeat DUI offenders), there has been considerable interest in developing or identifying biochemical parameters that could be used to determine if an individual is actively abusing alcohol or is regularly exposed. (Efforts to evaluate the genetic-based susceptibility an individual may have to alcoholism is beyond the scope of this text.)

There are, of course, many difficulties with attempting to evaluate alcohol abuse. First, of course, is the fact that simply drinking alcohol is not illegal, nor is the presence of alcohol in the blood or urine of an individual a valid indicator of abuse. Further, absence of alcohol is equally without value in that regular alcoholics may still have periods in which their blood alcohol concentration is below detectable limits.

Nevertheless, several parameters have been identified as potentially providing information regarding the magnitude of alcohol use or (in the case of individuals who have agreed not to ingest) whether alcohol is being used at all. While the history and scientific underpinnings for the different approaches would be a legitimate basis for a volume of just that topic, we will, in a very cursory manner, look at several of the various approaches being evaluated and (in some cases) used. Briefly, these consist of hepatic enzymes (e.g., γ-glutamyltransferase, or GGT; aspartate aminotransferase, or AST; and alanine aminotransferase, or ALT), mean corpuscular volume (MCV), N-acetyl-β-hexosaminidase (β-Hex), and carbohydrate-deficient transferrin (CDT).

Hepatic enzymes. GGT is a glycoprotein found in both hepatocytes and biliary epithelium. GGT levels tend to be elevated in response to hepatocellular stress and damage (which can, of course, be caused by large or frequent doses of alcohol and would be seen in consequence to the progression of cirrhosis). While elevated GGT levels can be an early indicator of hepatocellular damage, the parameter is not particularly specific nor sensitive. Similarly, AST and ALT are enzymes regularly used as a measure of hepatocellular damage and lack the specificity and sensitivity that would be required to rely on such values as indicators of regular or excessive alcohol use.

Mean corpuscular volume (MCV) is simply a measure of the average size of red blood cells. Curiously, the MCV tends to be somewhat larger in heavy drinkers than the expected average value. One negative factor is the length of time MCV remains elevated following cessation of drinking (can be several months). MCV can also be affected by other variables, making the marker somewhat less specific.

N-acetyl-β-hexosaminidase (Beta-Hex), an enzyme important in ganglioside metabolism, is elevated in heavy drinkers, and levels appear to return to normal levels following a week of abstinence. Unfortunately, β-hex can be elevated with other conditions (e.g., diabetes and hypertension).

Carbohydrate-deficient transferrin (CDT) refers to an incompletely sialylated version of the glycoprotein transferrin, which functions as an iron-transport molecule in the bloodstream. CDT normally has four to six sialic acyl residues, but alcohol apparently results in transferrin with an incomplete complement of carbohydrate residues. CDT has been widely used by clinicians in recent years to screen for heavy alcohol consumption, particularly in Europe. CDT has fairly good specificity for alcohol consumption, but analysis can be difficult (specifically, differentiating between the level of transferrin sialylation). Nevertheless, CDT remains a promising area of research for a sensitive and specific marker.

Alcohol screening methodologies generally utilize an enzymatic assay and measure the rate of formation of NADH in a reaction mix containing an abundance of ADH. In these assays, the rate of formation of product (NADH) will be proportional to the amount of substrate (ethyl alcohol) present. While the rate would be expected to decline as substrate is utilized, the initial velocity of the reaction is proportional to the amount of substrate. In the assay, the initial velocity of the reaction is extrapolated from the rate of NADH formation, and the concentration of ethanol in the sample is calculated from that value. The ADH reaction is reasonably specific, and the assay is surprisingly quantitatively accurate for an enzymatic assay. Screening using enzymatic assays is the basis of nearly all hospital-based testing. The sample used in the procedure is normally serum, and there is a slight difference between serum alcohol concentration and the "whole blood" that is evaluated in a forensic setting and is often specified in DUI statutes. As the cellular constituents of the blood are precipitated or filtered during the process of separation from the serum, the alcohol that would have been uniformly distributed throughout the blood is now differentially distributed between the two components. On average, the serum contains about 1.16 times more alcohol than the whole blood, and standard forensic practice is to correct a serum value by that number to yield a whole blood value (e.g., a 0.164 g/dL serum alcohol would correspond to a 0.141 g/dL whole blood alcohol).

Since the enzymatic assay correlates the rate of production of NADH with the amount of ethanol in the sample, any competing reaction that generates NADH could conceivably be the basis for erroneous results. However, in a practical sense, the large amount of ADH used in the assay ensures that in almost all cases, any endogenous NADH generation will be negligible. (In a practical sense, true false positives in the assay are rare.) One example reaction commonly cited is the potential for the action of lactate dehydrogenase (LDH) released by tissue damage (and thereby present in the blood sample) to generate NADH as a function of generation of pyruvate from lactate. This type of false positive result would require both a significant release of LDH from the body (e.g., significant trauma) and the presence of quantities of the substrate lactate in the blood. Both conditions, if occurring, are readily demonstrable in routine clinical testing. In practice, oxidation of lactate is not a particularly satisfactory explanation for an elevated serum alcohol level but remains a possible explanation in some cases. (Invoking such an explanation requires significant justification, providing a reasonable explanation for the presence of LDH and lactate and for the absence of alcohol.)

Forensic confirmatory analysis of alcohol is almost universally performed by headspace gas chromatography. This technique has the advantage of speed, accuracy, qualitative reliability, and the ability to readily identify other related volatile compounds that may be present in the sample, such as acetone, methanol, isopropanol, and so forth. This may be of considerable utility in the event a blood or vitreous sample is submitted for analysis that has been collected after the body has been embalmed.

12.2.7 Ethanol Consideration in Postmortem Cases

The basic question for the forensic toxicologist may differ significantly between postmortem cases involving alcohol and questions of cognitive/physical impairment that may arise in DUI or DFSA cases. In the former, the ability of alcohol to serve as a respiratory/CNS depressant must be considered in light of other drugs that may be present in the decedent, and the possibility of additive effects producing a lethal combination may be relevant, depending on the case circumstances. However, alcohol-based impairment, and the crashes or accidents that result, may unfortunately also arise in postmortem casework.

The ability of alcohol to cause cognitive impairment at relatively low levels (e.g., 0.04 g/dL and up) must be recognized. Clearly, in a DUI setting, the ability to perceive, react, and respond appropriately to an evolving or developing hazardous scenario may be an important consideration in understanding both a DUI arrest and a serious or even fatal crash.

The routine pathologic consequences of alcohol use are most often a consequence of accidents and injuries caused by the impact of alcohol on the ability of affected individuals to perform tasks. The primary toxic target for chronic exposure is the liver, discussed in Section 12.2.5.

12.2.7.1 Ethanol–Drug Combinations

The combination of ethanol and other drugs presents a frequent challenge to the forensic pathologist in the effort to understand the cause and manner of death. The responsible attribution of the cause of death requires careful consideration of drugs and chemicals in a person's system, and the extent to which their combined presence may have caused or contributed to death. In the case of ethyl alcohol, a high serum or blood level alone may be enough to have caused a lethal respiratory depression. However, more often the pathologist and toxicologist must understand combined effects of alcohol and one or more other drugs. The utility of tabulated therapeutic/toxic/lethal charts or tables becomes somewhat compromised when multiple drugs, operating through a common mechanism or producing a similar physiologic response, are present.

Clinical information (when available) in combination with laboratory data can facilitate an understanding of the role an alcohol–drug mix may have played in a given case. Even knowledge of the subject's drinking history can be of good use. For example, a naïve drinker whose alcohol-metabolizing enzyme level is not induced will achieve a higher BAC in a drinking experience than would an experienced drinker ingesting the same amount of alcohol. As such, a naïve drinker may sink into respiratory depression sooner than an experienced drinker. The presence of other drugs in the blood further complicates any such evaluation, particularly if the other drugs present have CNS-depressant capability.

12.3 Methanol

Methanol, also known as wood alcohol (as opposed to grain alcohol, or ethanol), is the simplest alcohol, with only a single carbon atom (CH_3OH). Methanol is a colorless liquid, with a mild, ethanol-like odor. Poisoning may occur following ingestion of methanol-containing liquids (e.g., "solid alcohol" fuel, some forms of antifreeze, solvents, window washing fluid, denatured alcohol, or methylated spirits). Methanol can be an inadvertent contaminant in "home-brew" whiskey and has historically been incorporated as an adulterant in moonshine as a cheap means of enhancing the apparent potency of the brew. While occasionally intentionally substituted for ethanol by alcoholics, methanol is not routinely ingested as a recreational drug. In the forensic environment, methanol is most often encountered as an unintended poison.

Endogenous levels of methanol in normal, unexposed and nonintoxicated individuals are minimal (well under 1.0 mg/dL) and are unlikely to be confused with a true toxic event.

12.3.1 Pharmacokinetics

Methanol is relatively slowly metabolized in the liver by alcohol dehydrogenase (at about one-tenth the rate of the ethanol) yielding formaldehyde, which is then rapidly metabolized ($t_{1/2}$ of 1–2 minutes in the blood) to formic acid by the action of formaldehyde dehydrogenase. Ultimately, formate can be oxidized to carbon dioxide by first forming 10-formyltetrahydrofolate, at the expense of an ATP by the action of formyltetrahydrofolate synthetase. The formyl carbon is then available for a multiplicity of reactions via formyl transferases. The slow initial oxidation of methanol results in an elimination rate longer than that of ethanol (because both methanol and ethanol exhibit zero-order kinetics, half-life for these species is a concentration-dependent variable). Induction of ADH will increase the rate of elimination for both species. The prolonged rate of methanol elimination, as compared with that of ethanol, can help explain the insidious nature of symptoms in some cases.

Methanol is rapidly absorbed from the GI tract, the skin, and the lungs, readily transiting the same aquaporin channels through which ethanol travels, as well as having significant membrane solubility. The peak serum concentration following an oral ingestion generally occurs between 30 and 90 minutes after a single exposure ingestion. Methanol, like ethanol, has a low volume of distribution (0.4–0.7 L/Kg), distributing with water, and is not actively concentrated in any tissues.

12.3.2 Methanol Toxicity

Methanol is well recognized as a potent toxic agent, and is a clear exception to the rule that the toxicity of alcohols increases with molecular weight. The basis for the toxic response is not a function of the structure of the parent alcohol per se, but rather of its metabolic products, formaldehyde and formate, produced by alcohol and aldehyde dehydrogenase respectively, in a manner analogous to acetaldehyde and acetate formation from ethanol.

12.3.2.1 Toxic Mechanism

In the case of a methanol ingestion, methanol and its metabolites, formaldehyde and formate, act as CNS depressants. The formation of formic acid contributes to acidosis, and formate can act as a chemical asphyxiant at the level of the mitochondria, inhibiting cytochrome oxidase in a manner similar to cyanide, thereby leading to a cellular hypoxia.

The accumulation of formic acid is thought to be directly responsible for irreversible damage to the retina and optic nerve, producing visual impairment or blindness in affected individuals. Although the exact mechanism has not been elucidated, formic acid appears to preferentially affect the ganglionic cells in the retina of the eye. Optic nerve damage occurs as mitochondrial cytochrome oxidase function is impaired, damaging the neuron and ultimately causing breakdown of myelin. Effects on the visual cortex may occur but are secondary to the optic nerve damage. Other parts of the brain may be affected as well when the methanol exposure is severe. Death as a consequence of methanol exposure is generally a function of a combined metabolic–respiratory acidosis, as a function both of respiratory depression and formation of formic acid. As a consequence of the CNS depressant effects of the drug, respiration rate and volume progressively decline, leading to reduced elimination of CO_2 from the blood and the resulting acidosis.

12.3.2.2 Clinical Presentation

Acute methanol ingestion is similar to that of ethyl alcohol intoxication in that the patient primarily exhibits CNS depression, gastrointestinal symptoms, and headache. Patients can exhibit a variety of features ranging from impaired coordination to coma. Toxic symptoms may be somewhat delayed following ingestion, because of the time needed for the formation of metabolic products (e.g., formaldehyde and formate) and because the rate of metabolism is slow relative to ethanol. Co-ingestion of ethanol may further prolong the time required for the expression of toxicity, since ethanol exhibits a higher affinity for the enzyme than does methanol. In this way, ethanol acts as a "competitive inhibitor" of methanol oxidation and is the basis for the use of ethanol as a treatment for methanol poisoning (slowing the rate of formation of formaldehyde and formate and allowing excretion or removal of the toxic metabolites). In some cases, a methanol poisoning can be distinguished from ethanol intoxication based on the presence of a visual disturbance generally present in about 50% of poisoning patients, with reports of blurring of the visual field analogous to looking into a snowstorm. Physical examination may reveal retinal edema, optic disc atrophy, and/or focal necrosis in the brain by computed tomography. A definitive diagnosis of methanol ingestion can be made by gas chromatographic identification in the blood. Clinical laboratory analyses can reveal a wide anion gap due to the increase in an unmeasured anion (formate) in the blood and metabolic/respiratory acidosis. The minimum blood methanol level considered lethal in adults, in the absence of therapy, is ~40 mg/dL.

12.3.2.3 Treatment

Because the toxic effects of methanol ingestion are caused by the metabolites, treatment of methanol poisoning is threefold: facilitate or enhance the rapid elimination of the parent compound, reduce or prevent the formation of formaldehyde and formate, and compensate for the metabolic–respiratory acidosis. Administration of bicarbonate will often ameliorate symptoms of acidosis to some extent and minimize physiologic damage while methanol and toxic metabolites are being eliminated. The administration of ethanol or fomepizole (an ADH inhibitor), used as competitive substrates for alcohol dehydrogenase, allows for the elimination of methanol unchanged in the urine. Hemodialysis can also help to rapidly eliminate methanol from the blood prior to oxidation and also to eliminate the toxic products that have already been formed. In the alcoholic patient who may be folate deficient, administration of the vitamin can be important as a cofactor for conversion of formic acid to carbon dioxide and water.

12.3.2.4 Pathology

At autopsy, death due to methanol poisoning may have no grossly discernable features. However, focal white matter necrosis has been reported following methanol poisoning, caused by accumulation and toxic action of formic acid. One major target appears to be the putamen, a portion of the central gray matter in the cerebrum, deep within the cerebral hemispheres. (Along with the globus pallidus and the caudate nucleus, these structures are collectively called the basal ganglia and with their connections form an associated motor system termed the extrapyramidal system. The extrapyramidal system affects involuntary movement and coordination of the musculature.) The putamen may be damaged as the result of metabolic acidosis, hypoxia, or hypotension rather than as a direct effect of formic acid on this area.

Damage to the putamen (and also to the white matter of the brain) may account for the parkinsonian syndrome sometimes reported in methanol poisoning as a consequence of the cells in the substantia nigra not receiving adequate or correct transmissions.

12.3.2.5 Forensic Toxicology Considerations

Methanol is only rarely encountered in forensic toxicology cases and is very unusual (if not unheard of) in the performance-testing and preemployment worlds. Methanol can of course play a role in death cases, as either a deliberate or an accidental poison, but is readily detected by headspace gas chromatography. Methanol is a component in many of the proficiency testing panels routinely used in the forensic laboratory.

Consideration of the role methanol may have played in a death can be challenging and complex and would certainly be facilitated by any antemortem clinical information that may be available. Finally, a practical and automatic question that should arise whenever methanol is detected in a postmortem sample is the obvious, Was this sample from an embalmed body? While seemingly unlikely, such cases arise with regularity, as fluid withdrawn postembalming may indeed have a blood-like appearance (more than one laboratory has been fooled). The presence of large amounts of some combination of acetone, ethanol, isopropanol, and methanol may be considered suggestive that the sample may not be a valid indicator of antemortem ingestion.

12.4 Isopropanol

Isopropanol is one of the two possible propanol isomers (the other being 1-propanol or "n-propanol"). This short-chain alcohol with a relatively strong odor is easily obtained by the general public as it is sold as rubbing alcohol (70% by volume) and may be used for a variety of household needs. While isopropanol is used industrially, the most common cause of poisonings is from commercially available consumer products. Toxicologically, isopropanol is not uncommonly encountered in both accidental and deliberate ingestions, and such ingestions may prove fatal. Isopropanol is also a major component of embalming fluid.

12.4.1 Pharmacokinetics

Isopropanol is easily absorbed from the lungs, the gastrointestinal tract, and transdermally, and metabolized to acetone by isopropyl dehydrogenase. Unlike ethanol, there is no subsequent oxidation beyond the carbonyl level (acetone) possible. Acetone is also produced endogenously in small amounts from acetoacetate and β-hydroxybutyrate and may be present in significantly higher concentrations in cases of ketoacidosis. Acetone is readily eliminated in the urine.

12.4.2 Toxicity

An acute lethal dose of isopropanol is approximately 2 mL/kg or about 150 mL for an adult (~220 mL of the commonly available 70% formulation). Isopropanol is about two times as toxic as ethanol and causes CNS depression (with respiratory depression, respiratory acidosis and ultimately cardiovascular collapse) as its fatal mechanism. Metabolic acidosis is not a feature of isopropanol intoxication, as the metabolite is not an acidic species, (accumulation of acetone, can however, contribute to the toxic effects). Like ethanol, the precise mechanism of action of isopropanol in the central nervous system (CNS) remains uncertain, but are thought to be caused by changes in membrane fluidity and function, and possible interactions with some neurotransmitter receptors. There is a linear relationship between the molecular weight of alcohols and their sedative effects: as size increases so does the degree of CNS depression. Clinically, isopropanol ingestions present with CNS depression similar to ethanol toxicity, but some gastrointestinal symptoms may also be present.

12.5 Ethylene Glycol

Ethylene glycol is a two-carbon di-alcohol (ethane-1,2-diol; $HO-CH_2-CH_2OH$) found commonly in automobile antifreeze solutions but is also a significant synthetic industrial chemical. Ethylene glycol is a slightly viscous, slightly sweet, colorless and odorless liquid. Commercial antifreeze solutions are generally iridescent green liquids. Because of the slightly sweet taste, ethylene glycol has been the cause of many accidental and deliberate poisoning events. Ethylene glycol poisonings are not uncommonly seen in animals, either accidental, usually a consequence of a leak or spill of antifreeze, or as a deliberate poisoning effort. Ethylene glycol is analogous to methanol in that the basis for toxicity of the molecule lies not entirely with the compound itself but also in the acidic species to which it is readily metabolized.

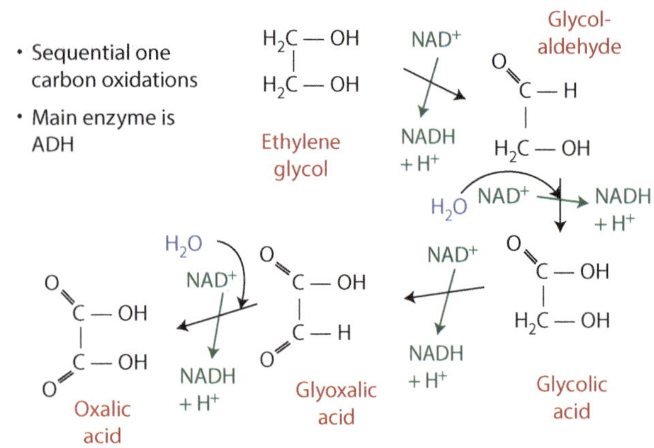

Figure 12.6 Ethylene glycol metabolism.

12.5.1 Pharmacokinetics

Ethylene glycol is water soluble and hence is readily absorbed in the GI tract following an ingestion. Like ethanol, ethylene glycol distributes in the total body water and has a volume of distribution of 0.5–0.8 L/kg. Ethylene glycol is a substrate for alcohol dehydrogenase, producing glycol-aldehyde, which may then be further oxidized to glycolic acid by aldehyde dehydrogenase. The remaining C–OH moiety may be similarly oxidized, yielding glyoxalic acid and ultimately oxalic acid, as shown in Figure 12.6. Approximately 80% of ingested ethylene glycol is oxidized, with the remainder eliminated in the urine. In contrast to ethanol, the oxidation of the aldehyde (glycoaldehyde) is the rate-limiting step.

12.5.2 Ethylene Glycol Toxicity

Ethylene glycol can cause an acutely toxic response as a function of the CNS depression caused by the parent compound and its metabolites and also due to the metabolic acidosis caused by formation of the acidic oxidative metabolites. A more insidious and delayed toxic response can occur as a consequence of the formation of oxalic acid (oxalate), which readily binds calcium to form insoluble crystals of calcium oxalate. The formation of such crystals may physically disrupt tissues (the kidneys seem particularly susceptible to such damage, as a function of the increased concentration of oxalate due to filtrate concentration and oxalate reuptake in the proximal tubule). The loss of extracellular calcium by salt formation with oxalic acid may contribute to a localized depletion, which may be of particular significance in the myocardium.

Victims of ethylene glycol poisoning will be neurologically impaired and may be comatose. Critically ill patients will have a widened anion gap, metabolic acidosis, and hyperosmolality. Many hospital laboratories do not routinely analyze blood or urine ethylene glycol, and clinicians rely on indirect laboratory findings to guide diagnosis and treatment. An easy procedure done in virtually all hospital laboratories is the microscopic inspection of a centrifuged urine sample, which may reveal the presence of calcium oxalate crystals. The presence of calcium oxalate crystals in the urine indicates that these have been formed in the blood, circulated through the kidney, and then excreted. While not diagnostic of ethylene glycol ingestion (calcium oxalate crystals may form and be present in acidic or neutral pH urine from oxalic acid in food), their presence is a strong clinical indicator, and treatment may be started before the toxicological analysis of blood is completed. Calcium oxalate crystals vary somewhat in appearance but are usually colorless and either dumbbell shaped or octahedral.

Treatment of ethylene glycol poisoning is similar to that of methanol poisoning: correct the acidosis, eliminate the parent compound, minimize the formation of toxic metabolites, and facilitate their elimination. As with methanol poisoning, the higher affinity of ethanol for ADH as compared to ethylene glycol can provide a protective window, allowing in some cases time for hemodialysis to remove the unmetabolized ethylene glycol and the opportunity to address the acidosis. In cases where substantial kidney damage is already present due to the physical consequences of oxalate crystal formation, few clinical options may be available.

An ethylene glycol dose of as little as 1 mL/kg is acutely fatal to humans, making this a potentially very dangerous material for small children. Significant toxic consequences can be realized in adults who consume even less than 1/2 cup (125 mL). The presence of polarizable crystals in the kidney is a characteristic pathologic finding (see Sidebars 12.11 and 12.12, respectively).

Autopsy examination of a person with either acute or chronic ethylene glycol poisoning is grossly benign. No characteristic findings are visible to the naked eye. Calcium oxalate crystals are too small to see without a microscope. Grossly, the kidneys do not appear unusual, except if they are affected by another disease process with grossly observable findings (e.g., hypertension, diabetes mellitus). Microscopically, there are polarizable crystals in the lumen of the tubules that may take on virtually any shape (usually dumbbell shaped or octahedral). Calcium oxalate crystals may be readily detected by the hematoxalyn and eosin stain (H&E, the typical stain used) or by polarized light microscopy; see Figures 12.7 and 12.8.

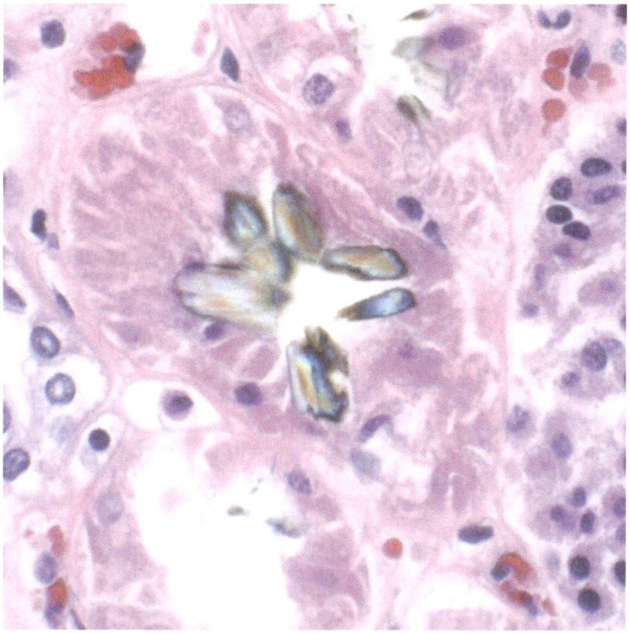

Figure 12.7 Calcium oxalate crystals in the kidney, 40×.

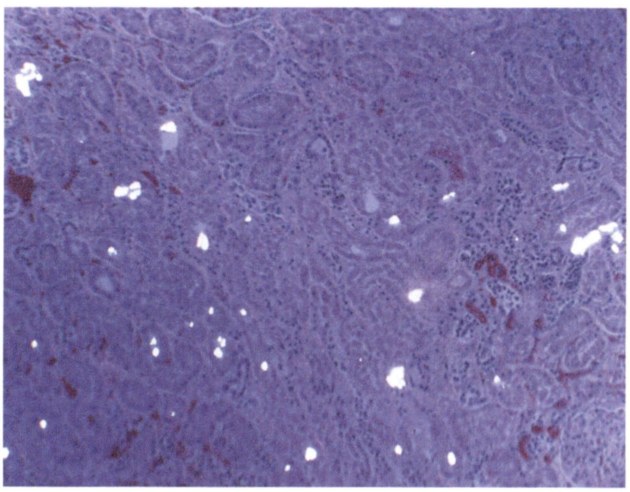

Figure 12.8 Calcium oxalate crystals in the kidney, polarized view 10×.

SIDEBAR 12.11 CASE OF ACUTE ETHYLENE GLYCOL INGESTION

A 53-year-old male with a long history of social anxiety and depression for which he had been receiving treatment was found dead in the garage of his home. Approximately one month prior to his death, his wife had left the home and filed for a divorce. The decedent had apparently gone to great lengths to disguise his suicide as an accident. Five suicide notes, written to his wife and children, had been hidden in a dresser drawer in the master bedroom but were discovered by ME investigators during scene investigation. Two empty gallon jugs of antifreeze were found in the garage but were not, however, readily observable. A vehicle was parked in front of the garage door with the hood raised and a pan beneath the front end. One of the notes stated, in part: "Tell them I was working on car and swallowed some antifreeze by accident...."

The autopsy procedure revealed a well-developed, middle-aged man (202 lbs., 91.7 kg), who looked to be in a good state of health. Several fresh abrasions were noted on one hand, knees, and forehead, presumably caused by minor impacts sustained as he became stuporous. The only other significant pathologic finding was hypertensive cardiovascular disease (heart weight 625 g, left ventricular wall thickness 2.0 cm).

Postmortem peripheral blood level of ethylene glycol was determined to be 29.8 mg/dL and ethanol was 0.028 g/dL. Calcium oxalate crystals were noted in the urine and numerous polarizable crystals observed in kidney sections. Based on the scene investigation and the postmortem blood level of ethylene glycol, the cause of death was determined to be ethylene glycol intoxication, and the manner of death, suicide.

SIDEBAR 12.12 A CHRONIC ETHYLENE GLYCOL EXPOSURE

A 40-year-old male was found dead in an easy chair at his residence by his parents during a well-being check. The decedent had complained of feeling ill for the previous few days while at work. Medical history was significant only for prior alcohol abuse.

The scene was completely benign with no signs of foul play, intoxicants, drug paraphernalia, or other forensic concerns. The decedent was not decomposed and was estimated to have died within the previous day or so. He became an ME case because of his relatively young age and lack of significant medical history.

The autopsy procedure revealed a relatively small male (65 inches tall, 112 lbs., body mass index 18.6 kg/m^2) with a heart size appropriate for his body (290 g). The lungs were markedly edematous at 1100 g combined. The most striking finding of the autopsy process was the presence of numerous polarizable crystals within the renal tubules ranging from amorphous to fan-shaped and from colorless to gray-blue to indigo. This finding prompted an analysis for ethylene glycol in blood (none detected and urine 130 mg/dL). No other volatile compounds or drugs were detected in the urine screen. The vitreous humor panel revealed an elevated glucose (153 mg/dL), a slightly elevated sodium (148 mEq/L), and a slightly elevated creatinine (1.8 mg/dL).

Further investigation revealed that the decedent had struggled with alcoholism and was thought to "do anything" to stay away from ethanol. He had apparently not consumed ethanol, at least to the knowledge of his family, in quite some time. However, a bottle of antifreeze located in his parents' garage (to which he had access) had a pinhole in the foil seal beneath the plastic top. Although no beverages were located at his apartment or in his vehicle, it was surmised that he made a little hole and poured some out over time into a beverage for his consumption. This assumption was based on the presence of urine ethylene glycol, numerous crystals in his kidneys, but no ethylene glycol detected in the blood, consistent with a series of small ingestions over time.

REVIEW QUESTIONS

1. How many standard drinks would you attribute to the ingestion of five 16 oz. beers and two shots of 80-proof liquor? (A shot is 1 oz.)
2. A 110 lb. female claims to have had three glasses of wine while at a bar for an hour or so. Her BAC, determined just after leaving the bar, is 0.082 g/dL. Is her story credible?
3. A heart blood alcohol level in a head trauma death is being challenged by an attorney, who is convinced the value represents postmortem redistribution. How do you respond?
4. An individual arrested for DUI provides two apparently legitimate breath alcohol samples, 20 min apart, the first being collected half an hour following his arrest: 0.217 and 0.211 g/210 L. The arrestee claims not to have had anything to drink for an hour prior to his arrest. Can you back-extrapolate to the time of arrest? If so, what would you conclude? If not, why not?
5. Which chemical would be more dangerous around small children, methanol or ethylene glycol? Why?
6. How could the two-sample approach to urine alcohol testing overestimate the true BAC? Could it underestimate the true BAC? If so, how?

TOPICS FOR DISCUSSION

1. In your opinion (and not in a legal sense), is operating a motor vehicle with a BAC of 0.06 g/dL impaired driving?
2. In a legal sense, what should the limit for DUI be?
3. Should urine alcohol testing results be admissible in DUI cases? If so, with what (if any) qualifications, criteria, or limitations?
4. What additional tests (if any) should be added to the standardized field sobriety tests (walk and turn, one leg stand, horizontal gaze nystagmus)?
5. What effects would you expect an acute ethylene glycol ingestion to have on the heart, assuming the CNS depression and metabolic and respiratory acidosis has been compensated for?

Bibliography

Fenton JJ. *The Laboratory and the Poisoned Patient, A Guidebook for Interpreting Laboratory Data.* Washington, DC: American Association for Clinical Chemistry, 1998.

Fenton JJ. *Toxicology: A Case Oriented Approach.* New York: CRC Press, 2002.

Garriott J, editor. *Garriot's Medicolegal Aspects of Alcohol.* 5th rev. ed. Tucson, AZ: Lawyers and Judges Publishing, 2008.

Schuckit MA. Ethanol and methanol. In: Brunton LL, editor. *Goodman and Gilman's The Pharmacological Basis of Therapeutics.* 12th rev. ed. New York: McGraw Hill Medical, 2011.

Widmark EMP. *Principles and Application of Medicolegal Alcohol Determination* (Translation of 1932 edition). Davis, CA: Biomedical Publications, 1981.

Opiates and Opioids

13

Contents

13.1 Introduction

The opiates are a group of structurally related, potent narcotic/analgesic and euphorogenic compounds, typified by morphine. Opiates have been used as both medicinal and recreational drugs for many centuries and continue to be extensively used throughout the world. Morphine has been and remains the standard by which the potency of medicinal analgesics are measured. Morphine is also unfortunately (in the form of its di-acetyl analog, heroin) the standard by which addictive and euphorogenic drug abuse is also commonly measured. (In recent years, however, methamphetamine and related compounds seem to be providing significant competition for that dubious honor.) Opiates and related drugs are perhaps the most common drug type the forensic toxicologist is called upon to deal with in explaining drug-related deaths, and shares with ethanol a long history of medicinal and recreational use (see Sidebar 13.1).

SIDEBAR 13.1 ROUTES OF ILLICIT DRUG ADMINISTRATION

It is not common that the manner in which a drug has been brought into the system is of forensic interest; however, such questions do occasionally arise. Although the methods of drug use (e.g., ingestion, inhalation, injection) are not limited to the opioids, because of the long history of this group and the variety of both legal and illicit preparations, a wide variety of usage schemes have been, currently are, and doubtless will continue to be demonstrated with the various opioids. While the various means and mechanisms of injection (and injection sites) are well known, the availability of opioids in pill and patch form has resulted in some novel drug use systems.

In some cases the question of how a particular amount of a drug could have gotten into a patient or decedent can be extremely important when the suggestion is that a dose or dose regime was inappropriate for a patient or medical situation (leading perhaps to civil or even criminal legal issues). The first question in such situations is often, how reliable is the drug quantitation information, recognizing that postmortem drug levels may not be truly reflective of antemortem concentrations. However, if there is reason to accept the validity of the postmortem drug results (e.g., levels are consistent with symptomology, antemortem levels or multiple determinations from various collections are internally consistent), then developing a reasonable explanation for how the necessary amount of drug got "on board" may be important.

Transdermal patches have been used for motion sickness (scopolamine), smoking cessation (nicotine), and analgesia (morphine, fentanyl, etc.). The rate of transfer of drug from a patch can be enhanced by heat, and abusers (whether of licit patches or not) will occasionally place a heating pad over a patch or patches in order to enhance the initial drug level and hence the associated high. Multiple patches can be used at a single time, thereby increasing the effective dose brought on board, and the contents of the patches can be removed and ingested or injected. (Whole or partial patches have been ingested as well. Ironically, removal of the contents of a patch to increase the availability of the dose is somewhat counteracted by ingestion, with the first-pass metabolism that would then occur in the liver.)

Pills or tablets may be crushed, suspended in an aqueous medium, and subsequently inhaled or injected. Either practice can leave identifiable particles in the lungs, providing indication of drug abuse. Similarly, multiple patches or injection sites can provide information to the effect that an abuse situation is being considered.

Morphine is a nitrogen-containing basic drug isolated from the opium poppy (*Papaver somniferum*) and defines the group of opiate functional and structural analogs with such well-recognized examples as codeine, hydrocodone, oxycodone, fentanyl, methadone, and meperidine. Naturally occurring structural analogs of morphine that possess similar biological activity are called the *opiates*, while *opioids* refers to all compounds that are able to function in whole or in a manner similar to morphine, regardless of structural similarity or lack thereof. (Thus, morphine is an opiate, hydrocodone is a semisynthetic opiate, and fentanyl is an opioid.)

Interpretation of toxicologic findings involving these compounds can be a challenging task, made more complicated by the variability of sensitivity of individuals to the opioids (a function of both their genetically related expression of receptors and development of tolerance with prolonged use). Such variability of sensitivity to the effects of the opioids also complicates the prescription process, in that a therapeutic level for one individual may be toxic in another, and the dose that was adequate for pain relief in a naïve user can become less effective or inadequate as tolerance develops. For this reason, opioid levels are generally not evaluated by therapeutic drug monitoring (TDM; the monitoring of drug levels in blood and adjustment of dose to achieve a targeted steady-state concentration range), despite the ready availability of relatively fast and accurate quantitative analytical procedures. Rather, opioid doses are adjusted to the individual patient (*titrated*) so as to achieve a requisite level of analgesia, while hopefully avoiding an unacceptable degree of side effects or potential for abuse. Further complicating the understanding and interpretation of opioid results for the forensic toxicologist and pathologist may be the presence of other drugs, both recreational and medicinal, as well as enterohepatic circulation and, of course in death cases, postmortem redistribution.

13.2 History

The opiates have a long and complex history. From the use of the poppy plant itself in the earliest days of recorded history as a medicinal and religious herb (and recreational drug), to the design of specific drugs based on three-dimensional receptor modeling, this family of drugs has played a significant role in Eastern and Western societies. With perhaps the sole exception of ethyl alcohol, or perhaps the penicillin-based antibiotics, one is hard pressed to identify a drug or family of drugs that have had a larger impact on human history.

Opium poppy cultivation, and use of the plant for medicinal and other purposes, dates back at least to the Sumerian culture in Mesopotamia, thousands of years BC. It has been suggested that opium use then spread to other cultures of the eastern Mediterranean region, and thence further east to India and China. Eventually, opium figured in folk medicine throughout the ancient world, including regions to the west of Greece. The word *opium* comes from the Greek word for juice, and it is the "juice" of the poppy plant (seed pod) from which morphine is derived. Opium played a significant role in Arabic medicine and was a factor in Arab-Indian/Chinese trade ~900 AD, and shortly thereafter was available to some degree in all parts of Europe. Ultimately, the opium trade became a significant commercial enterprise, leading to two wars between England and China and resulting in major economic and territorial concessions to the British. The active ingredient in opium was crudely isolated in 1806 by Sertürner and named *morphine* after Morpheus, the Greek god of dreams.

Efforts to develop a synthetic substitute for the anticholinergic atropine led to the discovery that meperidine was effective as an opiate analgesic, despite an apparent lack of structural similarity. Methadone, another functional (but not structural) analog, was discovered in 1946. Methadone was also discovered to be effective in ameliorating heroin or morphine withdrawal (with appropriate control of dose) and since that time has been extensively used as a treatment for morphine addiction. In recent years, methadone has seen increasing use as an analgesic for treatment of chronic pain.

One of the more interesting morphine analogs to be synthesized was N-allylnormorphine, or *nalorphine*, which, despite its structural similarity to morphine, could effectively reverse opiate-induced respiratory depression but also did have some analgesic capability itself, and was later recognized to be a *mixed agonist-antagonist*. Subsequently, pure antagonists, such as naloxone, were developed and remain in use today as first-line treatment for presumed opioid overdose.

The mechanism of action of morphine and related compounds were the subject of considerable research interest, and in the mid-1960s a specific opiate receptor was proposed as the basis for the actions of the drugs on the body. Shortly thereafter, opiate binding sites were identified in the CNS, and were further found to be differentially distributed. The presence of such receptors prompted the hypothesis of specific endogenous ligands and, ultimately then, the discovery of multiple such compounds, the enkephalins, endorphins, dynorphins, and endomorphins. Each family of endogenous opioids is derived from a specific protein, serving as a precursor for the group. Posttranslational modifications of the precursor peptides results in the production of the active species. The production of the opioid peptides occurs in specific locations, associated with specific neuron types. Interestingly, while markedly different in size and shape from morphine, the activity of the endogenous opioids can be reversed by opiate antagonists such as naloxone.

13.3 Chemistry

13.3.1 Morphine and Structural Analogs

Morphine is a substituted benzylisoquinoline alkaloid with a bridging bond and an ether linkage forming a fairly rigid five-ring structure. There are three active sites on the molecule, a tertiary amine and two hydroxyl groups (Figure 13.1). While morphine is the archetypal opiate molecule, structural modification can produce compounds of significantly greater agonist potential than morphine itself, for example, hydromorphone and etorphine. A great number of morphine functional analogs have been produced for the medicinal market, with varying degrees of strength, some hundreds of times more potent than morphine itself. Powerful antagonists have also been identified (e.g., naloxone, naltrexone, and nalorphine; see Table 13.1).

Morphine, as either a free base or hydrate, is only sparingly soluble in water, and as such, pharmaceutical preparations are usually formulated as hydrochloride or sulfate salts, although tartrate and citrate forms are not uncommon as well.

13.4 Pharmacokinetics

The pharmacokinetics of the opiates and their structural analogs are predictably determined by the facility with

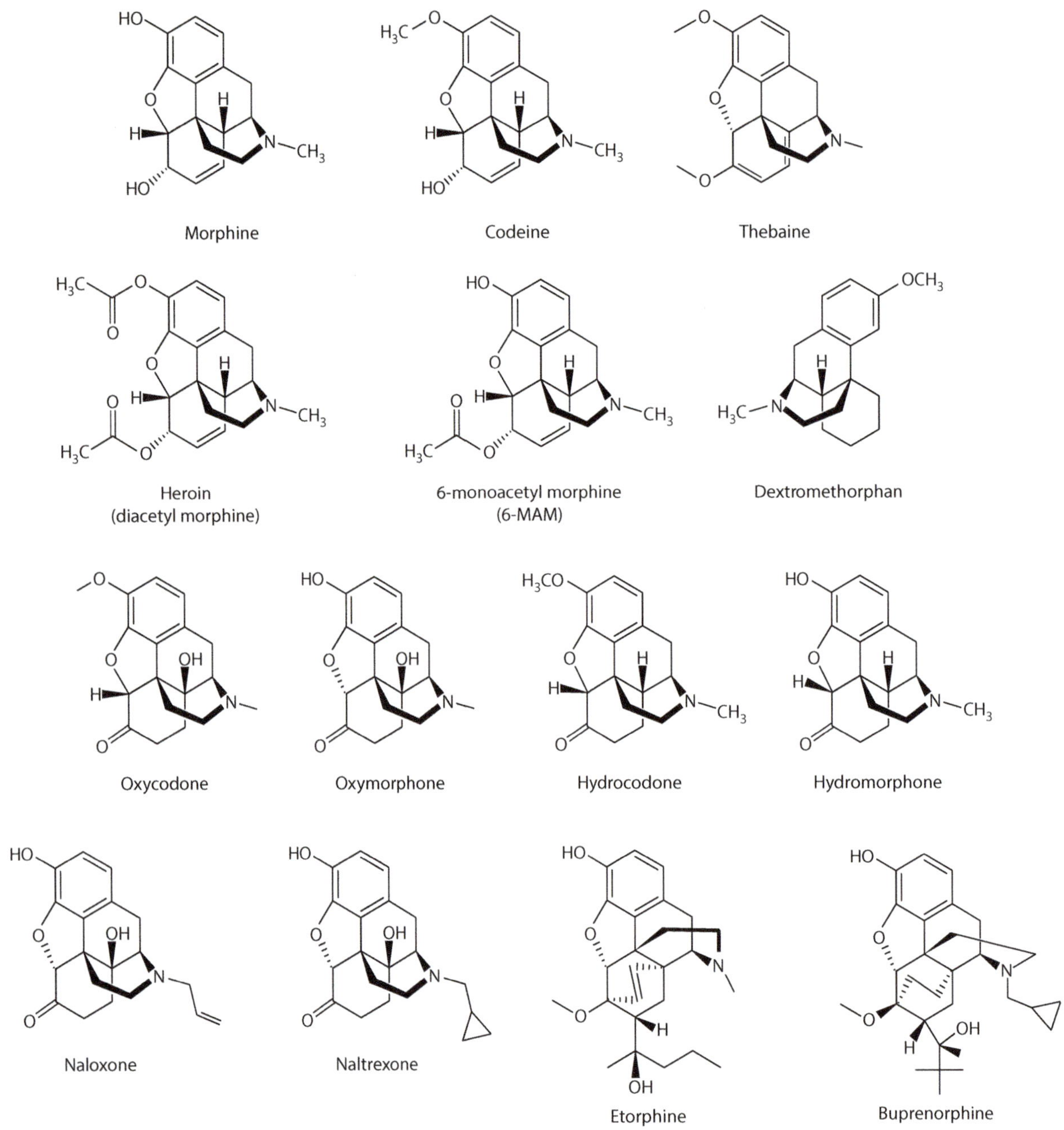

Figure 13.1 Morphine and related compounds.

which they undergo the transformations of morphine, specifically formation of glucuonides, and their susceptibility to phase I reactions. Opiate functional analogs must be evaluated on their own unique structure and therefore their susceptibility to both phase I and phase II metabolic transformations.

13.4.1 Absorption/Distribution

Morphine and the opiates are available for medical purposes in a wide variety of delivery systems, including oral, injectable, and transdermal. Delivery of opiates in a recreational or abuse setting is generally via injection or inhalation so as to avoid the loss of the active species associated with first-pass metabolism. The facility with which morphine is inactivated by the liver is impressive—only 40%–50% of an oral dose survives to reach the body. By any injection route, the time to C_{max} is relatively similar, with plasma morphine levels at their maximum in minutes. In contrast, the time to C_{max} from an oral administration is generally around 30 min.

13.4.2 Metabolism

Morphine is a substrate for phase II metabolism, via conjugation with glucuronic acid at primarily the 3-position

Table 13.1 Morphine Equivalent Dose

Analgesic	Dose Equivalent to 10 mg Morphine
D-Propoxyphene	130–200 mg
Codeine	100 mg
Tramadol	100 mg
Dihydrocodeine	50 mg
Meperidine	28 mg
Hydrocodone	10 mg
Pentazocine	10 mg (6.7–13.3 mg)
Morphine (oral)	(10 mg)
Oxycodone	5.0 mg
Morphine (IV/IM)	3.33 mg
Methadone (acute)	2.5–3.33 mg
Heroin; (IV/IM)	2–2.5 mg
Hydromorphone	2 mg
Oxymorphone	3.33 mg
Methadone (chronic)	1.35 mg
Levorphanol	1.3 mg
Buprenorphine	0.25 mg
Fentanyl	0.1–0.2 mg
Sufentanil	10–20 µg

with a much smaller percentage of morphine-6-glucuronide also formed. Both are the consequence of the action of UDP-morphine glucuronosyl transferases. Interestingly, while morphine-3-glucuronide (M3G) is without pharmacologic effect, its 6-analog (M6G) is able to bind to opiate receptors and is roughly half as potent as morphine itself. While morphine is not a significant substrate for phase I metabolism, a number of other opiates are, with a correspondingly complex pattern of metabolites formed and available for determination in forensic samples.

13.4.3 Elimination

Opiate elimination is somewhat different from many of the drugs the forensic toxicologist normally deals with, in that while urine is the primary mechanism of elimination (roughly 90% of a morphine dose is eliminated via the urine within 3 days of ingestion). An alternate parallel route is across the hepatocyte:biliary membrane, with ultimate elimination in the feces. Depending on the amount and nature of the gut microbiological contents, there may be a significant amount of enzymatic-catalyzed hydrolysis of the glucuronides, with subsequent release and resorption of the aglycone in the intestine. This enterohepatic circulation (discussed in Chapter 9) may comprise a major contributory mechanism to the levels of the morphine (or other aglycone) in the blood. Consideration of enterohepatic circulation is a routine factor for clinical toxicologists and treating physicians, since unanticipated contributions to circulating morphine levels may represent the difference between a therapeutic and a potentially toxic dose.

13.5 Mechanism of Action (Receptor, Mechanism at the Molecular Level)

At the molecular level, opiates and their analogs act on specific opiate receptors. These receptors are metabotropic, G-protein coupled systems and are found throughout the nervous system and GI tract, although the concentration is in the brain stem and cerebral cortex. The opiate receptors function in the dopaminergic reward and afferent nociceptive (pain) pathways and in the brain stem. The primary opiate receptors are the mu, delta, and kappa (μ, δ, and κ), with a *nociceptin receptor* part of the group in a sense, but generally insensitive to morphine and structural analogs (see Table 13.2).

Opiate agonists act as mimics of a group of endogenous peptide biomolecules, the endorphins (the name derived from *endogenous morphines*), which with related molecules (the enkephalins, dynorphins, and

Table 13.2 Physical Location of Opioid Receptors and Their Actions

Receptor	Locations	Actions
Mu	Brain	Analgesia
	Brainstem	Euphoria
	Spinal cord	Respiratory depression
	Peripheral sensory neurons	Miosis
	Intestinal tract (myenteric and submucosal plexi)	Reduced GI motility
		Nausea and vomiting
	Bladder wall	Urinary retention
	Peripheral nerves	Reduction of pancreatic and intestinal secretions
Kappa	Brain	Analgesia
	Spinal cord	Sedation
	Peripheral sensory neurons	Miosis
	Myenteric plexus of GI tract	Inhibition of ADH release
	Peripheral nerves	Dysphoria
		Delayed GI transit time
		Gastric stasis
		Reduction of pancreatic and intestinal secretions
Delta	Brain	Analgesia
	Peripheral sensory neurons	Antidepressant effects
	Myenteric plexus of GI tract	Delayed GI transit time
	Peripheral nerves	Reduction of pancreatic and intestinal secretions

endomorphins) act as natural agonists of the morphine receptors. Morphine and structurally related compounds are three-dimensionally similar; morphine functional analogs that are structurally dissimilar (e.g., methadone, fentanyl) are nevertheless able to assume a conformational orientation that allows binding to the active site of the receptor. Morphine acts as a strong receptor of the μ, and weak at δ and κ subtypes. Functionally, the receptors inhibit presynaptic inhibitory neurons by limiting calcium influx (thereby limiting inhibitory neurotransmitter release) and facilitating potassium efflux (thereby contributing to hyperpolarization).

13.5.1 Effect on the Nociceptive Response

The *nociceptive pathway* is the mechanism by which pain information is transferred from sensory pain receptors to the brain. The normal mechanistic action of the endogenous opioids is to act as agonists for presynaptic receptors, which inhibit Ca^{+2} influx in response to depolarization, thereby decreasing the magnitude of release of excitatory neurotransmitter, and hence, the nociceptive response. Postsynaptic agonism results in the activation of K^+ channels, allowing potassium efflux, thereby hyperpolarizing the membrane and making it less reactive to NT activation. The net effect is a diminution of the afferent (incoming) signal, and hence, analgesia. In the peripheral nervous system (PNS), opiate agonists result in a reduction in the release of a tachykinin neuropeptide, substance P (an 11 amino acid polypeptide), which functions as part of the excitatory neurotransmitter response to pain stimulation (Figure 13.2).

13.6 Physiological Effects

13.6.1 Analgesia

The primary medical uses for morphine and its analogs is for the relief of pain. Morphine has long been considered one of the most, if not *the* most, effective analgesic agents available (short of true anesthesia). Synthetic opiate agonists with considerably higher receptor affinities than morphine have been identified and have supplanted morphine as the most effective drug in the class (e.g., fentanyl, sufentanil, and related molecules).

13.6.2 Euphoria

It is nearly impossible to overstate the effect that the ability of opioids to elicit a euphoric response in abusers has had on lives in specific, and society in general, for thousands of years. The effect appears to be related to the activation of the dopaminergic reward system in the brain as a function of agonism of opiate receptors. Extensive efforts to parse out the analgesic effect from the euphoric effect have, so far, been unsuccessful. (An early effort in this area, named for its expected success, was the diacetyl derivative of morphine, called "heroic drug," or heroin for short.)

13.6.3 Respiratory Depression

Opioids act as both CNS depressants in the brain in general and as respiratory depressants through μ receptors located in the brain stem. In addition, opiates reduce the sensitivity of respiratory neurons to CO_2, thereby facilitating the downward spiral of depressed respiration,

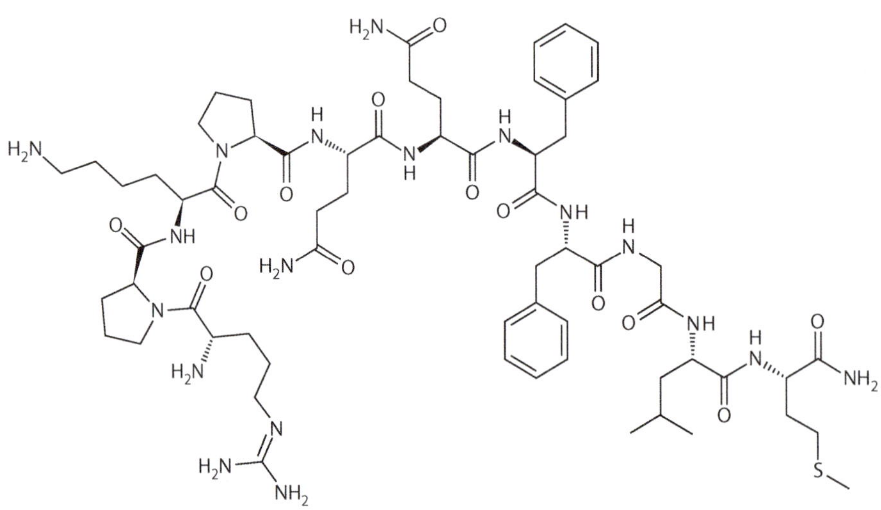

Figure 13.2 Substance P.

increased acidosis (see Sidebar 13.2), and biochemical stress that can ultimately lead to death.

SIDEBAR 13.2 RESPIRATORY ACIDOSIS

The respiratory depression associated with opiate overdose or toxicity can be a significant factor in causing or contributing to eventual death. A depressed respiratory rate is associated with a lowered blood pH, as a function of reduced elimination of CO_2, and the corresponding increase in the blood of bicarbonate and carbonate ions, with the release of their associated protons (see Section 11.4.1.1). The normal range for blood pH is ~7.35–7.45, and excursions into either the basic or acidic side can have devastating metabolic consequences.

From a toxicologic perspective, respiratory depression leading to respiratory acidosis, coupled with pulmonary edema in the lung accompanying the bradycardia associated with the opiates, provides some signposts supportive of, or calling into question, an assumption of opiate toxicity based on determined or inferred levels. In short, if an opioid overdose has occurred, one expects the physiological consequences expressed in terms of progressively slower and shallow breathing, unconsciousness, and eventual cardiac arrest, coupled with pronounced pulmonary edema. In some cases, an extensive collection of clinical chemistry parameters and data may be available to corroborate the circumstances surrounding the death. In some cases, there may be only pathological observation, in which case one expects in such a death edematous, heavy lungs.

Opioid overdose cases, often suggested because of an inappropriate interpretation of an opiate level from a postmortem heart blood sample (perhaps reflective of some degree of postmortem redistribution [PMR]), should prompt the toxicologist to look for corroboration in the clinical or pathological information prior to reaching the conclusion that an apparently elevated opiate level is necessarily the best explanation for death. It may well be so, but thoughtful, critical review can often be of great benefit.

13.6.4 Intestinal Motility

Agonism of opioid receptors located in the intestines can slow paristalysis, reducing intestinal motility and resulting in constipation. (The reduced motility causes delayed transit time, allowing more opportunity for water resorption, allowing the stool to become more solid.) Additionally, action on the intestinal μ receptors alleviates pain and spasm of the intestines that can be associated with diarrheal diseases. Opiates can be effective in the management of diarrhea in patients with chronic intestinal problems such as Crohn's disease and irritable bowel syndrome. A small dose of loperamide (a synthetic opiate agonist, not active in the CNS*) after watery stools is often sufficient to achieve normal bowel function.

13.6.5 Cardiovascular Effects

Overdose of opiates produces bradycardia and hypotension, which in combination with the respiratory depression noted above and the resulting acidosis can contribute to an opiate-mediated death. The process is not necessarily very quick, and in a hospital setting the pattern of depressed respiration and other clinical signs of opioid overdose may actually be clearly reflected in charted parameters, for example, blood pressure and respiration rate.

In contrast to the slow, downward spiral of respiration characterizing an opioid overdose, a well-recognized phenomenon in the postmortem community is heroin overdose in which the victim is found, quite literally, with a needle still in place in a vein. In such cases, a bolus dose of the drug has reached the right atria of the heart and resulted in a rapid death, via a mechanism distinct from the more common respiratory depression process. The exact mechanism of effect on the heart has not been identified, but is perhaps based on an electrical disturbance of cardiac rhythm. (As an aside, and in exception to the general rule, in such cases cardiac blood might very well be one of the better specimens for toxicologic examination.)

13.6.6 Miosis

Opiate agonists cause a contraction of the iris, producing pinpoint pupils, or *miosis*. Interestingly, this response is not diminished despite the development of tolerance to opiate effects elsewhere in the body. While shared with the cholinergic toxidrome, miosis is a key physiological clue to the presence of opioids, in both a clinical setting

* Loperamide does not effectively cross the blood–brain barrier, as it is a substrate for the action of P-glycoprotein, a member of the ATP-binding cassette family of transmembrane drug transporters, acting to remove foreign substances from cells. As might be expected, administration of loperamide with the P-glycoprotein inhibitor quinidine results in respiratory depression, typical of mu-receptor agonists, but not normally associated with loperamide.

and in assessment of suspected DUI arrestees by practitioners of the Drug Recognition Expert program.

13.6.7 Cough Suppression

The anticough (antitussive) ability of the opiates has long been recognized, although interestingly enough, these effects are probably not mediated through the μ, κ, Δ receptors. Codeine and dextromethorphan seem to be the more effective antitussive agents and are definitely not on the same scale for analgesic or euphorgenic potential with morphine.

13.7 Opiate/Opioid Toxicity

The toxicity of the opioids is, from a toxicogic perspective, twofold. First, consequential to the CNS depressant effects are impacts on driving and control of machinery or ability to function safely in a potentially hazardous environment. "Drugged driving" is increasingly recognized as having an impact on road safety, and law enforcement personnel are attuned to the potential for a DUI to actually be a function of drugs rather than alcohol. Second, there is the combination of CNS depressant effects, with the potential for respiratory depression and acidosis, leading ultimately to a terminal cardiac/respiratory arrest.

13.7.1 Toxic Mechanism

The usual cause of death in the opioid-overdosed patient is centrally mediated respiratory depression. The respiratory depression results not only in an impact on the availability of oxygen to tissues but also a respiratory acidosis. Ultimately, the combination of anoxia and ionic imbalance produces a terminal cardiac event. The patient slips into a coma, does not struggle (as would a patient experiencing an asthma attack), and dies. First responders may observe a colorless, white or blood-tinged cone of foam at the mouth, reflective of extensive pulmonary edema. Sometimes the foam cone does not appear until the body has been moved, allowing the mixing of air and liquid blood. Very rarely, the cause of death is bowel obstruction with ensuing rupture, peritonitis, and sepsis.

13.7.2 Clinical Presentation

The opioid-intoxicated patient has symptoms related to the physiologic effects, the most clinically significant being respiratory and CNS depression. Patients can exhibit a range of symptoms from euphoria through sedation to unconsciousness and deep coma, which can lead to death. Noncardiogenic pulmonary edema is classically present in cases of opiate overdose. Clinical and laboratory findings (depending on the state of intoxication) can show depressed respiratory rate and volume, low oxygen saturation, depressed cardiac rate, and acidosis. Urinary retention is also often a problem, and patients who cannot urinate must often be catheterized to relieve the distended bladder. (Opioids cause both a reduced sensation of bladder fullness and an increased tone of the bladder sphincter, making voiding difficult.) In fatal overdose cases the bladder may be greatly distended, with as much as 1000 mL of urine. Chronic opioid users generally have diminished intestinal function, but with some ability to resorb water. Therefore, the living patient is constipated and the deceased patient has very firm to rock-hard stool throughout the length of the colon. The contents of the small intestine are in the usual semiliquid form. Pupillary constriction combined with depressed consciousness and respirations is suggestive of an opioid toxidrome, and reversal of symptoms with a specific opiate antagonist (discussed below) is diagnostic.

13.7.3 Treatment

In comatose patients, supportive care with intubation allows medical control of respiration until the opiate is metabolized. A very elegant and effective treatment for overdose is the pure opiate antagonist naloxone (Narcan), administered intravenously. Its onset of action is only 1–2 minutes, but its half-life is short (approximately 1 hour); therefore a patient may need repeated doses until spontaneous respiration is restored. Naltrexone (Trexan) is an oral opiate antagonist with a much longer duration of action but may only be administered when the patient is not at risk for respiratory depression and aspiration of gastric contents. Overdose patients who are otherwise healthy will usually recover with adequate and timely therapy.

13.7.4 Withdrawal

Addiction to a number of psychotropically active drugs (e.g., morphine, cocaine, amphetamines, ethanol) can produce unpleasant symptoms when availability of the drug is restricted or terminated. However, the archetypal drug for withdrawal syndromes remains morphine, either as morphine proper, heroin, or opium in various forms. Addictive agents cause a physical dependence, in the sense that to at least some extent, use of the drug prevents withdrawal symptoms. Mild withdrawal symptoms may be expressed in some individuals having received opiates for analgesia. Withdrawal symptoms may include anxiety and agitation, aching muscles, cramps, diarrhea, nausea, and vomiting. While the withdrawal process can be very uncomfortable, it is not usually life threatening (although the fluid and electrolyte loss may be serious, and vomiting carries a risk of aspiration or asphyxiation). Expression of withdrawal can be most severe following a sudden complete cessation of availability, following a prolonged pattern of use (referred to as going cold turkey).

13.7.5 Postmortem Considerations

Cases in which opioids may have played a significant role in death can present some of the more interesting problems for toxicologists and forensic pathologists. Challenges can include *polypharmacy* cases with multiple medications, mixtures of prescribed and abused drugs, and drugs that can be difficult to identify and quantitate because of the low concentration in which they may be present (e.g., sufentanil). Postmortem redistribution is often a factor, and opiate concentrations in postmortem heart or central blood samples are not uncommonly misinterpreted as necessarily reflecting antemortem overdose concentrations. Interpreting the role that opiates may have played in deaths of elderly, very young, or patients that had significant natural disease can be particularly problematic (recognizing that literature reports of drug levels associated with toxicity in adults may be misleading with regard to the young or people with potentially compromised drug metabolism or elimination).

Some opioid overdose cases can be quite straightforward, as in that of an apparent drug abuser found shortly after death with a syringe and drug paraphernalia present. In the absence of anatomic disease and with toxicologic findings of morphine and 6-monoacetyl morphine (6-MAM; a metabolite of heroin not formed from morphine) in postmortem peripheral blood, the case would most likely be certified as an accidental, from heroin use.

Tolerance can be an additional confounding factor for interpretation, particularly in patients being treated for chronic pain. Occasionally, people who suffer from chronic pain from cancer or musculoskeletal derangement, especially those people who have been in a hospice program, come to the attention of the medical examiner. Such patients may have been taking one or more opioids for a time adequate to have developed physical tolerance to the drug(s). These patients require increasing amounts of drug to maintain a good quality of life and to function normally. Fairly large concentrations of morphine and other opiates may be provided to hospice or other patients in terminal or near-terminal status (even in such settings, dose levels are normally adjusted or provided on an as-needed basis so as to achieve a balance between the desired level of analgesia while keeping side effects to an acceptable level). Consequently, unlike antiseizure medication, there will usually be no antemortem blood level to which the postmortem level may be compared ("usually," because if the patient had been hospitalized just prior to death, a hospital sample drawn for other purposes may be salvaged and analyzed to resolve dose questions). Forensic practitioners should use considerable caution in evaluating hospice and high-dose analgesia patients.

Levels of opiates that may reasonably be considered therapeutic may still cause or contribute to death. Consider an elderly person with chronic obstructive pulmonary disease, sleep apnea, and osteoarthritis, who may require only a small dose of opiate to function normally and ambulate well. Should the patient take more of a prescribed medication for a new injury, or should there be a change in the metabolism or elimination rate of the drug, there may be an increase in blood concentrations sufficient to affect respiration and be a contributing factor in death. In any case, simple quantitative results will not, in many cases, provide an adequate basis for the determination of the role or lack thereof, that an opiate may have played in the cause and manner of death.

In some cases, the postmortem blood level of an opioid can be very low, or even undetectable, but the person clearly died as a consequence of opioid toxicity. In the case of a person who took or was given an overdose and then became comatose and died after a prolonged period, allowing for metabolism and elimination of the drug, there may simply be no drug on board to detect analytically. The physiologic sequence is straightforward—drug use, respiratory depression, coma, delayed death—but the problem is simply that the causative agent has been eliminated by the normal metabolic processes of the body. The pathologic consequences of this sequence of events are usually obvious at autopsy. If hospitalized, the patient will have received medical therapy including ventilator support of respiration, leading to what has been somewhat crudely named "respirator brain." The brain is swollen and extremely soft as a consequence of cerebral edema. The edema in such cases is not the result of the respirator use per se, but rather the brain's attempt to call in more oxygen after the hypoxic/anoxic insult of overdose. Other complications may be evident at autopsy, such as pressure-induced myoglobinemia from rhabdomyolysis (muscle breakdown) due to the maintenance of the person in one position for a prolonged time during the coma. In living patients, this is manifested as *compartment syndrome* (high pressure from edema in muscular compartments in the torso or limbs). Decubiti (bedsores) may also form from pressure on the skin and subcutaneous tissue over bony prominences. In such cases, the sample of choice for toxicologic analysis is not the postmortem blood, urine, or vitreous humor, but the earliest possible antemortem blood that had been drawn upon hospital admission.

In many cases, the decedent will be brought to the medical examiner's office having been found dead at home or some other location, and there is no antemortem sample to test. If the person lingered in a coma, the brain will be swollen, just as with the hospitalized patient. Without ventilator support, the person will probably not live as long, so the brain may not be as soft but will still be swollen, and cerebral edema in these cases will be obvious at autopsy. Decubiti and rhabdomyolysis may occur, but consequent ulcerations on the skin will probably not be present (decubiti begin with the internal structures of soft tissue and work toward the surface with time). Myoglobin in the blood and the urine may be detected analytically. A toxicologic analysis may not reveal the underlying opiate. If heroin was used, 6-MAM may be present in the vitreous fluid, cerebrospinal fluid, and urine (preferred sample in such cases, but for qualitative value only).

Interpretation of blood drug levels in polypharmacy cases can be a challenge. The potential for drug interaction should be considered, as well as indirect effects such as the consequences of enzyme induction or inhibition. Effects should be correlated with such pathologic or clinical information as might be available. One approach often useful in such cases is simply a *reductionist* approach, in which the potential for each drug or selected combinations of drugs to elicit the effects observed is evaluated in the absence of the other drugs present. This process can clarify which drugs were and which were not truly causative factors. Consider a case of a 37-year-old male discovered at home with multiple medications present, including alprazolam, oxycodone, gabapentin, and a cold medication mix including dextromethorphan. Assuming pathology consistent with an overdose (e.g., heavy lungs, no other compelling pathologic cause of death) and toxicologic levels from a properly collected femoral blood sample showing 37 ng/mL alprazolam, 650 ng/mL oxycodone, and 825 ng/mL gabapentin, one might reasonably expect a pathologist to cite a cause of death of combined drug overdose. However, upon reflection, a toxicologist might reason that in this case, in the absence of oxycodone, the combination of alprazolam and gabapentin would not really be an adequate explanation for the death. Further, the oxycodone, even in the absence of both other drugs, is an adequate explanation for the death. This approach, while not definitive, can in some cases help focus the evaluation of the case on the drug or drugs that were truly of significance in causation of the death.

13.8 Tolerance and Dependence

Tolerance to any drug is characterized by requiring more of the drug to achieve the same level of desired effect. Mechanistically, the body downregulates receptors in response to agonist exposure. As such, fewer receptors are expressed on the cell surface after an individual has developed tolerance, and a higher concentration of drug is required to achieve the same degree of receptor occupancy. For opioids, tolerance can be developed to all effects except constipation, miosis, and dysphoria. An increased tolerance to pain control is manifested by a need for a higher concentration of drug in the body to achieve the same degree of pain relief.

Dependence is defined as experiencing unpleasant side effects when the drug is abruptly withdrawn. For opiates, effects can include pain, nausea and vomiting, dysphoria, and fatigue. Some physicians prescribe progressively lower doses or shift the patient to a less potent opioid to help patients wean off the drugs and recover without developing dependence.

13.9 Morphine Analogs and Related Compounds

13.9.1 Heroin

Heroin is a diacetylated morphine analog, readily able to cross the blood–brain barrier, and as such, considerably more potent than morphine, particularly with regard to the induction of euphoria. Heroin is not available for medical use in the United States but is used in some European countries. The facility of first-pass hydrolysis and conjugation result in the abused drug community using heroin by injection or smoking.

13.9.2 6-Mono-Acetylmorphine

6-mono-acetylmorphine (6-MAM), which is simply the mono-deacetylated metabolic intermediate of heroin, is relatively rapidly converted to morphine in the body. Since morphine is not readily acetylated *in vivo*, the presence of 6-MAM in forensic samples is generally considered evidence that heroin was used. Detection of 6-MAM in blood can sometimes be problematic; however, it is often readily demonstrable in urine samples.

13.9.3 Codeine

Codeine is a popular analgesic, less potent than morphine but effective following oral dose, and is similar to morphine in antitussive effects. Codeine is less euphoragenic than morphine, with less abuse potential. Commonly formulated with an NSAID (e.g., aspirin, ibuprofen, or acetaminophen), codeine is commonly encountered in postmortem work. It is important to note that codeine can be metabolized (albeit relatively slowly) to morphine. As such, it is not uncommon to find a small amount of morphine present in a urine sample with codeine. In these cases, the amount of codeine generally exceeds that of morphine quite significantly.

13.9.4 Thebaine

Thebaine (also known as paramorphine) is, like morphine and codeine, a naturally occurring opiate; however, while structurally similar to morphine, thebaine is not an effective agonist for opiate receptors and does not have either CNS depressant or analgesic effects. Thebaine is the synthetic starting material for a number of semisynthetic opioids and related compounds, including oxycodone and oxymorphone, and the antagonists naloxone and naltrexone.

13.9.5 Hydrocodone, Hydromorphone, Oxycodone, Oxymorphone

These semisynthetic opioids are derived from the naturally occurring opiates codeine or thebaine. All are quite effective analgesics, with varying degrees of antitussive activities. Hydrocodone and oxycodone have become particularly popular in extended-release formulations. All of these compounds have significant abuse potential and are often the subject of illicit sales. Rather than swallowing tablets, users will occasionally crush and inject pills or tablets, resulting in a bolus dose that bypasses hepatic metabolism. (This practice also produces characteristic fragments in the alveolar capillaries of the lungs.)

13.9.6 Meperidine

Meperidine is a synthetic opioid, structurally unrelated to morphine, able to bind to and activate μ receptors, with some activity at κ receptors. Meperidine is not subject to the same degree of inactivation during first-pass metabolism as is morphine and as such can be given orally. When used in that fashion, meperidine can cause respiratory depression but does not generate the same degree of cardiovascular effects. Meperidine does not act as an antitussive. The demethylated metabolite (normeperidine) can accumulate in consequence to large and repeated doses and can cause anxiety and muscle tremor. Interestingly enough, in large doses, meperidine can cause mydriasis (pupillary dilation).

13.9.7 Methadone

Methadone is, like meperidine, a synthetic μ-opioid receptor agonist that is useful in an oral dosing regimen. Methadone has had a long history of use in treatment

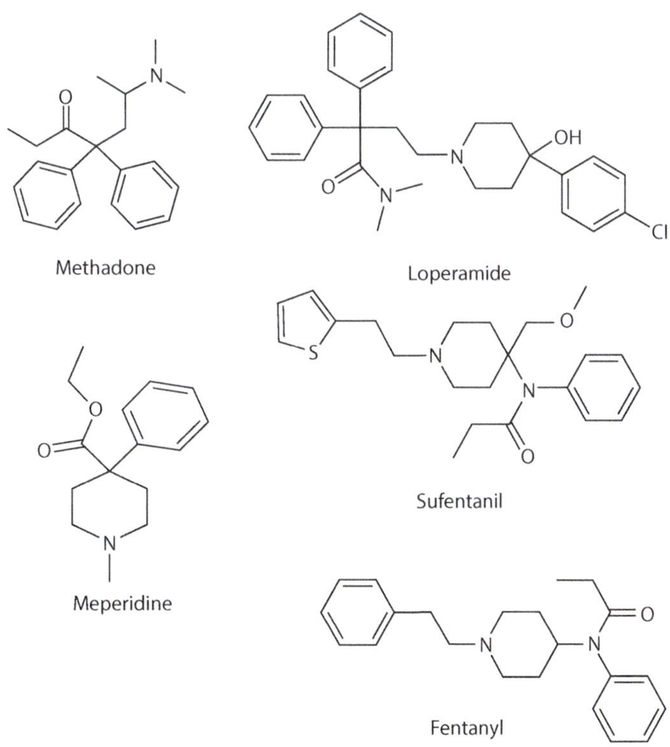

Figure 13.3 Example opioid molecules.

of opiate addiction, and relatively recently has been increasingly used as an analgesic for chronic pain situations. Methadone causes a similar constellation of effects as does morphine, including respiratory depression and miosis (Figure 13.3).

13.9.8 Fentanyl

Fentanyl (and a group of structurally related compounds) can be thought of as meperidine analogs. These compounds exhibit considerably greater affinity for the opioid mu receptor than does morphine and have been utilized in transdermal patches to facilitate prolonged analgesis. (Such patches have been the basis for abuse, either by ingestion, injection of contents, or extraction of drug for use.) Fentanyl is relatively rapidly metabolized by a CYP450 isozyme (3A4), with a correspondingly short duration of action. Because of the low concentration used, fentanyl and its analogs can sometimes represent an analytical challenge (Figure 13.3).

13.9.9 Buprenorphine

Buprenorphine is a semisynthetic opioid used both for analgesia and for treatment of opioid addiction. As an analgesic, buprenorphine can be used in individuals unable to tolerate other opiates. Buprenorphine is a μ-opioid receptor agonist with high affinity for the receptor, but relatively low activity when bound, and is therefore considered only a partial μ-opioid agonist. The combination of buprenorphine and naloxone (a full antagonist) is increasingly being used to treat opiate addiction, as Suboxone.

13.9.10 Naloxone and Naltrexone

The opiate receptor antagonists naloxone and naltrexone are commonly encountered in the forensic world. In cases where opiate toxicity is suspected, an antagonist will often be used, if only to rule out opiates. In cases of opiate-induced coma, recovery can be remarkably rapid. Mechanistically, the antagonists have a higher affinity for the μ, κ, and Δ receptors than the opiates, but do not activate the receptor complex.

REVIEW QUESTIONS

1. Describe the mechanism by which opioids produce analgesia.
2. Describe the mechanism by which opioids produce pulmonary edema.
3. Could naloxone or related opiate antagonists be used in a heroin treatment program? Why or why not?
4. What would be reasonable or expected pathologic findings at autopsy of an opioid-caused death?
5. How could individual sensitivity to opiates/opioids affect the validity of testing in a DUI situation? In other words, is it appropriate to equate a blood level of an opiate with impairment?
6. Discuss the mechanism of opiate/opioid analgesia.
7. How could morphine-6-glucuronide, a phase II metabolite, be active as a drug?
8. Would it be necessary to find heroin in a postmortem blood sample to determine a cause of death as heroin use? Why or why not?
9. How would an impaired ability to form glucuronide conjugates affect blood morphine levels from a particular dose?

TOPICS FOR DISCUSSION

1. What are the physiological implications of opioid-induced respiratory depression?
2. Should morphine levels be determined in postmortem blood samples in hospice patients? Why or why not?
3. What are the kinetic considerations for opiate overdose treatment by opiate antagonists?
4. Of what utility (if any) would a reductionist approach to drug effects be of value in DUI cases?
5. Morphine is the standard against which opiates and opioids are compared, yet it is far from the most potent. Should a more potent opiate agonist be used as a standard? If so, why?
6. A number of years ago, fentanyl was used in a hostage-rescue attempt. Is this a reasonable use for an opioid? Why or why not?
7. Oxycontin, a slow-release form of oxycodone, has been implicated in a number of overdose deaths. Is there something about this form that would make the drug particularly dangerous?
8. Why would opiates and opioids not be amenable to therapeutic drug monitoring?

Bibliography

Barile FA. *Clinical Toxicology: Principles and Mechanisms*. 2nd ed. New York: Informa Healthcare, 2010.

Drummer OH. *The Forensic Pharmacology of Drugs of Abuse*. London: Arnold, 2001.

Gilman AG, Rall TW, Nies AS, Taylor P, editors. *Goodman and Gilman's The Pharmacological Basis of Therapeutics*. 8th ed. New York: McGraw-Hill, 1990.

Klassen CD. *Casarett and Doull's Toxicology: The Basic Science of Poisons*. 8th rev. ed. New York: McGraw-Hill, 2013.

Reichl FX, Ritter L, editors. *Illustrated Handbook of Toxicology*. Stuttgart: Thieme, 2011.

Non-Opiate Sedative/Hypnotic Drugs

14

Contents

14.1 Introduction

From the perspective of the forensic toxicologist or pathologist, the distinction between sedative and hypnotic may often be trivial, particularly in the face of explaining either significant impairment or perhaps even a death. However, a sedative or tranquilizer can be thought of as a substance that has a calming effect, reducing excitement or activity level. In contrast, a hypnotic is a compound that induces sleep. The distinction is valid in a descriptive sense, but nevertheless, there may be considerable overlap in effects between the two types of compounds. In practice, the ability of these compounds to produce CNS depression is the underlying criteria for their function and for the effects that bring cases involving these drugs into the forensic world. While there are literally hundreds of compounds that could be considered as non-opiate sedatives or hypnotics, a brief overview of some selected groups and compounds can provide a working understanding of the group.

The non-opiate sedatives are a large group of disparate compounds, as simple as alcohol and as complex as the new Z-drug class of cyclopyrrolones and imidazopyridines (e.g., zopiclone and zolpidem). The major subgroups of this class, however, can be considered as the alcohols (see Chapter 12), barbiturates, benzodiazepines, and a wide variety of structurally distinct compounds. A very similar mechanistic basis underlies the action of many (albeit not all) compounds in this group, specifically, an ability to serve as either gamma-amino butyric acid (GABA) receptor agonists, or as allosteric activators (binding to the receptor in a location other than the active neurotransmitter [NT] binding site, but affecting the activity of the receptor). Many of these compounds can be of significance in forensic cases because of their ability to cause or contribute to significant central nervous system (CNS) depression. The consequences of even therapeutic use can, in some cases, affect the ability of an individual to safely drive, operate machinery, or otherwise capably function in tasks requiring cognitive function, motor control, or a combination of the two. In overdose, the consequences of these drugs can be of greater magnitude, even to the point of death. While this group of compounds may not be growing and changing as rapidly as some of the various stimulant classes, there is indeed a steady expansion of the number of drugs, in both the licit and illicit market, capable of producing the CNS depression typical of the group.

14.2 Barbiturates

The family of derivatives of barbituric acid, the barbiturates, were historically a very popular group of drugs

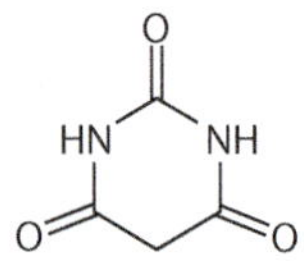

Figure 14.1 Barbituric acid.

(some of which are still of medical use) that have been largely supplanted by the functionally related benzodiazepines. Barbiturates are CNS depressants and can produce a spectrum of effects from mild sedation to anesthesia. In overdose barbiturates can readily cause death, particularly in combination with ethanol.

The basic structure of the group, barbituric acid (Figure 14.1), was synthesized in the late 1800s by Adolf von Baeyer but was not found to have any pharmacologic activity. The first indication of a potential medicinal role for substituted barbiturate structures was noted in the early 1900s when the ability of the C5 di-ethyl analog *barbital* to anesthetize dogs was discovered. Phenobarbital (5-ethyl-5-phenyl barbiturate) was introduced in 1912 and remains in use today as one of the more commonly prescribed anticonvulsant drugs (often in combination with the antiseizure medication phenytoin). Literally hundreds of other barbiturate analogs have been synthesized, many with pharmacologic activity and use as medicinal compounds. Barbiturates have been extensively employed as sleep aids, and the combination of alcohol and barbiturates has resulted in many accidental deaths (Figure 14.2).

Barbiturates are generally considered in three groups, based on how rapidly they produce effects in the body and how long-lasting those effects prove to be: ultrashort-, short/intermediate-, and long-acting. The ultrashort-acting barbiturates are used primarily for anesthesia, particularly in emergency situations, as they take only seconds following intravenous administration to become effective. These compounds (e.g., thiopental, hexobarbital, and methohexital) tend to be active in the body for only a relatively short time period, as short as 15 min to perhaps 3 hours, depending on the compound. The short/intermediate-acting barbiturates were generally used for anxiety or insomnia, although these uses have been significantly supplanted by the benzodiazepines and related compounds. Short-acting barbiturates (e.g., secobarbital and pentobarbital) have an onset of action of 10–15 min and have a duration of action of 2–4 hours. Intermediate-acting barbiturates (e.g., amobarbital and butabarbital) show an onset of action of 15–30 min with effects lasting for 4–6 hours. While barbiturates as a class are not commonly abused, it is the short and intermediate-acting compounds that tend to be misused. The long-acting barbiturates (e.g.,

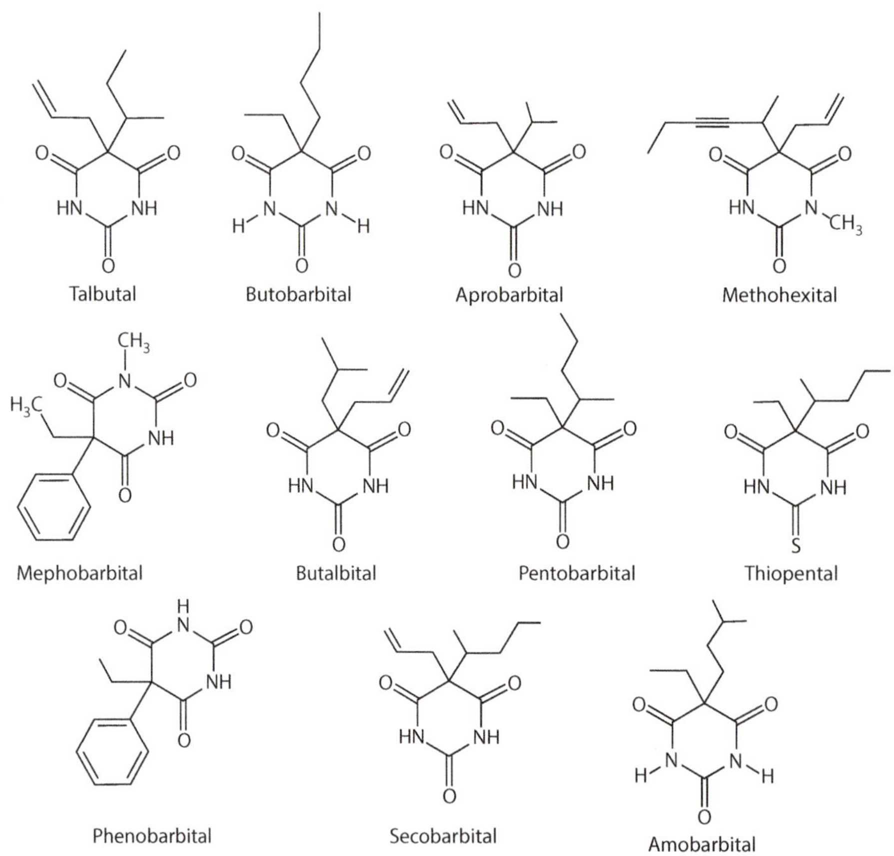

Figure 14.2 Example barbiturates.

phenobarbital and barbital) are primarily used as anticonvulsants and start to show an effect in 30–60 min with a duration of action of 6–8 hours (see Table 14.1).

Mechanistically, the barbiturates act as specific $GABA_A$-receptor agonists, binding to a specific barbiturate site (distinct from the GABA site) and are able to activate the receptor, resulting in a chloride influx and hyperpolarization of the postsynaptic neuron. The ability of this class of drugs to directly activate the $GABA_A$ receptor, thereby functioning independently of the level of endogenous GABA, is responsible for the risk associated with overdose, particularly in combination with ethanol.

Barbiturates are not now as commonly encountered in forensic casework as in the past. With the combination of effective immunoassays and the relatively large amounts of drug corresponding to an effective dose (therapeutic levels are often in excess of 10 mg/L), the analysis of the barbiturates in biological samples is straightforward. Barbiturates can be encountered in DUI cases (often as the combination of phenobarbital and phenytoin). While the potential for barbiturate CNS depressants to have a negative impact on performance is well recognized, it may be significant for the toxicologist to note the underlying medical condition for which the drugs have been prescribed. The phenytoin/phenobarbital combination is not uncommonly used with seizure disorders, and in a DUI setting that fact may be as important to understanding the case as the detection of the two drugs.

Barbiturates tend not to receive a lot of attention in the drug-facilitated sexual assault (DFSA) arena; however, the potential for these compounds to be used in this type of poisoning should not be underestimated.

Finally, of course, barbiturates may be a potential factor in accidental death, suicide, or even homicidal poisoning. Because of the relatively large amounts of drug involved, it is unlikely that such causative agent would go undetected. However, there is also the need to recognize the potiential for multiple drug effects, particularly when combined with other drugs acting as CNS depressants in general, and of course, as GABA agonists in specific.

Table 14.1 Example Barbiturates

Chemical	Brand Name	Half-Life
Methohexital	Brevital	Very short
Thiopental	Pentothal	Very short
Amobarbital	Amytal	Short
Aprobarbital	Alurate	Short
Butobarbital	Soneryl	Short
Pentobarbital	Nembutal	Short
Secobarbital	Seconal	Short
Butalbital	Fiorinal	Intermediate
Talbutal	Lotusate	Intermediate
Mephobarbital	Mebaral	Long
Phenobarbital	Luminal	Long

14.3 Benzodiazepines

Benzodiazepines are a class of drugs based on the chemical structure resulting from the fusion of a benzene and diazepine ring. The first benzodiazepine (chlordiazepoxide) was synthesized in 1955 and marketed in 1960 by the Hoffmann–La Roche company, which also then marketed the benzodiazepine diazepam (Valium) in 1963 (which subsequently became one of the most popular prescription drugs of all time). Used as antidepressants, anxiolytics, and sleeping aids, the basis for the success of the group was their efficacy and relative safety compared with the other alternatives available at the time (barbiturates and tricyclic antidepressants). Like the barbiturates, benzodiazepines can be categorized as either short-, intermediate-, or long-acting. Short- and intermediate-acting benzodiazepines are often used for short-term medical and dental procedures and treatment of insomnia; longer-acting benzodiazepines are generally prescribed as antidepressants and for the treatment of anxiety.

There are five classes of benzodiazepines: the 2-keto-compounds (e.g., diazepam), the 3-hydroxy compounds (e.g., lorazepam), the 7-nitro-compounds (e.g., clonazepam), the triazolo compounds (e.g., alprazolam), and the imidazo compounds (e.g., medazolam). However, benzodiazepines are not normally grouped by underlying structure, but rather by elimination half-life or speed of onset of action. Short-acting benzodiazepines have a half-life of under 12 hours. Intermediate-acting compounds have a half-life of 12–40 hours. Long-acting benzodiazepines have a half-life of more than 40 hours.

Mechanistically, benzodiazepines act as allosteric activators of the $GABA_A$ receptor, thereby enhancing the effect of the inhibitory NT GABA. It is important to note that benzodiazepines do not directly activate the receptor and are not agonists of the GABA binding site. Rather, benzodiazepines bind to and activate an allosteric site on the receptor, resulting in longer duration of chloride channel opening in response to GABA binding. The increased amount of chloride ions entering the postsynaptic neuron per receptor activation event results in a greater degree of hyperpolarization and an increased degree of inhibition of the neuron. Benzodiazepine activity therefore results in CNS depression, expressed as a sedative, hypnotic, or anxiolytic response. Because of the CNS depressant effects, benzodiazepines can be used as anticonvulsant agents.

The analysis of benzodiazepines can become of forensic interest in many types of cases. Benzodiazepines can, in the case of overdose, be dangerous, but fatal overdoses are usually the consequence of some degree of polypharmacy, or the combination of a benzodiazepine and alcohol. Because of the ability of these drugs to cause CNS depression, benzodiazepines can figure into impaired driving cases. Benzodiazepine abuse is normally associated with abuse of other drugs, and the use of benzodiazepines may represent efforts to self-medicate against withdrawal-associated depression.

Long-term use of benzodiazepines can be effectively addicting, and withdrawal can produce depression and anxiety. Finally, benzodiazepines have been used as agents for DFSA. One of the "date rape" drugs commonly requested by name in DFSA cases is Rohypnol (flunitrazepam; see Figure 14.3), which while not commercially available in the United States has nevertheless come to symbolize the ability of this class of drugs to facilitate such crimes. One undesirable side-effect of an overdose of benzodiazepines is retrograde amnesia, which may affect the ability of a victim to recall details and events in the time prior to the overdose event. Such memory effects can significantly complicate the investigation of DFSA events.

A specific antagonist to the activity of benzodiazepines is the structural analog flumazenil (see Figure 14.4). The use of this compound can be associated with significant side effects and, as such, is not commonly employed.

A number of benzodiazepines can be metabolized by cytochrome P450 (CYP450) enzymes, and therefore a potential exists for interactions with other drugs. Inhibition of CYP450 isozymes by other drugs present in the body can increase the half-life and area under the curve (AUC) for benzodiazepines. In many cases, depending on the sample matrix, the parent drug may not be readily detected, but metabolites can be present for some time (e.g., an ingestion of diazepam producing the metabolites nordiazepam, oxazepam, and temazepam in a urine sample, in which diazepam itself is undetected).

14.4 Z-Drugs

The so-called Z-drugs (zopiclone and zolpidem) are mechanistically identical to benzodiazepines and act as full agonists on the benzodiazepine binding site of the $GABA_A$ receptor, and are therefore allosteric modulators, with a similar potential to cause CNS depression. Initially introduced as sedatives, these drugs are relatively new to the market and have probably not yet seen the full extent of their use by the medical community. The Z-drugs are reported as capable of producing amnesia and, rarely, hallucinations. As with other drugs affecting the GABA receptor, the potential for producing CNS depression is associated with these drugs, either in frank overdose or simply as a consequence of an inadvertent overdose (e.g., medication error or use in association with ethanol or other sedative agents) (Figure 14.5).

14.5 Antihistamines

First-generation H1 antagonists, antihistamines, while not designed or primarily used for sedation, nevertheless often have such an effect. Mechanistically, these compounds do affect serotonin receptors, but the overall sedating effect may be more a function of actions on H1 receptors in the brain.* Diphenhydramine (DPH) is a commonly encountered example in forensic specimens, with both sedative and hypnotic effects, and is marketed as a nonprescription sleep aid. DPH is in a number of over-the-counter (OTC) cold medications and is also used as an antiemetic for motion sickness. High levels of DPH can cause cardiac effects (e.g., long QT interval and arrhythmia) and the mechanism for death in overdose is usually more a function of cardiac failure than CNS depression. DPH has historically been used as a hallucinogen but is not currently popular in that fashion. Another example of a sedating antihistamine is doxylamine, commonly formulated for nighttime allergy and cold relief. Promethazine is a phenothiazine, which, while functioning as an antihistamine, is also a strong sedative agent and not uncommonly encountered in forensic specimens. Interestingly, promethazine appears to have a potentiation effect on opiates (Figure 14.6).

14.6 Herbal Medications

Herbal medications often present a real challenge for the forensic toxicologist. In some cases, a psychotropically

* Histamine is a neurotransmitter that is involved in the immune/inflammatory response system and works through four metabotropic, g-protein coupled receptors, designated H1–H4. The H1 receptor is of toxicologic interest, in that in the CNS, it is related to the level of activity, while in the PNS, agonism causes bronchoconstriction (hence the use of H1 antagonists for asthma treatment), hives, pain, and itching. The H1 receptor is expressed in various tissues throughout the body including cardiac, vascular endothelium, and smooth muscle cell. (The H2 receptor is primarily involved in vasodilation, H3 in reduced CNS neurotransmitter release, and H4 in white blood cell motility.) Agonism of the H1 receptor in the brain inhibits cell membrane potassium channels, increasing the localized internal concentration of potassium, hypopolarizing the neuron, and bringing the resting voltage closer to the activation threshold. H1 receptor antagonists, or the antihistamines, produce drowsiness by blocking this action, allowing potassium efflux, hyperpolarizing the neuron, and making it less available for the excitation process.

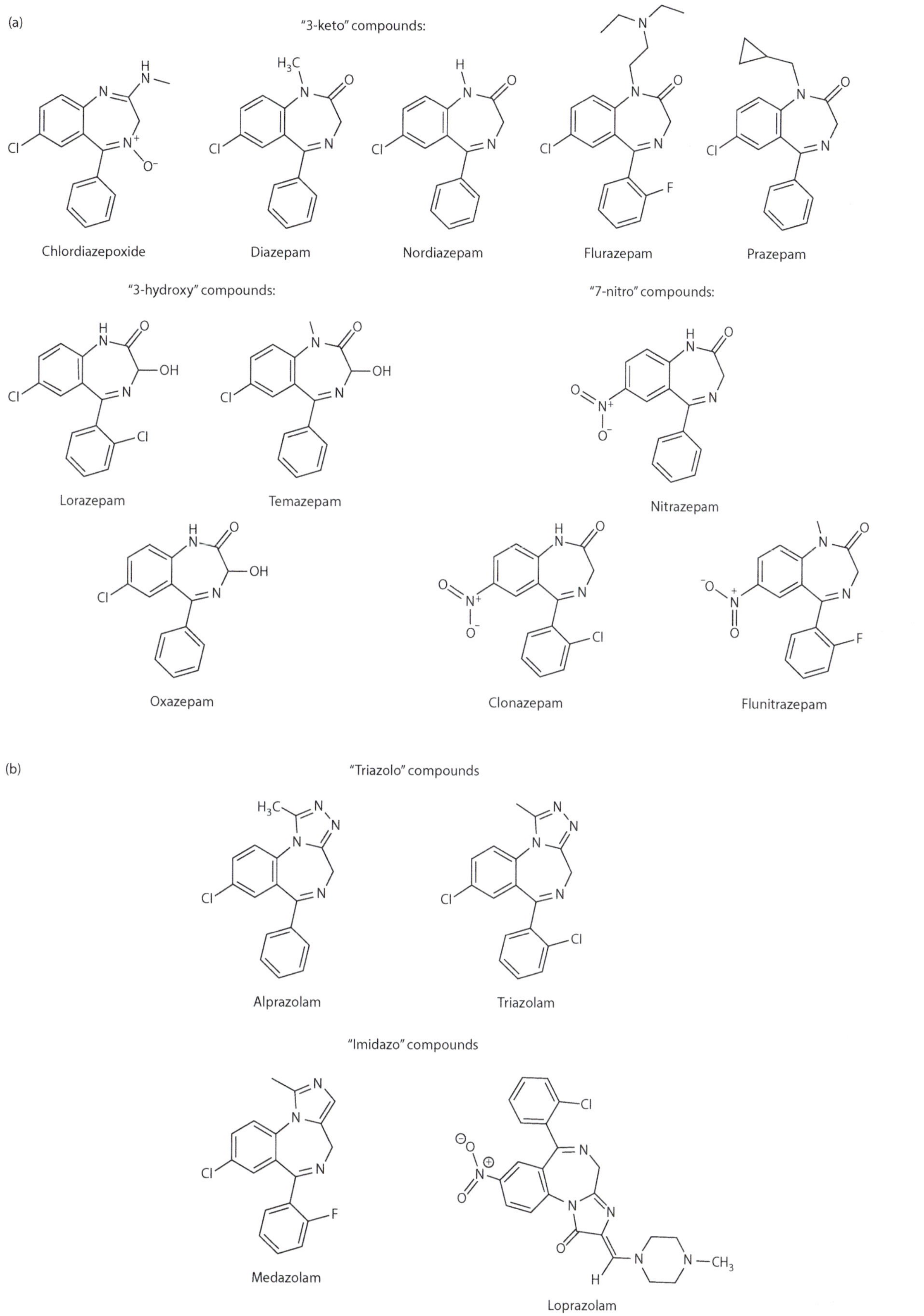

Figure 14.3 (a) Example 3-keto, 3-hydroxy, and 7-nitro benzodiazepine compounds. (b) Example triazolo and imidazo benzodiazepine compounds.

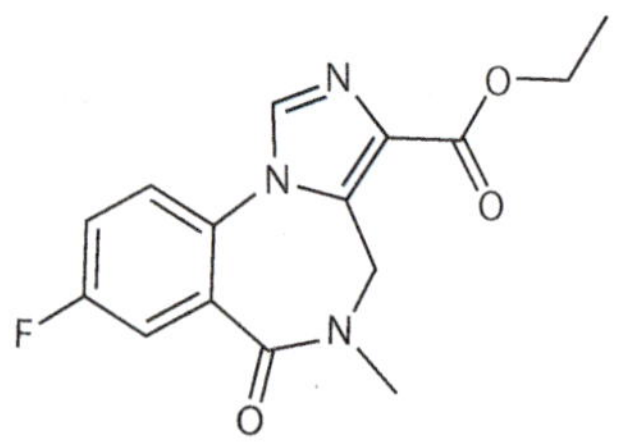

Figure 14.4 Flumazenil.

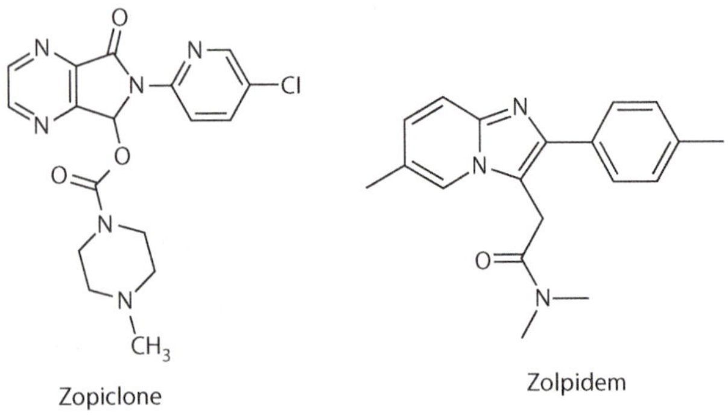

Figure 14.5 Zopiclone (PD) and zolpidem (PD).

active agent that has not yet been recognized or described (and hence, does not yet appear in mass spectral libraries) might be present in a case. More commonly, herbal preparations contain compounds that, while not particularly challenging analytically, are not necessarily recognized as medicinals. There is also the problem that some individuals may be more responsive to some preparations than others. Finally, the world of herbal medications is somewhat dynamic and changes in response to both market and societal factors, as well as current cultural trends. Despite all the challenges

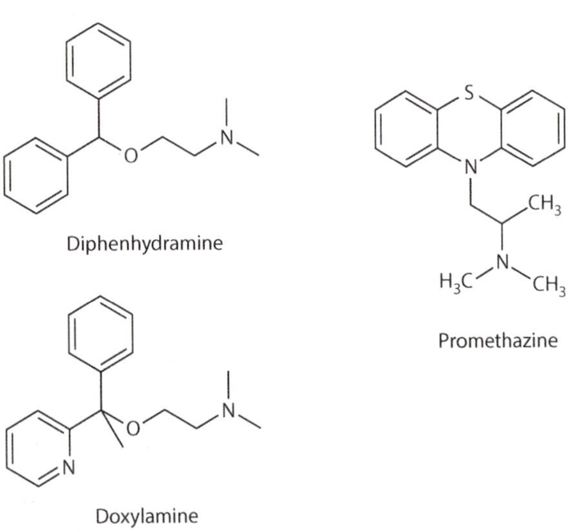

Figure 14.6 Diphenhydramine, doxylamine, and promethazine (all PD).

associated with dealing with herbal medication, and recognizing that a comprehensive listing would require its own volume, there are a number of interesting plants and compounds to consider for their sedating/hypnotic capability.

Chamomile is a catchall name for a number of plants resembling the daisy, of the Asteraceae family, commonly used to make an herbal tea associated with calming, sedating effects, and perhaps even mild hypnotic effects. A number of alkaloid compounds are present in chamomile, but with regard to the sedative/hypnotic effects, the ability of chamomile tea preparations to act on the GABA receptor suggests this as the mechanistic basis of action. Catnip (*Nepeta cataria*) is also used to make a calming herbal tea blend associated with sleep and sedation, although there seems to be considerable variability in the degree of individual sensitivity to the mix. Kava (*Piper methysticum*) is a plant of the Pacific Ocean islands, and the roots of the plant can be used to prepare a drink with some sedative properties. The active ingredients are a group of related psychoactive compounds, the *kavalactones*, which have been suggested to potentiate GABA activity in a manner analogous to the benzodiazepines. Interestingly, one of the kavalactones has been shown to be an agonist of the cannabinoid CB1 receptor (see Chapter 16), and may explain some of the additional psychoactive effects of the drink. Valerian (*Valeriana officinalis*) is a flowering plant widely distributed in Europe and Asia with a long history as a medicinal compound, which has been introduced in North America. Extracts of the roots of the valerian plant have sedative and perhaps anxiolytic properties, most likely a function of GABA receptor effects. However, by far the most popular herbal sedative would certainly be marijuana (*Cannabis* sp.), discussed in Chapter 16.

14.7 Tricyclic Antidepressants

The tricyclic antidepressants (TCAs; e.g., amitriptyline, nortriptyline, imipramine) have been quite popular as antidepressants; however, their use has largely been supplanted by newer compounds. Not uncommonly encountered in the forensic setting, TCAs can, in overdose, lead to potentially fatal cardiac arrhythmias. TCAs were among the first compounds in which the phenomenon of postmortem redistribution was noted. TCAs are colloquially named after their three-ring structure. (An analogous group of compounds, with four rings—hence tetracyclic antidepressants, also TCAs—have also seen extensive use.) Mechanistically, the TCAs act as serotonin and norepinephrine reuptake

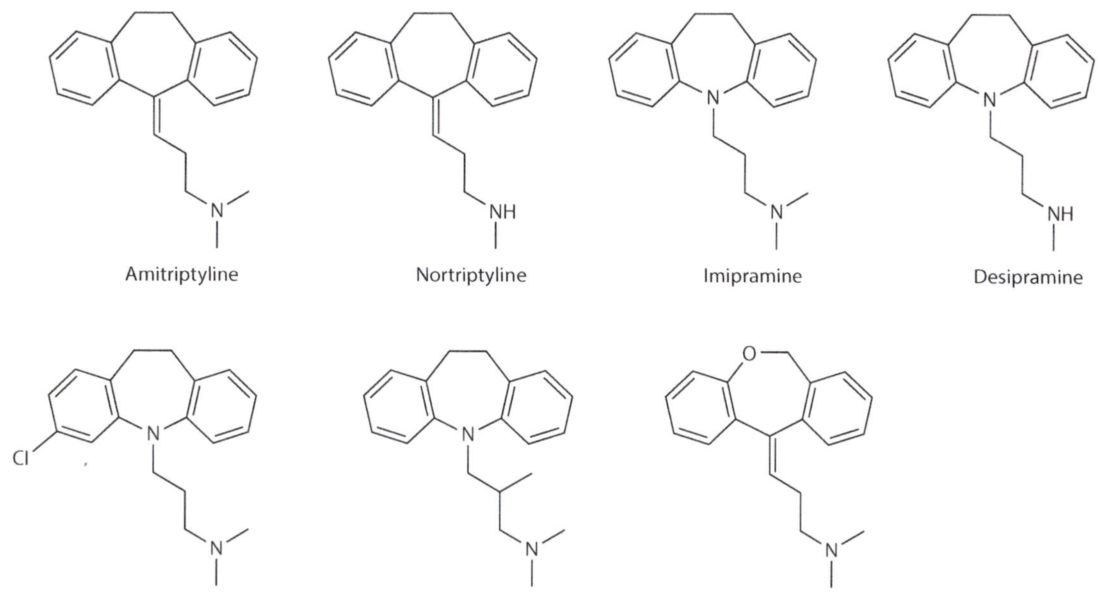

Figure 14.7 Example tricyclic antidepressants.

inhibitors. Interestingly, the TCAs do not have a significant affinity for the dopamine transporter and do not act as dopamine reuptake inhibitors. The TCAs can, at high concentrations, act as sodium and calcium channel blockers, thereby underlying their cardiotoxicity in overdose (Figure 14.7).

14.8 Antipsychotics

A wide variety of compounds are used in the treatment of psychosis, many of which have significant sedative/hypnotic effects. Some of the major classes of drugs include the phenothiazines (e.g., chlorpromazine, mesoridazine, perphenazine, thioridazine), thioxanthenes (e.g., chlorprothixene), butyrophenones (e.g., haloperidol), and newer *atypical antipsychotics* (e.g., loxapine, clozapine, olanzapine, quetiapine). All of the antipsychotics tend to block dopamine receptors in the brain, but a number also affect some serotonin receptors as well.

Antipsychotic medications are not uncommon in the forensic environment, in both postmortem as well as DUI cases. Often in postmortem cases, there is concern or interest as to the level of drugs, either adequate or in overdose. There may be a question of medication compliance or overprescription. As has been noted in numerous places in this text, the forensic toxicologist is well advised to be extremely cautious with any inferences of antemortem concentration or amount of drug taken to achieve that antemortem concentration, based on drug levels determined in postmortem samples. A good appreciation for the potential for uncertainty in the results is important to ensure that erroneous conclusions are not drawn. Multiple samples from multiple sites is one approach to help understand the potential for variability in a case, and antemortem samples (if available) can be of particular value (Figure 14.8).

14.9 Miscellaneous Compounds

14.9.1 Trazodone

Trazodone is an interesting antidepressant, a phenylpiperazine compound, related to the tricyclic antidepressants. Its primary action is as a serotonin receptor agonist, but it is not particularly active as a reuptake inhibitor. Trazodone has anxiolytic and hypnotic effects and is not uncommonly encounted in DUI cases (Figure 14.9).

14.9.2 Chloral Hydrate

Chloral hydrate is a relatively stable gem-diol water-addition product of trichloroacetaldehyde and historically was extensively used as a sedative, hypnotic, and anesthetic. The drug has a relatively narrow therapeutic index and because of the risk associated with use, has only limited medical applications. Outside of the medical arena, a solution of chloral hydrate in alcohol or added as an amendment to food or an alcoholic drink became known as a "Mickey Finn" or "knockout drops" and was reputed to render the person ingesting the drug

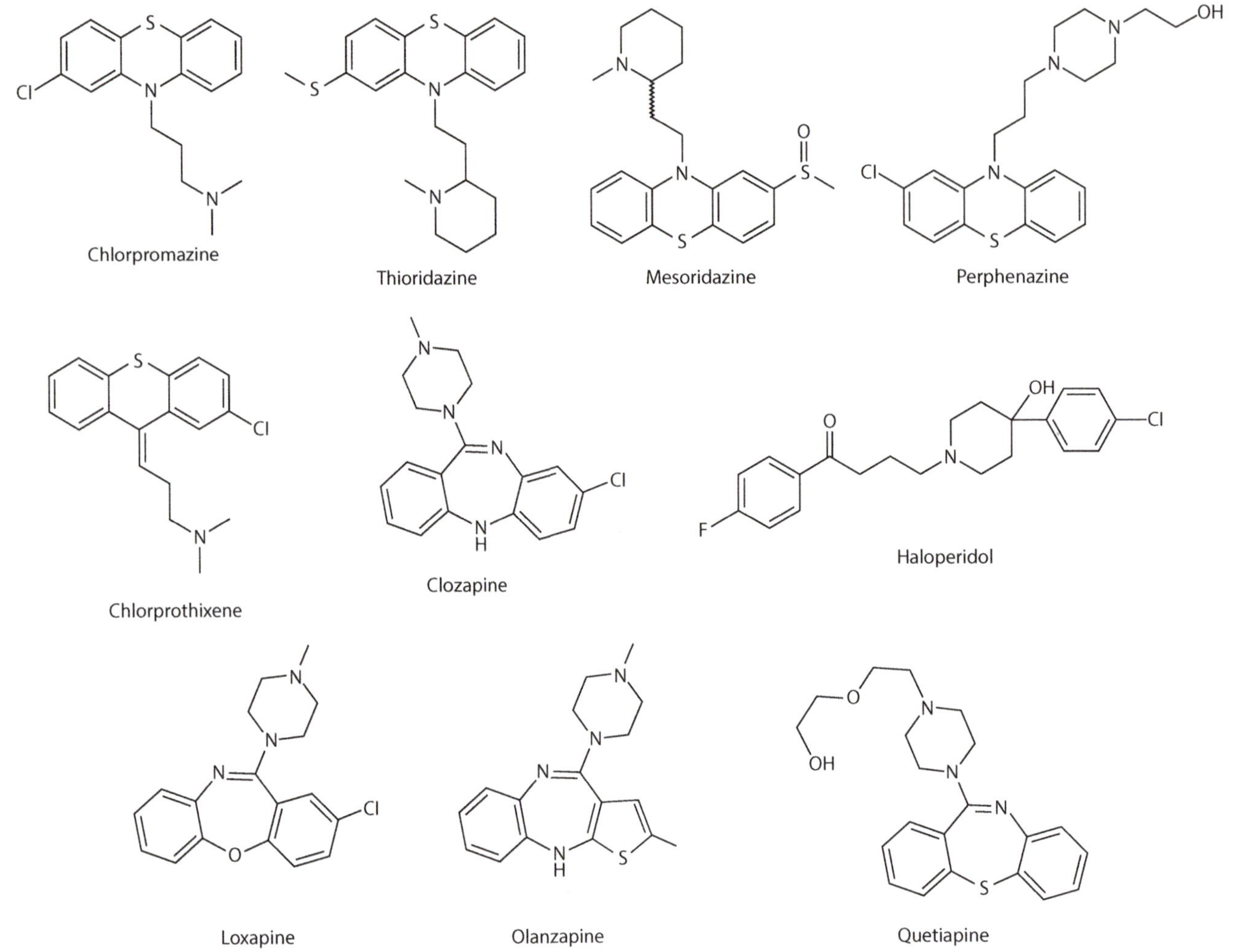

Figure 14.8 Example antipsychotic agents.

unconscious within seconds. The derivation of the term refers to a saloon proprietor in Chicago who reputedly used the compound as the basis for drugging and subsequently robbing patrons.

In the body, the gem-diol is rapidly metabolized to trichloroethanol, which is the active species. The compound is ultimately oxidized to trichloroacetate and eliminated via the kidneys. Mechanistically, trichloroethanol appears to functionally enhance the activity of the GABA receptor in a manner similar to ethanol, presumably affecting membrane function in a generalized sense.* Trichloroethanol may represent an analytical challenge in some laboratories, eluting after ethanol in headspace GC and yet before activation of the detector in some GCMS systems (Figure 14.9).

* The effective dose for chloral hydrate is considerably less on a molar basis than ethanol, suggesting that there may be a more focused mechanism of action, perhaps involving a more direct effect on the CNS inhibitory neurons (or the GABA receptors). At this point, however, a specific mechanism remains unidentified.

14.9.3 Glutethimide

Glutethimide is a substituted phenylpiperidine that was introduced in 1954, presumably as a safe alternative to the barbiturates. However, glutethimide had a significant addictive potential and can produce severe withdrawal symptoms upon cessation of use. Glutethimide is now only rarely encountered (Figure 14.9).

14.9.4 Methaqualone

Methaqualone, known as the brand name Quaalude, was a popular euphorogenic drug of abuse in the 1960s and 1970s but is only rarely encountered currently in the United States. Methaqualone acts as a functional GABA agonist. Interestingly, methaqualone was popular in nonalcoholic dance clubs in the 1970s and played a role in the drug culture that now seems to have been somewhat taken over by some of the sympathomimetic amines (SMAs) and γ-hydroxybutyric acid (GHB) in some "rave" and techno club venues (Figure 14.9).

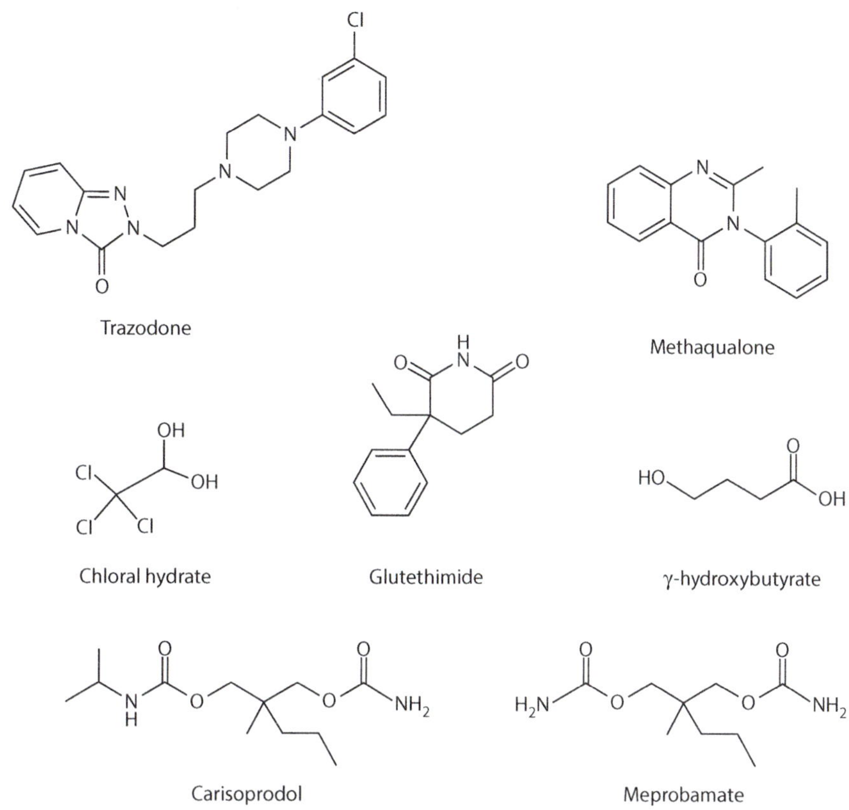

Figure 14.9 Miscellaneous sedative-hypnotic compounds.

14.9.5 Carisoprodol/Meprobamate

Carisoprodol is a dicarbamate with one carbamyl nitrogen carrying an isopropyl alkyl substituent. Meprobamate (also marketed as a stand-alone drug) is the N-dealkylated analog. While not often considered as recreational drugs, these (regionally) commonly prescribed drugs are usually used as skeletal muscle relaxants and often in the treatment of back pain. Carisoprodol/meprobamate can play a significant role in DUI casework because of their ability to relax and sedate. (Because of how rarely these drugs are included in hospital screening protocols, they provide a good example of the need for comprehensive forensic testing in DUI accident/fatality cases.) Interestingly, both carisoprodol and meprobamate have an additive effect with opiates, a factor that may be of significance in understanding cases where both are present. Both carisoprodol and meprobamate are postulated to act via $GABA_A$ receptors, with the suggestion of some degree of agonist activity at the barbiturate receptor. The actions of both drugs can be exacerbated by the co-ingestion of ethanol, opiates, or other CNS active drugs (Figure 14.9).

14.9.6 γ-Hydroxybutyric Acid

GHB, also known as 4-hydroxybutanoic acid, is a naturally occurring analog of the inhibitory neurotransmitter GABA. Originally investigated as a potential sleep aid, then thought to be a steroid-enhancing drug, GHB became popular as a club or rave drug. The ability of the drug to produce a pronounced sedation, or sleep, coupled with some degree of amnesia resulted in GHB being recognized and used as a date rape drug in cases of DFSA. This drug is often encountered in this capacity in the forensic community. Overdose of GHB can be fatal, and additive actions with other CNS depressant drugs can contribute to the effects of the drug.

Because of the structural similarity to GABA, the mechanism of action of GHB was originally thought to be agonism of the $GABA_A$ receptor, resulting in hyperpolarization of the postsynaptic neuron. However, GHB seems to act as a CNS depressant primarily through the $GABA_B$ metabotropic receptor, and results in hyperpolarization via activation of potassium channels. This allows gradient-driven egress, and hyperpolarization (to the point of approaching the equilibrium between gradient-driven flux, and potential-based resistance). The loss of potassium thereby achieves a similar end result (in terms of hyperpolarization) as the inward-directed chloride flux caused by GABA agonism of the $GABA_A$ receptor.

GHB appears to be generated in relatively small amounts as a consequence of the reduction of succinyl semialdehyde (SSA) and concurrent oxidation of

NADH + H^+. However, this enzyme system is reversible and in the presence of large amounts of GHB (such as may be ingested recreationally or in a DFSA case) serves to oxidize GHB to SSA, reducing NAD^+ in the process. SSA is subsequently rapidly oxidized to succinic acid, which can then become a substrate for the Krebs cycle. This facile reaction process results in a relatively short half-life in the body and, in a practical sense, severely limits the length of time following a potential DFSA event that samples can be reasonably analyzed for elevated levels of GHB. An additional confounder affects analysis in postmortem cases, specifically that after death, GHB can be produced in quantities that (erroneously) suggest antemortem exposure to the drug. (Postmortem GABA generation is most likely via a reverse transamination resulting in the amino group of GABA being replaced with a hydroxyl group, forming GHB.) Obviously, then, extreme caution should be taken whenever postmortem samples with GHB are being considered for forensic purposes (Figure 14.9).

REVIEW QUESTIONS

1. What are the three common mechanisms, by which the nonopiate sedative drugs act?
2. Would finding nordiazepam, lorazepam, oxazepam, and temazepam in a urine sample of an alleged DFSA victim be consistent with such a poisoning? Why or why not?
3. What significance could a finding of diphenhydramine have in a case of untimely death? What information would you want to know?
4. The tricyclic antidepressants are not generally associated with drugs of abuse. Why would that be so, if they are effective antidepressants?

TOPICS FOR DISCUSSION

1. GHB has been used in cases of DFSA. What characteristics of the drug make it amenable for such use? What factors make it problematic for such use? How do these factors affect efforts to investigate and prosecute the crime?
2. Many OTC cold medications have a sedative effect, exacerbated by ethanol. Should the presence of such medications be considered as an explanation for impairment in a DUI setting? What if ethanol is present as well?
3. What is the responsibility of the forensic laboratory with regard to herbal medications, particularly those whose effects seems to be somewhat variable between individuals?

Bibliography

Barile FA. *Clinical Toxicology: Principles and Mechanisms.* 2nd ed. New York: Informa Healthcare, 2010.

Drummer OH. *The Forensic Pharmacology of Drugs of Abuse.* London: Arnold, 2001.

Fenton JJ. *Toxicology: A Case-Oriented Approach.* Boca Raton, FL: CRC Press, 2002.

Klassen CD. *Casarett and Doull's Toxicology: The Basic Science of Poisons.* 8th rev. ed. New York: McGraw-Hill, 2013.

Reichl FX, Ritter L, editors. *Illustrated Handbook of Toxicology.* Stuttgart: Thieme, 2011.

Sympathomimetic Amines
Amphetamines and Related Compounds

15

Contents

15.1 Introduction

The amphetamines, or more broadly speaking, the class of sympathomimetic amines (SMAs), represents an important group of compounds for the forensic toxicologist. While many representatives of the class have been used as medicinal compounds, many others have been used as recreational drugs, with devastating long-term effects on some users. The history of the SMAs is complex and fascinating and, until relatively recently, primarily a story of ampethamine, methamphetamine, and cocaine. However, the SMAs are no longer a static group of drugs but rather an active and growing class with new species entering the legitimate and illegal market with some regularity. While many of the illicit-synthesis clandestine labs (see Sidebar 15.1) have focused on the relatively easily synthesized methamphetamine, an increasing scope and volume of new compounds is appearing in forensic samples on a regular basis. Many of the so-called designer drugs such as methylenedioxyamphetamine (MDA) and methylenedioxymethamphetamine (MDMA) and analogs can be made by only small molecular alterations to a more basic SMA structure, and as such can be relatively easily incorporated into existing synthetic schemes. Finally, as new drugs with similar effects are discovered and brought into the illicit market, there is an increasingly complex challenge for the toxicologist to identify and quantitate these new species (Figure 15.1).

SIDEBAR 15.1 CLANDESTINE LABORATORIES

While we may (somewhat justifiably) think of meth labs when the term *clan lab* is raised, hidden synthesis or purification processes have been carried out for as long as laws have made such processes illegal. Historically, alcohol distillation (particularly during Prohibition) has been commonplace, and laboratories processing opium resin for heroin and coca leaves for cocaine have been and remain the mainstay of the illegal drug trade. (Such laboratories are almost exclusively located outside the United States, and product reaches the North American market via various smuggling routes.) In recent years, however, the rise of numerous synthetic methamphetamine laboratories has become the focus of public attention, legal activities tracking or limiting availability to precursor molecules, and even popular television shows. Clandestine methamphetamine synthesis labs ("meth labs") are usually engaged in a rather inelegant synthesis of methamphetamine from (often) ephedrine/pseudoephedrine, providing significant challenges for those chemists who are asked to respond to the facility as part of specialized crime scene teams. The "clan lab" chemists act to safely terminate ongoing reactions and neutralize some of the chemicals associated with the synthetic schemes and chemicals that can represent a hazard (e.g., lye, lithium, ether), in addition to collecting appropriate evidentiary materials. While methamphetamine laboratories remain an active problem for law enforcement, from a toxicologic perspective, the analysis of the methamphetamine end product as well as the synthetic raw materials and intermediate mixtures is relatively straightforward.

As noted above, the "menu" of target analytes for the forensic toxicologist is rapidly changing, as the role of the clandestine laboratory now is expanded to include sophisticated synthetic operations capable of multiple complex reaction schemes in a production-level operation. Such labs may, depending on local laws, limit their activities and products to the legal (or not yet illegal) materials, and may therefore represent legitimate operations within the countries in which they are located. Again, the final products, from the synthetic cannabinoids to the various cathinones, tryptamines, and other varieties of currently popular psychotropic drugs, can then reach the North American market either via legitimate shipments or smuggling operations. The extent to which illicit synthesis activity is occurring in the United States remains an active area of interest for the Drug Enforcement Agency.

The challenge for the forensic toxicologist, in the face of a rapidly growing group of designer drugs, is simply to be able to recognize such compounds when they appear in casework. While we have historically relied on our GCMS library search programs to identify unknown peaks, the ability for new materials to appear on the drug scene prior to being recognized and incorporated in libraries remains an issue. A number of organizations (e.g., the Scientific Working Group for the Analysis of Seized Drugs [SWGDRUG]) maintain free and rapidly updated libraries of spectra that can be of assistance in the initial identification of new species. Ultimately, the skill of the analyst in recognizing that a certain spectra should be pursued will be the basis by which many of the newly synthesized materials will be recognized.

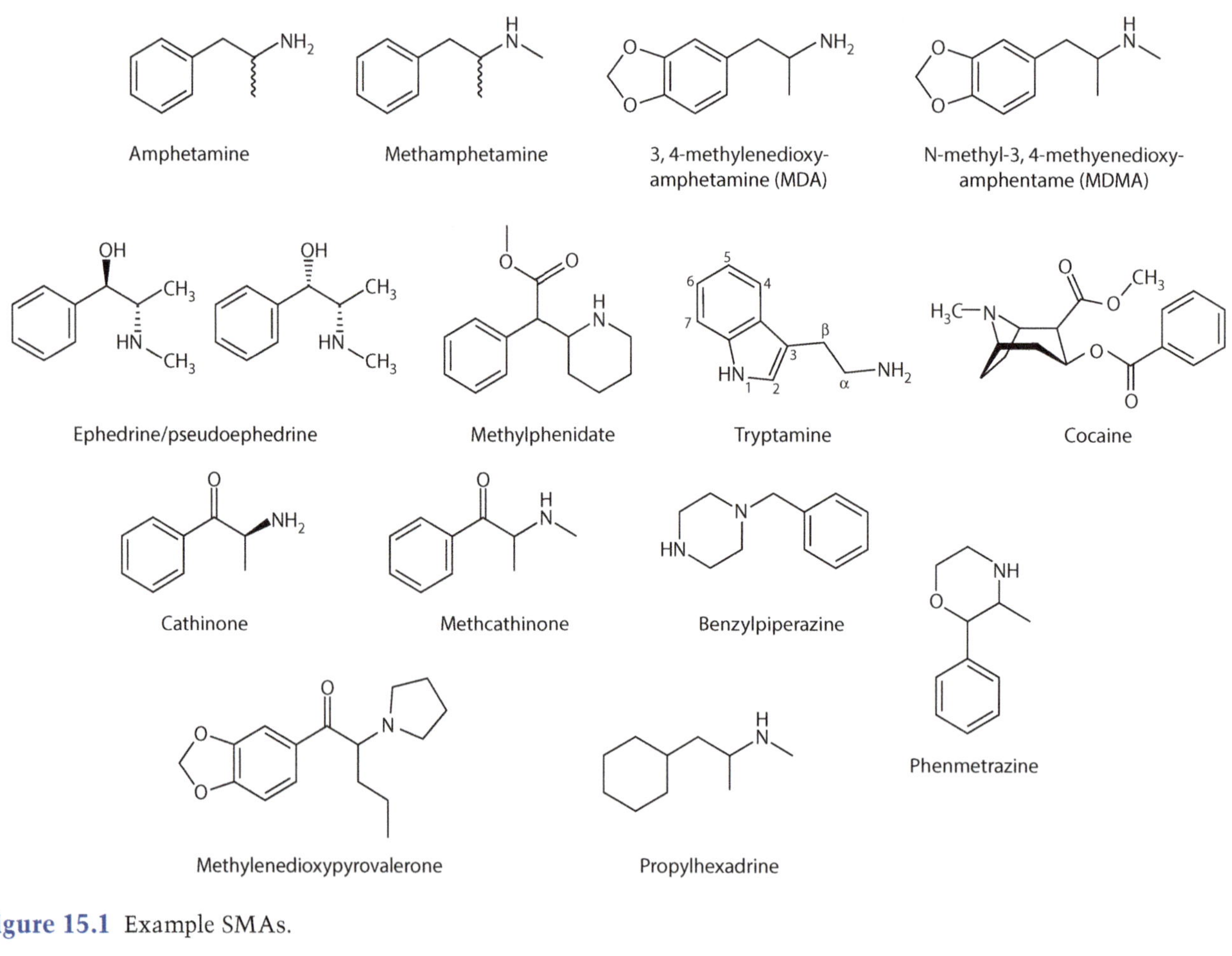

Figure 15.1 Example SMAs.

SMAs are also interesting mechanistically, in that effects are mediated in the nervous system via effects on postsynaptic receptors, and in the metabolism, storage, or reuptake of neurotransmitters (NTs). However, the specific mechanism of action differs slightly between the various members of the group. While the underlying common mode of action is CNS stimulation, some compounds (e.g., MDA and MDMA) depart a bit from the typical amphetamine/methamphetamine effects in that they can be described as *entactogens* or *empathogens* because of the degree to which they apparently induce feelings of empathy or an urge for social contact (emotional and physical).

The SMAs as a group can be of significance to the forensic toxicologist as an explanation for serious medical consequences, including death, as well as behavior, as in a particularly reckless or inappropriate driving or risk-taking behavior.

Finally, it would not be an overstatement to suggest that the sociological impact of these drugs is clearly of the same magnitude as the addictive opiates. The devastation that can be wreaked on an individual or a family (and by inference, larger communities) by SMA addictions (be it cocaine, meth, or some other species) touches all aspects of our society.

15.2 History

One prototypical compound of the SMA group is arguably ephedrine, the active component of the Chinese medicine *ma huang* with a recorded use as a medicinal compound of thousands of years (one can debate the inclusion of the β-hydroxy phenylethylamines, such as ephedrine, with the SMAs, as the hydroxyl substituent seems to preclude an amphetamine-like spectrum of effects). An undisputed example of the SMAs is amphetamine (α-methylphenylethylamine), which was first synthesized in the late 1800s but was not extensively used medicinally until the 1930s. SMAs were used by both sides in World War II to help combatants remain awake and alert during combat or when on long missions. (Interestingly, the Allies used amphetamine, while the Axis powers tended to use methamphetamine.) Following World War II, the combination of large stockpiles of the drugs, coupled with both legitimate medical and illicit recreational demands, resulted in extensive use and abuse. Since the 1950s there has been a consistent pattern of increasing restriction, regulation, and eventual removal of amphetamines from the legitimate medicinal market. Illicit production and sale has remained a significant issue worldwide, with methamphetamine synthesis and distribution rivaling, in many locations, the market for cocaine and heroin. Recently, there has been a veritable explosion of new SMAs in the form of designer drugs produced both in small clandestine laboratories as well as legal compounds made in industrial facilities in countries with less-restrictive drug laws.

The combination of the ready availability of synthetic capability and the current orientation of the legal system toward dealing with a single compound at a time has produced a system whereby a small, potentially innocuous or insignificant change in the structure of a molecule generates (in a legal sense) an entirely new compound. While such a system works to the advantage of pharmaceutical and industrial chemical synthesis companies for patent considerations, the legal inference is that a specific compound must be identified and determined uniquely to be illegal or a controlled substance. The process of controlling a new drug can take years, during which even newer drugs may have appeared on the scene.

Federally, the U.S. Analog Act passed in 1985 attempted to address this issue somewhat, by declaring essentially that analogs of controlled substances were also controlled. The law was clearly oriented toward the proliferation of newly created designer drugs, and three criteria were considered to identify a compound as an analog of an existing scheduled drug. First, was the material being sold or represented as if it were an illicit substance? Second, was the material structurally similar to an illicit substance? And finally, was there pharmacologic data to suggest the material was active in a manner similar to illicit substance? From a toxicologic perspective, the first point is generally not a concern of the laboratory or the toxicologist. The second point is patently flawed, in that structural similarity is no guarantee of activity, and by the same token, a lack of structural similarity is no guarantee of a lack of activity (see Section 15.4). Finally, the interpretation of pharmacologic data will doubtless be a contested issue in many cases, and to this end, toxicologists may be called upon to bring their knowledge of pharmacology, physiology, and mechanism of action to explain why a specific compound would reasonably be or not be considered an analog of a particular scheduled drug.

Nevertheless, the challenge of identification of newly synthesized drugs and determination of the legal status of these compounds will likely continue to represent a major area of interest and effort in forensic laboratories for some time to come.

15.3 Examples and Mechanisms

15.3.1 Amphetamine

Amphetamine (1-phenyl, 2-aminopropane; α-methyl phenylethylamine) is the simplest substituted phenylethylamine. Amphetamine is a stimulant psychotropic drug that produces an array of effects consequential to providing stimulation and reward to the brain. Amphetamine and related compounds have been used to treat attention deficit disorder and narcolepsy and have been used as effective appetite suppressants.

Amphetamine continues to be used as a recreational drug, both for its capability to function as a performance enhancer (both physical and cognitive) and for the psychotropic effects, which include euphoria, mental focus, self-esteem, and confidence. Less desireable side effects of use can include irritability and aggression, obsessive behavior, and paranoia. A characteristic psychosis typified by delusional interpretation of normal stimuli (bordering on hallucination), often expressed as paranoia, is often associated with chronic use.

Amphetamine overdose can result in psychotic symptoms, nausea, tachypnea, fever, tremors, and restlessness. Potentially lethal seizures, hyperthermia, hypertension, and cardiac arrhythmias may also occur. Renal failure can be caused by dehydration and rhabdomyolysis that can result from amphetamine toxicity. Withdrawal from amphetamine can produce depression and an inability to function cognitively at normal levels.

Amphetamine functions to increase the effective concentration of the excitatory NTs, dopamine (DA), serotonin, and norepinephrine in the nervous system (more specifically, the synaptic space). The ability to elevate dopamine levels is typical of addictive drugs. Mechanistically, this process appears to be caused by an effect by amphetamine on the concentration of dopamine in the presynaptic NT vesicle. Uptake of dopamine into the vesicle is mediated by the vesicle monoamine transport protein (VMAT), which can, in the presence of amphetamine, exchange amphetamine for dopamine, resulting in increased dopamine concentrations in the cytosol. The resulting elevated dopamine concentrations in the cytosol causes the dopamine reuptake transport protein (DAT) to act in reverse and allow dopamine to leak back into the synaptic space. Alternatively (or coincidentally), amphetamine appears to affect the function of the DAT, facilitating release of dopamine from the presynaptic neuron and blocking reuptake. In this fashion, amphetamine functionally alters the DAT from a sodium-dopamine symport to a dopamine-amphetamine antiport. In normal operation, the sodium gradient (concentrated on the exterior of the cells, as a function of the cell membrane potential, generated by the sodium-potassium ATPase) provides the energy required to facilitate transport of a DA molecule into the cell (hence upgradient) along with a sodium ion moving downgradient. In the presence of amphetamine, the transporter brings an amphetamine molecule into the cell, in exchange for a DA molecule exiting. The ability of amphetamine to affect both serotonin and norepinephrine seems to be based on similar mechanistic effects on their transport protein (Figure 15.2).

Amphetamine also acts as an inhibitor of monoamine oxidase, and that activity contributes to the increases in intracellular dopamine concentration. Effects similar to dopamine are noted with serotonin as well, with reversal of the action of the serotonin transport protein in the presence of amphetamine, leading to increased serotonin concentrations in the synaptic space. Amphetamine may also affect the activity of norepinephrine, again by interference with the norepinephrine reuptake transporter.

A significant fraction of ingested amphetamine is excreted into the urine unchanged, and because of the weak-base nature of the molecule, that process can be significantly affected by the pH of the urine (as the urinary pH is decreased, a higher percentage of amphetamine molecules will be ionized and tend to remain in the aqueous renal filtrate, ultimately to be eliminated in the urine). Hydroxylation of either the phenyl ring of the molecule or the β-carbon, mediated by the cytochrome P450 system, accounts for only a relatively small percentage of metabolic products (<10%). Deamination and oxidation, leading to phenylacetone, benzoic acid, and ultimately hippuric acid, accounts for ~40% of excreted metabolites. Half-life is a function of age and, to an extent, enzyme induction, being roughly 12 hours for adults and somewhat less for children.

15.3.2 Methamphetamine

Methamphetamine is simply the N-methyl analog of amphetamine and is a similar, potent CNS-stimulant drug, capable of affecting heart rate and rhythm, blood pressure, body temperature, appetite, attention, alertness, and emotional state. Methamphetamine also produces the enhanced sense of focus, alertness and reduction in fatigue, and appetite suppression seen with amphetamine. Interestingly, methamphetamine is slightly more lipophilic than amphetamine, resulting in a somewhat faster transit into the brain and a somewhat slower rate of degradation by monoamine oxidase (MAO). Methamphetamine is a significant drug of abuse, with large amounts appearing in the illicit market from both

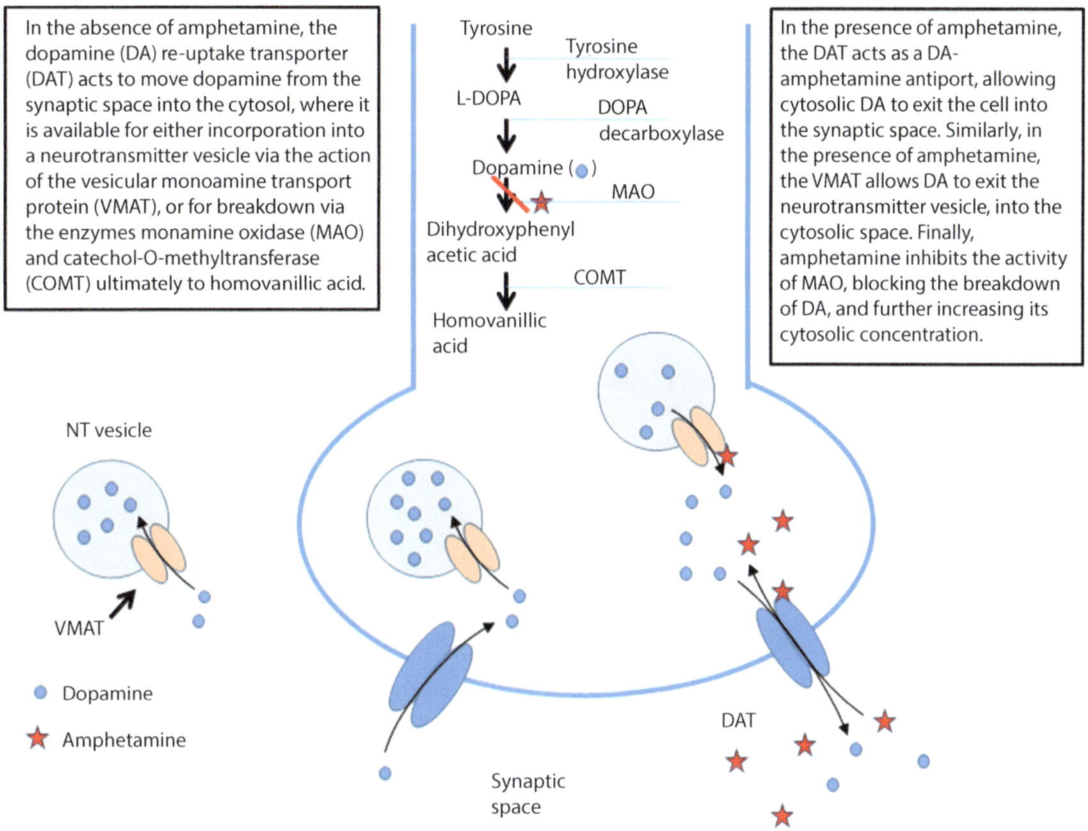

Figure 15.2 Amphetamine mechanism.

domestic clandestine laboratory production and importation from foreign synthetic operations. Long-term methamphetamine use can be particularly deleterious to users, with significant physical and mental deterioration.

Effects associated with methamphetamine include euphoria, heightened sensory awareness, increased wakefulness, hyperactivity, pupil dilation, flushed skin, tachycardia, increased respiratory rate, dry mouth, excessive perspiration, cardiac arrhythmias, hypertension, hyperexcitability, suppression of appetite, and hyperthermia. Long-term use can lead to anorexia, bruxism (teeth grinding), acne, and other skin disorders. High doses can be fatal, with seizures, cardiac events, stroke, or hyperthermia leading to death (see Sidebar 15.2).

SIDEBAR 15.2 HYPERTHERMIA, LIVER FAILURE, AND DISSEMINATED INTRAVASCULAR COAGULATION

The use of amphetamines and similar drugs can be related to significant health risks including liver failure, renal failure, and neurotoxicity. SMA users may receive emergency medical attention for symptoms of agitation, delirium, hallucinations, and more seriously debilitating conditions. While SMA overdoses can indeed be fatal, the basic action of the drug is not directly threatening (as in contrast to the action of, e.g., opiates or barbiturates). Of the serious medical consequences due to SMA overdose, autopsy findings can be variable, but hyperthermia (elevated core body temperature) and its consequences is often identified as the underlying cause. As such, in death cases, an elevated core temperature coupled with the presence of SMAs may point to a rampant hyperthermia and, by inference, the cause of death.

For deaths outside a hospital and unattended by medical personnel, scene investigators will generally obtain and document the core body temperature as soon as possible. Hyperthermia can cause massive hepatic necrosis detected at autopsy as an enlarged, soft liver with breakdown of hepatocytes and bile stasis microscopically observable.

Hyperthermia can also be caused by the increased muscle activity during the excitation phase of SMA use. Increased muscle activity may lead to muscle tissue breakdown (rhabdomyolysis). Necrotic muscle cell debris then enters the bloodstream where it can be trapped by the kidney, leading to renal failure. The urine of such patients, even at autopsy, may be red tinged. Myoglobin may be detected in the urine, and creatinine kinase may be elevated in the blood. Increased myolobin, necrotic tissue, and intracellular ions in the bloodstream may initiate the coagulation cascade using up the available coagulation factors. The medical syndrome is termed disseminated intravascular coagulation (DIC). This phrase can be deceiving because the patient appears to experience uncontrolled bleeding, not coagulation. Uncontrolled bleeding is the end result when coagulation factors are used faster than they can be made, most of which are made in the liver.

SMA use may also stimulate seizure activity, which in itself, may raise body temperature. Seizure activity may also cause muscular contractions (tonic-clonic-type seizures).

SMA use also causes catecholamine release, which may lead to cardiotoxicity manifested as accelerated coronary artery disease (large coronary arteries are more narrowed by plaque at a younger age than cohorts) and thickening of the media of the small arteries embedded within the myocardium.

In a manner similar to amphetamine, methamphetamine causes either depressed activity or actual reversal of flow in the dopamine, norepinephrine, and serotonin vesicular transporters, leading to elevated cytoplasmic levels. This elevation of cytoplasmic NT level results in the release into the synaptic space, thereby increasing the concentration of NT consequential to normal depolarization-triggered NT release. Methamphetamine also inhibits NT reuptake, further increasing the concentration in the synaptic space. Methamphetamine has a neurotoxic effect, possibly a consequence of dopamine release from the NT vesicle and intracellular catabolism (via MAO oxidase) leading to the formation of reactive oxygen species. Oxidative stress as a consequence of this process could then lead to cellular death.

Methamphetamine is quickly absorbed into the bloodstream, regardless of route of administration and is rapidly distributed throughout the body. As noted above, the lipophilic nature of the drug allows rapid uptake into the brain and seems to be somewhat protective against degradation by (the cytosolic) MAO system. Methamphetamine is primarily metabolized by N-demethylation in the liver, yielding amphetamine, with the subsequent metabolism as noted above. Roughly 30–50% of ingested, insufflated, or injected methamphetamine is excreted as unchanged drug, with ~10% as amphetamine.

15.3.3 MDA and MDMA

Both 3,4-methylenedioxyamphetamine (MDA) and N-methyl-3,4-methylendioxyamphetamine (MDMA) are popular recreational drugs, with amphetamine-like effects, but are also associated with an increased level of "empathy" or socially oriented feelings. MDMA is commonly referred to as *ecstasy*, although in the real world of substance abuse, the term is applied to a number of functionally similar compounds. It is the slightly different sensations associated with these drugs that led to the terms *entactogen* and *entheogen*, suggesting an increased focus on social contact and awareness experienced with the drugs. Mechanistically, MDA and MDMA act in a manner analogous to amphetamine and methamphetamine, in that they serve to inhibit reuptake of dopamine, serotonin, and norepinephrine. MDA seems to be more toxic than MDMA, with overdose producing the expected consequences of amphetamine-type overdose, hypertension and tachycardia, hyperthermia, and ultimately, seizures, coma, and death (Figure 15.3).

15.3.4 Ephedrine, Pseudoephedrine, and Related β-Hydroxyphenylethylamines

The β-hydroxyphenylethylamines have a long history as medicinal compounds, being used as stimulants, appetite suppressants, cold medications, and constituents in various herbal medications. Ephedrine is known as *ma huang* in traditional Chinese medicine and has been used for more than 2000 years as an antiasthmatic compound. In relatively recent times, the association with ephedrine in dietary supplements with cardiac events resulted in restrictions and regulations. The illicit use of the drug as a basis for methamphetamine synthesis via reduction of the hydroxyl group resulted in the severe restrictions on the availability of ephedrine and pseudoephedrine. While the β-hydroxyphenylethylamines are structurally similar to amphetamine, methamphetamine, and related compounds, the presence of the hydroxyl function apparently precludes members of the group from acting on the NT transport proteins in a manner similar to amphetamine and related compounds.

The mechanism of action of ephedrine and pseudoephedrine seems to be a function of stimulation of release of norepinephrine from presynaptic neuron vesicles, resulting in the activation of postsynaptic adrenergic receptors. The adrenergic receptors are located on vesicular walls, causing vasoconstriction, and hence, less

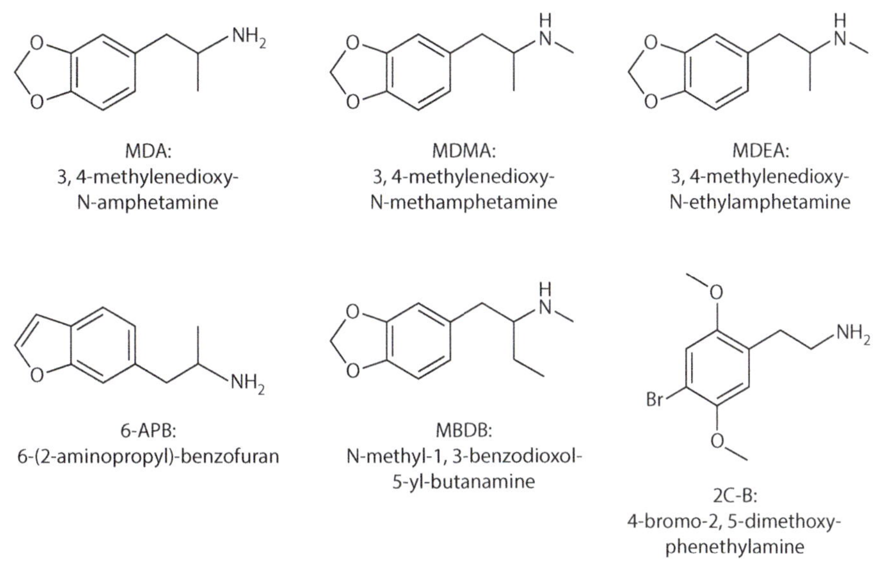

Figure 15.3 Example entactogens.

blood flow to inflamed tissues (e.g., nasal membranes) and corresponding relief of nasal congestion.

Ephedrine and pseudoephedrine are primarily excreted in the urine. Both compounds are subject to N-demethylation producing norephedrine and norpseudoephedrine respectively. The half-life for ephedrine is relatively short, 3–6 hours; pseudoephedrine is slightly longer.

15.3.5 Methylphenidate

Methylphenidate is a sympathomimetic amine analog that has seen significant successful utilization in the treatment of attention-deficit hyperactivity disorder (ADHD), particularly in children. ADHD is believed to be related to subadequate performance of dopamine and norepinephrine-linked processes in the brain. The ability of SMA-type compounds to increase functional NT levels seems a reasonable explanation for the use of the drug. Methylphenidate is of interest to the forensic toxicologist in that behavioral consequences can arise from the use of the drug as an SMA, and there is some abuse potential among adults. Methylphenidate is a commonly prescribed CNS stimulant. As might be expected based on its mechanistic similarity to amphetamine, the drug increases alertness, reduces fatigue, and improves ability to focus and maintain attention.

Methylphenidate is a dopamine reuptake inhibitor with a somewhat lesser effect on norepinephrine reuptake. Unlike amphetamine (but like cocaine) methylphenidate does not appear to reverse dopamine flow at the level of the DAT and hence does not act as a dopamine releasing agent.

15.3.6 Cocaine

Cocaine is arguably one of the most important compounds the forensic toxicologist deals with, having a long and interesting history of use in both the old and new worlds (see Karch 2006). Cocaine is a highly addictive psychotropic drug, producing a pronounced euphoria that may last as long as half an hour. There is an extensive illicit trade in the drug, as both the salt form and the free base (one form of which is crack cocaine).

The ability of cocaine to cause a potentially fatal cardiac event is well recognized. The presence of cocaine in a deceased body will often be cited as a causative or contributory factor in the death, particularly if there is a corresponding cardiac hypertrophy, suggestive of chronic bouts of hypertension. Interestingly, the presence of cocaine in a DUI case can also be of considerable significance, despite the fact that the drug is not a CNS depressant. One of the characteristics of the SMAs is their ability to cause the user to feel empowered and capable of dealing with risks and challenges. In some cases, the belief may not be consistent with the reality of a hazardous or risky situation. Such inappropriate assessment of risk can occur because of a distorted view of reality, or from the distorted sense of power and capability of the user, and can result in tragic consequences. Individuals experiencing a cocaine high may therefore make decisions that place themselves or those around them at risk. This is in contrast to a similar outcome from CNS depressants, where the underlying cause of an accident or crash can be a consequence of an inability to adequately process the available information.

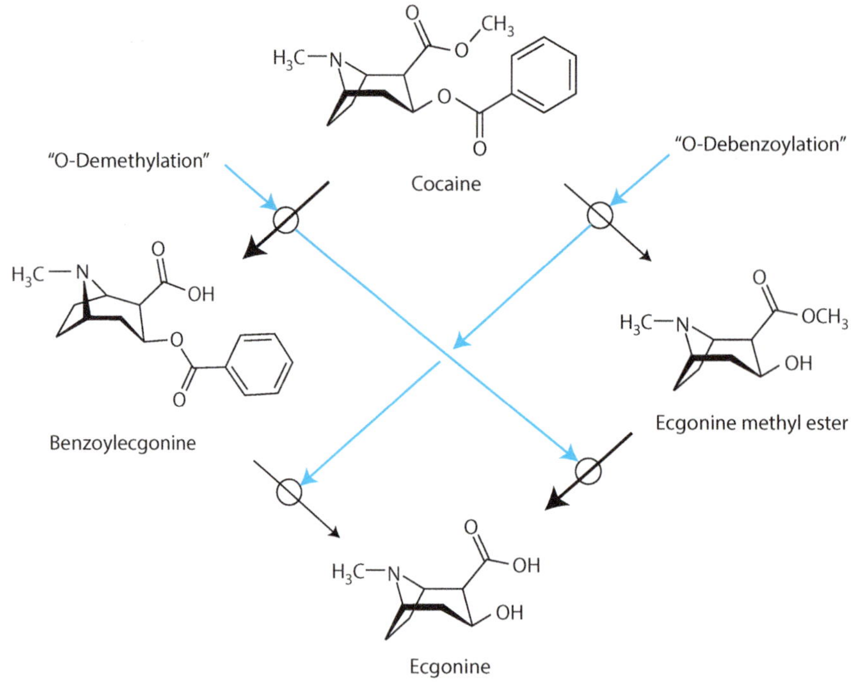

Figure 15.4 Cocaine biotransformation.

Mechanistically, as one might expect from a drug in the SMA category, cocaine acts on NT release and reuptake. Cocaine binds to the dopamine transporter (DAT), thereby blocking the reuptake ability of the protein. Unlike amphetamine, however, cocaine does not seem to reverse the action of the transporter and does not cause an outward flow of DA from the neuron via the DAT. (In other words, unlike amphetamine, cocaine does not apparently change the DAT from a DA-sodium symport to a DA-drug antiport configuration.) Frequent cocaine use does result in a downregulation of the DAT, with implications for both addiction and the depression that may accompany withdrawal from the drug. Cocaine inhibits the serotonin and norepinephrine reuptake transport protein as well. The pattern of effects on norepinephrine, serotonin, and dopamine, and the specific tissues in which those effects are expressed, is probably the basis for the subtle differences between subjective effects caused by the drugs many users associate with the SMAs.

Cocaine, rather uniquely of the SMAs, is also an anesthetic agent, acting as a voltage-gated sodium channel blocking agent. Cocaine has historically been utilized as the anesthetic of choice for localized surgical procedures of the face, scalp, and neck, although in recent years that function has been replaced by other agents.

Cocaine is rapidly metabolized in the body, with hydrolysis of the methyl ester moiety producing benzoylecgonine (BE) and hydrolysis of the benzoyl ester yielding ecgonine methyl ester (EME). Hydrolysis of either BE or EME yields ecgonine (see Figure 15.4). Many forensic laboratories quantitate and report only cocaine, the psychotropically active species of the group, and BE, the predominant metabolite (readily detectable both in blood and urine). BE can be detected in urine for as many as 3 days after use in some cases.

Cocaethylene is a hepatic transesterification product that can be formed when alcohol and cocaine are present in the liver at the same time. Cocaethylene is recognized as a potent psychotropic drug, acting in the same manner as cocaine and perhaps with a somewhat greater effect.

15.3.7 Cathinones

The cathinones are a huge group of drugs built on the basic substructure of cathinone, benzoylethanamine. With few exceptions, the drugs are CNS stimulants, but with perhaps somewhat lessened effects as compared with the analogous amphetamine compounds. The archetypal compounds are cathinone itself, and the synthetic analogs mephedrone, methylone, and MDPV (methylenedioxypyrovalerone). Many of these compounds are currently being sold as bath salts or plant food and often marked somewhat hypocritically as "not for human consumption" (Figures 15.5 and 15.6).

Cathione is a monamine alkaloid and is the psychotropically active component contained in the flowering plant khat (*Catha edulis*), native to the Horn of Africa and the Arabian Peninsula. Cathinone is a mild,

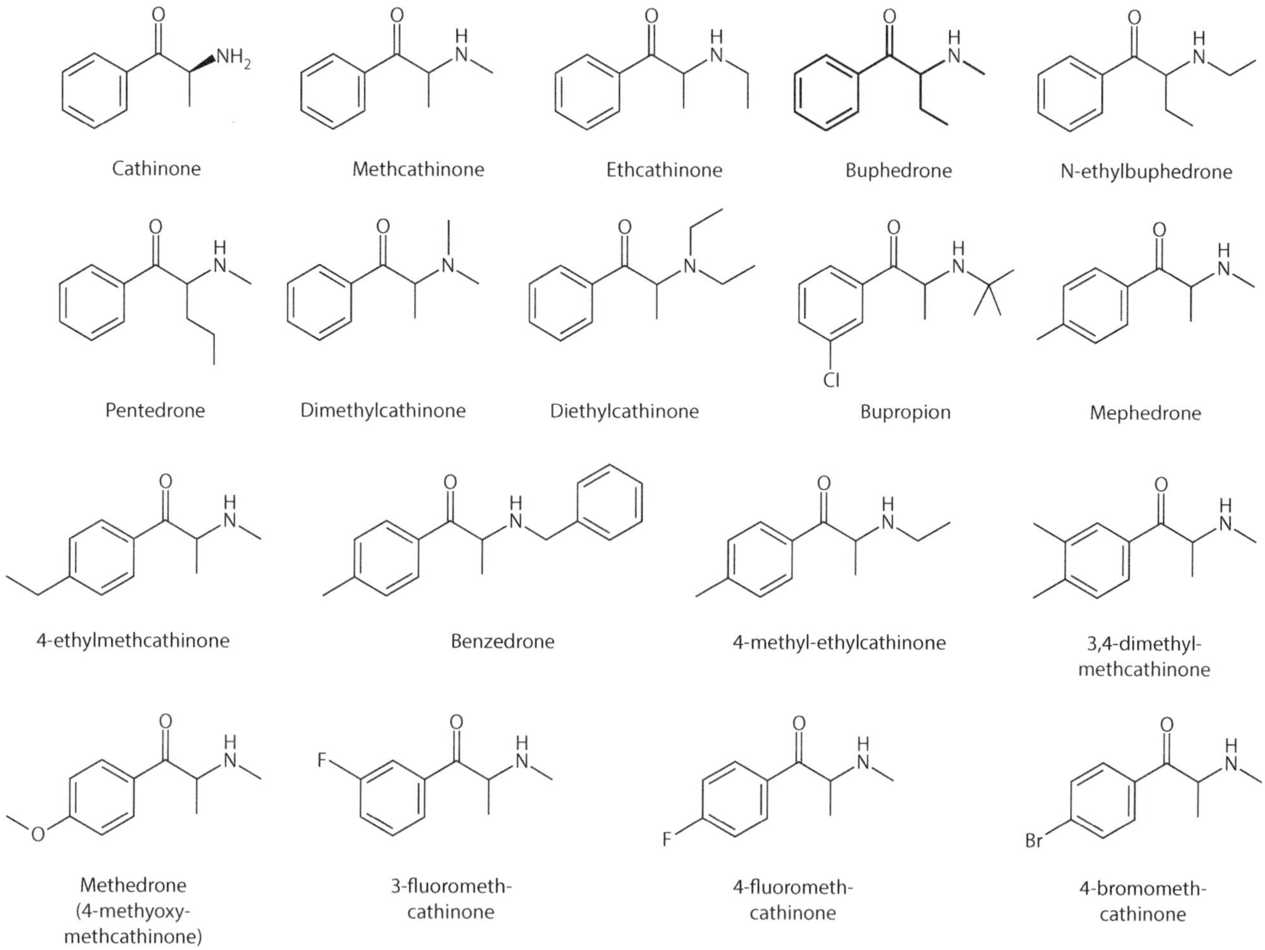

Figure 15.5 Cathinone and related compounds.

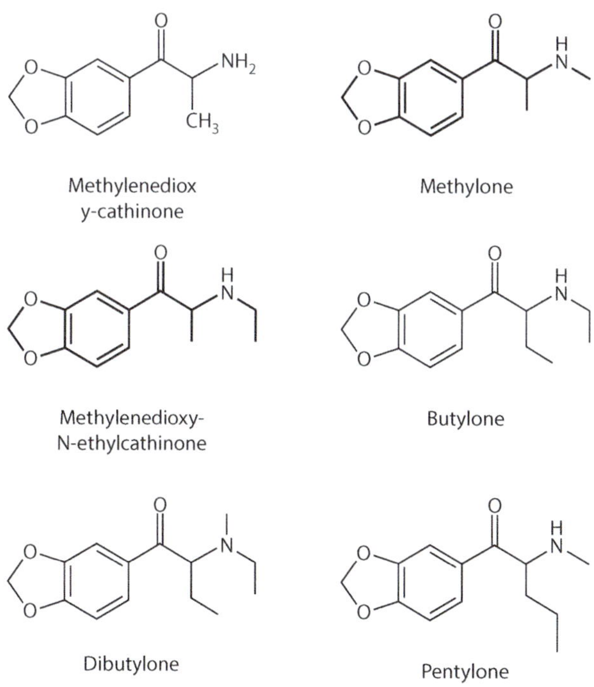

Figure 15.6 Methylenedioxycathinones.

amphetamine-like stimulant. The significance of the compound lies in the tremendous number of structurally related compounds that can be readily synthesized on the cathinone substructure and by substituents on the phenyl group (including the dimethoxy structure characterized by MDA and MDMA).

The cathinones are reputed to be euphorogenic and produce an enhanced mood and mental function and capability, similar to the effects of other SMAs. Unintended side effects are reported to include teeth grinding (again characteristic of many of the SMAs), short-term memory problems, hallucinations, and delusions. Perhaps more seriously are elevation in heart rate and core body temperature. The cathinone derivatives appear to act in a manner similar to amphetamines, in that they can bind to and block norepinephrine, dopamine and serotonin reuptake, and transport proteins. Differences between specific molecules are likely to be a function of relative binding affinities for the various receptors rather than mechanistic distinctions.

The cathinones are ready substrates for multiple phase 1 metabolism, including demethylation, oxidation, and hydroxylation. Glucuronide and sulfate conjugates can be generated by phase II reactions and can therefore be expected to be detectable in urine samples.

15.3.8 Benzyl- and Phenylpiperazines

The benzylpiperazines and phenylpiperazines are large classes of structurally diverse drugs based on the benzyl- or phenylpiperazine core. A number of varied pharmacologic agents are in this group, including antipsychotics, antibiotics, antidepressant, antifungal, antihypertensive, and other drugs. Trazodone is an example regularly seen in forensic samples (Chapter 14). Drugs in this class are relatively simplistic in structure, meaning the substituent groups are not too large and tend to act as sympathomimetics.

Benzylpiperazine (BZP) was fairly popular as a designer drug in the 1990s in its own right, and to some extent as an adulterant in some drug mixes. BZP is the archetypal compound for the group of "benzylpiperazines" currently serving as a basis for a multiplicity of related drugs built upon the BZP structure, both legitimate pharmaceuticals (including antidepressants, antipsychotic, antihistamine, antiparkinsonian, cardiac medications, and illicit species). A few of the designer drugs include 4-methyl-1-benzylpiperazine (MBZP), 4-bromo-2,5-dimethoxy-1-benzylpiperazine (2C-B-BZP), 1,4-dibenzylpiperazine (DBZP), and 3,4-methylenedioxy-1-benzylpiperazine (MDBZP). Effects produced by the BZPs are similar to those produced by amphetamine and similarly acting compounds. The BZPs act on the serotonin and dopamine receptors, in a manner similar to MDMA and amphetamine but with less efficacy on the norepinephrine reuptake transporter.

Similarly, there are a multiplicity of phenylpiperazines, including many pharmaceutical compounds (e.g., ciprofloxin, ketoconazole, and trazodone). The ability of the prototypical compound phenylpiperazine to serve as a synthetic basis for modification is demonstrated in a variety of designer drugs currently represented in the club drug arena, for example, dichlorophenylpiperazine (DCPP), methoxyphenylpiperazine (PFPP), and trifluoromethylphenylpiperazine (TFMPP) (Figure 15.7).

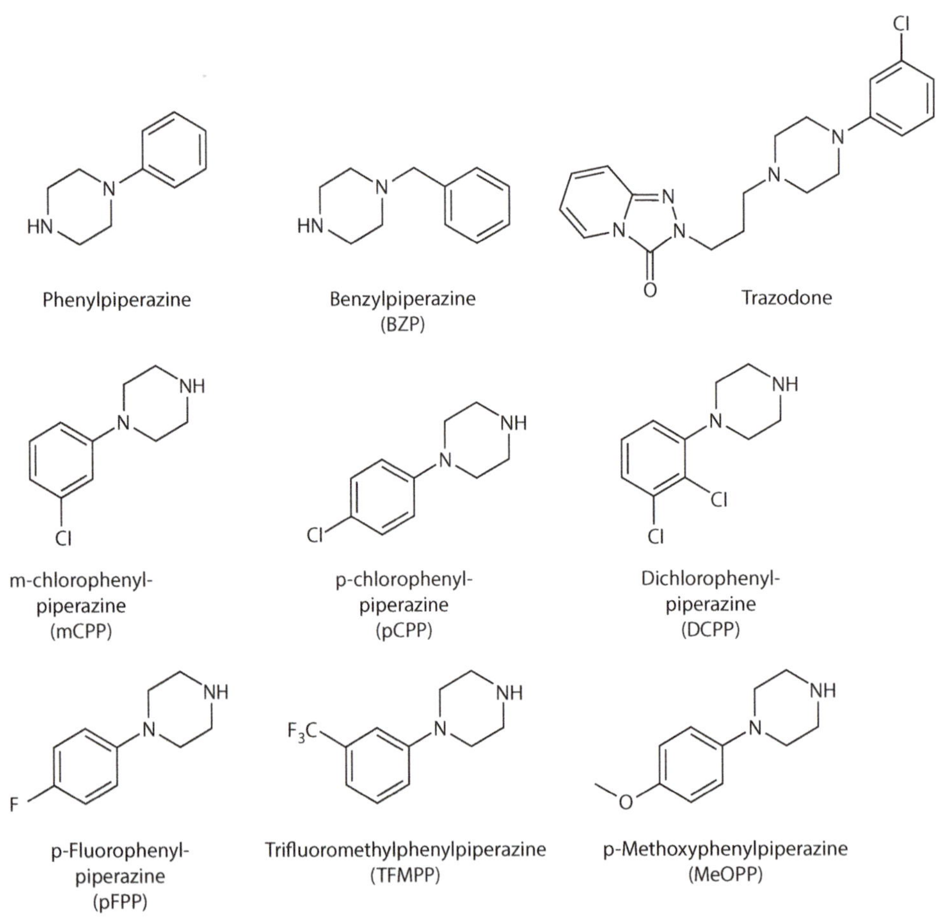

Figure 15.7 Phenylpiperazines.

15.4 Analysis and Interpretation of SMA Results

The analysis of the well-recognized SMAs such as cocaine, amphetamine, methamphetamine, MDA, and MDMA is fairly straightforward. However, the massive influx of functional analogs of the cathinones, piperazines, pyrovalerones, and others represents a significant analytical challenge for many laboratories. For those laboratories that rely on computerized mass spectral identification as a first step in a quantitative analytical process, libraries constantly need to be updated. Many laboratories also rely to some extent on the skill, experience, and ability of analysts to determine that a peak observed on a chromatogram may actually represent a drug, and then to follow up with a focused identification process. Finally, most laboratories insist on having an actual standard of a compound identified in a sample prior to reporting the presence or a quantitative result for that compound. While forensically desirable, this can represent a significant burden, both in terms of the costs for maintaining the necessary inventory of standard materials but also the difficulty that can exist in finding reliable sources for new compounds. In some cases, drugs appear in a local market prior to a standard source being available at all.

Interpretation of SMA results can be difficult, depending on the nature of the question being asked. DUI cases may depend on behavior, and relation of that behavior to drugs that may have been identified in blood or urine. While quantitate levels of drugs in blood can be the basis for a legitimate inference of effect on the body, the identification of a drug in a urine sample is (in most cases) no guarantee that the drug was present in the body at a level that could produce a physiological effect. In short, the presence of a drug in urine can be used to explain impairment, but cannot be used to infer impairment. It is difficult in the extreme to envision a circumstance that would allow a valid inference of a blood drug concentration based on a urine level.

Toxicologists are increasingly being asked to determine whether a specific new, perhaps designer drug qualifies as an analog of an existing, scheduled compound. Historically, structural similarity, as evident in two-dimensional molecular representations, might have been considered adequate for a reasonable inference of analog status. It is important, however, to recognize that structural similarity is simply not a valid basis for an inference of functional analogy, and by the same token, the lack of structural similarity is equally not a valid basis for concluding that a molecule is unable to elicit a specific pharmacologic effect. Consider morphine, naloxone, and fentanyl. Morphine and fentanyl are potent opioid agonists, with no two-dimensional structural similarity. However, fentanyl is able to adopt a three-dimensional configuration such that it can fit in and act as an agonist at morphine receptors, and as such can reasonably be described as a morphine functional analog. In contrast, naloxone has considerable structural similarity to morphine and yet is a receptor antagonist, able to block the actions of morphine and similar drugs. Naloxone, then, could reasonably be defined as a structural, but not a functional morphine analog.

Interpretation of SMA results in postmortem cases can also be difficult. Effects and the potential for lethality of the common SMAs is of course well known and recognized among forensic pathologists. Typically cited are the hypertensive effects, with the resultant cardiac hypertrophy associated with prolonged use, but also the potential for "excited delirium" that has been discussed and debated in the field for some time. Information provided to the case pathologist in cases of cocaine, amphetamines, and so forth will in most cases be limited to the drugs identified and the concentrations thereof. However, in some cases, particularly those with drugs that are relatively new to the forensic world, the forensic toxicologist may be able to provide information and insight with regard to the mechanism of action, effects, and potential for lethality.

REVIEW QUESTIONS

1. Differentiate the mechanism of cocaine and methamphetamine in terms of presynaptic neuron effects.
2. What inference can you draw from the presence of cocaethylene in a DUI case? In a death case?
3. How can use of cocaine cause death?
4. Why were amphetamines used as diet pills?
5. Why doesn't ephedrine act like methamphetamine?
6. What behavioral effects seem to associate with methylene dioxy ring substitution on the phenylethylamine substructure?

TOPICS FOR DISCUSSION

1. Currently, specific compounds are scheduled and are therefore illegal to possess or require a legitimate prescription. Should entire drug classes (e.g., SMAs) as opposed to specific compounds be available for the schedule process?
2. Ephedrine (*ma huang*) has been used medicinally for centuries but is currently not legal in

the United States. Should it be? What are the risks/benefits?

3. Can (or should) structural similarity be utilized as a basis for analog designation? Why or why not?
4. What would you expect the combination of cocaine and alcohol to produce in terms of psychotropic effects? Would they cancel each other out (depressant v. stimulant)? If not, why not?
5. Khat is a natural, organic plant containing a mild stimulant. Should it be made legal? Why or why not?

Bibliography

Barile FA. *Clinical Toxicology: Principles and Mechanisms.* 2nd ed. New York: Informa Healthcare, 2010.

Drummer OH. *The Forensic Pharmacology of Drugs of Abuse.* London: Arnold, 2001.

Karch SB. *A Brief History of Cocaine.* 2nd ed. Boca Raton, FL: Taylor & Francis, 2006.

Klassen CD. *Casarett and Doull's Toxicology: The Basic Science of Poisons.* 8th rev. ed. New York: McGraw-Hill, 2013.

Levine B, editor. *Principles of Forensic Toxicology.* Washington, DC: American Association for Clinical Chemistry, 1998.

Reichl FX, and Ritter L, editors. *Illustrated Handbook of Toxicology.* Stuttgart: Thieme, 2011.

Hallucinogens, Psychedelics, and Cannabinoids

16

Contents

16.1 Introduction

Hallucinogens represent a rather broad grouping of drugs that can distort or affect the manner in which the brain perceives reality. These drugs can affect the cognitive, perceptual, and emotional aspects of the brain. A true hallucination is a perception that is not based in reality but nevertheless appears realistic to the drug user. A classic, or archetypal, hallucinogen is lysergic acid diethylamide (LSD), producing in users highly intensified sensations of colors, smells, and sounds, associated with distortions of perception and time. In common terminology, *hallucinogen* is often used to refer specifically to LSD-type drugs and experiences, and *psychedelic* is often considered a broader term, with hallucinogen being as a subclass of mind-altering or psychodelic substances thereof. However, in the current formal approach to nomenclature of these compounds, that model is reversed; the three generalized categories of hallocinogens are psychedelics, dissociative agents, and deliriants. As is often the case with classification schemes, the categories can significantly overlap. The cannabinoids represent a particular classification problem, in that while marijuana could be described as a mild psychedelic, some of the synthetic cannabinoids can have a much more stimulatory, sympathomimetic amine (SMA)-type effect.

Drugs that are classified as hallucinogenic agents generally exert their primary impact and effect on cognition, perception, and emotion, without a significant CNS depressant effect (thereby excluding narcotic compounds from consideration). Autonomic effects (the unconscious or involuntary processes, e.g., heartbeat, respiration, etc.) are generally minimal, and while there may be an effect of these compounds on excitatory neurotransmission, that effect is relatively minimal and addiction is not normally associated with hallucinogenic species (although there may also be long-term consequences to the use of these compounds).

From a forensic sense, while these drugs are not generally toxic in the sense of cellular or organ toxicity, they can clearly have a negative effect on the ability of an individual to safely operate machinery, or function safely in a potentially hazardous environment. The presence of hallucinogens may therefore be of forensic significance in a driving under the influence (DUI) or accidental death scenario. With the tremendous increase in the appearance and use of new or novel designer drugs, and the willingness of many people to experiment with such compounds (whether synthetic or naturally occurring), the potential of a particular psychotropic agent to cause a significant and detrimental physiologic effect must be recognized in forensic casework.

Many of these new compounds can be relatively innocuous in use, but others can be debilitating in the extreme, essentially removing the user from the real perceptual world around them (e.g., in a manner analogous to PCP). Individuals using these drugs may be at risk (depending on the circumstances) from their setting and environment rather than from a particular toxic impact of the drug.

The forensic challenges represented by these species is formidable, a function of the variability of the mix of specific drugs that are available for use in a given geographic region and the frequency with which new drugs are introduced and move into use. A well-recognized example of this phenomenon is the appearance of many different synthetic marijuana compounds and the rapid change in the pattern of particular species available and marketed, as the producers respond to changes in federal and state scheduling of particular drugs and local laws. One challenge then from the analytical perspective is simply being able to recognize the presence of such a drug when it appears in an analytical scheme for the first time, particularly if the compound has not yet been included in the spectral library in use by the laboratory. A second challenge is the mechanistic consideration of a new compound and any expectation of effects, based on similarity to existing species (i.e., whether a new structure qualifies as a functional analog of a recognized, scheduled drug). While structural similarity between species can indeed be suggestive of a similar mechanism of action, it is not a guarantee of efficacy. Great care and caution should be exercised in consideration of any opinion regarding activity that is based solely on structural similarity between species, in the absence of pharmacokinetic or other experimental evidence suggesting functional or mechanistic similarity. In a related vein, the toxicologist should be extremely cautious in associating any particular symptom or pattern of effects with a new species in the absence of a sound structure-activity basis for such an association, or better still, definitive research supporting either a mechanistic or functional basis for the opinion. The appearance of structural similarity (particularly as determined from a 2-D presentation) is generally an unreliable basis from which to infer pharmacologic activity.

16.2 Psychedelics

The term *psychedelic* is generally applied to a drug that can produce significant perceptual distortions, such as LSD, psilocybin, mescaline, a number of the tryptamine compounds, and even at least one amphetamine-type compound (e.g., 2,5-dimethoxy-4-bromoamphetamine, or DOB).

16.2.1 Serotonin-Releasing Agents and Receptor Agonists

While generally classified as sympathomimetic amines, the substituted methylenedioxyphenethylamines (e.g., MDA, MDMA, MDEA), because of their particular spectrum of effects (similar to the amphetamines but emphasizing the euphorogenic and entactogenic responses), are often classified as psychedelics (further emphasizing the somewhat arbitrary and overlapping nature of the classification schemes). (See also MDA and MDMA in Chapter 15.) Of course, many species are able to stimulate or cause serotonin release from the presynaptic neuron. The particular pattern of that release, in relation to the other excitatory neurotransmitters (dopamine [DA] and norepinephrine [NE]), characterizes the psychedelic behavior of specific drugs.

The serotonin receptors are a large and complex family of receptor proteins, functional as both agonist-gated ion channels, and G-coupled protein receptors (GCPRs) with serotonin as the endogenous agonist. The 5-HT2A subtype is a GCPR and is activated by the serotonergic psychedelic drugs, such as LSD (serotonin is 5-hydroxytryptamine, or 5-HT, so 5-HT2A is the 2A serotonin receptor). Upon agonist activation, subunits of the protein dissociate from the receptor complex and initiate multiple intracellular reactions primarily through the action of phospholipase and protein kinase activity (e.g., phospholipase C), including formation of inositol triphosphate (IP3) and diacylglyceral (DAG). The IP3/DAG pathway allows mobilization of calcium ions from the smooth endoplasmic reticulum (ER) into the cytosol, enhancing neurotransmitter packaging and release.

16.2.2 Tryptamines

The tryptamine class includes the endogenous neurotransmitter serotonin (5-HT), and many members of the group are functional as psychedelic drugs due to their ability to act as serotonin receptor agonists. The basic tryptamine structure is commonly found in many living species of both the plant and animal kingdoms. Many naturally occurring members of the class have been used specifically for their psychotropic effects (e.g., psilocybin, dimethyltryptamine, ibogaine, and yohimbine). The class has become much more "populated" in recent decades with synthetic or partially synthetic examples. An extensive investigatory compilation of synthetic tryptamines was published by Alexander Shulgin as *TiHKAL* (Tryptamines I Have Known and Loved) in 1997. Many of the compounds discussed in the text have appeared or are appearing on the forensic scene and can represent an analytical challenge, in part at least because of their similarity in many cases to endogenous biomolecules. The class is large and still growing, in part due to the ease with which the basic structure can be synthetically modified (Figure 16.1).

16.2.3 Lysergic Acid and Related Structures

Lysergic acid is the core molecule upon which a number of derivatives, the ergoline alkaloids, are synthesized.

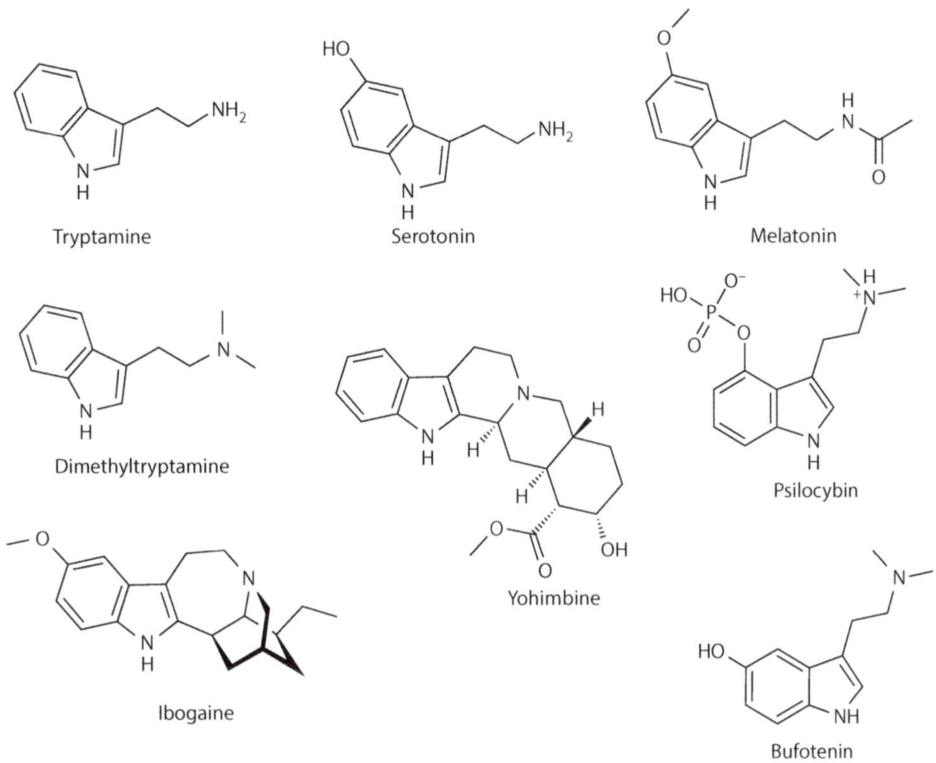

Figure 16.1 Examples of naturally occurring tryptamines (tryptamine, serotonin, melatonin, dimethyltryptamine, yohimbine, psilocybin, ibogaine, and bufotenin).

Lysergic amides are known as lysergamides, characterized by the diethylamide LSD. LSD was first synthesized in 1938 from ergotamine and is an extremely potent hallucinogen, with effective doses in the range of roughly 100 micrograms in an adult human (see Sidebar 16.1).

Mechanistically, LSD affects multiple G-coupled proteins, including those agonized by dopamine and serotonin. Specifically, LSD is an agonist of 5-HT2A receptors (see Section 16.2.1). The exact mechanism by which LSD is hallucinogenic remains an active topic of investigation (Figure 16.2).

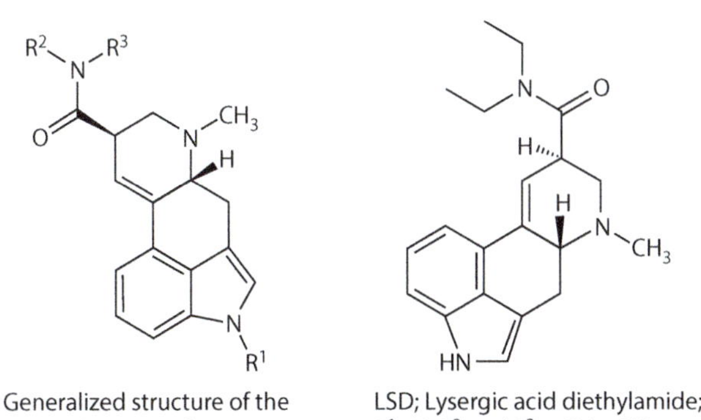

Figure 16.2 Lysergamides and LSD.

SIDEBAR 16.1 ERGOT ALKALOIDS IN HISTORY

Examples of some texts from the Middle Ages contain descriptions of towns where seemingly, "all hell breaks loose." People are reported as complaining of "hot fires" in their extremities, some seeing visions and others writhing in pain. Concurrently, an increase in the number of spontaneous abortions appeared to increase. In such chaotic circumstances, supernatural explanations were quickly invoked.

The descriptions of these events, however, seem more descriptive of an outbreak of "ergotism," a poisoning resulting from the consumption of grains (often rye, although wheat and other grains can be involved, and foodstuffs made from these grains) that had been infected with the fungus *Claviceps purpurea*. This fungus thrives in damp conditions and affects seed grains, producing black sclera (and hence black rot fungus). The fungus produces mycotoxins responsible for ergotism—the ergot alkaloids—notably ergotamine, ergonovine, lysergic acid, and bromocriptine.

Ergot poisoning seems to be categorized into two main types of symptoms. The first is gangrenous ergotism and is characterized by feelings of fire in limbs. The physiologic explanation for this burning described is increased lactic acid production as a consequence of vasospastic ischemia. Ergot alkaloids are potent alpha-adrenoreceptor blockers that cause constriction of peripheral veins and arteries leading to a significant decrease in oxygen reaching peripheral tissues. As oxygen is less available, the tissues shift toward anaerobic energy generation. The consequence of this change manifests as immediate pain, inflammation, and the extremities adopting a burned appearance. Prolonged vasospasms can result in the digits, toes, or whole limbs becoming gangrenous. The increased rate of spontaneous abortions can best be explained by the alkaloids stimulating the smooth muscle of the uterus into premature contractions.

A second focus of the symptoms of ergot poisoning is the CNS stimulation caused by the ergot alkaloids interacting at dopamine and serotonin receptors. Symptoms observed included tremors, seizures, writhing, blindness, dementia, and vivid hallucinations. It is interesting to note that these symptoms may or may not present themselves with the ischemic related symptoms. This variety of symptoms is the result of diversity in the strains of the fungus, and hence the pattern of alkaloids generated. It is easy to understand that such symptoms, particularly in the absence of any manifestation of physical disease, could lead observers to believe afflicted individuals were either "possessed" or practicing witchcraft.

If left untreated, ergot poisoning can lead to death. Symptoms of ergotism were termed St. Anthony's Fire, and in some areas it was believed that appeals to the saint could take away the pain. (There are numerous records speaking of the healing properties of pilgrimages to Padua to visit the bones of St. Anthony. Presumably, a diet based on uncontaminated foodstuffs may have played a role in the healing process.)

16.2.4 Phenethylamines

The phenethylamine core is the basic structure underlying the amphetamines and related compounds and are therefore discussed in Chapter 15. To the extent that the drugs are able to agonize the 5-HT2A receptor, they may exhibit hallucinogenic activity.

16.2.5 Cannabinoids

Until relatively recently, *cannabinoids* meant the psychotropically active compounds derived from the marijuana plant, primarily Δ-9 tetrahydrocannabinol (THC), and the other related active compounds (and some inactive species) derived from the marijuana plant. One of the most popular recreational drugs, marijuana has been the subject of much of the routine testing in forensic laboratories. Smuggling and domestic production has continued to make marijuana a readily-available illicit drug, and with the increasing use of marijuana in a medical setting and the relaxation of many laws associated with possession of the drug, the forensic community will certainly be continuing to devote considerable efforts to the demonstration of the presence, or history of use, of marijuana.

In contrast to ethanol, blood levels of marijuana are not generally a reliable indicator of drug level in the target tissue, being the CNS. The active species, tetrahydrocannabinol, is highly lipophilic, with a large volume of distribution (Vd) and is extensively distributed. Elimination kinetics from the blood are biphasic with an early phase representing both metabolism and distribution, and a later, long phase representing mobilization, from lipophilic tissues, and metabolism, ultimately to the carboxylic acid aglycone, and eventually the glucuronidated form. Both the acyl and glucuronide species appear in the urine and can be detected for several days following usage (how long is actually a function of the amount and frequency of use in the time prior to sample collection).

Marijuana is not a particularly toxic species, and the consequences of use tend to be expressed in terms of impairment. As such, marijuana use is of considerable importance in DUI situations but not a major factor as a potential cause of death (beyond, of course, contributing to a fatal accident).

In 2004, the concept of synthetic marijuana began to emerge, the idea being that with the right combination of herbs (legal, but with some psychotropic activity, e.g., Wild Dagga, Honeyweed, Dwarf Skullcap, Egyptian Water Lily, Lotus, etc.), the right balance of effects could be achieved so that a marijuana-like high could be experienced without the actual presence of the active component of the marijuana plant. These mixes were often marketed as some variation of "herbal incense" and achieved considerable popularity among certain drug-using communities. However, in 2008, chemists at the University of Freiburg (Germany) discovered the presence of CP 47,497 (a synthetic analog of tetrahydrocannabinol) in one of the herbal incense mixes. This finding suggested, of course, that the true explanation for the cannabinoid-like effects of the herbal mix was not a mystical proportion of exotic herbs but rather … a cannabinoid.

While seeming to simplify matters, the presence of synthetic cannabinoid compound (of which quite a number had been synthesized) in the herbal mixes instead further emphasized the problem of analysis for the forensic toxicologist as a function of the routine approach to the detection and determination of drugs. The common approach, following immunologically based screen assays, is confirmation of screen-positive results for drugs or drug group components by gas chromatography/mass spectrometry (GCMS) technology, often looking for a defined group of target analytes via selected ion monitoring (SIM) technology. While this approach is fast, accurate, and reliable, it is nevertheless limited to those drugs already identified, characterized, and present in calibrator and control materials. In many cases there are no screen-positive results to guide confirmatory procedures, and a generalized GCMS program will be run in Scan mode, with chromatographic peaks identified by retention time, with spectral comparison to libraries and/or standards. Compounds new to the laboratory may be detected by such an approach, if the operator selects an unknown peak for a library search, and the compound generating the peak is already included in the instrument spectral library. Herein lies much of the problem with the new synthetic cannabinoids, both in a specific and a general sense, with many of the new designer drugs appearing within our forensic samples. Our ability to detect drugs is to a great extent dependent upon the quality of the spectra libraries we use and the ability of our analysts to recognize that the spectrum associated with a particular peak most likely represents a drug (rather than either an endogenous or otherwise innocuous biomolecule). The analyst must then carry out a library spectrum search.

The spectra libraries of most utility to the forensic toxicologist are actually being updated and populated by the controlled substances (CS) chemists, who, based on seizures of (relatively) pure materials, have an adequate supply of material so as to characterize the specific structure. Depending on the mechanism by which the material came to the laboratory, there may also be synthetic information, starting materials, intermediates, and synthetic reagents that can be used to help determine the target molecule for synthesis. Larger CS laboratories generally have access to instrumentation not usually used for biological samples (e.g., infrared or nuclear resonance spectroscopy [IR or NMR]) that can, given relatively pure materials, provide a wealth of structural information. The end point of this of course is that the spectra libraries generated by the CS community can be of tremendous use and utility to the forensic laboratory. (Specifically, the community-generated library maintained by SWGDRUG is of particular relevance and value.)

There is another contrast as a function of the appearance of the synthetic cannabinoids on the drug market, and that is the subtle distinction in mechanistic action of the various compounds, as compared to the mix of compounds, psychotropic and not contained in marijuana itself.

The active component in marijuana, THC, acts as a partial agonist for two "cannabinoid receptors," CB1 and CB2. CB1 is thought to be primarily responsible for the psychotropic actions of the drug. Both CB1 and CB2 are GPCRs, part of a large family of transmembrane receptors, which in consequence to agonist binding on the extracellular part of the protein, then activate reactions within the cell, ultimately leading to the physiological consequences of the specific activating species. GPCRs are active in many endogenous signal pathways, as well as the mechanistic basis for the action of many pharmaceutical agents (see Sidebar 16.2).

SIDEBAR 16.2 G-PROTEIN COUPLED RECEPTORS

G-protein coupled receptors (GPCRs) provide an elegant mechanism by which the body is able to translate biochemical signals into reactions, actions, and changes at the cellular level, primarily via the cyclic adenosine monophosphate (cAMP) and phosphatidylinositol signal pathways. The GPCRs are a large family of cellular transmembrane receptors, acting to mediate a multitude of physiological processes. Roles of toxicologic significance include response to a number of neurotransmitters, pharmacologic and psychotropic agents, and within the autonomic nervous system, both sympathetic and parasympathetic functions.

Mechanistically, the resting state of the receptor is a heterotrimeric transmembrane protein, associated with α, β, and γ subunits, and a guanosine diphosphate (GDP) molecule bound to the α subunit. In consequence to ligand binding to the external, glycosylated aspect of the protein, a conformational change is induced in the GPCR, which then allows the associated G protein to exchange the α-subunit bound GDP molecule for a guanosine triphosphate (GTP). Binding of GTP to the α subunit causes dissociation from the β and γ subunits. The GTP α-subunit complex and the β and γ subunits diffuse away from the transmembrane portion of the complex and act as allosteric modulators of various effector proteins. (Diffusion of the subunits away from the transmembrane portion of the receptor is limited by affinity to the membrane.) The nature of the α subunit then determines the nature of the subsequent intracellular reactions. The GTP binding site of the α complex hydrolyzes GTP to GDP, though relatively slowly. Many of the molecules that are allosterically modulated by the α subunit also have GTP-ase phosphoryl hydrolase activity. The hydrolysis of the GTP triphosphoryl group inactivates the α subunit and initiates the process of reformation with the β and γ subunits, eventually leading to the reconstitution of the GPCR in the resting state.

The main pathways by which the activated α subunit functions within the cell are as an allosteric activator of adenylyl cyclase, forming cyclic AMP (cAMP) from ATP. The cellular second messenger cAMP is active in many cellular pathways, including acting as an allosteric activator of the phosphorylating enzyme protein kinase A. (Interestingly, inhibitory GPCR α subunits function to inhibit adenylyl cyclase.) A second major pathway is the activation of phospholipase C, which functions to hydrolyze phosphatidylinositol 4,5-bisphosphate (PIP2), yielding inositol 1,4,5-triphosphate (IP3) and diacylglycerol (DAG), which act as second messengers. IP3 facilitates the intracellular release of Ca^{+2} from endoplasmic reticulum and mitochondria, which can then combine with the calcium-binding protein calmodulin, activating calmodulin kinase II, which is active in the phosphorylation and regulation of many enzyme systems within the cell. Calcium, in combination with DAG, also activates protein kinase C (PKC), leading to the phosphorylation and activation of other enzymatic pathways in the cell (Figure 16.3).

Agonist binding to CB1 activates multiple intracellular pathways, the most important of which are likely the inhibition of adenylate cyclase (limiting the production of the intracellular messenger cyclic AMP), voltage-gated calcium channels, and the positive modulation of inwardly rectifying potassium channels, the net effect of which is to inhibit presynaptic inhibitory neurons. This presynaptic inhibition normally occurs in the body when the postsynaptic neuron releases endocannabinoids, which then, diffusing from the postsynaptic to the presynaptic neuron, bind to and activate CB1 receptors.

Two distinctions between many of the synthetic cannabinoids, and the mix of cannabinoids found in marijuana, is simply that unlike many of the synthetic analogs, which are full agonists of CB1, THC is a partial agonist, unable to elicit the full magnitude of effect from binding to the CB1 as would a full agonist. Second, among the mix of compounds contained in marijuana are a number of species that act as antagonists of the cannabinoid receptors. The mix of partial activators and some inhibitors seems to modulate the nature of the overall response to marijuana, so as to produce the characteristic high associated with the drug, yet without an excessive CNS stimulation. In contrast, a number of the synthetic compounds, as full agonists of CB1 and without any inhibiting activity, can produce a qualitatively different experience in the user and may produce symptoms more characteristic of an SMA-type drug than would be expected from a cannabinoid mix.

The consequences of this distinction may be important for the forensic toxicologist. While the ability of marijuana to impair the functional capability of the user is well established, one does not normally associate the potential for severe physiologic consequences as a function of marijuana use. In contrast, the use of synthetic cannabinoid species has been associated with rapid heart rate, hypertension, psychotic behavior, seizures, and death. Mechanistically, the synthetic cannabinoids generally act as full CB1 agonists and as such are able to elicit a much stronger inhibition of GABA neurotransmission than THC, with the associated physiologic consequences expected from reduced CNS inhibition.

The challenge for the forensic toxicologist is twofold. First, to the extent that the cannabinoid effects in a case are a function of marijuana, an ability to understand the effects of THC in the context of impairment (e.g., DUI, accidents, etc.) is important. However, the ability for the laboratory to be able to detect the synthetic cannabinoids used in the region is equally important and may represent a significantly greater analytical challenge than the demonstration or quantitation of THC. Not only must the drug be recognized (usually by reference to a spectral library) but there must be a valid standard available to facilitate a quantitative analysis (Figure 16.4).

16.3 Dissociative Agents

Dissociative agents are often also referred to as *dissociative anesthetics* in that the sense of detachment from the physical body can produce a sense of anesthesia as well. At subanesthetic levels, these drugs affect cognition and perceptual processing in a manner similar to hallucinogenic drugs. There are two general classifications of drugs that can act in this fashion: the NMDA

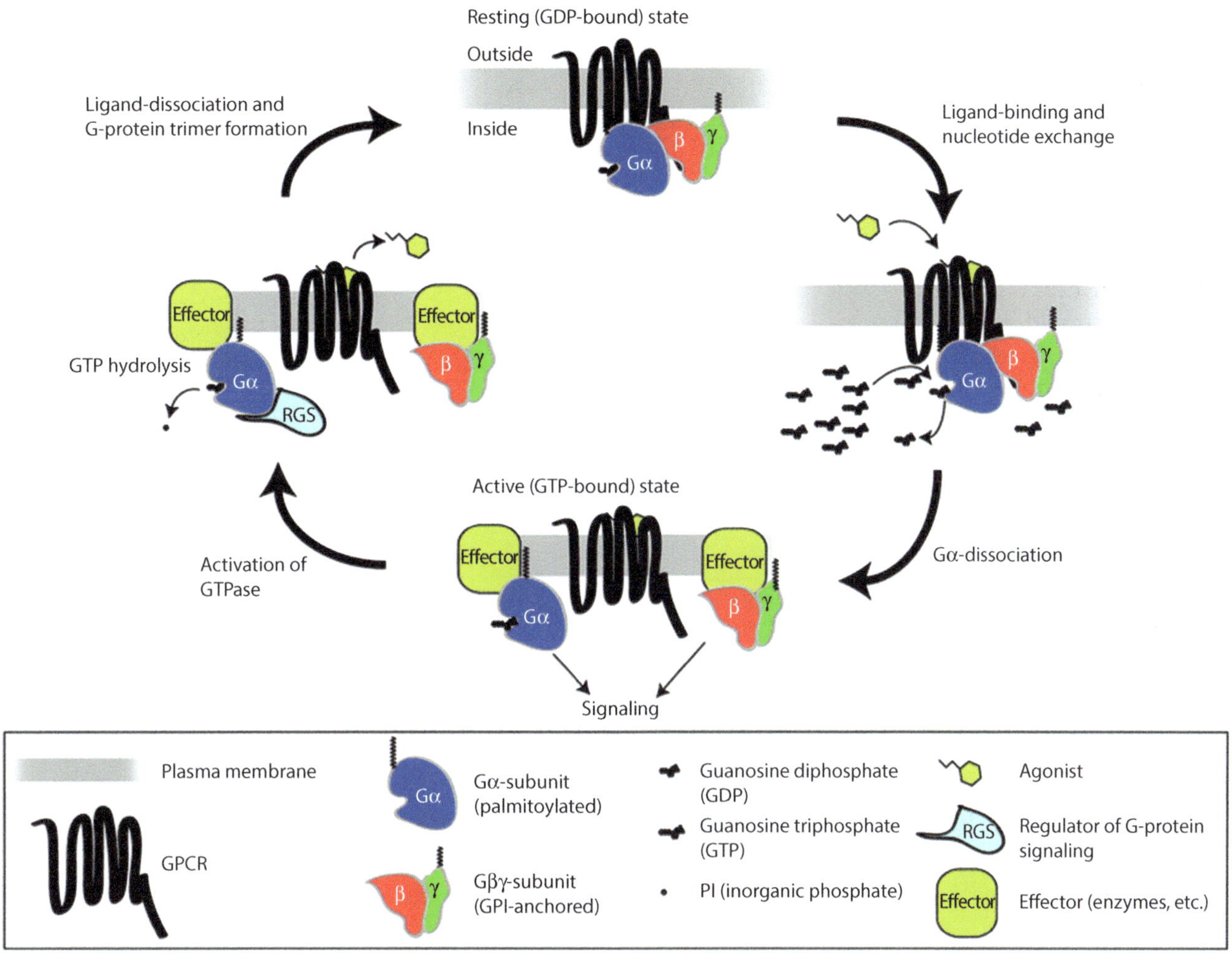

Figure 16.3 G-coupled protein GPCR-G-protein activation/deactivation cycle. In the resting state the receptor may be found associated with a heterotrimeric G-protein with GDP bound to its alpha subunit. Agonist binding to the GPCR induces a cascade of conformational changes first in the receptor and then in the bound G-alpha subunit of the G-protein. This results in release of GDP, which is soon replaced by GTP. The cell maintains a 10:1 ratio of cytosolic GTP:GDP so exchange for GTP is ensured. GTP-bound G-alpha takes yet another conformation that has low affinity for the GPCR as well as the β-γ complex, so all three dissociate from one another. GTP-G-alpha and the G-β/γ complex then go on to allosterically modulate the activities of various downstream effector proteins, but diffusion is usually limited to the membrane surface due to the presence of palmitoyl and a GPI-anchor, respectively. The GTP-binding site of G-alpha is also capable of hydrolyzing GTP to GDP, albeit at a relatively slow rate. This rate can be increased by binding to various GTPase-activating proteins (GAPs) such as those of the RGS family. Many effector molecules modulated by G-alpha also have GAP activity. Upon GTP hydrolysis the G-alpha subunit is rendered inactive and once again may bind G-beta/gamma and form a heterotrimeric G-protein, which will often be found associated with an unliganded GPCR. (Figure caption and image retrieved from Wikipedia Commons April 2, 2015. Image made available and published under the Creative Commons Attribution-Share Alike 3.0 Unported license by user and author Repapetilto. Original upload date June 23, 2010. License can be found here and no changes were made to the image: http://creativecommons.org/licenses/by-sa/3.0/legalcode.)

(N-methyl-D-aspartate) receptor antagonists and the opioid κ-receptor agonists.

Classic drugs producing this effect via NMDA receptor antagonism are ketamine and PCP, members of the arylcyclohexylamine group. The mechanism of action appears to be a function of the noncompetitive antagonist action of the drugs at a binding site in the central channel of the (NMDA) receptor, a relatively nonselective cation channel, allowing a potentially depolarizing sodium and calcium influx, and potassium efflux from the postsynaptic neuron when activated. The NMDA receptor is associated with synaptic plasticity (modulation of the connection between neurons as a function of signal frequency). Antagonists of the receptor bind to an active site within the ion channel, physically preventing the transit of cations either in or out of the cell (Figure 16.5).

Opioid κ receptor agonists have the potential to cause dissociative and delirium-inducing effects. An endogenous agonist is the opioid peptide dynorphin, and a

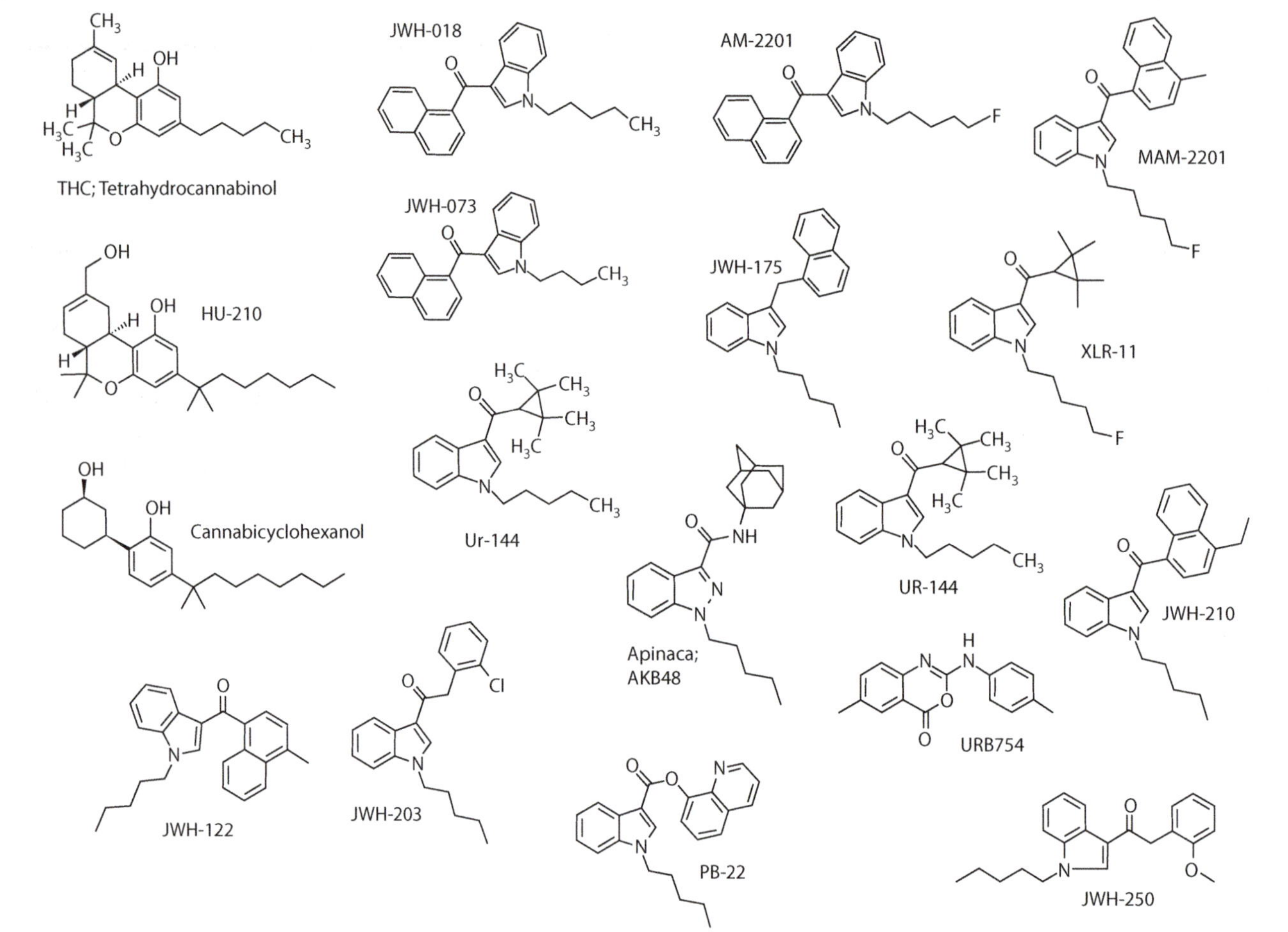

Figure 16.4 THC and example synthetic cannabinoids.

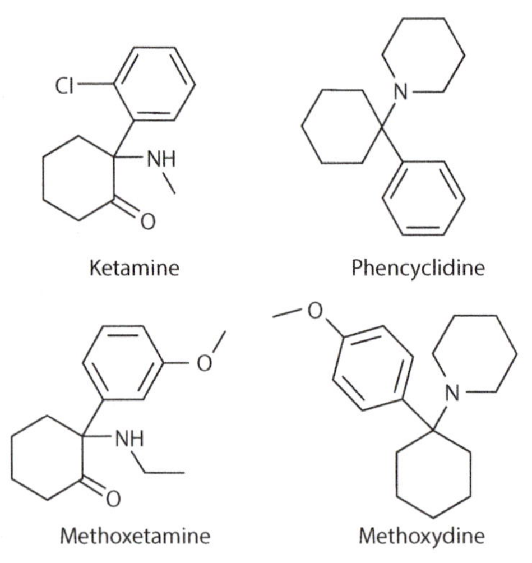

Figure 16.5 Dissociative arylcyclohexylamines (ketamine, phencyclidine, phenylhexylcyclopyrrolidine, methoxydine 4-MeO-PCP).

number of alkaloids have been shown to act as agonists. The κ-receptor is metabotropic, activating the phosphodiesterase activity in the cell, causing a more rapid breakdown of cAMP. The overall effect is inhibitory. κ-opioid receptor agonists include dextromethorphan, dextrorphan, methorphan, morphanol, and the natural compounds menthol, ibogaine, and salvia divinorum (see Sidebar 16.3 and Figure 16.6).

SIDEBAR 16.3 SALVIA DIVINORUM

Salvia divinorum is a plant that has a long history of use in folk medicine and ritualistic practices in Mexico and Central America and has relatively recently emerged onto the recreational drug scene, albeit in a relatively small way. The plant produces the psychoactive diterpenoid drug salvinorin A, associated with dissociative effects. Mechanistically, salvinorin A is a κ-opioid and dopaminergic agonist.

Leaves of the plant may be chewed, or dried and smoked. An alternate dosing mechanism consists of preparation of tincture (alcohol extract), which is then ingested.

The use of the plant as a recreational drug has received some negative publicity, and while

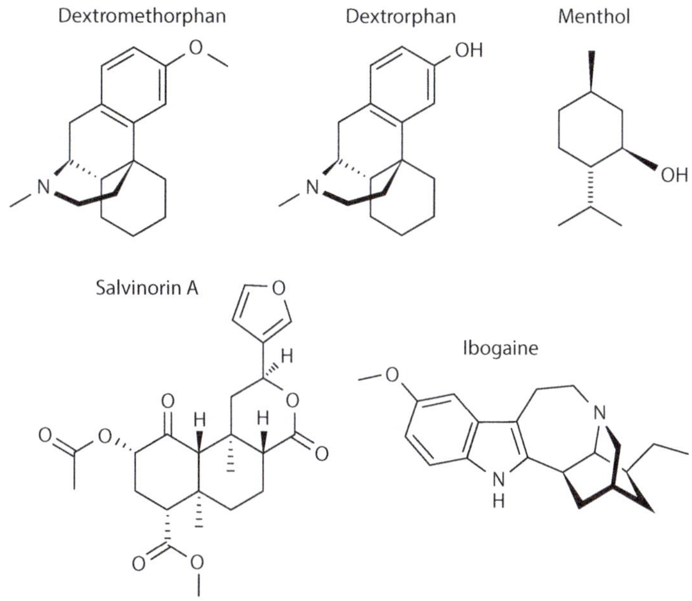

Figure 16.6 Example κ-opioid receptor agonists (dextromethorphan, dextrorphan, menthol, salvinorin A, and ibogaine).

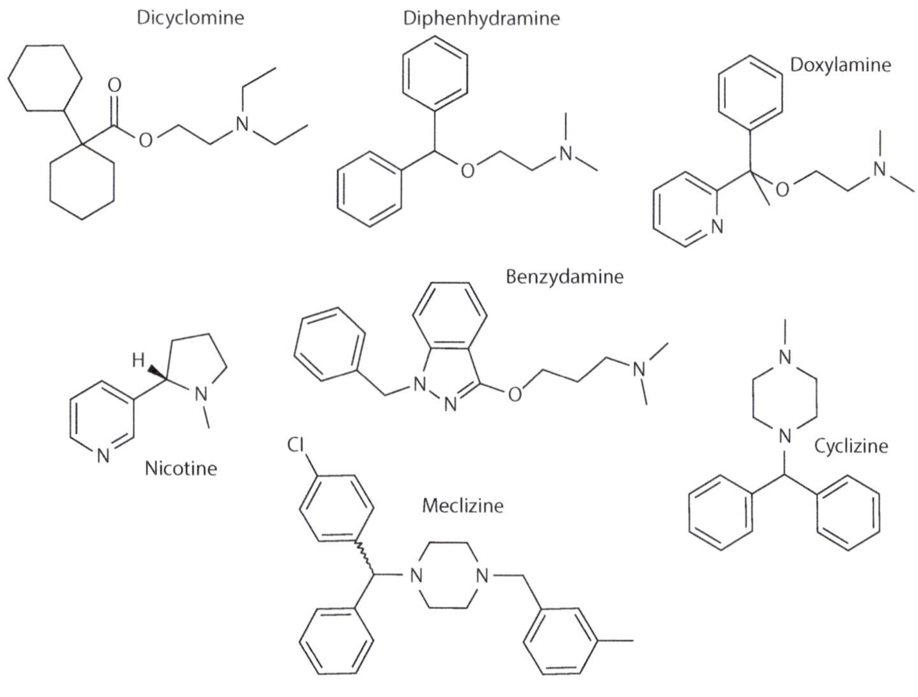

Figure 16.7 Example deliriants (dicyclomine, diphenhydramine, doxylamine, meclizine, benzydamine, cyclizine, and nicotine).

popular in some locales, the drug is not widely available. Significant toxicity is not associated with the drug, and the inherent risks with use seem to be primarily a function of the altered sense of reality the drug evokes.

16.4 Deliriants

The distinction between deliriants and hallucinogens seems to lie greatly with the degree to which the affected individual is dissociated from reality. The deliriant state has been described as a "psychotic episode." Affected users may carry on conversations with imaginary people, become stuporous and confused, or perform disconnected stages of a complex multistep process. Often, the user will have no recollection of their experiences. While occasionally encountered in forensic toxicology and may play a role in some casework, deliriants tend not to be deliberately abused. Many of these compounds are anticholinergic agents and are therefore discussed in Chapter 17. A number of synthetic antihistamine compounds (e.g., diphenhydramine, doxylamine) are deliriants in high enough doses. Interestingly, nicotine, if ingested in adequate dose, also functions as a deliriant (Figure 16.7).

REVIEW QUESTIONS

1. A number of forensic toxicologists and pathologists consider the synthetic cannabinoids to be more dangerous than marijuana. Why would that be?
2. What is the natural agonist for the NMDA receptor, and how does that system function?
3. Would the presence of LSD be recognized in a DUI situation? If so, how? If not, why not? How about a death case?
4. Can the substituted tryptamine analogs cause death? If so, what would the likely mechanism be? How would such compounds be recognized in that scenario?
5. Would you expect the various classes of hallucinogens and related drugs to be addictive? Why or why not?

TOPICS FOR DISCUSSION

1. In some areas of the country, PCP is commonly seen in combination with THC-carboxylic metabolite in the urine of drivers arrested for DUI. There is generally not, however, the aggressive, or psychotic behavior sometimes associated with PCP. Comment? What would you expect the effect of synthetic cannabinoids to be (if any)?
2. While LSD has had some periods of general interest, the level of use of the drug has never even remotely approached that of the SMAs or opiates. Why would that be?
3. Many states are legalizing marijuana to some degree. Should the synthetic compounds be legalized as well? Why or why not?
4. Discuss the statement, Structural similarity is not a valid basis for inference of functional similarity.
5. Should the entactogens be considered as a class distinct from the SMAs (e.g., amphetamine, methamphetamine, cocaine)? Why or why not?
6. Could there be a connection between the "monster mythology" of northern Europe and the ergot fungus?

Bibliography

Ellenhorn MJ. *Ellenhorn's Medical Toxicology: Diagnosis and Treatment of Human Poisoning*. 2nd ed. Baltimore: Williams & Wilkins, 1997.

Klassen CD. *Casarett and Doull's Toxicology: The Basic Science of Poisons*. 8th rev. ed. New York: McGraw-Hill, 2013.

Laing R, editor. *Hallucinogens: A Forensic Drug Handbook*. New York: Academic Press, 2003.

Reichl FX, Ritter L, editors. *Illustrated Handbook of Toxicology*. Stuttgart: Thieme, 2011.

Shulgin A, Shulgin A. *PIHKAL: A Chemical Love Story*. Berkeley, CA: Transform Press, 1991.

Shulgin A, Shulgin, A. *TiHKAL: The Continuation*. Berkeley, CA: Transform Press, 1997.

Viccellio P, editor. *Emergency Toxicology*. 2nd ed. Philadelphia: Lippencott-Raven, 1998.

Cholinergic and Anticholinergic Toxins 17

Contents

17.1 Introduction

Acetylcholine (ACh) is a major neurotransmitter (NT) of the body, utilized at *cholinergic synapses* in both the peripheral nervous system (PNS) and central nervous system (CNS). ACh is active at neuromuscular junctions and thereby controls muscle contractions throughout the body, both sympathetic (under conscious control) and parasympathetic (e.g., breathing and heart function), and also controls glandular secretion. Binding of ACh to postsynaptic receptors produces muscle contraction by causing a localized depolarization, which activates voltage-gated calcium channels, both at the cellular surface and intracellularly at the sarcoplasmic reticulum. Overactivation of the system can result in inappropriate muscle contraction or spasm, and blockage can produce paralysis. In the extreme, either scenario can be fatal.

Drugs that affect cholinergic transmission have long been recognized both for their commercial applications, pharmacological utility, and (of course) their potential as toxins or poisons. Drugs that result in excessive ACh-based muscle contractions and glandular secretions are *cholinergic* and cause the cholinergic toxidrome. In contrast, drugs that block the action of acetylcholine are *anticholinergic* and produce the anticholinergic toxidrome (Figure 17.1).

17.2 History

Plants containing anticholinergic agents, such as mandrake (*Mandragora* spp.) and henbane (*Hyoscyamus* spp.), were identified in some of the earliest societies (e.g., Ancient Egyptians and Greeks) as containing medicinal properties. In Roman society, a woman was believed to appear more attractive with large, dilated pupils. To achieve this desired effect, an extract of the deadly nightshade plant (*Atropa belladonna*) would be applied to the eyes, where the anticholinergic muscle paralysis would prevent the contraction of the muscles controlling the iris in the eye, producing the desired pupil dilation (and hence, from *bella donna* or "beautiful woman" in Italian, our modern systematic name for the species). Natives of Central and South American countries have learned to fashion arrowheads and blowgun darts coated with the anticholinergic *curare*, causing rapid paralysis and death in their prey. Curare is the collective name for a group of paralytic poisons extracted from a climbing vine (*Chonndrodendron tomentosum*), whose active component is d-tubocurarine. Another natural cholinergic toxin, physostigmine can be found in the Calabar bean (from *Physostigma venenosum*) and has been used as an "ordeal agent" where survival of the ingestion of the bean was performed as a primitive proof of innocence. Today, many cholinergic agents are employed in pesticides, such as nicotine, although their use is being phased out.

One of the first organophosphates to be synthesized was tri-ortho-cresyl phosphate, and while not active on cholinergic neurons, this line of research led quickly to the development of organophosphate compounds as military nerve gas agents in preparation for World War II. This was in response to the use of chlorine and other toxic gases to devastating effect in World War I. (However,

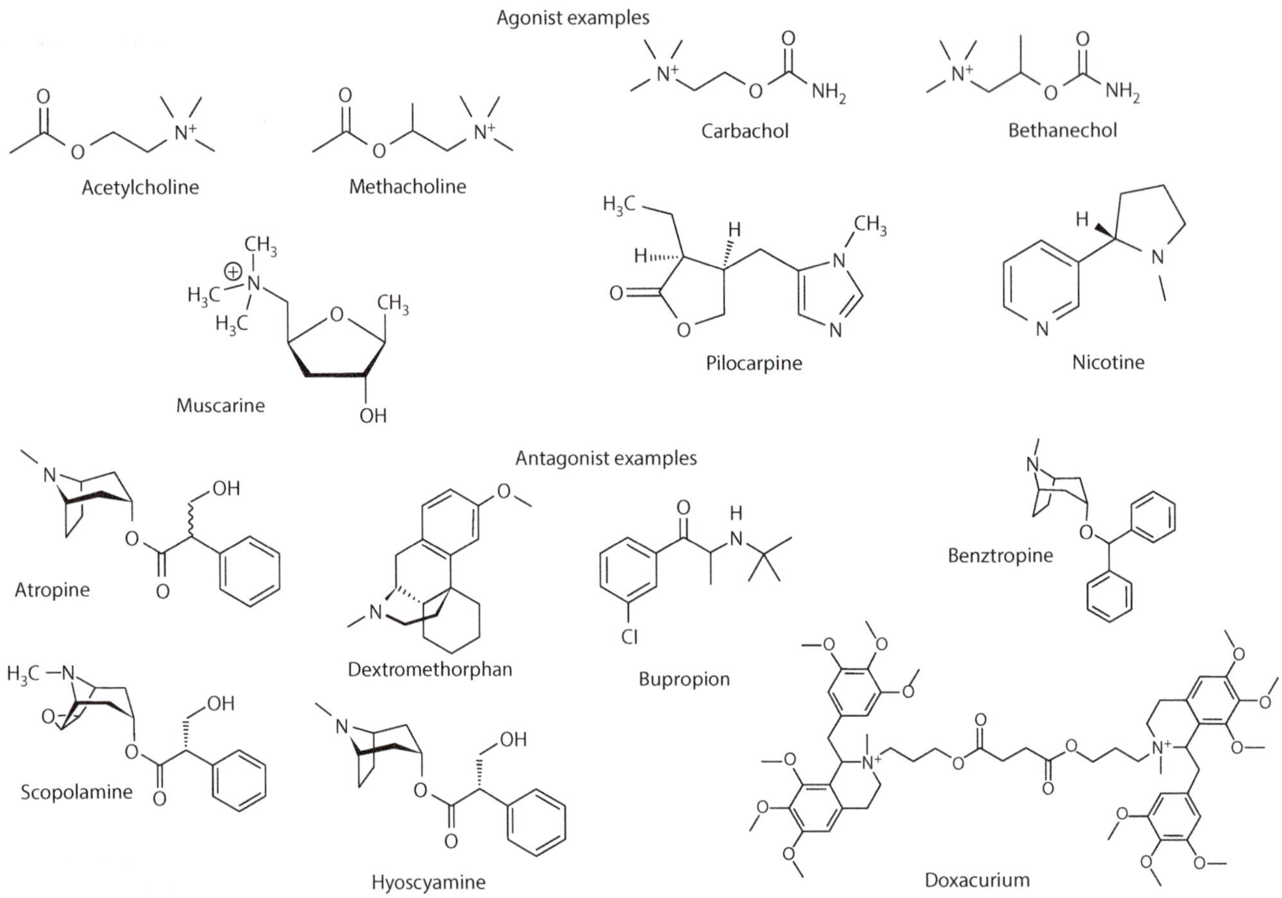

Figure 17.1 Example cholinergic agonists and antagonists.

nerve gases were not used in World War II, at least as battlefield weapons.) The effectiveness of the organophosphates and the broad scope of their action led to their introduction as insecticides in the decades following the war. With the demise of chlorinated hydrocarbon insecticides, such as DDT (because of the environmental consequences of their long half-life, and toxicity to nontarget species), the organophosphates became increasingly popular. Further development of military-grade cholinergic-syndrome-inducing nerve agents (along with their military-grade anticholinergic antidotes) continued to be investigated and remain an issue today, both in terms of military actions and as a bioterrorist threat. (In 1995, passengers on the Tokyo subway system were attacked by the terrorist group Aum Shinrikyo by using the organophosphate nerve gas sarin, with a number of fatalities.) Use of modern weaponized nerve gas preparations seems to have occurred in the Syrian Civil War (2013), with a significant number of casualties (Figure 17.1).

17.3 Cholinergic Synapse

ACh is the most abundant of the neurotransmitters in the body. Cholinergic synapses can be found in both the CNS and the PNS and form the neuromuscular junctions in the somatic nervous system. Cholinergic neurotransmission is responsible for a variety of physiological actions, including voluntary and involuntary muscle contractions, glandular secretions, and some central nervous functions.

17.3.1 Normal Cholinergic Neurotransmission

ACh is synthesized from choline and acetyl coenzyme A (acetyl CoA), an anabolic process catalyzed by the enzyme choline acetyltransferase. ACh molecules are then packaged into vesicles by an ACh vesicular transport protein, in a process that will load about 10,000 molecules of ACh into a single cholinergic presynaptic vesicle. NT release into the synaptic space is triggered by neuron depolarization and, if the magnitude is adequate to exceed the action potential of the postsynaptic neuron, triggers depolarization (as discussed in Chapter 7). If the downstream cell is a myocyte (muscle cell), adequate postsynaptic ACh binding triggers the influx of sodium and calcium ions that leads to muscle contraction.

Under normal physiological conditions, free ACh in the synapse is quickly degraded by the enzyme acetylcholinesterase (AChE). ACh binds to the enzyme creating an acetylcholine-enzyme intermediate that is rapidly hydrolyzed, yielding choline and acetate, along with regenerated active enzyme. Choline liberated from this hydrolysis is then transported back into the presynaptic terminal for incorporation into a new molecule of ACh. In this manner, the body regulates the amount of ACh present in the synapse and at the same time recycles the components used to make this important NT.

ACh receptors are divided into two classes based on whether or not they are sensitive to muscarine or nicotine. Muscarine is an alkaloid found in the toxic mushroom *Amanita muscaria*, and the receptors where muscarine can act as an agonist are termed *muscarinic*. In a similar fashion, nicotine (from the tobacco plant, *Nicotiana* spp.) is able to activate a separate set of ACh receptors, called *nicotinic*. Muscarinic receptors predominate in the parasympathetic nervous system and are associated with smooth muscle and glandular function. While nicotinic receptors are found in large quantities in the sympathetic nervous system, with effects most evident associated with the ACh receptors located at neuromuscular junctions in the somatic nervous system. While it is valuable to remember the distinction of these two groups, it is equally important to remember that both sets of receptors are agonized by their natural neurotransmitter, ACh.

17.3.2 Cholinergic Toxins and Mechanisms

The magnitude of a neuronal signal (and hence whether the signal is propagated) is a function of the amount of NT released and already present (if any) in the cholinergic synapse. Should the concentration of ACh in the synapse be either too high or too low, toxic symptoms will ensue, either from an inability for signal propagation and muscle contraction to occur when and as it should, or the converse, an excess amount of signal leading to inappropriate muscle contraction.

Excessive stimulation of the cholinergic system, either by direct ACh agonists or toxin-amplified levels of ACh release, or concentration in the synaptic space results in the *cholinergic syndrome* characterized by symptoms corresponding to the mnemonic SLUDGE (salivation, lacrimation, urination, defecation, gastric sounds, emesis). The cholinergic response can be accompanied by the "killer B's" of bronchorrhea, bronchospasm, and bradycardia. The spasmodic contraction of air passages (bronchospasms), are the result of nicotinic stimulation, compounded with increased bronchial watery secretions (bronchorrhea), and a slower-pumping heart (bradycardia). The resulting bronchiolar contractions, coupled with the filling of air passages, can result in major respiratory distress, which may quickly lead to death in the absence of medical intervention. Weakening respiratory muscles as a consequence of nicotinic overstimulation can further compromise the pulmonary capability of the victim. Other nicotinic symptoms (muscle fasciculation and weakness) as well as varied and nonspecific CNS findings (tremors, headache, seizures) can also present in cholinergic syndrome cases.

17.3.2.1 *Presynaptic Toxicity*

A number of compounds affect ACh release from the presynaptic neuron. Latrotoxins are the primary component of toxins found in the venom of spiders of the genus *Latrodectus*, or the "widow" spiders, (among which is the black widow). α-Latrotoxin is a 130 kDa protein, which adopts a tetrameric conformation that inserts itself into the cell membranes of presynaptic cholinergic neurons. The tetrameric form is able to bind to and form Ca^{2+}-permeable pores in the presynaptic cholinergic neuron. The subsequent calcium ion influx results in the phosphorylation of NT vesicles and the inappropriate release of ACh into the synaptic space. Depending on the amount of toxin present, a cholinergic response can be elicited. Since the normal endogenous neurotransmitter is released, as opposed to an exogenous agonist being present, both nicotinic and muscarinic receptors will be activated as a consequence of latrotoxin envenomation. Victims can display, along with systemic pain, autonomic nervous system toxicity manifesting itself as muscle fasciculation (nicotinic), facial grimacing (nicotinic), tachycardia (nicotinic), diaphoresis (muscarinic), and hypertension (nicotinic).

17.3.2.2 *Synaptic Toxicity*

Some of the most common and certainly some of the most deadly cholinergic agents to be encountered by the forensic toxicologist are the organophosphate and carbamate insecticides and the organophosphate nerve gases. All of these agents are toxic because of their ability to inhibit the acetylcholinesterase (AChE)-mediated breakdown of ACh in the neuronal synaptic gap. Mechanistically, these compounds effectively bind at the active site of acteylcholinesterase and function as competitive inhibitors of ACh hydrolysis. ACh concentrations in the synaptic space and neuroeffector (neuromuscular) junctions rise, increasing the frequency of postsynaptic stimulation and depolarization, and ultimately evoking a cholinergic response. As seen with latrotoxins, since elevation of levels of ACh in the synapse is the vehicle for toxicity, both nicotinic and muscarinic receptors will be stimulated.

Commonly encountered organophosphate-based pesticides include parathion, diazinon, chlorpyrifos,

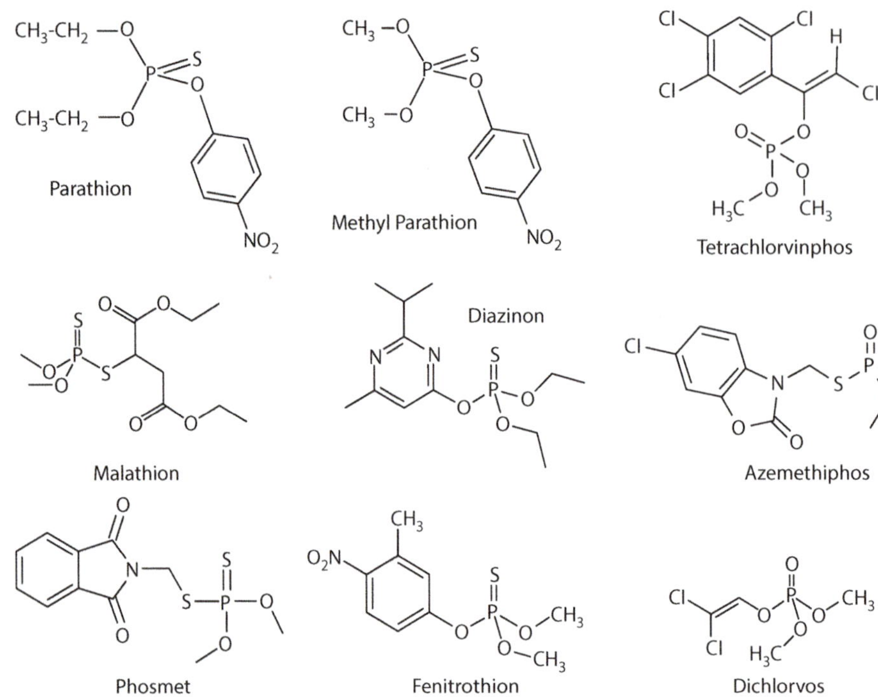

Figure 17.2 Example organophosphate pesticides.

malathion (a clinical insecticide), and dichlorvos, among others. Organophosphates have additional forensic relevance as they are the chemical backbone for a number of nerve warfare agents, such as sarin, VX, soman, and tabun, that have been employed by militaries and terrorist organizations (Figures 17.2 and 17.3).

Beyond simply binding to AChE, if given adequate time of exposure, organophosphates can actually form a covalent bond with the hydroxyl group of a serine residue in the active site of the enzyme, thereby phosphorylating the protein in an irreversible manner. The initial formation of the bond is not particularly strong and can be reversed by treatment with an oxime (e.g., pralidoxime). However, formation of the serine–O–P bond facilitates dealkylation of the alkylphosphate group, strengthening the bond to the protein. This step is referred to as aging of the enzyme-phosphate combination and effectively strengthens the O–P bond such that the enzyme is then irreversibly inhibited. The amount of time required for the aging reaction is highly compound specific. Most

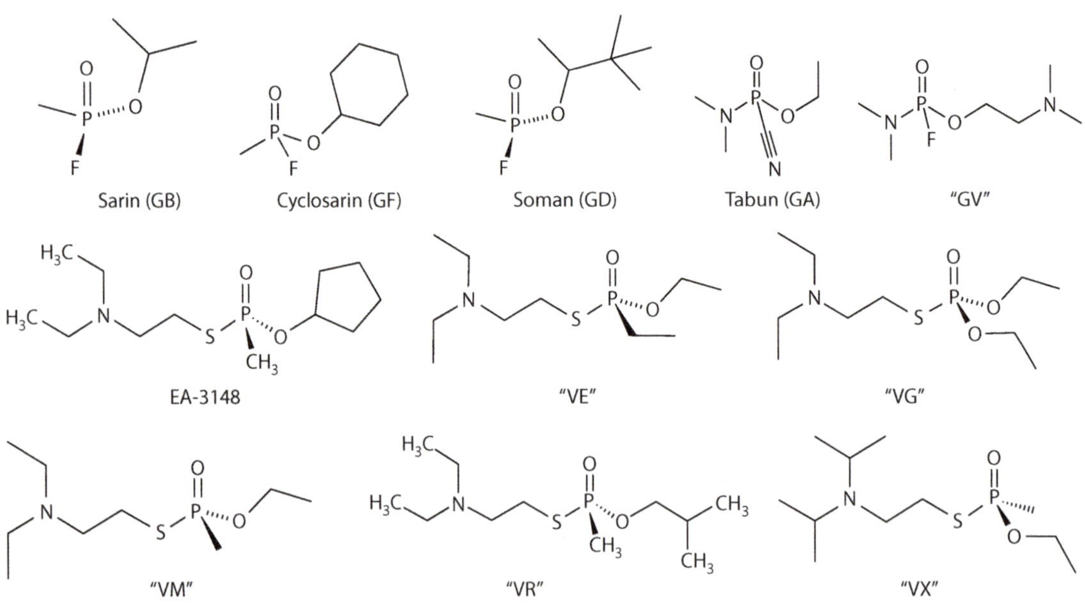

Figure 17.3 Example organophosphate nerve agents.

organophosphate agents take hours to react and dealkylate (and hence a therapeutic window for pralidoxime treatment exists); aging in the case of exposure to some species (e.g., the highly toxic soman) can occur in minutes (see Sidebar 17.1).

A number of carbamate insecticides are in use, and the class is an effective alternative to the organophosphates, with a somewhat lessened potential for toxicity. Phyostigmine (noted above) is a naturally occurring carbamate and is used for the treatment of Alzheimer's disease, glaucoma, and as a treatment for symptoms resulting from anticholinergic drug (e.g., atropine, scopolamine) overdose. Although carbamates and organophosphate compounds share the same toxic mechanism of action (inhibition of AChE, resulting in ACh excess), the chemical structure of carbamates dictates a slight, but important, difference in its inhibition. The carbamates' interaction with the AChE active-site serine results in the transient formation of a carbamoyl bond ($R_1R_2NC–O$) that is relatively unstable, thereby returning the functionality of the AChE enzyme. In contrast to organophosphate-mediated inhibition, this carbamoylation is reversible and does not exhibit the aging phenomenon (Figure 17.4).

SIDEBAR 17.1 THE MECHANISM OF 2-PAM REGENERATION

In cases of organophosphate poisonings, it is critical to restore the functionality of ACh as soon as possible. This can be accomplished clinically through the use of oximes, strong nucleophiles that are able to break the serine-organophosphate bond, thus regenerating a functional AChE enzyme. The most frequently prescribed oxime is pralodoxime, known clinically as 2-PAM (see mechanism detailed in Figure 17.5).

As discussed in Section 17.3.2.2, 2-PAM treatment must be initiated before the serine O-P bond has aged,—loss of an alkyl substituent group from the phosphate. It is worth noting that the organophosphates are a vast and diverse group whose different chemical structures greatly affect the ability of 2-PAM to regenerate the active enzyme. As such, some organophosphates respond poorly to 2-PAM even before aging has occurred.

Both organophosphates and carbamates cause the classic symptoms of the cholinergic syndrome. These muscarinic effects can be effectively treated with atropine, but this compound will not alleviate nicotinic symptoms such as facial fasciculations. Nicotinic symptoms must be treated with an oxime (e.g., pralidoxime) as noted above.

17.3.2.3 Postsynaptic Toxicity

17.3.2.3.1 General Mechanism As noted above, ACh receptors can be functionally divided based on their sensitivity to either muscarine or nicotine (see Sidebar 17.2). The action of nicotine highlights the variety of locations in which cholinergic neurons exist, exhibiting a binding preference for receptors in the CNS over those in the somatic nervous system as well as binding to the postganglionic receptor in the adrenal medulla. Agonism of these receptors causes many symptoms that do not coincide with the classic (more muscarinic driven) symptoms of the cholinergic syndrome.

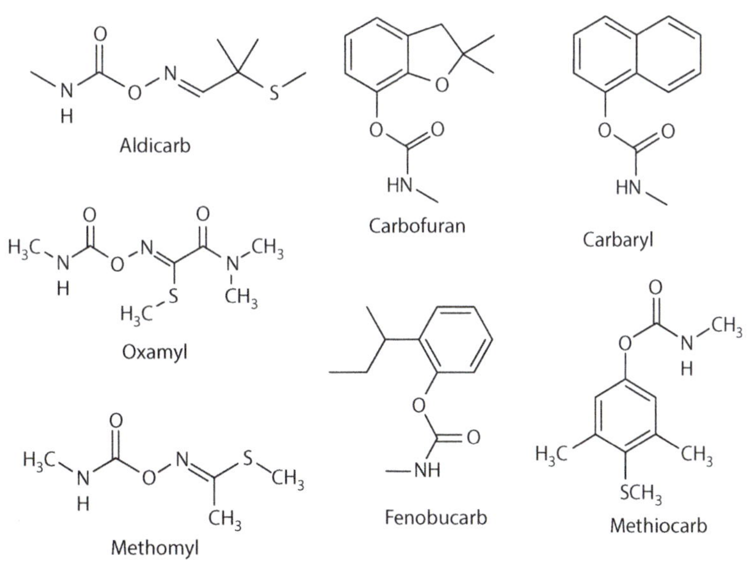

Figure 17.4 Example carbamate insecticides.

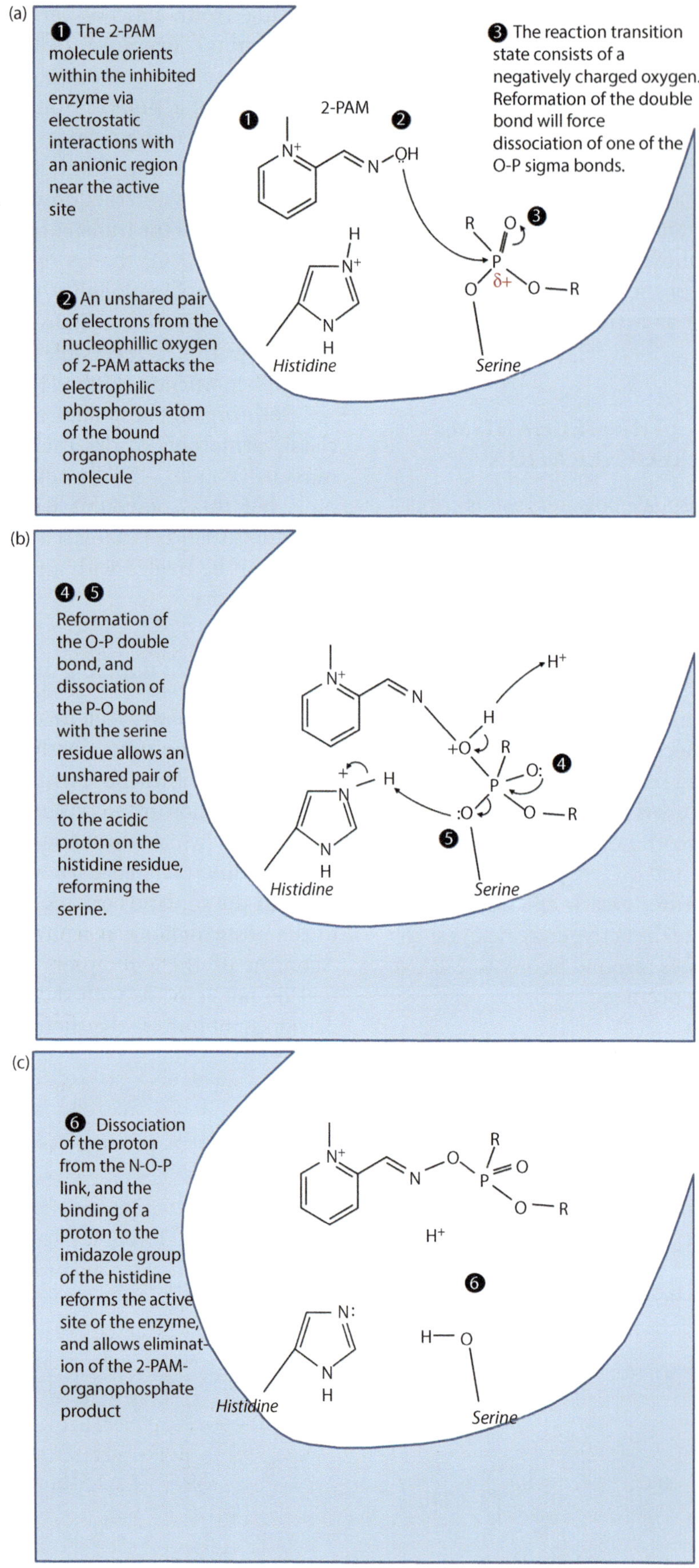

Figure 17.5 (a, b, and c) Mechanistic diagram of pralidoxime-mediated acetylcholinesterase regeneration.

SIDEBAR 17.2 NICOTINIC VS. MUSCARINIC ACETYLCHOLINE RECEPTORS

ACh is a primary neurotransmitter, active in both the sympathetic and parasympathetic nervous systems and in multiple organs and tissues. The two types of ACh receptors are muscarinic and nicotinic. In structural terms, muscarinic receptors are G-coupled protein receptors, while nicotinic receptors are ligand-gated ion channels. They can be found on both sides of the synaptic cleft (presynaptic and postsynaptic). Both muscarinic and nicotinic receptors are located in the central and autonomic systems, while only nicotinic receptors are found at neuromuscular junctions. Both the sympathetic and parasympathetic systems are cholinergic (utilizing ACh as neurotransmitter) at the preganglionic level. In the sympathetic system, the postganglionic NT is norepinephrine, while in the parasympathetic system, the NT remains ACh (Figure 17.2).

Muscarinic Receptors

The muscarinic type of ACh receptors were so named for their ability to bind both ACh and muscarine, a toxic alkaloid found in a number of poisonous mushroom species, particularly of the *Amanita* genus. Muscarinic receptors are metabotropic, or G-protein coupled receptors (GCPRs), which function by activating a second messenger (usually cAMP or cGMP) within the postsynaptic cell, thereby leading to reactions within the cell. Muscarinic receptors are found in the organs innervated by the autonomic parasympathetic system and in the CNS itself. There are five subclasses of muscarinic receptor, M_{1-5}. The M_2 receptor is of particular interest from a toxicologic perspective in that activation lowers conduction velocity at the sinus and atrioventricular nodes, resulting in a lowered heart rate.

Nicotinic Receptors

Nicotinic receptors are ligand-gated sodium ion channels. Activation by ligand (ACh) binding induces a conformational change that allows gradient-driven entry of sodium ions into the postsynaptic cell, which, depending on signal magnitude, may result in depolarization. Nicotinic receptors can be generally divided into subtypes, with one type (N_m) found at neuromuscular junctions and the other (N_n) found in the CNS, at both cholinergic and adrenergic ganglia.

Nicotinic stimulation of the adrenal medulla results in the release of several catecholamines, including norepinephrine, which is responsible for the familiar tachycardia and hypertension associated with smoking and chewing tobacco. Binding of ACh to nicotinic receptors in the brain releases dopamine that in turn is linked to the limbic reward pathway and associated with euphoria and addiction. However, sweating, vomiting, and tremors are observed in higher, more concentrated doses, such as when contact is made with nicotinic pesticides. Death can result from cardiovascular and respiratory failure from muscle weakness.

In contrast to nicotine, muscarine is a quaternary ammonium compound that therefore cannot readily cross the blood–brain barrier, and hence, effects are more peripheral than central. The symptoms of muscarinic ingestion include increased urination, lacrimation, sweating, and stimulation of involuntary muscles in the GI tract, resulting in increased bowel sounds and diarrhea.

In a general sense, ACh receptor agonists, including nicotine and muscarine, can be generally classified in two types: choline esters (e.g., methacholine, carbachol, and bethanechol) and naturally occurring alkaloids (e.g., epibatidine pilocarpine). The scope of effects of the drugs will be a function of the selectivity exhibited between the nicotinic and muscarinic receptors and, of course, the time the drugs are available in the body, a function of the pharmacokinetics of the drugs (Figure 17.6).

17.3.3 Anticholinergic Toxins and Mechanisms

In contrast to the cholinergic consequences of too much ACh, or molecules that mimic ACh activity, toxins that limit ACh release or interfere with the action of the NT can also have serious harmful effects. ACh, when released in inadequate amounts in response to depolarization or interference with agonist activity of the NT, can result in symptoms of an *anticholinergic syndrome*. A useful mnemonic used to describe the symptoms of this toxidrome is as follows:

Blind as a bat (fully dilated pupils—mydriasis)
Fast as a hare (tachycardia)
Mad as a hatter (disorientation and agitation)
Dry as a bone (dry mucosal membranes and skin)
Red as a beet (flushed skin)
Hot as Hades (hyperthermia due to inability to sweat—anhydrosis)
Full as a tick (urinary retention, decreased GI motility)

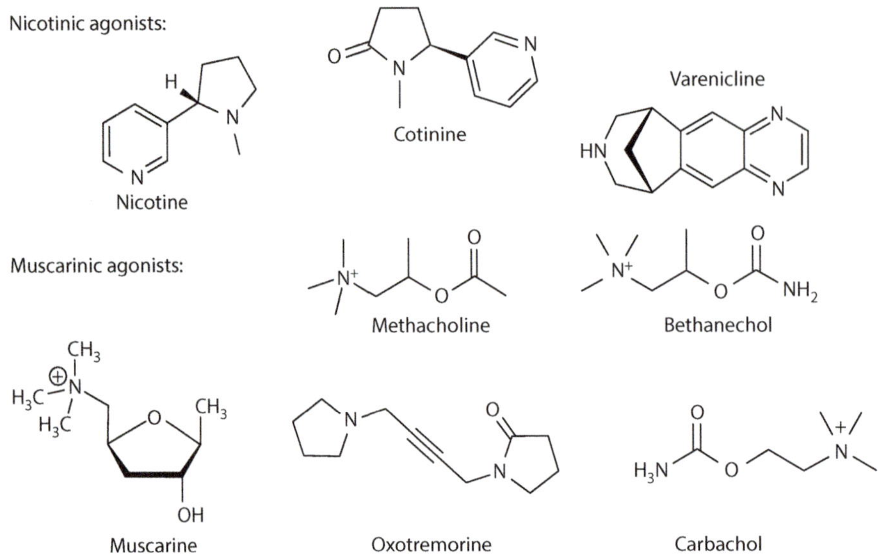

Figure 17.6 Example ACh receptor agonists.

The anticholinergic syndrome can be as life-threatening as the cholinergic syndrome, with symptoms ranging from agitation and delirium to seizures, coma, and death. Effects of the lack of ACh will be expressed in both muscarinic and nicotinic systems, although the more prominent symptoms are antimuscarinic.

Many of the classic anticholinergic agents are well-recognized for their toxic potential, such as atropine, scopolamine, and tubocurarine. There are many other important classes of drugs whose toxic symptoms overlap with the anticholinergic toxidrome, including some antidepressants (TCAs, MAOIs), antihistamines, and antipsychotics. These classes of drugs differ in that their primary antagonist target is not at ACh neural or neuromuscular junction receptors and are therefore not discussed in this chapter (Figure 17.7).

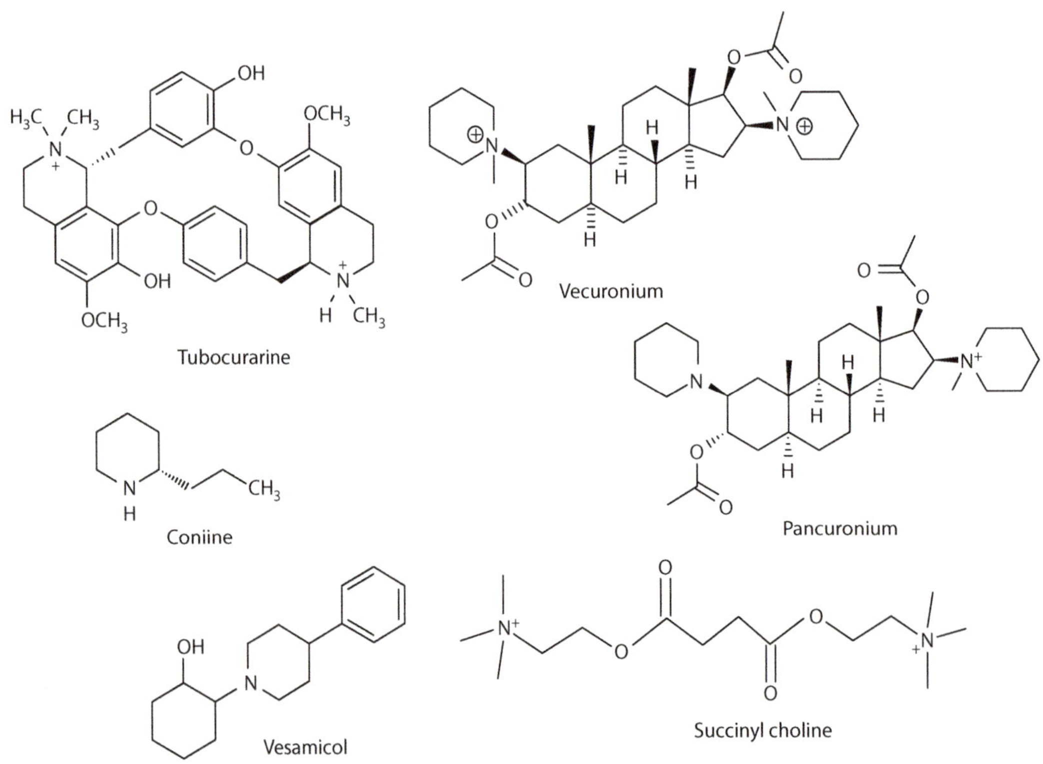

Figure 17.7 Example anticholinergic and related drugs.

17.3.3.1 Presynaptic Toxicity

A classic example of anticholinergic, presynaptic toxicity is botulism, primarily caused by contaminated food that has been improperly canned or otherwise preserved. The botulin toxin is produced by the anaerobic bacteria *Clostridium botulinum*. The toxin functionally inhibits the release of ACh at the synapse of cholinergic neurons, resulting in muscular paralysis. Botulin toxin is one of the most toxic known compounds, with a lethal dose in humans estimated at ~2 ng/kg. Once the toxin enters the bloodstream, it is taken up via endocytosis into presynaptic neuronal terminals at peripheral cholinergic neuromuscular junctions. The toxin is a heat-sensitive polypeptide chain consisting of a heavy and light chain, that denatures at ~80°C. The heavy chain (~100 kDa) binds to and facilitates endocytosis of the toxin into the presynaptic neuron at the synaptic membrane. The toxin then undergoes proteolysis, freeing the lighter chain (~50 kDa), a zinc endopeptidase that targets the SNARE (soluble N-ethylmaleimide-sensitive factor protein attachment receptor) "fusion" proteins involved in NT vesicle docking to the presynaptic membrane, as part of NT release. Several different forms of the botulin toxin have been discovered, targeting one of the various SNARE proteins: VAMP (vesicle-associated membrane protein), SNAP-25 (25 Kdal synaptosome-associated protein), syntaxin, or synaptobrevin. The toxin's endopeptidase function efficiently cleaves and inactivates these proteins, thereby limiting the ability for vesicles to fuse with the presynaptic plasma membrane and, ultimately, ACh release in response to depolarization. The primary clinical manifestations of the signal loss are acute symmetric voluntary muscle dysfunction and muscle paralysis, characterized as a flaccid paralysis. Paralysis of muscles needed for respiratory function can rapidly lead to death. Other symptoms include dry tongue, dry mouth, constipation, double vision, and difficulty swallowing. Interestingly, while botulin is one of the most lethal toxins known, its use in small doses as a localized muscle paralytic agent (Botox) in cosmetic procedures remains popular.

The experimental drug vesamicol also functions as a cholinergic inhibitor (and hence anticholinergic agent) and, like botulinum, the mechanism of action lies within the presynaptic neuron. Vesamicol binds to and inactivates the vesicular ACh transport protein responsible for incorporation of ACh molecules into the presynaptic vesicle. This interaction is noncompetitive in that the binding site is distinct from the ACh binding/transport side. The effect of the drug is that NT vesicles then contain less ACh than they would normally, and the response to a depolarizing event is therefore less (in terms of synaptic ACh) than would be the case in the absence of the drug. The physiologic response is that of an anticholinergic agent or cholinergic receptor antagonist.

A third presynaptic mechanism affecting synaptic ACh concentration is demonstrated by hemicholine, an experimental drug that acts by blocking the presynaptic reuptake of choline by the specific choline transport protein. The reuptake is a rate-limiting step in ACh synthesis, and limitation in choline reuptake ultimately affects the amount of ACh synthesized and available for incorporation in presynaptic vesicles and, as such, the magnitude of ACh release in response to depolarization of the neuron.

17.3.3.2 Postsynaptic

The more commonly encountered mechanism of anticholinergic activity is classic antagonism of the ACh receptor, molecules that can bind to the ACh postsynaptic receptor but do not activate the molecule, and hence do not initiate the depolarization of the postsynaptic neuron or contraction of the muscle cell.

Curare is the collective name for a group of paralytic arrow poisons used by natives in the Amazon Basin in South America. The pharmacologically active compound is d-tubocurarine and can be isolated from the plants *Strychnos toxifera* and *Chondrodendron tomentosum*. Curare poisons are potent nicotinic receptor antagonists. Nicotinic receptors, at neuromuscular junctions, are responsible for the depolarization of muscle cells that results in somatic muscle contractions. Therefore, the primary consequences of curare toxicity are muscle weakness (from constant contractions) leading to rapid muscle paralysis and death generally due to paralysis of the diaphragm with the resulting asphyxia.

Coniine, the toxic alkaloid found in poison hemlock (*Conium maculatum*), is another nicotinic antagonist. Symptoms of coniine poisonings mirror that of curare intoxications with the acute clinical consequence being that of flaccid muscle paralysis. Death results from hypoxia as a consequence of respiratory paralysis. Sudden hypoxic convulsions are associated with such poisonings, known as "death rattles." This was, of course, the poison by which Socrates was executed in 399 BC. The notable absence of the death rattles in Aristotle's description of Socrates' death has led some to speculate that the hemlock preparation Socrates was given had been mixed with opium.

While generating a similar effect, vecuronium and pancuronium are nicotinic antagonists that are employed therapeutically as nondepolarizing muscle relaxants. With the use of these agents, the postsynaptic myocyte remains polarized and does not contract. In contrast, the depolarizing muscle relaxant, succinylcholine, is unique in that it results in the continual depolarization or desensitization of the cell, by allowing continued sodium influx through the ligand-gated sodium channel. Succinylcholine is not a substrate for neuronal ACh-ase but instead is metabolized by a related hydrolytic enzyme, pseudocholinesterase, or more formally, butyrylcholinesterase. Pseudocholinesterase is a plasma enzyme not present in high concentration in the synapse; therefore succinylcholine is not as quickly degraded in the synaptic space as is ACh, and is able to continue to interact with the postsynaptic nicotinic receptor, precluding the repolarization of the cell for a comparatively long time. Succinylcholine is extremely fast acting (effects felt between 30 and 60 seconds) but the paralytic effects from a normal dose last for only 10 minutes.

Atropine is perhaps *the* classic anticholinergic compound. Found in nature as a racemic mixture of d- and l-hyoscyamine (not to be confused with hyoscine, an old term for scopolamine), this tropane alkaloid can be extracted from the plant *Atropos belladonna* (deadly nightshade) as well as various species of the genus *Datura*. Atropine is a competitive muscarinic antagonist that can cross the blood–brain barrier resulting in mydriasis, tachycardia, anhydrosis, dry mucosa, and decreased peristalsis. Lack of CNS ACh receptor stimulation can cause hallucinations, delirium, coma, and death. One interesting aspect of atropine CNS toxicity is that a person can awake from an atropine-induced coma and still be experiencing delirium symptoms (as opposed to GHB or other GABAergic-agent-induced comas). Atropine poisonings can be treated with physostigmine, which unlike neostigmine (a related quaternary amine compound used in treatment of myasthenia gravis, and to reverse effects of nondepolarizing muscle relaxants, e.g., vecuronium), is able to cross the blood–brain barrier. Therefore, physostigmine can alleviate not only muscarinic effects but also return the patient back to normal CNS function. Atropine itself is the classic clinical antidote to reverse the increased secretions and other symptoms associated with muscarinic hyperstimulation caused by anticholinesterase (organophosphate or carbamate) exposure (see Sidebar 17.3).

Scopolamine is an alkaloid very similar to atropine in structure and function. Like atropine, scopolamine is a muscarinic antagonist and is found in combination with atropine in such plants as henbane (*Hyocyamus niger*), mandrake (*Mandragora* spp.), and jimsonweed (*Datura stramonium*). The anticholinergic effects of scopolamine on CNS muscarinic receptors have been exploited for both therapeutic and criminal purposes. Scopolamine is a front-line treatment for postoperative vomiting and is one of the few effective treatments for motion sickness (generally used as a transdermal patch). Scopolamine use has been associated with recent criminal enterprises in South America where scopolamine is used to induce a coma that can last up to 24 hours, during which the victim may be assaulted or robbed. Concerns of scopolamine-aided crimes prompted the US State Department to issue a warning in March 2012 to travelers in Colombia (Figure 17.7).

SIDEBAR 17.3 THE ATROPINE/PRALODOXIME INJECTOR

Near the end of the 1996 film *The Rock*, the biochemist protagonist Dr. Stanley Goodspeed (played by Nicholas Cage) injects atropine into his heart in response to an exposure to the organophosphate nerve gas VX. Atropine had been introduced as an antidote earlier in the film, when Dr. Goodspeed and a trainee encounter (allegedly) sarin nerve gas. They are instructed to inject atropine into their hearts in order to stay alive; the request is met with understandable hesitation. (While the atropine injector represents a real and practical device, the location of the injections may be somewhat more reflective of the need for Hollywood to embellish reality than to need to beat the VX to the right atrium.)

In Operation Desert Storm, US ground soldiers were issued the "Mark 1 nerve agent antidote kit" containing two syringes to be administered simultaneously; one contained atropine sulfate and the other pralidoxime chloride (providing therefore a cholinergic antagonist and a protection against organophosphate-acetylcholinesterase aging). Since then, technology has allowed for both atropine and pralidoxime to be administered in one syringe, called the "antidote treatment nerve agent auto-injector." Per military guidelines, the injection is to occur in the lateral thigh muscle or buttocks, and as the name "auto-injector" implies, it requires the user to only firmly press the syringe onto the leg and the needle will automatically deploy and inject.

REVIEW QUESTIONS

1. How is ACh functionally different from NE, 5HT, and DA?
2. What is the mechanism for ACh-mediated muscle contraction?
3. Functionally differentiate the nicotinic and muscarinic receptors.
4. Mechanistically distinguish between latrotoxin and botulinum toxin.

5. Discuss the acetylcholinesterase aging process when bound to an organophosphate.
6. Differentiate the three mechanisms of anticholinergic toxin action.

TOPICS FOR DISCUSSION

1. Could spider venom (latrotoxin) be a basis for a neurotoxic weapon?
2. Succinylcholine is often cited in dramatic and fictional works as an "ideal poison." Why would that be?
3. Drug abuse is not normally associated with the cholinergic/anticholinergic drugs. Why not?
4. Should organophosphate nerve gases be allowed as weapons of war?
5. Why weren't poison gases used in World War II (as battlefield weapons)?

Bibliography

Ellenhorn MJ. *Ellenhorn's Medical Toxicology: Diagnosis and Treatment of Human Poisoning.* 2nd ed. Baltimore: Williams & Wilkins, 1997.

Fenton JJ. *Toxicology: A Case-Oriented Approach.* Boca Raton, FL: CRC Press, 2002.

Gilman AG, Rall TW, Nies AS, Taylor P, editors. *Goodman and Gilman's The Pharmacological Basis of Therapeutics.* 8th ed. New York: McGraw-Hill, 1990.

Klassen CD. *Casarett and Doull's Toxicology: The Basic Science of Poisons.* 8th rev. ed. New York: McGraw-Hill, 2013.

Reichl, FX, Ritter L, editors. *Illustrated Handbook of Toxicology.* Stuttgart: Thieme, 2011.

Metals

18

Contents

18.1 Introduction

Casework involving metals is relatively uncommon in most forensic toxicology laboratories. (Occasionally a legitimate postmortem issue, metals are almost never addressed in driving under the influence [DUI] or routine drug-testing cases.) Metals are not associated with any psychotropic potential (with the arguable exception of lithium) and are not in the "menu" of society's abused drugs. Nevertheless, metals and metallic elements have had a long history in accidental and deliberate poisonings, as well as in both short- and long-term environmental exposures and contamination. It is well worth having an understanding of the biochemical havoc that can be caused when the amount of these species in the body exceeds its ability to detoxify or eliminate them.

Metal poisoning can present a particular challenge in the postmortem setting. First of all, the symptomology associated with the various types of metal toxicity is often readily mistaken for other conditions (e.g., flu or food poisoning) and may have (most reasonably) gone unrecognized prior to death. Second, as noted above, metal poisoning or toxicity is relatively unusual. Finally, most forensic laboratories tend to be oriented toward the detection of organic pharmaceuticals, psychotropics, and poisons. As such, the necessary analytical equipment for metals analysis (e.g., atomic absorption spectroscopy or ion-coupled plasma atomic emission spectroscopy) is usually accessed via environmental or public health laboratories or in the contract analytical world. On the positive side, the nature of these analytes as elemental species means that even if there has been degradation of an organometallic form, the elemental metal will be available for analysis as long as there are biologic samples to test.

Occasionally, testing of heavy metals is performed on individuals who may have sustained environmental or workplace exposures or may otherwise be concerned about the level of toxins in their bodies. While such testing can in many cases be legitimate, providing useful and instructive clinical information, such is not always the case. There are many examples of metal levels determined in 6, 12, or 24 h urine samples collected following administration of a chelator, with the results compared with "normal ranges" derived from unchallenged individuals. Clearly, comparison of urine metal levels following chelation (thereby driving the equilibrium toward the blood, and hence the urine) to levels without such treatment is misleading at best and provides a disservice to the concerned patient.

The metals (and metalloids) represent a wide and disparate group of toxic mechanisms and effects. While most of the metals are encountered in an elemental form, many of the more toxic forms are organometal or organometalloid compounds. Environmental exposures can of course be either the metal species themselves or one of many possible mineralized or other combination forms, perhaps including multiple metal species.

A number of different biochemical mechanisms are associated with metals and metallic species; however, there is also one mechanism common to many metals by which the body is able to rid itself of these elements. Specifically, many of the metals can be complexed, or chelated (from the Greek *chelos*, meaning "claw," a reference to the manner in which the molecule wraps itself around the metal atom), by a rather small protein, *metallothionein*, which can subsequently be eliminated following filtration in the kidney. This mechanism is responsible for the routine elimination of a number of metallic species that are regularly present in our normal diet.

An in-depth exploration of the mechanistic effects of all of the metals would be beyond the scope of this text. Nevertheless, we will discuss several compounds of historical (and occasionally current) interest commonly recognized as having significant toxic potential: arsenic, antimony, cadmium, mercury, and lead.

18.2 Arsenic

Historically, arsenic has been perhaps one of the most widely recognized (and perhaps used) components of homicidal poison concoctions, long considered the "king of poisons" (or the poison of kings; see Sidebar 18.1). The utility of arsenic for this purpose was brought to, if not an end, at least some limitation by the analytical capability represented by the Marsh and Reinsh tests, and ultimately, more specific and sensitive analytical instrumentation. The ability of forensic scientists to readily detect arsenic in suspected poisonings in the late 1800s made the element less attractive as a potential homicidal poison. Nevertheless, arsenic continues to be a factor in some homicide cases, and a familiarity with the toxic potential of the element can be of value and relevance to the forensic toxicologist.

SIDEBAR 18.1 LA CANTARELLA

Historically, countless preparations and concoctions have been used as poisons. The ancient world did not lack for toxins, but arsenic figured in many deadly preparations. The common form of arsenic, in the +5 valence state, is reported to have a marked taste and could readily be detected in foodstuffs (thereby providing steady employment for food tasters). However, the +3 valence forms of arsenic were generally tasteless and were therefore the optimal choice for the poisoner. Arsenic lay at the base of a toxic preparation associated with the infamous Borgia family of medieval Italy. A number of politically based assassinations have been blamed on the brother and sister Cesare and Lucrezia. Their poison of choice, "la Cantarella," is reputed to have included As^{+3} as a primary ingredient. The problem, of course, lay in the preparation of having a mechanism that could reduce the rather abundant As^{+5} to the desired +3 valence. In a world of oxidative metabolism, a decaying carcass is one of the few places where reduction can occur. Through the process of putrefaction, pentavalent arsenic could be successfully reduced to its more deadly trivalent species. As such, the "recipe" reputedly used by the family involved killing a pig or hog with arsenic, then further salting the animal's abdominal cavity with more arsenic (+5) and allowing the carcass to decay (usually an anaerobic, reductive process). The fluid resulting from the decay process would be collected, from which arsenic trioxide could be precipitated, washed, and preserved.

Arsenic is often thought of as an industrial chemical or homicidal poison; however, most of the arsenic-related maladies that occur are actually a consequence of environmental contamination of drinking water rather than a consequence of deliberate or even accidental poisoning. This is a worldwide problem as a chronic, debilitating condition, rather than a result of an acute toxic exposure. Arsenic is a relatively common crustal element, appearing in a number of mineral forms, often in conjunction with sulfur and other metals, for example, antimony.

Historical uses of arsenic were mostly of the sulfide and oxide forms. Arsenic sulfide ores (orpiment, realgar) and oxides have been known and used since ancient times. Arsenic was alloyed with copper and tin during the Bronze Age, producing a useful hard alloy known as *arsenical bronze*. Arsenical compounds have been used medicinally for an equally long time, and with some success as a treatment for syphilis and trypanosomiasis. Such use has been discontinued in the face of modern antibiotics with less toxic potential.

Arsenic is commonly found in the +5, pentavalent form, but can readily be reduced to the more toxic +3 form by a number of mechanisms. The biochemical mechanism of arsenic involves the pentavalent form acting as an uncoupler of oxidative phosphorylation in the mitochondria by substituting for phosphate during the formation of ATP (thereby producing an unstable arsenate ester that is rapidly hydrolyzed and therefore unable to be used by the body as an energy source).

The more potent trivalent form of arsenic binds to and inhibits many enzymes with available -SH groups at catalytic or allosteric sites. One specific and important site is the pyruvate dehydrogenase complex, which functions to transfer two carbons from pyruvate via lipoic acid, to coenzyme A, forming acetylCoA. This enzyme complex links glycolysis with the citric acid cycle, and as such is essential to the ability of the cell to convert energy (in the form of glucose) to forms usable in the cell (ATP and reducing equivalents, e.g., NADH, NADPH, $FADH_2$). Lipoic acid (an eight-carbon carboxylic acid with sulfhydryl groups at C6 and C8) plays a central role in the process, transferring an acetate equivalent from pyruvate to coenzyme A (in the process, oxidized lipoic acid is reduced, and reoxidation generates $NADH/H^+$). Arsenic is able to bind to the two sulfydryl groups of lipoic acid, thereby blocking its ability to accept an acetyl residue from pyruvate. Because of the generalized nature of this effect, many systems in the body are affected.

Acute arsenic poisoning can initially appear as flu-like symptoms, but can be quite severe, with nausea, vomiting, bloody diarrhea, and abdominal pain. Arsenic acts as a mild vasodilator at low doses and can cause edema. Larger doses of the metal can cause increased capillary permeability to the point of transudation of plasma, producing copious fluid in the GI tract, along with epithelial sloughing. Peristalsis is enhanced, and the resulting watery diarrhea is characterized as "rice water stools." Hypotension and bradycardia can also be expressed, and other cardiac symptoms can include electrocardiogram (EKG) abnormalities (e.g., prolonged Q-T interval) and ultimately with adequate dose, convulsions, coma, and death.

A gaseous form of arsenic, arsine (AsH_3), was discovered in 1775 by reduction of As3O2 with zinc (thereby forming the basis of the Marsh test, discussed in Chapter 2). Arsine is a highly toxic gas, currently used in semiconductor and organoarsencial synthesis. Arsine affects the hemoglobin molecules in red blood cells, resulting in lysis and leading to hemolytic anemia and kidney damage. Arsine concentrations in the 100 ppm range can be fatal in minutes, with lower concentrations producing effects in a longer time scale. Even exposure of 1 ppm can lead to expression of toxic symptoms.

Following World War I, arsine was considered as a potential chemical warfare agent, as the situation in Europe following the end of the war was such that a second confrontation between Germany and the Western powers seemed increasingly inevitable, with both sides armed and prepared for the next round (see Sidebar 18.2).

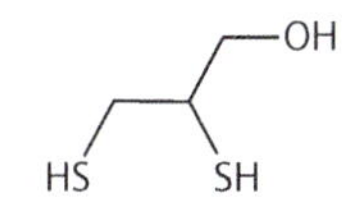

Figure 18.1 Dimercaprol.

SIDEBAR 18.2 LEWISITE AND BRITISH ANTI-LEWISITE

Lewisite is an arsine, 2-chloroethenyldichloroarsine, developed as a chemical weapon between World Wars I and II. While its primary mechanism of action is the inhibition of pyruvate dehydrogenase, lewisite is also vesicant (blistering agent) and a lung irritant. In its pure state, lewisite is colorless and odorless, but impure preparations are yellowish with an odor resembling geraniums.

Dimercaprol (Figure 18.1), or British anti-lewisite (BAL), was developed as an antidote for lewisite and can be thought of as an analog of lipoic acid (with which arsenic reacts so readily in the body). While lewisite has essentially disappeared as a potential toxin, BAL has been used to treat other metal poisonings (e.g., mercury, lead, and antimony), and has become one of a number of metal chelating agents used in routine treatment regimens.

18.3 Antimony

Antimony (Sb) is a metalloid element found in the periodic table beneath arsenic, with a very similar electrical structure, and with a valence shell d^{10}, s^2, p^3 electron configuration in addition to the noble gas core (argon for As, and krypton for Sb). Antimony is often found in nature in close association with arsenic ores, and symptoms of antimony poisoning closely mirror those of arsenic. Like arsenic, antimony can appear as a trivalent or pentavalent ion as well as *stibine*, its hydride gas (SbH_3). Commercial uses of antimony include cosmetic pigments, semiconductor materials, and a constituent of cartridge primer for ammunition (antimony along with lead and barium are the hallmarks of gunshot residue). Antimony has been used as an emetic (as antimony potassium tartrate) and a constituent of antiparasitics. In terms of acute toxicity, stibine is the most toxic form, trivalent is next, and pentavalent compounds are the least dangerous.

Acute inhalation of stibine produces respiratory distress and profuse vomiting as well as the more serious consequence of red blood cell lysis (hemolysis), which can cause kidney and liver complications. Acute oral ingestions of antimony compounds result in gastrointestinal irritation with severe vomiting. Antimonials are rapidly absorbed from the GI tract. The +5 valence form of the metal is predominantly excreted in the urine, while the +3 form appears in the feces. Antimony +3 can participate in enterohepatic recirculation, exacerbating both hepatotoxicity and kidney damage. Chronic symptoms of antimony poisoning also can involve intense episodes of vomiting and hepatic injury leading to hepatic encephalopathy (damage to the brain, caused by a failure of the liver to adequately eliminate toxic species, such as ammonia).

The underlying mechanism of Sb toxicity is, like As^{+3}, a function of its binding to enzyme sulfhydryl groups inhibiting carbohydrate and protein metabolism, specifically the pyruvate dehydrogenase complex. Antimony has been shown to inhibit succinic oxidase, pyruvate oxidase, and phosphofructokinase. Its effect on phosphofructokinase is the basis for antimony compounds to be used clinically to treat leishmaniasis and schistosomiasis. Differences that may aid in distinguishing between an As and Sb exposure (before instrumental identification confirmation) are identification of "antimony spots" and the time with which symptoms of vomiting occur. Antimony produces emesis almost immediately, while arsenic preparations delay vomiting up to an hour after ingestion. In some antimony poisonings, pustules or "spots" will erupt around sebaceous glands.

18.4 Cadmium

Cadmium (Cd) is a rare-earth element released into the environment primarily through human activities. It has no endogenous use or purpose in the body. Unlike other metals, cadmium has a single valence state (+2), with no known organometallic compounds of toxicological significance formed. Cadmium is most commonly found in nature in association with lead and zinc, and industrial processes involved in the extraction and processing of these metals can result in cadmium release (generally by leaching) into the environment. Commercial uses include the production of nickel-cadmium batteries, pigments, ceramics, and glasses. The most common route of industrial exposure is inhalation of dust.

Nonoccupational exposures can occur through ingestion of water and food products (fish, shellfish, meat, vegetables, cereals) in addition to cigarette smoking. Plants, including tobacco, can concentrate cadmium from soil. A pack-a-day smoker can be exposed to 1–3 μg cadmium per day, in addition to that which may be ingested in their regular diet.

Acute cadmium exposures and toxicity can cause flu-like symptoms, including fever, chills, and muscle aches, which may resolve as the exposure is eliminated. Severe inhalation-based exposures can cause bronchitis, pneumonitis, and pulmonary edema. Cadmium (at relatively high doses) is also toxic to the liver, but particularly so to the kidneys, as the primary target organ. Cadmium affects the ability of the kidneys to function, specifically in the proximal tubule, and such damage is generally irreversible. Depending on the degree of damage to the tubules, the magnitude of kidney failure may be fatal. While there is no treatment for organ damage, cadmium may be removed (if indeed identified as a source of toxicity) via chelation, often with EDTA (ethylenediamine tetraacetate).

Chronic exposure and toxicity are primarily expressed in the kidney. The symptoms of cadmium exposure are nonspecific, yet clinical testing can indicate the presence of a damaged organ system. β-2 microglobulin is a small molecule (11.8 kDal) that, while filtered in the glomerulus, should normally be reabsorbed in the proximal convoluted tubule in normal, healthy kidneys. Detection of the molecule in the urine can be an early and sensitive marker for kidney damage but is nonspecific in that levels will increase in any condition where tubules are damaged.

Cadmium in the body, whether entering via ingestion or inhalation, stimulates the production of metallothionein (MT) in the liver. Metallothioneins are a group of low molecular-weight (<15 KDal) cysteine-rich proteins with free sulfhydryl groups that effectively bind and sequester cadmium (and other heavy metals) forming a Cd-MT complex. Normally, metal-MT chelated complexes are readily filtered in the kidneys, and most are eliminated from the body through the urine. However, the cadmium-MT complex is not readily excreted but is rather reabsorbed in the proximal tubules. The cause of this may be that cadmium's electronic structure ($[Kr]+4d^{10}5s^2$), isovalent with zinc ($[Ar]+3d^{10}4s^2$), divalent nature, and size allow it to mimic a zinc-MT complex. (Zinc-MT complex has been shown to be an important regulator of homeostasis, thus explaining their proximal tubule reabsorption.)

Upon reabsorption, the Cd-MT complex enters the cells of the proximal tubule via endocytosis and is subjected to degradation in the lysosome, cleaving the complex and releasing free cadmium into the organelle and ultimately into the cytosol. Cadmium can then be bound by proximal tubular MT to reform the protective Cd-MT complex. However, cellular injury occurs when the amount of cadmium entering the cell overwhelms the binding capabilities of the renal MT. Cadmium cytotoxicity, resulting from free cadmium, has been associated with the generation of active oxygen species (e.g., superoxide and hydroxyl radical) as well as the inhibition of antioxidant enzymes like superoxide dismutase, and interference with lysosomal enzymes. The combination of these effects lead to proximal tubular cell death and the release of the cellular contents into the blood and tubule (with potential for resorption). A consequence of proximal tubule necrosis is the presence of protein, amino acids, and glucose in the urine (proteinuria, aminoaciduria, glucosuria, respectively) as the kidneys' filtration processes and reabsorption abilities are increasingly compromised. Notably, any cadmium released into the bloodstream will be re-complexed and again taken up in functional proximal tubules. This cycle of complexation and reuptake underlies the extremely long half-life of cadmium in the body (10–30 years) and is ultimately the basis for the expression of chronic toxicity of the element.

Nephropathy is the main consequence of chronic cadmium exposure, most notably seen as proximal tubule injury. The consequences to the tubular epithelium loss affect the critical processes of the reabsorption of water, electrolytes, and organic molecules, causing an acid-base disturbance (metabolic acidosis) and hypophosphatemia (low blood phosphates).

Cadmium toxicity became an international issue in the 1950s when a group of women living in the Toyama Prefecture of Japan's main Honshu island (located on the northern coast) presented with intense back and shoulder pain that continued to spread across the body to the point where the patient was bedridden for the rest of her life. This devastating disease was called *itai-itai* disease in reference to the pain caused in the victim (its name in English translates to "ouch-ouch") in response to bone degeneration leading to fractures and injuries. The cause of these problems was linked to high cadmium concentrations in the local Jinzu River, as a result of runoff from a zinc-lead mine upstream. This extremely painful bone disease is characterized by bone softening (osteomalacia) and osteoporosis as cadmium replaced calcium in the bone. The weakened bones had a high risk and incidence of spontaneous fractures. Cadmium has also been observed to promote bone resorption (a process that removes calcium from the bones) and concurrently inhibits new bone formation. As would be expected of a cadmium exposure, renal tubular degeneration and kidney failure characterized the disease as well.

18.5 Lead

Lead is an insidiously toxic element that, both as an element and in mixtures, has been responsible for toxicity from ancient European civilizations to the modern day. Historically, examples of exposures ranged from lead-containing syrups in wines (see Sidebar 18.3) to runoff and fumes from mines and smelting operations. Lead has been used for many purposes including munitions (as both projectile material and a component in primers), basic building materials, ship and boat ballast, x-ray and radiation shielding, piping (including drinking water pipes), preparation of pewter and other alloys, and multiple other uses. Lead has been mined in both the old and new world and is readily purified from ore. One of the most widespread sources of environmental lead was the use of tetraethyl lead as gasoline additive up until the 1970s (lead concentration in the soil is still demonstrably related to roadway proximity).

In the last few decades, lead exposure has been increasingly recognized as a potential toxin in low levels

SIDEBAR 18.3 LEAD, WINE, AND THE ROMAN EMPIRE

The discovery of relatively high levels of lead in the remains of presumably upper-class Roman citizens has fueled speculation, not only that lead toxicity in some fashion contributed to the decline and fall of that civilization, but of more immediate implication, that the source of the lead was the pewter goblets in which the wine was often served. (Pewter is a rather soft alloy, consisting primarily of tin but containing other elements, generally copper, antimony, and often lead.) The assumption was that the mildly acidic wine would dissolve some of the lead comprising the goblet, leading ultimately to the ingestion and accumulation of the metal and its toxicity. While seemingly plausible, such an explanation requires the transfer of significant quantities of lead by this solvation process and may not provide an adequate basis for the amount of lead required for the levels observed. (Nevertheless, in response to concerns of lead toxicity, pewterware no longer contains lead!) One fact that is lost in the discussion of lead toxicity is the fact that lead salts have a sweet taste (and hence the reason for children eating lead-paint chips). One reasonable thought is that rather than lead being leached out of pewter goblets by wine, the lead may well have been actually added in the form of the sweet-tasting lead salts to enhance the wine, and providing a dose of lead at the same time. Syrup prepared from grape juice was generated by cooking down the juice in lead vats. The end product, *sapa*, contained a considerable level of lead acetate, providing both a sweetening agent for wine and a mechanism for a dose of lead.

and concentrations. As such, the various exposure limits and recommendations for elimination of exposure risks have steadily moved toward lower concentrations. While lead is not well recognized by the general public as a potential acute toxin, there is an understanding that chronic low-level exposure can be a legitimate risk for brain development and cognitive function.

Part of the recognition of the toxic potential of lead is related to the observation, in the decades following World War II, that inner-city children would occasionally express relatively high blood lead levels, correlated with cognitive deficits. Eventually, an exposure source was identified as the chewing and ingestion of paint chips. Lead oxide (red) and lead carbonate (white) were popular pigments used in a variety of paints, including both interior and exterior house paints until their elimination in 1978. Lead salts have a sweet taste, and so chips of lead-based paint were a common source for elevated lead levels and frank toxicity in juveniles. Recognition of the potential for the toxicity of lead paint and the elimination of lead-based pigments has considerably reduced the occurrence of this problem.

Children are especially vulnerable to lead as a toxin, as they have an increased ability for GI absorption as well as less-developed blood–brain barrier (BBB) to protect their CNS. Lead ions attack a variety of enzyme systems with a high affinity for sulfhydryl groups. Lead is especially toxic to zinc and calcium-dependent enzyme systems as it can replace these vital elemental co-factors. Chronic lead poisoning is pervasive, with symptoms observed in many organ systems.

18.5.1 Gastrointestinal Toxicity

Acute lead toxicity affects the smooth muscle responsible for peristalsis in the abdomen. The first symptoms are muscular discomfort and a metallic taste, accompanied by a headache. As the toxicity progresses, pronounced constipation and anorexia occur. Excruciating intestinal spasms can occur, causing severe abdominal pain, or "lead colic," marking the advanced abdominal stage of toxicity. ("Devonshire colic," a GI affliction of the 1600–1700s, was caused by lead in cider, a traditional drink of the Devon region, and is a classic example of both the potential for toxicity linked to lead intake and—denied vociferously by the producer—the degree to which commercial interests will occasionally go to deny inconvenient truths.)

18.5.2 Heme Synthesis Toxicity

Two enzymes directly inhibited by lead are involved in the synthesis of heme: Δ-aminolevulinic acid dehydratase (ALAD) and ferrochelatase. These different enzymes contain sulfhydryl groups to which lead binds, inhibiting their normal functions. Inhibition of the activities of these two enzymes results in nonfunctional hemoglobin, resulting in anemia (microcytic hypochromic anemia, characterized by small, immature red blood cells with low hemoglobin content). ALAD catalyzes the conversion of delta-aminolevulinate to porphobilinogen, while ferrochelatase is responsible at the terminal step for the incorporation of the divalent ferrous ion into protoporphyrin, forming the final heme molecule. Inhibition of this enzyme leads to the incorporation of zinc instead of iron, forming zinc protoporphyrin, the appearance of which can be used to diagnose lead poisoning. Heme synthesis is also integral to the formation of cytochrome proteins that compose the mitochondrial electron transport chain leading to the reduction of molecular oxygen and energy generation. In this manner, lead can indirectly impact oxidative metabolism, resulting in energy-deficient cells.

18.5.3 Neurotoxicity

The CNS symptoms of lead toxicity are so extensive that the consequences has been termed "lead encephalopathy." Lead is able to enter the brain very rapidly compared with other metals, due to its ability to mimic calcium ion. Ca^{+2} ATPase transmembrane pumps are able to transport lead across the BBB. Lead in the brain appears to alter the permeability of the BBB, causing cerebral edema as the brain fills and swells with excess fluid. Early signs of the effects of lead can be clumsiness, ataxia, vertigo, falling, headache, restlessness, and irritability. The patient can become excited and confused; delirium followed by a coma is common. As the intoxication progresses, cerebral edema proliferates along with meningitis, hemorrhages, and areas of focal necrosis. Seizures, optic atrophy, and mental retardation are possible long-term consequences of lead encephalopathy if the exposure is nonfatal.

Lead can cause major damage in the peripheral nervous system (PNS) as well, targeting motor axons, causing degeneration and segmental demyelination. Highly active muscle groups are therefore those most affected, such as the extensors of the forearm, wrist, fingers, and extraocular muscles. Damage to the nerves responsible for innervation of these extensor muscles manifests itself in the commonly observed "wrist-drop" and, to a lesser extent, "foot drop" phenomena. The mechanism for the neurotoxicity caused by lead has not been conclusively identified.

Lead also interferes with the ability of calcium ions to trigger neurotransmitter exocytosis as well as activate calmodulin and calcium-dependent kinase C, both of which translate to disruptions in normal nerve signal transmission. Kinase C has been linked to the regulation of long-term memory and is believed to play a role in the learning disability and behavior deficits seen in children diagnosed with lead poisoning.

18.6 Mercury

Another metal of ancient history, mercury, has been employed as a component of antibacterials, laxatives, and skin ointments for centuries. In the present day, these uses have been replaced with safer alternatives; however, due to its important industrial applications (thermometers, thermostats, electric) and occupational and environmental exposures, it is not a forgotten toxin. The toxicity associated with a mercury exposure is a function of the species of mercury involved: elemental, inorganic, or organic.

The mechanism of action of mercury in the body is based on its strong affinity for sulfur, leading to covalent bond formation. Many enzymes have free sulfhydryl groups as part of the active or catalytic sites, and thereby provide multiple locations for the formation of mercaptide bonds, effectively inhibiting the enzyme. Mercury, in addition, can bind amides, amines, carboxyl, and phosphoryl groups, meaning that virtually any host protein is subject to mercurial inactivation and explains the wide-reaching effects in a variety of biological systems affected by this metal.

18.6.1 Elemental Mercury Toxicity

Elemental mercury as a liquid is not well absorbed and poses a minimal threat if orally ingested with an intact GI system. (Historically, elemental mercury was employed as an emetic.) Dermal absorption is also minimal. However, elemental mercury can pose a dangerous threat if the liquid is volatilized and inhaled (see Sidebar 18.4). Acute inhalation can result in chemical pneumonitis that can progress to respiratory failure. Chronic inhalation of vapor results in a much more sinister form of poisoning. The gaseous nature allows for a faster distribution of the toxin across membranes including those protecting the brain. As a result, significant CNS symptoms occur. Chronic mercury inhalations result in neuropathies including loss of coordination and tremors of the face and hands. Psychiatric personality disorders also develop, including symptoms of insomnia, poor concentration, memory loss, and emotional instability.

SIDEBAR 18.4 "MAD AS A HATTER"

Contrary to popular belief, the phrase "mad as a hatter" existed before Lewis Carroll would pen his own Mad Hatter in *Alice's Adventures in Wonderland*, first published in 1865. The history of how mercury became involved in the hat-making process may be as notable as the mad hatters themselves. Felt hats for gentlemen were highly fashionable during the seventeenth to nineteenth centuries. The process of making the felt began with obtaining pelts from small animals, such as beaver or rabbit. The fur itself then needed to be separated from the hide, before it could be further used to make felt. At first, urea was used to denature the animal hair proteins, allowing the fur to be separated from the animal skin. The most convenient source of urea was of course, urine. Curiously enough, it was found that urine from factory workers suffering from syphilis made the best felt for the hat. The reason had nothing to do with the disease per se, but rather the medicine prescribed at the time for treatment: mercury (II) chloride.

Around 1840, pelts began being subjected to solutions of mercuric nitrate that would remove the fur from the skin as well as coil and shrink the fur, making it more pliable. This process was called "carroting" due to the orange color produced in the underlying hide. The heat of the factories often increased the fumes arising from the mercuric nitrate, and thereby the exposure of the workers. The hat makers, or hatters, then suffered from the insidious symptoms of chronic mercury vapor toxicity. In 1941, mercury was finally banned from the felting industry in the United States due to the severe neurotoxic effects demonstrable in hat makers. The phrase "mad as a hatter" was a popular and (tragically) accurate phrase to describe someone who was absentminded, irritable, and suffered from tremors.

18.6.2 Organic Mercury Toxicity

Organic short-chain mercurials (methyl and ethyl) are responsible for the majority of mercury toxic exposure in humans. Their use as insecticides and fungicides has led to some devastating mass poisoning incidents in Pakistan, Ghana, Guatemala, and Iraq as the result of consumption of mercury-poisoned grain. Organomercurial can rapidly diffuse across the GI tract into the blood and CNS, causing tremors, loss of muscle control, loss of speech muscles, and paresthesias.

In nature, organomercurials are formed when inorganic mercury, a by-product of natural off-gassing from the earth's crust, is methylated by algae and bacteria, whereby it makes its way into the food chain, eventually entering humans, who represent the top level. Through bioaccumulation, fish can also concentrate mercury that is the result of human pollution. A major mercury poisoning event occurred in Minamata Bay in Japan (western coast of Kyushu island) in the 1950s and 1960s, where consumption of fish with high levels of methyl mercury caused those affected to suffer tremors, difficulties in speech, and severe ocular, auditory, and tactile sensory impairment.

18.6.3 Inorganic Mercury Toxicity

The inorganic mercury salts exist in two forms: the monovalent mercurous and the divalent mercuric. These charged species cannot easily penetrate membranes and therefore tend to reside in the GI tract, acting as extremely caustic agents causing vomiting, nausea, and intense abdominal pain. An ashen gray appearance of the mucosa of the mouth, throat, and intestine appear as a result of mercurial protein precipitation of mucosal proteins. Renal failure frequently accompanies chronic exposure to these salts, with glomerular injury predominating.

REVIEW QUESTIONS

1. What is the mechanism for acute arsenic toxicity?
2. Explain the basis for the unusually long half-life of cadmium in the body.
3. What would be the basis for a patient suffering from some symptoms of mercury toxicity but without CNS involvement?

TOPICS FOR DISCUSSION

1. The Devonshire colic was notable for both the scientific proof of the link to lead toxicity and also the rebuttals to the proposed link, supported by cider makers. How far have we come in separating commercial and scientific interests?
2. How likely is it that an arsenic poisoning could be overlooked or written off as a natural death?

Bibilography

Barile FA. *Clinical Toxicology: Principles and Mechanisms.* 2nd ed. New York: Informa Healthcare, 2010.

Byrns MC, Penning TM. Environment toxicology: Carcinogens and heavy metals. In: Brunton LL, editor. *Goodman and Gilman's The Pharmacological Basis of Therapeutics.* 12th rev. ed. New York: McGraw Hill Medical, 2011.

Dart RC, editor. *Medical Toxicology.* 3rd rev. ed. Philadelphia: Lippincott Williams & Wilkins, 2004.

Klassen CD. Casarett and Doull's *Toxicology: The Basic Science of Poisons.* 8th rev. ed. New York: McGraw-Hill, 2013.

Osterhoudt KC, Perrone J, DeRoos F, Henretic FM. *Toxicology Pearls.* Philadelphia: Elsevier Mosby, 2004.

Reichl FX, and Ritter L, editors. *Illustrated Handbook of Toxicology.* Stuttgart: Thieme, 2011.

Index

D

E

U

V

W

Y

Z

For Product Safety Concerns and Information please contact our EU representative GPSR@taylorandfrancis.com Taylor & Francis Verlag GmbH, Kaufingerstraße 24, 80331 München, Germany

Batch number: 10732794

Printed by Printforce, the Netherlands